KU-023-573

The Member States of the European Union

SECOND EDITION

Edited by

Simon Bulmer
Christian Lequesne

OXFORD
UNIVERSITY PRESS

OXFORD
UNIVERSITY PRESS

Great Clarendon Street, Oxford OX2 6DP,
United Kingdom

Oxford University Press is a department of the University of Oxford.
It furthers the University's objective of excellence in research, scholarship,
and education by publishing worldwide. Oxford is a registered trade mark of
Oxford University Press in the UK and in certain other countries

© The several contributors and in this collection Oxford University Press 2013

The moral rights of the authors have been asserted

First edition published 2005

Impression: 1

All rights reserved. No part of this publication may be reproduced, stored in
a retrieval system, or transmitted, in any form or by any means, without the
prior permission in writing of Oxford University Press, or as expressly permitted
by law, by licence or under terms agreed with the appropriate reprographics
rights organization. Enquiries concerning reproduction outside the scope of the
above should be sent to the Rights Department, Oxford University Press, at the
address above

You must not circulate this work in any other form
and you must impose this same condition on any acquirer

British Library Cataloguing in Publication Data
Data available

ISBN 978-0-19-954483-7

Printed in Great Britain by
Ashford Colour Press Ltd, Gosport, Hampshire

Links to third party websites are provided by Oxford in good faith and
for information only. Oxford disclaims any responsibility for the materials
contained in any third party website referenced in this work.

QM LIBRARY
(MILE END)

QM Library

23 1420323 9

The Member States of the European Union

WITHDRAWN
FROM STOCK
QMUL LIBRARY

THE NEW EUROPEAN UNION SERIES

Series Editors: John Peterson and Helen Wallace

The European Union is both the most successful experiment in modern international cooperation and a daunting analytical challenge to students of politics, economics, history, law, and the social sciences.

The EU of the twenty-first century continues to respond to expanding membership and new policy challenges – particularly in transnational arenas such as climate change, energy security, and crisis management – as well as political and institutional controversies. The result is a truly new European Union that requires continuous reassessment.

THE NEW EUROPEAN UNION SERIES brings together the expertise of leading scholars writing on major aspects of EU politics for an international readership.

The series offers lively, accessible, reader-friendly, research-based textbooks on:

POLICY-MAKING IN THE
EUROPEAN UNION

THE INSTITUTIONS OF THE
EUROPEAN UNION

THE EUROPEAN UNION:
HOW DOES IT WORK?

ORIGINS AND EVOLUTION
OF THE EUROPEAN UNION

INTERNATIONAL RELATIONS AND
THE EUROPEAN UNION

THE MEMBER STATES OF THE
EUROPEAN UNION

OUTLINE CONTENTS

DETAILED CONTENTS vii
PREFACE xvii
LIST OF BOXES xx
LIST OF FIGURES xxi
LIST OF TABLES xxii
LIST OF ABBREVIATIONS AND ACRONYMS xxiii
LIST OF CONTRIBUTORS xxvii

1 The European Union and its Member States: An Overview 1
Simon Bulmer and Christian Lequesne

PART I **Analysis**

2 Europeanization: Concept, Theory, and Methods 31
Paolo R. Graziano and Maarten P. Vink

PART II **The Member States**

3 France: Genuine Europeanization or Monnet for Nothing? 57
Olivier Rozenberg

4 Germany: In Search of a New Balance 85
Timm Beichelt

5 The United Kingdom: Towards Isolation and a Parting of the Ways? 108
David Allen

119-141

6 Spain: Modernization Through Europeanization 134
Francesc Morata

7 Sweden: From Scepticism to Pragmatic Support 161
Anna Michalski

8 Poland: An Awkward Partner Redeemed 186
Nathaniel Copsey

9 Estonia: Excelling at Self-Exertion 213
Piret Ehin

▍DETAILED CONTENTS

PART II   The Member States

3   France: Genuine Europeanization or Monnet for Nothing?   57

PART III Europeanization

▌PREFACE

This is the second edition of our book that was first published in 2005 in the New European Union series edited by John Peterson and Helen Wallace and inspired by *Policy-Making in the European Union*, now in its sixth edition.

For this second edition, we have undertaken a fairly fundamental re-think. The first edition was originally conceived in the context of a European Union with fifteen member states and covered the accession states of 2004 and 2007 in a single chapter. For the second edition, coverage of all the member states as well as including thematic chapters on Europeanization was no longer tenable without extending the book into two volumes. We therefore took advice through Oxford University Press's market research on how to take the volume forward, and we take this opportunity to thank those who contributed to this exercise. Several options were available to us. In one scenario we could cover all states in detail but omit the chapters on Europeanization. Another option was to extend the practice in the first edition and have more multi-country chapters, along the lines of the coverage of the Nordic countries in a single chapter in the 2005 book. Finally, we could be selective in our country coverage in order to maintain and develop the thematic coverage of Europeanization. In the event, we chose the last of these in order to maintain the philosophy behind the first edition as well as to provide analytical depth on the countries selected. We also elected to emphasize the theme of Europeanization.

Our original philosophy was to offer something different from the existing books on member state–EU relations. At the time of the first edition, these books tended to be comparative studies of EU policymaking in member states. In the meantime, several books have been published that contain thematic coverage of Europeanization. The basic idea of our distinctive coverage is to cover analysis, member states, and thematic aspects of Europeanization. The book thus comprises three parts. The first explores the key analytical issues associated with the Europeanization literature. The second puts the member states under the spotlight. Here we have sought to have coverage of key states, notably France and Germany, as well as one from each round of the rounds of enlargement. We have a spread of states ranging in size from Germany to Estonia. Our Chapter 11 aims to highlight some of the issues relating to member state adaptation that can be applied to states not specifically covered in the volume. The third part comprises thematic coverage. Here we have made some changes by adding a chapter on sub-national authorities as well as splitting parties and interest groups into two separate chapters.

As a consequence of the re-shaping of our book, we would like to thank outgoing contributors to the first edition and welcome those new to this edition. We are very grateful to our colleagues from Oxford University Press for helping us to realize the project. For this edition we thank our editors, Catherine Page and, subsequently, Martha Bailes. Thanks are also due to the production team of Joanna Hardern. We also thank Helen Wallace and John Peterson, the series editors, for their support. Finally, we thank Eurostat for permission to reproduce the data contained in Table 16.1.

Our authors have worked with high professionalism, accepting to rewrite parts of the manuscript in short periods of time. We are very grateful to each of them for their contribution to make the book—we hope—a success. Sadly, while the manuscript was in production, one of our contributors, David Allen, passed away after a short illness. Not only was Dave a contributor to both editions of this book and a long-standing analyst of Britain's relationship with the EU, but poignantly he was the academic who introduced Simon Bulmer to European integration as an undergraduate students at Loughborough University in 1974–5. We take the opportunity to pay tribute to his academic contributions and friendship over the years.

Simon Bulmer would like to thank students at the University of Sheffield and at the Autonomous University of Barcelona, where he has gained feedback from teaching graduate students on Europeanization. Christian Lequesne would also like to thank students at the London School of Economics and at Sciences Po for their feedback on the member state—EU relationship. Finally, we thank our series editors, John Peterson and Helen Wallace, for their confidence, help, and patience. Our final expression of thanks goes to our families: Helen Bulmer in Glossop, Monique, Matthieu, and Juliette Lequesne in Fontainebleau.

Simon Bulmer, *University of Sheffield and* Christian Lequesne, *CERI-Sciences-Po Paris*

▌ New to this edition

- The second edition has been thoroughly updated to include the latest round of EU enlargement and to reflect the increasing significance of Europeanization.
  - Five new member-state chapters: Spain, Poland, Estonia, Sweden, and Romania.
  - More coverage of Europeanization with three new thematic chapters.

▌ LIST OF BOXES

▍LIST OF FIGURES

■ LIST OF TABLES

■ LIST OF ABBREVIATIONS AND ACRONYMS

AC	Autonomous community
AWS	*Akcja Wyborcza Solidarność* (Solidarity Electoral Action)
BNP	British National Party
BSE	Bovine spongiform encephalopathy
CAP	Common Agricultural Policy
CARCE	Conference on Issues Related to the European Communities
CC	Constitutional Council
CDU	Christian Democratic Union
CEE	Central and Eastern European
CEEC	Central and Eastern European country
CFDT	*Confédération Française Démocratique du Travail*
CFP	Common Fisheries Policy
CFSP	Common Foreign and Security Policy
CiU	Convergència i Unió (Convergence and Union)
CONCORD	*Confederation d'ONG pour l'aide d'urgence et le développement*
COPA	Committee of Farmers' organizations in the EU
COREPER	Committee of Permanent Representatives
COSAC	Conference of Representatives of European Affairs Committees
CPNT	*Chasse Pêche Nature et Traditions*
CSF	Community Supporting Framework
CSO	Council of Senior Officials
CSU	Christian Social Union
CT	Constitutional Treaty
DA	Justice and Truth Alliance
DEFRA	Department for the Environment, Food and Rural Affairs
DG	Directorate General
DTI	Department of Trade and Industry
ECAS	European Citizen Action Service
ECB	European Central Bank
ECOFIN	Council of Economic and Finance Ministers
ECSC	European Coal and Steel Community
EC	European Community/ies

ECJ	European Court of Justice
EDC	European Defence Community
EEA	European Economic Area
EEC	European Economic Community
EFPIA	European Federation of Pharmaceutical Industry Associations
EFSF	European Financial Stability Facility
EFTA	European Free Trade Association
EIA	Environmental impact assessment
EIoP	European Integration online Papers
EMS	European Monetary System
EMU	European Monetary Union/Economic and Monetary Union
ENP	European Neighbourhood Policy
EP	European Parliament
EPC	European Political Cooperation
EPP	European People's Party
ERM	Exchange Rate Mechanism
ESDP	European Security and Defence Policy
ETUC	European Trade Union Confederation
EU	European Union
EUAC	European Union Affairs Committee
FCC	Federal Constitutional Court
FCO	Foreign and Commonwealth Office
FDI	Foreign Direct Investment
FDP	Free Democratic Party
FPÖ	Freedom Party
FSN	National Salvation Front
GATT	General Agreement on Tariffs and Trade
GDP	Gross Domestic Product
GNP	Gross National Product
GO	Government Offices
GUE/NGL	Group of the European United Left – Nordic Green Left
HI	Historical institutionalism
HR	High Representative
IGC	Intergovernmental Conference
IMF	International Monetary Fund
INTERREG	Inter-regional cooperation initiative of the EU
IR	International relations

IU	United Left
JC	Congress-Senate Joint Committee
JHA	Justice and Home Affairs
KERM	European Committee of the Council of Ministers
KPRM	Office of the Prime Minister
LEADER	Rural development programme
LI	Liberal intergovernmentalism
M&A	Mergers and acquisitions
MEDA	Programme of measures as part of the Euro-Mediterranean partnership
MEP	Member of the European Parliament
MFA	Ministry of Foreign Affairs
MSZ	Ministry of Foreign Affairs
NATO	North Atlantic Treaty Organization
NGO	Non-governmental organization
NUTS	Nomenclature of Territorial Units for Statistics
ODS	Civic Democratic Party
OECD	Organization for Economic Cooperation and Development
OEI	Office of European Integration
OMC	Open Method of Coordination
OSCE	Organization for Security and Cooperation in Europe
PACO	Support Programme for Co-finance schemes
PCA	Partnership and Cooperation Agreement
PD	Democratic Party
PDL	Democratic Liberal Party
PDSR	Party of Social Democracy in Romania
PHARE	Poland and Hungary Assistance for Reconstruction of Economy
PIIGS	Portugal, Ireland, Italy, Greece, and Spain
PiS	*Prawo i Sprawiedliwość* (Law and Justice)
PM	Prime Minister
PMO	Prime Minister's Office
PNL	Party of National Liberals
PNV	Basque National Party
PO	*Platforma Obywatelska* (Civic Platform)
PP	*Partido Popular* (People's Party)
PRM	Greater Romania Party
PRODER	Rural Development Programme
PSD	Party of Social Democrats

PSL	*Polskie Stroictwo Ludowe* (Polish People's Party)
PSOE	*Partido Socialista Obrero Español* (Spanish Socialist Workers' Party)
QMV	Qualified Majority Voting
PVV	Party of Freedom
PZPR	*Polska Zjednoczona Partia Robotnicza* (Polish Communist Party)
RCI	Rational choice institutionalism
REPER	Permanent Representative of Spain to the European Union
SEA	Single European Act
SEUE	State Secretary for the EU
SGAE	General Secretariat for European Affairs
SGP	Stability and Growth Pact
SI	Sociological institutionalism
SLD	*Sojusz Lewicy Demokratycznej* (Democratic Left Alliance)
Smer-SD	Direction—Social Democracy
SMO	Social movement organization
SMP	Single Market Programme
SNA	Sub-national authority
SNP	Scottish National Party
SPD	Social Democratic Party
SSIER	State Secretariat for Integration and Foreign Economic Relations
SUD	*Solidaires, Unitaires et Démocratiques*
TABD	Transatlantic Business Dialogue
TEU	Treaty on European Union
TFEU	Treaty on the Functioning of the European Union
TINA	There is no alternative
UDMR	Democratic Union of Hungarians in Romania
UK	United Kingdom
UKIE	Office of the Committee for European Integration
UKIP	UK Independence Party
UKREP	UK Permanent Representation to the European Union
UMP	Union pour un Mouvement Populaire
UN	United Nations
USSR	Soviet Union
VAT	Value Added Tax
UNICE	Union of Industries of the European Community
WEU	Western European Union
WTO	World Trade Organization

■ LIST OF CONTRIBUTORS

DAVID ALLEN	Loughborough University
TIMM BEICHELT	European University Viadrina, Frankfurt (Oder)
SIMON J. BULMER	University of Sheffield
PETER BURSENS	University of Antwerp
NATHANIEL COPSEY	Aston University
PIRET EHIN	University of Tartu
PAOLO R. GRAZIANO	Bocconi University, Milan
HUSSEIN KASSIM	University of East Anglia
ROBERT LADRECH	Keele University
CHRISTIAN LEQUESNE	CERI-Sciences Po, Paris
ANNA MICHALSKI	Uppsala University
FRANCESC MORATA	Autonomous University of Barcelona
DIMITRIS PAPADIMITRIOU	University of Manchester
DAVID PHINNEMORE	Queen's University, Belfast
CLAUDIO M. RADAELLI	University of Exeter
OLIVIER ROZENBERG	Sciences Po, Paris
SABINE SAURUGGER	Sciences Po, Grenoble
VIVIEN A. SCHMIDT	Boston University
MAARTEN P. VINK	University of Maastricht

LIST OF CONTRIBUTORS

CHAPTER 1

The European Union and its Member States: An Overview

Simon Bulmer and Christian Lequesne

▌ Summary

The European Union (EU), like other international institutions, is composed of a set of member states. Despite the EU's distinctive supranational institutions, such as the European Commission and the European Court of Justice (ECJ), the member states remain key actors in making EU policy, and their role in this process is central to understanding the integration process and EU governance. At the same time, European integration has had an important impact upon the member states: the phenomenon that has come to be termed 'Europeanization'. In this chapter we examine, first of all, why the member states matter in the EU. We then review the analytical issues raised and the theoretical perspectives deployed in exploring the impact of member states on the EU and the Europeanization of the member states. Finally, we explain the logic and structure of this volume: how the relationship between the EU and its member states will be portrayed in the chapters and parts of the book that follow.

Introduction: Why Member States Matter

The European Union is built upon foundations made up of its member states. However, the early years of studying European integration were characterized by a preoccupation with supranational institutions and with theories of integration that made little effort to make connections between developments *within* member states and those at EU level. James Caporaso (2007) has identified three different broad research agendas on European integration that have emerged at different phases of its development. The first phase held sway from the beginning of theorizing on integration in the 1950s and was dominated by international relations theories. The focus was on explaining the trajectory of integration and was 'dominated by bottom-up thinking' (Caporaso 2007: 24). Central to this phase of theorizing were two competing accounts of integration: neo-functionalism and intergovernmentalism. Whilst the former placed emphasis on the role of non-state and supranational actors, the latter emphasized the importance of state power in the integration process. Neither, however, sought to open up the 'black box' of the member states to widen analysis of the domestic level of the integration process. In a second phase of research the focus shifted to understanding the EU as a political system. Two particular characteristics of this second phase can be identified: a shift towards the toolkit of comparative politics (Hix 1994); and an understanding of the EU as a polity. This new focus developed in the 1980s and gathered pace with the so-called 'governance turn', which is reviewed by Kohler-Koch and Rittberger (2006). It was from the 1990s, though, that the member states really became the focus of the research agenda, as the growing impact of EU legislation, such as that arising from the single market programme, impacted on the member states. The resultant Europeanization research agenda, a central concern of this volume, has been a major research concern of analysts of the EU in the twenty-first century.

One of the remarkable characteristics of this evolving research agenda has been the shift in underlying assumptions. Those underpinning the first, 'bottom-up' research agenda were competing hypotheses from international relations (IR). The second research agenda, focused on the EU level, utilized competing analytical frameworks from comparative politics and governance. The 'top-down' Europeanization research agenda has been intertwined with mainstream debates in IR and political science concerning the role of interests, institutions and identity.

The bottom-up research focus did not end in the 1980s; indeed, it experienced a revival in the 1990s. From different disciplinary perspectives, Alan Milward, an economic historian, and Andrew Moravcsik, a political scientist, explored the relationships between the member states and the EU through detailed analyses of particular episodes of European integration (Milward 1995; Moravcsik 1993; 1998). Both these analysts took the member state as the unit of analysis. The member state—and specifically its national government—was seen as a gatekeeper aggregating national interests before representing them in EU-level debates.

The centrality of the nation state in this interpretation prompted others to offer a more multi-layered approach that also identified connections between regional and other actors within states and the dynamics of the EU (Marks *et al.* 1996a; Kohler-Koch 1996; Bache and Flinders 2004). The state itself became problematized, as commentators argued that traditional notions of statehood were weakening. For analysts working within comparative politics frameworks this broad phenomenon was characterized as the 'hollowing out of the state'—from above and below—as international and sub-national pressures simultaneously reduced the autonomy of the nation state. For many IR analysts developments such as globalization and European integration were seen as heralding the end of the traditional, all-powerful, 'Westphalian' state (see Caporaso 1996). The security challenges posed by terrorist groups highlighted additional threats to a model of IR based around the nation state.

The emergence of Europeanization as a concern in the literature re-examines many of these themes, except viewed from the other end of the telescope, as it were. This literature has wide concerns: with the impact of the EU on state institutions, on public policy, on political forces, and so on. In the Europeanization literature national governments have never been regarded as gatekeepers, controlling the effects of integration within the member state. Nevertheless, different analytical approaches have been developed, as we shall see.

Before exploring these issues we need to clarify some preliminary questions.

- What exactly is meant by the term 'member state'?
- How and why do member states matter to understanding the EU?

Here we use the term 'member states' as shorthand to comprise *all* political actors and institutions within a member state. We are not using it as a synonym for national governments. The latter usage, prominent in early intergovernmentalist accounts of the EU, brings with it a number of problems. First of all, such accounts understood the EU as the interplay of national governments and ignored the process of preference formation beneath the governments. Second, another legacy of cruder variants of intergovernmentalism is that member governments were seen as unitary actors. This assumption, we believe, was a matter for empirical exploration and not a prior assumption. Third, and also a legacy of early intergovernmentalist thinking, was the understanding of national governments as the 'gatekeepers' of integration. In other words, as gatekeepers they were presumed to have control over contacts between national actors and the EU political system. In the heavily populated EU policy-making arena of the contemporary era this assumption looks highly problematic. This is why we have used a definition of member states that is more neutral as regards the different theoretical approaches to understanding the EU.

Member governments matter as key actors in EU decision-making. They are key players in the strategic decisions of the European Council, in Intergovernmental Conferences (IGCs) on the 'architecture' of the EU, and on enlargement. They are key participants in the more routine policy decisions of the Council and its support-ing committee structure. However, it is not just member governments, for other public authorities are also engaged. For instance, government agencies and regional/local government are key actors in the implementation of European policy: in pro-viding the administrative sub-structure on which the EU depends in most areas, if its policies are to achieve their goals. Helen Wallace (2010: 89) summarizes the situa-tion thus: 'in a real and tangible sense national governments, and other authorities and agencies, provide much of the operating life-blood of the EU.' An earlier obser-vation is also worth repeating:

Most of the policy-makers who devise and operate EU rules and legislation are from the member states themselves. They are people who spend the majority of their time as national policy-makers, for whom the European dimension is an extended policy arena, not a separate activity. Indeed much of EU policy is prepared and carried out by national policy-makers and agents who do not spend much, if any, time in Brussels.

(Wallace 2000: 7)

As indicated already, member states also matter in the theoretical and analytical debates concerning integration and governance. They are attributed varying levels of importance by different approaches. But how do member states matter in the real world of the EU?

First, the 'state of the European Union' at any one time is reflective of a balance of unifying (EU) and territorial forces/institutions. This balance represents the interplay of national and integrationist forces. They are not diametrically opposed forces in a zero-sum game but interact to find creative policy solutions. This interaction finds expression in the routine decision-making of the so-called Ordinary Legislative Proc-ess, where the Commission proposes legislation and the Council and European Parlia-ment co-decide. The 'state of the EU' is also a function of the balance of the member states of the EU. For example, the character of the structural funds has been altered right from the creation of the European Regional Development Fund in the aftermath of the 1973 accession of the United Kingdom and Ireland, through to their re-orienta-tion ahead of the 2001 eastern enlargement. The pattern of financial transfers has changed with each successive enlargement, but so has the overall balance of interests.

Second, territoriality matters in the EU: it is the main organizing principle. Iden-tity, democracy, and legitimacy tend to be located at the member state level (albeit often with a layering of these within the state concerned). Similarly, the predominant form of institutional organization within the EU is along national lines: whether, most obviously, in the Council hierarchy or in the distribution of commissioners or MEPs. The territoriality principle predominates in the institutions of policy making, policy-implementation, and of the judicial system.

However, European integration has made the territoriality of politics more permeable, as have forces in the global economy, patterns of technological change and so on. Thus, the importance of territoriality does not mean that the era of the Westphalian state has been 'frozen' into the EU. On the contrary, European integration has gone hand-in-hand with a number of transformative changes to the state system: the erosion of national boundaries; some hollowing out from below as a result of internal regionalism; the emergence of new forms of governance which have altered traditional boundaries between the public and private spheres (for instance, so-called networked governance); and the growth of para-public agencies, that is, bodies that have autonomy from government, and are responsible for regulatory governance (for instance, the European Central Bank). European integration has not been the sole cause of these developments; indeed, in some cases it may not have been the cause at all. But the key point here is that changes in patterns of governance within member states are closely inter-linked with the development of the EU. In many cases the EU is simply regarded by national governments as an additional resource to address global policy challenges.

Third, member states (that is not just governments) are key players in the politics of the EU. Territorial-based interests are articulated *upwards* into EU arenas. Empirical and analytical study of this process of upward articulation may be concerned with the role of actors, institutions, and the attempt to project national policy preferences into the EU arena. This upward projection of domestic interests has been clearly demonstrated in the euro-zone crisis. For states such as Greece, Portugal and Ireland the unsustainability of their fiscal debt has presented the EU and particularly the other euro-zone countries with major challenges to provide financial support to avoid the break-up of the currency. However, the domestic interests arising from the indebted states have collided with the conflicting preferences of other states, most clearly Germany, that would need to agree such financial solidarity. Long-standing adherence to principles of fiscal rectitude, opposition on the part of public opinion to bailing out states with lax fiscal practices, and the need to secure parliamentary approval and avoid the possibility of actions being brought before the Federal Constitutional Court resulted in lengthy periods of deadlock at EU level in the search for solutions. This deadlock arose from the conflicting preferences amongst the different euro-zone member states.

Fourth, at the same time, the EU is an important factor in member state politics. Its activities impinge upon political actors, institutions, policies, and identities at this level. This *downwards* direction of flow—often termed 'Europeanization'—may be studied in isolation or as part of an iterative (that is repeated) and interactive process. Iteration and interaction mean that the upwards and downwards flows between the two levels of governance are related to one another.

The dynamic interaction of member states and the EU is important in a number of specific ways.

- National governments and other actors must devise ways of making effective inputs into the political process at the supranational level.

- National governments and other actors must devise ways of incorporating EU business into their organization of business at the national level.

- For all actors within a member state—whether governmental, institutional, parties, interest groups, or less formal parts of civil society—the EU creates a changing opportunity structure. New tactical and strategic opportunities are opened up in terms of 'projection' for all these types of political actor.

- However, these new opportunities do not come without cost, for all these types of political actor are also subject to new constraints: policy commitments, legal obligations and so on emanating from the EU level.

- This interaction raises questions of logics: should the 'logic' of political action in Brussels prevail, or that of political action in the member state concerned? Does the EU act as a centripetal force, causing convergence in member states' patterns of governance and policies? Or is it compatible with the continuance of distinctive national patterns? In other words, should domestic political actors seeking to influence the EU do so according to their standard domestic 'script' or should they adapt to the logic of the EU policy process?

- The types of actors confronted with these issues in their interaction with the EU are national governments (ministers and officials), para-public agencies (for instance, national competition agencies), national parliaments, sub-national government, political parties, interest groups, and civil society. Also affected, albeit in a slightly different way, are national courts, through the judicial process, and, in a more diffuse sense, public opinion and conceptions of identity.

- Finally, are the EU institutions the agents of national governments? Or are national government institutions becoming administrative arms of the EU's institutions as components of what Morten Egeberg (2006) has termed a European administrative space? Similar questions may be asked of transnational political parties or transnational interest groups: do they remain the agents of their national constituent member organizations?

These are amongst the key questions with which the theoretical and empirical literatures on the relationship between the member states and the EU are concerned. Of course, there are other perspectives on the European Union apart from the territorial focus of EU–member state relations. However, many contemporary issues in the EU benefit from a territorial analysis, not least because national governments retain important powers in the EU institutional system. In the next section we explore the different ways in which the member states' role in the EU system can be understood in theoretical terms.

Analysing the Role of Member States in the EU

As noted earlier, the early theoretical debates about European integration, starting in the 1950s, were initially a quasi-monopoly of IR theorists. The principal debate was between neo-functionalists and intergovernmentalists (for a review, see Rosamond 2000: chapters 3 and 6). Neo-functionalists looked at the dynamics behind the accumulation of powers at supranational level. The main weakness of this theory proved to be its assumption that national governments would readily give up their authority to the EU. In 1965, a dispute between the French President, Charles de Gaulle, and the European Commission as well as other national governments made plain that this assumption was flawed. Whilst it enjoyed a small revival from the late-1980s, neo-functionalism does not really have much to offer to understanding EU–member state relations. The dynamic account of integration that was offered by neo-functionalism—based upon the notion of spillover—neglected a member state focus. Functional spillover emphasized the interconnectedness of economic sectors. Political spillover emphasized the accumulation of political pressure for further integrative steps but focused particularly on the role of interest groups. Finally, cultivated spillover focused on the role of the supranational institutions in fostering further integration. In short, the role of national governments as the drivers of further integration was neglected, since that was the premise of a rival theory, intergovernmentalism, which placed the member state at the centre of bargaining.

Intergovernmentalism: the Member State at the Centre of EU Bargaining

For many years the principal representative of intergovernmentalism was Stanley Hoffmann. The main foundations of his approach were set out in a string of publications, re-stated in a collection (Hoffmann 1995).

- The EU is seen first of all as a venture in cooperation amongst states, which are rational actors and whose domestic functioning is governed by principles of authority and hierarchy.

- In a context of generalized economic interdependence, the EU constitutes a more profound form of 'international regime'—defined as a set of common norms, institutions, and policies allowing those states to manage more efficiently specific issue areas such as trade, agriculture, or the environment (Hoffmann 1982; Levy, Young, and Zürn 1995).

- The resulting 'pooled sovereignty' does not lead to a diminution of the role of the states, but on the contrary to a strengthening of that role, encouraging their adaptation to constraints imposed by the international environment.

- The creation of one regime does not necessarily lead to the creation of others by an automatic spillover effect, as supposed by neo-functionalists.

In terms of international relations (IR) theory, Hoffmann was never a neo-realist asserting, like Kenneth Waltz for instance (Waltz 1979), that a state's national interest derives solely from its position in the international system. Rather, he worked on the basis that member states—and specifically national governments—jealously guarded their power for sound domestic reasons.

While variants of intergovernmentalism were above all the work of an American IR theorist, their spread in Europe was later facilitated by work on the economic history of integration. Alan Milward considered that the heavy interdependence of markets in coal, agriculture, and trade left European welfare states after 1945 with hardly any alternative to organizing themselves collectively in order to bestow welfare policies on their citizens (Milward 1995). Refuting the thesis that states renounced part of their sovereignty in creating common EU institutions, Milward asserted, on the contrary, that this was a means for each of them to recover individually.

The revival of intergovernmentalist approaches also came about through the theory of rational choice, which gained substantial ground in American political science from the 1980s. Starting from the hypothesis that states desire to cut transaction costs in an open economy, rational choice theorists consider European integration above all as a collective action whose aim, for each state, is to optimize gains. Geoffrey Garrett's work on the establishment of the single market is a good example (Garrett 1992). Member states' political preferences were accorded importance, although in practical terms this meant central governments' preferences, since he did not explore their origins in the societies composing them.

It was out of concern to restore the relationship between state and society that Andrew Moravcsik devised, in the early 1990s, another approach: 'liberal intergovernmentalism'. This has become an established reference in the literature and cannot be ignored by anyone interested in European integration (Moravcsik 1993, 1998; Moravcsik and Schimmelfennig 2009). In pursuit of the ambitious project of building a theory of European integration, Moravcsik starts from three research postulates:

- The state is a rational actor in Europe.
- Power in the EU is the result of bargaining amongst states.
- Liberal theory is needed to explain the formation of national preferences within the state.

The first two hypotheses are quite similar to assumptions made by Stanley Hoffmann, although Moravcsik's work has also entailed extensive empirical illustration (see Moravcsik 1998). The formation of national preferences constitutes liberal intergovernmentalism's (LI) most original contribution. While LI sees bargaining among states as a confrontation of national interests, it also sees in those interests demands addressed by domestic societal actors to 'their' national government. In developing this model, Moravcsik was influenced by Robert Putnam's two-level game approach: an analytical framework which has its own independent value for understanding the role of member governments in EU negotiations (Putnam 1988). Putnam's two-level game approach drew on the bargaining literature from industrial relations to highlight the different dynamics that exist in upper tier negotiations (international organizations or the EU) and the interplay with the domestic politics of the participating states.

LI is insightful into EU–member state relations even though Moravcsik is using them to explain European integration rather than looking at those relations in their own right. However, LI is not without its critics and rivals. Here we mention four criticisms, which are particularly relevant to the concerns of this book. First, in seeing the EU member states through the prism of central governments alone, Moravcsik neglects their internal diversity (multi-party coalitions, relations between central executives and regional authorities, rivalry amongst agencies and bureaucracies, presidential versus parliamentary systems, and so on). As Part II of this book shows, this diversity between member states is great. That diversity is indispensable for understanding their different positions within the EU. Next, in assuming that the EU is an arena where *large* member states exercise power, Moravcsik simplifies the decision-making games considerably. Let's take a concrete example. It is not at all certain that the convergence of domestic policy preferences in Germany, France, and the United Kingdom (UK) on the single market carried more weight in the adoption of the Single European Act than the doubling of structural funds desired by the Mediterranean states and Ireland and institutional reforms to which the Benelux countries were very attached (Moravcsik 1998). Third, Moravcsik sees in EU institutions only agencies created by the member states with the purpose of increasing the initiative and influence of national governments, although they are also organizations which develop their own ideas and interests in relation to the states that have set them up. Lastly, as regards preference formation within states, there is a strong assumption that interests can only be advanced via national governments rather than via other routes, such as direct lobbying in Brussels.

Criticisms of this nature led to the emergence of alternative approaches to understanding European integration and EU governance. We now turn to two such alternatives—institutionalism and new governance approaches—and the insights offered by them into the study of member state–EU relations.

Institutionalism and Member State–EU Relations

Although both neo-functionalism and LI had their origins in broader theoretical developments in the study of IR, from the 1980s analytical perspectives on the EU moved away from these grand theories towards the application of more mainstream approaches from political science. The first such development came with the emergence of the so-called new institutionalism, which was based on two simple assertions (March and Olsen 1995).

- Institutions are more than the reflections of underlying social forces.
- Institutions do more than produce a neutral arena for political interaction.

In short, institutions *matter*. However, that assertion gave rise to further questions about *how* they matter, triggering the emergence of distinct variants of new institutionalism (see Hall and Taylor 1996; and, in the EU context, Schneider and Aspinwall 2001 for reviews). Three variants predominated: rational choice institutionalism (RCI), sociological institutionalism (SI) and historical institutionalism (HI). What are the insights of these variants into EU–member state relations?

RCI shared many of the underlying assumptions of Moravcsik's LI. Just as Moravcsik's approach could comprehend member states' rational action in delegating policy responsibilities to the EU level in order to reduce transaction costs and improve economic efficiency, so RCI analysts focused on the delegation of authority to the supranational institutions. Mark Pollack's work, for example, explored the delegation of authority, holding supranational institutions to be 'agents' created by 'principals' (the member states) to reduce the transaction costs in the functioning (or governance) of the EU (Pollack 1997). Principal–agent analysis opened up exploration of the extent to which supranational institutions had discretion in undertaking the tasks assigned to them by the member governments (see Pollack 2003); and how such discretion might be limited (see Hix and Høyland 2011: 23–7 for a review).

SI offered a different research agenda, influenced by a broader understanding of institutions beyond formal rules to include cultural aspects, such as administrative culture, norms, and values. For instance, Jeff Lewis (1998, 2000) explored whether member state negotiators in the Council hierarchy of institutions departed from their national interests and became socialized into a more collective European outlook as a result of repeated interaction with their counterparts from the other member states. The SI research agenda thus opened up issues such as identity and culture in member states' relations with the EU. German governments have been seen as flying in the face of a straightforward interpretation of national interests, for instance through giving up the Deutsche Mark and the well-established central banking principles of its central bank (the Bundesbank) in favour of the inevitable compromises associated with monetary union. SI analysts might attribute this behaviour to a set of pro-European norms modifying material national interests. Similarly, observers of British European policy might regard the frequent appeal of (prime) ministers to the symbolism of sovereignty as indicative of a cultural or identity-based aspect of domestic politics rather than reflecting the UK's material interests.

Historical institutionalists, by contrast, are alert to the role of time. Two implications emerged for the study of the EU:

- Politics at the EU level is no longer seen as a series of strategic decisions made by national governments, but as a 'path dependent' process with a series of critical situations and unforeseen consequences.

- Institutions at supranational and national levels should no longer be regarded only as instruments in the service of outside pressures, but as structures capable of integrating experiences and norms over the course of time.

Although these observations are targeted at the EU as a whole, it is not difficult to see how they can be applied to relations between member states and the EU by taking the level of analysis downwards. For instance, it is possible to see how different historical and institutional legacies have impacted on the way member states conduct their European policy (see Bulmer and Burch 2001 for an Anglo-German comparison). So, like sociological institutionalists, they argued that national European policy could be interpreted as not just the product of the interplay of material interests. The contrast lies in the emphasis on historical legacies.

The three new institutionalisms can thus offer insights into the way in which member states interact with the EU: the character of their policies and how they are formulated domestically. Institutionalism also encompasses longer-standing ways of understanding EU–member state relations. Federalism was an important strategy for the development of European integration for those who wished to see the abandonment of the nation state as the basis of a new international order. However, beyond this normative approach, comparative political analysis of the EU's territoriality has offered valuable insights into EU–member state relations (see Sbragia 1993; Nicolaidis and Howse 2001). Amongst the factors making comparative federal analysis relevant, Sbragia mentioned the continuing problem of balance between territorial interests and functional interests within the EU. Federal analysis offers useful trails for researchers who wish to conceptualize the two dynamics—at EU and inter-state levels—which have been present since the early years of the EU's formation (Quermonne 2001). Similarly, it makes it possible to develop theories about the dialectical relationship between a de-territorialized political project and interests that remain firmly rooted in member states' territories, as one can see empirically in studying EU policies and politics (Lequesne 2004).

The fact that federal political systems have tended in recent decades to develop from their original dualist form towards an ever increasing overlap between the levels of government ('cooperative federalism') is also a pertinent element for analysing the ongoing obligation to find consensus between the different member states' institutions at one level, and the EU institutions at the other level (Scharpf 1988; Croisat and Quermonne 1999). Cooperative federalism also makes it possible to reflect on the exercise of democracy in political systems which tend to attach importance to interaction among executive authorities (ministers, specialized committees of civil servants) at the expense of control by parliaments and societies. Works inspired by federalism have the advantage of studying not only EU member state relations as a process but also as a 'political order'.

Governance Approaches and Member State–EU Relations

From the 1990s there has been quite a strong convergence between IR and comparative politics theorists in moving from the idea of nation states being powerful in both the international and domestic spheres. Instead, governing has been presented as the interaction of a large number of actors: public and private (Leca 1996). Authors adopting this standpoint have often resorted to the notion of *governance*. While this notion was quickly taken up by the EU institutions themselves (European Commission 2001) to push for the pluralist engagement of civil society in the running of politics, its primary sense is analytical. James Rosenau, for instance, resorts to governance to describe how international politics concerns not only the activities of states but also of informal, non-governmental mechanisms whereby those persons and organizations move ahead, satisfy their needs, and pursue their wants (Rosenau 1992). Similarly, Renate Mayntz uses the concept of governance to stress that the dynamics of Western societies tend to give ever greater autonomy to social groups, and that analysis of the state therefore implies identifying modes of horizontal coordination among sub-systems rather than traditional patterns of hierarchical authority and vertical administration (Mayntz 1993).

Given the absence of a single 'ruler' and of a clear divide between 'public' and 'private' actors in the EU, it is quite understandable that some researchers, wanting to distance themselves from state-centric thinking, should have chosen to analyse the EU as a governance model (Hooghe 1996; Marks *et al.* 1996b; Armstrong and Bulmer 1998; Kohler-Koch 1996; Kohler-Koch and Rittberger 2006; Kohler-Koch and Larat 2009). In these works, the member state is no longer in a situation of monopoly or of hierarchical superiority. EU politics and policies are the results of interactions between the Commission, the member states, regions, and interest groups. Understanding the EU in terms of governance raises questions about the conditions for the emergence of the political agenda. On the one hand, in an ever increasing number of fields, the process of problem definition has been transferred away from national governments to the European level (Muller 1996). On the other hand, at the member state level, policy making has become more technocratic such that specialized experts (civil servants of national ministries, interest group representatives) exercise more power than in the 'traditional' European state. Conflicts therefore centre less on problems of representation than around control of expertise (Radaelli 1999).

A further contribution made by the new governance approach to the EU is to explore policy networks: pluralist networks as configurations of actors (including national officials, Commission officials, representatives of interest groups, etc.) which do not conform to a single institutional model but, on the contrary, tend to become differentiated through the gradual emergence of internal rules of the game in each sector. Reproducing the type-casting used for the study of policy making in the UK (Marsh and Rhodes 1992), writers distinguished different types of policy networks at the EU level according to their stability and the elements underlying transactions by their members (Peterson 2009; Peterson and Bomberg 1999). Member state actors are not excluded from the policy networks. They share the transactions with other member state actors and with supranational actors. Moreover, policy networks make negotiation the dominant mode of political transaction at the European level. This permanence of negotiation is strengthened by the fact that the main EU policies are regulatory ones (Majone 1996). Regulatory policies encourage actors subjected to them (especially national administrations and interest groups) to negotiate with the EU Commission the precise obligations involved.

The new governance approach has shed light on a wide array of issues in European integration. For example, it has made it possible to redefine the relationships between European integration and democracy. Through the diffuse nature of the EU polity comes the question of democratic accountability. 'Who is accountable for what?' has been a frequent question in the national debates on the EU (Jachtenfuchs and Kohler-Koch 1996, 2004). This question played a role in the debate about the EU's constitution and survived through to the listing of the EU's competences in Articles 3–6 of the Treaty on the Functioning of the European Union, as introduced by the Lisbon Treaty. The principal drawback of the governance approach has been that the 'shedding of light' has not entailed the creation of any *theory* of member state–EU relations providing the clear reference points, however criticized they may be, of LI.

Towards a Domestic Politics of the EU?

One of the striking things to emerge from this review of analytical perspectives on the upstream relationship between member states and the EU is that it remains an under-explored theoretical agenda. Most of the frameworks reviewed thus far have focused on the EU level. However, after implementation of the Lisbon Treaty, integration seems to have reached a plateau of development, although the fate of the euro-zone could lead either to a reversal of the process in the event of the currency breaking up or to further integration through a fiscal union. In addition, economic weakness across many member states has placed domestic politics at the forefront in the member states, even in Germany, the longest-standing proponent of integration. Defence of the euro has been a protracted process owing to Chancellor Merkel's attentiveness to domestic public opinion, to parliamentary process, and to potential legal challenges. Is the time perhaps not ripe for greater focus on the domestic politics approach to understanding the EU? One contribution along these lines was Helen Wallace's (2005) chapter in the first edition of this book, where she explored the stages in the EU policy process at which member states could seek influence and the means whereby they could do so. This is an important facet to the member state-EU linkage but the agenda of a domestic politics approach is rather wider because it extends to include domestic party politics, public opinion, and the wider factors which can help explain whether member governments wish to be influential in the EU in the first place.

The basic tenet of the domestic politics approach is that it is impossible to understand the EU without considering domestic politics (Bulmer 1983). This approach shared some of the assumptions of Moravcsik's later LI and these are re-stated here in the context of the present EU (for the original statement, see Bulmer 1983: 354). The national polities were considered to be the basic units of the EU. Yet the economics and politics of the 27 polities differ considerably, and it is important to have these variations in mind since they are at the root of the states' European policies. And these European policies are each deeply enmeshed in a wider set of domestic and foreign policies in the member state concerned. Whilst national governments are held to be of key importance, the centrality attributed to them by intergovernmentalists was challenged and, with the subsequent development of European integration, globalization, new modes of domestic governance and so on, is even more disputed than in the early 1980s. Finally, the specific concept of 'policy styles' was advanced as a way of encapsulating the variation in policy patterns between states, taking account of differing institutional structures and the varying political forces they were mediating.

Of course, it might be argued that the domestic politics approach has been superseded by Moravcsik's LI. The counter-argument is that LI was engaged in a different exercise. First, Moravcsik was not concerned with in-depth exploration of the mainsprings of European policy in individual member states. Second, his privileging of economic interests over political ones in shaping member governments' negotiating positions is open to challenge. Similarly, the lack of attention to domestic institutions opens the door for an institutionalist challenge. However, the analytical challenge has not yet been met: that is where space is available for further elaboration of the domestic politics approach (for an empirical analysis of the domestic politics of the negotiations leading to the Lisbon Treaty, see Carbone 2010). That this approach has not been developed is doubtless in part attributable to the extensive analysis over the last two decades to the opposite direction of influence, namely the EU's impact on member states. Which brings us to *Europeanization*.

Analysing Europeanization

Exploring the impact of integration upon the member states as well as applicants or near-neighbours of the EU is generally termed 'Europeanization'. However, there are three other developments in the literature which deserve prior exploration because they provide an important context for the Europeanization literature. They relate to three propositions:

- that integration strengthens the state;
- that integration creates a new multi-level politics thereby recalibrating how domestic actors respond to integration; and
- that the EU has transformed governance.

In a 1994 paper, Andrew Moravcsik developed the first of these arguments, namely that the European Community strengthens the nation state (Moravcsik 1994). This argument chimed with his own 'bottom-up' liberal intergovernmentalist analysis of integration; the link being provided by the centrality of 'the state'. Little further exploration of this argument has been undertaken. But, just as Moravcsik's theoretical interpretation of integration was contested, so too was this paper.

One of his 'adversaries' on integration theory, Wayne Sandholtz, argued for an alternative interpretation of the impact of integration upon member states (Sandholtz 1996). He suggested that integration could create new 'options for domestic actors in their choice of allies and arenas' (multi-level politics), and induce changes in domestic institutions and policies. What Sandholtz was making clear by 'multi-level politics' was much the same point as that made by Gary Marks and his collaborators (for example Marks *et al.* 1996a), namely that national governments neither represent the sole objects of integration nor the exclusive link between national politics and the EU (Sandholtz 1996: 412). Essentially he was arguing that domestic actors—governmental or societal—recalibrate their goals as a result of EU membership. His concern was not with domestic change per se, but with reinforcing a non-state-centred understanding of integration. However, he went further and argued that domestic actors could exploit the supranational situation to secure domestic change. Anticipating later analyses, he pointed to the French and Italian governments exploiting the requirements of the European Monetary System and European Monetary Union respectively to secure domestic policy reform (Sandholtz 1996: 423–6).

The 'transformation of governance' argument is especially associated with Beate Kohler-Koch and her collaborators. Her argument is that integration has not only shifted the distribution of power between multiple levels of authority, but has also shifted the boundary between the public and private spheres (Kohler-Koch 1996: 360). The character of the state—its institutional structures and political processes—is transformed as part of this process (also see Jachtenfuchs and Kohler-Koch 1996: 22–3; Kohler-Koch and Eising 2000): quite the reverse of Moravcsik's argument.

The three propositions outlined above may be seen as precursors to the literature explicitly termed 'Europeanization'. They formed a link from integration theory through governance analysis to the terrain that the Europeanization literature has occupied. The Europeanization literature proceeded cautiously from using the term as a loose background concept to one which is more precisely defined (Featherstone and Radaelli 2003; Graziano and Vink 2007; Ladrech, 2010). Paolo Graziano and Maarten Vink offer a fuller review of Europeanization in Chapter 2. Here we confine ourselves to an introduction to the literature by highlighting its origins and usages, as well as some brief observations relating to conceptual, theoretical, and methodological aspects, and finally to what might be termed 'directionality'.

Origins

The origins of the Europeanization research agenda can be attributed to the gathering momentum of integration from the middle of the 1980s, with agreement on completion of the single market and ratification of the Single European Act. These steps were augmented with the broadening of European integration in the Maastricht Treaty to include monetary union as well as justice and home affairs cooperation. All these advances had significant implications—political, economic, and legal—for the member states. Unsurprisingly, these impacts became a growing research agenda, not only for those with a long-standing interest in EU studies, but also for domestic public policy specialists and others who came to recognise the growing impact of the EU on their field of study. In addition to the deepening impact of the EU upon the member states, the impact of its widening upon prospective member states became a further research agenda associated especially with the enlargements of 2004 and 2007 (see Glenn 2004; Grabbe 2005; Hughes *et al.* 2004, 2005; Schimmelfennig and Sedelmeier 2004, 2005; Schimmelfennig 2008).

Usages

Spurred on by these developments at EU level, Europeanization enjoyed a period of growing attention, expanding out of Robert Ladrech's early definition (1994: 17) of it as 'an incremental process reorienting the direction and shape of politics to the degree that EC political and economic dynamics become part of the organizational logic of national politics and policy-making'. Johan Olsen (2002: 923–4) sought to map the research area and identified five different usages of the term (see Bache and Jordan 2006: 20–21 for a different mapping of usages).

- First, Europeanization arising from '*changes in external boundaries*'. The most obvious example is the extension of the policies, rules, institutional requirements and values in the new member states which acceded in 2004 and 2007.

- Second, he identified Europeanization as '*developing institutions at the European level*'. This usage relates to the development of a central governance capacity in the EU, with its implications of constraints and opportunities for political actors at the domestic level.

- Third, he saw the classic definition of Europeanization as the '*central penetration of national systems of governance*'. This is arguably the core usage of Europeanization and covers adjustment processes in respect of institutional structure, policy, patterns of political behaviour and so on at lower levels of the multi-levelled European political system.

- A fourth usage is Europeanization as '*exporting forms of political organization*'. Here the term is deployed where the EU seeks to export its values, such as through the Lomé/Cotonou Conventions or through its foreign policy to non-member states.

- A final variant is Europeanization as '*a political unification project*'. Like the earlier second definition, this one is about the development of capacity at the EU level. The distinction here is that it is interpreted more widely, namely in terms of political integration [emphasis in original].

One of the difficulties of the second and fifth definitions is that they come close to being synonymous with the term European integration. European integration may well be a pre-requisite for Europeanization—see under Concept below—but the terms cannot be synonymous without serious risk of 'concept-stretching'. In other words, Europeanization is best confined to encompassing the consequences of integration so that its distinctive focus is not lost.

How may these different understandings of Europeanization be compared and contrasted? Kevin Featherstone (2003) undertook a useful early review plotting the origins of the literature and its coverage. He drew up a fivefold classification of areas covered: historical processes, cultural diffusion, institutional adaptation, and policy (or policy process) adaptation. His reference to historical processes is significant because one of the key features of the literature is the assumption that the EU is the independent variable, that is, the source of Europeanization. Of course, there are other European organizations that could serve as the independent variable, such as the Strasbourg-based Council of Europe. In reality, Europeanization is normally a synonym for 'EU-ization'. However, taking a longer historical time-frame draws attention to much wider interpretations of Europeanization. Trine Flockhart (2010) has taken this unconventional viewpoint on Europeanization from the perspective of historical sociology. In her work, she identifies five phases of Europeanization starting with 'European Self-Realization' in the period up to 1450. Only her fifth phase covers the period since 1945 and thus corresponding to the mainstream literature. It is therefore important in using Europeanization to be clear on definitions and what is the independent variable. Whilst noting this historical sociological perspective is an atypical understanding of the term, it does find wider resonance in some of the contemporary research agenda. For instance, studies of Europeanization in the Turkish context are not always confined to the EU's impact but also encompass aspects of westernization and modernization.

The empirical literature on Europeanization deals with a range of subject matter. A typical classification of the impact of Europeanization distinguishes between that on polity (that is, the institutions and patterns of governance), on policy, and on politics (including parties, political parties, public opinion, and identity). Our thematic chapters in Part III of this book present a slightly different set of categories, adding interest groups, sub-national government and political economy as separate areas of impact (see also Chapter 2). An alternative perspective is not to look at the subject matter that Europeanization affects, but to consider more abstract categories of adjustment. Vivien Schmidt (2002) distinguished between economic, institutional, and ideational adaptation. Another way of looking at things is to draw on the new institutionalism discussed earlier in this chapter. Rational choice institutionalists would emphasize the material incentives offered by Europeanization, whereas socio-logical institutionalists would focus on the EU's impact in terms of norms, ideas, or identity. The contrast between these two forms of Europeanization lies at the heart of Schimmelfennig and Sedelmeier's work on accession states (2004, 2005; Schimmelfennig 2008).

Concept

As we pointed out earlier, it is important that in using Europeanization analysts make clear *how* they are using it. There seems little point using Europeanization as a synonym for European integration, although the term was sometimes deployed in this way during the early stages of the literature and it is occasionally still used in this way colloquially. The distinction is this: where European integration is concerned with political and policy development at the supranational level, Europeanization is concerned with the consequences of this process for the member states as well as non-members who are the targets of EU policy, such as applicant states or members of the European Economic Area. However, while an aspiration to have a precise definition of Europeanization sounds attractive in theory, the reality of social science research is that concepts and definitions are always contested. Hence if we follow Graziano and Vink (2007: 7) and define the concept relatively concisely as 'domestic adaptation to European regional integration', we find that this would not satisfy the historical sociological usage of Flockhart (2010). Another reasonably concise definition of Europeanization has been offered by Ian Bache and Andrew Jordan (2006: 30), namely as:

the reorientation or reshaping of politics in the domestic arena in ways that reflect policies, practices and preferences advanced through the EU system of governance.

This definition would not satisfy the small number of authors who look at cases where the Council of Europe is the origin of adaptional pressure (e.g. see Checkel 2001).

Definitional issues matter, of course, for Europeanization as for other concepts (see Chapter 2; also Radaelli and Pasquier 2007 for further discussion). They bear upon understanding and identifying the different ways in which Europeanization can have an impact. First, it can be an intended impact of initiative at EU level. Second, it can be an inadvertent impact. These are termed *direct* and *indirect* Europeanization respectively by Bache and Jordan (2006: 27). A third variant is the discursive creation of an 'impact narrative'. For example, Hay and Rosamond (2002) have contrasted a tendency in France to see Europeanization as resistance to globalization with a tendency in the UK to see it as facilitating globalization. In other words, the *discourse* on impact has to be taken into account alongside, and may indeed be more significant than, the *material* impact. Finally, the work of Woll and Jacquot (2010) is illustrative of research which looks at 'usages of Europe': how domestic actors may appropriate EU rules or norms and exploit them in barely related domestic political debates.

Theory

Of fundamental importance in this context is that there is no 'theory' of Europeanization. This characteristic has one benefit, namely that it avoids one of the pitfalls of some of the EU studies literature, for instance neo-functionalism, in that it has been developed around one set of circumstances and has little comparative applicability. Instead, Europeanization has generally relied on new institutionalism (and its variants) for operationalization (see Chapter 2; also Bulmer 2007). This pre-dominance of new institutionalism has arisen from the literature's focus on explaining the obstacles to, and facilitators of, change; that is, the 'missing link' between the EU and the domestic adaptation processes (e.g. see Risse *et al.* 2001).

The new institutionalist theoretical underpinning has put Europeanization into the mainstream of comparative political analysis. Johan Olsen has offered a clear statement expounding why the institutionalist account of adjustment is so prominent:

> The most standard institutional response to novelty is to find a routine in the existing repertoire of routines that can be used. . . . External changes are interpreted and responded to through existing institutional frameworks, including existing causal and normative beliefs about legitimate institutions and the appropriate distribution, exercise and control of power.

(Olsen 2002: 933)

New institutionalism identifies institutions as being important to domestic adjustment, but this literature fragments once attention is focused on *how* institutions matter, resulting in different perspectives on Europeanization emerging from the different brands of institutionalism. RCI analysts explore how EU rules may create new opportunity structures, veto points, or incentives for domestic political action. SI analysts, by contrast, explore how the EU may lead to a re-orientation in domestic norms and values (*cognitive* Europeanization). Börzel and Risse (2003) were influential in advocating using these two variants of institutionalism as parallel, or competing, means of explaining domestic adaptation. Historical institutionalists, finally, are particularly interested in the time, timing, and tempo of domestic Europeanization (Bulmer and Burch 2009).

Methodological issues

A number of methodological issues arise with the Europeanization literature and have culminated in increasing attention to research design (Exadaktylos and Radaelli 2012). A key issue has been to ensure that research design does test whether Europeanization—as opposed to other potential independent variables, such as globalization—can be identified as the cause of domestic change. A recurrent bias in some of the literature is to set up a research design that privileges Europeanization over (or even excludes) other potential explanations. Markus Haverland (2005, 2007) underlined the problems associated with this approach, especially if combined with the analysis of a single case study. He argued for comparative case studies and the use of counter-factual explanations to test the validity of an explanation based on Europeanization. Another problem has been the relative absence of quantitative data, except in the case of domestic compliance with European law. Exadaktylos and Radaelli's volume (2012) has taken up this methodological agenda to address issues of causality, mechanisms of change, and the choice of methods. Whilst their research agenda is designed to inject greater rigour into the analysis of Europeanization, contributors come from different research traditions to offer diverse diagnoses and prescriptions for taking research design seriously.

Directionality

On the face of it, if Europeanization is about the EU's impact at domestic level, as suggested above, then directionality would appear not to be an issue in the literature. However, the Europeanization literature has tended also to emphasize the interactive nature of the relationship between EU and domestic levels. Tanja Börzel (2005) was prominent in arguing that Europeanization comprised not only the domestic adjustment of member states to the EU (which she termed 'downloading') but also the process whereby member states seek to 'upload' policy to the EU level. In other words, the states should not be seen as 'merely passive receivers of European demands for domestic change' (Börzel 2005: 62). Rather, they were likely to be active in seeking to 'upload' their demands to the EU level, not least with a view to reducing the domestic adjustment costs at the downloading stage. Thus, according to Klaus Goetz (2002: 4), Europeanization is 'circular rather than unidirectional, and cyclical rather than one off'.

These observations opened up discussion of what we here refer to as directionality in Europeanization research. It has revealed new ways of applying the concept, but it has raised some problems relating particularly to methodology and research design. First, it is worth noting that some of the issues of directionality have been tackled in the literature on policy transfer (Bomberg and Peterson 2000; Bulmer *et al.* 2007: Chapter 1; Bulmer and Padgett 2005; Radaelli 2000). The policy transfer literature, with its origins in inter- or intra-state studies was consequently very familiar with the idea of horizontal Europeanization (sometimes termed 'crossloading') that came to be added to the lexicon of directionality. Specifically, horizontal Europeanization concerned the transfer of concepts and policies between member states under circumstances where the EU has not played a legislative role. Accordingly, it was particularly associated with newer governance mechanisms in the EU, notably the Open Method of Coordination (see Chapter 15).

Further challenges to understanding Europeanization in the 'vertical' terms of uploading and downloading arose from when the research subject matter shifted from the EU's effect on public policy to its impact on structures of governance or wider political forces. In such cases there was no EU-level template to be downloaded. This is one of the reasons why the findings of Hussein Kassim (see Chapter 12) are that member state institutions have tended to maintain very distinct approaches to governance even if faced with the same challenges of working within an EU context. The EU does not prescribe an 'identikit' form of governance across the member states, for that would be seen as intrusive. The terminology of downloading and uploading did not seem appropriate; instead Bulmer and Burch (2001: 78) utilized the terminology of projection and reception as roles that national executives played in relation to the EU (see also Laffan 2007: 129–30). Horizontal Europeanization can also be seen to a degree in studies of national governments' adaptation to the EU because the successful projection of policy proposals often relies on bilateral alliance-building, such as was typically practiced through the Franco-German relationship.

Whilst observations such as these offered important insights into the concept and application of Europeanization, they did raise problems. Specifically, how could this complex directionality be compatible with clear research design? How could the EU be the independent variable at one time-point (downloading) and then the dependent variable at another (uploading)? Questions such as these raise fundamental issues relating to political analysis—on structure-agency relationships and time, for instance—as well as how to accommodate these issues into practical research design (see Radaelli 2012; Bache *et al.* 2012). For the more casual student of EU–member state relations, these developments may mean a loss of trusted reference points. Thus it may be necessary to find a pragmatic solution, such as regarding the top-down understanding of Europeanization (downloading) as the core focus of the research design, while keeping other directionalities in mind as the research context.

By way of conclusion, it is clear that theoretical debate about Europeanization has not yet reached the end of the road. However, it might be running out of road for two reasons. First, the pace of integration has slackened, and this might shift academic analysis to other issues; perhaps to domestic politics approaches, as discussed earlier in the chapter. Similarly, enlargement looks likely to become less important on the EU agenda after agreement at the end of 2011 on Croatia's accession and with the prospects for Turkish membership unclear. The long-standing twin dynamics of deepening and widening lay behind the emergence of the Europeanization research agenda and a slackening of them is likely to impact on academic debates. One further, final, observation relates to the potential for challenges to some of the orthodoxies of the Europeanization literature. In particular, Europeanization has typically been seen positively except in a few member states with significant 'pockets' of Euro-scepticism, such as Britain. The likelihood of a prolonged period of economic austerity in some member states of the euro-zone, as their public finances are brought into balance as part of the rescue of the single currency, is likely to result in a growth of criticism of the EU and in the growth of more critical approaches to Europeanization.

Previewing the book

The themes identified here all feature in the chapters and parts that follow. In Part I Europeanization is discussed in greater depth. Europeanization is the way in which this edition of the book has been framed, and it is therefore important that the 'state of the art' is reviewed in greater detail. In Part II the Europeanization perspective takes on a geographical focus. Unlike in the first edition (Bulmer and Lequesne 2005), space precludes covering all member states while addressing thematic aspects of Europeanization as well. Consequently, we have selected our coverage of member states on three criteria. First, we decided it was vital to cover the two member states that have been at the heart of integration, Germany and France. Second, we opted to select states from different rounds of enlargement. The UK is thus the representative of the 1973 enlargement; Spain of the southern enlargements of the 1980s; and Sweden of the 1995 accessions. The 2004 enlargement was large, introducing ten new states, and we have selected Poland and Estonia in order to have variation in size. Finally, Romania represents the 2007 enlargement. Of course, we have had to omit some important states but we did not wish to sacrifice depth by covering multiple states in single chapters, nor to sacrifice the book's combined geographical and thematic approach. In Part III, the focus is on Europeanization, with the chapters adopting a thematic approach. The themes addressed are the impact of Europeanization on member state institutions, political parties, interest groups and social movements, public policy, sub-national authorities, and the European political economy. Through these chapters, our aim has been to cover the key issues as well as to give illustrative applications of the Europeanization literature.

The volume aims to present a twin-track approach to the relationships between member states and the EU. It cannot be exhaustive. Nevertheless, our approach is distinctive from existing studies, which *either* adopt a geographical approach (for instance, Wessels *et al.* 2003; Zeff and Pirro 2006) *or* a thematic one (for instance, Cowles, Caporaso, and Risse 2001; Featherstone and Radaelli 2003; Graziano and Vink 2007; Ladrech 2010) rather than bringing both together. Finally, we have sought to contextualize the three parts of the book, including through giving a brief guide to existing literature.

 FURTHER READING

A good overview of the analytical and theoretical literature on European integration is offered by Rosamond (2000). For major treatments of European integration 'from below' that take a nation state-centred, or intergovernmentalist, perspective, see

Hoffmann (1982), Moravcsik (1998), and Milward (1995). For important critiques of the intergovernmental interpretation, see Marks *et al.* (1996a), Pierson (1996). A good starting-point for exploring the Europeanization literature is Ladrech (2010), while Graziano and Vink (2007) provide a very good 'handbook' covering the various theoretical and thematic areas of Europeanization. Further guidance on the Europeanization literature is available at the end of subsequent chapters.

WEB LINKS

General websites on EU–member state relations scarcely exist, although later chapters identify more specific sites for individual countries or themes. However, a good source of scholarship, that brings together several series of working papers, including specifically on Europeanization is available at **http://eiop.or.at/erpa/**. The ARENA series and the Queen's Papers on Europeanization, accessed via this site, are particularly valuable but relevant papers can be found in the others as well. The EU's own website is also a huge resource **http://europa.eu**.

REFERENCES

Armstrong, K. and Bulmer, S. (1998), *The Governance of the Single European Market*, Manchester: Manchester University Press.

Bache, I. and Flinders, M. (eds) (2004), *Multi-Level Governance*, Oxford: Oxford University Press.

Bache, I. and Jordan, A. (2006), 'Europeanization and Domestic Change', in I. Bache and A. Jordan (eds), *The Europeanization of British Politics*, Basingstoke: Palgrave Macmillan, 17–33.

Bache, I., Bulmer, S., and Gunay, D. (2012), 'Europeanization: A Critical Realist Perspective', in T. Exadaktylos and C. M. Radaelli (eds), *Research Design in European Studies: Establishing Causality in Europeanization*, Basingstoke: Palgrave Macmillan, 64–84.

Bomberg, E. and Peterson, J. (2000), 'Policy Transfer and Europeanization: Passing the Heineken Test?', Queen's Papers on Europeanization, No. 2/2000, available at: http://www.qub.ac.uk/schools/SchoolofPoliticsInternationalStudiesandPhilosophy/FileStore/EuropeanisationFiles/Filetoupload,38445,en.pdf

Börzel, T. (2005), 'Europeanization: How the European Union Interacts with its Member States', in S. Bulmer and C. Lequesne, *The Member States of the European Union*, Oxford: Oxford University Press, 45–69.

Börzel, T. and Risse, T. (2003), 'Conceptualizing the Domestic Impact of Europe', in Featherstone, K. and Radaelli, C. (eds), *The Politics of Europeanization*, Oxford: Oxford University Press, 57–80.

Bulmer, S. (1983), 'Domestic Politics and EC Policy-making', *Journal of Common Market Studies*, 21: 4, 349–63.

Bulmer, S. (2007), 'Theorizing Europeanization', in P. Graziano and M. Vink (eds), *Europeanization: New Research Agendas*, Basingstoke: Palgrave Macmillan, 46–58.

Bulmer, S. and Burch, M. (2001), 'The "Europeanisation" of Central Government: The UK and Germany in Historical Institutionalist Perspective', in G. Schneider and M. Aspinwall (eds), *The Rules of Integration: Institutionalist Approaches to the Study of Europe*, Manchester: Manchester University Press, 73–96.

Bulmer, S. and Burch, M. (2009), *The Europeanisation of Whitehall: UK Central Government and the European Union*, Manchester: Manchester University Press.

Bulmer, S. and Lequesne, C. (2005), *The Member States of the European Union*, Oxford: Oxford University Press.

Bulmer, S. and Padgett, S. (2005), 'Policy Transfer in the European Union: An Institutionalist Perspective', *British Journal of Political Science*: 35: 1, 103–26.

Bulmer, S., Dolowitz, D., Humphreys, P., and Padgett, S. (2007), *Policy Transfer in European Union Governance: Regulating the Utilities*, Abingdon: Routledge.

Carbone, M. (2010), *National Politics and European Integration: From the Constitution to the Lisbon Treaty*, Cheltenham: Edward Elgar.

Caporaso, J. (1996), 'The European Union and Forms of State: Westphalian, Regulatory or Post-Modern', *Journal of Common Market Studies*, 34: 1, 29–52.

Caporaso, J. (2007), 'The Three Worlds of Regional Integration Theory', in P. Graziano and M. Vink (eds), *Europeanization: New Research Agendas*, Basingstoke: Palgrave Macmillan, 23–34.

Checkel, J. (2001), 'The Europeanization of Citizenship?', in Cowles, M. G., Caporaso, J., and Risse, T. (eds), *Transforming Europe: Europeanization and Domestic Change*, Ithaca, NY: Cornell University Press, 180–97.

Cowles, M. G., Caporaso, J., and Risse, T. (eds) (2001), *Transforming Europe: Europeanization and Domestic Change*, Ithaca, NY: Cornell University Press.

Croisat, M. and Quermonne, J-L. (1999), *L'Europe et le fédéralisme*, Paris: Montchrestien.

Egeberg, M. (ed.) (2006), *Multilevel Union Administration: The Transformation of Executive Politics in Europe*, Basingstoke: Palgrave.

European Commission (2001), *White Paper on European Governance*, Brussels: OOPEC.

Exadaktylos, T. and Radaelli, C. (eds) (2012), *Research Design in European Studies: Establishing Causality in Europeanization*, Basingstoke: Palgrave Macmillan.

Featherstone, K. (2003), 'Introduction: In the Name of "Europe"', in Featherstone and Radaelli, *The Politics of Europeanization*, Oxford: Oxford University Press, 3–26.

Featherstone, K. and Radaelli, C. (eds) (2003), *The Politics of Europeanization*, Oxford: Oxford University Press.

Flockhart, T. (2010), 'Europeanization or EU-ization? The Transfer of European Norms across Time and Space', *Journal of Common Market Studies*, 48: 4, 787–810.

Garrett, G. (1992), 'International Cooperation and International Choice: The European Community's Internal Market', *International Organization* 46: 2, 533–60.

Glenn, J. K. (2004), 'From Nation-states to Member States: Accession Negotiations as an Instrument of Europeanisation', *Comparative European Politics* 2: 1, 3–28.

Goetz, K. H. (2002), 'Four Worlds of Europeanization', paper prepared for the ECPR Joint Sessions of Workshops, Turin, Italy, 22–27 March.

Grabbe, H. (2005), *The EU's Transformative Power: Europeanization Through Conditionality in Central and Eastern Europe*, Basingstoke: Palgrave Macmillan.

Graziano, P. and Vink, M. (eds) (2007), *Europeanization: New Research Agendas*, Basingstoke: Palgrave Macmillan.

Hall, P. and Taylor, C. R. (1996), 'Political Science and the Three New Institutionalisms', *Political Studies*, 44: 5, 936–57.

Haverland, M. (2005), 'Does the EU Cause Domestic Developments? The Problem of Case Selection in Europeanization Research', *Europeanization Integration online Papers (EIoP)*, 9, http://eiop.or.at/eiop/pdf/2005-002.pdf

Haverland, M. (2007), 'Methodology', in Graziano, P. and Vink, M. (eds), *Europeanization: New Research Agendas*, Basingstoke: Palgrave Macmillan, 59–70.

Hay, C. and Rosamond, B. (2002), 'Globalisation, European Integration and the Discursive Construction of Economic Imperatives', *Journal of European Public Policy* 9: 2, 147–67.

Hix, S. (1994), 'The Study of the European Community: The Challenge to Comparative Politics', *West European Politics*, 17: 1, 1–30.

Hix, S. and Høyland, B. (2011), *The Political System of the European Union*, 3rd edn, Basingstoke: Palgrave Macmillan.

Hoffmann, S. (1982), 'Reflection on the Nation-state in Western Europe Today', *Journal of Common Market Studies*, 21: 21–37.

Hoffmann, S. (1995), *The European Sisyphus. Essays on Europe, 1964–1994*, Boulder, CO: Westview Press.

Hooghe, L. (ed.) (1996), *Cohesion Policy and European Integration*, Oxford: Oxford University Press.

Hughes, J., Sasse, G., and Gordon, C. (2004), 'Conditionality and Compliance in the EU's Eastward Enlargement', *Journal of Common Market Studies* 42: 3, 523–51.

Hughes, J., Sasse, G., and Gordon, C. (2005), *Europeanization and Regionalization in the EU's Enlargement to Central and Eastern Europe: The Myth of Conditionality*, Basingstoke: Palgrave Macmillan.

Jachtenfuchs, M. and Kohler-Koch, B. (1996), 'Regieren im dynamischen Mehrebenensystem', in M. Jachtenfuchs and B. Kohler-Koch (eds), *Europäische Integration*, Opladen: Leske and Budrich, 15–44.

Jachtenfuchs, M. and Kohler-Koch, B. (2004), 'Governance and Institutional Development', in A. Wiener and T. Diez (eds), *European Integration Theory*, Oxford: Oxford University Press, 97–115.

Kohler-Koch, B. (1996), 'Catching up with Change: The Transformation of Governance in the European Union', *Journal of European Public Policy*, 3: 3, 359–80.

Kohler-Koch, B. and Eising, R. (eds) (2000), *The Transformation of Governance*, London: Routledge.

Kohler-Koch, B. and Larat, F. (eds) (2009), *European Multi-Level Governance: Contrasting Images in National Research*, Cheltenham: Edward Elgar.

Kohler-Koch, B. and Rittberger, B. (2006), 'The "Governance Turn" in EU Studies'. *Journal of Common Market Studies: Annual Review*, 44: 27–49.

Ladrech, R. (1994), 'Europeanization of Domestic Politics and Institutions: The Case of France', *Journal of Common Market Studies*, 32: 1, 69–88.

Ladrech, R. (2010), *Europeanization and National Politics*, Basingstoke: Palgrave Macmillan.

Laffan, B. (2007), 'Core Executives', in Graziano, P. and Vink, M. (eds), *Europeanization: New Research Agendas*, Basingstoke: Palgrave Macmillan, 128–40.

Leca, J. (1996), 'La Gouvernance de l'Union Européenne sous la Ve République. Une Perspective de Sociologie Comparative', in F. d'Arcy and L. Rouban (eds), *De la Ve République à l'Europe. Hommage à Jean-Louis Quermonne*, Paris: Presses de Sciences Po.

Lequesne, C. (2004), *The Politics of Fisheries in the European Union*, Manchester: Manchester University Press.

Levy, M., Young, O., and Zürn, M. (1995), 'The Study of International Regimes', *European Journal of International Relations*, 1: 267–330.

Lewis, J. (1998), 'Is the "Hard Bargaining" Image of the Council Misleading? The Committee of Permanent Representatives and the Local Elections Directive', *Journal of Common Market Studies*, 36: 479–504.

Lewis, J. (2000), 'The Methods of Community in EU Decision-making and Administrative Rivalry in the Council's Infrastructure', *Journal of European Public Policy*, 7: 261–89.

Majone, G. (1996), *La Communauté Européenne: Un Etat Régulateur*, Paris: Montchrestien.

March, J., and Olsen, James (1995), *Rediscovering Institutions: The Organisational Basis of Politics*, New York: Free Press.

Marks, G., Hooghe, L., and Blank, K. (1996a), 'European Integration from the 1980s', *Journal of Common Market Studies*, 34: 3, 341–78.

Marks, G. Scharpf, F., Schmitter, P., and Streeck, W. (1996b), *Governance in the European Union*, London: SAGE.

Marsh, D. and Rhodes, R. A. W. (eds) (1992), *Policy Networks in British Government*, Oxford: Clarendon Press.

Mayntz, R. (1993), 'Governing Failures and the Problem of Governability: Some Comments on a Theoretical Paradigm', in J. Kooiman (ed.), *Modern Governance*, London: SAGE.

Milward, A. (1995), *The European Rescue of the Nation–State*, London: Routledge; Berkeley: University of California Press.

Moravcsik, A. (1993), 'Preferences and Power in the European Community: A Liberal Intergovernmentalist Approach', *Journal of Common Market Studies*, 31: 4, 473–524.

Moravcsik, A. (1994), 'Why the European Community Strengthens the State: Domestic Politics and International Co-operation', Working Paper No. 52, Harvard University: Center for European Studies.

Moravcsik, A. (1998), *The Choice for Europe: Social Purpose and State Power from Messina to Maastricht*, Ithaca, NY: Cornell University Press.

Moravcsik, A. and Schimmelfennig, F. (2009), 'Liberal Intergovernmentalism', in A. Wiener and T. Diez (eds), *European Integration Theory*, 2nd edn, Oxford: Oxford University Press, 67–87.

Muller, P. (1996), 'Un Espace Européen de Politiques Publiques', in Y. Mény, P. Muller, and J. L. Quermonne (eds), *Politiques Publiques en Europe*, Paris: L'Harmattan, 11–24.

Nicolaidis, K. and Howse, R. (2001), *The Federal Vision: Legitimacy and Levels of Governance in the United States and the European Union*, Oxford: Oxford University Press.

Olsen, J. (1996), 'Europeanization and Nation State Dynamics', in S. Gustavsson and L. Lewin (eds), *The Future of the Nation State*, Stockholm: Nerenius and Santerus, 245–85.

Olsen, J. (2002), 'The Many Faces of Europeanization', *Journal of Common Market Studies*, 40: 5, 921–52.

Peterson, J. (2009), 'Policy Networks', in A. Wiener and T. Diez (eds), *European Integration Theory*, 2nd edn, Oxford: Oxford University Press, 105–24.

Peterson, J. and Bomberg, E. (1999), *Decision-Making in the European Union*, Basingstoke: Palgrave Macmillan.

Pierson, P. (1996), 'The Path to European Integration. A Historical Institutionalist Analysis', *Comparative Political Studies*, 29: 2, 123–63.

Pollack, M. (1997), 'Delegation, Agency and Agenda Setting in the European Community', *International Organization*, 51: 1, 99–135.

Pollack, M. (2003), *The Engines of European Integration: Delegation, Agency and Agenda Setting in the EU*. Oxford: Oxford University Press.

Putnam R. (1988), 'Diplomacy and Domestic Politics: The Logic of Two-Level Games', *International Organization*, 42: 427–60.

Quermonne, J-L. (2001), *Le Système Politique de l'Union Européenne*, Paris: Montchrestien.

Radaelli, C. (1999), *Technocracy in the European Union*, London: Longman.

Radaelli, C. (2000), 'Policy Transfer in the European Union: Institutional Isomorphism as a Source of Legitimacy', *Governance*, 13: 1, 25–43.

Radaelli, C. (2012), 'Europeanization: The Challenge of Establishing Causality', in Exadaktylos, T. and Radaelli, C. (eds), *Research Design in European Studies: Establishing Causality in Europeanization*, Basingstoke: Palgrave Macmillan.

Radaelli, C. and Pasquier, R. (2007), 'Conceptual Issues', in P. Graziano and M. Vink (eds), *Europeanization: New Research Agendas*, Basingstoke: Palgrave Macmillan, 35–45.

Risse, T., Cowles, M. G., and Caporaso, J. (2001), 'Europeanization and Domestic Change: Introduction', in Cowles, M. G., Caporaso, J., and Risse, T. (eds), *Transforming Europe: Europeanization and Domestic Change*, Ithaca, NY: Cornell University Press, 1–20.

Rosamond, B. (2000), *Theories of European Integration*, Basingstoke: Macmillan Press Ltd.

Rosenau, J. (1992), 'Governance, Order and Change in World Politics', in J. Rosenau and E-O. Czempiel (eds), *Governance without Government. Order and Change in World Politics*, Cambridge: Cambridge University Press.

Sandholtz, W. (1996), 'Membership Matters: Limits of the Functional Approach to European Institutions', *Journal of Common Market Studies*, 34: 3, 403–29.

Sbragia, A. (1993), 'The European Community: A Balancing Act', *Publius: The Journal of Federalism*, 23: 23–38.

Scharpf, F. (1988), 'The Joint Decision Trap: Lessons from German Federalism and European Integration', *Public Administration*, 66: 95–128.

Schimmelfennig, F. (2008), 'EU Political Accession Conditionality after the 2004 Enlargement: Consistency and Effectiveness', *Journal of European Public Policy* 15: 6, 918–37.

Schimmelfennig, F. and Sedelmeier, U. (2004) 'Governance by Conditionality: EU Rule Transfer to the Candidate Countries of Central and Eastern Europe', *Journal of European Public Policy*, 11: 4, 661–79.

Schimmelfennig, F. and Sedelmeier, U. (eds) (2005), *The Europeanization of Central and Eastern Europe*, Ithaca, NY: Cornell University Press.

Schmidt, V. (2002), 'Europeanization and the Dynamics and Mechanics of Economic Policy Adjustment', *Journal of European Public Policy*, 9: 6, 894–912.

Schneider, G. and Aspinwall, M. (eds) (2001), *The Rules of Integration: Institutionalist Approaches to the Study of Europe*, Manchester: Manchester University Press.

Wallace, H. (2000), 'The Institutional Setting', in H. Wallace and W. Wallace (eds) (2000), *Policy-Making in the European Union*, 4th edn, Oxford: Oxford University Press, 3–37.

Wallace, H. (2005), 'Exercising Power and Influence in the EU: The Roles of Member States', in S. Bulmer and C. Lequesne (eds), *The Member States of the European Union*, Oxford: Oxford University Press, 25–44.

Wallace, H. (2010), 'An Institutional Anatomy and Five Policy Modes', in H. Wallace, M. Pollack, and A. Young (eds), *Policy-Making in the European Union*, 6th edn, Oxford: Oxford University Press, 69–104.

Waltz, K. (1979), *Theory of International Politics*, New York: McGraw Hill.

Wessels, W., Maurer, A., and Mittag, J. (eds) (2003), *Fifteen into One? The European Union and its Member States*, Manchester: Manchester University Press.

Woll, C. and Jacquot, S. (2010), 'Using Europe: Strategic Action in Multi-level Politics' *Comparative European Politics*, 8: 1, 110–26.

Zeff, E. and Pirro, E. (2006), *The European Union and the Member States*, 2nd edn, Boulder, Co.: Lynne Rienner.

PART I

Analysis

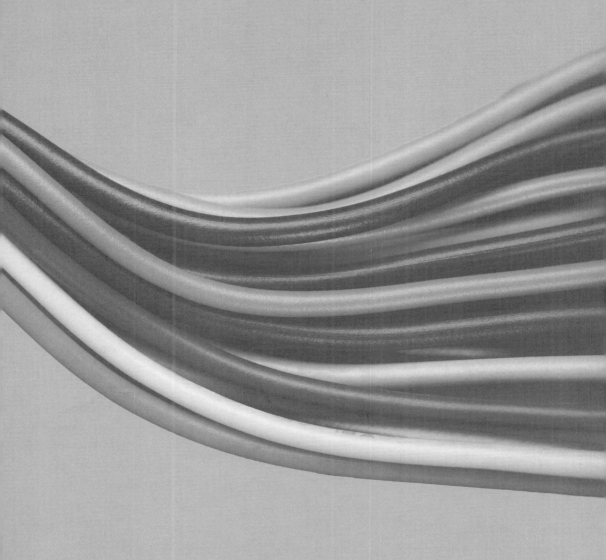

CHAPTER 2

Europeanization: Concept, Theory, and Methods

Paolo R. Graziano and Maarten P. Vink

▍ Summary

Membership of the European Union demands a fundamental reorganization of the way politics is organized in the member states of the EU. Europeanization studies focus on the impact of EU membership on member states. In this chapter we discuss a number of fundamental issues that arise when studying Europeanization. What actually is Europeanization? And what is not? How can we explain why some parts of political life seem more affected by the process of European integration than others? How do we explain variation between member states? These questions are important if we want to understand what Europeanization means with respect to the evolution of national democratic political regimes and their decision-making processes. We provide examples of Europeanization studies and also discuss how to design a good Europeanization study.

Introduction: The Europeanization Turn in EU Studies: Beyond Grand Theory

Since the late fifties, European studies became increasingly relevant first in international relations and then in comparative politics (Risse-Kappen, 1996). The main theoretical focus for almost forty years regarded the formation of the new European polity. On the one hand, the 'neofunctionalist' reading of Europe, provided initially by Haas (1958), focused on the societal driving forces of European political integration. Haas defined political integration as a 'process whereby political actors in several distinct national settings are persuaded to shift their loyalties, expectations, and political activities toward a new centre, whose institutions possess or demand jurisdiction over the pre-existing national states' (Haas 1958: 16). In the original analysis provided by Haas, European integration was fuelled by the 'loyalty shift' expressed by non-state elites—such as the new 'regional' bureaucracy and interest associations formed at the level of the 'new' region—who considered a new (European) supranational setting to be in line with their predefined social and economic preferences. The key motors of European integration, in this view, were non-state actors seeking a new centre which could be beneficial to their selected interests. In the words of a 'proud' neofunctionalist:

regional integration is an intrinsically sporadic and conflictual process, but one in which, under conditions of democracy and pluralistic representation, national governments will find themselves increasingly entangled in regional pressures and end up resolving their conflicts by conceding a wider scope and devolving more authority to the regional organizations they have created.

(Schmitter 2004: 47)

Put differently, in the neofunctionalist reading, European integration follows an 'expansive logic of sector integration' in the form of inevitable 'spillovers' from one economic sector to the other (functional spillover) which eventually also leads to (European) political integration (political spillover).

On the other hand, the 'intergovernmentalists'—such as Stanley Hoffmann (1966, 1982)—or the 'liberal' pioneers of intergovernmentalism (Moravcsik 1993, 1998) challenged both the empirical and theoretical strengths of neofunctionalism since, as for the former, it increasingly appeared that neofunctionalism 'mispredicted both the trajectory and the process of EC evolution' (Moravcsik 1993: 476) and, as for the latter, neofunctionalism 'lacked a theoretical core clearly enough specified to provide a sound basis for precise empirical testing and improvement' (Moravcsik 1993: 476). In fact, the main claim of intergovernmentalists was that after years of European integration still the state was 'alive and kicking' and capable of shaping further the process of supranational integration. As Hoffmann notes in his 1982 contribution: 'the most striking reality is not the frequent and well-noted impotence of the so-called sovereign state. It is its survival' (Hoffmann, 1982, 21).

And, according to the intergovernmentalist reading of the process of regional integration, the main motors of European integration traditionally were not non-state actors but rather national governments.

The best way of analyzing the EEC is not in the traditional terms of integration theory, which assumes that the members are engaged in the formation of a new, supranational political entity superseding the old nations . . . and that there is a zero-sum game between the nation-states on the one hand, the EEC on the other. . . . It is to look at the EEC as an international regime.

(Hoffmann 1982: 33)

Therefore, intergovernmentalism focuses on the enduring presence of 'rational' governments which domestically form their preferences and subsequently negotiate at the regional (i.e. European) level.

We will not dwell here on a discussion of the two main contrasting theoretical understandings of European integration, but we argue that it is relevant to better understand the 'Europeanization turn' in EU studies in connection with the loss of attractiveness of other approaches which have been mainstream for decades. In fact, until the end of the nineties—with few exceptions (Bulmer 1983; Ladrech 1994)—the main focus of European studies scholars was the description and explanation of the European integration process whereas very limited space was left for a systematic analysis of the ongoing relationship between regional and domestic political regimes. And this is where Europeanization comes in as a new phase in European integration studies or a 'third step' in a European-based regional integration theory (Caporaso 2007).

Europeanization research builds on the above mentioned classic integration perspectives. First, with respect to neofunctionalism and its more recent variants—supranational governance (Sandholtz and Stone Sweet 1998) and multilevel governance (Hooghe and Marks 2001; Piattoni 2009)—the Europeanization literature is inspired by the notion of 'uploading' domestic societal preferences at the EU level. Second, with respect to the intergovernmentalist approach, Europeanization is inspired by the focus on the domestic state-related sources of European decision making and their consequences on the nature of EU institutions and policies.

Nevertheless, the Europeanization approach goes clearly beyond this European centred orientation of 'classic' integration theories by focusing primarily on a different target: the domestic level. To be sure, since the mid-nineties the domestic 'shift' was inbuilt in the administrative oriented analysis of domestic patterns of adaptation to EU membership (Rometsch and Wessels 1996; Meny, Muller, and Quermonne 1996; Hanf and Soetendorp 1998; Börzel 1999; Kassim *et al.* 2000; Héritier *et al.* 2001; Zeff and Pirro 2001). This reorientation was clearly connected to the expansion of EU powers which followed the adoption (and ratification) of the Maastricht Treaty which reinvigorated the EU political arena as a provider of new political opportunities for both domestic governments and societal actors involved in national decision making. The above mentioned contributions, together with the first, more explicit, Europeanization studies (Olsen 1996; Harmsen 1999), are characterized by a clear change of focus since they are primarily centred on domestic administrative adaptation, although others have considered also the changes in the 'organizational logic of national politics and policy-making' induced by EU membership (Ladrech 1994) or, more broadly, changes that occurred within 'national political systems' connected to European integration (Goetz and Hix 2000).

In the early stages of the development of Europeanization research, the main analytical core of the studies was the domestic implementation of EU policies, which also shared several substantive—but not methodological—features with the 'EU directive transposition' research agenda (Boerzel 2001; Mastenbroek 2003; Kaeding 2006). The implementation studies originated from the idea that European integration remains an incomplete political project as long as European rules are not implemented according to their intentions (Sverdrup 2007). In fact, the first main empirical focus of Europeanization research was in the most developed European policy domains such as environmental policy (Knill 1998), transport policy (Héritier *et al.* 2001), and cohesion policy (Conzelmann 1998; Benz and Eberlein 1999). Among the 'classic' European policies, only agricultural policy has been relatively absent from early Europeanization research, arguably because it is probably the policy domain par excellence that has been virtually completely 'European' on account of the integrated character of the Common Agricultural Policy. Yet, as Roederer-Rynning (2007) demonstrates, even in the field of agricultural policy the domestic impact of European policies—for example with regard to state-farmer relations—is far from self-evident. In the early 2000s also, other policy domains where the involvement of the EU was of lesser importance were investigated, such as social policy (Graziano 2003), refugee policy (Lavenex 2001), or even citizenship policy (Checkel 2001; Vink 2001). These studies contain mainly qualitative case studies or focused policy-based comparisons of a limited number of countries, whereas another set of contributions were more country-based analysis which went beyond a mere sectoral analysis (Falkner 2001; Grabbe 2001).

Furthermore, Europeanization research has also provided more focused 'European' analytical lenses for the study of domestic politics and policy making. Both political scientists and political sociologists have increasingly realized that the EU, as an advanced instance of regional integration, has become a significant part of national politics. Especially with regard to policy making, it is currently very rare to find domestic policies which are not somehow connected to European ones. Without considering the European sources of domestic policies, today any domestic-centred policy analysis would neglect important international constraints and opportunities for political actors. This observation holds true beyond policy analysis and applies to changing domestic opportunity structures and political environments more generally. First, the study of the domestic executives could not be carried out without a clear understanding of how the governments developed and coordinated domestic preferences in EU negotiations and increasingly tried to oversee domestic implementation of EU policies (Zeff and Pirro

BOX 2.1	Europeanization: twelve key publications

Ladrech 1994, Europeanization of Domestic Politics and Institutions
Path-breaking study that focuses on the case of France

Bulmer and Burch 1998, Organising for Europe
Study of the Europeanization of British central government

Börzel 1999, Towards Convergence in Europe?
Study of the EU and regional government in Germany and Spain

Knill and Lehmkuhl 1999, How Europe Matters
Study of three different mechanisms of Europeanization

Haverland 2000, National Adaptation to European Integration
Study that points at the importance of institutional veto points

Radaelli 2000, Whither Europeanization
Seminal paper on the concept of Europeanization

Goetz and Hix 2000, Europeanised Politics?
Edited volume with important studies by scholars of comparative politics

Green Cowles *et al.* 2001, Transforming Europe
Edited volume which advocated a 'three-step' approach to Europeanization

Olsen 2002, The Many Faces of Europeanization
Study of the different ways in which Europeanization can be conceived

Schmidt 2006, Democracy in Europe
Study about the impact of European integration on national democracies

Graziano and Vink 2007, Europeanization
Edited volume (25 chapters) on the state-of-the-art in Europeanization research

Ladrech 2010, Europeanization and National Politics
First single-authored textbook on Europeanization, with a strong comparative politics focus

See References at the end of this chapter for full references.

2001). Second, other aspects of national politics have also been increasingly investigated adopting—more or less explicitly—Europeanization analytical lenses: domestic parliaments (Holzhacker 2002), political parties (Ladrech 2002), party systems (Mair 2000), interest groups (Grote and Lang 2003), and local governments (Pasquier 2005).

When we consider the development of the Europeanization literature, a peak of important publications emerges at the end of the 1990s and in the early 2000s (see Box 2.1; see also Featherstone for a bibliometric analysis of the period 1981–2001, Featherstone 2003: 5). Why did the Europeanization turn in European integration studies emerge during the second half of the nineties? Mainly on account of two fundamental reasons: the first is endogenous to EU studies, and the second is exogenous. The first motivation is connected to the loss of analytical appeal of the almost four decades-long debate between 'neofunctionalists' and 'intergovernmentalists' and the need to move onto a new stage in EU studies. As the authors of the path-breaking contribution on Europeanization (*Transforming Europe: Europeanization and Domestic Change*) point out in the introduction to their book, it was the result of a 'joint research project [that wanted to] examine the "next phase" of European integration studies: the impact of the European Union on the members states' (Green Cowles *et al.* 2001: ix). Put differently, by the end of the nineties it clearly emerged—at least to some inspired scholars—that European integration studies needed to enter into a new phase which would focus on different topics with respect to the more consolidated European integration literature. The somewhat sterile contraposition between the two leading interpretations of the EU needed to be overcome by shifting the analytical focus. The second reason is connected to the emerging relevance of EU policies and institutions after the ratification of the Maastricht Treaty. As in the case of national parliaments, during the second half of the nineties the political actors were discovering the new domestic obligations connected to the expansion of EU powers and therefore needed to adapt to a new multilevel political game. Also, domestic political actors had increasingly to cope with the consolidation of, or new competencies emerging in, numerous policy fields such as social policy (Graziano 2003), immigration policy (Vink 2001), or foreign policy (Tonra 2001). To be sure, the importance of European integration for domestic affairs has been a long-lasting phenomenon, since domestic courts have applied and interpreted European law, for over thirty years (Stone Sweet 2004) and more recently rulings have had an increasing impact also on poorly regulated EU policies (for example, social policy; see Ferrera 2005). The judicial construction of Europe may be well acknowledged now, but until very recent times empirical evidence has been lacking of how national judges have made (and are still making) use of EU law both in 'old' EU countries and 'new' ones (Nyikos 2007; Piana 2009).

In sum, Europeanization as a research agenda has managed to end the exhausted debate between (neo)intergovernmentalists and neofunctionalists by widening the research spectrum to previously under-researched topics such as the impact of EU institutions and policies on domestic political systems. Of course, although highly fashionable, this new research agenda has been striving to gain a well reputed scientific standing since, over the years, some scholars started to question its analytical validity or, more precisely, its theoretical value (Olsen 2002: 27) or innovativeness (Radaelli 2004). As we shall see in the next sections (and also in other chapters of this volume, namely Chapters 1 and 15), the Europeanization research agenda has primarily reframed old questions regarding the mechanisms of European integration and focused on the emerging relevance of the EU for national political systems. But, before we take stock of the promises and pitfalls of Europeanization research, let us turn to the main conceptual and theoretical issues which have been raised by Europeanization.

Defining Europeanization: Conceptual Debates

The seminal contribution by Radaelli (2000) started a long-lasting debate on the 'nature of the beast' which, in this case, is not the European political organization as in Puchala's analysis (1972) but the analytical devices used in order to study the EU. From this standpoint, we are still in the middle of the 'ontological' phase in Europeanization studies since we can still find many different definitions in the literature. But before the definitional debate fully developed (late nineties) in the European integration literature there were some attempts to define the notion of Europeanization. The first acknowledged definition of Europeanization is the one provided by Ladrech in his 1994 contribution where Europeanization is defined as an 'incremental process re-orienting the direction and shape of politics to the degree that EC political and economic dynamics become part of the organizational logic of national politics and policy-making' (Ladrech 1994: 69). By 'organizational logic' the author refers to the 'adaptive processes of organizations to a changed or changing environment' (Ladrech 1994: 71). A few years later, when the Europeanization literature was just about to take off, in the first systematic and comparative attempt to look at Europeanization processes the definition of Europeanization became 'the emergence and development at the European level of distinct structures of governance, that is, of political, legal, and social institutions associated with political problem solving that formalize interactions among the actors, and of policy networks specializing in the creation of authoritative European rules' (Risse *et al.* 2001: 3). In 2003—in the final version of Radaelli's above mentioned contribution—Europeanization was defined as a set of,

processes of (a) construction (b) diffusion and (c) institutionalization of formal and informal rules, procedures, policy paradigms, styles, "ways of doing things" and shared beliefs and norms which are first defined and consolidated in the making of EU decisions and then incorporated in the logic of domestic discourse, identities, political structures and public policies.

(Radaelli 2003: 30)

Finally, in a 'state of the art' contribution, Vink and Graziano provided a broad definition of Europeanization as a process of 'domestic adaptation to European regional integration' (Vink and Graziano 2007: 7).

Bottom-up vs. Top-down

The first definition captures the most innovative feature of Europeanization: the domestic 'adaptive processes' connected to the 'changed or changing [European] environment'. In his study on France, Ladrech (1994) focuses on politics and institutions in a broad sense and carries out an empirical investigation of how the French institutional setting has been affected by the increasing role of EU institutions. Nevertheless, the definition seems to be particularly useful for institutional analysis rather than decision-making studies because of its privileged focus on the notion of 'organizational logic' rather than, more broadly, behaviour of political actors. The second definition (by Risse *et al.* 2001) is strikingly similar to the (European) political integration definition provided by Haas which is focused on the 'loyalty shift' to the European level. But, as noticed by Radaelli (2000), we should not confuse Europeanization with European integration since there would, in fact, be no need to invent new concepts with old meanings. To be sure, the various contributions which are inspired by the above mentioned definition treat Europeanization in 'top-down' fashion rather than in the advocated 'bottom-up' one, generating some conceptual confusion notwithstanding the overall empirical richness of the study. The last two definitions try to combine both set of processes (bottom-up and top-down) in order to provide a more detailed (albeit complex) characterization of Europeanization. In this respect, Radaelli's definition is quite explicit since it embodies both the construction and diffusion of a set of EU-related phenomena. In the Vink-Graziano definition, the notion of 'domestic adaptation' draws heavily on the 'adaptive processes' researched by Ladrech. As stated in the discussion of the concept, 'in order to study Europeanization we need to start at the domestic level, analyze how policies or institutions [or other political phenomena] are formed at the EU level, and subsequently determine the effects of political challenges and pressures exerted by the diffusion of European integration at the domestic level' (Vink and Graziano 2007: 7–8).

Conceptual Boundaries: What is *not* Europeanization?

To avoid the danger of conceptual stretching, as Radaelli (2003) rightly notes, we need to specify not only what Europeanization is, but also what it is *not*. Europeanization should not be confused with convergence, neither with harmonization, nor with political integration. This can be clarified as follows. *Convergence* can be a consequence of European integration, but it must not be used synonymously with Europeanization because there is a difference between a process and its consequences (Radaelli 2003: 33). There may have been convergence in monetary policies towards monetarist policy and away from Keynesianism in the member states that joined European Monetary Union (EMU) (Sbragia 2001). Yet, European regimes may be converging, as in the case of citizenship policies, however, not as a result of initiatives emanating from Brussels, but as a response to domestic considerations (Freeman and Ögelman 1998). *Harmonization* of national policies is often seen as an important goal of European integration, but empirical research suggests that Europeanization is often manifest in a 'differential' impact of European requirements on domestic policies (Héritier *et al.* 2001). European directives aimed at harmonization in, for example, gender equality policy, in effect often leave much room for continued national diversity (Caporaso and Jupille 2001). Understanding, finally, why countries pool and delegate sovereignty (Milward 1994; Moravcsik 1998) is not equal to understanding the specific dynamics, or even the unexpected consequences, this process of *political integration* brings about at the domestic level.

In recent years, Europeanization research has moved beyond these conceptual debates to a phase where '[m]ost scholars *de facto* favour a definition of Europeanization either as the domestic impact *of* the EU, and/or the domestic impact *on* the EU' (Flockhart 2010: 790). This does not mean that there is a universally shared acceptance of such definitions, but clearly much of the empirical work that has been carried out over the past years departs from an understanding of Europeanization as a process of both construction and diffusion of discourses, political strategies, institutions, and public policies. Moving beyond these conceptual discussions has also allowed the research agenda of Europeanization to move to a phase where there is more explicit attention for methodological concerns. These concerns related in particular to the question of causality: how can we show that European integration actually *causes* domestic changes? Haverland (2005) has been investigating the methodological problems connected causality in Europeanization research, and, more recently, Exadaktylos and Radaelli have taken stock of its (limited) research design capacities (Exadaktylos and Radaelli 2009). To a certain extent, at least with respect to the conceptual dimension, Europeanization has come of age.

Explaining Europeanization: Theoretical Debates

Europeanization may represent a new step in European integration theory (see also Caporaso 2007). Surprisingly, however, more conventional studies of European integration and Europeanization studies have not often been clearly linked. And this relates not only to Europeanization scholars, but also to those of European integration. It is, for example, remarkable that a recent article devoted to the development of a 'postfunctionalist theory of European integration' does not even mention Europeanization as a theoretical advancement in European integration research (Hooghe and Marks 2009).

New institutionalism

Although, theoretically, there may be a striking continuity in European integration-Europeanization studies, many authors seem not to address the issue and consider Europeanization as a mere phenomenon which needs to be (domestically) explained. In fact, as Bulmer (2007) argues, Europeanization as such is not a theory but rather a phenomenon that needs to be explained.

The theoretical added value of Europeanization lies primarily in the need to generalize on the mechanisms through which European political discourses, strategies, institutions and policies have affected domestic political systems, i.e. have led to political change. In this respect, Europeanization scholars have looked much into a 'new institutionalist' perspective (Goetz and Hix 2000). More specifically, it is well known that institutional approaches put at the centre of their object of enquiry the role of institutions in decision-making processes and, more generally, in the functioning of political systems; and institutions are classically understood as formal rules, standard operating procedures, and governmental structures. From this standpoint, Europeanization studies have mobilized all strands of the 'new institutionalist approaches'—historical, rational choice, and sociological (Hall and Taylor 1996). Historical institutionalist analysis in Europeanization research has been at the heart of several studies (Bulmer and Burch 1998; Bulmer 2009), in line with the other historical institutionalist studies beyond Europeanization (Hall and Taylor 1996: 938). The main focus of this strand of research was—and still is—the analysis of the sequences of domestic adaptations in connection to the evolution of European political discourses, strategies, institutions, and policies. Domestic political change— limited or greater—is explained in connection to concepts derived from historical institutionalism such as 'path dependency', 'increasing returns', 'positive feedbacks'. The rational choice orientation, strongly connected with more traditional studies of European integration (Moravcsik 1993, 1998), emphasizes the increasing political opportunities provided by European integration. Several studies have shown the strategic organizational adaptation displayed by interest groups which, since the early nineties, have tried to profit from the new multilevel European power structure (for further details, see Saurugger in this volume). Political change occurs primarily when domestic political actors 'rationally' use European resources in order to support predefined preferences. Finally, sociological institutionalism has been particularly used in connection to the analysis of 'cognitive' Europeanization, i.e. changes occurred in the mental frameworks of domestic political actors. The construction and diffusion of EU ideas, and the socialization provided by EU institutions and policies, have constituted a motor of change in their own right. Political change may be less visible than in the other cases, but several authors have argued—especially in those fields where the competences of the EU remain limited—that this form of Europeanization may be as powerful as more conventional forms of Europeanization in more 'classic' institutional and policy domains of the EU (Checkel 2001).

Goodness of Fit

If we turn to the theoretical relevance of Europeanization, however, what can be said after over a decade of empirical research? Europeanization has by no means obtained a strong theoretical status until now probably because it is more concerned with *domestic political change* rather than *EU political development*. Therefore, Europeanization has been used as an analytical approach to understand domestic changes, being more relevant for country specialists and comparative politics scholars. In fact, from this standpoint, some theoretical elements can be found in the Europeanization literature, which regard specifically the mechanisms of domestic political change. Probably the most interesting (and well investigated) theoretical contributions of the Europeanization literature regard, on the one hand, the 'goodness of fit' and, on the other, the 'mediating factors' concepts (Risse *et al.* 2001). The goodness

of fit hypothesis sets a clear link between the development of EU 'institutional settings, rules and practices' and the possible 'adaptational pressure' exerted on the
domestic levels when the domestic 'institutional settings, rules and practices' differ.
More specifically, 'the degree of adaptational pressure generated by Europeanization
depends on the "fit" or "misfit" between European institutions and the domestic
structures. The lower the compatibility (fit) between European institutions, on the
one hand, and national institutions on the other, the higher the adaptational pressures' (Risse *et al.* 2001: 7). We will thus expect domestic change, especially in those
cases where the 'misfit' is high and therefore the adaptational pressures are strong.

Mediating Factors

Even relevant adaptational pressures, though, do not trigger domestic change automatically. Risse, Cowles, and Caporaso continue in their theoretical analysis and
suggest that, 'in cases of high adaptational pressures, the presence or absence of mediating factors is crucial for the degree to which domestic change adjusting to Europeanization should be expected' (Risse *et al.* 2001: 9). They then continue by
identifying five mediating factors (three 'structural' and two related to 'agency'):
multiple veto points; mediating formal institutions; political and organizational cultures; differential empowerment of actors; and learning.

If we try to place these analytical tools—which can easily generate specific
hypotheses—in a broader theoretical framework, we can read Europeanization as a
possible *theory of multilevel institutional change* (in Europe) rather than a *political*
(i.e. *European*) *integration theory*. In fact, the above mentioned analytical framework
may 'travel' beyond Europe if we consider the European Union as a *species* of a
broader *genus* which is regional integration. Certainly, the EU as a regional institution has very specific features, such as a high degree of supranational authority,
which cannot easily be found in other parts of the world. Yet, if we consider that
adaptational pressures may differ significantly as a function of the institutionalization of a supranational entity, we could successfully study Europeanization as a variant of a broader, extra-EU trend of *regionalization* and apply similar analytical tools
for the study of other supranational political organizations, albeit less developed
than the European one. The prerequisite for a well equipped research strategy is to
mobilize competitive, sometimes counterfactual, explanations of possible change
(see Haverland 2007). Although not always easy to do, this exercise may strengthen
the empirical findings of any research devoted to the analysis of Europeanization (or
regionalization more in general) and its effects.

Worlds of Compliance

Building on these previous approaches, Falkner *et al.* (2005) and Falkner *et al.*
(2007) argue that existing theories to explain domestic compliance have weak explanatory power and are, at best, only 'sometimes-true theories'. Instead, a more

context-sensitive approach is needed which explains why different compliance mechanisms matter in different contexts. In particular, they argue that countries cluster into different 'worlds of compliance': the world of law observance, the world of domestic politics, and the world of transposition neglect.

In the world of law observance, abiding by EU rules is usually the dominant goal in both the administrative and the political systems. The same is only true for the administrative system when it comes to the world of domestic politics. There, the process can easily be blocked or diverted during the phase of political contestation. In the world of transposition neglect, by contrast, not even the administration acts in a dutiful way when it comes to the implementation of EU Directives. Therefore, the political process is typically not even started when it should be

(Falkner *et al.* 2007: 407)

In a more recent study, Falkner and Treib (2008) compare the new EU member states with the fifteen 'old' member states that they investigated earlier and ask whether these countries constitute a fourth world of compliance. The expectation, after all, could be that the new member states might behave according to their own specific logic, such as significantly decreasing their compliance efforts after accession in order to take 'revenge' for the strong pressure of conditionality. They investigate four case studies—Czech Republic, Hungary, Slovakia, and Slovenia—and conclude that all four new member states appear to fall within their original third group, the 'world of dead letters'. See Box 2.2 for a discussion of the debate around the worlds of compliance.

Analysing Europeanization: Empirical Examples

In this section, we provide research examples covering both older and newer EU countries, as well as non-EU countries (through the European Economic Area and European Neighbourhood Policy), and focus specifically on Europeanization and public opinion and parties, political institutions and governance, and public policy. We also discuss methodological issues such as operationalization, the use of counterfactuals, and different qualitative, quantitative, and mixed approaches.

Polity

If we focus on the main polity dimensions (governments, parliaments, bureaucracies, political parties, interest groups, social movements, courts), we can understand more easily how relevant Europeanization studies have been with respect to the understanding of institutional change. Although the variance in research design makes general remarks on the empirical findings not an easy task, it is possible to identify some basic trends which have been detected by the available literature.

BOX 2.2   **The 'worlds of compliance' debate**

Gerda Falkner, an Austrian political scientist, certainly struck a chord when she and her collaborators presented a typology of different clusters of countries in the book *Complying with Europe: EU Harmonisation and Soft Law in the Member States*, published in 2005. This book is based on a large-scale qualitative project on the transposition, enforcement, and application of six EU labour law directives in fifteen member states. The comparative scope and the fact that 'compliance' was not restricted to just transposition, as is the case with many Europeanization studies, highlighted the ambition of the project, and the 'worlds of compliance' argument stood out as the most remarkable part of the study.

The 'worlds of compliance' argument was clearly a provocative one and led to considerable debate in the literature. On the one hand, it probably relates closely to intuitions that scholars might have about the extent to which non-compliance is a cultural phenomenon. Even common-sense observers would not expect compliance processes to be similar between, for example, countries from Catholic Southern Europe and those from Protestant Nordic Europe. Yet, although Falkner *et al.* are careful to avoid reifying these existing cultural stereotypes, they argue that culture matters in the implementation process, at least as one factor amongst several. To be sure, this link is hard to prove with existing data. Toshkov (2007) tested individual attitudes regarding law-abidingness as expressed in survey data with reference to the 90 cases of the 'Complying with Europe' study. He finds no direct relation with the three types of worlds, and concludes that additional work has to be done in order to specify the casual mechanism distinguishing between the types. Thomson (2009) uses selective data from the Falkner *et al.* study and argues that the misfit hypothesis in fact does hold across the different worlds of compliance: 'medium and high levels of misfit are associated with a significantly lower risk of transposition at any given time point' (2009: 14). Both tests, though, rely on small extracts of the data presented by Falkner *et al.* In short, compliance research has so far resulted in highly contradictory findings.

Gerda Falkner, Oliver Treib, Miriam Hartlapp, and Simone Leiber (2005) *Complying with Europe. EU Minimum Harmonisation and Soft Law in the Member States*. Cambridge: Cambridge University Press.

Dimiter Toshkov (2007) 'In search of the worlds of compliance: Culture and transposition performance in the European Union', *Journal of European Public Policy*, 14/6: 933–54. See also brief reply by Falkner *et al.* in same issue (14/6: 954–8).

Robert Thomson (2009) 'Same effects in different worlds: The transposition of EU directives.' *Journal of European Public Policy* 16/1: 1–18.

With regard to organization of government, two main aspects have been investigated: centre–periphery relations and the structure of the executives. The analysis of centre–periphery relations has primarily shown that 'the EU is not causing any convergence between the member states [since t]he impact of the EU is strongly mediated by pre-existing domestic power balances' (Bursens 2007: 119) which mostly means that strong—and not largely funded by EU policies—regions have been empowered by the EU. Furthermore, a recent special issue of *Regional & Federal Studies* has also addressed the ways through which Europeanization opens up new 'spaces for politics' and it also provides new political opportunities for non-institutional actors (such as social partners and NGOs) to perform institutional and policy functions at the regional level (Carter and Pasquier 2010). The changing structures of domestic governments have also been an object of empirical enquiry over the past years. Again, despite the common development of new governmental offices specialized in EU matters, research has provided unchallenged evidence of institutional variance rather than institutional convergence towards a EU-driven model. Another key research focus regarded the coordination modes in the various domestic government structures. For example, Kassim identifies two key dimensions of variance in national coordination systems, namely *coordination ambition* and *coordination centralization*. Putting the two dimensions on a grid produces four basic coordination types: comprehensive centralizers, comprehensive decentralized, selective centralizers, and selective decentralized (Kassim 2003: 92).

Also, political parties have been affected by Europeanization. Mair (2007) has extensively discussed the mechanisms of penetration and institutionalization through which Europeanization has exercised a direct or indirect impact on party politics and party systems. More specifically, Mair (2007: 157) suggests that the Europeanization literature on party politics has identified four possible (and empirically detected) outcomes of Europeanization: the emergence of new anti-European parties, or anti-European sentiments within existing political parties (such as in the case of the Italian Lega Nord, Albertazzi and McDonnell 2005); the creation and consolidation of pan-European party coalitions (Külahci 2010); the hollowing out of national party competition, constraints on domestic decision making, and devaluation of national electoral competition such as in the case of central and eastern countries who accessed the EU in early two-thousands (Grabbe 2001); and the emergence of alternative and non-partisan channels of representation, as in the analysis provided by Beyers and Kerremans (2004).

The Europeanization of interest groups and social movements has also been an increasingly researched topic in the literature. Although the general balance is clearly in favour of interest groups rather than of social movements, there are some noteworthy exceptions. In the analysis coordinated by Imig and Tarrow (2001), Europeanization—somewhat in disguise since it focused on the European dimension of social movements' activities—was already at the centre of their research agenda. The findings show that social movements have not been particularly affected by Europeanization with respect to their mobilization capacity, although they have clearly contributed to building a European public sphere space (della Porta and Caiani 2009). Interest groups were at the heart of the neofunctionalist account of European integration, and also the Europeanization literature has been focusing on the topic: recently two special issues were devoted to the European dimension of interest group representation (Coen 2007; Beyers *et al.* 2008). The main findings (also discussed in Eising 2007) demonstrate that Europeanization has strongly affected interest groups by promoting new 'political opportunities structures' both at the EU and at the national level. Recent research has further qualified the previous research: in the words of Beyers and Kerremans, 'although the EU creates many new opportunities for domestic groups to adapt, Europeanization is not a natural or immediate response' (2007: 477). What becomes particularly relevant in explaining EU-induced interest groups' empowerment is the degree of dependency on governmental or EU resources: the more dependent an interest group is on domestic resources, the less 'Europeanized' it will be (Beyers and Kerremans 2007).

Europeanization has also affected the judiciary's powers at the domestic level. As with the other polity dimensions, the courts' adaptation to European law has been a differentiated one. Some courts have easily incorporated the supremacy of European law (such as in the case of the Netherlands) whereas others 'have yet to bow their heads to the complete superiority of EC law' (Nyikos 2007: 185). But why has such a differential adaptation process occurred? In principle, all the courts could have benefitted from the reference to European law since it may provide further opportunities for judicial empowerment. Empirical research, though, has shown that, in several cases, domestic courts refer to European law and to the ECJ rulings primarily for organizational reasons since 'outsourcing is desirable when actors within an organization face problems that only appear infrequently and thus from which it makes no sense that someone within the organization develops the knowledge necessary to confront them' (Ramos 2002: 11). Furthermore, on account of the domestic variance in legal traditions, in several cases domestic courts had to cope with growing inconsistencies between European and national law and therefore a growing set of disputes arose with reference to the compatibility of the two law sources—European and domestic. These inconsistencies have led to greater domestic courts' reference to European law—thus increasing EU-induced changes in the functioning of domestic courts.

Finally, important research connecting Europeanization and enlargement has been carried out by several scholars (see Schimmelfennig and Sedelmeier 2005; Sedelmeier 2006) who have pointed out that the influence of EU candidate countries in the context of eastern enlargement was greater than on member states, and was conducive to some convergence—although the adaptation to the EU was differentiated since diversity still persists 'both between eastern and western Europe and within the new member states' (Sedelmeier 2006: 14).

Policy Domains

The political dimension which has been empirically investigated the most is the domain of public policy (see also Bulmer and Radaelli in this volume). Following the increasing competences of European institutions, numerous domestic policies have been reshaped by the growing EU multilevel political system. Initially, mainly European 'market-making' policies (i.e. policies aimed at the development of a European single market) were concerned. Since the late eighties, virtually all domestic policy areas have been affected by Europeanization. Clearly, the most developed EU policy domains were also the policies which offered the most relevant opportunities and constraints to domestic policy settings: agriculture, cohesion, economic, and environmental national policies became increasingly linked to the evolution of EU decision making (Roederer-Rynning 2007; Börzel 2007; Bache 2007; Dyson 2007). Also, in the case of public policy, domestic pressures gave birth to differential adaptation processes at the domestic level. Furthermore, the policy domain has proven to be probably the best case to test the 'goodness of fit' hypothesis. More specifically, much empirical research grounded in the new institutionalist process tracing approach, has pointed out that a) the more binding the EU policies are (i.e. supported by 'hard law' such as regulations and directives), the more probable it is—in cases of 'policy misfit'—for domestic policies to be subject to strong adaptational pressures; b) the more 'mediating factors' (i.e. domestic actors such as governments, political parties, interest groups, and the like) support EU policies, the more intense and rapid the policy change will be. In fact, empirical findings in various policy areas have provided support for these overall hypotheses. More recently, policies regulated by 'soft law' (such as recommendations and communications) have also been scrutinized, such as social policy (Falkner 2007), and the results—although not unilateral— have been consistent overall with the 'goodness of fit hypothesis' (Thomson 2009; Graziano *et al.* 2011). Also, other policies, which still lie at the heart of national sovereignty, have been affected somewhat by the 'Open Method of Coordination' (explicitly or implicitly) which has been increasingly used in fiscal and foreign policy domains (Hallerberg *et al.* 2009; Wong 2007).

Research design

If we look at the existing literature on Europeanization, what is striking is the limited use of coherent research designs (Exadaktylos and Radaelli 2009). One key problem of much of the Europeanization literature is what can be called an over-determination of the European factor when explaining domestic change. In other words: Europeanization researches focus too much on the importance of 'Europe' when explaining domestic change. Especially when looking at policy changes at the national level, we should carefully try to distinguish Europeanization from, for instance, developments which are embedded rather in a wider globalization process (Graziano 2003). At the same time, plausible alternative explanations for domestic change may not only be derived by looking beyond European pressures, but also by taking into account endogenous processes within national political systems. A change of government, to use a simple example, could well be a better explanation for, say, a restriction of immigration policy than a still vague notion of 'fortress Europe' (Vink 2005).

What matters for domestic actors and institutions is how the delegation to the European level affects policy outcomes in the domestic arena. Put another way, who are the winners and losers from the EU? At face value, such an approach would imply that we need to look at domestic policy A, domestic institution B, or domestic actor C, and analyse change in terms of policy substance, institutional set-up, or political behaviour between the time before (t_0) and after (t_1) a specific European dimension is introduced in a given policy area or a new European agency or coordination mechanism is created. In this way one can, as it were, analyse Europeanization by observing the 'net change' at the domestic level between t_0 and t_1.

In reality, things are, of course, not so simplistic as increasingly intertwined political systems make it difficult to detect what causes what (Mair 2007). Yet, if one thing becomes clear quickly it is that, even in this simplistic modelling, there is nothing inherently 'top-down' about Europeanization research (see Figure 2.1). On the contrary, to assess the 'net result' of European regional integration without making that European factor 'a cause in search of an effect' (Goetz and Hix 2000), domestic change can only be accounted for by starting from a—hypothesized—domestic situation *ex ante* (the t_0 situation). This means that in order to study Europeanization we need to start at the domestic level, analyse how policies or institutions are formed at the EU level, and subsequently determine the effects of political challenges and pressures exerted by the diffusion of European integration at the domestic level (see Börzel 2002: 193). Such a 'bottom-up-down' research design is probably the only guarantee, if any, for a due consideration of the European factor as one of several alternative explanations. In addition, as also visualized in Figure 2.1, Europeanization needs to be understood not only as 'vertical' processes (bottom-up versus top-down) but also as a 'horizontal' process. Such horizontal Europeanization results from the fact that, in an integrated Europe, actors—civil servants, lobbyists, entrepreneurs etc.—increasingly have cross-border contacts and exchange information and expertise. In such a conception, Europeanization is not about a Brussels-induced 'top-down' domestic adaptation, but rather about change induced by policy learning and diffusion.

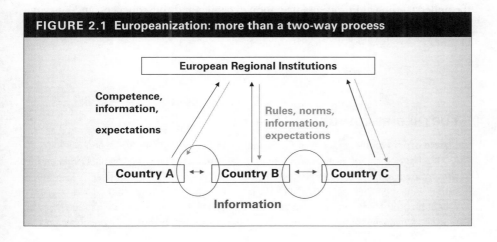

FIGURE 2.1 Europeanization: more than a two-way process

European Regional Institutions

Competence, information, expectations

Rules, norms, information, expectations

Country A ↔ Country B ↔ Country C

Information

Conclusion: Future Challenges in Analysing Europeanization

Europeanization, despite its enduring 'pitfalls' (Lehmkuhl 2007), not only has come of age but has also allowed European studies to better understand the politics of European integration. By focusing on both the EU construction and domestic diffusion processes, Europeanization has provided new analytical and empirical pathways to unveil the dynamics of the EU multilevel political system. The current 'post-ontological' phase in Europeanization studies may not have to focus on defining what Europeanization is (or is not) but still needs to become more sophisticated with respect to research design and research methods, as briefly discussed in the previous section. Cautiously designed and comparative research efforts may allow Europeanization to move from the realm of 'fashion', and consolidate itself as a useful analytical tool which could 'travel' also beyond Europe by focusing on broader research questions such as institutional change, policy change, (supranational) political development, and regionalization.

Currently, the most problematic, yet promising, challenge is twofold. First, to take seriously the 'uploading' and 'downloading' dimensions of Europeanization. This implies that the research focus cannot be confined to the analysis of the impact of the EU—as in the first stages on Europeanization research, despite the bottom-up definitions—but needs to develop greater links between the two (equally important) sides of the Europeanization coin. Second, more sophisticated hypotheses linking these two aspects need to be formulated. For example, what are the relationships between preference formation and negotiation capacity at the EU level, on the one hand, and the mechanisms of 'downloading' on the other? Put differently, sound hypotheses are needed linking actors' and institutions' behaviour in both phases of Europeanization. By enriching the research hypotheses, and going beyond the now well established 'goodness of fit' one (which is primarily focused on the 'downloading' phase), Europeanization research may mature even more and become even more promising with respect to the understanding of European integration dynamics and consequences, and—beyond the EU—shed new light on the growing regional integration research agenda.

FURTHER READING

Classic papers on the concept of Europeanization are by Radaelli (2000) and Olsen (2002). For original theoretical arguments, see work by Knill and Lehmkuhl (1999) and Green Cowles, Caporaso, and Risse (2001). For an overview of theoretical discussions, see Bulmer (2007). Haverland (2005) is a good starting point for a reflection on the key methodological issue of 'causality'. Graziano and Vink (2007) provide an overview of the core research questions and key findings in Europeanization research. Chapters by Radaelli and Pasquier, and Bulmer and Haverland in that volume are particularly useful overviews of conceptual, theoretical, and methodological discussions. See also Box 2.1 with twelve key 'Europeanization' publications.

WEB LINKS

The most relevant website for issues relating to Europeanization is offered by the web portal that brings together various online papers on EU studies, (**http://eiop.or.at/ erpa/**). Several of the published chapters and articles on Europeanization were first available at this site, notably as European Integration online Papers (EIoP). This is a working paper series that has now been officially recognized as a peer-reviewed academic journal and is included in the authoritative Social Science Citation Index.

REFERENCES

Albertazzi, D. and McDonnell, D. (2005), 'The Lega Nord in the Second Berlusconi Government: In a League of Its Own', *West European Politics*, 28/5: 952–72.

Bache, I. (2007), 'Cohesion Policy', in P. Graziano and M. P. Vink (eds), *Europeanization: New Research Agendas*, Basingstoke: Palgrave Macmillan, 239–52.

Benz, A. and Eberlein, T. (1999), 'The Europeanization of Regional Policies: Patterns of Multi-level Governance', *Journal of European Public Policy*, 6/2: 329–48.

Beyers, J. and Kerremans, B. (2004), 'Bureaucrats, Politicians, and Societal Interests: How is European Policy Making Politicized?', *Comparative Political Studies*, 37/10: 1119–51.

Beyers, J. and Kerremans, B. (2007), 'Critical Resource Dependencies and the Europeanization of Domestic Interest Groups', *Journal of European Public Policy*, 14/3: 460–81.

Beyers, J., Eising, R., and Maloney, W. (2008), 'Researching Interest Groups' Politics in Europe and Elsewhere: Much We Study, Little We Know?', *West European Politics*, 31/6: 1103–28.

Börzel, T. (1999), 'Towards Convergence in Europe? Institutional Adaptation to Europeanization in Germany and Spain', *Journal of Common Market Studies*, 37/ 4: 573–96.

Börzel, T. (2001), 'Non-compliance in the European Union: Pathology or Statistical Artefact?', *Journal of European Public Policy*, 8/5: 803–24.

Börzel, T. (2002), 'Pace-Setting, Foot-Dragging, and Fence-Sitting: Members States Responses to Europeanization', *Journal of Common Market Studies*, 40/2: 193–214.

Börzel, T. (2007), 'Environmental Policy', in P. Graziano and M. P. Vink (eds), *Europeanization: New Research Agendas*, Basingstoke: Palgrave Macmillan, 226–38.

Bulmer, S. (1983), 'Domestic Politics and European Community Policy-Making', *Journal of Common Market Studies*, 21/4: 349–64.

Bulmer, S. (2007), 'Theorizing Europeanization', in P. Graziano and M. P. Vink (eds), *Europeanization: New Research Agendas*, Basingstoke: Palgrave Macmillan, 46–58.

Bulmer, S. (2009), 'Politics in Time meets the Politics of Time: Historical Institutionalism and the EU Timescape', *Journal of European Public Policy*, 16/2: 307–24.

Bulmer, S. and Burch, M. (1998), 'Organising for Europe: Whitehall, the British State and the European Union', *Public Administration*, 76/4: 601–28.

Bursens, P. (2007), 'State Structures', in P. Graziano and M. P. Vink (eds), *Europeanization: New Research Agendas*, Basingstoke: Palgrave Macmillan, 115–27.

Caporaso, J. (2007), 'The Three Worlds of Regional Integration Theory', in P. Graziano and M. P. Vink, *Europeanization: New Research Agendas*, Basingstoke: Palgrave Macmillan, 23–34.

Caporaso, J. and Jupille, J. (2001), 'The Europeanization of Gender Equality Policy and Domestic Structural Change', in M. Green Cowles, J. Caporaso, and T. Risse (eds), *Transforming Europe? Europeanization and Domestic Change*, Ithaca: Cornell University Press, 21–43.

Carter, C. and Pasquier, R. (2010), 'Studying Regions as "Spaces for Politics": Territory, Mobilization and Political Change', *Regional and Federal Studies*, Special Issue, 20/3.

Checkel, J. (2001), 'The Europeanization of Citizenship?', in M. Green Cowles, J. Caporaso, and T. Risse (eds), *Transforming Europe? Europeanization and Domestic Change*, Ithaca: Cornell University Press, 180–97.

Coen, D. (2007), 'Empirical and Theoretical Studies in EU Lobbying', *Journal of European Public Policy*, 14/3: 333–45.

Conzelmann, T. (1998), '"Europeanization" of Regional Development Policies? Linking the Multi-level Approach with Theories of Policy Learning and Policy Change', *European Integration online Papers*, 4/2.

della Porta, D. and Caiani, M. (2009), *Social Movements and Europeanization*, Oxford: Oxford University Press.

Dyson, K. (2007), 'Economic Policy', in P. Graziano and M. P. Vink (eds), *Europeanization: New Research Agendas*, Basingstoke: Palgrave Macmillan, 281–94.

Eising, R. (2007), 'Interest Groups and Social Movements', in P. Graziano and M. P. Vink (eds), *Europeanization: New Research Agendas*, Basingstoke: Palgrave Macmillan.

Exadaktylos, T. and Radaelli, C. (2009), 'Research Design in European Studies: The Case of Europeanization', *Journal of Common Market Studies*, 47/3: 507–30.

Falkner, G. (2001), 'The Europeanization of Austria: Misfit, Adaptation and Controversies', *European Integration online Papers*, 5/13.

Falkner, G. (2007), 'Social Policy', in P. Graziano and M. P. Vink (eds), *Europeanization: New Research Agendas*, Basingstoke: Palgrave Macmillan, 253–65.

Falkner, G. and Treib, O. (2008), 'Three Worlds of Compliance or Four? The EU-15 Compared to New Member States', *Journal of Common Market Studies*, 46/2: 293–313.

Falkner, G., Hartlapp, M., and Treib, O. (2007), 'Worlds of Compliance: Why Leading Approaches to European Union Implementation are only "Sometimes-True Theories"', *European Journal of Political Research*, 46/3: 395–416.

Falkner, G., Treib, O., Hartlapp, M., and Leiber, S. (2005), *Complying with Europe: EU Harmonisation and Soft Law in the Member States*, Cambridge: Cambridge University Press.

Featherstone, K. (2003), 'Introduction. In the Name of "Europe"', in K. Featherstone and C. Radaelli, *The Politics of Europeanization*, Oxford: Oxford University Press.

Ferrera, M. (2005), *The Boundaries of Welfare*, Oxford: Oxford University Press.

Flockhart, T. (2010), 'Europeanization or Eu-ization? The Transfer of European Norms across Time and Space', *Journal of Common Market Studies*, 48/4: 787–810.

Freeman, G. P. and Ögelman, N. (1998), 'Homeland Citizenship Policies and the Status of Third Country Nationals in the European Union', *Journal of Ethnic and Migration Studies*, 24/4: 769–88.

Goetz, K. and Hix, S. (eds) (2000), *Europeanised Politics? European Integration and National Political Systems*, London: Frank Cass.

Grabbe, H. (2001), 'How Does Europeanization Affect CEE Governance? Conditionality, Diffusion and Diversity', *Journal of European Public Policy*, 8/6: 1013–31.

Graziano, P. (2003), 'Europeanization or Globalization? A Framework for Empirical Research (with some evidence from the Italian case)', *Global Social Policy*, 3/2: 173–94.

Graziano, P. and Vink, M. P. (eds) (2007), *Europeanization: New Research Agendas*, Basingstoke: Palgrave Macmillan.

Graziano, P. R., Jacquot, S., and Palier, B. (2011), 'Letting Europe In. The Domestic Usages of Europe in (Re)conciliation Policies', *European Journal of Social Security*, Special Issue, 13: 1–2.

Green Cowles, M., Caporaso, J., and Risse, T. (eds) (2001), *Transforming Europe: Europeanization and Domestic Change*, Ithaca: Cornell University Press.

Grote, J. and Lang, J. (2003), 'Europeanization and Organizational Change in National Trade Associations: An Organizational Ecology Perspective', in K. Featherstone and C. Radaelli (eds), *The Politics of Europeanization*, Oxford: Oxford University Press.

Haas, E. B. (1958), *The Uniting of Europe: Political, Social and Economic Forces, 1950–1957*, Stanford, CA: Stanford University Press.

Hall, P. A. and Taylor, R. C. R. (1996), 'Political Science and the Three New Institutionalisms', *Political Studies*, 44/5: 936–57.

Hallerberg, M., Strauch, R. R., and von Hagen, J. (2009), *Fiscal Governance in Europe*, Cambridge: Cambridge University Press.

Hanf, K. and Soetendorp, B. (eds) (1998), *Adapting to European Integration: Small States and the European Union*, London and New York: Longman.

Harmsen, R. (1999), 'The Europeanization of National Administrations: A Comparative Study of France and the Netherlands', *Governance*, 12/1: 81–113.

Haverland, M. (2000), 'National Adaptation to European Integration. The Importance of Institutional Veto Points', *Journal of Public Policy*, 20/1: 83–103.

Haverland, M. (2007), 'Does the EU Cause Domestic Developments? The Problem of Case Selection', *European Integration online Papers*, 9/2.

Héritier, A., Kerwer, D., Knill, C., Lehmkuhl, D., Teutsch, M., and Douillet, A.-C. (2001), *Differential Europe: The European Union Impact on National Policymaking*, Boulder, CO: Rowman and Littlefield.

Hoffmann, S. (1966), 'Obstinate or Obsolete? The Fate of the Nation-State and the Case of Western Europe', *Daedalus*, 95/3: 862–915.

Hoffmann, S. (1982), 'Reflections on the Nation-State in Western Europe Today', *Journal of Common Market Studies*, 20/1: 21–38.

Holzhacker, R. L. (2002), 'National Parliamentary Scrutiny over EU Issues: Comparing the Goals and Methods of Governing and Opposition Parties', *European Union Politics*, 3/4: 459–79.

Hooghe, L. and Marks, G. (2001), *Multi-Level Governance and European Integration*, Lanham, ML: Rowman and Littlefield.

Hooghe, L. and Marks, G. (2009), 'A Postfunctionalist Theory of European Integration', *British Journal of Political Science*, 39/1: 1–23.

Imig, D. and Tarrow, S. (eds) (2001), *Contentious Europeans: Protest and Politics in an Emerging Polity*, Lanham: Rowman and Littlefield.

Kaeding, M. (2006), 'Determinants of Transposition Delay in the European Union', *Journal of Public Policy*, 26/3: 229–53.

Kassim, H. (2003), 'Meeting the Demands of EU Membership: The Europeanization of National Administration Systems', in K. Featherstone and C. M. Radaelli, *The Politics of Europeanization*, Oxford: Oxford University Press.

Kassim, H., Menon, A., Peters, B. G., and Wright, V. (eds) (2000), *The National Co-ordination of EU Policy: The National Level*, Oxford: Oxford University Press.

Knill, C. (1998), 'European Policies: The Impact of National Administrative Traditions', *Journal of Public Policy*, 18/1: 1–28.

Knill, C. and Lehmkuhl, D. (1999), 'How Europe Matters: Different Mechanisms of Europeanization', *European Integration online Papers*, 3/7.

Külahci, E. (2010), 'Europarties: Agenda-Setter or Agenda-Follower? Social Democracy and the Disincentives for Tax Harmonization', *Journal of Common Market Studies*, 48/5: 1283–306.

Ladrech, R. (1994), 'Europeanization of Domestic Politics and Institutions: The Case of France', *Journal of Common Market Studies*, 32/1: 69–88.

Ladrech, R. (2002), 'Europeanization and Political Parties: Towards a Framework for Analysis', *Party Politics*, 8/4: 389–403.

Ladrech, R. (2010), *Europeanization and National Politics*, Basingstoke: Palgrave Macmillan.

Lavenex, S. (2001), *The Europeanization of Refugee Policies: Between Human Rights and Internal Security*, Aldershot: Ashgate.

Lehmkuhl, D. (2007), 'Some Promises and Pitfalls of Europeanization Research', in P. Graziano and M. P. Vink (eds), *Europeanization: New Research Agendas*, Basingstoke: Palgrave Macmillan, 337–53.

Mair, P. (2000), 'The Limited Impact of Europe on National Party Systems', *West European Politics*, 23/4: 27–51.

Mair, P. (2007), 'Political Parties and Party Systems', in P. Graziano and M. P. Vink (eds), *Europeanization: New Research Agendas*, Basingstoke: Palgrave Macmillan, 154–66.

Mastenbroek, E. (2003), 'Surviving the Deadline: The Transposition of EU Directives in the Netherlands', *European Union Politics*, 4/4: 371–95.

Meny, Y., Muller, P., and Quermonne, J.-L. (eds) (1996), *Adjusting to Europe: Impact of the European Union on National Institutions and Policies*, London: Routledge.

Milward, A. S. (1994), *The European Rescue of the Nation-State*, London: Routledge.

Moravcsik, A. (1993), 'Preferences and Power in the European Community: A Liberal Intergovernmentalist Approach', *Journal of Common Market Studies*, 31/4: 473–524.

Moravcsik, A. (1998), *The Choice for Europe: Social Purpose and State Power from Messina to Maastricht*, Ithaca, NY: Cornell University Press.

Nyikos, S. A. (2007), 'Courts', in P. Graziano and M. P. Vink (eds), *Europeanization: New Research Agendas*, Basingstoke: Palgrave Macmillan.

Olsen, J. P. (1996), 'Europeanization and Nation-State Dynamics', in S. Gustavsson and L. Lewin (eds), *The Future of the Nation-State*, London: Routledge, 245–85.

Olsen, J. P. (2002), 'The Many Faces of Europeanization', *Journal of Common Market Studies*, 40/5: 921–52.

Pasquier, R. (2005), 'Cognitive Europeanization and the Territorial Effects of Multi-Level Policy Transfer. The Case of Local Development in French and Spanish Regions', *Regional and Federal Studies*, 15/3: 295–310.

Piana, D. (2009), 'The Power Knocks at the Courts' Back Door: Two Waves of Postcommunist Judicial Reforms', *Comparative Political Studies*, 42/6: 816–40.

Piattoni, S. (2009), *The Theory of Multi-level Governance*, Oxford: Oxford University Press.

Puchala, D. J. (1972), 'Of Blind Men, Elephants and International Integration', *Journal of Common Market Studies*, 10/3: 267–85.

Radaelli, C. (2000), 'Whither Europeanization? Concept Stretching and Substantive Change', *European Integration online Papers*, 4/8.

Radaelli, C. (2003), 'The Europeanization of Public Policy', in K. Featherstone. and C. Radaelli, *The Politics of Europeanization*, Oxford: Oxford University Press, 27–56.

Radaelli, C. (2004), 'Europeanization: Solution or Problem?', *European Integration online Papers*, 8/4.

Ramos, F. (2002), 'Judicial Cooperation in the European Courts: Testing Three Models of Judicial Behaviour', *Global Judicial Frontiers*, 2/1: Article 4.

Risse-Kappen, T. (1996), 'Exploring the Nature of the Beast: International Relations Theory and Comparative Policy Analysis meet the European Union', *Journal of Common Market Studies*, 34/1: 53–80.

Risse, T., Green Cowles, M., and Caporaso, J. (2001), 'Europeanization and Domestic Change: Introduction', in M. Green Cowles, J. Caporaso, and T. Risse, *Europeanization and Domestic Change*, Ithaca: Cornell University Press, 1–20.

Roederer-Rynning, C. (2007), 'Agricultural Policy', in P. Graziano and M. P. Vink, *Europeanization: New Research Agendas*, Basingstoke: Palgrave Macmillan, 212–25.

Rometsch, D. and Wessels, W. (eds) (1996), *The European Union and Member States: Towards Institutional Fusion?*, Manchester, Manchester University Press.

Sandholtz, W. and Stone Sweet, A. (1998), *European Integration and Supranational Governance*, Oxford: Oxford University Press.

Sbragia, A. (2001), 'Italy Pays for Europe: Political Leadership, Political Choice, and Institutional Adaptation', in M. Green Cowles, J. Caporaso, and T. Risse (eds), *Transforming Europe: Europeanization and Domestic Change*, Ithaca: Cornell University Press, 79–96.

Schimmelfennig, F. and Sedelmeier, U. (eds) (2005), *The Europeanization of Central and Eastern Europe*, Cornell: Cornell University Press.

Schmidt, V. A. (2006), *Democracy in Europe: The EU and National Politics*, Oxford: Oxford University Press.

Schmitter, P. (2004), 'Neo-neo-Functionalism?', in A. Wiener and T. Diez (eds), *European Integration Theory*, Oxford: Oxford University Press, 45–74.

Sedelmeier, U. (2006), 'Europeanisation in New Member and Candidate States', *Living Reviews in European Governance*, 1/3.

Stone Sweet, A. (2004), *The Judicial Construction of Europe*, Oxford: Oxford University Press.

Sverdrup, U. (2007), 'Implementation', in P. Graziano and M. P. Vink, *Europeanization: New Research Agendas*, Basingstoke: Palgrave Macmillan, 197–211.

Thomson, R. (2009), 'Same Effects in Different Worlds: The Transposition of EU Directives', *Journal of European Public Policy*, 16/1: 1–18.

Tonra, B. (2001), *The Europeanization of National Foreign Policy: Dutch, Danish and Irish Foreign Policy in the European Union*, Aldershot: Ashgate.

Toshkov, D. (2007), 'In Search of the Worlds of Compliance: Culture and Transposition Performance in the European Union', *Journal of European Public Policy*, 14/6: 933–54.

Vink, M. P. (2001), 'The Limited Europeanization of Domestic Citizenship Policy: Evidence from the Netherlands', *Journal of Common Market Studies*, 39/5: 875—96.

Vink, M. (2005), *Limits of European Citizenship: European Integration and Domestic Immigration Policies*, Basingstoke: Palgrave Macmillan.

Vink, M. P. and Graziano, P. (2007), 'Challenges of a New Research Agenda', in P. Graziano and M. P. Vink (eds), *Europeanization: New Research Agendas?*, Basingstoke: Palgrave Macmillan, 3–20.

Wong, R. (2007), 'Foreign Policy', in P. Graziano and M. P. Vink (eds), *Europeanization: New Research Agendas*, Basingstoke: Palgrave Macmillan, 321–34.

Zeff, E. E. and Pirro, E. B. (eds) (2001), *The European Union and the Member States: Co-operation, Co-ordination and Compromise*, Boulder, CO: Lynne Rienner.

PART II

The Member States

CHAPTER 3

France: Genuine Europeanization or Monnet for Nothing?

Olivier Rozenberg

■ Summary

France's relationship with the EU appears paradoxical given the contrast between the traditional pro-EU involvement of French elites and regular expressions of reticence, such as the opposition to the draft Constitutional Treaty by referendum in 2005. This chapter offers an account of this paradoxical relationship by highlighting the heterogeneity of adaptation to the EU. While public policy and legislation are becoming increasingly Europeanized, the EU has a limited impact on political life and the domestic institutional system. As a result of this mixed situation, the national narratives for supporting French membership of the EU suffer from progressive erosion and Euroscepticism subtly gaining ground.

Introduction

Making generalized statements about the relationship between a Member State and the EU involves the risk of neglecting the variety of actors and aspects that shape this relationship. In the case of France, the risk can be even greater given that the relationship between France and the EU is undoubtedly paradoxical. On the one hand, France is one of the pro-European forces in Europe. It is one of the founding members of the EU, as indicated by the French background of one of the most preeminent founding fathers of Europe, Jean Monnet (1888–1979). French political elites contributed to the building of the EU and still manifest a high level of support for the European project. With the idea of *Europe puissance* (i.e. power through Europe), both Right-wing and Left-wing leaders have spread the idea that the European level of governance can help France restore some of its lost prestige. From de Gaulle to Sarkozy, there has been continuity in the commitment of the French Presidents to a special relationship with Germany—in contrast with French politicians' attitudes after World War One (Cole 2001). To some extent, the factors that traditionally accounted for France's singularity from the EU appear much less determinant nowadays: French public policies have become more market-friendly and contribute to picture a *Changing France* (Culpepper *et al.* 2006), the governing Socialists accepted a more liberal orthodoxy since the turning-point of 1983 (Clift 2003), and the Gaullist distinctiveness of the Right is progressively disappearing after a last-ditch stand during the 1990s (Haegel 2009).

On the other hand, other elements sketch a less pro-European picture. Since the very beginning, France's elites and citizens have wavered about the loss of sovereignty to Europe that they were willing to accept (Drake 2010). In key episodes during the European integration process they said 'no': in 1954 when the National Assembly refused the European Defence Community; in 1965–66 when de Gaulle provoked the empty-chair crisis; almost, in 1992 when only 51 per cent of the voters approved the Maastricht Treaty; and in 2005 when a large majority of citizens refused the Draft Constitutional Treaty. The feeling of distance between France and the EU has been particularly acute during the 2000s, with the muffling effect of the divided executive (*cohabitation*) up to 2002, and the huge turnover of ministers for the EU (more than ten over the past decade). Furthermore, the reluctance shown by the political leaders towards the 2004 and 2007 enlargements, the difficulties of coping with the Growth and Stability Pact, the lack of dynamism of the Franco–German relationship, the cyclical tensions with the European Commission, and the loss of influence of French MPs within the European Parliament have all added to a sense of division between France and the EU. A more recent example of France's attachment to its national prerogatives was the controversy over the deportations of Roma migrants in September 2010, which created an exceptional clash between French officials and the European Commission. The response of European Affairs Minister, Pierre Lellouche, to the European Commissioner for Justice was particularly illustrative of the intergovernmental approach to the EU of the French government. He told French radio: 'It is not the manner one uses to address a great state like France, which is the mother of human rights. We are not the naughty pupil of the class whom the teacher tells off and we are not the criminal before the prosecutor' (Davies 2010).

The key to understanding the paradoxical relationship between France and the EU has to be found in the divergent aspects of France's Europeanization. This chapter argues that the ambiguity and unpredictability of France's relationship with the EU is rooted in the impact of the EU on France's domestic social and political structures. In other words, to understand France's 'bottom-up' European policy, we need to adopt a 'top-down' perspective that focuses on the effects of the EU on France's domestic policies, politics, and polity. More precisely, the comparison between different aspects of political life will clarify how divergent the extent and direction of the Europeanization process is and will shed light on the causes of the country's political ambivalence towards the EU. The first section of this chapter sketches the patterns of France's membership in the EU. The next sections evaluate the impact of EU membership on public opinion and political parties, then with regard to political institutions, and finally on public policies.

Patterns in France's Membership of the EU

France's priorities in the EU are characterized by a high level of continuity in the defence of a few positions: keeping an ambitious Common Agricultural Policy (CAP), developing an intergovernmental Common Foreign and Security Policy (CFSP), braking EU enlargements, and supporting a European economic government. The convergence between Left- and Right-wing governing parties on those priorities is indicated by the lack of tension between the Right-wing President Chirac and the Left-wing Prime Minister Jospin on most of the European dossiers from 1997 to 2002. Such remarkable convergence can be explained by the fact that the definition of France's priorities was not only dictated by the defence of domestic interests but also by a shared neo-Gaullist vision of the world. According to that vision, France should use the European megaphone to voice an autonomous and distinctive message to the world.

Elected in 2007 by promoting a rupture in Chirac's presidencies (1995–2007), Sarkozy did not really break with that logic even if he made some amendments and introduced new issues to the agenda. He defended significant spending for agriculture and fisheries. This traditional credo was voiced even more strongly as the general elections approached. The willingness to develop an independent voice in the world through CFSP first appeared less accurate given Sarkozy's good relationship with President Bush and, more importantly, given the full reintegration of France within North Atlantic Treaty Organization (NATO) military structures in 2009. Yet, his diplomacy progressively appeared more path-dependent as indicated by France's reluctance towards NATO's official participation in the bombing of Libya in March 2011. In late 2010, the return of neo-Gaullist leaders to the Ministry of Foreign and European Affairs, successively Michèle Alliot-Marie and Alain Juppé, confirmed that continuity. Proof of Sarkozy's pragmatism in EU issues was provided during the Turkish candidacy to the EU. He strongly opposed Turkey's membership during Chirac's presidency and the 2007 electoral campaign, but he did not try to stop the negotiations after being elected. Yet, he publicly recalled his position that 'Turkey was not European'. With regard to support for a European economic government, France continued to adopt an ambiguous position. On the one hand, a greater economic convergence and cohesion is officially supported, as illustrated by Sarkozy's call for solidarity towards Greece in 2010. On the other hand, France has continued not to cope with the criteria of the stability pact. But Sarkozy also introduced new issues to the agenda, as illustrated by the priorities of the French presidency of the EU Council during the second semester of 2008. Cooperation and common standards were supported regarding migration. An ambitious pro-environment position was promoted, notably in the preparation of the Copenhagen summit of 2009. The Union for the Mediterranean was officially launched in Paris in 2008. Implicitly promoted both as an alternative to the Turkish membership and unofficially seen as a way of counter-balancing the German influence in eastern Europe, the Union for the Mediterranean was rather unsuccessful on account of the geopolitical divisions of the region. Yet, the 2011 Arab Spring, and Sarkozy's willingness to appear proactive in that region, could change the situation in the future.

Recent developments in France's bilateral relationships with its main partners continue the trends of the past decade. First, the significance of the Franco–German tandem has been maintained, both regarding France's policy and the whole governance of the EU (Cole 2001). In that respect, the remarkable aspect of Sarkozy's presidency was not that his relationship with Chancellor Merkel was seemingly tense but that, despite the personal feelings of the two leaders, they needed to agree to give the EU the capacity to face forthcoming challenges. A demonstration was indisputably made in 2010 and 2011 in the design of the common mechanism aimed at providing financial stability for the euro-zone members. After initial German reluctance, Sarkozy and Merkel agreed on common positions and played a key role in the development of the

European Financial Stability Facility in 2010 and the Competiveness Pact in 2011. This indicates that, far from eroding the leadership of the two countries, the 2004 and 2007 enlargements could be analysed as an opportunity to enhance the tandem. As stated by Joachim Schild, 'in an enlarged Union, France and Germany might use enhanced co-operation inside or outside the Treaty framework in order to overcome political deadlock in the Council or the unwillingness of partners to move the EU into new policy fields' (2010: 1387). Yet, some new aspects of the Franco–German tandem can be noted. First, the initial divergences between the two partners are more publicly voiced than before. Second, the German economic balance and growth tend to give its leaders greater influence to the detriment of the French decision makers. Official discourses by French authorities indicate that Germany is increasingly regarded as *the* model to follow, as illustrated by the governmental rhetoric used to promote the 2010 pension reform in France. Third, the tandem is not less influential but probably less proactive and less imaginative than before (Cole 2008a). For instance, as noted with humour by Renaud Dehousse (2005: 140), the two main outputs of their relationship had been first the stability pact in 1997, and second the decision to soften it in 2005 when both countries were unable to respect it.

The progressive awakening of the Franco–British *entente cordiale* has been confirmed in the past few years as indicated by Sarkozy's official visit to London in 2008. In November 2010, twelve years after the Saint Malo declaration, Sarkozy and Cameron signed a treaty for defence and security cooperation at Lancaster House. This ambitious text mentions the possibility of 'pooling forces and capabilities for military operations and employment of forces'. The treaty results from a long-term convergence of the security doctrine of both countries but also, more pragmatically, from the search for savings in a context of state spending cuts. In March 2011, the leadership taken jointly by the two countries in Libya brought confirmation of their willingness to play an active role in promoting a European defence identity. The development of relationships with Germany on the one hand and the UK on the other locates France in a pivotal position within the EU. France certainly lost some of its leadership in a Union of twenty-seven members but, in comparison with Germany and the UK, it appears to be the most complete large member whose contribution to economic, budgetary and diplomatic files is still essential. It is, therefore, all the more important to question the attitudes of elites and citizens towards the EU.

Public Opinion and Political Parties: A Contained Destabilization

The rejection of the draft Constitutional Treaty could suggest that the European issue has become increasingly controversial in France. Yet, a historical look at France and empirical data point to a different conclusion: despite the 'no' vote on the Constitutional Treaty in 2005, Europe has not realigned with the French electorate, nor has the European issue had the effect of de-freezing the party system. The political system has demonstrated a large degree of resilience to the progressive increase in Euroscepticism, primarily among Right-wing voters, but also among Left-wing voters.

The Toing and Froing of Opposition to European Integration

Opposition to the European project in France did not start with the Maastricht referendum of 1992 (Guyomarch *et al.* 1998; Parsons 2003; Balme and Woll 2005a; Guieu and Le Dréau 2009). In the beginning, the European project faced strong opposition both from the Gaullists and the Communists, as illustrated by mobilization against the European Defence Community (EDC) in 1954. Even as the Gaullists' views evolved (when they acceded to power in 1959 and after de Gaulle's withdrawal in 1969), and the Communists started to decline in the late 1970s, the European project remained questionable in French public debate throughout the Vth Republic. A longitudinal analysis of the parties' manifestos (from 1958 to 1997, Sauger 2005) indicates that positive or negative views about Europe were present in the manifestos since 1958 and had the most structuring effects from 1978 to 1986. During the 1980s, political evolution specific to France forged a pro-European consensus among governing parties. Indeed, the alternation of power between parties in 1981 (when the Socialists came to power after more than two decades of opposition), the realist shift of the Left in 1983 (when Mitterrand decided to stay within the European Monetary System) and the unprecedented experience of a divided executive in 1986 (repeated in 1993 and 1997) can all be seen as factors that bestowed political parties with the expediency to avoid confrontation with each other on EU issues. From the Single Act in 1986 to the Convention on the Future of Europe in 2002, all treaty amendments have been negotiated, ratified, or implemented either by a divided executive or during alternation periods.

The 1992 referendum constituted a major shift in elite and public perception of the European issue. Indeed, comparative studies highlight a greater impact of the EU after Maastricht on the French party system (Mair 2000) and public opinion (Down and Wilson 2008) than in other countries. The *souverainisme* (a term borrowed from Quebec's emancipation movement against Canadian tutelage) emerged during the campaign as a catch-all term for opponents to EU treaties. Ideologically, the *souverainisme* was close to other movements in Europe willing to fight for restoration of national independence—the nation being viewed as the only possible locus for democracy. What was specific to France was, first, the ideological foundation of this kind of Euroscepticism. French *souverainisme* was rooted in French history, claiming the legacy of republicanism and/or Gaullism (Hainsworth *et al.* 2004). Second, the *souverainisme* found support not only at the extreme of the political spectrum but within each political family as well, including the Left—even if the movement was more marginal there. Several *souverainist* leaders created their own political formations, the most durable one being the Member of the European Parliament

(MEP) Philippe de Villiers's movement (the 'Movement for France' created in 1994), and the most significant split concerning the Gaullist family (with the 'Rally for France' created in 1999). Indeed, Chirac's choice to support the Maastricht Treaty in 1992 and, once elected President in 1995, to fulfil the Maastricht criteria for the European Monetary Union (EMU) was actually disputed by nearly half of the Gaullist MPs, followed by activists and supporters. The political groups that derived from the *souverainist* divisions enjoyed some electoral success: 13 per cent at the European elections (thirteen MEPs) both in 1994 and 1999 (when the Eurosceptic list finished first in front of the official Gaullist one) and 5 per cent at the first round of the French presidential elections of 1995 and 2002, with different candidates. One side effect of the *souverainist* success was to foster the opposition to Europe of the extreme Right party, the Front National.

In addition to the *souverainisme*, two other structured oppositions to the EU emerged in the aftermath of Maastricht. The first one praised hunting activities, localism and rural ways of life. This group concentrated on opposition to the European legislation on bird protection. However, it aimed more generally to protect local and rural specificities against Brussels' interference. Despite its relatively narrow focus, illustrated by the name of the party *Hunting Fishing Nature and Traditions*, the movement was relatively successful during European elections (six MEPs in 1994) and presidential elections (4 per cent in 2002). The second one came from the Left in the mid-2000s. For ideological, but also geopolitical reasons, the Communists and the extreme Left have long opposed the European treaties. In 2004/05, those criticisms acquired larger proportions during the referendum campaign on the draft Constitutional Treaty, when some Socialist leaders, as well as significant numbers of Socialist activists and supporters, positioned themselves against the Constitution. The denunciation of the pro laissez-faire features of European policies and the regret of the lack of *Europe sociale* were central to the discourse of these leftist movements, which remain, in other respects, highly divided internally.

A French Euroscepticism Based on Two Kinds of Anti-liberalism

French public opinion has not become Eurosceptical. Nor has it remained indifferent to the political movements presented above. Since its creation, the *Eurobarometer* survey has asked French citizens whether France's membership in the EU is 'a good thing', 'a bad thing', or 'neither good nor bad'. Figure 3.1 summarizes the results of this survey, presenting a trend measure of support for the EU, derived from data collected twice a year for nearly forty years.

Figure 3.1 makes it clear that the support for France's membership dominates despite long-term erosion. Since the peak, reached in 1987, support for the EU has declined by thirty points while opposition has increased by twenty points and indifference has increased by ten points. During the decade that followed the referendum of 1992, indecisiveness rather than opposition to the EU increased—as indicated by

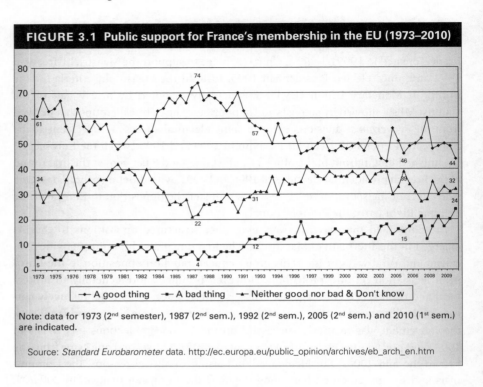

FIGURE 3.1 Public support for France's membership in the EU (1973–2010)

Note: data for 1973 (2nd semester), 1987 (2nd sem.), 1992 (2nd sem.), 2005 (2nd sem.) and 2010 (1st sem.) are indicated.

Source: *Standard Eurobarometer* data. http://ec.europa.eu/public_opinion/archives/eb_arch_en.htm

the number of 'neither good nor bad' and 'I don't know' responses. The trends following the 2005 referendum are less clear: the support for the EU increased with Sarkozy's victory in 2007 and has decreased since in a context of economic crisis. France is not considered to be one of the most Eurosceptical countries; however, it can no longer be counted among the most pro-EU countries. From Sarkozy's election in 2007 to 2010, rejection of France's membership has increased by twelve points, against the EU mean of five points.

Scholars are divided on the salience of the EU issue within French opinion. Some studies point to the 'Euroindifference' of ordinary citizens (Van Ingelgom 2010). Sophie Duchesne *et al.* (2010) organized several focus groups on the European issue and observed that, only six months after the 2005 referendum, no participant group mentioned the victory of the 'no', with the exception of political activists. Indifference and resignation sum up French citizens' attitudes towards the EU. The perception of the EU tends to be shaped by a post-colonial narrative and by a negative emphasis put on globalization. Yet, other studies point out that citizens' opinions towards Europe group into two broad sets of attitude. First, European opinions are correlated with citizens' relationship with authority and cultural liberalism. Opinions can indeed be analysed as the expression of universalistic or anti-universalistic attitudes, independently of the Left–Right divide (Grunberg and Schweisguth 1997, 2003). Thus, the analysis of the 2008 data from the Value Survey states an existing negative correlation between support for the EU and attitudes related to xenophobia, the death penalty and authoritarianism, as well as a positive one between support and tolerance towards homosexuality and soft drug consumption (Belot 2009).

Second, opinions of Europe also express citizens' attitudes towards globalization and the market economy. Independently of the evaluation of Europe in terms of (loss) of sovereignty and national independence, several studies indicate that voters' views about the EU are also organized by fears around the social consequences of European policies and rules (Belot and Cautrès 2004; Brouard and Tiberj 2006; Sauger *et al.* 2007). During the 2005 referendum, those social worries were so significant that they dictated a 'no' vote from some Left-wing supporters who were otherwise keen on sharing sovereignty: one-fifth of the opponents to the European Draft Constitution were among the more pro-European citizens (Sauger *et al.* 2007: 99). The salience of the social question and distrust towards economic liberalism are not specific to French citizens. They are also important issues of concern for their political elites. It is not only that 'few politicians of the political mainstream openly advocated the benefits of the market as pro-European argument', as Hussein Kassim puts it (2008: 266), but also that they seem to partly doubt the economic advantages of the Single Market and the EMU. For instance, the political elites' reluctance towards the 2004 and 2007 enlargements was expressed in terms of the assimilation of eastern European countries to economic liberalism. An EU of twenty-seven members was criticized by French politicians as being a 'laissez-faire Europe', which gives an idea of their lack of trust towards the free-market economy (Lequesne 2008; Bickerton 2009).

The Resilience of the Political System

Each side of the political spectrum has been destabilized by the EU issue. Right-wing voters, but also activists and leaders, were particularly divided during the 1992 referendum, while Left-wing voters were similarly divided during the 2005 referendum. However, it appears that both camps have been able to successfully overcome their respective divisions.

Euroscepticism decreased within the Right from Maastricht to the European Constitution, which may have been partially because of the partisan organization of the Right. Despite some ephemeral successes, *souverainist* leaders and MPs became marginalized on account of the choice of hazardous strategies and/or the radicalization of their discourse. In contrast, during both Chirac's presidency (1995–2007) and Sarkozy's (since 2007), the main leaders of the Right stood by a pro-EU commitment. This consistency of commitment has also been facilitated by the duration of political dominance of the Right (the Right has led for fourteen years, from 1993 to 2012). Yet, empirical analyses are not available to explain such a shift at the level of the voter. Right-wing supporters may regard the EU as a way of modernizing France's economy by going beyond domestic political and social constrictions.

Regarding the Left, the division of the Socialists in 2005 evoked the division of the Gaullists in 1992. However, the destabilization of the Left following the 2005 referendum was less severe than the destabilization of the Right after 1992. The explanation for the limited extent of the disturbing effect of the European issue rests, again, on the structure of the party system. The leaders of the 'no' were particularly divided, in organizational but also ideological terms (Crespy 2008; Wagner 2008; Heine 2009). Thus, they comprised Communists, some Socialists, conflicting Trotskyites and so-called civil society representatives. In addition, the traditional logic of the Left–Right divide became decisive during the 2007 presidential election campaign, given Sarkozy's radicalization and the enduring trauma for Left-wing supporters caused by the previous presidential election, when the division of the Left prevented Jospin being selected for a second term.

The successive evolution of the Right after Maastricht, and of the Left after the European Constitution, shows how resilient the French political system is. The limited Europeanization can be explained by reasons specific to each political party but also by the tendency of governing parties to circumscribe an issue that divided them internally. The avoidance or 'muffling' (Parsons 2007) strategy of the main parties can be observed through the limited space devoted to Europe in platforms and speeches,[1] but also through modification of institutional rules. Indeed, the regionalization of the European elections in 2004 enabled governing parties to limit the most disturbing effects of these elections. Regionalization has permitted a reduction in the number of seats obtained by EU treaty opponents and diminished the political significance of the campaign and of the results.

The Silent Europeanization of French Politics

A new clear-cut European cleavage has not emerged within the French political system. However, the way of doing politics in France has changed slightly within the European context. Three processes of Europeanization are particularly noticeable. First, governing parties can justify painful and unpopular decisions by arguing that they are imposed by Brussels. This case of blame avoidance has been largely used by successive Left-wing and Right-wing majorities, one recent example being, in 2009, the justification of the domestic decision to privatize part of *La Poste* in the name of the EU directive of liberalization of the mail market. Yet with the greater number of domestic—political or private—actors monitoring EU affairs, the use of Europe as a scapegoat tends to be less efficient (Grossman 2007).

Second, the EU card has come to constitute a strategic resource insofar as it can be played by a political opponent to challenge the leadership of his/her party or coalition. The strategy of the challenger will thus consist of voicing criticisms against the European position of the incumbent party leader. In some circumstances, this may lead to the creation of a new party. Most of the time, pro-EU views are criticized in the name of ideological purity and of the resolute opposition to the other side of the political spectrum. For the Right, this included the cases of Chirac against President Giscard in 1979, the *souverainistes* against Chirac's pro-Maastricht position in the 1990s, and Sarkozy against Chirac's pro-Turkish policy in the mid-2000s. For the Left, former

Prime Minister Fabius' opposition to the European Constitution in 2004 has also been understood in terms of a strategic anticipation of the 2007 presidential election, in a period when the leadership of the Left was still uncertain.[2] More rarely, the challenger can claim a more pro-EU orientation, as has been the case since 2002 of the refusal of the centre-Right leader, François Bayrou, to join Chirac's party, the UMP (*Union pour un Mouvement Populaire*). Among other justifications, Bayrou refused to join the UMP by stressing the pro-EU commitment of the Christian–Democrat family. Yet, the lack of emphasis put on EU issues by Bayrou during the 2009 European elections supports the idea of a strategic use of the EU card (Rozenberg 2011).

Third, an unexpected and indirect effect of the EU could be the stronger opposition of pro-EU parties regarding non-EU issues (Parsons 2007). It can be hypothesized that the difficulty arising from the Socialists and the UMP opposing each other about the EMU or the end of public monopoly, for instance, has resulted in their stronger opposition regarding domestic cultural and societal issues. The hypothesis would shed light both on the phenomenon of radicalization of the French Right with Sarkozy (Tiberj 2007) and on the Socialist resistance to the reformist social-democrat paradigm (Grunberg and Laïdi 2007). Yet, Brussels' criticisms of Sarkozy's Roma policy evoked in the introduction show that no policy field can now be totally alien to the EU sphere. Ironically, radicalization around non-EU issues could feed Euroscepticism in the future.

The Impact of EU Membership on French Institutions: Europeanization Equals Hyper-presidentialization

The participation in EU affairs has strengthened original institutional features of the French political system. The paradox here is striking. The consensual, horizontal, and painstakingly institutional style of the EU is utterly opposed to the majoritarian and presidential features of the Vth Republic. In principle, we would expect that the influence of the EU would result in the softening of these features. On the contrary, France's participation in EU affairs constitutes a remarkable illustration of how the institutional model of the Vth Republic operates. We will see, however, that this adaptive capacity does not necessarily translate into a healthy institutional system. To a large extent, this system is increasingly deadlocked.

The Primacy of the President and the Centrality of the Prime Minister

The President of the Republic is in charge of defining the main objectives of the French European policy and of making ultimate decisions in cases of governmental conflict (Guyomarch 2001; Menon 2001). EU issues thus occupy a significant part of the priorities, conduct and evaluation of each presidency. European issues were particularly central to the agendas of President Giscard (1974–1981) and President Mitterrand during his second term (1988–1995). Both presidents acted as if they considered their commitment towards the building of a single currency essential to their personal historical legacy. This interest in European issues is indicative of the significance of diplomatic and symbolic functions of the presidential institution. With his Cypriot and Lithuanian counterparts, the French President is the only European Head of State that leads a national delegation during European Councils. The European summits constitute one of the few occasions in which the French President can physically incarnate the whole country (Foret 2008). Since de Gaulle, the personal involvement of the President has been particularly central in setting the stage of Franco–German relations (Nourry 2005). More recently, we have witnessed how Sarkozy has strengthened the primacy of the institution of the President in EU affairs. In July 2007, he went in person to the Eurogroup meeting to justify France's economic policy rather than sending his minister for the economy. During the French Presidency of the European Council of the second semester of 2008, the priorities of the agenda and the official communications were also focused on him, as illustrated by his express trip to Moscow during the Georgia crisis. The implicit message of this behaviour was to contrast the personal energy, voluntarism, and commitment of a political leader to the alleged lack of dynamism of EU procedures and institutions (Lequesne and Rozenberg 2008). The only aspect with which Sarkozy, as Chirac before him, has proven to be ill at ease during EU summits is the obligation to deliver press conferences, a democratic exercise that is usually avoided in France.

The primacy of the President regarding major priorities should not lead to neglect of the central role played by the Prime Minister in the management of day-to-day Community business. The actual execution of the President's decisions, the preparation of the French position regarding EU draft legislation, and the transposition of EU rules into domestic legislation are realized under the authority of the Prime Minister. This is illustrated by his direct responsibility over the SGAE (General Secretariat for European Affairs). This bureaucratic body, in charge of conducting intergovernmental negotiations on EU issues, is led by the Prime Minister's adviser for EU affairs. Contrary to theses prospecting important institutional changes in France (Kassim 2008), the domestic management of EU affairs is characterized by significant continuity over time and by remarkable administrative centralization (Lanceron 2007; Lequesne 2010). The density of the administrative networks managed by the SGAE, as well as the generalist (rather than expert) profile of high civil servants have contributed to limit the participation of ministers and politicians in EU affairs (Eymeri 2002). Attempts to get ministers involved more personally in EU affairs have been rather unsuccessful. Thus, after the 'no' to the European Constitution in 2005, the Inter-Ministerial Committee on Europe was created. This committee holds specific ministerial meetings dedicated to EU issues, under the authority of the Prime Minister. Initially, the committee met monthly and then, during the 2008 presidency, weekly. However, since then, these meetings have been far more irregular.

The French Parliament: Still Lazy After All These Years?

The French Parliament has obtained important formal prerogatives in the past few decades, such as the right to be informed of EU documents (1990), the right for each assembly to submit non-binding opinions (called resolutions) on EU draft legislation (1992), and the obligation on ministers to not give their official position in the Council until parliamentary scrutiny is completed (1994) (Sprungk 2007). The constitutional right to adopt resolutions on EU documents was originally limited, given the material division between statute law and regulation specified in the French Constitution. However, this initial restraint was progressively abandoned in 1999, 2005, and 2008. In fact, the new version of Article 88-4 of the Constitution allows the National Assembly and the Senate to adopt EU resolutions on any Community draft legislation or even on 'any document issuing from a European Union Institution'.[3] As a result of the implementation of this article, the number of EU documents sent to both assemblies for which resolutions can be made has doubled from 2007 to 2009, as indicated in Figure 3.2.

Organizationally, both assemblies have adapted themselves to the EU by developing specific bodies devoted to scrutinising EU draft legislation and organizing hearings. The EU affairs parliamentary committees created in 1979 were considerably empowered during the 1990s in terms of prerogative and human resources.[4] Since 2008, they have also had more autonomy for adopting resolutions without having to consult other exclusive parliamentary committees.[5] In addition, other constitutional amendments adopted in 2008 have transposed the prerogatives given to national parliaments by the Lisbon Treaty: the right to send reasoned opinions as to the conformity of a proposal with the principle of subsidiarity (Article 88-6 of the French Constitution),

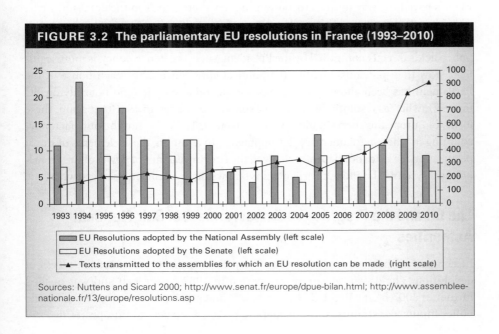

FIGURE 3.2 The parliamentary EU resolutions in France (1993–2010)

Legend:
- EU Resolutions adopted by the National Assembly (left scale)
- EU Resolutions adopted by the Senate (left scale)
- Texts transmitted to the assemblies for which an EU resolution can be made (right scale)

Sources: Nuttens and Sicard 2000; http://www.senat.fr/europe/dpue-bilan.html; http://www.assemblee-nationale.fr/13/europe/resolutions.asp

the right to institute proceedings before the ECJ for the same matter[6] (Article 88-6), and the right to oppose use of the Simplified Revision Procedure for treaty amendment (Article 88-7). These elements are certainly not negligible. The National Assembly enacts a mean of eleven EU resolutions a year, and the Senate nine. In 2009, the Senate EU Committee organized fifty-two meetings and published fifteen reports.

However, the level of Europeanization of the French Parliament still appears to be modest both in comparative and concrete terms. Indeed, the legal prerogative given to the assemblies stands in considerable contrast with the modest involvement of MPs. Outside the small club of EU Committee members, French MPs do not appear to be concerned about the EU and hardly ever deal with Community matters. The enactment of EU resolutions is irregular, Committee hearings are poorly attended, and floor debates are scarce. Examples of parliamentary influence in the European field are hard to find. To a certain extent, the reasons for this lack of involvement are constitutional and institutional. Major orientations of the European policy are difficult to control, given the central role played by the President and its lack of parliamentary accountability (Grossman and Sauger 2007). Non-binding opinions can easily be ignored. The *ex ante* involvement in EU committees (i.e. before the passing of EU laws) is disconnected both from floor debates (Auel 2007) and from the transposition phase of the legislative process (Sprungk 2011). But the main reason for the modest involvement of the Parliament is the lack of personal incentives for MPs to dedicate time and energy to EU business–irrespective of whether they are vote, policy, or office seekers (Rozenberg 2009).

Beyond the involvement of the French Parliament in the EU legislative process, we can identify other elements of Europeanization of the legislative branch of the French political system. Since 1992, the formal empowerment of the Parliament regarding the EU has paved the way for the attributions of new prerogatives in the domestic arena. Thus, non-legislative committees have been created after the EU model, to deal with issues such as women's rights. The idea that the Parliament should give its opinion in policy fields directly controlled by the President, such as defence policy, is more legitimate now than previously within the political elite. Since 2008, each house of the Parliament has been allowed to pass resolutions on any topic (and not only on EU matters), whereas resolutions had been expressly forbidden in 1958. Yet again, these forms of Europeanization should not be overstated. The EU is not the only factor accounting for these parliamentary developments. In addition, these elements of Europeanization have not dramatically changed the existing balance of power of the French political system. The French Parliament is still weak, in EU business as elsewhere.

The EU and the Progressive Empowerment of Sub-National Authorities

In contrast with its strong centralist legacy, France has experienced a process of devolution. The decentralization was started in 1982 by the Left and was pushed further in 2003 by the Right. The process was first and foremost driven by domestic policy inputs, constraints, and considerations. Yet, references to European rules and practices have persistently called for more devolution (Ladrech 1994). For instance, regional leaders claimed for a long time that French regions were too small compared with their European homologues. In 2010, a bill significantly re-organizing local and regional governments eventually allowed regional and *départemental* merging, a change that could be made in Normandy and Alsace in the near future. French metropolitan majors frequently lobby Brussels authorities (Le Galès 2011) and French regions are involved in 'new networks of regional paradiplomacy' (Pasquier 2009). However, in EU matters, local authorities' power remains limited because of the sustained mediation by the central state, as indicated by the management of structural funds by regional prefects rather than by elected regional councillors (Cole 2008b: 91).

A Deadlocked Institutional Model

The institutions of the Vth Republic have adapted to the EU by perpetuating and often strengthening their defining domestic traits. Yet, the domestic institutional setting is increasingly inefficient both in terms of national influence in decision making and from a democratic point of view. Regarding efficiency first, there are some cases in which the primacy of the President regarding EU affairs does not promote national interests. In comparison with the British Prime Minister, who needs to secure a majority in the Commons, or to the German Chancellor, who needs the support both from within her coalition and from the Länder, the French President is often free from domestic veto players. Paradoxically, such strength may occasionally weaken France's negotiation position, as indicated by Chirac's shift towards compromise on institutional questions, from Nice in 2000 to the European Convention in 2003 (Jabko 2004). When the President has a clear agenda with firm priorities, the lack of domestic red lines can be an asset. This had been the case for some presidents, who defined their European policy with major domestic problems in mind. Thus, de Gaulle's *grandeur* international agenda allowed him to go beyond the profound internal political divisions of post-war France. Mitterrand's European vision elegantly hid his renunciation of a neo-Marxist agenda. However, in the current period, the European policy does not seem to be such a useful mechanism for the President to solve domestic issues. As a result, French Presidents are more inclined to compromise in Brussels and more concerned with short-term success in the French press. The domestic strength of the President makes him weak in Brussels.[7]

Regarding the domestic public debate about Europe, the presidential and majoritarian institutional culture of the Vth Republic makes it difficult for French citizens and the elite to fully understand the Community method of decision making and the patient quest of the EU decisional system for large consensus. Ordinary French citizens tend to perceive the EU through the filter of the French presidential setting. Political leaders also have difficulty understanding the institutional philosophy of the EU, as indicated by their long disdain towards the European Parliament and by the emphasis put on the European Council (a French initiative) to the detriment of the Council of Ministers of the EU. In the 2000s, the diffuse diagnosis among politicians and high civil servants that the EU was suffering from a lack of leadership, and therefore needed a permanent President, was rooted in the presidentialism *à la française*. Likewise, the French EU Presidency of 2008, regarded in France as a success, was rather severely judged outside France, and mostly seen as a product of Sarkozy's unilateral and personal style (Dimitrakopoulos *et al.* 2009). More generally, it can be said that the decision-making process that defines the French European position suffers from a lack of accountability. The influence of the President on EU decision making contributes to present EU affairs as foreign policy issues, rather than domestic issues (Drake and Milner 1999). Many European dossiers do not find an institutional venue where they can be justified, discussed, and criticized. The deficit in adequate institutional channels results in latent Euroscepticism and, in some cases, in irruptive mobilizations against EU rules (Balme 2009: 149). The lack of enthusiasm towards the 2004 and 2007 waves of enlargement to the EU can be understood under this perspective. Political elites failed to build a positive narrative toward the enlargements not only because they were nostalgic of 'small Europe' or, as mentioned before, afraid of economic liberalism, but also because the issue had remained unquestioned publicly for more than a decade. Indeed, the absence of parliamentary debates accompanying the Council meetings during the pre-accession phase of the enlargement played a fundamental role in the creation of the scapegoat of the 'Polish plumber' (Grossman and Woll 2011).

The Impact of EU Membership on Public Policy: Between 20 and 80 per cent

In France, EU membership has generated a change in public policies both in substantive and procedural terms. First of all, France is not, or is no longer, the EU's lame duck, as indicated by French jurisdictions' decisions or by transposition rate. Even if several recent studies have played down the impact of the EU on French policies, its influence appears to be massive.

A Very Progressive Acknowledgement of EU Rules

The story of the Europeanization of French public policies is full of clichés—France is reluctant to acknowledge the primacy of Community laws, the French State has always been late in transposing EU legislation, French citizens only like EU policies when they correspond with existing French ones. While these might have been true in the past, several elements indicate that this is less and less the case. French judges, politicians, and civil servants now take EU rules seriously.

At first, regarding domestic respect of EU legislation, the decisions of the highest French jurisdictions are convergent and increasingly similar to the ECJ doctrine (Masclet *et al.* 2010). Early on, France recognized the immediate applicability of EU laws and their primacy over existing French law (i.e. French law that was adopted before a given EU directive or regulation). That recognition has been favoured by the monist judicial order, built on Article 55 of the French Constitution that foresees an automatic integration of international norms. Tensions between the ECJ and French jurisdictions remained for a long time on two points. On the one hand, they dealt with the direct effect of EU law: it was only in 2009 (arrêt Perreux) that the Council of State, the highest administrative jurisdiction, recognized the invocation by individual citizens of a directive not transposed in due time against an individual administrative act. On the other hand, the divergences regarded the primacy of EU rules on French posterior laws (i.e. French law that was adopted after a given EU directive or regulation). The two highest courts recognized the full primacy of EU legislation over French posterior laws in 1975 (arrêt Jacques Vabre) for the *Cour de cassation* (the highest court of the French judiciary for civil, commercial, social, or criminal cases) and in 1989 (arrêt Nicolo) for the Council of State. The changes in decisions of the Council of State resulted from the pressure of ECJ decisions, but can also be understood strategically: the highest administrative court found a role as domestic guardian of the EU treaties (Mangenot 2005). In a context of empowerment of the Constitutional Council (CC), the Council of State could differentiate through Europe since the CC refused, at least up to 2006, to control the respect of EU rules by domestic laws. A similar strategic game was played in 2010 when the *Cour de cassation* tried, unsuccessfully, to block the implementation of the new constitutional right of citizens to initiate proceedings before the CC, arguing that it could be damaging to the procedure of requesting preliminary rulings by the ECJ.

The evolution of the CC decisions also strengthened the legal foundation of France's participation in the EU. In 2004, the Council argued that the primacy of EU rules was not only based on international obligations (Article 55 of the Constitution) but on Article 88-1, which stipulates: 'The Republic shall participate in the European Union constituted by States which have freely chosen to exercise some of their powers in common by virtue of the Treaty on European Union [. . .]'. This meant that the Council recognized the EU judicial order as a part of the national, but distinct from the international, judicial order. As a result, transposing EU rules is regarded as a constitutional obligation and not only as a convention. A tension still exists between the French courts and the ECJ concerning the primacy of EU laws over the French Constitution. In a 2006 decision, the CC indicated that it was responsible for monitoring the respect of 'France's constitutional identity' by laws transposing EU legislation. The notion is vague but recalls that the Council does not consider EU treaties and rules as superior to the French Constitution. According to French judges, EU rules are supreme only because the French Constitution says so; therefore, the French Constitution cannot be inferior to those rules. Such a theoretical conflict has been avoided so far by amending the Constitution whenever the Council find conflicts between the Constitution and

TABLE 3.1 Constitutional amendments with EU dimension

	EU norm	Fields and contents
1992	Maastricht	City elections for EU citizens, EMU, visa policy, French language, parliamentary resolutions
1993	Schengen agreements amended	Asylum
1999	Amsterdam	Asylum, migration and borders, parliamentary resolutions
2003	European Arrest Warrant	Justice
2005	Draft Constitutional Treaty	Compulsory referendum on EU accessions, parliamentary resolutions (not implemented)
2008	Lisbon	New competencies, parliamentary rights (subsidiarity, simplified revision procedure)
2008	(none)	EU parliamentary committees, parliamentary resolutions, no more compulsory referendum on EU accessions[9]

EU primary and even secondary legislation.[8] A new Title was added to the Constitution in 1992 and seven of the eighteen constitutional amendments passed since 1992 had a European dimension (see Table 3.1).

The second dimension of the progressive acknowledgement of Community laws rests on the improvement of the domestic transposition rate. France was for a long time dysfunctional in dealing with EU laws. If the actions for failure of a Member State to fulfil its obligation are added since the creation of the ECJ (1952–2009), France is the second deficient Member State behind Italy, with 389 actions versus 258 for Germany.[10] The reasons are numerous. Ministerial departments occasionally changed the meaning of a directive when transposing it. The multiplication of alternating majorities from 1981 to 2002 also gave greater priority to the domestic agenda. In a few cases, such as wild bird hunting or women's work at night, the lack of transposition also came from political or social blockages. Ultimately, the French delay illustrated a more global lack of consideration for the EU both with politicians and high civil servants. It should be noted that the French Parliament cannot be made responsible for this deficit given that the assemblies do not control their agenda and half of the directives adopted by the Council are transposed by statutory means (Bertoncini 2009: 28). The National Assembly has rather put pressure on the government by producing annual reports on transposition since 2003.

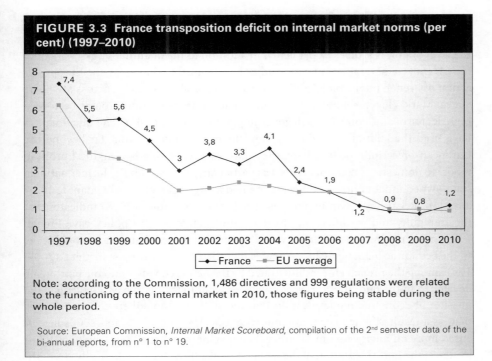

FIGURE 3.3 France transposition deficit on internal market norms (per cent) (1997–2010)

Note: according to the Commission, 1,486 directives and 999 regulations were related to the functioning of the internal market in 2010, those figures being stable during the whole period.

Source: European Commission, *Internal Market Scoreboard*, compilation of the 2nd semester data of the bi-annual reports, from n° 1 to n° 19.

To a large extent, France's transposition deficit is over. Figure 3.3, which presents data for the internal market only, provides evidence of a real improvement in the second half of the 2000s. As a result, France is now close to the EU mean.

Some contextual factors—political stability since 2002 and greater official concern for EU issues after the 2005 referendum—may partly explain why France caught up. Yet, the awareness came, above all, from the first financial penalties by the ECJ in 2005 (about fisheries) and 2006 (about liability for defective products). It should also be noted that France's improvement remains partial: the number of pending infringement cases is decreasing quickly but, with eighty cases in late 2010, it is still high compared with other Member States (the EU average is forty-six cases, internal market only).[11]

The Disputed Assessment of the Impact of the EU on French Policies

Whereas European studies were originally developed in France with the credo that EU public policies matter (Hassenteufel and Surel 2008), a series of recent quantitative studies aimed to challenge this idea, or, more exactly, Jacques Delors's false prediction (made in the late 1980s) that in the future, 80 per cent of the economic legislation will originate from the EU (Bertoncini 2009; Fekl 2010; Brouard *et al.*

2012). Thus, Fekl estimated that one-quarter of the laws and ordinances passed between 1999 and 2008 aimed to transpose EU rules—the rate is far less significant if the level of unit is articles (7 per cent). In addition to the quantitative assessment of the EU impact, several recent case studies have tended to downplay the Europeanization of French public policies. By comparing several policy fields across Members States, Mark Thatcher (2007a) concludes that the transposition process bestows a high degree of autonomy on each government. In some cases, French policy-makers have used the alibi of a directive to implement dramatic reforms, far beyond the European prescriptions. In others, they have succeeded in adapting the European model to domestic constraints. This was particularly the case for the former national state-owned monopolies, which were granted a large span of time to adapt to liberalization. Regarding environmental issues, Pierre Lascoumes (2008) indicates that the ambiguity and modification of the main objectives of this policy gave French policy-makers a margin of manoeuvre when they translated them to a national scale. In the economic field, Ben Clift estimates that there is still a 'dirigist instinct' (2009: 164) among the French elite, as illustrated by the new credo of 'economic patriotism' developed in the mid-2000s. He acknowledges that EU policies have challenged the mission of economic modernization that the state used to adhere to but observes that, as a result, 'French economic interventionism in the 1990s and 2000s has focused more on microeconomic, rather than macroeconomic policy' (ibid: 166). For instance, the implementation of the 2004 take-over directive paradoxically strengthened the anti-takeover opportunities of domestic firms. The merger policy in the field of energy particularly illustrates the unforeseen impact of market liberalization. At a more sociological level, continuity in the policy-makers' identity can also be observed. The members of the regulatory agencies, for instance, still originate from high civil service, particularly from the state's *grands corps* (Baudy and Varone 2007; Thatcher 2007b).

Another point raised to express the minimal impact of Europe is the congruence between EU and French pieces of legislation (Brouard *et al.* 2012). This fitness first and foremost derives from France's influence within the EU. Thus, in his analysis of Chirac's presidency (1995–2007), Kassim (2008) challenges the thesis of a French malaise (Keeler and Schain 1996; Grossman 2007) and estimates that, especially through the strategic partnership with Germany, France can still minimize EU constraints. The avoidance of a sanction for excessive deficit in 2003 and even the reform of the Stability Pact negotiated in 2005 give credit to this point of view. Since the Greek financial crisis of spring 2010, French officials have appeared more concerned about a downgrade of France's financial ratings than hypothetical EU sanctions. In policy fields in which it has become more difficult for France to get full satisfaction, like the CAP, regional aids, and environment, there are some indications that 're-nationalization' is ongoing (Smith 2008).

Finally, it should be said that, as for public opinion and political parties, minimizing the EU impact should not be led too far. There are indeed some risks of replacing Delors's '80 per cent myth' with a 'new 20 per cent myth'[12] given that a large part of the Europeanization process is impossible to assess quantitatively. References to 'Europe' can take a great variety of forms from EU legislation, to the praise of national champions (Denmark for instance), transnational networks, or even geopolitical considerations. Precisely thanks to this great heterogeneity, Europe can matter, i.e. help or constrain policy-makers. Thus, several case studies have established that the reference to Europe has been central to some policy enterprises in fields where EU competencies were limited or nonexistent, such as the welfare reforms of 1995 (Palier 2002), the professionalization of the French army in 1996 (Irondelle 2003), the parity laws in favour of female representation in 1999 (Bereni 2004) or the University curriculum reform since 2002 (Ravinet 2008). As regards more specifically the implementation of EU norms, the idea that EU norms are adapted nationally rather than merely dictated, should not lead to neglect that EU rules matter, and they do so especially in a country where the state has historically played a unique role in shaping the nation and the economy. To give one example, the ECJ definition of the civil service narrowly focused on the exercise of government authority contributions to a full redefinition of who civil servants are, and indirectly of what the French State's missions should be (Eymeri 2006). Pierre Muller *et al.*'s (1996) seminal intuition, that the production of constraining legal rules by a non-statist system constitutes a radical innovation, is still relevant (see also Balme and Woll 2005b).

Conclusion

This general overview of the impact of EU membership on France enables the conclusion that France has changed by participating in the EU. Such a conclusion stands in contrast with a large body of recent work that has tended to downplay the impact of the EU on French domestic politics and policies, after an initial period of enthusiasm in the 1980s and 1990s. Certainly, Monnet did not act for nothing. Yet, this chapter has also highlighted how mixed the Europeanization process is. Public policies and policy-making have changed dramatically even if the domestic legislation is not dictated by EU institutions. Domestic institutions have also evolved, but mostly in order to strengthen France's distinctiveness. The impact of the EU is more limited with regard to public opinion and politics. The EU has occasionally destabilized the party system and offered new tips for political entrepreneurs, but most of the political leaders have chosen a strategy of avoidance of EU issues. Therefore, the inner European cleavages within public opinion are not activated by political leaders. They have only been expressed on a few occasions, such as the 2005 referendum. For the rest of the time, the 'threatening indifference' of political elites and citizens feed each other.

To a large extent, the uncertainty of France's commitment towards the EU described in the introduction can be explained by this mixed aspect of the Europeanization process. The contrast between the impact of the EU on public policies and the relative torpor of the public debate on Europe is certainly not specific to France. What is more specific is that national institutional systems reinforce this contrast: parliamentary debates are rare, the President is not held accountable for his EU policy, EU bargains are perceived as diplomatic, and high civil servants do their best to circumscribe politicians' involvement. The institutional features of the Vth Republic have been strengthened by France's EU membership, but do not contribute to politicize that membership.

In a sense, the resilience of the French institutional and party system makes France's European policy more regular and constant. The stability of the political system contributed, for instance, to minimize both the external and the internal effects of the 2005 referendum. Yet, the mixed nature of the Europeanization process also leads to the development of two other phenomena that could, in the future, impact on France's European policy. First, the Europeanization process is increasingly silent. As observed by Richard Balme (2009: 142), 'European integration lost the prominent position it occupied on public policy agendas during the 1970s and 1980s'. While Europe was used by governing leaders to camouflage domestic renunciations for the best, or as a scapegoat for the worst, the mobilizing potential of the European reference is less and less efficient. The narrative of the *Europe puissance* has been eroded. As a result, and this is the second aspect, mainstream political parties and leaders tend to develop a catch-all discourse integrating pro- and anti-EU elements, as seen in the European elections in 2009 (Rozenberg 2011). So far, such a way of playing softly with Euroscepticism has remained discursive and has not impacted on France's EU policy. Among other elements, the September 2010 clash between Sarkozy and Barroso over Roma migrants indicates that this might no longer be the case in the future.[13]

 FURTHER READING

Even if a comprehensive monograph on the French relation to the EU is still needed, the literature is abundant. For an historical overview, Parsons (2003) is a must. The Balme and Woll (2005a) contribution from the previous edition of this book also offers an historical account. The complex question of public opinion is clearly presented in Sauger (2008). Borraz and Guiraudon (2008) propose an overview of public policy issues. For the last developments of France's European policy, see Kassim (2008) and Balme (2009). Grossman's special issue of the *Journal of European Public Policy* (2007) covers most of those aspects. On the Franco–German relationship, see Cole (2001) for the main aspects and Cole (2008a) and Schild (2010) for updates.

WEB LINKS

The French Government has developed a specific online section about Europe: **http://www.gouvernement.fr/gouvernement/europe** as well as the National Assembly **http://www.assemblee-nationale.fr/europe/**. Official information about the Franco–German relationship can be found at **http://www.france-allemagne.fr/-France-.html**. The governmental platforms **http://www.vie-publique.fr/** and **http://www.ladocumentationfrancaise.fr/** propose much information about a range of political issues. French universities provide online working papers on the EU at **http://prisme.u-strasbg.fr/working-papers/** (University of Strasbourg) and **http://www.cee.sciences-po.fr/fr/publications/les-cahiers-europeens.html** (Sciences Po). The French Political Science Association has developed a European section **http://see-afsp.webou.net/**. A French journalist in Brussels has developed an interesting blog at **http://bruxelles.blogs.liberation.fr/coulisses/**.

REFERENCES

Auel, K. (2007), 'Adapting to Europe: Strategic Europeanization of National Parliaments', in R. Holzhacker and E. Albaek (eds), *Democratic Governance and European Integration*, Aldershot: Edward Elgar, 157–79.

Balme, R. (2009), 'France, Europe and the World: Foreign Policy and the Political Regime of the Fifth Republic', in S. Brouard, A. M. Appelton, and A. G. Mazur (eds), *The French Fifth Republic at Fifty*, Basingstoke: Palgrave Macmillan, 136–50.

Balme, R. and Woll, C. (2005a), 'France: Between Integration and National Sovereignty', in S. Bulmer and C. Lequesne (eds), *The Member States of the European Union*, Oxford: Oxford University Press, 97–118.

Balme, R. and Woll, C. (2005b), 'Europe and the Transformation of French Policy-Making: A Cross-Sectoral Approach', *Zeitschrift für Staats- und Europawissenschaften*, 3/3: 388–409.

Baudy, P. and Varone, F. (2007), 'Europeanization of the French Electricity Policy: Four Paradoxes', *Journal of European Public Policy*, 14/7: 1048–60.

Belot, C. (2009), 'Europe: De la Confiance aux Peurs', in P. Bréchon and J. F. Tchernia (eds), *La France à Travers ses Valeurs*, Paris: Armand Colin, 305–9.

Belot, C. and Cautrès, B. (2004), 'L'Europe, Invisible Mais Omniprésente', in B. Cautrès and N. Mayer (eds), *Le Nouveau Désordre Electoral. Les Leçons du 21 Avril 2002*, Paris: Presses de Sciences Po, 119–41.

Bereni, L. (2004), 'Le Mouvement Français pour la Parité et l'Europe', in S. Jacquot and C. Woll (eds), *Les usages de l'Europe. Acteurs et Transformations Européennes*, Paris: L'Harmattan, 33–54.

Bertoncini, Y. (2009), 'Les Interventions de l'UE au Niveau National: Quel Impact?', *Etude et Recherche, Notre Europe*, 73 (http://www.notre-europe.eu/uploads/tx_publication/Etud73-Y_Bertoncini-fr.pdf).

Bickerton, C. J. (2009), 'Arrogance or Ambivalence? Rethinking France's Role in a Europe of Twenty-seven', *French Politics*, 7/2: 194–205.

Borraz, O. and Guiraudon V. (eds) (2008), *Politiques Publiques. 1, La France dans la Gouvernance Européenne*, Paris: Presses de Sciences Po.

Brouard, S. and Tiberj, V. (2006), 'The French Referendum: The Not So Simple Act of Saying Nay', *PS: Political Science & Politics*, 39/2: 261–8.

Brouard, S., Costa, O., and Kerrouche, E. (2012), 'Are French Laws Written in Brussels? The Limited Europeanization of Lawmaking in France and its Implications', in S. Brouard, O. Costa, and T. König (eds), *The Europeanization of Domestic Legislatures: The Empirical Implications of the Delors' Myth in Nine Countries*, New York: Springer, 75–93.

Clift, B. (2003), *French Socialism in a Global Era*, New York: Continuum.

Clift, B. (2009), 'Economic Interventionism in the Fifth Republic', in Brouard, S., Appleton, A., and Mazur, A., *The French Fifth Republic at Fifty*, Basingstoke: Palgrave Macmillan, 153–73.

Cole, A. (2001), *Franco–German Relations*, Harlow: Longman.

Cole, A. (2008a), 'Franco–German Relations: From Active to Reactive Co-operation', in J. Hayward (ed.), *Leaderless Europe*, Oxford: Oxford University Press, 147–66.

Cole, A. (2008b), *Governing and Governance in France*, Cambridge: Cambridge University Press.

Crespy, A. (2008), 'Dissent Over the European Constitutional Treaty Within the French Socialist Party: Between Response to Anti-Globalization Protest and Intra-Party Tactics', *French Politics*, 6/1: 23–44.

Culpepper, P. D., Hall, P. A., and Palier, B. (eds) (2006), *Changing France. The Politics that Markets Make*, Basingstoke: Palgrave Macmillan.

Davies, L. (2010), 'France Defends Roma Expulsion Policy', *Financial Times*, 15 September, available on www.ft.com.

Dehousse, R. (2005), *La fin de l'Europe*, Paris: Flammarion.

Dimitrakopoulos, D. G., Menon, A., and Passas, A. G. (2009), 'France and the EU Under Sarkozy: Between European Ambitions and National Objectives?', *Modern & Contemporary France*, 17/4: 451–65.

Down, I. and Wilson, C. J. (2008), 'From "Permissive Consensus" to "Constraining Dissensus": A Polarizing Union?', *Acta Politica*, 43: 26–49.

Drake, H. (2010), 'France in Europe, Europe in France: The Politics of Exceptionalism and Their Limits', in T. Chafer and E. Godin (eds), *The End of the French Exception? Decline and Revival of the 'French Model'*, Basingstoke: Palgrave Macmillan, 187–202.

Drake, H. and Milner, S. (1999), 'Change and Resistance to Change: The Political Management of Europeanisation in France', *Modern & Contemporary France*, 7/2: 165–78.

Duchesne, S., Haegel, F., Frazer, E., Van Ingelgom, V., Garcia, G., and Frognier, A. (2010), 'Europe Between Integration and Globalisation Social Differences and National Frames in the Analysis of Focus Groups Conducted in France, Francophone Belgium and the United Kingdom', *Politique Européenne*, 30/1: 67–105.

Eymeri, J. M. (2002), 'Définir "La Position de la France", dans l'Union Européenne. La Médiation Interministérielle des Généralistes du SGCI', in O. Nay and A. Smith (eds), *Le Gouvernement de Compromis. Courtiers et Généralistes dans L'action Politique*, Paris: Economica, 149–76.

Eymeri, J. M. (2006), 'La Fonction Publique aux Prises avec une Double Européanisa-tion', *Pouvoirs*, 117: 121–36.

Fekl, M. (2010), 'Normes Européennes, Loi Française: Le Mythe des 80%', *Terra Nova* (http://www.tnova.fr/sites/default/files/mythe_0.pdf).

Foret, F. (2008), *Légitimer l'Europe. Pouvoir et Symbolique à l'ère de la Gouvernance*, Paris: Presses de Sciences Po.

Grossman, E. (2007), 'Introduction: France and the EU: From Opportunity to Con-straint', *Journal of European Public Policy*, 14/7: 983–91.

Grossman, E. (2008), 'La Résistance Comme Opportunité: Les Stratégies des Insti-tutions Politiques Françaises Face à l'Europe', *Revue Internationale de Politique Comparée*, 15/4: 667–78.

Grossman, E. and Sauger, N. (2007), 'Political Institutions Under Stress? Assessing the Impact of European Integration on French Political Institutions', *Journal of European Public Policy*, 14/7: 1117–34.

Grossman, E. and Woll, C. (2011), 'The French Debate on the Bolkestein Directive', *Comparative European Politics*, 9/3: 344–66.

Grunberg, G. and Laïdi, Z. (2007), *Sortir du Pessimisme Social: Essai sur l'identité de la Gauche*, Paris: Hachette Littérature and Presses de Sciences Po.

Grunberg, G. and Schweisguth, E. (1997), 'Vers une Tripartition de l'espace Politique', in D. Boy and N. Mayer (eds), *L'électeur a ses Raisons*, Paris: Presses de Sciences Po, 331–47.

Grunberg, G. and Schweisguth, E. (2003), 'French Political Space: Two, Three or Four Blocs?', *French Politics*, 1/3: 331–47.

Guieu, J.M. and Le Dréau, C. (eds) (2009), 'Anti-européens, Eurosceptiques et Sou-verainistes. Une Histoire des Résistances à l'Europe (1919–1992)', *Les cahiers Irice*, 4.

Guyomarch, A. (2001), 'The Europeanization of Policy Making', in A. Guyomarch, H. Machin, P. Hall, and J. Hayward (eds), *Developments in French Politics 2*, Basing-stoke: Palgrave Macmillan.

Guyomarch, A., Machin, H., and Ritchie, E. (eds) (1998), *France in the European Union*, London: Palgrave Macmillan.

Haegel, F. (2009), 'Right-wing Parties in France and in Europe', in P. Perrineau and L. Rouban (eds), *Politics in France and Europe*, Basingstoke: Palgrave Macmillan, 217–33.

Hainsworth, P., O'Brien, C., and Mitchell, P. (2004), 'Defending the Nation: The Politics of Euroscepticism on the French Right', *European Studies*, 20: 37–58.

Hassenteufel, P. and Surel, Y. (2008), 'Politiques publiques', in C. Belot, P. Magnette, and S. Saurugger (eds), *Science politique de l'Union européenne*, Paris: Economica, 81–105.

Heine, S. (2009), *Une gauche contre l'Europe?*, Brussels: édition de l'Université de Bruxelles.

Irondelle, B. (2003), 'Europeanisation Without the European Union? French Military Reforms 1991–1996', *Journal of European Public Policy*, 10/2: 208–26.

Jabko, N. (2004), 'The Importance of Being Nice: An Institutionalist Analysis of French Preferences on the Nature of Europe', *Comparative European Politics*, 2/3: 282–301.

Kassim, H. (2008), 'France and the European Union under the Chirac Presidency', in A. Cole, P. Le Galès, and J. Levy (eds), *Developments in French Politics 4*, Basingstoke: Palgrave Macmillan, 258–76.

Keeler, J. and Schain, M. (eds) (1996), *Chirac's Challenge. Liberalization, Europeanization and Malaise in France*, New York: St Martin's Press.

Kriesi, H.-P. (2007), 'The Role of European Integration in National Election Campaigns', *European Union Politics*, 8/1: 83–108.

Ladrech, R. (1994), 'Europeanization of Domestic Politics and Institutions: The Case of France', *Journal of Commons Market Studies*, 32/1: 69–88.

Lanceron, V. (2007), *Du SGCI au SGAE. Evolution d'une administration de coordination au cœur de la politique européenne de la France*, Paris: l'Harmattan.

Lascoumes, P. (2008), 'Les politiques environnementales', in Borraz *et al.* (eds), *Politiques publiques* 1: 29–67.

Le Galès, P. (2011), *Le retour des villes européennes*, 2nd edn, Paris: Presses de Sciences Po.

Lequesne, C. (2008), *La France dans la nouvelle Europe*, Paris: Presses de Sciences Po.

Lequesne, C. (2010), 'l'Administration Centrale Française et l'Union Européenne', in Y. Doutriaux and C. Lequesne (eds), *Les Institutions de l'Union Européenne Après le Traité de Lisbonne* 8th edn, Paris: La documentation française, 145–87.

Lequesne, C. and Rozenberg, O. (2008), 'The 2008 French EU Presidency: The Unexpected Agenda', *Swedish Institute for European Policy Studies*, 3 op.

Leuffen, D. (2009), 'Does Cohabitation Matter? French European Policy-Making in the Context of Divided Government', *West European Politics*, 32/6: 1140–60.

Mair, P. (2000), 'The Limited Impact of Europe on the National Party Systems', *West European Politics*, 23/4: 27–51.

Mangenot, M. (2005), 'Le Conseil d'Etat and Europe', in H. Drake (ed.), *French Relations with the European Union*, Abingdon: Routledge, 86–104.

Masclet, J. C., Fabri, H. R., Boutayeb, C., and Rodrigues, S. (eds) (2010), *L'Union Européenne: Union de Droit, Union des Droits. Mélanges en l'Honneur de Philippe Manin*, Paris: Editions A. Pedone.

Menon, A. (2001), 'The French Administration in Brussels', in H. Kassim, A. Menon, B. G. Peters, and V. Wright (eds), *The National Coordination of EU Policy: The Domestic Level*, Oxford: Oxford University Press, 75–100.

Muller, P., Quermonne, J. L., and Mény, Y. (eds) (1996), *Adjusting to Europe: The Impact of the European Union on National Institutions and Policies*, London: Routledge.

Nourry, C. (2005), *Le Couple 'Franco-Allemand': Une Symbolique Européenne*, Brussels: Bruylant.

Nuttens, J.-D. and Sicard, F. (2000), *Assemblées Parlementaires et Organisations Européennes*, Paris: La Documentation française.

Palier, B. (2002), *Gouverner la Sécurité Sociale*, Paris: PUF.

Parsons, C. (2003), *A Certain Idea of Europe*, Ithaca, NY: Cornell University Press.

Parsons, C. (2007), 'Puzzling out the EU Role in National Politics', *Journal of European Public Policy*, 14/7: 1135–49.

Pasquier, R. (2009), 'The Europeanisation of French Regions', *French Politics*, 7/2: 123–44.

Ravinet, P. (2008), 'From Voluntary Participation to Monitored Coordination: Why European Countries Feel Increasingly Bound by Their Commitment to the Bologna Process', *European Journal of Education*, 43/3: 353–67.

Rozenberg, O. (2009), 'Présider par Plaisir. L'examen des Affaires Européennes à l'Assemblée Nationale et à la Chambre des Communes depuis Maastricht', *Revue française de science politique*, 59/3: 401–27.

Rozenberg, O. (2011), 'Playing Softly with Euroscepticism. The 2009 European Elections in France', in R. Harmsen and J. Schild (eds), *Debating Europe: The 2009 European Parliament Elections and Beyond*, Baden-Baden: Nomos, 51–68.

Sauger, N. (2005), 'Sur la Mutation Contemporaine des Structures de la Compétition Partisane en France: Les Partis de Droite Face à l'Intégration Européenne', *Politique européenne*, 16: 103–26.

Sauger, N. (2008), 'Attitudes Towards Europe in France', in Cole *et al.* (eds), *Developments in French Politics* 4: 60–73.

Sauger, N., Brouard, S., and Grossman, E. (2007), *Les Français contre l'Europe? Les sens du Référendum du 29 Mai 2005*, Paris: Presses de Sciences Po.

Schild, J. (2010), 'Mission Impossible? The Potential for Franco–German Leadership in the Enlarged EU', *Journal of Common Market Studies*, 48/5: 1367–90.

Smith, A. (2008), 'L'intégration Européenne des Politiques Françaises', in Borraz *et al.* (eds), *Politiques publiques 1*: 197–214.

Sprungk, C. (2007), 'The French Assemblée Nationale and the German Bundestag in the European Union. Towards Convergence in the "Old" Europe?', in J. O'Brennan and T. Raunio (eds), *National Parliaments in the Enlarged European Union*, London: Routledge, 132–62.

Sprungk, C. (2011), 'How Policy-Shaping Might (not) Affect Policy-Taking: The Case of National Parliaments in the European Union', *Journal of European Integration*, 3/3: 323–40.

Thatcher, M. (2007a), *Internationalisation and Economic Institutions. Comparing European Experiences*, Oxford: Oxford University Press.

Thatcher, M. (2007b), 'Regulatory Agencies, the State and Markets: A Franco–British Comparison', *Journal of European Public Policy*, 14/7: 1028–47.

Tiberj, V. (2007), *La Crispation Hexagonale: France Fermée Contre « France Plurielle », 2001–2007*, Paris: Plon.

Van Ingelgom, V. (2010), *Intégrer l'Indifférence. Une Approche Comparative, Qualitative et Quantitative, de la Légitimité de l'Intégration Européenne*, doctoral thesis: Sciences Po, Université catholique de Louvain.

Wagner, M. (2008), 'Debating Europe in the French Socialist Party: The 2004 Internal Referendum on the EU Constitution', *French Politics*: 6, 257–79.

ENDNOTES

1. Hans-Peter Kriesi (2007) notes that the frequency with which party positions on Europe were mentioned in the press during the election campaigns was multiplied by two from the 1970s to the 1990s, but remained twice below the UK or Switzerland.

2. The fact that criticising EU Treaties can be damaging for the statesperson image of a political leader suggests that challengers face a trade-off when positioning themselves on EU issues.

3. Article 88–4 says: 'The government shall lay before the National Assembly and the Senate drafts of European legislative acts as well as other drafts of or proposals for acts of the European Union as soon as they have been transmitted to the Council of the European Union. / In the manner laid down by the Rules of Procedure of each House, European resolutions may be passed, even if Parliament is not in session, on the drafts or proposals referred to in the preceding paragraph, as well as on any document issuing from a European Union Institution. / A committee in charge of European affairs shall be set up in each of the Houses of Parliament'.

4. Created in 1979 as 'delegations', they have been called 'committees' since 2008. Contrary to Grossman's analysis (2008), it does not seem that the lack of resources of the EU committees explain the modest involvement of the French Parliament in EU affairs. Rather, the high number of clerks has enabled those structures to camouflage the lack of personal involvement of the MPs.

5. EU committees are actually the only committees specifically mentioned in the Constitution. Yet, they are not similar to the eight select committees, since mutual belonging is possible, and even compulsory, for EU committees.

6. This right is open to the political opposition as sixty MPs can activate the procedure.

7. In addition, the occasional periods of divided governments (*cohabitation*) call for a specific comment. They appear to be upsetting both regarding the European policy of France and the electoral arena. The Constitutional ambiguity about who—the President or the Prime Minister—should have the last word concerning EU major bargains favours the status quo (Leuffen 2009). Moreover, the relative share of responsibility between the two political opponents shadows the democratic game. Situations of divided government, however, are less likely given the limitation of the Presidential term to five years in 2000, even if they are still possible.

8. Regarding the statutory acts resulting from the transposition of EU laws, the requests for preliminary ruling by the Council of State have also prevented such conflicts.

9. The compulsory referendum on EU accessions was introduced in the Constitution before the 2005 referendum in view of disarming the opponents to the Turkish accession. Despite his initial objective, Sarkozy did not succeed in totally suppressing this clause in 2008. Contrary to what is said in the literature (Lequesne 2008: 65; Dimitrakopoulos *et al.* 2009: 462), referendums on accession are no longer compulsory as they can be avoided by the votes of each assembly, separately and then jointly, with a majority of three-fifths.

10. Source: *Annual Report of the Court of Justice*, 2009.

11. Source: European Commission, *Internal Market Scoreboard*, n° 19, 2010.

12. I borrow the expression from Katrin Auel, used at a conference at Sciences Po Paris, 18 January 2010.

13. I am grateful to the editors of the volume and Richard Balme, Yves Doutriaux, Sophie Duchesne, Cesar Garcia Perez de Leon, Angela Tacea, Virginie Van Ingelgom, and Cornelia Woll for their assistance.

CHAPTER 4

Germany: In Search of a New Balance

Timm Beichelt

▌ Summary

This chapter will offer different perspectives on Germany as an EU member state. In the first section, an overview of the patterns of Germany–EU relations will use the traditional approach of discussing the German voice within the concert of European states. Subsequent sections will then use the comparative politics paradigm by investigating public opinion on Europe, the European dimension of party politics, and the Federal Republic's major political institutions and their role in European policy. Finally, the policy performance of Germany as an EU member state will be discussed. Here, the German government as one of the major actors reappears as a national agent in international affairs.

Introduction: Germany and European Integration

The relationship between Germany and the European Union (EU) has been captured by two different paradigms. In one part of the pertinent literature, the status of the Federal Republic as a member state is conceived through the lens of international relations. From that perspective, Germany has been characterized as a 'tamed power' (Katzenstein 1997) which has been able to shape its regional milieu through the means of European diplomacy (Bulmer *et al.* 2000; Bulmer and Paterson 2010). The other part of the literature approaches Germany in the EU by the means of domestic analysis. Germany's capacities to be present in European politics then depend less on the country's international status than on the institutional resources to be used within the EU multilevel system (Börzel 2006; Lankowski 2001; Sturm and Pehle 2006).

Going along with the conception of this book (see Chapter 1), this chapter will use both approaches alongside each other in order to track Germany's profile as an EU member state. The diplomacy model, suggesting an intergovernmentalist arena of perpetual negotiations, serves its purpose when focusing on Germany's trajectory during the history of European integration. The same holds true for certain contemporary periods of European politics like treaty revisions, enlargement processes, or negotiations on the fiscal framework of the EU. Beyond these incidents of high EU politics, however, the day-to-day level of European affairs is inextricably integrated into the whole of the domestic German political system. As in other member states, the interlocking nature of domestic and EU structures has not been internalized by all political elites, let alone by all voters. Consequently, we can observe a setting in which long-term adaptations from a domestic to a transnational regime are still taking place. German approaches to the European level need to be analysed as a bundle of societal and institutional preferences that go far beyond the government's reach. Many EU related issues are dealt with by tight interlocking with the EU level and therefore involve other modes of interaction than just negotiation.

Patterns of Germany–EU Relations

It is a commonplace that Western integration after World War II had the aim of preventing a revival of German power on the European continent. The evolving security architecture was established by the Allies in order to 'keep the Germans down' (a quote from the British diplomat, Hastings Ismay), and economic integration had the aim to 'bind France, Germany, and the other countries that join', as Robert Schuman expressed in a speech on 9 May 1950.[1] Germany started into European integration as an object, more a dangerous thug that needed to be roped in than a valued partner or even friend. In the early years after the war, Germany depended on the goodwill of other European governments in almost all matters of the European 'order' (Thränhardt 1996).

Konrad Adenauer—the first chancellor of the Federal Republic from 1949 to 1963—developed a twofold strategy in order to re-establish Germany as an economic power and diplomatic player in Europe. On the one hand, his government invested in real and symbolic acts of reconciliation with the most important Western powers—France and the United States. On the other, active steps towards reconstructing the economy and to establishing an international political standing were usually carried out in coordination with Western partners. Strengthened by the pressure of the Soviet Union on Berlin, and on Germany as a whole, all relevant political elites of the Federal Republic took over the essence of Adenauer's early policy decisions. By the time of German reunification, the country had become a fully integrated member of the EU, of Western security structures, and of global politics and institutions (Hellmann 2006).

From this perspective, the Federal Republic is indeed to be understood as an actor in international politics. Europe and European integration play an important role but need to be contextualized by the broader developments of world politics. Thus the European vocation of the Federal Republic was less a policy perspective born from free will, and rather the choice of Western integration following the necessities of the Cold War (Hanrieder 1967). On the one hand, West Germany was, in a strong sense, dependent on the Western Allies. Its state sovereignty remained restricted, its re-armament was completely intertwined with Western security organizations, and its trade relations were focused on the West. On the other hand, the Soviet Union and its satellite state on East German territory were tacitly hostile on good days and openly aggressive on bad days. West European integration served as a very good solution to the many problems which came out of the confrontational international setting. It represented the basis for trust building in the West in order to be able to resist fierce pressure from the East.

In order to follow this interest, West German diplomacy developed a style which distinguished it from all Western powers of comparable economic and—increasingly—political weight. Restricted in its potential to formulate and pursue a completely autonomous foreign policy, Germany not only followed multilateral patterns of international politics, but declared multilateralism as a foreign policy aim as such. The best example of this general approach was represented by the establishment of the Franco–German relationship which consisted of a very close relationship between the governments of the two countries. During some phases, the Franco–German axis openly declared a leadership position with regard to the European integration process as a whole. With the growing number of member states within the EU, especially after Eastern enlargement in 2004, Franco–German leadership capacities have, however, eroded (Schild 2010).

Within the framework of European integration, the German strategy of multilateralism had the additional virtue of pulling medium and small size EC/EU member states to the German camp in many policy areas. Therefore, it is no surprise that the traditional West German doctrine of acting as an honest broker between all EC/EU member states continued well into the post-unification framework (Erb 2003;

Rittberger 2001). At the same time, we can observe a growing number of incidents where German governments get into open conflict with European neighbour states. Many of them started during the Schröder government of 1998–2005: the construction of a Russian–German gas pipeline around Poland, and the European divisions over the Iraq war serve as prime examples (Hacke 2005). Other examples—this time from the Merkel government, which started in 2009—are the fierce resistance to an easy bail-out during the Greek fiscal crisis of 2010–12 and, in general, the principled approach in the struggle for a stable euro (Barysch 2010). The accumulation of such incidents tells us that German governments are less timid to voice their interests than in earlier years. Still, the issue should be treated with more nuances than just a rise of national assertiveness (Paterson 2010). Section 6 will return to that discussion.

EU Membership and Public Opinion

In the first decades of European integration, the German population is said to have taken the position of a permissive consensus—as was the case in other member states (Lindberg and Scheingold 1970). The support for EU membership was especially high around the period of German reunification when more than 70 per cent of Germans labelled EU membership 'a good thing'. This has been explained by the feeling of Germans that European integration served as a major element of stabilization within the critical process of overcoming German, and at the same time European, division. In that sense, the population followed its political elites of the time. For example, Chancellor Helmut Kohl had categorically linked German and European unification (see, for example, Kohl 1996).

In later years, however, public support for EU membership and European integration as a whole fell dramatically (see Figure 4.1). By 1997, less than 40 per cent of Germans were ready to announce EU membership a 'good thing'. About 35 per cent expressed the opinion that Germany had 'on balance benefited' from EU membership, but more than 40 per cent took the opposite position. The huge fall in popularity is accredited to the mostly critical domestic discussion, namely on the single European currency replacing the Deutsche Mark. This explains why levels of public support remained modest for some years until experience showed that inflation—as the main fear connected to giving up the D-Mark—did not result from the introduction of the euro. The next steep fall in public support in 2004 is connected to fears related to Eastern enlargement. The latest fall in support for the EU, during 2009 and 2010, is related to expected negative results of the financial crisis and its effects on the euro. All in all, public support for European integration has become much more nuanced than in recent years (see overviews in Hrbek 2002; Seidendorf 2010).

Also beyond the question of explicit support for European integration, German public opinion on Europe is characterized by diversity. On the surface, we find

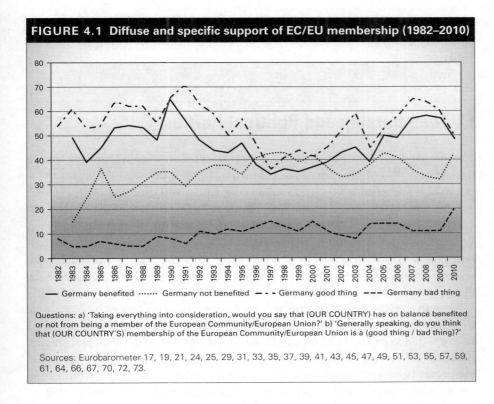

FIGURE 4.1 Diffuse and specific support of EC/EU membership (1982–2010)

—— Germany benefited ⋯⋯ Germany not benefited — - — Germany good thing – – – Germany bad thing

Questions: a) 'Taking everything into consideration, would you say that (OUR COUNTRY) has on balance benefited or not from being a member of the European Community/European Union?' b) 'Generally speaking, do you think that (OUR COUNTRY'S) membership of the European Community/European Union is a (good thing / bad thing)?'

Sources: Eurobarometer 17, 19, 21, 24, 25, 29, 31, 33, 35, 37, 39, 41, 43, 45, 47, 49, 51, 53, 55, 57, 59, 61, 64, 66, 67, 70, 72, 73.

attitudes that confirm considerable openness to the Europeanization of formerly national elements of society and politics. For example, Eurobarometer findings show that significantly more than 50 per cent of the German population accredit themselves an either partial or completely 'European' identity. In other words, only a minority of Germans identify their own political existence mainly with Germany. As the historian, Hartmut Kaelble (2005), has shown, Germans as well as other Europeans live a good proportion of their lives in transnational contexts. Two thirds of young Germans between 15 and 24 manage to actively speak a foreign language. Germans are also among the more than 30 per cent of young Europeans that have spent at least a three-month period in another country than their own. Fifteen per cent of all marriages in Germany take place between EU-Europeans of different nationalities (figures, taken from different sources, are cited in Beichelt 2009: 140–1).

However, these facts should not be translated into a statement that Germany mainly consists of Europhiles. To all data just mentioned we have to be aware of mirror-image contrast groups. A good minority of a third of the population maintains an exclusively national identity. Older generations and less educated population groups are less open to European or other international societal contacts (again, see Kaelble 2005). Also, Figure 4.1 exhibits a solid minority of more than 10 per cent of the population which explicitly judges EU membership to be a 'bad thing'. In the logic of party politics, these minorities are able to wield a considerable blackmail potential (Sartori 1976) which makes them an important cornerstone of German EU policy.

EU Membership and Political Parties

The international setting after 1945 left German elites little room for manoeuvre to deviate from the pro-Western course pursued by Konrad Adenauer during his chancellorship. The main adversary to Adenauer's Christian Democratic Party (CDU) was the Social Democratic Party (SPD). During the first decade of the Federal Republic, the SPD aimed for German unification beyond the firm commitment on Western integration including the possibility of German neutrality on the international scene. This changed in 1959, when a new party programme was much more open to capitalist market democracy, and made the party's agenda compatible with the type of economic integration practised within the EC (see Rosolowsky 1987).

From the 1960s, then, the German party system was characterized by consensus. European integration was seen by all relevant party elites as something that should be supported as an end in its own right. Besides the CDU and the SPD, four smaller parties should be mentioned. The liberal Free Democratic Party (FDP) was a relevant actor because it served as a minor coalition partner in many governments. There, it often occupied the foreign minister post and produced several politicians with a Europe-wide reputation; Walter Scheel (1969–74) and Hans-Dietrich Genscher (1974–92) are the main examples. The conservative Christian Social Party (CSU) is a party restricted to the southern region of Bavaria (where the CDU leaves the field to its sister party). The CSU is sometimes characterized as a EU-sceptic party, not least because one of its deputies challenged the Lisbon Treaty before the German Constitutional Court. However, the CSU's leaders have in the end always supported the German policy of widening and deepening; the EU-sceptic reputation is more fuelled from public rhetoric than from empirical evidence. After their appearance on the parliamentary stage in the 1980s, the German Green party elites soon joined the pro-integrationist consensus of the German party system. For example, Joschka Fischer and Hans-Jürgen Trittin—two ministers of the Red-Green government from 1998–2005—belonged to the most outspoken supporters of the European Constitution and the Treaty of Lisbon. Finally, the Leftist Party (Linkspartei) should be mentioned as the most EU-sceptic player in the German Bundestag. The party challenges the allegedly neo-liberal policy of EU elites and criticizes most of the EU's external action as overly militaristic.

As a whole, party politics play a limited role for German EU policy. Even in the European debt and financial crisis of 2010–2012, most decisions have been taken consensually between the major parties of the political system. The strong position of government in the institutional system leads to some detachment of German politicians from their respective party bases once they enter government. Since large proportions of a country's EU policy are addressed in the Council, politicians in power largely have to stick within their governmental role. Not only organizational aspects, but also programmatic elements of EU related political action are better understood by focusing on the government level.

However, beyond the dimension of government action, party-related aspects play a considerable role in German EU policy. First and foremost, the level of contestation with regard to EU policy has risen dramatically during the last twenty years. This is true for landmark decisions as well as for day-to-day politics. For example, the ratification of the Lisbon Treaty was embedded in a fierce debate on the consequences of the Europeanization of German economic, foreign, and security policies. In the end, the Bundestag faction of the Leftist Party brought in a constitutional challenge against the treaty which was partly accepted and led to a revised form of the law into the parliamentary involvement in European affairs.

Beyond milestone decisions, there are other arenas of conflict which concern those parties whose leaders have in recent epochs cultivated the consensus style of European policy. Two authors have listed programme statements of German political parties (Sturm and Pehle 2006: 193–203), and found that considerable EU related policy conflicts can be found in the following areas: social policy, economic policy, security policy, agrarian policy, cohesion policy, consumer protection policy, as well as enlargement policy. The list shows why contestation has entered German EU policy. Common market principles have infiltrated policy areas beyond foreign trade and competition policy, and hence the central cleavages of German politics—liberal versus state regulated economic and social policy, pacifist versus Western integrated security policy—spill over on the European arena.

Consequently, EU related party competition is torn between two principles which, for the time being, co-exist. On the one hand, those parts of European policy making connected to the Council are treated as foreign policy. Therefore, party politicians from the opposition today respect executive dominance. The administrative predominance in policy development is not generally contested, and German policy makers on the EU level are somewhat protected from opposition attacks in order to close German ranks during and after Council negotiations. On the other hand, the domestic relevance of many issues causes party politicians of all camps to enter into public debate and policy making where possible. Here we find one arena in which Europe and the EU are still in the process of changing German politics. In the long run, we may expect domestic conflicts to enter the Council also (which would then weaken our understanding of politics in the EU as 'EU diplomacy').

Indications of such a development can already be found (Beichelt 2009: 185–206). One option of opposition parties consists in voicing protest through members of the European Parliament. Although this type of multilevel parliamentarism is not fully developed and suffers from structural restrictions, the bigger parties, especially, are usually capable of using their resources accordingly. A second field of party competition is opened after the Council phase. Typically during the transposition of directives into national legislation, parliamentarians of all camps have the opportunity to refer to the EU level. The constellation is always tricky. Since major elements of legislation are fixed by a directive, the scope for domestic interpretation remains limited. Opposition to the substance of a directive to be transposed easily crosses over into abstract criticism of EU procedures. Still, controversial debates between coalition and opposition parties appear. Third, the restriction on domestic contestation during the Council phase of a project does not apply to coalition parties. Therefore, it is quite often possible to observe substantial EU policy conflicts between coalition partners, which then possibly encourage other actors to engage in the debate as well. Taken together, these three patterns of party conflict reveal that party politics have started to play a significant role in German EU policy. All political parties have consequently built up specific structures to deal with EU affairs (for details, see Poguntke 2007).

EU Membership and Political Institutions

If the multilevel system terminology is employed with regard to the European polity, political institutions need to be understood in a specific way. Within a system, institutions fulfil certain functions, for example interest articulation and aggregation (Almond *et al.* 1996). Originally, these terms were developed for national political systems—they were even explicitly designed to isolate national systems from the international environment. In the reality of the European polity, however, elements of international politics have penetrated national politics. The articulation and aggregation of interests as well as other system functions therefore take place on several levels. As a whole, this multi-stage setting can be viewed as a European policy cycle (Beichelt 2009; Maurer and Mittag 2003).

The EU policy cycle consists, depending on the type of legal act at the EU level, of two or three stages. The three stage setting applies to directives. The first stage takes place on the EU level and can be characterized as the run-up to, and the substance of, decision taking[2] in the Council and, where granted by treaty provisions, the European Parliament. The second round of decision making repeats this procedure on the national level. The third stage consists of implementation and is usually carried out by national bureaucracies. If we are not dealing with directives, but with other legal acts as foreseen by the Treaty of Lisbon, stage 2 of the policy cycle is omitted.

Stage 1: EU Level Decision Making

In the first phase of decision making on the EU level, a lot of attention goes to the Commission which collects opinions and positions with regard to their initiatives. This process is often characterized as a playground for EU lobbyists, be it from national or EU interest groups (Greenwood 2011). Accordingly, German 'Verbände' play a major role here. Additionally, it is often overlooked that the preparation of Commission initiatives bears a strong component of inter-executive coordination. A handbook for the German administration lists more than 1,702 expert groups which are relevant for members of German executives of all levels (Thomas and Wessels 2006: 86–7). We also find that the German administration cooperates 'intensively' with the Commission at that stage. Much of the consultation preceding initiatives bears a technical character. In the German federal system, implementation is usually carried through by the sixteen Länder administrations. For many of the technical consultations, it will therefore be Länder officials taking part in the expert groups.

The considerable potential for executive action contrasts with parliamentary absence at this stage. In general, national parliaments do not have institutionalized access to EU interest articulation. German parliamentarians are rather used to this constellation from the national context where most legislative proposals are also prepared by the executive. There is, however, a categorical difference which seems overly neglected. In the national system, the executive is at least by idea controlled through the elected government. Such a political element is absent from the EU level where the Commission follows the general concept of enlightened technocracy. The only scope for parliamentary influence at this stage comes via German MEPs.

After a Commission initiative is on the table, Council negotiations between member governments start officially. For that purpose, about 250 working groups, which cover all policy areas of EU legislation, meet more or less regularly. The Federal Republic equips these working groups mainly with staff of the Permanent Representation in Brussels (sometimes also called 'EU embassy'). In the German Representation, about 90–100 officials have their offices. Not all of them are drafted from the foreign office (Auswärtiges Amt). Many official members of the Representation are delegated from other Berlin ministries, and also from Länder ministries. This recruitment style mirrors domestic administrative structures and usually means that German officials in Council working groups know their files comparatively well and have a direct link to those ministries where legislation is actually managed (Beichelt 2007).

Simultaneously with Council negotiations, the European Parliament (EP) gets involved in many policy areas. Some countries show a clear profile of EP deputies who focus almost completely on issues which are relevant for respective national arenas. For Germany, this is not the case (Weßels 2003). Despite the sporadic interaction mentioned in the previous section, the two parliamentary arenas co-exist rather than being equipped with firmly institutionalized interlocking mechanisms. Therefore, interest aggregation by German deputies in the EP by and large follows an EP-related logic rather than that of German national politics (again, see Poguntke 2007).

Next, we get to the stage of Brussels procedures where decisions are actually taken. Here, the profile of involvement of both the German executive and German MEPs changes in intensity, but not by character. In the Council, issues are now dealt with on the level of the two Committees of Permanent Representatives

(COREPER) and ministerial meetings. Consequently, higher ranks in the Berlin ministries get involved, and consequently 'political' aspects gain ground vis-à-vis the 'technical' components of legislative acts. In order to deal with the complex necessities of German federal administration and Council negotiations in Brussels, a hierarchical setting of conflict management has been set up in Berlin (Beichelt 2009: 219–34). In general, all EU issues are dealt with on the level of the respective administrative unit which is officially responsible for this or that piece of legislation. Higher levels in the ministries, for example heads of whole sections or state secretaries, only get involved in the case of conflict. Final decisions in EU policy usually take place on the cabinet level of German government. This, however, is almost always a formal element. In fact, a committee of state secretaries is the instance where most decisions are taken.

All these process properties underline the generally technocratic character of German EU policy. Negotiators on all levels are usually recruited from top civil servants rather than from elected politicians. German level political parties or members of parliament play a minor role not only during interest articulation and aggregation, but also during the phase of decision taking. Other German actors, for example in the Commission or in the EP often dispose an image of following their institutions' interests rather than explicitly feeling responsible for 'German' positions (Weßels 2005).

Stage 2: German Level Decision Making

On the next level, the process of decision making largely follows a specific form of the German parliamentary regime. Its core elements are party dominance, coalition government, a working parliament based on a largely non-political administration and, last not least, federal bicameralism (Hesse and Ellwein 2004). They translate into specific procedures of decision making which have been characterized as 'semi-sovereignty' or 'middle way' (Katzenstein 1987; Schmidt 1987). This concerns not only a rather continuous profile between the poles of market liberalism and state-oriented welfare policy, the metaphors are also used for a style of decision making which refrains from sharply polarized party conflict and is calibrated around consensual decision making in the federal dimension. Of course, these core elements of the parliamentary regime also apply to pieces of legislation which originate from the EU level. Although the major properties of German legislation can consequently be found with regard to EU bills as well, there are a few additional elements which need further discussion.

First and probably most importantly, initiatives reach the parliamentary stage after they have gone through a regular phase of preparation in the responsible ministry. Since the time frame between a Council decision and the deadline for its transposition may easily last several years, it would be an exaggeration to expect the same civil servant who already put the directive through the Council to be responsible for its enactment in Germany. But still, most likely it will be the same ministry and the same internal division which drafts the respective German law. Therefore, the executive dominance on EU bills is re-enacted on the domestic level. Any legislation which has a previous EU history is solidly fenced in by executive actors before intermediary actors and parliament get the bill on the table.

The transposition of EU legislation, and this is the second point, is usually deprived of open party competition. This has to do with the fact that directives only leave limited room for the interpretation of an EU bill; substantial changes are not possible. The only opportunity for conflict evolves when so called 'saddling-up' takes place in the sense that EU directives are combined with domestic legal rules which add up to the regulations as proposed by the EU. A prominent case where this happened was the antidiscrimination bill of 2006.[3] The discussion which followed focused on the allegedly exaggerated influence of the EU on German politics. In the end, German parliamentarians advocated there should not be further incidents of saddling-up onto EU acts in general.[4] While the effect for public acceptance of the EU may be positive, this agreement further confines actors on the national level.

Third, the existence of EU bills further minimizes conflict in the federal arena. Formally the Bundesrat—the second chamber of German parliament—is involved through its European affairs committee. However, it should not be forgotten that the Bundesrat is not made up of elected parliamentarians, but of delegated officials from Länder executives. Therefore, we find a high continuity between Länder positions on a given project on the EU level (where they have been involved through interest aggregation in the Permanent Representation) and during the German legislative phase. Conflicts with an explicitly federal dimension have most likely already been tackled during the first phase of EU decision making.

Fourth and last, EU secondary legislation is often of very limited interest for the public sphere, especially the media. If there has been no particular conflict on the EU level, for the already given reasons it is not to be expected that one occurs on the German level. In these cases, EU affairs enter into German legislation without wider public debate. If a conflict has not been solved during the EU decision making phase, the issue may appear in the German media. However, its appearance is then likely to bear an EU-sceptic overtone—it means that an unpopular issue has not been settled completely and is now to be transposed despite its contentiousness in the German sphere. In the end, the transposition of EU bills into German legislation is only rarely linked to the European public sphere in constructive terms.

Stage 3: German Level Implementation

Post-legislative implementation is often seen as a purely administrative task where political aspects only play a minor role. This is somewhat contradictory to theoretical expectations which see quite some scope for national executives to transform undesirable legislation into more agreeable rules on the ground (Garrett and Weingast 1993). At first sight, Germany could be a case where such practices might play a role as executive actors are involved into EU policy making from the very first until the very last stage. However, political considerations are limited by nature in the German system because of the specific style of administrative implementation which is characterized by a federal division of labour. For almost all matters (including those where the central state is exclusively responsible for decision making), Länder administrations are responsible for the implementation of legislative acts. Both the German constitution and the administrative culture hold to a tight notion of federal allegiance ('Bundestreue') which makes most administrative bodies in the Federal Republic non-autonomous agents of the political elite.

Summary: Institutions

In the analysis of European politics, the characteristics of national institutions can be summarized as follows:

- German *government* is the only actor which is present at all stages of EU related decision making. It is therefore adequate to name the German government as major legislator in EU decision making. In sum, administrative action dominates its style. Political aspects play a role too, but rather with regard to conflicts with other EU governments or EU institutions (Commission, EP) than with regard to other political actors on the domestic stage.

- The *Bundestag* has often been described as a weak institution with a secondary role in European politics (Auel 2006). On the one hand, that has to do with the logic of action unfolding on the EU level, where governments are the sovereign representatives of a state. On the other, the Bundestag has only in recent years started to see itself as an actor in its own right in EU affairs. Since 2006, parliament opened a liaison office in Brussels and considerably strengthened its administrative capacity to deal with EU bills. In the Lisbon Treaty, national parliaments have been accorded additional rights with regard to the subsidiarity clause (Schröder *et al.* 2009). Therefore the coming years may well show a certain revival of the Bundestag in EU legislation.

- The *Bundesrat* can be characterized as an institution involved in EU legislation but one which rarely plays an autonomous role in EU policy (Grünhage 2007). Following its structure as a body made up of administrative actors, the Bundesrat's activities largely unfold in the bureaucratic sphere of technical advice. Political competition only plays a role in one constellation, namely if the party-political make-up of the majority of the Länder governments in the Bundesrat is at odds with the composition of the coalition ruling in Berlin. In that case, party politics may even dominate federal relations (Scharpf 1985). Empirically, such constellations have been rare in German politics, and they have never lasted more than a few years. Since many EU bills have a longer time horizon, effects for the EU level have so far been modest.

- An institution which is important despite its absence during Brussels and Berlin decision making is the German *Constitutional Court*. It has proved decisive during integration history by determining the degree to which the German constitutional order may be penetrated by transnational elements (Schwarze 2001). Major verdicts concerned the constitutional compatibility of the Maastricht and Lisbon Treaties with the German Basic Law. The Constitutional Court has, in these decisions, insisted that the substance of political decision making in Europe has to remain in the national sphere, in particular with regard to the Bundestag. Some authors have used this evidence to claim a general hostility of the Constitutional Court to the pro-integration decisions of German political elites (Höpner *et al.* 2010). However, such statements may be exaggerated. By and large, the Court has insisted on the general legality of EU integration. In the Lisbon Treaty case, it stated the friendliness of the German constitution to Europe ('Europafreundlichkeit') and explicitly valued the principle of openness towards European law (again, see Schröder *et al.* 2009).

All in all, the institutional setting which has evolved in the field of EU politics differs significantly from the parliamentary model which is constitutive to the Federal Republic of Germany. The core arenas of deliberation, legislative preparation, and decision taking have shifted away from the public sphere, from political parties and parliament to government and the executive in general.

EU Membership and Public Policy

If we stay in the framework of the EU policy cycle, nations and their governments face the specific problem of influencing EU institutions and other member governments in the direction of their preferences. As a big member state, Germany is generally able to exert considerable influence on other institutions within the multilevel system. It is therefore no surprise to see characterizations of Germany as a 'major player' in EU politics (Lankowski 2001). After restrictions on account of a limited sovereignty disappeared in 1990, many authors expected a more self-confident foreign and European policy, paired with the will to push through national interests even against European partners (Rittberger and Wagner 2001). And, indeed, recent analyses have shown that there seems to be a new balance between national interests and a genuinely European vocation (Chandler 2010; Paterson 2010). However, there are also other voices judging Germany's capacity to actively shape EU policies in more pessimistic terms ('weaker, meaner, leaner', see Harnisch and Schieder 2006).

However tempting it may be to subsume German EU policy under one formula, the multidimensional character of EU policy makes it hard to find a clear trend on German performance within the EU. Many hypotheses focus on landmark events like enlargement rounds or the financial perspective. Here, negotiations in the EU have in general become more public than previously, and therefore all EU governments have to present successes to their respective national audiences. In this context, it is probably hard to find any government of an EU state that has not become more outspoken on conflict issues or matters of special interest.

In the German case, it is certainly possible to confirm a corresponding change in style. The evolving multilevel system opens a field of transnational communication beyond single decisions on this or that issue in this or that policy area. Political leaders have become aware of this to a growing extent, and they increasingly use it for all kinds of decisions beyond landmark issues. For example, German politicians regularly meet with their French counterparts in order to influence the EU agenda on issues important to both countries. Examples are common suggestions around the Iraq war, the Lisbon Treaty crisis, the global financial crisis, and in connection with plans to address the euro-zone crisis. By doing this, German politicians have developed a style of voicing the country's interests which is quite different from their official commitments to multilateral decision making. On the one hand, there is consultation going on. On the other, even beyond the Franco–German relationship, the government consciously seeks to close ranks with those governments that share its own interests before opening the black box of EU negotiations. Being purposeful and explicit on one's policy aims does not necessarily mean, however, that the aim itself is more likely to be achieved. The German strategy of self-assertiveness did not work well with regard to Iraq, it partly worked during the financial crisis, and it was more or less successful on the Lisbon Treaty. Therefore, the issue of a new German EU style and German effectiveness in pushing through its interests should not be confused.

As for policy effectiveness, further differentiation is necessary. The treaties have established different types of procedures for different policy areas. In some of the deeply integrated areas, like agricultural or foreign trade policy, actors from national executives have been pushed back in favour of the EU level executive and (national as well as EU level) interest groups. In policy areas where intergovernmentalist practices prevail, the German government is able to employ the comparatively strong weight it has in comparison to many other EU governments. The effectiveness of German EU policy making then depends on the character of policy outcomes against the background of previously formulated policy preferences. As in all member state governments, one basic difference always consists in the will (or capacity) to apply a mainly national or an EU problem horizon when trying to achieve policy goals. Here, we find different approaches which are determined by the level of integration of a given policy area, by the salience of the given issue, and by the will of political leaders to play political games on one or several levels of the multilevel system.

Approach 1: The Politics of Constructing a European Framework

German performance in the EU has often been characterized as exceptionally integrationist and multilateral (Anderson and Goodman 1993; Erb 2003). While this judgement is not wrong, a closer look tells us that it has usually been associated with the historic landmark decisions of German EU integration. Until 1989/90, the pro-integrationist profile presented the only rational path of preventing Soviet domination during the Cold War. After the fall of the Berlin Wall, there was again no alternative to EU integration because France and Great Britain needed to be convinced to agree to German reunification. Decisions taken during this period—the continuous strengthening of EU institutions, the ever closer coordination of Foreign and Security Policy, the introduction of the euro—therefore represent long-term policy goals that were meant to establish a European political order to encapsulate Germany in order to liberate it from the ties of post-war Europe. In a way, German governments have been able to upload their preferences to the EU level on a broad scale by shaping an EU political system which fits German interests very well.

This strategy of 'western integration' left a strong legacy on policy makers especially in all domains of traditional foreign policy. Until today, Germany will habitually try to gather most EU member states behind most foreign policy initiatives. Multilateralism is usually combined with a focus on complementing robust means of foreign policy with 'civilian' elements (Maull 2007); one primary example is German engagement in the Western Balkans (Calic 2007). German multilateralism also materializes with regard to EU institutions. For example, the Commission lead in foreign trade policy is completely accepted despite the status of Germany as the biggest industrial power in the EU. Also, with regard to other long-term strategies like EU enlargement, Germany has tried to establish a common EU approach rather than trying to seek a national profile within that policy area. Here, the question of Turkish EU accession may prove an interesting test case for the enduring capability of Germany to upload its preferences to the EU level—the Merkel government has repeatedly voiced the policy goal of offering Turkey the status of a 'privileged partner' rather than full EU membership.

Another area in which Germany has continuously been able to export political aims and institutions to the EU level is monetary policy. It is no secret that the European Central Bank has largely been designed from the Bundesbank model (see Dyson 2002). However, that is not the only instance of uploading. In 2004, the Schröder government talked a majority of its European partners into loosening the same stability pact that had been dictated by the Kohl government a few years earlier. In all these cases, it was German preferences which decisively shaped the monetary order of the EU—from the idea of a European economic government in the early 1990s, to strict monetarism in the wake of the euro, to permissive government spending in the early 2000s. Only the euro-zone crisis caught the Merkel government on the wrong foot as the reaction to the crisis called to different logics of action on the domestic and the EU level: the necessity to downsize public expenses domestically; and the need to invest in a stable monetary setting on the EU level (see Approach 2). Therefore, monetary policy belongs to different approaches, depending on the phase.

Approach 2: Securing Electoral Support in the Multilevel Regime

While the 'constructing Europe approach' is still propagated by the German government as being at the core of German EU policy, the rapidly growing number of transnationalized policy areas has in the last twenty years added another layer to German action within the EU. Crudely, it consists of the political struggle on the EU level in arenas of domestic and/or EU-internal conflict. In the institutional order of the EU, any national government has to secure its legitimation primarily vis-à-vis the national electorate. Two important areas where the national election game extends onto the EU level are migration and asylum policy as well as cohesion policy.

The former Justice and Home Affairs section of the European treaties presented the first instance—notably after reunification—where a German government openly challenged other member states' aims to further integrate a policy area. This happened on open stage during the intergovernmental conference leading to the Treaty of Amsterdam, when the government of Helmut Kohl tried to prevent the integration of asylum and migration policy fully into the Community structures (Gimbal 2001). Back at the time, the policy area was of high domestic priority to the German government because of considerable migration waves during the 1990s (Thränhardt 2007). Even today, Germany will usually try to resist an asylum policy which shares the burden equally between EU member states. Rather, German governments of all colours have tried to insist on the given legal framework which allocates asylum seekers and refugees to those countries where they enter the EU—an inexpensive position for a country which, after Eastern enlargement, has become landlocked within the EU. In general, German migration policy on the EU level follows its outline on the domestic level, which is characterized by moderate modernization of residence rights and strong pressure on further migration influx. In following these aims, Germany has used the EU level largely in instrumental terms; Simon Bulmer has characterized the approach as 'venue shopping' (Bulmer 2011).

Another example for open and returning conflict is cohesion policy. In the past, the policy area served as proof for Germany's quest for EU integration even at high financial cost (Bulmer *et al.* 2010: 6). Since the mid-1990s, when German reunification proved to be a heavy burden on public budgets, the tough position during negotiations on the financial perspectives of 2000–2006 and 2007–2013 were, in contrast, seen as an indicator of a more self-confident or national interest driven approach of German EU policy as a whole. In a narrow perspective, it is certainly true that the German government applies a national horizon when formulating aims in cohesion policy. However, a look at the cohesion policy shows that member state governments have in general chosen to use cohesion policy in order to satisfy domestic demands (Allen 2005: 223). In that sense, the conflict-oriented approach of Germany with regard to structural funds should be seen as a consequence of a generally more politicized institutional order in EU politics.

Approach 3: Reacting to 'Europe' on the National Scene

The first two approaches visible in German EU policy are characterized by a consensus among German elites as well as the population that political problems should be solved through the involvement of EU institutions—regardless of previous successes or failures in uploading national preferences to the EU level. The third approach differs from that pattern in the sense that EU politics are not a regular part of a policy area. While this applies to a wider range of policy fields, the most debated area in this regard is that part of economic policy that deals with correcting market mechanisms. Of course, the common market policy and parts of social policy are today integrated. However, in the area of welfare state policy (for example, labour market, pensions, and social subsidies) most relevant actors have an almost exclusively domestic horizon. EU institutions in these fields are not seen as the main locus of solution finding even if—as is the case in parts of social policy—competencies have partly been deferred to the EU (Schmidt 2006).

Scholars of German politics come to quite different conclusions on the weight of European integration with regard to its economic and welfare policy. Some authors completely disregard the European dimension (Schmid 2006; Zohlnhöfer 2006), others define the European political order mainly as a constraint on domestic policy (Scharpf 2002), still others see Europeanization as a major element of German economic governance (Green 2010). The decision on how to conceptualize 'Europe' with regard to economic and welfare policy has a considerable impact on the interpretation of German government action in times of economic crisis. During the euro-zone crisis, the Merkel government has been subject to divergent judgements. On the one hand, it has been accused of a negligent attitude towards European stability by being too hesitant to help out, notably, the Greek and Irish governments (Habermas 2010). On the other, almost 200 German professors of economics openly criticized the financial stability package the EU had agreed upon in February 2011.[5]

It would be premature to categorize this debate as a mere reflection of pro-integrationist and Europhobe forces within German society, the one side being afraid of 'too little', the other of 'too much' German engagement in the direction of a European economic government. Rather, we find two different interpretations on the legitimacy of governing the European economic space. Only one—supported by authors like Habermas or Scharpf—argues in the context of a truly European economic space. The prevailing tendency in German economic governance, however, consists of defending the alleged German stability culture.[6] However, it should not be overlooked that advocates of this position usually belong to the camp of critics of the traditional German 'politics of the middle way' (Schmidt 2010) in which governments pay as much attention to social balancing as to economic competitiveness. In that sense, the economic policy of Germany within the EU context often bears a momentum of using the EU level in order to better influence domestic debates and decision making. This pattern of reacting to Europe—rather than trying to shape it—can also be found in other policy areas with a low degree of EU integration, for example in education or energy policy.

Conclusion

At the end of this chapter, it should have become clear that the classification of Germany as an EU member state to a large extent depends on preliminary methodological decisions. Within the framework of international politics, Germany has ceded much of its sovereignty and become ever more integrated into European and transatlantic frameworks. During that process, its potential to autonomously exert power has naturally been diminished. At the same time, German interests in the fields of international security and socioeconomic development have been massively served by European integration. German diplomacy—characterized by multi-lateralist practices and domestic interest orientation at the same time—can be characterized as a major success story but is at the same time under pressure in a political system where intergovernmentalist practices play a role in a diminishing number of policy areas. The 'success' of German EU policy increasingly depends on other modes of action than negotiation between governments.

This development has yielded far reaching consequences if we look from the perspective of the domestic system. On the input side, the Europeanization of politics has almost completely overturned the tradition of the Federal Republic to organize decision making and communication around political parties. To be sure, the predominance of parties in German political life has been widely criticized (starting with Leibholz 1958). With the current system, however, wide parts of interest articulation, interest aggregation, and decision taking have been relocated to non-elected executives and interest groups. It is not at all clear if that construction will be able to withhold pressure in times of real crisis. Also, the German government—pulling the strings in Brussels—has not undertaken visible steps to legitimize its real position as a legislator in respect of the traditional legislative institutions of the German system.

With regard to the EU as a whole, these latent elements of future 'system stress' (David Easton) have translated into a somewhat inconsistent profile of EU policy making. In some areas, Europeanization and transnationalization have broken through and refocused elites to the new European centre that was once hoped for (Haas 1958: 16). Other fields are characterized by intractable national glue, and neither political actors nor the public seem close to accepting the transnationalized structures which legally apply. Sometimes a European problem horizon exists, sometimes not. For the time being, Germany as an EU member state remains in search of a new balance between a tamed, normalized, or indeed convoluted power in Europe.

FURTHER READING

Much of the more recent literature on Germany's European perspective is published in German. Three edited volumes in English offering an overview are: Simon Bulmer, Charles Jeffery, and Stephen Padgett (2010) *Rethinking Germany and Europe: Democracy and Diplomacy in a Semi-Sovereign State* (Basingstoke: Palgrave Macmillan); from Kenneth Dyson and Klaus H. Goetz (2004), *Germany, Europe, and the Politics of Constraint* (Oxford: Oxford University Press); and, for the earlier post-Cold War period, Peter Katzenstein (ed.) (1997), *Tamed Power – Germany in Europe* (Ithaca/London: Cornell University Press).

WEB LINKS

The federal government's website is an important source of official information (**www.bundesregierung.de**), and so is the Bundestag's homepage with many products of the Bundestag's scientific service online (mostly in German, **www.bundestag.de**). Important think tanks with useful online publications are the Stiftung Wissenschaft und Politik (**www.swp-berlin.org**), the Institut für Europäische Politik (**www.iep-berlin.de**), and the Zentrum für Europäische Wirtschaftsforschung (**www.zei.de**). Another useful source is the Max Planck Institut für Gesellschaftsforschung in Cologne (**www.mpifg.de**). Information mainly oriented to political science scholars can be found at the Deutsche Vereinigung für Politikwissenschaft (**https://www.dvpw.de**) and the American Institute for Contemporary German Studies (**www.aicgs.org**).

REFERENCES

Allen, David (2005), 'Cohesion and the Structural Funds', in Helen Wallace, William Wallace, and Mark A. Pollack (eds), *Policy-Making in the European Union. Fifth Edition*, Oxford: Oxford University Press, 213–42.

Almond, Gabriel, A. Powell, G. Bingham, and Robert J. Mundt (1996), *Comparative Politics. A Theoretical Framework. 2nd edition*, New York: Harper Collins.

Anderson, Jeffrey J. and Goodman, John B. (1993), 'Mars or Minerva? A United Germany in a Post-Cold War Europe', in Robert O. Keohane, Joseph S. Nye, and Stanley Hoffmann (eds), *After the Cold War: International Institutions and State Strategies in Europe, 1989–1991*, Cambridge: Harvard University Press, 23–62.

Auel, Katrin (2006), 'The Europeanisation of the German Bundestag: Institutional Change and Informal Adaptation', *German Politics*, 15/3: 249–68.

Barysch, Katinka (2010), *Germany, the euro and the Politics of the Bail-out*, London: Centre for European Reform briefing note, June 2010 (http://www.cer.org.uk/pdf/bn_barysch_germanyandeurope_28jun10.pdf).

Beichelt, Timm (2007), 'Over-efficiency in German EU Policy Coordination', *German Politics*, 16/4: 421–32.

——— (2009), *Deutschland und Europa. Die Europäisierung des Politischen Systems*, Wiesbaden: VS Verlag für Sozialwissenschaft.

Börzel, Tanja (2006), 'Europäisierung der Deutschen Politik?', in Manfred G. Schmidt and Reimut Zohlnhöfer (eds), *Regieren in der Bundesrepublik Deutschland*, Wiesbaden: VS Verlag für Sozialwissenschaft, 491–509.

Bulmer, Simon (2011), 'Shop Till You Drop? The German Executive as Venue-shopper in Justice and Home Affairs', in Petra Bendel, Andreas Ette, and Roderick Parkes (eds), *The Europeanisation of Control*, Münster: LIT, 41–76.

Bulmer, Simon and Paterson, William E. (2010), 'Germany and the European Union: From "Tamed Power" to Normalized Power?', *International Affairs*, 86/5: 1051–73.

Bulmer, Simon, Jeffery, Charlie, and Paterson, William (2000), *Germany´s European Diplomacy. Shaping the Regional Milieu*, Manchester: Manchester University Press.

Bulmer, Simon, Jeffery, Charles, and Padgett, Stephen (2010), 'Democracy and Diplomacy, Germany and Europe', in Simon Bulmer, Charles Jeffery, and Stephen Padgett (eds), *Rethinking Germany and Europe: Democracy and Diplomacy in a Semi-Sovereign State*, Basingstoke: Palgrave Macmillan, 1–21.

Calic, Marie-Janine (2007), 'Ex-Jugoslawien', in Siegmar Schmidt, Gunther Hellmann, and Reinhard Wolf (eds), *Handbuch zur Deutschen Außenpolitik*, Wiesbaden: VS Verlag für Sozialwissenschaft, 468–81.

Chandler, William M. (2010), 'European Leadership in Transition: Angela Merkel and Nicolas Sarkozy', in Simon Bulmer, Charles Jeffery, and Stephen Padgett (eds), *Rethinking Germany and Europe: Democracy and Diplomacy in a Semi-Sovereign State*, Basingstoke: Palgrave Macmillan.

Dyson, Kenneth (2002), 'Germany and the Euro: Redefining EMU, Handling Paradox, and Managing Uncertainty and Contingency', in Kenneth Dyson (ed.), *European States and the Euro. Europeanization, Variation, and Convergence*, Oxford: Oxford University Press, 173–211.

Erb, Scott (2003), *German Foreign Policy. Navigating a New Era*, Colorado: Lynne Rienner Publishers.

Garrett, Geoffrey and Weingast, Barry R. (1993), 'Ideas, Interests, and Institutions: Constructing the European Community's Internal Market', in Judith Goldstein and Robert O. Keohane (eds), *Ideas and Foreign Policy. Beliefs, Institutions and Political Change*, Ithaca: Cornell University Press, 173–206.

Gimbal, Anke (2001), 'Deutsche Suche nach europäischen Lösungen im Rahmen der Zusammenarbeit in den Bereichen Justiz und Inneres', in Heinrich Schneider, Mathias Jopp, and Uwe Schmalz (eds), *Eine neue deutsche Europapolitik? Rahmenbedingungen - Problemfelder - Optionen*, Bonn: Europa Union Verlag.

Green, Simon (2010), 'Beyond Semi-Sovereignty?: Economic Governance in Germany', in Simon Bulmer, Charles Jeffery, and Stephen Padgett (eds), *Rethinking Germany and Europe: Democracy and Diplomacy in a Semi-Sovereign State*, Basingstoke: Palgrave Macmillan, 85–96.

Greenwood, Sean (2011), *Interest Representation in the European Union*, Houndmills: Palgrave Macmillan.

Grünhage, Jan (2007), *Entscheidungsprozesse in der Europapolitik Deutschlands*, Baden-Baden: Nomos.

Haas, Ernst B. (1958), *The Uniting of Europe: Political, Social and Economic Forces*, Stanford: Stanford University Press.

Habermas, Jürgen (2010), 'Germany and the Euro-Crisis', *The Nation*, 28 June, 2010: 18–20.

Hacke, Christian (2005), 'Die Außenpolitik der Regierung Schröder/Fischer', *Aus Politik und Zeitgeschichte*, 32–33: 9–15.

Hanrieder, Wolfram F. (1967), *West German Foreign Policy 1949-1963. International Pressure and Domestic Response*, Standford: Standford University Press.

Harnisch, Sebastian and Schieder, Siegfried (2006), 'Germany's New European Policy: Weaker, Leaner, Meaner', in Hanns W. Maull (ed.), *German Foreign Policy in the 1990s*, New York: Palgrave Macmillan, 95–108.

Hellmann, Gunther (2006), *Deutsche Außenpolitik*, Wiesbaden: VS Verlag für Sozialwissenschaft.

Hesse, Joachim Jens and Ellwein, Thomas (2004), *Das Regierungssystem der Bundesrepublik Deutschland. 9. Auflage. 2 Bände*, Berlin: de Gruyter.

Höpner, Martin, Leibfried, Stephan, Höreth, Marcus, Scharpf, Fritz W., Zürn, Michael. (2010), 'Kampf um Souveränität?', *Politische Vierteljahresschrift*, 51/2 323–55.

Hrbek, Rudolf (2002), 'Europa', in Martin Greiffenhagen and Sylvia Greiffenhagen (eds), *Handwörterbuch zur Politischen Kultur der Bundesrepublik Deutschland. 2. Auflage*, Wiesbaden: Westdeutscher Verlag, 110–14.

Kaelble, Hartmut (2005), 'Eine europäische Gesellschaft?', in Gunnar Folke Schuppert, Ingolf Pernice, and Ulrich Haltern (eds), *Europawissenschaft*, Baden-Baden: Nomos, 299–330.

Katzenstein, Peter (1987), *Policy and Politics in West Germany. The Growth of a Semisovereign State*, Philadelphia: Temple University Press.

Katzenstein, Peter J. (ed.) (1997), *Tamed Power – Germany in Europe*, Ithaca/London: Cornell University Press.

Kohl, Helmut (1996), *Ich wollte Deutschlands Einheit*, Berlin: Propyläen.

Lankowski, Carl (2001), 'Germany: A Major Player', in Eleanor E. Zeff and Ellen B. Pirro (eds), *The European Union and the Member States. Cooperation, Coordination, and Compromise*, Boulder: Lynne Rienner, 89–114.

Leibholz, Gerhard (1958), *Strukturprobleme der modernen Demokratie*, Karlsruhe: Müller.

Lindberg, Leon and Scheingold, Stuart (1970), *Europe's Would-Be Polity: Patterns of Change in the European Community*, Englewood Cliffs: Prentice Hall.

Maull, Hanns W. (2007), 'Deutschland als Zivilmacht', in Siegmar Schmidt, Gunther Hellmann, and Reinhard Wolf (eds), *Handbuch zur deutschen Außenpolitik*, Wiesbaden: VS Verlag für Sozialwissenschaften, 73–84.

Maurer, Andreas and Mittag, Jürgen (2003), 'The "One" and the "Fifteen": The Member States between Procedural Adaptation and Structural Revolution', in Wolfgang Wessels, Andreas Maurer, and Jürgen Mittag (eds), *Fifteen Into One? The European Union and its Member States*, Manchester: Manchester University Press, 413–54.

McNamara, Kathleen R. (2005), 'Economic and Monetary Union', in Helen Wallace, William Wallace, and Mark A. Pollack (eds), *Policy-Making in the European Union. Fifth Edition*, Oxford: Oxford University Press, 141–60.

Paterson, William (2010), 'Does Germany Still Have a European Vocation?', *German Politics*, 19/1: 41–52.

Poguntke, Thomas (2007), 'Europeanization in a Consensual Environment? German Political Parties and the European Union', in Poguntke, T., Aylott, N., Carter, E., Ladrech, R., and Luther, K. R. (eds), *The Europeanization of National Political Parties*, London: Routledge, 108–33.

Rittberger, Volker (ed.) (2001), *German Foreign Policy Since Unification. Theories and Case Studies*, Manchester: Manchester University Press.

Rittberger, Volker and Wagner, Wolfgang (2001), 'German Foreign Policy Since Unification: Theories Meet Reality', in Volker Rittberger (ed.), *German Foreign Policy Since Unification*, Manchester/ New York: Manchester University Press, 299–326.

Rosolowsky, Diane (1987), *West Germany's Foreign Policy. The Impact of the Social Democrats and the Greens*, New York: Greenwood.

Sartori, Giovanni (1976), *Parties and Party Systems*, Cambridge: Cambridge University Press.

Scharpf, Fritz W. (1985), 'Die Politikverflechtungsfalle: Europäische Integration und deutscher Föderalismus im Vergleich', *Politische Vierteljahresschrift* 26/4: 323–56.

———— (2002), 'The European Social Model: Coping with the Challenges of Diversity', *Journal of Common Market Studies*, 40/4: 645–70.

Schild, Joachim (2010), 'Mission Impossible? The Potential for Franco–German Leadership in the Enlarged EU', *Journal of Common Market Studies*, 48/5: 1367–90.

Schmid, Günther (2006), 'Der kurze Traum der Vollbeschäftigung: Was lehren 55 Jahre deutsche Arbeitsmarkt- und Beschäftigungspolitik', in Manfred G. Schmidt and Reimut Zohlnhöfer (eds), *Regieren in der Bundesrepublik Deutschland*, Wiesbaden: VS Verlag für Sozialwissenschaft, 177–202.

Schmidt, Manfred G. (1987), 'West Germany: The Policy of the Middle Way', *Journal of Public Policy*, 7/1: 135–77.

———— (2006), 'Wenn zwei Sozialstaatsparteien konkurrieren: Sozialpolitik in Deutschland', in Manfred G. Schmidt and Reimut Zohlnhöfer (eds), *Regieren in der Bundesrepublik Deutschland*, Wiesbaden: VS Verlag für Sozialwissenschaft, 137–58.

———— (2010), 'The Policy of the Middle Way: Germany since 1990', in Simon Bulmer, Charlie Jeffery, and Stephen Padgett (eds), *Rethinking Germany and Europe. Democracy and Diplomacy in a Semi-Sovereign State*, London: Palgrave Macmillan, 73–84.

Schröder, Birgit, Hapel, Simone, and Last, Christina (2009), *The Treaty of Lisbon: The 'Accompanying Laws'*, Berlin: Wissenschaftliche Analysen, Nr. 75/09 (http://www.bundestag.de/dokumente/analysen/2009/begleitgesetzgebung_engl__uebersetzung.pdf).

Schwarze, Jürgen (2001), 'Germany', in Jürgen Schwarze (ed.), *The birth of a European Constitutional Order. The Interaction of National and European Constitutional Law*, Baden-Baden: Nomos, 109–204.

Seidendorf, Stefan (2010), 'German Public Opinion and EU Membership' in Renaud Dehousse and Elvire Fabry (eds), *Where is Germany Heading?*, Paris: Notre Europe, 29–36.

Sturm, Roland and Pehle, Heinrich (2006), *Das neue deutsche Regierungssystem. Zweite Auflage* Wiesbaden: VS Verlag für Sozialwissenschaft.

Thomas, Anja and Wessels, Wolfgang (2006), *Die deutsche Verwaltung und die Europäische Union*, Brühl: Bundesakademie für öffentliche Verwaltung.

Thränhardt, Dietrich (1996), *Geschichte der Bundesrepublik Deutschland*, Frankfurt: Suhrkamp.

—— (2007), 'Einwanderungs- und Flüchtlingspolitik', in Siegmar Schmidt, Gunther Hellmann, and Reinhard Wolf (eds), *Handbuch zur Deutschen Außenpolitik*, Wiesbaden: VS Verlag für Sozialwissenschaft, 684–9.

Weßels, Bernhard (2003), 'Parlamentarier in Europa und europäische Integration: Einstellungen zur zukünftigen politischen Ordnung und zum institutionellen Wandel der Europäischen Union', in Frank Brettschneider, Jan van Deth, and Edeltraut Roller (eds), *Europäische Integration in der öffentlichen Meinung*, Opladen: Leske+Budrich, 363–94.

—— (2005), 'Roles and Orientations of Members of Parliament in the EU Context: Congruence or difference? Europeanisation or Not?', *Journal of Legislative Studies*, 11/3-4: 446–65.

Zohlnhöfer, Reimut (2006), 'Vom Wirtschaftswunder zum kranken Mann Europas? Wirtschaftspolitik seit 1945', in Manfred G. Schmidt and Reimut Zohlnhöfer (eds), *Regieren in der Bundesrepublik Deutschland*, Wiesbaden: VS Verlag für Sozialwissenschaft, 285–314.

 ENDNOTES

1. Citation from http://www.historiasiglo20.org/europe/monnet.htm, downloaded 7 October, 2010.
2. The term 'decision taking' is in this text reserved for those events where decisions are actually taken. In contrast, the notion of 'decision making' (German 'Willensbildung') refers to the whole of societal and institutional input to a given phase of the policy cycle.
3. See Bundesgesetzblatt I, p. 1897, 1910 (14 August 2006).
4. The decision went into the coalition agreement of 2009: http://www.cdu.de/doc/pdfc/091026-koalitionsvertrag-cducsu-fdp.pdf, p. 116.
5. The Open letter can be found in the electronic version of the Frankfurter Allgemeine Zeitung, 24 February 2011 (www.faz.net).
6. 'Alleged' because of the breach of the first European Stability Pact exactly by a German government in 2004; Kathleen R. McNamara, 'Economic and Monetary Union', in Helen Wallace, William Wallace, and Mark A. Pollack (eds), *Policy-Making in the European Union*. *Fifth Edition*, Oxford: Oxford University Press, 2005, 141–60, 156.

CHAPTER 5

The United Kingdom: Towards Isolation and a Parting of the Ways?

David Allen

▌ Summary

Britain's relationship with the EU continues to be characterized by partial Europeanization. The British ruling elite, notably the civil service, has been Europeanized. However, the political parties have been characterized by internal divisions on European integration, while public opinion has been amongst—if not *the*—least supportive of integration amongst the member states. The crisis in the euro-zone and the ongoing mood of Euroscepticism suggests that Britain may be destined to play a lesser role in a two-tier EU in the future. This chapter first of all explores the history of Britain's relationship with the integration process. It then turns to Europeanization, exploring in turn the impact of the EU on British politics, its policy machinery and policy content, highlighting the differing levels of accommodation with European integration and taking note of the changes that have accompanied the coming to power in 2010 of the Conservative–Liberal Democrat coalition after a lengthy period of Labour rule (1997–2010). A brief comparative perspective precedes the conclusion.

Introduction

In the first edition of this book we argued that whilst the British government and significant sections of the British ruling elite had become 'Europeanized', the same could not be said of the wider British polity (Allen 2005). Nothing has occurred in the years since 2005 to change this view, indeed the events of late 2011 served to further confirm it, which means that successive Labour governments failed during their time in office (1997–2010) to achieve the stated objective of creating a domestic consensus in support of pro-European policies. Instead, after the general election of May 2010, Britain found itself governed under David Cameron, by a coalition of Conservatives and Liberal Democrats who hold broadly opposite views about the European Union and Britain's place within it. Events surrounding the crisis of the euro-zone in late 2011, which culminated in Prime Minister Cameron exercising the British veto over attempts to reinforce the Lisbon Treaty, suggested that the European issue had the potential to put both the future of the coalition and the UK's relationship with the EU in doubt. In 1975, the British people voted in a referendum by two to one to remain within the European Economic Community but by 2010, it was clear that there was no prospect that they would support in a referendum either the Lisbon Treaty or UK membership of the euro and it seemed quite likely that they might also reject continued UK membership of the EU. As we shall see, the new government has passed legislation to ensure that any future changes to the powers or legal basis of the European Union would have to be the subject of a referendum in the UK.

Although Britain has been a member of the European Union for nearly forty years, it remains an uncertain member state; uncertain about the advantages of membership, uncertain about its relationship with the other leading member states, and uncertain about the direction that it would like the European Union to take following its eastern enlargement and the recent economic and financial crises (Allen 2003b; Menon 2004; Rachman 2010; Miller 2011). These uncertainties about the consequences and future of EU membership all essentially relate to the failure of successive British governments to build a supportive consensus amongst the British public for the EU policies that they wish to pursue, and raise some doubts about whether such a consensus could ever be constructed. The European Union Act (2011; Federal Trust 2011a) now provides a referendum 'lock' designed to ensure that, without that consensus, the present and future British governments will be unable to participate in any further enhancement of the EU's powers. Although there have been significant differences in the negotiating *style* of British governments towards the EU since 1973, there have always been significant continuities in the *substance* of British policy—not least a preference for an intergovernmental European Union of 'independent' states open to further enlargement. This preference has, until recently, led governments of both political persuasions to distort and emphatically reject all notions of a 'federal' European Union with a view to limiting the extent of European integration and thus making continued UK participation in it acceptable to the British people. This policy of effectively restraining the integrative ambitions of some of the other EU member states so as to keep the EU 'comfortable' for the UK may now be changing. Because the UK government has an interest in the crisis of the euro-zone being resolved, it, ironically, now finds itself advocating closer political and fiscal integration for the euro-zone members whilst at the same time responding to the growth of Euroscepticism at home by making it clear that the UK will not participate itself. This is potentially a recipe for the sort of two-tier EU that previous UK governments have always sought to prevent and it could be argued that this recent shift in UK policy, combined with a likely intensification of integration amongst the euro-zone countries, marks the start of a process that has the potential to lead to a more substantial parting of the ways between the UK and the EU. The UK's long history of ambivalence about its place in the EU may be about to be characterized by a move from managed interdependence towards a more isolationist stance.

Britain's European Diplomacy

In 1950, Britain supported the proposal to create a European Coal and Steel Community (ECSC) but made it clear that it would not join such an organization with supranational powers. A similar response was given to the 1952 proposal for a European Defence Community (EDC). Whilst the ECSC was established, the EDC plan was not credible without Britain and failed but it was replaced by a British inspired intergovernmental organization—the Western European Union (WEU). When the six members of the ECSC proposed the creation of a general common market in 1955, Britain both refused to consider participation and argued the case against further integration of this kind.

In response to the Treaty of Rome and the establishment of the European Economic Community (EEC), the UK created the European Free Trade Association (EFTA) as an intergovernmental alternative. However, in 1961 the Conservative government of Harold Macmillan reversed Britain's position and applied to join the EEC along with Denmark, Ireland, and Norway. Britain's application appeared to be an acceptance that the other circles of British influence—the Commonwealth and the special relationship with the United States—were no longer realistic alternatives to the EEC. De Gaulle rejected the 1961 application on the grounds that the UK was too close to the US to be trusted within the EEC. Since then all British prime ministers have at one time or another faced difficulties in managing and balancing the transatlantic and European dimensions of diplomacy.

Under the Labour governments of Harold Wilson (1964–1970), a second entry bid was also rejected by De Gaulle whose resignation in 1968 paved the way for a final successful application by the government of Edward Heath (1970–1974). Britain entered the EEC in 1973, with Denmark and Ireland, but when Harold Wilson returned to power in 1974 he undertook an essentially spurious 'renegotiation' of the terms of EEC membership (Allen 2004: 53–7) which culminated in 1975 in a referendum that supported continuing UK membership. During the global recession of the late 1970s, British enthusiasm for the EEC significantly declined even while a British President of the European Commission (Roy Jenkins) worked with the leaders of France and Germany to advance the cause of monetary integration. (For a fuller account of the 1950–1979 period see Allen: 2005: 120–23.)

Under Margaret Thatcher, a clearly definable EC strategy emerged as the British government sought to restrain plans to progress the EC until the question of Britain's net EC budget contribution was addressed. The Fontainebleau settlement, which included an ongoing budget rebate for the UK, paved the way for the mid-1980s revival of the EC's fortunes which owed their success in part to British policy. The Single Market Programme (SMP) was advocated by Thatcher as an alternative to other members' preferences for progress towards a single currency and political union, and was taken forward in the Delors Commission by a British Commissioner, Lord Cockfield. Mrs Thatcher, albeit reluctantly, signed up to the Single European Act (SEA) and thus to a reformed EU decision-making system which combined more qualified majority voting in the Council with increased legislative powers for the European Parliament, but she had not allowed for the dynamic impact of the SEA and the SMP on the evolution of the EC. As Delors, with the support of France and Germany, pushed ahead towards the goal of economic and monetary union, so Mrs Thatcher sought to revert to the UK policy of resistance, but in so doing brought about her own downfall. This was greeted with relief by Britain's EC partners and by pro-European forces within the UK who made the mistake of believing her hesitations about the future direction of the EC to be unique to her rather than, as they were, an extreme version of a more deep seated and ongoing British unease about further integration.

Nevertheless, the Major government promised, and at first delivered, a new approach. He remained stubbornly determined to place Britain 'at the heart of Europe' and to insist on full account being taken of Britain's concerns. This policy enabled the UK to extract a number of concessions (the limitation of supranationalism by the preservation of the pillar structure, an 'opt in' to EMU at a time of its own choosing and an 'opt out' of the Social Chapter), which enabled John Major to proclaim on his return from Maastricht that the new Treaty on European Union was 'game set and match' to Britain (Seldon 1997: 243). Major subsequently won the 1992 UK election and an apparent domestic endorsement for his European policies, which put the immediate focus on the completion of the single market and enlargement to include the states of Eastern Europe rather than any further deepening of integration.

However the Danish rejection of the TEU in a referendum, and the UK's unceremonious departure from the Exchange Rate Mechanism (ERM), soon undermined domestic support for the Major government's attempts to normalize Britain's relations with its European partners. At Edinburgh in December 1992, collective fear for the future of the Union ensured a degree of success for a weak British Presidency (Ludlow 1993). The atmosphere of agreement and solidarity was, however, illusory and between 1992 and 1997 Britain once again became isolated in its European diplomacy as the Major government became increasingly weakened by the attacks of the Eurosceptics at home, and thus reneged on its commitments to its EU partners. Britain found itself in dispute with them over the timing of its ratification of the Maastricht Treaty, institutional arrangements for the 1995 enlargement, the appointment of a new Commission President, and the 1996 'mad cow' crisis. Britain's response to efforts to organize a new intergovernmental conference (IGC) was to reject every proposal for reform of the treaties and, on the beef export ban resulting from the BSE crisis, to pursue a policy of non-cooperation in the Council of Ministers. It became clear to Britain's partners that no new treaty could be progressed until the Major government had departed.

In 1997, the Blair government was elected with an overwhelming majority and once again an incoming British prime minister promised a fresh approach to the EU. At Amsterdam, shortly after his election, Blair opted into the Social Chapter, went along with a degree of communitization of the Justice and Home Affairs (JHA) pillar, and accepted a significant extension of qualified majority voting whilst generally seeking to reassure Britain's partners that things had changed for the better. At the time, however, he resisted any progress on defence and, under pressure from Gordon Brown, he rejected, in the autumn of 1997, the opportunity to move quickly towards British participation in the euro. During the 1998 British Presidency, the euro-zone countries, as they prepared for the introduction of the euro, excluded Britain from their deliberations and made it clear that, whilst they welcomed the improved British attitude, they were not going to allow Britain influence over the new currency if it was not going to participate in it.

Britain's response was a rather surprising bilateral defence initiative agreed with France at St Malo in 1998, which eventually led to the establishment and rapid development of the EU's European Security and Defence Policy (ESDP)—a significant development in the evolution of the EU's external stance. Blair's stated ambition for Britain to be a 'pivot' or a 'bridge' between the EU and the US was always likely to be challenged once the Clinton administration was replaced by that of George W. Bush. After '9/11', as the US began to put serious pressure on its European allies over Afghanistan and Iraq, a more familiar British stance re-emerged. Faced with a choice between supporting Bush's determination to bring down Saddam Hussein by force and aligning itself with the opposition to this course of action that was led by France and Germany, Britain once again went with the US. This time, however, Britain was not as isolated as it had been in the past, with both Spain and Italy providing a measure of support along with most of the (then) applicant states from Eastern Europe and the former Soviet Union.

Their differences over the war in Iraq, over the Stability and Growth Pact, and the proposed Constitutional Treaty, all suggested that France and Germany's ability to drive the EU forward in partnership was diminished. Under Blair, the UK sought to take on the Franco–German duo both by attempting to divide them and by seeking new bilateral relationships within the EU. Whilst Germany looked like a natural partner for Britain over CAP reform, restricting the EU budget and enlargement (Grabbe and Munchau 2002), defence issues found Britain in partnership with

France, and Germany an increasingly concerned onlooker. Blair sought to engage Spain and, more controversially, Berlusconi's Italian government, as partners in the drive to make Europe competitive, and the UK worked hard with both the Swedish and Danish Presidencies to maintain the enlargement momentum when it looked like faltering in 2001–02. Under Blair, only the attempt to negotiate with Iran gave any hope to those who saw the leadership problem in the EU being resolved by a *directoire* of Britain, France, and Germany.

The handover from Tony Blair to Gordon Brown took place in 2007 and was greeted with some apprehension by Britain's partners, who had become accustomed to Brown's brusqueness at meetings of the Council of Economic and Finance Ministers and to his tendency to brief the UK press on the failings of those in the EU who did not sign up to his own 'Atlanticist' take on global economic and financial management. For his part, Brown had kept a keen, some might argue paranoid, eye on Blair as he attended his last European Council at which the final details of the Lisbon Treaty were thrashed out (without Blair conceding any of the UK 'red lines'). In fact, Brown surprised many of his detractors, first of all by standing firm on the question of not holding a referendum in the UK on the Lisbon Treaty even after the Irish had initially rejected it, but mainly by his positive leadership role (Seldon and Lodge 2010: 190–243) and his enthusiastic embrace of his EU colleagues as the financial crisis took hold after 2008. Before the G20 meeting in London, in 2009, he argued that Britain could leverage its global influence via Brussels and astonished many by stating that he was proud to be British and proud to be European and that Britain's place was not in Europe's slipstream but firmly in the mainstream.

Whilst Brown had not proved to be as difficult as many EU leaders feared, it was also becoming clear that he was unlikely to retain power in the British general election scheduled for the spring of 2010. The leader of the Conservative Party, and most likely winner, was David Cameron and he had only secured this position by appeasing his Eurosceptic Right wing with the promise that he would take his MEPs out of the mainstream European People's Party (EPP) in the European Parliament after the 2009 EP elections. This he duly did to the annoyance of both President Sarkozy and Chancellor Merkel whose own political parties belong to the EPP, and whose influence within the EU was considerably diminished by the absence of the British Conservatives. Although Cameron's actions momentarily appeased the Conservative Eurosceptics, he annoyed them again when the Lisbon Treaty was eventually ratified by stating that he regarded this as a done deal and that he would not now call a retrospective UK referendum if he became prime minister. This despite the fact that Cameron had also alienated his future EU partners by encouraging the Czech President not to back down on his own refusal to agree to the new treaty. Both Cameron and his shadow foreign minister, William Hague, also made it clear that they would seek to both repatriate certain powers from the EU and pass legislation to ensure that no further EU treaties could be agreed without a referendum in the UK.

The ratification of the Lisbon Treaty led to negotiations to fill the new post of President of the European Council and to find a replacement for Javier Solana as

High Representative (HR). The Brown government advocated Tony Blair for the post of President of the Council and many British names, including those of Chris Patten and David Miliband, were also touted for the HR post. William Hague was opposed to Blair, whom he claimed would divert power away from national leaders, and argued instead that the UK should focus its attention on securing one of the important economic portfolios in the new Commission. In the end, the UK was rewarded with the unlikely appointment of Baroness Ashton as the HR who, by the curious logic of EU bargaining, qualified as a Left leaning female from a large member state who nicely counter balanced the appointment of Herman Van Rompuy, a Right leaning male from a small member state, as President of the European Council.

In the event, concern about the EU policies of a Cameron administration were lessened by the fact that the Conservatives did not win an outright majority in the 2010 election and David Cameron was only able to become prime minister by negotiating a coalition agreement with the Liberal Democrat party. The agreement (Guardian 2010) provided a measure of reassurance to the UK's partners that the Liberal Democrats presence would moderate Conservative policy, which a leaked memo from Hague to Cameron just after the election suggested would have been a very hard line towards the EU (Miller 2011: 6–7). Instead, Cameron appointed David Lidington, an EU moderate, to be his Minister for Europe and frequently sent Nick Clegg, his Liberal Democrats deputy prime minister, to charm European leaders with his EU background and his impressive linguistic skills. However, despite the superficial pleasantries and despite dropping their immediate plans for demanding the repatriation of certain powers from the EU to the UK in their first year in government, Cameron and Hague did progress the passage of the European Act with its referendum lock on any future EU treaty changes. They also ruled out any consideration of UK membership of the euro for at least ten years. Furthermore, Cameron and his Chancellor, George Osborne, made it clear that, unlike their Labour predecessors, they were not prepared to involve the UK in paying for any further euro-zone bail outs. Interestingly, Cameron did actively progress the strictly bilateral talks on defence collaboration that Labour had initiated with France, but outside the established ESDP framework. This improved defence relationship with France manifested itself further in the Anglo–French led military action against Gadaffi's Libya, which took place within a NATO rather than EU framework. The Libyan intervention, which was resisted by Germany, was a success for both Cameron and Sarkozy and also reflected the reality of the emerging US position, namely to leave such action in future to the Europeans. The fact that only NATO (rather than the EU) could provide the necessary organizational basis for such operations meant that it was well received by Conservative Eurosceptics, who would have been concerned had the action taken place under the EU banner.

At the end of 2011, a dramatic meeting of the European Council took place at which the UK Prime Minister, David Cameron, used the veto to prevent a proposed amendment to the Lisbon Treaty, sought by Germany in particular, to underpin arrangements by the euro-zone countries to stabilize the currency. On the day itself he was opposed by all the other EU member states (the seventeen euro-zone states plus nine states not yet in the euro) who announced that they would pursue their plans by an alternative route—an intergovernmental treaty that was France's preferred vehicle. Some commentators (Stephens 2011; Freedland 2011) saw this as an historic turning point in the evolution of Britain's relationship with the EU, with the potential to lead to Britain's isolation and eventual departure. Others saw it as yet another temporary and redeemable spat in a turbulent relationship. Whatever the eventual outcome, there seemed to be general agreement that the use of the veto represented a significant failure of British diplomacy (Rawnsley 2011; Barber 2011) as the UK lost the support even of the group of 'northern' EU states such as Denmark, Sweden, Finland, and the Baltic states that Cameron had been cultivating as sympathetic to British thinking on the EU. At a meeting with the German Chancellor a few weeks before the December summit, the British Prime Minister (PM) believed that he had extracted assurances that, in exchange for Britain's agreement to the necessary adjustments to the Lisbon Treaty (which would not directly impact on the UK and would therefore not require a referendum under the provisions of the European Union Act), additional measures would be agreed favouring the UK and, in particular, exempting the City of London from restrictive regulation at the EU level. In fact, the full details of the British demands (which were clearly seen by David Cameron as necessary to appease his Eurosceptic backbenchers) had not been spelt out to the Germans. They were, however, considered at a meeting of the EPP leaders in Marseilles on the eve of the summit (a meeting that ironically David Cameron had excluded himself from by his 2009 decision to take the UK Conservatives out of the EPP). The UK's attempt to divide France and Germany over the rescue of the euro was rejected by President Sarkozy's absolute refusal to countenance any exemptions for the UK from regulation of a financial sector which French rhetoric held primarily responsible for the post 2008 financial crisis. In the UK, Cameron's use of the veto was generally well received by the public but provoked outrage amongst his Liberal Democrats coalition partners whilst at the same time encouraging the Conservative Eurosceptics to demand more. The balance of informed opinion was that Cameron had blundered mainly because he sought advice only from his Foreign Secretary, William Hague, and his newly appointed Ambassador to the EU, Sir Jon Cunliffe (Parker and Blitz 2011), whose training in international diplomacy bore the mark of his Treasury origins. Inside the UK this episode highlighted once again the growing impact of domestic factors on the UK's European diplomacy.

Europeanization and British Politics

The EU has had a major impact on British politics, but to date no government has been able to create a supportive consensus for whole-hearted EU membership. Whilst all governments since 1964 have fundamentally supported British membership of the

EU, they have all fallen foul in one way or another of adverse domestic opinion. Similarly, there have been significant periods of time when leading parties in opposition (Labour from 1980–1983 under Michael Foot and the Conservatives from 1997–2005 under William Hague, Ian Duncan Smith, and Michael Howard) have sought to build a consensus around a fundamental challenge to British membership but they have fared no better. The British people seem reluctant to support either a government that advances Britain's role in the EU or elect one that seeks to abandon it.

By the late 1960s, both major political parties had sought membership whilst in office. However, even before entry was achieved, the European question proved internally divisive with significant minorities in both the Conservative and Labour parties opposing the views of their party leadership. These divisions have intersected with a fundamentally adversarial political system with the result that the major parties have usually resisted making the EU a significant electoral issue and have been reluctant to publicly debate how they would like the EU to evolve (Allen 2003b). In the post-1945 era, questions relating to European integration have been ever present in British politics and they have had a significant impact on the fate of several governments. But the EU has rarely featured strongly in national election campaigns (Geddes 2004: 214) and it typically languishes low on the political agendas at election time. Since 1979, direct elections have been held for seats in the European Parliament but these too have failed to ignite any short term, let alone sustained interest in the European Union.

The West European states that created the European Community were led by governments whose leaders were confident that their electorates would endorse the deals that they made with one another. This was how Britain eventually negotiated its way into the EEC in 1973, with parliament alone endorsing the relevant treaties. The electorate as a whole only gained a say after the event as a result of divisions within the Labour Party. In the referendum of 1975, the Labour government gained overwhelming support for its 'renegotiated terms' even though the negotiations had produced no change whatsoever to the Accession Treaty. This was essentially also how Margaret Thatcher approached the debate about the revival of the EEC that culminated in the SEA. She was prepared to bargain hard at the European level for her limited vision of Europe, but she expected the British people, and indeed her own Cabinet, to accept whatever deal she struck—as they did.

John Major's approach to the Maastricht negotiations was slightly less confident because he understood that he would be closely scrutinized, both by the broad British electorate and the official opposition, but especially by Eurosceptics in his own party. John Major sought to use this domestic ambivalence about the EU as a bargaining tool when it came to issues such as endorsing the principle of subsidiarity and rejecting federalism where he was able to argue that British concerns had to be heeded if the treaty was to be accepted by the British people. Maastricht was the turning point, however, and ever since British negotiators in the EU have been driven fundamentally by their sensitivity to domestic public opinion—both mass and elite—rather than by their perception of the British national interest.

Thanks to Mrs Thatcher's success in arguing that a federal Europe symbolized the relentless advance of a European superstate, any British government now faces an enormous challenge in separating the two ideas. Blair's awareness of this problem is to be seen in his strange portrayal of the EU as 'a superpower but not a superstate' (Blair 2000). However, the image of the latter continues to feature in British perceptions even as the EU flounders in the face of the economic crisis, and it remains a real barrier to any informed discussion of the EU in the UK. The result is that British politicians now know that they are addressing two audiences—the EU member states and also the UK electorate. This explains in part the Major government's spectacularly negative public performance at the 1996 Intergovernmental Conference (IGC), Blair's constant backtracking on his stated EU ambitions, and Cameron's delicate balancing act between EU expectations and domestic restraints.

Although the Labour Party had a more constructive agenda than its predecessors, there was little European policy debate during or after the general elections in 1997, 2001, and 2005. In effect, both major political parties have reversed their positions. During the 1980s, the Labour Party was torn apart over the issue of policy toward Europe, with almost fatal consequences as the pro-European Right wing of the party departed to form the Social Democratic Party. This left Mrs Thatcher to preside over a fundamentally pro-European government while gaining considerable political capital from her obstruction of wider EU ambitions. By the end of her premiership, however, she had become much more resistant to further integration.

In the 1990s, Labour sought, won, and retained power by shifting to a pro-European stance as the Conservative Party enthusiastically embarked on a fatal internal battle over Europe. As a result, Labour currently retains a large majority of predominately pro-European MPs in contrast to the Conservative Party, which has become dominated by the Eurosceptic Right whose hardliners are now convinced that withdrawal from the EU is a desirable and viable option for the Cameron government to consider despite the objections of the Liberal Democrats.

Public opinion about the EU is, and always has been, negative with European views often argued passionately but usually held weakly. In the regular Eurobarometer polls published by the Commission over the years since British entry, Britain has always come at or close to the bottom of any ranking of member states by enthusiasm for the EU or belief that the EU has done any material good (Geddes 2004: 211–24). In an analysis of recent polls (Gallup 2009: 5), respondents were evenly divided about their perception of the EU with 37 per cent having a positive image and 40 per cent a negative image, whilst 37 per cent felt the EU economically benefited the UK whilst 40 per cent felt the opposite. In all recent polls a significant majority (over 70 per cent) are opposed to UK membership of the euro. However, the Gallup survey also showed that only 18 per cent of UK respondents felt informed about the EU (up a little on the 12 per cent who felt this in 2002), whilst 83 per cent said that they knew little or nothing about the EU. Only a few (4 per cent) strongly agreed that information on EU affairs was simple and clear and almost half (48 per cent) perceived a negative bias in press reports, although 54 per cent indicated that they did not want to receive more information about the EU. These figures might suggest that the electorate could be open to persuasion about an issue it cares little about, but the image of an all-powerful, predominantly anti-European media would seem to counter that view (Wilkes and Wring 1998).

Undoubtedly, the British popular press has done little to inform the public debate about the EU. The Murdoch-owned News International Group broadly supported Labour in the breakthrough 1997 election, but it has not softened its opposition to the EU in general, and the euro in particular, and the recent memoirs of Labour politicians suggest that this always impacted on Blair and Brown's calculations. Today, most of the British tabloid press remains hostile to the EU and seeks mainly to sensationalize rather than impartially report the activities of the various European institutions. *The Sun* and the *Daily Mail* continue to wage a nationalistic campaign against Brussels and all things foreign, while *The Daily Telegraph, The Times*, and *The Sunday Times* report the EU from a sceptical perspective. Of the daily broadsheets, only the *Financial Times, The Guardian*, and *The Independent* offer in-depth and broadly sympathetic reporting on the EU; the weekly *The Economist* does so as well. In 2005, faced with the prospect of a referendum on the Constitutional Treaty, the BBC commissioned a report on its EU coverage (BBC 2005) which found it to be poorly informed with a tendency to oversimplify issues and perceived by a wide section of UK public opinion to be biased in favour of the EU. Much has been said about the alleged power of the British press to affect government policy, and the government is certainly sensitive to the press's ability to influence its overall popularity. It has been argued that the main impact of a more intrusive press is to divert ministers' attention from substantive policy matters to mere policy presentation (Coles 2000: 100) but Daddow (2007: 595) claims that the UK press also has the power to counter attempts (in this case by Blair) to change the terms of the UK discourse on Europe. Evidence suggests, however, that, when the government is clear about its European policy direction, the press will usually follow as was the case for a brief period after John Major won the 1992 general election with a mandate to put Britain at the 'heart of Europe'. In the light of this experience, which ended in September 1992 when the UK was forced to leave the ERM, Blair's pro-European colleagues constantly urged him to take the lead on Europe, forcing the press to follow him, and Labour initially made serious efforts to improve the British public's perception of Europe. However, the determination of the Blair government to create a domestic consensus was neither sustained nor successful. Blair made numerous public announcements to the effect that the government sought a step change in its approach to the EU, but, whilst the style of British policy changed under Blair, he still failed to bring about any significant change in public attitudes towards the EU (Daddow 2007, 2010).

Nevertheless, the question of Europe has clearly had its impact on British political life. In the end her European policy contributed to Mrs Thatcher's downfall, John Major's government first triumphed and then faltered before being fatally wounded by the European issue, and Tony Blair, once so cocksure and optimistic about Europe, was quick to downgrade his ambitions whenever he felt that they might damage his electoral chances. Since the 2010 election, David Cameron has been forced to plot a delicate path between the opposing views of the Liberal Democrats and the Conservative Eurosceptics at a time when the euro-zone crisis means that the pressures from Brussels are difficult to ignore. Even the elections to the European Parliament, that have been held every five years since 1979, have failed to arouse much interest amongst the British people. Turnout has always been low (never more than 40 per cent, and in 1999 only 24 per cent rising back to 34.7 per cent in 2009) compared to both the EU average and to turnout in British General Elections (65.1 per cent in 2010). The elections are accorded a low priority by the major political parties who prefer to spend their limited resources on national, regional, and even local elections rather than European elections. Furthermore, 'European' issues are rarely debated at the hustings. Instead, European elections in the UK turn into national by-elections with those who do turn out to vote using the opportunity to express their frustrations with the government in office.

Until 1999, the use of the 'first past the post' simple majority system of voting in single member constituencies meant that Britain (the only member state not to use a system of proportional representation) was significantly out of step with its partners, predominately returning members drawn from the two major political parties. All this changed in 1999 when Labour introduced a system of proportional representation. Under this system, Britain was divided up into large multi-member regional constituencies and, for the first time, the Liberal Democrats party had (ten) MEPs elected, and several minority parties, such as the Greens, the UK Independence Party (UKIP), and, in 2009, the British National Party (BNP) also achieved a measure of success with UKIP notably gaining the same number of seats as Labour (thirteen) and one more than the Liberal Democrats. In this way, the EU has indeed impacted on British politics because the success of UKIP and of the BNP, combined with the need to form a coalition with the Liberal Democrats in Westminster, means that David Cameron has a very difficult task to hold the Eurosceptics at bay while maintaining UK influence in the EU mainstream (Hug 2011, Federal Trust 2011b).

Europeanization and British Institutional Adaptation

Britain's governance institutions have made a successful adaptation to EU membership and the adjustment has been steady and incremental rather than radical (Schmidt 2006; Wall 2008; Bulmer and Burch 2009). Under Labour since 1997, the pace of institutional change both quickened and deepened although this may now be reversed in the changed climate of relations between the UK and the EU.

For Britain, EU membership presented a potential coordination problem and raised the question of how governmental procedures would best deal with the 'blurring' of the boundaries between the domestic and the foreign that characterizes EU business. Membership had implications for all of the UK's major institutions and procedures; the office of prime minister, the cabinet system, the 'pecking order' of government departments, the civil and diplomatic services, the legislative, budgetary, and scrutiny powers of the parliament, the principle of sovereignty, the judiciary, the electoral system, and the relationship between the various parts of the United Kingdom.

British adaptation to the need to both project to and receive from the EU has been pragmatic and effective on a day-to-day basis, with British negotiators seen as formidable and effective in Brussels. However, the system has been criticized for its failure to develop long-term strategies built around a clear vision of the European future (Schmidt 2006: 25–6). Most British governments have entered office determined to 'start afresh' with the EU, but most have at one time or another been branded as 'awkward' by their partners. This is partly to be explained by the failure of successive governments to create a supportive domestic consensus, partly by a consistent antipathy to supranationalism and talk of federalism, but also by a certain 'style' which is a product of the adversarial British political culture. British negotiators at all levels and at all times have been unwilling to subsume their concern about the specifics of EU policies or procedures to a general enthusiasm for European integration. In addition, and more positively, British awkwardness can be explained by a seriousness of intent to both implement and enforce any agreements that are reached (Wall 2008: 202–3).

Britain's policy towards the EU is coordinated in at least three different places: the Cabinet Office, whose European Secretariat has in recent years been headed by the PM's personal adviser on EU matters; the Foreign and Commonwealth Office; and UKREP—Britain's Permanent Representation to the EU, based in Brussels. At the heart of the British system of government is the cabinet system presided over by a PM who is constitutionally regarded as being no more than *primus inter pares* but who is often perceived to have ambitions to make the British system more presidential, in particular by building up his or her office in Downing Street.

The PM's central role has grown, partly out of choice and partly because the EU itself is increasingly driven by the European Council where the PM meets with his or her fellow EU leaders. Prime ministers with EU leadership aspirations, such as Margaret Thatcher and Tony Blair, have chosen to enhance the power of Downing Street on EU matters whereas Harold Wilson, James Callaghan, John Major, and, to a certain extent, David Cameron, were content to leave the general direction of EU business in the hands of their foreign secretaries and thus the Foreign and Commonwealth Office (FCO). Under Blair, the Downing Street Office grew steadily to support the direct involvement of the PM in foreign policy in general and the EU in particular (Wall 2008: 195–7), and he was criticized, as was Thatcher before him, by those (Owen 2003) who fear that the erosion of collective cabinet decision making impacts adversely on the quality of Britain's EU policy. Whilst the cabinet as a decision-making forum on Europe was undoubtedly diminished under Blair, the Treasury, under Gordon Brown, exercised significant countervailing power to Downing Street by maintaining a stranglehold over British policy on the euro. Cameron, Hague, and

Osborne have to date presented a relatively united front on EU matters and can be expected to prevail even if the Liberal Democrats do seek wider discussions about EU policy within the cabinet.

Whilst membership of the EU has enabled the British PM to enhance his power, the foreign secretary has struggled to maintain FCO control over contacts, both formal and informal, between the British government and its EU partners (Allen 2003a; Aktipis and Oliver 2011: 78–9). A great deal of EU business concerns single government departments and they are, in the main, left alone to determine British interests and negotiate the detail of policy. The Foreign Office plays a key coordinating role and, in recent years, it has been organized on functional as well as geographical lines. This coordinating role is nowadays much prized by the FCO, which has always resisted more radical suggestions that EU policy coordination should be entrusted to a Ministry for Europe.

Similarly, successive foreign secretaries have resisted the idea that the post of Minister for Europe (currently a junior ministerial appointment under the direction of the foreign secretary) should be elevated to cabinet rank. Whilst the FCO might relish the prospect of having two seats in the cabinet, the foreign secretary is understandably reluctant to contemplate the downgrading of his own role that this might imply.

The British Cabinet rarely discusses EU business; at political level this is mainly done in a sub-committee of the cabinet chaired by the foreign secretary. Most coordination is carried out at official level within the European Secretariat of the Cabinet Office which provides a forum in which any interdepartmental disputes on EU policy are ironed out (Forster and Blair 2002; Wall 2008: 185–203). A particular feature of this process is an interdepartmental meeting held each Friday in the Cabinet Office which used to be attended by the British Ambassador (Permanent Representative) to the EU in person but which now relies more often on a live video link. The work of UKREP is generally admired within the British system, although senior officials are sometimes heard to complain that the British EU Ambassador both represents Britain in Brussels and Brussels in Britain and those from home departments increasingly tend to see the Ambassador as primarily a representative of the FCO despite the fact that significantly more than 50 per cent of UKREP staff are drawn from the home civil service.

EU membership used to involve a few key ministries such as the FCO, the Department of Trade and Industry (DTI), the Treasury, and the Department for the Environment, Food and Rural Affairs (DEFRA) all of whom, but in particular the FCO, came to value their role in EU business where once they found it a tiresome distraction. However, in recent years, as the scope of EU activity has widened, almost all UK departments have come to play a role with the most notable changes affecting the Home Office, with the development of EU JHA competences, and the Ministry of Defence, whose rapid transformation from being an exclusively NATO-orientated department to one with substantial EU concerns as a result of the development of ESDP surprised incoming Conservative ministers in 2010 (Aktipis and Oliver 2011: 80–81; Dover 2007).

The British civil service had little difficulty in handling EU business in Britain, but resisted at first the idea that British officials might move effortlessly between London and Brussels. This changed with the introduction of a European dimension to both the home and diplomatic 'fast stream' via which Britain sought to 'place' some of its best officials in Brussels. This system was successful as far as senior posts are concerned, but when he became foreign secretary, William Hague was dismayed to discover a lack of 'bright British officials' in EU institutions. He noted that the UK represents 12 per cent of the EU population but that, at entry-level policy grades in the Commission, only 1.8 per cent of the staff were British and that since 2007 the number of British officials at Director level has fallen by a third with 205 fewer UK officials in the Commission overall (Hague 2010).

The British legal system took its time to accept and adjust to the primacy of EU law over UK national law because of sensitivity to the principle of UK parliamentary sovereignty which meant that UK courts derive the right to apply EU law from the European Communities Act of 1972 rather than from Community law itself. British law firms have developed highly lucrative EU legal practices, and the British government has always accepted ECJ judgments even when they run counter to its own estimation of British interests.

The British Parliament has adapted less easily than the core executive to EU business, although Britain has one of the most effective systems in the EU for parliamentary scrutiny of EU legislation. When Britain first joined the EU, the then government pledged the Scrutiny Reserve stating that it would never agree to legislation in the EU Council of Ministers that had not first been considered by the British Parliament. Successive governments have adhered to this commitment and, over the years, extended it to include UK government agreements under the non-legislative intergovernmental procedures that underpin all EU foreign policy activities and which initially underpinned actions involving JHA. In recent times, the government has also agreed that all relevant EU documentation will be made subject to the scrutiny procedures (House of Commons Information Office 2011).

In the House of Commons this involves sending all EU legislative proposals and working papers to the European Scrutiny Committee with an explanatory memorandum. The Scrutiny Committee, which has three standing committees, assesses the legal and political implications of each proposal, decides which ones should be subject to no further action, which should be considered in a sub-committee, and which debated in the House. It reports in detail those matters it considers significant, it monitors the activities of British ministers in the Council, and it works in partnership with the European Union Committee of the House of Lords, which conducts detailed enquiries into specific policy areas. The problem with this scrutiny system is that it is liable to be swamped by the sheer (and growing) volume of EU material that it has to process and by lack of time. It is also the case that, despite the high quality of the UK scrutiny procedures, those who are exercised about Britain's membership of the EU tend to hold their fire for the big set piece debates that occur when new treaties are ratified, and national MPs show little interest in the detail of EU business or in the activities of their colleagues in the European Parliament. The work of the European Union Committee in the House of Lords, which conducts very effective inquiries into EU issues, takes evidence from every incoming EU Presidency and from the government after every European Council meeting, reaches a wider audience outside as well as inside Westminster because its reports are highly valued by those who seek to influence, study, or report on EU policy matters.

Since 1997, there have been a number of significant constitutional changes which are only indirectly linked to EU membership but which have subsequently impacted on Britain's relationship with the EU. The most important of these changes (which also include the introduction of proportional representation for the 1999 elections to the European Parliament) is devolution. The devolution of governance to Scotland, but also to Wales and Northern Ireland, raises significant issues about UK policy-making and representation on EU matters (Schnapper 2011). At present, although significant powers have been transferred to the devolved authorities, British EU policy is determined in London and there are complex agreements and procedures that are designed to ensure that devolved interests are considered by the government of the UK. Although this system worked reasonably well at first, problems have subsequently arisen in Scotland, in particular following the 2010 UK election of a Conservative-dominated coalition government and the 2011 election of a Scottish government with an outright Scottish National Party majority. First of all, the question of independence, and thus of the future of the UK as an EU member state, has become more immediately relevant, but the new Scottish government is also pressing for amendments to the Scotland Bill to give it statutory rights so that its members can attend EU Council of Ministers meetings and its officials can attend Commission and Council working groups (at present Scottish government representatives can attend only by invitation of the UK government). Scotland in particular has stepped up its representation in Brussels where it and the Scottish parliament office work within UKREP to represent Scottish interests as well as to provide information back to the Scottish government in Edinburgh, which has a Minister for European Affairs, and the Scottish parliament, which has an European and External Relations Committee. Thus the joint 'institutional' impact of UK devolution combined with UK membership of the EU is an active British participation in an evolving system of multilevel governance in Europe (Bulmer *et al.* 2002). Although the British government has become an effective player at the EU level, continuing ambivalence about Britain's EU membership, and the more recent questioning of the long-term existence of the United Kingdom, remains a limiting factor.

Europeanization and Policy Issues

The substantive policy issues that first caused the UK problems with the EU persist as negative factors for the British government and for the wider public. For most British citizens, the EU raises the issue of cost, whether it be the overall cost of membership as indicated by Britain's continuing role as a major net contributor to the EU budget, or the immeasurable costs that EU 'red tape' (a constant complaint) and policies like the common agricultural and fisheries policy are believed to have inflicted on Britain over the years of membership. Under Blair and Brown, attempts, albeit half-hearted, were made to be positive about the appropriateness of the EU as a framework within which the UK could and should pursue its policy objectives. Under the present government, and despite the efforts of the Liberal Democrats, Euroscepticism, both within the Conservative Party and in the wider polity, is more widespread with little attempt being made to highlight the policy advantages to the UK of EU membership. Although the repatriation of powers in the area of employment and social welfare is off the agenda at the moment, it remains a key objective of the Conservative Eurosceptic Right, who are keen that the government should exploit any opportunities provided by the need for the EU as a whole to accommodate any euro-zone rescue package.

Although the scope of the EU's policy agenda has increased considerably in recent years, the desire to, wherever possible, restrain this increase and thus limit the competences of the EU remains a key feature of the UK approach to integration, although on some issues, the CAP and the Budget, the UK is not as isolated as it once was. The *Coalition Agreement* itself (Guardian 2010) had a policy component and stated that Britain would be a 'positive participant' in the EU with the goal of ensuring that the UK was equipped to face the challenges of 'global competitiveness, global warming and global poverty'. However this was to be achieved without any further transfers of power from the UK to Brussels, and existing EU competences would be 'examined' with a view in particular to limiting the application of the Working Time Directive in the UK. The UK interest would be 'strongly defended' in both the annual budget negotiations and in the resolution of the financial perspective for 2013–2020. The coalition was in agreement that the EU budget should only focus on those areas where the EU could 'add value'. EU legislation in the criminal justice area would be approached by the UK on a case-by-case basis (which is softer than the original Conservative intention to reject it on principle), and further enlargement would be supported.

The creation and preservation of the 'Single Market', and the desire to make it as competitive as possible, has always been a core UK interest, but this is essentially an interest in 'negative' integration by which is meant the removal of barriers. Successive British governments have also been willing to accept an element of competition policy at the EU level as necessary to preserve the essential market freedoms, but attempts to develop social and industrial policy to counter market irregularities have always been resisted—this is partly a resistance to furthering 'positive' integration, but also a particularly Conservative interest in resisting what is sometimes referred to as 'supranational socialism'. This position led Margaret Thatcher and John Major to resist and opt out of the idea of a Social Chapter in the Maastricht Treaty, and contemporary Conservatives would ideally like to reverse the acceptance of most of the contents of that Chapter which Blair conceded at the time of the Amsterdam

Treaty. The present government shares with its predecessors a desire to reduce single market related regulation at the EU level (ideally removing an old EU regulation for every new one added) and to keep the single market as open to the outside world as possible in international trade negotiations. British governments have never shared the French desire to ring-fence the European market as a defence against globalization; instead they have always seen the single market as an important step towards greater globalization. Under Blair, the determination to make the EU single market the most competitive in the world by 2010 was seen as a way of further developing the single market that could be supported by the UK. The Lisbon Agenda and its use of the 'open method of cooperation' was attractive to Britain because it downgraded the use of EU legislation in favour of individual EU member states, agreeing 'best practice' at the EU level but seeking to implement it by individual national action—a policy process that seemed to fit British preferences for intergovernmental as opposed to supranational policy practices.

Although the Lisbon Agenda failed to deliver its ambitious target on European economic competitiveness, UK interest in developing its conception of the single market remains. To that end, following a Baltic–Nordic summit which he convened in London early in 2011, David Cameron has sought to build an alliance with 'northern' EU member states to keep the single market free of overregulation, but better encompassing services, energy, and the digital economy.

Britain opposed the CAP, with its reliance on Community preference and a guaranteed price, from the very beginning, preferring its own method of agricultural support. British governments' efforts to reform the CAP have achieved a measure of success with a steady move in recent years from price support to direct payments to farmers, and the abolition of direct export subsidies designed to support the offloading of EU overproduction. The UK remains fundamentally opposed to a policy that continues to consume around 40 per cent of the total EU budget, and whose protectionist attitude towards the outside world remains as a considerable barrier to acceptance of EU trade objectives within the framework of the World Trade Organization's Doha Round.

In the case of the CAP and of the budgetary arrangements, Britain paid the price of late entry. Had Britain managed to enter the EU in 1963, then the arrangements would most certainly have been different, but attempts to reform these early policy agreements (to which could be added the Common Fisheries Policy) have not been easy. Whilst the funding of the EU budget has moved from reliance on agricultural levies and import duties towards direct payments linked to member states, since 1984 the UK has enjoyed significant rebates to lower its net contribution. However, it remains the case that, for the past forty years, successive UK governments have been frustrated by the fact that 80 per cent of the EU budget has been devoted to agricultural support and to the structural funds. Because the UK has always insisted that the overall size of the EU budget should not be increased much beyond 1 per cent of EU GNP, Britain has tended to argue that new budget lines can only be introduced if significant reductions can be made in the funds allocated to agricultural and structural funding. Although the structural funds originated in the 1970s as a way of reducing the UK's net contribution (Allen 2010: 231), the British government now argues that such funding was always meant to be transitional and that it should now be limited only to the new member states and then gradually phased out altogether leaving the member states themselves to deal with any remaining regional disparities. In 2005, the UK Presidency oversaw negotiations on the 2007–2013 financial perspective during which Blair made some concessions on the previously untouchable UK rebate but failed to press home his desire for a fundamental review of the CAP, mainly because of the determination of France and Germany to preserve it. Instead, Blair was promised a mid-term (2010) review, but Britain ended up opposing the Commission's subsequent plans to cap direct payments to the EU's richest agricultural producers (many of whom are British). Since coming to power, the Cameron government argued strongly for either a reduction or a freeze on both the 2011 and 2012 annual EU budgets, but still claimed victory when the inevitable increases were agreed, albeit at a lower level than requested by the Commission. The UK is a leading member of a group of member states that includes France and Germany, who are determined to resist the Commission's argument for significant budget increases in the 2013–2020 financial perspective. Whilst Britain is not alone in wanting to prevent increased EU funding, it is probably still relatively isolated in its wish to dramatically reduce the overall level of expenditure at the EU level by fundamentally challenging the CAP and the system of structural funding.

Although Blair paid lip service to the long-term possibility of eventual 'membership of the euro', aloofness from the euro has always had popular support in the UK. Since all political parties became committed to winning a referendum as a prerequisite to joining the euro, it seems unlikely that membership will be viable in the immediate or medium term future. Indeed the coalition agreement not to even prepare for euro membership in the lifetime of the current parliament would seem to rule out membership before 2020 (it would take a minimum of five years to prepare for entry).

There are some EU policy areas, most particularly environmental policy, where the EU has provided the major legal framework for domestic policy and the major forum for the international pursuit of UK objectives on matters such as the management of climate change. On the other hand, the UK has been reluctant to fully embrace the potential of cooperation in the areas of JHA, particularly as attempts to keep policy making in this area intergovernmental failed and it became 'communitized'. This led to the UK seeking and achieving a degree of flexibility under the Lisbon Treaty, which at present enables it to opt in or out of EU legislation relating to immigration and asylum matters as well as proposals affecting the police or criminal justice on a case-by-case basis (Grant 2009: 16–19). To date the Cameron government has opted into about 50 per cent of all recent legislation in this area, but a crunch will come in 2014 when a decision will need to be made as to whether the UK accepts legislation in this area or opts out entirely.

Whilst Labour under Brown sought initially to take a leading role in managing the EU's response to the financial crisis that started in 2008, as soon as the major focus of attention became the euro-zone itself the UK's influence rapidly waned, and since 2010 Cameron and Osborne have been at pains to make it clear that the UK is opposed to contributing financially to any euro rescue plans. This again is popular within the UK, but has not made Britain many friends amongst its EU partners, and in part led to the UK's isolation in December 2011. Apart from not being prepared to offer financial support to EU attempts to better manage its economy and currency, the UK government is also determined to protect the City of London from what it sees as the EU's determination to diminish its power and influence. Cameron's objection to EU regulation of financial practices reflects a fear that the UK will suffer at the hands of EU regulators, but it can also be seen as a concern by UK regulators that EU legislation will not be tough enough compared with what they would ideally implement at the national level. In this, and other areas, the UK does have somewhat of a reputation for using the national implementation process to 'gold plate' EU directives by adding to rather than diminishing their regulatory impact.

One of the major reasons for the original 'Six' finally welcoming and accepting Britain's EU membership bid related to the external dimension of European integration, and it was an awareness of its own diminished role in the world that was one of the major factors that explained Britain's turn to Europe after 1961. With regard to EU competence in trade, aid, and development, Britain has always been a major player in the evolution of policy and, particularly in the trade field, has accepted the principle of EU primacy over national policy as a price worth paying for the combined power that the EU can exercise. When Britain joined the EU in 1973, the EU's aid and development policy was primarily targeted at francophone Africa. British membership extended this, as did the subsequent membership of Spain and Portugal. Britain has always been a firm supporter of the pooling of a certain amount of national aid as EU aid, and Britain has supported the idea of collective decision making and of the effectiveness of multilateral aid programming. What the British have never accepted is the way that the European Commission administers EU aid, arguing instead that this would be better done by an independent EU agency. Britain's unenthusiastic reception for the new European External Action Service partly reflects its annoyance that development remains formally in the hands of the European Commission.

Britain has always been a keen advocate of European Political Cooperation (EPC) and the CFSP, and has always been in the forefront of those countries determined to preserve their established intergovernmental procedures (in the Lisbon Treaty for example) whilst still trying to make them work more effectively. Whilst Britain has always been determined to maintain a separate national foreign policy (uploaded if possible to the EU level) and diplomatic service, it was more prepared under Labour than it is under the current coalition to recognize the fact that the EU is Britain's 'point of departure' when it comes to foreign policy rather than the first thing that Britain bumps into. Under the stewardship of William Hague, the clear emphasis has been on British rather than European foreign policy and there has been a preference stated for ad hoc bilateral arrangements (such as those that were developed under Gordon Brown with France in the defence area, and which have been enthusiastically developed further under Cameron, whose stated aim of limiting the role of the EU and of ESDP in defence matters is necessary to keep the Eurosceptic Right at bay). Under Hague, decisions have been taken to reduce the number of diplomats dealing with the EU and its member states, and to increase the number dealing with India, China, and other emerging powers. Under Cameron and Hague, the UK has, if anything, become less convinced than under Blair of both the desirability and viability of moves to forge a common foreign policy amongst the twenty-seven member states, even though it is clear that, under President Obama, the US no longer offers a viable alternative for the UK to foreign policy cooperation within the EU framework. Finally, in contrast to France but in common with Germany, the UK has supported every enlargement of the EU hitherto, although it is clear that the British support for enlargement is often seen as a device for limiting the intensity of European integration.

The UK in Comparative Perspective

Britain joined the EEC in 1973 along with Ireland and Denmark. Negotiations had also included Norway, and accession terms were agreed by the government and passed by the Norwegian parliament but then rejected by its people in a referendum. Both Ireland and Denmark applied to join the EEC at the same time as the UK primarily because their economies were interdependent with that of the UK. Ireland in particular could not at the time contemplate breaking its close trading links with Britain.

All three of the states who joined in 1973 have subsequently experienced the same problem that prevented Norway joining—that of persuading their electorate to endorse the government's EU policy. The Irish people have twice rejected new treaties (in 2001 and 2008) in referenda, only for the decision to be subsequently reversed in repeat referenda. The Danish people, in addition to rejecting membership of the euro in a referendum in 2000, also initially rejected the Maastricht Treaty in 1992 only to subsequently accept it when the question was put a second time one year later. Although the British people agreed to stay in the EEC in the referendum of 1975, commitments by the Labour government to hold a referendum on euro membership or acceptance of the Constitutional Treaty would likely have resulted in a negative vote, had the votes been held.

All three states that joined in 1973 have experienced a successful Europeanization of their governance processes, although they have perhaps been less successful when it comes to the Europeanization of their politics. All three have attracted resistance to further integration in their electorates, as is reflected in the emergence of anti-EU parties (UKIP in the UK, Libertas in Ireland, and Unity and the Danish Peoples Party in Denmark). It is generally accepted that the UK and Denmark have developed the most effective systems of national parliamentary scrutiny of EU legislation. Ireland is one of the few member states whose Council Presidencies have consistently attracted favourable comment.

On policy issues, the UK and Denmark have favoured restrictions on the growth in size of the EU budget and the UK has campaigned consistently for the reform of the CAP. Ireland on the other hand, as a major net recipient from the EU budget and as a member state that derives a significant proportion of its agricultural income from the CAP, has been less critical. The UK and Demark have not joined the euro, but Ireland did. Although the recent problems in the euro-zone have hit Ireland hard, its ability to join the euro when the UK remained outside indicated that it was no longer so inextricably bound to the UK economy. All three member states have been very cautious about the development of the EU's foreign and security policy. Ireland remains sensitive about its neutrality, which means that it is cautious about military policy and a closer relationship between the EU and NATO, whilst both the UK and Denmark remain determined to preserve the intergovernmental nature of the policy process. Britain, Ireland, and Denmark are, however, divided by the fact that the UK is one of the small group of highly influential large member states, whilst Ireland and Denmark are part of the much bigger group of smaller, and therefore less influential, member states.

Conclusions

The broad conclusion of this chapter is that Britain's relationship with the European Union is at a significant turning point, primarily because of the crisis in the euro-zone that has the potential to lead to some form of enhanced integration between some but not all of the current member states. Partly because of the failure of successive UK governments to build a permissive domestic consensus for British participation in the full range of European Union activities, and partly because of the impact of the crisis in the euro-zone, there is a distinct possibility that a two-tier European construction might emerge with Britain relatively isolated in the lower tier whilst the remaining major European states continue to work closely together in the top tier. It seems unlikely at present that any combination of UK political parties could be brought together into a coalition that could persuade the UK electorate of the virtues of full participation in the closer Union that might emerge.

Although, under Labour, Britain became superficially more EU-friendly, the commitment to further integration was never there. The aim of whole-hearted participation in what already existed was never really followed through so that the ambiguity and ambivalence of the relationship soon resurfaced under the pressures generated first by the attempt to establish the Constitutional Treaty (Menon 2004) and then by the economic and financial crisis that has consumed the EU since 2008. If the European Union and the euro are to survive the current crisis, then it seems likely that European integration will intensify to a degree that will be unacceptable to the British government and electorate for a considerable time to come.

FURTHER READING

Hugo Young's politico-historical account of Britain's relationship with the EU (1999) remains essential contextual reading whilst Geddes (2004) provides a useful single-authored overview of the impact of membership on British politics. The special issue of The British Journal of Politics and International Relations entitled *Rethinking Britain and Europe* (BJPIR 2006) is useful, whilst the Europeanization of British Politics is well covered by Bache and Jordan (2006). There have of course been a plethora of biographical and autobiographical works about the major figures of the two Labour administrations (Cook 2003: Blair 2010: Seldon and Lodge 2010: Mandelson 2010: Rawnsley 2010), but by far the most informative of the recent publications is that of Stephen Wall (2008). Rosamond (2002), Forster and Blair (2002), Allen (2003b), Gamble (2005), Bulmer (2008), Bulmer and Burch (2009), Daddow, (2010), Daddow and Gaskarth (2011), Federal Trust (2011b), Hug (2011), Miller (2011), Allen (2011) and Nugent and Phinnemore (2010) provide good overviews of the relationship between Britain and Europe in recent years.

WEB LINKS

The FCO website **http://www.fco.gov.uk/en/global-issues/european-union/** has a very useful section on Britain and Europe and the prime minister's EU activities can be followed at **http://www.number10.gov.uk/**. The UK Delegation to the EU can be found at **http://ukeu.fco.gov.uk/en/**. The Federal Trust **http://www.fedtrust.co.uk/** is a good source on the British debate about the EU, as is Chatham House **http://www.chathamhouse.org/research/europe**. The House of Lords European Committee publishes excellent reports on most aspects of the UK's relationship with the EU and can be found at **http://www.parliament.uk/hleu**. The European Movement **http://www.euromove.org.uk/** works for the European idea, and the Bruges Group **http://www.brugesgroup.com/** works against it. *European Voice* is a weekly newspaper specialising in reporting on the EU **http://www.europeanvoice.com/** and good coverage can also be found in the weekly *The Economist* **http://www.economist.com/world/europe**. The BBC coverage of the EU can be found at **http://www.bbc.co.uk/news/world/europe/**. Links to the websites of all British newspapers can be found at **http://www.thebigproject.co.uk/news/**.

REFERENCES

Aktipis, M. And Oliver, T. (2011), 'Europeanization and British Foreign Policy', in R. Wong and C. Hill (eds), *National and European Foreign Policies*, London and New York: Routledge, 72–92.

Allen, D. (2003a), 'The Foreign and Commonwealth Office: Adapting to Change within a Transformed World', in B. Hocking and D. Spence (eds), *Integrating Diplomats: Foreign Ministries in the European Union*, Basingstoke: Palgrave Macmillan.

Allen, D. (2003b), 'Great Britain and the Future of the European Union: Not Quite There Yet', in S. Serfaty (ed.), *The European Finality and its National Dimensions*, Washington, DC: Center for Strategic and International Studies, 77–105.

Allen, D. (2004), 'James Callaghan', in K. Theakston (ed.), *British Foreign Secretaries since 1974*, London: Routledge.

Allen, D. (2005), 'The United Kingdom: A *Europeanized* Government in a *non-Europeanized* Polity', in Bulmer, S. and Lequesne, C. (eds), *The Member States of the European Union*, Oxford: Oxford University Press, 119–41.

Allen, D. (2010), 'The Structural Funds and Cohesion Policy: Extending the Bargain to Meet the Challenges of Enlargement', in Wallace, H., Pollack, M., and Young, A. (eds), *Policy-Making in the European Union*, Sixth Edition, Oxford: Oxford University Press, 229–52.

Allen, D. (2011), 'Die EU-Politik der britischen Koalitionsregierung: Distanz vor Pragmatismus', (The UK Coalition Government's European Policy), *Integration*, 3/2011: 197–213.

Bache, I. and Jordan, A. (2006), *The Europeanization of British Politics*, Basingstoke and New York.

Barber, T. (2011), 'Summit was a Disaster for British Diplomacy', *Financial Times*, 14 December.

BBC (2005), *BBC News Coverage of the European Union*. Independent Panel Report, January 2005.

Blair, T. (2000), Speech to the Polish Stock Exchange, 6 October, http://www.number-10.gov.uk/ (Speeches).

Blair, T. (2010), *A Journey*, London: Hutchinson.

BJPIR, (2006), 'After the Constitutional Treaty: Rethinking Britain and Europe', *The British Journal of Politics and International Relations*, 8/1 February.

Bulmer, S. (2008), 'New Labour, New European Policy? Blair, Brown and Utilitarian Supranationalism', *Parliamentary Affairs*, 61/4: 597–620.

Bulmer, S. and Burch, M. (2009), *The Europeanisation of Whitehall: UK Central Government and the European Union*, Manchester: Manchester University Press.

Bulmer, S., Burch, M., Carter, C., Hogwood, P., and Scott, A. (2002), *European Policy-Making under Devolution: Transforming Britain into Multi-Level Governance*, Basingstoke: Palgrave Macmillan.

Coles, J. (2000), *Making Foreign Policy: A Certain Idea of Britain*, London: John Murray.

Cook, R. (2003), *The Point of Departure*, London, New York, Sydney, Tokyo, Singapore, Toronto, and Dublin: Simon and Schuster.

Daddow, O. (2007), 'Playing Games with History: Tony Blair's European Policy in the Press', *The British Journal of Politics, and International Relations*, 9/4: 582–98.

Daddow, O. (2010), *New Labour and the European Union: Blair and Brown's Logic of History*, Manchester and New York: Manchester University Press.

Daddow, O. and Gaskarth, J. (eds) (2011), *British Foreign Policy: The New Labour Years*, Basingstoke: Palgrave Macmillan.

Dover, R. (2007), *The Europeanisation of British Defence Policy*, Aldershot: Ashgate.

European Union Act, (2011) available at http://www.legislation.gov.uk/ukpga/2011/12/contents/enacted/data.htm.

Federal Trust, (2011a), *The European Union Bill: A Federal Trust Briefing*, London: Federal Trust.

Federal Trust (2011b), *The Coalition and Europe – After the Honeymoon*, London: Federal Trust.

Forster, A. and Blair, A. (2002), *The Making of Britain's European Foreign Policy*, London: Longman.

Freedland, J. (2011),'The Two-Speed Europe Is Here. With UK Alone in the Slow Lane', *The Guardian*, 10 December.

Gallup (2009), *Flash Eurobarometer Attitudes toward the EU in the United Kingdom; Analytical Report*, The Gallup Organisation for the Directorate General for Communication of the European Commission, Flash EB Series # 274, July 2009.

Gamble, A. (2005), *Between Europe and America: The Future of British Politics*, London: Palgrave Macmillan.

Geddes, A. (2004), *The European Union and British Politics*, Basingstoke: Palgrave Macmillan.

Grabbe, H. and Munchau, W. (2002), *Germany and Britain: An Alliance of Necessity*, London: Centre for European Reform.

Grant, C. (2009), *Cameron's Europe: Can the Conservatives achieve their EU objectives?*, London: Centre for European Reform.

Guardian (2010), 'The Coalition Agreement', *The Guardian*, 15 May 2010.

Hague, W. (2010), 'Britain's Foreign Policy in a Networked World', 1 July, available at http://www.fco.gov.uk/en/news/latest-news/?view=Speech&id=22472881

House of Commons Information Office (2011), *EU Legislation and Scrutiny Procedures*, Factsheet L11 Legislation Series, Revised September 2011.

Hug, A. (2011), (ed.), *The New British Politics and Europe: Conflict or Cooperation?*, London: The Foreign Policy Centre.

Ludlow, P. (1993), 'The UK Presidency: A View from Brussels', *Journal of Common Market Studies*, 31/2: 246–60.

Mandelson, P. (2010), *The Third Man: Life at the Heart of New Labour*, London: Harper Press.

Menon, A. (2004), *Leading from Behind: Britain and the European Constitutional Treaty*, Paris: Notre Europe, Research and European Issues No 31, January.

Miller, V. (2011), *The Government's Policy on Europe*, House of Commons Library, Standard Note, SN/1A/5b54, 7 February.

Nugent, N. and Phinnemore, D. (2010), 'United Kingdom: Red Lines Defended', in Carbone, M. (ed.), *National Politics and European Integration: From the Constitution to the Lisbon Treaty*, Cheltenham: Edward Elgar, 71–89.

Owen, D. (2003), 'Two-Man Government', *Prospect*, 93, 14–16 December.

Parker, G. and Blitz, J. (2011), 'Cameron Appoints Opponent of Euro Entry as Envoy to EU', *Financial Times*, 25/26 June.

Rachman, G. (2010), 'The Fear that unites Britain and Europe', *Financial Times*, 15/16 May 11.

Rawnsley, A. (2010), *The End of the Party: The Rise and Fall of New Labour*, London: Viking/Penguin Books.

Rawnsley, A. (2011), 'Now it's three-speed Europe and we're left on the hard shoulder', *The Observer*, 11 December, 43.

Rosamond, B. (2002), 'Britain's European Future', in C. Hay (ed.), *British Politics Today*, Cambridge: Polity, 185–215.

Schmidt, V. (2006), 'Adapting to Europe: Is it Harder for Britain?', *British Journal of Politics and International Relations*, 8/1: 15–33.

Schnapper, P. (2011), 'New Labour, Devolution and British Identity: The Foreign Policy Consequences', in Daddow, O. and Gaskarth, J. (eds), *British Foreign Policy: The New Labour Years*, Basingstoke: Palgrave Macmillan, 48–62.

Scottish Government (2011), 'Scotland Bill-EU Involvement', available at http://www.scotland.gov.uk/Topics/International/Europe/About/Scotland-in-EU

Seldon, A. (1997), *Major: A Political Life*, London: Weidenfeld & Nicolson.

Seldon, A. and Lodge, G. (2010), *Brown at 10*, London: Biteback.

Stephens, P. (2011), 'Was this the moment we stumbled out of Europe?', *Financial Times*, 13 December.

Wall, S. (2008), *A Stranger in Europe: Britain and the EU from Thatcher to Blair*, Oxford and New York: Oxford University Press.

Wilkes, G. and Wring, D. (1998), 'The British Press and European Integration: 1948–1996', in D. Baker and D. Seawright (eds), *Britain For and Against Europe: British Politics and the Question of European Integration*, Oxford: Oxford University Press, 185–205.

Young, H. (1999), *This Blessed Plot: Britain and Europe from Churchill to Blair*, London: PaperMac.

CHAPTER 6

Spain: Modernization Through Europeanization

Francesc Morata

Summary

Spain is the only country among all those which have joined the EU after 1958 whose political parties and citizenry were in complete agreement on the issue. Expectations have been broadly satisfied in terms of economic, social, and administrative modernization. In a multi-national country of conflicting identities, belonging to Europe was also perceived as an opportunity to merge in a common project beyond the nation-state. EU membership has prompted institutional adjustments both at the central and the regional level fostering new modes of multilevel governance. At the same time, to a larger or lesser extent, Europeanization has affected most policy areas, and particularly economic and social policies in response to EU pressures during the financial crisis.

Introduction

Spain and Portugal joined the European Community (EC) in 1986. Symbolically, this date put an end to the international isolation of Spain after Franco's dictatorship (1939–1975). European membership meant a golden opportunity to allow the country to recover its lost place in Europe (Morata 1998; Powell 2007). Since then, the combination of democracy, political decentralization, and European membership has led to the fastest process of transformation in modern Spanish history. Before the global financial crisis, Spain was one of the countries with the highest economic growth in the EU, ranking as the eighth economy in the world with a GDP per capita comparable to the EU-15 average. Despite high structural unemployment, it had achieved a considerable reduction of its public deficit and a rapid modernization of infrastructure and public services. As a less developed country in the European context, Spain has been relying largely on EU subsidies to develop its regions and to modernize its infrastructures. With €100 billion, it was the member state which most benefited from the Structural and Cohesion funds between 1989 and 2006, and it is the second biggest recipient of agricultural subsidies. Meanwhile, for a country unaccustomed to protecting public health or preserving natural areas, European environmental policy has been crucial. With regard to regional and local administrations, many of them have learned to carry out new modes of governance and to participate in European networks that facilitate the sharing of interests, experiences, and knowledge.

One of the transformations that best reflects the nature of changes in Spain since 1986 is that it is no longer a country of emigration. On the contrary, it has turned into the largest recipient of immigrants throughout the EU.[1] Another notable feature is the international dynamism of Spanish firms. Spain ranked as the second private investor in Latin America from 1996 to 2008, just behind the US. Although it would be unreasonable to attribute all these achievements to Spain's EU membership, 'they hardly would have occurred without it' (Powell 2007: 65). Moreover, Spain is most likely the member state where the dual process of state restructuring from 'above' and 'below' has been most intense as a result of both European integration and political decentralization.

Until the post-Maastricht period, Spanish European politics were based on a nationwide consensus rather than on partisan preferences (Closa 2001: 10). Spain's entrance into the EC was almost unanimously supported by political parties, interest groups, the media, and public opinion. The consensus style of the Spanish transition to democracy contributed to this general agreement (Ruiz Jiménez and Egea de Haro 2011). Significantly, Spain is the only country among all those which have joined the EU after 1958 whose political parties were in complete agreement on this issue (Alvarez Miranda 1996). In a multi-national country of conflicting identities, belonging to Europe was also perceived as an opportunity to share a 'common identity' based on non-nationalist values. Finally, EU membership has led to adjustments of both the institutional framework and domestic policy making to face EU requirements, although these have not always been appropriate or effective (Hanf and Soetendorp 1998: 7).

In what follows, we will examine in more depth the different aspects of Spanish adaptation to the EU according to the common analytical framework set up in this volume.

The Pattern of Relations with the EU

Commitment and Funding

Since its entry into the EC, Spain has seen itself as one of the large member states (Powell 2002). Under the Lisbon Treaty provisions, until November 2014, it will continue to enjoy twenty-seven votes in the EU Council, just two less than Germany, France, Italy, and the UK. From 1999 to 2009, the former Spanish Minister of Foreign Affairs and Secretary General of the NATO, Javier Solana, served as Secretary General of the Council and High Representative for the Common Foreign and Security Policy (CFSP), while three Spaniards have been president of the European Parliament since 1989. To play a major role in the EU, Spain has also sought to take advantage of its historical relations with Latin American and Arab countries. However, some of the problems faced by Spain as an EU partner might be better explained because it 'does not fit into any of the categories into which all others may be grouped: the very prosperous and large; the very prosperous and small; the less prosperous and small' (Powell 2002: 13).

Notwithstanding agreement on a number of fundamental issues (i.e. preserving Spain's institutional weight; rejecting a 'two-speed' Europe; claiming more cohesion; strengthening EU relations with Latin America; supporting Mediterranean partnership), socialist and conservative strategies towards European integration have been rather different. Until 1996, under the leadership of the socialist Premier, Felipe Gonzalez, Spain combined commitment to European integration with an increasingly clear-cut definition of national interests. From 1996 to 2004, with the conservative

José M. Aznar, it shifted to reactive attitudes based on self-interest alongside emphasis on market liberalization, terrorism, and alignment with the USA on sensitive issues like the invasion of Iraq. From 2004–2011, under the socialist government of José L. Rodríguez Zapatero, Spain re-joined the hardcore of pro-integration member states, especially the Franco-German axis.

Gonzalez (1982–1996) attached high priority to building a strong alliance with Mitterrand and Kohl[2] with a view to participating in the Community's hard core while promoting initiatives such as subsidiarity, European citizenship, and closer economic relations with Latin America. His good relations with Jacques Delors led also to important outcomes related to cohesion policy and the integration of Spanish agriculture and fisheries sooner than initially established. By framing European priorities in compatible terms with national aspirations and vice versa, the latecomer Spain was able to gain a reputation as a reliable member state (Morata and Fernandez 2003).

Gonzalez displayed a twofold entrepreneurial and bargaining strategy, which combined commitment to far-reaching European integration and the claim for Community funding to enable the country to close the gap with the large member states. In 1989, Spain vetoed the EC budget in order to force agreement on doubling the Structural Funds as a side-payment for accepting the single market. Again, in 1991, it threatened to block agreement on Political Union if the new Cohesion Fund was not included in the Maastricht Treaty. While the Spanish negotiators did not succeed in imposing their views on the need to create a federal compensatory fund to reduce disparities among member states, they managed to build a winning coalition with Portugal, Greece, and Ireland to get additional resources (Cohesion Fund) aimed at improving transport and environmental infrastructures. In exchange for the agreement, the Spanish government was ready to accept qualified majority voting (QMV) for a number of policies, especially for environmental decisions, a very sensitive issue for the government and domestic economic interests (López-Novo and Morata 2000).

National interests re-emerged at the Ioannina summit of 1994, when the Spanish government, together with the UK, opposed the increase, from twenty-three to twenty-six, of the votes needed to form a blocking minority in the Council decisions as a result of the entrance of Austria, Finland, and Sweden into the EU. Spain clearly feared that the centre of gravity would shift northwards, so that the country would find it difficult to grab the lion's share of the EU regional funds (Morata and Fernandez 2003). Putting the Spanish economy on the fast track towards the euro was another achievement of Gonzalez's term.

Domestic Consensus Break-down

The initial consensus among political elites, and especially between the two main parties (PSOE, the Spanish Socialist Workers' Party, and PP, People's Party), began to break down in the early nineties when Aznar took over the PP leadership. While the conservative leader had criticized Gonzalez's efforts to get additional financing at the Edinburgh summit in 1992, ironically, in the Berlin summit on Agenda 2000, he blocked the final agreement until he obtained an increase in the Spanish share of the Cohesion Fund. However, only when the PP came into power, in 1996, did European issues related to institutional architecture, social policies, and the free market become matters of political contention in day-to-day politics. The debate about the Constitutional Treaty ultimately deepened these differences when Aznar, supported by Poland, blocked agreement on the double majority voting in the EU Council, arguing that Spain would have lost the influence it had gained in Nice. In 2003, his support for the invasion of Iraq also broke the traditional domestic consensus on foreign policy.

Aznar's strategy was twofold: building alternative coalitions of member states to counteract the Franco-German axis, and strongly supporting neo-liberal policies. In 2000, in concert with Blair, he promoted the Lisbon Strategy on strengthening European competitiveness. Both also took common initiatives against terrorism and illegal immigration. Together with Blair and Berlusconi, Aznar was one of the most fervent European supporters of the US global strategy after 11 September 2001. He was also among the initiators of the so-called 'letter of the eight', signed by the Prime Ministers of the UK, Italy, Spain, Portugal, Denmark, Poland, and Hungary and the President of the Czech Republic, supporting the George W. Bush administration's plans to invade Iraq. Against the overwhelming majority of Spanish public opinion, Aznar joined the US-led military coalition.

With regard to institutional issues, the PP government took an obstructionist stance during the negotiation of the Amsterdam and Nice treaties. In Amsterdam it threatened to block the agreement on the overall reform if the other partners would not accept its claims regarding the re-weighting of votes in the Council. Spain would only accept the loss of one of 'its' two commissioners in exchange for a substantial increase of votes in the Council. With respect to the other issues at stake, Spain's main objective was to prevent any decision that would harm Spanish financial advantages or bring about any increase in domestic expenditures. Thus Spanish negotiators fiercely opposed the extension of QMV to Structural and Cohesion Funds as well as, together with Britain and Denmark, to social security decisions. A similar strategy was deployed during the Nice Intergovernmental Conference (IGC). Aznar succeeded in increasing the Spanish weight in the EU Council (twenty-seven votes, two below the larger member states) but failed to avoid a reduction in the share of Spanish MEPs (Closa and Heywood 2004). As to the extension of QMV, Spain retained its veto power on the Structural and the Cohesion Funds until 2006 (Morata and Fernández 2003).

With regard to the European Convention on the Future of Europe, Aznar's main concern was to maintain the benefits achieved in Nice. He also refused to change the balance of power between member states and the supranational institutions and to recognize the role of the regions in European integration. Instead, the Spanish representatives put much emphasis on the inclusion of an explicit reference to respect by the EU of 'state functions, including ensuring the territorial integrity of the State, maintaining law and order and safeguarding national security' (Article I-5). Despite their efforts, however, they failed to gain inclusion in the preamble of a reference to the 'Judean-Christian roots of Europe'. During the IGC on the Constitutional Treaty (CT), Spain, together with Poland, blocked agreement on the double majority—and then, in the whole treaty draft, lost the power achieved in Nice.

Europeanization of Domestic Financial Crisis

The victory of the PSOE in the general elections on March 2004 made it possible to conclude the negotiations on the CT. Considering the EU as 'the natural platform of Spain', the new prime minister, Zapatero, declared that 'Europe should see us again as a friendly country, a pro-European country which makes no division between the new and the old Europe'. As the Premier was ready to reach a compromise on the CT, Poland desisted from further blocking the agreement. In the end, Spain accepted the double majority system with some tweaks: decisions should be taken at least by 55 per cent of the member states representing 65 per cent of the population, rather than the initial percentages of 50 per cent and 60 per cent, respectively. At the same time, the blocking minority should be formed by at least four member states. With this result, Spain improved its ability to form blocking coalitions and, above all, facilitated the most satisfactory agreement possible. Spain was also one of the eight member states that voluntarily held a referendum to ratify the CT (see under Political Parties and European Elections below).

During the crisis of the CT, the self-styled 'Friends of the European Constitution', led by Spain and Luxembourg, met in Madrid in late January 2007 with the aim of overcoming the crisis. These countries were ready to make concessions without distorting the institutional achievements. They also enriched the EU agenda with pressing issues: re-defining the criteria for the accession of new member states; reviewing mechanisms for controlling subsidiarity; fostering immigration, energy, and climate change policies; greater coordination of national economic policies; development of a European social space; and an enhanced European Security and defence policy.

Spain held its fourth European Presidency in 2010 with the responsibility to manage the implementation of the Lisbon Treaty. It also had to face the impact of the Greek financial crisis on the euro-zone. From the outset, Zapatero gave prominence to the newly appointed president of the European Council, Herman Van Rompuy, and the High Representative for Foreign and Security Policy, Catherine Ashton, opting to maintain a discreet position in the background. The Spanish government displayed a more active role on issues that most directly coincided with the 'national interest', such as economic recovery (the 2020 Strategy for Growth and Employment), gender violence, and trans-Atlantic relations, especially the Mediterranean and Latin America. Whilst fighting against the global financial crisis was at the top of the Spanish agenda, the economic collapse of Greece and its dramatic implications for the euro-zone—and especially for Spain—eventually prevailed. Pressures from Germany forced the Spanish government to launch a hard adjustment plan. Ironically, it was the gravity of the global crisis that had prompted the Spanish agenda move towards 'creating a genuine economic government of the EU and in particular, the Euro-zone'.[3]

Public Opinion and Political Parties

Public Opinion

The overall assessment of Spain's EU membership among public opinion has been positive since 1986, ranging between 54 per cent (1995) and 76 per cent (2004), always above the European average (Diez Medrano 2007). In 2009, 64 per cent of Spaniards considered belonging to the EU a 'good thing' (EU average: 53 per cent) close to 1999 (62 per cent) and 1989 (68 per cent) figures (Eurobarometer 2009, 1999, 1989). Similarly, two out of three Spanish citizens felt that they had benefited from European membership. Meanwhile, despite the impact of the economic crisis, and declining confidence with regard to domestic institutions, confidence towards the EU scored 56 per cent, five points above the previous year (EU average: 46 per cent) (Eurobarometer Standard 72, 2009). In terms of the impact of the different levels of government on their lives, as in all member states, Spaniards gave priority to the national government (49 per cent), ahead of regional or local authorities (34 per cent) and EU institutions (12 per cent). It is interesting to note that 68 per cent of the respondents claimed that decision making in the EU does not take sufficient account of regional and local governments.

On a variety of topics (combating terrorism, environmental protection, defence and foreign policy, and immigration), a majority of Spaniards preferred decisions to be made at the EU level and not by the individual governments. By contrast, they believed that economic issues such as pensions and taxes should remain within the national realm. Nevertheless, the EU was viewed as somewhat better equipped than the national government to address the economic and financial crisis. Significantly, just over half of respondents stated in 2009 that Spain would be better protected against the crisis if it had kept the 'peseta' (the former Spanish currency) although 43 per cent considered that the euro had mitigated the effects of the crisis. Spaniards also acknowledged that European issues affect national policies and that EU decisions impact on their everyday life.

Spanish literature on public opinion attitudes towards European integration generally agrees on utilitarian approaches as the most important explanatory factor of citizens' loyalty towards the EU (Szmolka 2008). However, feelings based on trust in European institutions and identification with Europe as a whole are also significant. In general, citizens who trust the European institutional system have a more positive attitude towards the EU. Likewise, citizens who recognize themselves as Spanish (and/or Basques, Catalans, etc.) and European develop more favourable attitudes towards the EU. Finally, the influence of domestic political factors on European attitudes is significant to the extent that satisfaction with the functioning of democracy in Spain is positively correlated with EU integration (Szmolka 2008).

Although, as already said, negative attitudes towards the Union are lower in Spain than in the other member states, the percentage of citizens with no clear/defined attitude towards the EU exceeds the EU average, as well as ignorance and lack of interest about European issues (Diez Medrano 2007). There is also significant resistance to ceding sovereignty to the EU, while concerns regarding losses of national identity as a consequence of integration are more important in Spain than in the EU as a whole (Ruiz Jiménez and Egea de Haro 2007).

Political Parties and European Elections

Spanish political parties began to 'discover' Europe only in the 1990s in the aftermath of the Maastricht Treaty. The PSOE was one of the most active promoters of the European Socialist Party, while the PP managed to make a late entry into the European People's Party (EPP) after having overcome the resistance of the Catalan and Basque Christian Democrats. The successive defeats of the Right in the larger member states during the 1990s indirectly contributed to enhancing the political status of Aznar, who became a reference point for the centre-Right leaders of the EPP.

In line with the Lisbon Treaty, Spain is to elect fifty-four MEPs (2009 = fifty). European election rules follow the same criteria as domestic elections (corrected proportional d'Hondt formula and closed lists) with two significant differences: a single constituency instead of provincial ones, and no threshold (3 per cent in the Congress). A single constituency tends to benefit the two larger state parties and hinders the regional parties that are obliged to coalesce in order to achieve higher representation (instrumental coalitions). The six European elections held in Spain since 1987 show a set of trends common to most of the member states: 1) 'second order' elections and higher abstention rates, 2) a predominantly domestic approach (low profile of European issues and nationalist discourses), 3) 'mid-term referendums' on the ruling party, and 4) higher levels of volatility and fragmentation (Rodriguez Aguilera 2007) (see Table 6.1). Voter turnout has always been lower in comparison with domestic elections, except in 1987 and 1999, when the European elections coincided with other domestic electoral processes.

The referendum on the Constitutional Treaty of February 2005 reveals some interesting characteristics of citizen and political elite attitudes towards European integration. Aznar had committed himself to hold a referendum during the debates of the European Convention. Zapatero took up the challenge for a number of reasons: to be the first European leader to convene a consultation process, to strengthen his popularity after a year of government, and to reorient the European policy of Spain (Rodriguez Aguilera and Morata 2008). It was the second referendum in nineteen

TABLE 6.1 Voter turnout in European elections

Year		1987*	1989	1994	1999	2004	2009
Spain		68.52	54.71	59.14	63.05	45.14	44.90
EU average	-		58.41	56.67	49.51	45.47	43.00

*only in Spain
Source: European Parliament (2010)

years (the first one, in 1986, dealt with entry into NATO), and the first consultation on the EU (Marcet 2006: 13).

Although the 'yes' votes (76.73 per cent) outperformed the 'no' votes (17.24 per cent), abstention reached 57 per cent, with a significant 6 per cent of unmarked ballots. Abstention was particularly high among 18–39 year old people, workers, people with lower educational skills, and in smaller cities and towns. The degree of rejection of the CT was higher in the regions with greater presence of nationalist parties—Basque Country and Catalonia—that did not support the treaty.

During the campaign, one crucial political event was the break-down of the traditional European consensus amongst the parties, something which was already hinted at the time of the Maastricht Treaty. The two major Spanish parties (PSOE and PP), the Catalan centre-Right nationalist party (Converence and Union: CiU), and the Basque National Party (PNV) supported the treaty, while the former communists (IU—United Left) and a wide range of left parties from Catalonia and the Basque Country opposed it (Torreblanca 2005).

Impacts on political institutions and governance

Central Administration Restructuring

Like most member states, Spain has not established a ministry responsible for the EU. From 1986 to 1996, the Secretary of State for EC, located in the Ministry of Foreign Affairs, was responsible for coordinating the Spanish positions in the EU, while the General Secretariat of Foreign Policy took charge of CFSP and JHA issues. In 1996, the PP government decided to integrate the General Secretariat of Foreign Policy in a newly created office of State Secretary of Foreign Policy and the European Union. In 2004, under the new government of Zapatero, European responsibilities were merged under a new State Secretary for the EU (SEUE) entrusted with assisting the Minister of Foreign Affairs and Cooperation in the formulation and the implementation of Spanish European policy. The SEUE also coordinates the activities of domestic public administrations in the EU, including the regions and local authorities. The SEUE instructs the Permanent Representative of Spain to the European Union (REPER). The State Secretary also directs the General Secretariat for the EU, the Directorate of Integration and Coordination of General and Economic Affairs of the European Union, and the General Direction for the Internal Market Coordination and other EU Policies. Finally, the Secretary of State chairs the Inter-ministerial Committee for Economic Affairs related to the EU, established in September 1985 with the aim of speeding up intra-governmental coordination.

The Inter-ministerial Committee includes two vice chairmen, shared between the SEUE and the Ministry of Economy and Finance, and representatives (usually Secretaries of State or General Secretaries) of the Presidency (i.e. the prime minister), Industry and Energy, Rural Development and Environment, Labour, Economy and Finance, and Trade. In general, meetings are held every three weeks to debate items on the agenda of the next EU Council, European issues of general interest and decisions taken in earlier Council sessions. Most activity is focused on channelling information from Brussels, exchanging of information, and, when necessary, resolving interdepartmental conflicts. However, the main task of the Committee is consensus-building in the short term, particularly on economic issues rather than on defining strategic positions.

The Committee carries out a systematic evaluation of the administrative implications of EU documents. Its instructions are mandatory for the officials involved in the working groups of the EU Council and to be considered as general guidelines by the Ministers and Secretaries of State who attend the EU Council meetings. This organizational structure is intended to channel Spanish positions through a single actor—the SEUE—while preserving the specific powers and political influence of each individual ministry. However, it is not always possible to prevent the emergence of inter-ministerial conflicts related to issues of particular importance. Sometimes, the committee finds it difficult to define the Spanish position regarding outstanding issues on the agenda of the COREPER and the Spanish Council of Ministers (the cabinet). In these cases, negotiation takes place mainly through informal contacts between the REPER, the Secretary of State, and the Ministries concerned. When its members fail to reach a common position, the decision rests with the Committee for Economic Affairs, chaired by a vice-president of the government or, as a last resort, the Council of Ministers.

Another ad hoc structure is the Monitoring and Coordination Committee for Affairs referred to the European Court of Justice (ECJ). This committee, made of representatives of the Cabinet of the Presidency, the SEUE, the Ministries of Justice and Economy and Finance, and any other department concerned, reviews proceedings against Spain or affecting national interests, including the regions.

All ministries are involved to a greater or lesser extent in EU policy making. The various departments rely on policy experts, lawyers and economists generally with the rank of deputy director general, and advisers. When Spain holds the EU Presidency, an ad hoc task force, comprising officials from the various ministries, takes responsibility for preparation and coordination tasks.

The Spanish REPER is one of the most numerous in Brussels. It consists of about fifty diplomats and almost sixty ministerial experts, and reproduces the organizational structure of the central government. According to the specific requirements of the negotiation process, ministerial experts participate in the consultative committees of the European Commission and the working groups of the Council while the permanent representatives also attend, when required, coordination meetings in Madrid. However, the procedure has not been institutionalized, so in the absence of specific instructions the formulation of the Spanish position rests with the permanent representatives. This does not seem to be particularly troublesome. Given its composition, the REPER works in close connection with each one of the ministries and acts as an informal inter-ministerial coordination mechanism, including also two representatives of the autonomous communities (regions).

Spain's membership of the EU has also entailed the creation or remodelling of ministries in order to strengthen policy coherence between European and domestic structures. As an example, in 1990, criticism from the European Commission regarding the growing number of proceedings against Spain for breach of environmental directives led to the creation of a General Secretariat of the Environment attached to the Ministry of Infrastructures and Transports. In 1996, a Ministry of the Environment was established. However, in 2008, the environment was integrated into a new Ministry of Environmental, Rural and Marine Affairs. The decision to merge the three policy areas, mainly in reaction to the new Common Agricultural Policy (CAP) and the common fisheries policy, generated strong criticisms from environmental groups.

Infrastructures is another Ministry that has been subject to major changes. In 1991, the ministries of Public Works and Transport and Telecommunications merged in a single Ministry (renamed 'Infrastructures' since 1996) as a result of EU pressures to improve the internal coordination of the Structural Funds (Closa and Heywood 2004). Since the 1990s, the Ministry of Industry has also had to adapt to the administrative requirements of the Internal Market. The aim of the reform was to achieve greater competitiveness on the part of Spanish companies and to provide an institutional response to the EU commitments to strengthen policies in the fields of scientific research and knowledge development (Closa and Heywood 2004).

Economy and Finance has also undertaken substantial changes to adapt to EU membership. This department is responsible for coordinating the implementation and the management of Structural and Cohesion Funds through the General Directorate of Community Funds and the General Secretariat of Budget and Expenditure. Beyond negotiating the Spanish share of EU Funds, the Directorate General performs general programming, monitoring, and evaluation functions in coordination with the various departments and regions responsible for the management of Structural Funds. It is also in charge of selecting and monitoring projects from the Cohesion Fund and the European Economic Area.

Parliament's Incremental Adaptation

The Spanish Parliament (Congress and Senate) is not directly involved in EU decision making although, over the years, some improvements have been made in order to follow up the formulation of Spanish positions. Yet, its role remains largely symbolic, except for the new subsidiarity procedure foreseen in the Treaty of Lisbon. Parliamentary intervention is articulated primarily through a Congress-Senate Joint Committee (JC) on the EU established in 1985. However, the role of the JC has been relatively insignificant since it was not competent either to scrutinize the formulation of Spain's European policy or to assess the decrees and other regulations usually set up by the executive to transpose Community rules. In 1988, the information procedure was expanded to all EU initiatives. Moreover, the JC can now prepare reports on the proposals put forward by the European Commission and also submit reports to the plenary sessions of the parliament.

A second phase aimed at enhancing the responsiveness of the JC started after the entry into force of the Maastricht Treaty. A 1994 law provided the JC with new additional functions such as the right to debate EU drafts, the possibility of moving discussions to the Plenary of the Congress, and the convening of Spanish MEPs. However, the most interesting innovation was the executive's obligation to give account to the JC for the negotiation and the outcomes of EU proposals in the Council. Governmental reports on EU proposals had to include an assessment of their legal, political and economic implications. At the same time, the government pledged to include reports on the most relevant issues raised during the six-month Presidency of the EU before the European Councils.

The last step coincided with the Lisbon Treaty. A new law of December 2007 adapted the JC to the requirements of the early warning system included in the Protocol on subsidiarity. The Act gives the JC the power to issue opinions based on the principle of subsidiarity. It also provides for the immediate transmission of all EU proposals to the parliaments of the autonomous communities which may issue a reasoned opinion. In that case, the JC shall incorporate the regional opinion and submit it to the European institutions. In addition, the law gives the JC and the two branches of the parliament the right to bring actions before the Court of Justice, via the government, on the grounds of infringement of the subsidiarity principle. However, the government may rule against the request although it has to justify its refusal.

Beyond the JC, EU developments are also raised during the annual debate on 'the state of the nation' which entails the adoption of resolutions and recommendations addressed to the executive. The Premier keeps the plenary regularly informed about the outcomes of each European Council, albeit ensuing discussions lack any effective impact. The role of the Congress is more important, at least formally, when Spain holds the EU Presidency. Before each presidential turn, a debate takes place about priorities and the work programme. Once completed, the results are set out.

Beyond the presence of its representatives in the JC, the Senate is not directly involved in European affairs, except for issues of interest to the autonomous communities. In 1995, the Upper House entrusted the General Committee of the Autonomous Communities with the monitoring of regional participation in the EU. However, due to the institutional weakness of the Senate, its role remains almost irrelevant.

Regional Participation in the EU

Regional participation in EU decisions has been a permanent matter of dispute and negotiation between the central state and the autonomous communities (ACs) since 1986 (Börzel 2002; Morata 2007). It is also an interesting example of how sub-state actors can take advantage of domestic institutional resources to face the negative impacts of EU integration on the constitutional balance of power (Morata 2006; Bursens 2008).

In 1988, in view of the first EC Spanish Presidency, regional claims led to the creation of a so-called 'sectoral—intergovernmental—Conference on Issues Related to the European Communities' (CARCE). Its main task was to communicate information about the 1989 Spanish Presidency and, after that, to serve as a mechanism for the exchange of information between both levels of government. However, the horizontal character and the lack of pre-eminence of the CARCE with regard to the other sectoral conferences weakened its effectiveness.

The tight electoral victory of the PP in the 1996 elections turned the Catalan nationalists (CiU) into central players to guarantee political stability. Both parties subscribed to an agreement which included the improvement of regional participation in the EU, embodied in the empowerment of the CARCE; the intervention of the ACs in the formulation of the European positions of the Spanish Government; the inclusion of a regional adviser in the REPER; and finally, the participation of regional representatives in the consultative committees of the Commission and the working groups of the Council. A bilateral state-Catalonia committee on the EU was also set up. However, the central government did not fully respect its commitments, vetoing the presence of regional representatives in the EU Council and its working groups.

Though the socialists won the general elections of March 2004, they fell short of an absolute majority. The need to gain parliamentary support from the Catalan Left wing parties paved the way for regional participation in the EU Council. Two intergovernmental agreements of December 2004 made possible the integration in the Spanish delegation—in four of the nine formations of the Council[4]—of a regional minister acting as the ACs' representative for matters affecting their competences. The agreements also required the presence of two regional advisers appointed as members of the Spanish REPER. Their main duties consist of transmitting information about EU developments that can affect regional competences through their delegations in Brussels, and to assist, or replace, regional representatives in the Council working groups as members of the Spanish delegation. On the basis of a 'good practices agreement' of December 2006, the REPER is entrusted with providing the ACs with information regarding the meetings of the four Council formations, the Council agendas and an evaluation of the issues at stake.[5] Moreover the regional delegations in Brussels can get access at any moment to additional information from the REPER. As a current practice, the members of the REPER regularly meet with the experts of the regional delegations on multilateral or bilateral basis or with regional ministers.

Alongside this general top-down procedure for information exchange, the agreements foresee the channelling of specific information and the debating of EU issues within the nine sectoral conferences affected by the four Council formations.[6] These are responsible for establishing the procedure of regional representation for each Council formation, the selection of regional priorities among the items of the Council agenda and the appointment of the region in charge of representation and coordination tasks.

Horizontal coordination among the regions is twofold: deciding about the opportunity to participate in the Council meetings (which is the rule), and reaching a common position on the points of the agenda affecting regional competences or interests. The AC in charge of coordination formulates a proposal for a common position to be sent to the other regions, which may react within a short deadline. In general, the final decision regarding the common position expressed by the ACs is taken in an informal meeting, two or three weeks before the Council meeting, and then communicated to the central Ministry.

The implementation of the agreement reveals a number of shortcomings (Hanf and Morata 2010). First of all, the central government is neither legally obliged to integrate the regional position into the Spanish one, nor to justify any refusal to do so. Since there are no mandatory guidelines, each minister makes his/her own interpretation and, therefore, the 2004 agreements are not fully respected. According to regional observers, some central ministries are reluctant to accept regional positions or to enable the active involvement—or even the presence—of regional ministers in the Council meetings. Since the agreement does not benefit from any legal support, the regions cannot appeal before the Constitutional Court. Thus, effective participation ultimately depends on the goodwill of each central minister.

Beyond this political problem, the real impact of regional positions is hardly relevant because, in general, they are formulated a few days before the Council meetings. Clearly, the common positions of the ACs could be better integrated in the discussions of the working groups at the EU level between each Council meeting. Consequently, the regions are now striving to accelerate the decision-making process.

Third, leaving aside cohesion policy and the CAP, some regions still do not consider European issues relevant enough to allocate financial and administrative resources to follow up the policy process. As a result, they are not able to put forward policy positions or do not do so in due time. Because of the lack of expertise and, sometimes, also linguistic skills, some regional authorities do not participate actively in the Council working groups.

Fourth, regarding the domestic formulation of common positions, there is not a single coordination procedure among the regions, but six discrete ones (one for each Council configuration).[7]

Finally, although the two regional experts assigned to the Spanish REPER participate in the COREPER meetings, they are hardly able to follow up on the ever growing number of issues at stake for regional interests.

In sum, the new procedure entails a series of political and technical challenges. The most important one remains the regional ability to influence EU decision making from the early phases and not just at the end of the process, when the game is already over. On the whole, irrespective of the problems connected with the formal institutional arrangements, effective mobilization of regional actors, during the determination of the national positions, ultimately depends on the political relevance attached by the regions to EU proposals and, especially on the efforts deployed by the AC responsible for coordination.

However, regional experts agree that the procedure has meant a significant involvement of the autonomous governments at the EU level, including the drafting of new legislation. Work by the units of the regional ministries, for example, enables better forecasting and direct knowledge of EU decision-making mechanisms. Furthermore, the meetings of all the regional representatives prior to each Council of Ministers have created important working relationships, both at the European and the domestic level.

As in the German case (Benz 2006), regional participation in the EU through the state strengthens the power of the executives to the detriment of the autonomous parliaments which remain almost excluded from the procedure. As the regional minister who participates in the Council meetings embodies all of the regional authorities, he/she is not accountable to his/her respective parliament.

With regard to organizational issues, besides the creation of official delegations in Brussels, the autonomous governments have set up administrative structures and procedures to face EU policies. As an example, the Secretary for the EU of the Catalan government, located in the Presidency cabinet, is entrusted with monitoring, promoting, and coordinating the participation of the Catalan government in the EU Council. It also performs other functions, such as supporting the implementation of Catalan policy within the EU; monitoring and coordinating policies related to it; assuming the representation of the President and coordinating the government's participation in the Committee of the Regions. As for the regional ministries most involved in EU policy making and implementation (Agriculture, Environment, Economy, Transport, Industry, Social Affairs, and Universities and Research), in general they have adapted their organizational structure and improved European expertise.

Judicial Politics

Despite the obvious impact of EU law on Spanish society, there are still some doubts about the judicial system's ability to enforce the European rules. Assuming that the preliminary rulings are a reliable indicator of the degree of implementation of

TABLE 6.2 Preliminary rulings 1986–2009 (by court or tribunal)	
Supreme Court	24
National Audience Tribunal	1
Central Criminal Court	7
Other courts	190
Total	222

Community law, until 2009 the number of procedures brought by the Spanish courts to the ECJ was only 222, below the average of the larger member states (see Table 6.2). This situation does not seem to reflect any reluctance from the national courts to enforce Community law, but simply ignorance or lack of technical training, especially in the first years of membership. At the same time, it is interesting to note that both the Supreme Court and the Constitutional Court have expressed serious doubts about their competence to bring cases before the ECJ. In particular, the Constitutional Court has declared itself incompetent to rule about the compatibility of Community law with domestic law, except in regard to the protection of fundamental rights. The High Court has settled conflicts of jurisdiction between the central government and the ACs with regard to the internal implementation of Community law, establishing the principle that EU membership cannot entail an internal reallocation of responsibilities at the expense of the regions. A different problem arises from infringement proceedings or even judgments of the ECJ against Spain for breaches of European law by the ACs (see Table 6.3). In these cases, the central government can only negotiate the resolution of the problem with the region concerned, but cannot force it to act.

Policy Adaptation

In Spain, almost all policy sectors are affected by EU policies, although the extent of the impact obviously varies across areas and governmental levels according to European powers. Here we will briefly review eight areas: CAP, Cohesion policy, Environmental policy, Energy, Telecommunications, the Lisbon Strategy, JHA, and CFSP.

Common Agricultural Policy

The dual process of decentralization and Europeanization of agricultural policy has entailed deep transformations. Since the regions are the effective managers of the CAP, there is no longer policy implementation at the national level. The Spanish Ministry simply acts as national negotiator of EU legislation—since 2005 with the

TABLE 6.3 Number of steps taken in infringement proceedings within a year, broken down by member state[1]

Member state	Formal Notice					Reasoned Opinion					Referral to the Court				
	2007	2006	2005	2004	2003	2007	2006	2005	2004	2003	2007	2006	2005	2004	2003
GERMANY	56	55	63	91	116	18	35	27	39	31	15	10	12	14	18
SPAIN	61	69	73	69	108	28	44	35	17	32	21	18	6	13	23
FRANCE	76	84	77	84	120	20	41	48	41	48	12	7	12	23	21
ITALY	101	126	136	123	152	34	65	93	74	70	24	25	24	26	18
UK	73	65	60	68	113	17	27	28	22	28	2	5	7	11	11
TOTAL EU	1760	1536	1623	1946	1552	423	680	737	454	533	211	189	166	202	215

[1] The formal steps in infringement proceedings are: letter of formal notice, reasoned opinion, and referral to the ECJ.
Source: European Commission (2008: 9).

regions—while most decisions related to the regional distribution of EU funding are taken in the intergovernmental Conference of Agricultural Policy. Even though the domestic institutional framework has considerably strengthened the role of the regions, these have not been able to establish their own agricultural policies beyond promoting Community programmes of rural development under the LEADER initiative and the rural development programme (PRODER). According to recent assessments, the lack of specific agricultural policies tailored to the individual regions has had a negative impact on the sector (Ramon 2007). At the same time, devolution in this field has favoured the emergence of policy communities in connection with the CAP through which the regional governments seek to enhance the agricultural interests of their own territories at the EU level without effective horizontal (interregional) and vertical (central-regional) coordination (Ramon 2007).

Cohesion Policy

Regarding cohesion policy, Spain's membership has had a significant impact on regional development, a policy almost irrelevant in 1986 (Morata and Popartan 2008). According to some estimates (Sosvilla and Herce 2004), in some regions Community funding generated approximately 4–6 per cent of the regional GDP during the 1989–2004 period. Since the introduction of cohesion policy regulations in 1988, the ACs have played a greater role in regional development policy (Morata and Popartan 2008). They participate in programming functions on both bilateral and multilateral bases, under the coordination of the relevant central ministries, and are also involved in multilevel monitoring tasks. During the first cohesion policy round (1989–1993), the internal distribution of funds among the various levels was a permanent matter of contention on account of the refusal of the Spanish Ministry of Economy and Finance to regionalize the central state's funds and those allocated to local government. The central state took advantage of its institutional prerogatives to allocate funds according to its own criteria, curtailing regional autonomy (Morata and Muñoz 1996). Nevertheless, after 1996, and especially during the 2000–2006 round, the central government progressively adapted to European requirements. Partnership with the regions has been improved, along with the creation of a single Community Supporting Framework (CSF), and almost fully regionalized. In the 2007–2013 round of cohesion policy, the ACs were confronted with the challenge of using their expertise to achieve a more efficient use of increasingly limited resources.

Environmental Policy

Environmental policy is a highly sensitive policy area in the Spanish context. In many instances, economic growth has put strong pressures on the environment. In 1986, Spain lacked any consistent environmental policy. Therefore, the development of this policy field is closely linked to its European membership in terms of regulation, financial and cognitive resources, and pressure from the European Commission (Fernández *et al.* 2010). At the same time, Spain has often complained about the low salience of Mediterranean environmental specificities on the EU agenda. Regarding the policy process, the central government is entrusted with negotiating at the EU level in collaboration with the regions, and also with transposing EU directives and establishing general standards and programmes to be implemented at the regional level (Font and Morata 1998). However, the ACs may also anticipate the transposition of EU legislation when the central government is not complying with its obligations. The complex multilevel character of environmental policy has required the establishment of coordination mechanisms for promoting intergovernmental cooperation. Through the sectoral conference on the environment, central and regional representatives meet on a regular basis to exchange information and agree on common issues, including the formulation of common positions at the EU level.

The lack of effective integration of environmental considerations into other policies—especially cohesion policy—has given rise to a network of environmental authorities made up of the European Commission, central, regional, and local representatives.[8] At the same time, environmental governance promoted by the EU has facilitated the involvement of non-governmental actors in policymaking, especially at the local and the regional level. However, EU requirements are not always fulfilled in a country characterized until recently by rapid economic development. In most of coastal, mountain, and urban areas environmental preservation has not been a priority among regional and local authorities, giving rise to scandals of political corruption. Consequently, over the years, the European Commission has taken legal actions against Spain. These include non-compliance with directives on air quality, uncontrolled and illegal waste landfills, environmental impact assessment, protected areas and habitats, the protection of wild birds, and the Water Framework Directive.

Energy Policy

Spain provides an interesting example of institutional 'fitness' between the EU and the domestic renewable energies policy (Solorio 2009). When the 2001/77/EC directive on renewable energies was adopted, Spain already had developed technical-administrative capacities in this area and its implementation did not entail institutional adaptation costs. European funding provided additional resources to accelerate the development of innovative solar and wind-power technologies to supply the energy market up to 12.3 per cent of total consumption (2010), in line with the overall EU target. As a result, Spanish companies are also becoming world leaders in this emerging field.

Telecommunications

As for the impact of the internal market on telecommunications in Spain, the establishment of a European regime after 1993 coincided with the gradual liberalization of the sector in Spain. This dynamic led to the creation, in 1997, of an independent regulator: the Telecom Market Authority. It was a decisive step towards the process of liberalization sponsored by the European Commission. However, the central government maintained control and regulatory powers to protect 'national interests' on the basis of a national champion—Telefonica—which would later become one of the biggest global players (Jordana and Sancho 2007). Rather than determining the configuration of telecommunications in Spain, the European regulatory structure was perceived as a window of opportunity to modernize the sector. Therefore, Europeanization as a key driver of the liberalization of telecommunications in Spain is questionable. In fact, liberalization was part of a global process in most of the world during the nineties. While the EU prompted a common regulatory alignment across the member states, national governments carried out telecommunications policies based on national interests (Jordana and Sancho 2007).

The Lisbon Strategy

Spain was among the *pace setters* of the Lisbon Strategy. As a model of support for structural reforms and liberalization of the economy, it fitted well with the economic policies advocated by the PP government. Spain aligned with the UK, the Nordic countries, and the Netherlands on the idea of 'exporting' to other member states the reforms carried out at the domestic level. The strategy also pursued the type of European (intergovernmental) governance—the Open Method of Coordination (OMC)—supported by Aznar (Yañiz and De Lecea 2007). However, the domestic outcomes were rather disappointing. It is worth recalling that the characteristics of Spanish economic growth during the 2000s, with high profits in the construction sector, reduced the attractiveness for investment in other sectors. In the first phase of the strategy, the decisions taken at the European Council often were not translated into policy reforms at the national level and, since 2005, the Spanish government, like most European partners, was reluctant to implement those aspects of the strategy that could have entailed electoral costs. The 'spirit of Lisbon' therefore did not permeate the economic and social actors to whom it was intended (Yañiz and De Lecea 2007).

Justice and Home Affairs

Cooperation in JHA is another sensitive policy area for a country confronted with endogenous and exogenous terrorism and illegal immigration. The traditional Spanish proactive approach at the EU level is rooted in the willingness to achieve a common policy framework to strengthen domestic action in these fields. Regarding immigration policy management, initially Spain 'imported' ideas from France, the UK, and Germany. After 2000, with the massive arrival of immigrants, it transferred its own challenges and, increasingly, its policy approach to Europe, often clashing with German positions on illegal immigration. On the other hand, since its entry into the EU Spain was able to transfer its own experience in combating terrorism.

Beyond effective accomplishments in these areas, the EU has become also a support-ing argument for the various Spanish governments in the political debate to legiti-mize domestic policies (Delgado 2007).

Common Foreign and Security Policy

The EU has had a crucial influence on Spanish foreign policy. As a first impact, ac-cession brought about a rapid process of modernization and socialization of Span-ish diplomacy (Barbé 2007). Since the beginning, Felipe Gonzalez strongly supported CFSP as the best means to enhance European and international influ-ence. In Maastricht, Spain backed the proposals championed by Kohl and Mitter-rand, although it opted for the intergovernmental method against the Community one. In terms of preferences, during the 1990s, the Spanish government strongly encouraged the European partners' interests towards the Mediterranean area (Gillespie, 1999). The main policy outcomes were the Barcelona Process (1995) and the MEDA programme offering support for economic reform in Mediterranean non-member states of the EU. Unlike the policy on the Mediterranean, that on Latin America reflects a divergence between domestic preferences and those of most of Spain's European partners for which this region does not have a comparable economic and strategic relevance. The invasion of Iraq was the dramatic breaking point of domestic consensus on European foreign policy. While Gonzalez sought to maximize the international role of Spain through the EU, as we have seen, Aznar opted to align with the Bush administration in search of a global role for Spain (Barbé 2007). The Spanish pro-European stance on CFSP was restored by Zapate-ro's government in 2004.

A Comparative Appraisal

Comparing Spain with other member states is not an easy task. In terms of surface area, it ranks as the second largest member state after France with the fifth largest population (45.5 million). Along with Poland, it occupies an intermediate position between the four larger and the medium-small member states. As previously dis-cussed, in terms of wealth, its GDP per capita is roughly equivalent to the EU-15 average, close to the Italian level. In institutional terms, Spain is a parliamentary democracy and a highly decentralized state divided into seventeen ACs, three of which contain national minorities (Basques, Catalans, and Galicians). The constitu-tional need to cope with cultural and linguistic diversity makes Spain a particular case in the European context, comparable only to Belgium and, to a lesser extent, Italy. Given its historical characteristics and geographical location, it seems more appealing to compare the European course of the two Iberian countries that simul-taneously joined the EU.

Spain and Portugal have recent histories of dictatorship. From 1926 until 1974, Portugal was ruled by an authoritarian regime, while Spain was under Franco's dictatorship from 1939 to 1975. Portugal has a smaller population of ten million. Both economies largely rely on tourism and agriculture, although Spain has a more sophisticated economic structure based on telecommunications, transport, energy, banking, and other services. Spain is also the third largest investor and the main trade partner of Portugal. Both countries suffered greatly during the global economic downturn that began in 2008.

Since joining the EU, the two countries have always fully participated in key EU projects. Both Spain and Portugal were founder members of the euro in 1998. The former played a key supporting role in reviving the EU Constitutional project, while the latter carried forward the resultant Treaty of Lisbon when it took over the EU Presidency in June 2007.

Yet, these countries' membership was not without initial controversy. Until Spain and Portugal joined the EC—except for southern Italy and Ireland—it had been largely a club of prosperous, northern European industrialized countries. The new members represented Mediterranean Europe and had much poorer, more agricultural economies. Their membership meant that the EC had to alter the way it saw itself. Since joining the EU in 1986, both Iberian countries have benefited from a variety of EU programmes intended to improve agriculture, infrastructure, and help economies converge. Spanish and Portuguese membership also led to a substantial alteration of the Common Fisheries Policy (CFP) to accommodate their large fishing fleets.

Yet the results have been vastly different. While Spain has developed an efficient infrastructure network, Portugal has failed to connect its highway systems to those in Spain, leaving it isolated from the main currents of European trade. Unlike Spain, Portugal remains a highly centralized country that only recognizes the autonomy of its two Atlantic archipelagos (Azores and Madeira). This has entailed territorial tensions between the less developed northern area and the central government regarding the allocation and management of European funds. As in Spain, some European environmental directives have proved difficult to implement in Portugal (e.g. in the fields of water quality, nature conservation, and environmental impact assessment (EIA)) (OECD 2001).

In addition to having provided both countries with additional funding for economic and social development and a common policymaking framework, European membership has significantly boosted cross-border cooperation through the INTERREG initiative and, more recently, the Territorial Cooperation objective. If we consider Portugal's traditional suspicion of Spain, and the relative indifference of the latter vis-à-vis Portugal, this cross-border collaboration must be seen as a crucial improvement in the process of rapprochement between both countries.

Finally, regarding budget discipline, Portugal has been reprimanded twice by the European Commission for excessive deficits, while Spain has been a model member. In 2008, with the collapse of the global economy came the collapse of Spain's housing bubble and of Portugal's economic growth. Both were struggling under strong pressure from the EU to get out of the recession and had cut public expenditure considerably.

Conclusions

Spain's entry into the EC raised great expectations in a country eager to join the European project after long decades of dictatorship. Popular support was virtually unanimous and still remains above the EU average despite ups and downs. No doubt, the initial condition of being a lesser-developed country in the EU context boosted the expectations of the political elite and the general public, for which Europe was mainly perceived as a source of benefits and modernization.

From 1986 to 1996, successive socialist governments played the European card generally aligning with Franco-German positions on institutional and economic reforms while adopting a proactive stance on issues such as subsidiarity, European citizenship, and relations with Latin America and the Mediterranean. Moreover, Spain took the leadership of the least developed countries seeking additional funding to close the gap with the large member states and to reach the EMU targets. The conservative PP government (1996–2004) shifted to a more nationalist approach coupled with confrontational positions on highly sensitive issues (CT, Iraq). At the EU level, priority was given to market liberalization and fighting against terrorism. After the 2004 elections, Spain joined back the core of pro-integration member states. However, in 2010, the financial crisis revealed the extreme fragility of its main economic drivers. The socialist government had to bow to EU (German) pressures in terms of hard expenditure cuts along with financial institutions and labour market reforms to avoid endangering the stability of the euro-zone. As a result, domestic economic policy was 'Europeanized' and Spain had to regain credibility among its partners.

Regarding institutional impacts and governance, the same organizational pattern to cope with EU affairs has prevailed since 1986 with some incremental changes. Membership of the EU has also brought about the restructuring—and sometimes, the creation—of domestic structures and procedures to adapt to policy changes at the European level or to face implementation failures. The most affected ministries include Environment, Agriculture, Infrastructures, Industry, and Economy and Finance.

EU membership deeply affected the internal distribution of functions, both horizontally and vertically. Although the Spanish parliament has improved its monitoring functions over the executive's European policy, its role remains symbolic. However, the need to mitigate the impact of EU membership on the domestic balance of powers has caused major political disputes between the central state and the regions. Because of the lack of political consensus on the issue, regional participation in EU decision making through the central state only resulted from the veto power of national minorities' parties in the Spanish parliament.

The need for adaptation in terms of ideas, values, and instruments has also affected most policy areas. This is particularly true for agriculture, cohesion policy, and the environment—in which the regions play a central role too. Before 1986, some of these policies did not exist (environment, cohesion) while others were scarcely developed or far away from Community requirements. In some cases, Europeanization has provided additional arguments to carry out ongoing reforms at the domestic level (i.e. telecommunications, labour market). However, the most significant policy change arose, in July 2012, from the obligation to carry out drastic spending cuts and tax increases in the face of an ultimatum by the EU to get a bailout for Spanish banks. It should be also noted that promoting Europeanization via the Lisbon Agenda did not necessarily entail effective policy implementation. JHA is a good example of policy transfer from the EU to the domestic level (immigration) and vice versa (fighting terrorism), whilst CFSP shows the difficulty of matching national interests (Latin America) with the European ones.

FURTHER READING

The following studies offer different perspectives on Spain's relationship with the EU: T. Börzel (2002), *States and Regions in the European Union. Institutional Adaptation in Germany and Spain* (Cambridge: Cambridge University Press); C. Closa and P. Heywood (2004), *Spain and the European Union* (Basingstoke: Palgrave Macmillan); J. Díez Medrano (2003), *Framing Europe: Empire, WWII and Attitudes toward European Integration in Germany, Spain, and the United Kingdom* (Princeton: Princeton University Press); R. Gillespie, (1999), *Spain and the Mediterranean. Developing a European Policy towards the South* (London: Macmillan); C. Rodríguez-Aguilera de Prat (2009), *Political Parties and European Integration* (Brussels: Peter Lang). For a Spanish-language study, see F. Morata and F. Mateo (eds.), *España en Europa. Europa en España* (Barcelona: CIDOB).

WEB LINKS

Research institutes and think tanks that publish reports and working papers in English: European Council on Foreign Relations (Madrid Office) (**http://ecfr.eu/content/entry/madrid**).

FRIDE (European Think Tank for Global Action) (**http://www.fride.org/**)

Fundación Alternativas (**http://www.falternativas.org/**)

Institut Barcelona d'Estudis Internacionals (IBEI) (**http://www.ibei.org/**)

Institut Universitari d'Estudis Europeus (IUEE)
(**http://www.iuee.eu/**)

Real Instituto El Cano
(**http://www.realinstitutoelcano.org/wps/portal**)

 REFERENCES

Alvarez Miranda, B. (1996), *El sur de Europa y la adhesión a la Comunidad: los Debates Políticos*, Madrid: CIS.

Barbé, E. (2007), 'España en la Política Exterior y de Seguridad Común (PESC)', in F. Morata and G. Mateo (eds), *España en Europa. Europa en España*, Barcelona: CIDOB, 373–98.

Benz, A. (2006), 'Policy-making and Accountability in EU Multilevel Governance', in Benz, A. and Papadopoulos, Y. (eds), *Governance and Democracy: Comparing National, European and International Experiences*, Abingdon: Routledge, 99–114.

Börzel, T. (2002), *States and Regions in the European Union. Institutional Adaptation in Germany and Spain*, Cambridge: Cambridge University Press.

Bursens, P. (2008), 'State Structures', in P. Graziano and M. P. Vink (eds), *Europeanization. New Research Agendas*, Basingstoke: Palgrave Macmillan, 115–27.

Closa, C. (2001), 'Las Raíces Domésticas de la Política Europea de España y la Presidencia de 2002', *Etudes et Recherches*, 16, Paris: Fondation Notre Europe.

Closa, C. and Heywood, P. M. (2004), *Spain and the European Union*, Basingstoke: Palgrave Macmillan.

Delgado, L. (2007), 'España y la Política de Justicia e Interior', in F. Morata and G. Mateo (eds), *España en Europa. Europa en España*, Barcelona: CIDOB, 291–318.

Díez Medrano, J. (2003), *Framing Europe: Empire, WWII and Attitudes toward European Integration in Germany, Spain, and the United Kingdom*, Princeton: Princeton University Press.

Díez Medrano, J. (2007), 'La Opinión Pública Española y la Integración Europea', in F. Morata and G. Mateo (eds), *España en Europa. Europa en España*, Barcelona: CIDOB, 205–36.

European Commission (2008), 'Commission Staff Working Document accompanying the 25th Annual Report from the Commission on Monitoring the Application of Community Law (2007)', *Statistical Annex*. Annexes I to III COM(2008) 777. SEC(2008) 2854.

Fernández, A. M, Font, N., and Koutalakis, C. (2010), 'Environmental Governance in Southern Europe: The Domestic Filters of Europeanisation', *Environmental Politics*, 19/4: 557–77.

Font, N. and Morata, F. (1998), 'Spain: Environmental Policy and Public Administration. A Marriage of Convenience Officiated by the EU?', in K. Hanf and A. I. Jansen (eds), *Governance and Environment in Western Europe*, Harlow: Addison Longman, 208—29.

Gillespie, R. (1999), *Spain and the Mediterranean. Developing a European Policy towards the South*, London: Macmillan.

Hanf, K. and Morata, F. (2010), 'Spanish Autonomous Communities and Multi-Level Strategic Planning of Sustainable Development', Paper presented at the Workshop on Comparative Sub-national Sustainable Development Politics, Flemish Policy Research Centre for Sustainable Development, 23 June, Leuven.

Hanf, K. and Soetendorp, B. (eds), *Adapting to European Integration: Small States and the European Union*, Harlow: Longman.

Jordana, J. and Sancho, D. (2007), 'España y la Política de Telecomunicaciones', in F. Morata and G. Mateo (eds), *España en Europa. Europa en España*, Barcelona: CIDOB, 237–66.

López-Novo, J. and Morata, F. (2000), 'The Implementation of IEAs in Spain: From National Energy Considerations to EU Environmental Constraints', in K. Hanf and A. Underdal (eds), *International Environmental Agreements and Domestic Politics: The Case of Acid Rain*, Aldershot, Hants: Ashgate, 183–206.

Marcet, J. (2006), 'Un 'Oui' Clair et Fort Majoritaire', in J. Marcet (ed.), *La Constitution Européenne à Référendum. Espagne et France*, Barcelona: ICPS, 24–42.

Morata, F. (1998), 'Spain: Modernization Through Integration', in K. Hanf and B. Soetendorp (eds), *Adapting to European Integration: Small States and the European Union*, Harlow: Longman, 116–26.

Morata, F. (2006), 'European Integration and the Spanish "State of the Autonomies",' *ZSE Journal for Comparative Government and European Policy*, Vol. 4/4: 507–28.

Morata, F. (2007), 'La Europeización del Estado Autonómico', in F. Morata and G. Mateo (eds), *España en Europa. Europa en España*, Barcelona: CIDOB, 149–78.

Morata, F. and Fernández, A. M. (2003), 'The Spanish Presidencies of 1989, 1995 and 2001: From Commitment to Reluctance Towards European Integration', in O. Elgstrom (ed.), *European Union Council Presidencies. A Comparative Perspective*, London-New York: Routledge, 173–90.

Morata, F. and Mateo, G. (eds) (2007), *España en Europa. Europa en España*, Barcelona: CIDOB.

Morata, F. and Muñoz, X. (1996), 'Vying for European Funds', in L. Hooghe (ed.), *Cohesion Policy and European Integration. Building Multi-level Governance*, Oxford: Oxford University Press, 195–218.

Morata, F. and Popartan, L. A. (2008), 'Spain', in M. Baun and D. Marek (eds), *EU Cohesion Policy after Enlargement*, Houndmills: Palgrave Macmillan, 73–95.

OECD (2001), *OECD Environmental Performance Review of Portugal*, Paris: OECD.

Powell, C. (2002), 'Spanish Membership of the European Union Revisited', *Working paper 2002/2*, Madrid: Real Instituto Elcano.

Powell, C. (2007), 'La larga marcha hacia Europa', in F. Morata and G. Mateo (eds), *España en Europa. Europa en España*, Barcelona: CIDOB, 41–67.

Ramon, R. (2007), 'España y la Política Agrícola Común', in F. Morata and G. Mateo (eds), *España en Europa. Europa en España*, Barcelona: CIDOB, 237–66.

Rodríguez-Aguilera, C. (2007), 'Elecciones Europeas y Partidos en España', in F. Morata and G. Mateo (eds), *España en Europa. Europa en España*, Barcelona: CIDOB, 179–204.

Rodríguez-Aguilera, C. and Morata, F. (2008), 'Europa en la Refriega Politica Española', in H. J. Trenz, A. J Menéndez, and F. Losada (eds), *¿Y por fin Somos Europeos? La Comunicación Política en el Debate Constituyente Europeo*, Madrid: Dykinson.

Rodríguez-Aguilera de Prat, C. (2009), *Political Parties and European Integration*, Brussels: Peter Lang.

Royo, S. (2010), 'Portugal and Spain: Paths of Economic Divergence (2000-2007)', *Análise Social*, vol. XLV (195): 209–54.

Ruiz Jiménez, A. M. and Egea de Haro, A. (2011), 'Spain: Euroscepticism in a pro-European Country?', *South European Society and Politics*, 16/1: 105–31.

Solorio, I. (2009), 'Framing the Europeanization Footprint: A Follow-up of the EU Renewable Electricity Directive and its Impacts in Spain', *EUGov Working-Paper* 25, Bellaterra: IUEE.

Sosvilla, S. and Herce, J. (2004), 'La Política de Cohesión Europea y la Economía Española: Evaluación y Prospectiva', *Documento de Trabajo* 142/2004, Madrid: Real Instituto El Cano.

Szmolka (2008), 'El Apoyo de los Españoles al Proceso de Integración Europea: Factores Afectivos, Utilitaristas y Políticos', *Revista Española de Investigaciones Sociológicas REIS*, 122: 55–88.

Torreblanca, I. (2005), 'El Referéndum Sobre la Constitución Europea en España: Una doble Decepción', *ARI*, 27, Madrid: Real Instituto El Cano.

Yañiz Igal, J. and De Lecea, A. (2007), 'España y la Agenda de Lisboa', in F. Morata and G. Mateo (eds), *Europa en España. España en Europa*, Barcelona: CIDOB, 349–72.

ENDNOTES

1. According to Royo (2010), between 2000–2007, some five million immigrants settled in Spain (8.7 per cent of the population compared with 3.7 per cent in the EU-15). However, the migration trend has reversed with the economic crisis since 2011.

2. In 1989, Gonzalez was almost the only European leader who strongly supported German re-unification.

3. In July 2012, the new conservative prime minister, Mariano Rajoy, introduced a drastic package of austerity measures as a condition to receive EU emergency assistance aimed at counteracting the Spanish banking debt crisis.

4. These are: Employment, Social Policy, Health and Consumers; Agriculture and Fisheries; Environment; and Education, Youth and Culture. Although the Basque Country and Catalonia, according to their competences, could participate in more Council formations, the idea behind the agreement was that regional participation should only include matters affecting all the autonomous communities. However, an agreement of 2010 between the socialist government and the Basque PNV foresees the participation of the Basque minister of Economy and Finance in the ECOFIN meetings when regional competencies are at stake.

5. The same information is communicated at the domestic level through the CARCE's secretariat.

6. Social Affairs; Labour Affairs; Health System; Consumers; Agriculture and Rural Development; Fisheries; Environment; Education; Culture. These nine SCs are supported by fourteen different working groups.

7. Alphabetical order or special regional interests (Agriculture); random decision (Public Health and Consumers); special interests (Fisheries); rotation (Environment); economically active population (Employment and Social Affairs); population combined with political criteria (Education, Youth and Culture).

8. For details see: **http://www.mma.es/secciones/info_estadistica_ambiental/estadisticas_info/memorias/2006/pdf/mem06_5_3_redautoridadesambientales.pdf**.

CHAPTER 7

Sweden: From Scepticism to Pragmatic Support

Anna Michalski

▌ Summary

Sweden became a member of the EU on 1 January 1995 after a long period of hesitation. At the time, EU membership was surrounded by quite significant misgivings about the implications of political integration on national sovereignty and democracy. Membership was also deemed problematic for Sweden's long tradition of neutrality in armed conflicts and its extensive welfare state. After fifteen years of membership, reticence has given way to a more positive stance, best characterized as pragmatic support. This chapter offers an account of the adaptations that have occurred in Sweden's political and administrative system, its public policies, and the evolving attitudes among the public and political parties.

Introduction

Since the early 1960s, the Swedish political elite has mulled over the imperative of access to European markets and the constraints of EU membership. The creation of a free trade zone in Western Europe led by Great Britain secured at least temporary access to Sweden's most vital markets. Sweden therefore became a founding member of the European Free Trade Association (EFTA) in 1960. In the wake of the accession of Denmark, Ireland, and the UK to the EEC, Sweden signed a bilateral free trade agreement to ensure access to the enlarged Common Market. As European integration picked up speed in the second half of the 1980s, the prospect of being excluded from the internal market prompted Sweden, together with the other EFTA countries, to seek a comprehensive association agreement with the EU, the European Economic Area (EEA), signed in 1992. In parallel to the EEA negotiations, momentous changes were taking place in Europe with the reunification of Germany and the dissolution of the Soviet Union, which changed the underlying constraints of Sweden's traditional neutrality. Moreover, the prospect of enlargement of the EU to a number of countries in Central and Eastern Europe not only made membership appear more urgent but also renewed the significance of European integration. Furthermore, Sweden was not entirely satisfied with the provisions of the EEA as the agreement was based on the EFTA countries' compliance to the evolving body of law of the EU without right of meaningful participation in the decision-making process. Nonetheless, the announcement by a Social Democratic government in 1990 of Sweden's intention to seek membership of the EU came as a surprise. Although the membership application was supported by a majority of the political parties in parliament, the volte-face of the Social Democrats appeared hasty and had not been preceded by debate on either the political or the public level. The decision was presented more as an after-thought to a long list of measures to handle the deep economic crisis that besieged the country rather than a carefully thought through decision heralding a new political orientation. Ambivalence, therefore, was quite strong when Sweden acceded to the EU in 1995 and this significantly impacted on the country's pattern of adaptation in the first decade of membership. Since 2005, however, a number of indications show that the initial reluctance has given way to pragmatism and attitudes towards the EU among the elite and the public are no longer polarized according to a 'for-or-against' logic but considered on a case-by-case basis.

In this chapter, I investigate the reasons behind Sweden's initial reticence towards the EU and the internal and external conditions that paved the way for a change. I lay out the country's position to various aspects of European integration and the pattern of interaction with the EU. I deal in detail with the impact of membership on Swedish public opinion, political parties, public governance, and local and regional administration as well as on Swedish public policy. The aim of the chapter is to shed light on the role played by Europeanization in changing Sweden's stance on membership from reluctance to pragmatic support. Europeanization of Sweden's political and administrative system and public policy is a two-way process that has resulted in intentional reforms of policies and structures as well as unanticipated adaptations and underlying trends of convergence. Sweden constitutes an interesting case for scholars of Europeanization since it illustrates the effects of EU membership on an initially sceptical country which for a long time held on to a perception of 'misfit' between its domestic policy regimes and those of the EU. Today, Sweden still remains sceptical of certain EU policies and institutional practices but on the whole takes a more positive attitude actively trying to influence the direction of the EU's policy orientation and prevailing norms on the European level.

Patterns of Sweden's Membership of the EU

In the first decade of membership, Sweden was often described as a reluctant, foot-dragging, sceptic which firmly believed in its own exceptionalism (Dinkelspiel 2009; Andersen 2001). The ambivalence rested on a perception of the EU as a threat to national sovereignty and identity combined by a widespread fear of the country losing its 'Swedishness'. These deep-seated fears were particularly prevalent in three dimensions: foreign and security policy; democratic norms and principles; and the welfare state and the ability to pursue an independent economic policy. In these three dimensions, Sweden's policy norms and orientation were seen as more advanced than in the EU and therefore membership constituted a 'misfit'.

Traditionally, Sweden conducts a normative foreign policy with a strong internationalist inclination. During the Cold War, Sweden stood out as a normative international actor often punching above its weight advocating universal human rights and multilateralism against super-power confrontation and the nuclear arms race. It strongly supported the UN system, spoke in defence of developing countries in Africa and Asia, and donated generously to the third world. A key feature of Sweden's stance in international politics is its long-standing policy of neutrality in armed conflicts, which for many decades was seen as incompatible with the obligations of EU membership with its implicit links to NATO. The end of the Cold War led to a less tense geopolitical situation in Europe and cancelled the obligation of neutrality between two ideological blocs. However, the steps taken by EU leaders to strengthen the Common Foreign and Security Policy (CFSP) in the negotiations on the Maastricht Treaty, signed in 1992, were initially problematic for the Swedish political elite as it gave ammunition to those who argued that EU membership remained incompatible with the policy of neutrality. Despite quite vocal domestic misgivings, the Swedish government signed up to the aims and principles of the CFSP with the motivation that the policy area was intergovernmental in nature and the decision on creating a common defence policy was postponed to the future when Sweden, as a member, would have a say. In the end, therefore, neutrality did not get in the way of Sweden's accession to the EU. Fifteen years after accession, Sweden is actively involved in EU foreign policy and the EU has provided an arena in which Swedish interests are actively pursued. Sweden has influenced the CFSP to adopt a more forceful policy on the prevention and resolution of conflicts and on the civilian aspects of post-conflict management. Sweden is one of the strongest supporters of strengthening the EU's policy of democracy promotion and human rights in the context of enlargement and relations with third countries and has recently aligned its national development aid policy with the goals of the European development agenda. It strongly supports EU enlargement as a means to extend peace, stability, democracy, and economic prosperity to the EU's neighbourhood and therefore promotes the accession of the countries in the Balkans and Turkey. Sweden has adopted a foreign policy stance that is less based on exceptionalism and more concerned with fulfilling international obligations, be they to the EU, UN, or NATO. The normative dimension of Sweden's foreign policy has remained a key characteristic, which today is couched in terms of a European community based on shared values. The EU has also become a platform from which Sweden may advance normative standpoints as well as gain leverage on the international level.

Among the strongest arguments against membership of the EU was the threat to Swedish sovereignty and democracy founded on consensual politics and closeness between the political elite and the electorate. The EU with its elitist political culture, opaque bureaucracy, and complex decision making was seen as a threat to Swedish democratic principles and traditions. Such misgivings were at the heart of the reticent attitude of Swedish governments to revisions of EU treaties. Since accession, Sweden has participated in three intergovernmental conferences where its involvement has ranged from sceptical on issues of a constitutional/institutional character to supportive of proposals to enhance the EU's decision-making capacity in areas of Swedish interest, such as the environment or employment. In the domestic arena, successive governments have invariably downplayed the implications of treaty reform in order to avoid a polarization of the public debate, and there is a strong preference to ratify new treaties through a parliamentary vote rather than by referendum as witnessed in the ratification of the Lisbon Treaty in 2009.

Successive governments have championed the principle of open government and the public's ability to hold national government and EU institutions accountable. Since accession, Sweden has consciously pursued a policy of improving openness and transparency of EU institutions and giving the public a statutory right of access to EU documents. The regulation (1049/2001) on public access to documents of the EP, the Council, and the Commission has been portrayed as a successful outcome of Swedish efforts to improve open government on the European level. As part of its quest to influence the prevailing norms of the EU, the government has pursued the issue of gender equality on the European level, partly as a response to the hostility of a large proportion of Swedish women who feared that EU membership would erode Sweden's gender equality policy. Hence, the Social Democratic government supported the inclusion of gender equality as a fundamental principle of the EU in the Amsterdam Treaty of 1997 (Anderson 2001). Swedish governments also have a long-standing commitment to increase the number of women appointed to political posts in the EU institutions and hitherto all Swedish commissioners have been women. When holding the rotating presidency of the EU in the autumn of 2009, the government actively promoted the appointment of a woman to one of the four vacant top jobs in the EU institutions.

Access to the internal market was the main motivation for the Swedish elite to seek closer ties with the EU. However, as long as membership of the EU has been contemplated, there have been concerns over the possible impact of European integration on Sweden's extensive welfare state and its ability to pursue an independent economic policy. Such fears might appear somewhat paradoxical as Sweden has, ever since the deep recession in the 1990s, pursued a prudent economic policy governed within the rules of the Stability and Growth Pact (SGP). Rather than a rebuttal of the economic rationale of the SGP, Swedish reticence towards adopting the euro derives from a fear of losing control over the ability to regulate the public economy and scepticism towards some euro countries' sincerity in respecting the rules of the SGP. Despite a rejection of the euro in a referendum in 2003 (see Table 7.1), the debate on a possible adoption of the euro has never really died down, although the question is off the political agenda since the onset of the sovereign debt crisis in the euro-zone. As the emphasis of economic policy has shifted to the coordination of economic reform in the framework of the Lisbon Strategy, the Swedish model's successful combination of economic competitiveness and a generous welfare state has gained relevance. With Sweden persistently among the best performing national economies, successive governments have been able to promote national policy solutions as best practices. The Social Democratic government, in power between 1996 and 2006, was particularly keen to promote active employment at the European level by including a European Employment Strategy in the Amsterdam Treaty and championed active labour market policies in the Lisbon Strategy. The Right-wing government in power since 2006 has put more stress on pursuing competitiveness and innovation as factors of job creation on the European level.

The Public and the Party Political System

Public Opinion

Sweden is generally regarded as one of the most Eurosceptic member states of the EU. However, Swedish public opinion has recently undergone a noticeable transformation and in 2005, for the first time since accession, more Swedes were in favour of membership than against. This upward trend has continued despite the economic crisis with over 50 per cent of the population supporting EU membership in 2009. The Swedish population still holds quite critical views on certain aspects of integration, but Sweden's membership is now fully accepted as part of economic, social, and political life with only a declining proportion of the population (20 per cent) still supporting a withdrawal from the EU (Holmberg 2010).

Swedish public opinion has experienced substantial swings since the early 1990s reflecting the evolving relationship between Sweden and the EU (see Figure 7.1). Periods of support are found before membership negotiations started in 1993, in 2002–2003 in the wake of Sweden's presidency in 2001, and recently in a steady upward trend beginning in 2005. Periods of opposition are linked to the deep recession in the first half of the 1990s, whose effects, particularly on employment, lasted well into the following decade. In other words, all through the 1990s and the first half of the 2000s, membership of the EU was not widely supported among the population and the country was not seen as being better off as a member. In this perspective, the outcome of the referendum in 1994, when 52.3 per cent of the population voted in favour of EU membership, appears as a short-lived phenomenon, attributable to an intense and ultimately successful campaign in which membership was depicted as a necessary step to lead the country out of recession. The surveys of the Eurobarometer (1995, 2005, and 2010a) show a pattern of support among the Swedish population of EU membership being 'a good thing' starting at a low level at 39 per cent in 1995, increasing to 44 per cent in 2005 and to 54 per cent in 2010 (above the EU average of 49 per cent). When asked whether Sweden benefits from membership of the EU, only 22 per cent of the respondents answered affirmatively in 1995, in 2005 the proportion had increased somewhat (36 per cent) while in 2010 a majority (52 per cent) believed membership was beneficial.

What are the reasons for increasingly positive public attitudes towards the EU? First, Swedish people have grown accustomed to, and appreciate, the tangible

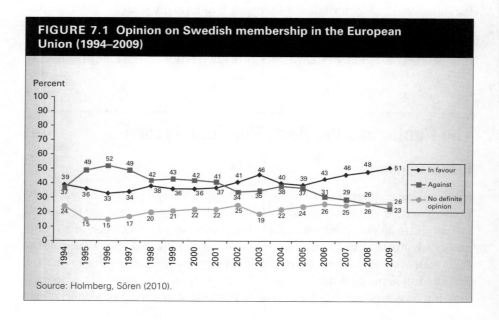

FIGURE 7.1 Opinion on Swedish membership in the European Union (1994–2009)

Source: Holmberg, Sören (2010).

opportunities that membership offers in terms of travelling, studying, or looking for a job (Eurobarometer 2010b). Second, the EU was previously a strongly polarizing issue that pitted different social groups against each other: women against men; the countryside and towns against big cities; the north against the south; people with low education against those with high; the public sector against the private; and blue-collar workers against white-collar workers. Today, social cleavages in the EU persist but have shifted across the board to more favourable attitudes reducing the degree of polarization (Holmberg 2010). Third, the ideological polarization, prevalent in referenda and election campaigns to the EP, has also declined over time while keeping to the same pattern. Ideologically, the strongest opposition to the EU is found among those who vote on parties to the Left and the extreme Right, whereas support is found among the parties to the centre Right and Left. EU membership is definitely de-dramatized among public opinion and Swedes are today prepared to take a much more pragmatic attitude to the EU, supporting or opposing aspects of European integration on a case-by-case basis.

With public opinion in Sweden becoming more favourable to membership, what does the EU mean for Swedish people and what do they expect from it? Many Swedes link the EU to peace in Europe. This normative belief was present in the campaign in the run-up to the referendum of 1994 and is often used by those who advocate further enlargement of the EU. The EU is also linked to concrete outcomes such as travel, study, and work in Europe, but not to social protection which is considered a national competence. Swedes have negative views on the EU's bureaucracy, but are not worried about the impact of membership on cultural identity and do not link it to unemployment (Eurobarometer 2010a). Overall, Swedish public opinion believes to a greater degree than Europeans do that, on average, the EU takes national interests into account (Eurobarometer 2010b). Also the EU's democratic deficit, which has long belonged to the contentious issues in the Swedish debate, seems to have lost in salience as the public appears to be relatively content with how democracy functions—trust in European institutions, albeit on a much lower level than trust in national political institutions, is on a par with the EU average (Eurobarometer 2010b).

Political Parties

The Swedish party political system is characterized by stability and predictability. Since the early nineteenth century, there has been little change among the parties represented in parliament, and the ideological division into a Left-wing and a Right-wing block has remained surprisingly stable. Despite the heated public debate in the run-up to the referendum in 1994, Sweden's accession to the EU did not result in an upheaval of the party political system—contrary to its neighbour, Denmark. Scholars have argued that the ensuing politicization of the EU in a one-dimensional debate should be seen as an attempt to win votes and mobilize the electorate rather than an expression of a profound disagreement over the EU, as a majority of political parties represented in parliament accepted membership after accession (Tallberg *et al.* 2010). The de-politicization of Sweden's membership of the EU is noticeable also in national general elections, as the electorate has ranked the EU furthest down in the list of priorities in the five elections after accession (Tallberg *et al.* 2010; Holmberg and Oscarsson 2008).

The Right-wing of the political spectrum is composed of the Conservatives (*Moderaterna*), the Liberals (*Folkpartiet*), the Agrarians (*Centerpartiet*), and the Christian Democrats (*Kristdemokraterna*). The Conservatives and the Liberals, traditionally the most pro-European political parties in Sweden, have consistently advocated a more active involvement of Sweden in the EU by supporting reforms to the treaties, the adoption of the euro, and closer integration in areas such as Justice and Home Affairs (JHA) and foreign and security policy. The Agrarians and the Christian Democrats were initially divided on the question of membership worrying about the impact on democracy, local and regional self-governance, the effect on the countryside, and small and medium size companies. The Christian Democrats also raised concerns of a normative nature chiefly against the European Security and Defence Policy. Both parties have gradually adopted a more pronounced pro-European profile, a move that has met with the support of their members. These four parties formed an electoral alliance and won the national election in 2006. With the Right-wing coalition, Sweden got, for the first time, a government that publicly declared support for Sweden's membership of the EU and pledged to work actively and constructively to promote national interests in Brussels. In the election of September 2010, the extreme Right-wing Swedish National Party (*Sverigedemokraterna*) was elected to parliament for the first time. It advocates Sweden's withdrawal from the EU chiefly on grounds of national sovereignty and the costs of membership through Sweden's contribution to the EU budget.

The Left wing in Swedish politics is composed of the Social Democrats, the Green Party (*Miljöpartiet*), and the Left Party (*Vänsterpartiet*). The Social Democrats occupy a special place in Swedish politics, being the biggest party in parliament and holding power for seventy-three years in the period since 1920. Ever since EU membership was first on the agenda, the Social Democratic Party has had to manage quite strong internal divisions between those who supported membership and those who were against. Recent Social Democratic prime ministers (Palme, Carlsson, and Persson) held quite positive views on European integration but the threat of an open conflict within the party led the leadership to adopt a wait-and-see attitude, isolate the EU from domestic politics and, at crucial moments, insist on referendums to decide on EU membership and the euro. The internal division of the party goes deep and cuts right across the voters, party fractions, and top leadership. Recently, Social Democratic voters have become more favourable to EU membership but the party still has to balance a desire to see the EU adopting stronger social policy with a strong resistance against interference of Brussels on Swedish labour market traditions. For the same reason, the trade union movement's relationship to the EU is ambivalent and, despite being one of the strongest in Europe, the Trade Union Congress has remained somewhat reluctant to get too closely involved in European policymaking. Further to the Left, the Green Party used to advocate Sweden's withdrawal from the EU, a policy that the party abandoned in a radical political shift in 2008. The shift was motivated by the necessity to work on the European level for a more ambitious environmental policy and a forceful stance on the international scene in the fight against climate change. The Left Party's hostility to the EU is predominantly ideological in nature ranging from hostility to market integration to aversion to co-operation in foreign, security, and defence policies. It sees the EU as an organization of capitalist countries with strong links to NATO and the US and a threat to Sweden's traditional welfare state model, internationalist development policy, and neutrality. The Left Party advocates Sweden's withdrawal from the EU.

Sweden's membership of the EU has added a European dimension to the party political system. Nonetheless, fifteen years after accession the impact on the national level remains modest (Tallberg *et al.* 2010). National political parties have been reluctant to go beyond the 'for-or-against' dialectic to include a European dimension to public debate. Voters still make a distinction between politics on the national and sub-national level and the European level, which is clearly demonstrated in elections to the EP where maverick parties and parties of discontent have gained representation, including the Eurosceptic June-list and the Pirate Party, whereas the same parties have been unable to gain enough seats to enter the *Riksdag*. Another important difference between national and European elections is the turnout which in the former attracts well above 80 per cent of the electorate while in the latter barely 40 per cent bother to vote (see Table 7.1). The election to the EP in 2009 recorded a small but significant increase in turnout (7.5 per cent) as 45.5 per cent of the electorate cast their vote. This turnout is still considerably lower than in national elections but represents a break with the declining voter participation in the rest of the EU. Nevertheless, the elections to the EP show all the characteristics of a second order election.

Swedish members of the EP lack a high profile in the Swedish political arena although increasingly their actions are noted in the media, particularly on 'hot' political issues, such as file-sharing or the treatment of ethnic and sexual minorities in the EU. The links between MEPs and their 'mother' party on the national level are not strong, although the national party organizations keep tight control over the selection of candidates to the EP and the drafting of the parties' election manifestos (Blomgren 2009). Recently, Swedish political parties have stepped up their participation in the European political families.

Political Institutions, Public Administration, and Sub-National Actors

Since accession in 1995, there have been a number of changes in Sweden's political system and administration. Today, there is hardly any aspect of the Swedish political system and administration that has not been affected by EU membership.

TABLE 7.1   Referenda and elections to the European Parliament

	In favour	Against	Turnout
Referendum on membership			
1994	52.3	46.8	83.3
Referendum on the euro			
2003	42.0	55.9	82.6
Elections to EP			
-1995			41.6
-1999			38.8
-2004			37.8
-2009			45.5

Source: Statistics Sweden http://www.scb.se/

Governance on the Political Level

According to the Swedish constitution, power rests with parliament (*Riksdag*) as the institution representing the people. However, the government (*Regering*) traditionally holds a strong position of power on account of the functioning of the parliamentary system and the historic dominance of the Social Democratic Party. The prime minister, chosen from the party with the greatest number of votes and/or representing a stable electoral alliance, has extensive powers over the composition and organization of government and the central administration (Persson 2007). Sweden's accession to the EU has not resulted in a weakening of the government's ability to exercise power despite considerable Euro-scepticism in several political parties. In fact, one of the most noted changes in Sweden's political system, directly attributed to EU membership, is the significant strengthening of the executive at the expense of the legislative and in particular the 'presidentialization' of the office of the prime minister whose incumbents have gradually come to enjoy increasing power and prestige (Johansson and Tallberg 2010; Persson 2007). The elevation of the European Council as the supreme decision body of the EU, supported by recurrent summitry, presents arguably the single most important development for the balance of power in the national political system. In Sweden, it has led to changes in the relationship between parliament and the government and a centralization of the coordination of EU affairs, particularly its political dimension.

Relations between parliament and the government

In the decades preceding Sweden's accession to the EU, Right-wing and Left-wing governments took consultation with parliament on relations with the EU seriously. During the accession negotiations, the European Affairs Minister, Ulf

Dinkelspiel, and the Chief Negotiator, Frank Belfrage, held regular consultations with the then EFTA delegation. There were also informal talks between the minister and senior Social Democrats as the support of the latter was indispensable in the up-coming referendum (Dinkelspiel 2009). The form and extent of parliamentary oversight of government was much debated as a prerequisite for upholding Swedish democratic traditions. In the end, however, Sweden did not opt for the Danish system of parliamentary scrutiny with binding mandates as it was seen as too much of a constraint on the government's 'room for manoeuvre' in negotiations in the council (Jungar and Ahlbäck Öberg 2004). Parliament's body for monitoring the executive, the Committee on EU Affairs, is therefore technically an advisory committee that does not give formal mandates to government, although a government chooses to disregard the committee's directives at its peril. Contrary to parliament's standing committees, the EU Affairs Committee has the task to review all proposals on the council's agenda and the government is obliged by the constitution to supply the committee with information on all matters relevant to Sweden's policy on the EU. In addition, the committee can request consultations with members of the government on its own initiative. Given the wide range of matters the committee must consider, its seventeen permanent members and forty-two substitutes also sit on one or more standing committees of parliament. Members of government appear roughly once a week before the committee and the ministerial presence varies according to the subject area. Successive governments have ensured adequate ministerial presence, both on the level of prime minister and specialized ministers.

Despite regular consultations with members of the government, the EU Affairs Committee's monitoring of the actions taken by ministers in Brussels is hampered by structural factors. Among the most serious is the problem of influencing the position of the government as the committee consults with the government at a very late stage in the process when the negotiations are so far advanced in the Council that substantial changes are difficult or the matter has already been settled in COREPER. This applies in particular to CFSP issues, which need to be dealt with in a short time given the nature of the policy area. Another related problem is the division of the dossiers between the EU Affairs Committee and the standing committees, which in principle are responsible for discussing EU dossiers related to their policy area. In reality, debates on individual dossiers are postponed until the stage when the proposal reaches the Council, and are then brought up in the EU Affairs Committee rather than in a standing committee, which objectively is best placed to consider the issue (Larue 2006). Moreover, the *Riksdag*, just as any other national parliament in the EU, suffers from time constraints and information deficits. Because members of parliament have to make a choice as to which issues to invest time in, EU affairs are seldom prioritized over domestic policy. Despite these shortcomings, how strong is the EU Affairs Committee's control over the government? Has the committee been able to influence the government's positions? In 2007, the prime minister's practice to appear in front of the committee ahead of European Council summits was given statutory weight by a revision to the Government Act giving the committee increased formal power to control a prime minister who does not respect the views of the committee. Additional reforms sought to 'mainstream' EU affairs by bringing in specialized committees earlier in the process in order to scrutinize ministers with sector portfolios (Johansson and Tallberg 2010). Nevertheless, the *Riksdag* has been reluctant to bind the hands of Swedish representatives in the Council and the European Council because defending national interests and showing a united national front in negotiations have been seen as more important than the desire to hold individual ministers to account. In autumn 2010, the *Riksdag* showed its willingness to test the 'yellow card' system brought in by the Lisbon Treaty by rejecting a proposal for new legislation on bank deposit guarantees to which the government had already given its support.

Political coordination of EU affairs

At the outset of Sweden's membership of the EU, there was a desire on behalf of the then prime minister, Ingvar Carlsson, to maintain the Prime Minister's Office (PMO) as a small unit of a handful of political advisers and support staff. Carlsson decided to keep the post of minister for European affairs in the foreign ministry, which also came to house and staff the EU Secretariat. Carlsson regarded EU matters as foreign policy (Persson 2007). His successor, Göran Persson, on the other hand, came to power with the view that EU affairs are domestic policy and should be subjected to the same stringent budgetary restrictions as any other public policy. He set about a process of gradual reform of the coordination of EU policy: first, the political control of the PMO was strengthened by the elevation of the prime minister's adviser on foreign policy and European affairs to the rank of state secretary. During the premiership of Persson, 1996–2006, the incumbent, Lars Danielsson, had substantial power over the coordination of Sweden's EU policy from more technical positions in the various councils to political issues such as negotiations on the financial framework and reforms to the EU treaties (Danielsson 2007). The prime minister's role in foreign policy was strengthened through his participation in the European Council meetings, and the PMO's knowledge and competence was reinforced to serve his needs. To this end, an International and EU Affairs Division was set up in 2004 located in the prime minister's secretariat (Johansson 2008) under the political guidance of the state secretary, who subsequently came to act as an informal EU minister. Second, the Ministry of Foreign Affairs saw its involvement in EU affairs reduced through the transfer of the EU Secretariat, which coordinates the day-to-day activities of Sweden's EU policy, to the PMO.

As a result of the centralization of the political coordination of EU policy in the PMO, relations among members of the government also changed. In Sweden, the government is collectively responsible for EU policy which means that extensive consultation and coordination is required before a decision is adopted to which subsequently all cabinet members are bound (Johansson and Tallberg 2010). In view of the increasingly important role played by the European Council in the orientation and prioritization of EU policy, as well as intervening in conflicts between specialized councils, the position of the prime minister has been strengthened vis-à-vis members of the government. The successive reforms of the EU treaties, the on-going enlargement, and negotiations of financial frameworks have further strengthened the prime minister's role in EU affairs leaving other ministers with little influence over matters of high political salience with the exception of the finance minister who keeps a tight hold on the purse strings. The rotating presidency of the EU has had a decisive impact on national EU coordination and the role of the prime minister. The demands of the presidency were deemed to require strong political leadership and spearheaded the centralization of EU coordination to the PMO. For Göran Persson, whose government held the first Swedish EU presidency in 2001, the experience of being at the helm of the EU for six months had a major impact on a personal and political level (Ruin 2002). In the same vein, Fredrik Reinfeldt saw Sweden's presidency of the EU in 2009 as an opportunity to raise his profile as a statesman and increase his popularity at home (Johansson *et al.* 2010).

The Right-wing government which swept to power in 2006 further strengthened the central position of the PMO as the locus of coordination of Sweden's EU policy by reinstating the post of Minister for EU Affairs in the PMO. During the Reinfeldt government, there was a certain overlap in responsibilities between the state secretaries of the prime minister and the EU minister. Moreover, the political coordination on EU affairs became somewhat more cumbersome because of the necessity to coordinate Sweden's positions, including COREPER instructions, with the political state secretaries representing the four coalition partners. However, coordination with the party political state secretaries was necessary for all new policy, not on-going policy dossiers, and therefore did not impact adversely on the smooth policy-making in the PMO during the EU presidency (Johansson *et al.* 2010).

The Civil Service

Sweden is a decentralized unitary state. According to Swedish basic law, all levels and functions of government are organized into a single structure. The civil service, including the public agencies, is subordinate to the government and so are, in principle, the regional and local authorities. However, the basic law also establishes the principle of local self-government whereby municipalities, in particular, enjoy substantial autonomy.

The Swedish public service is characterized by small Government Offices (GO) and large central government agencies that are organizationally and legally independent of the government. To illustrate the difference in size, the GO employed 4,693 people in 2009 while employees in public authorities and agencies numbered 240,000.[1] The Swedish civil service rests on a constitutional principle of dualism which separates politics from public administration, thereby separating the formulation of policy from its implementation. From this principle follows a prohibition of ministerial encroachment in the execution of policy as well as the interpretation of the implementation of different instruments of law. In view of EU membership, the impact on the division of competence between the GO and the public service was much discussed. Today, 15 years after Sweden's entry we detect a number of gradual changes to these principles. The increased centralization of the political dimension of EU coordination to the PMO was discussed above, but a number of potentially equally important changes have taken place on the level of the civil service.

The central administration

The GO (*regeringskansliet*) was brought into one organizational unit in 1997 under the leadership of the prime minister. The objective was to improve the internal coordination between ministries, to 'tear down "firewalls" between units' within the GO as well as realizing efficiency gains and economies of scale by sharing support functions. Just as for the gradual relocation of the coordination of EU policy to the PMO, 'this comprehensive organizational transformation' was justified by the demands of EU membership (Persson 2007: 223). In 2009, the GO comprised the twelve ministries, the PMO, and an administrative division. Each ministry is responsible for EU policy that falls under their policy remit and has dedicated EU coordination offices, which include at least one liaison officer who constitutes the formal link between the ministry and the EU Secretariat of the PMO. To assist these officers in drawing up and preparing draft instructions/positions on specific dossiers, each ministry has a drafting or reference group (Larue 2006).

The ministries have developed quite different organizational practices and structures regarding their work on European affairs, depending on the nature of their policy on the EU level. The Ministry for the Environment and the Ministry for Agriculture are regarded as having a 'heavy' workload because of the extensive activity in the EU. The Ministry of Finance has a special position through its budget department, which monitors and ultimately vets the budgetary impact of EU dossiers that fall under the remit of other ministries. The involvement of the Finance Ministry in EU policymaking related to financial and monetary affairs has increased in recent years and overall the ministry occupies a central position in domestic policymaking. The Ministry of Foreign Affairs, on the other hand, has seen its influence decline since the EU Secretariat was moved to the PMO, but it still retains the formal responsibility over the Permanent Representation in Brussels, and supplies most of the non-political staff to the PMO's European affairs units. Today, the Foreign Ministry's EU Unit coordinates activities of the CFSP.

The EU Secretariat of the PMO sits as the spider in the cobweb of Sweden's EU coordination. It has the overall responsibility for ensuring that Swedish interests are presented as early and effectively as possible in the policy process. To this effect, it coordinates the Swedish positions in COREPER I and II meetings, the General Affairs Council, and assists the prime minister's staff in preparing European Council summits. It liaises with the EU desk officers in specialized ministries and intervenes when disputes occur between ministries, but as a general rule it tries to push issues back down in the organization and lets only genuinely contentious issues be dealt with at higher levels (Larue 2006). Political leadership is not provided by the EU Secretariat, a task that under the Persson governments fell to the state secretary for EU and international affairs. The then incumbent led weekly meetings with EU liaison officers in the ministries, which dealt not only with day-to-day coordination but also discussed general developments in the EU as well as Sweden's position vis-à-vis 'political' processes, such as treaty reform, budget negotiations, and foreign policy. During the Reinfeldt government, political responsibility for coordination of EU affairs was divided between the state secretaries of the prime minister, the EU minister, and the political parties with a special role played by the prime minister's state secretary. The EU Secretariat retained a key coordinating role but it was rather more administrative than in previous governments.

The Permanent Representation in Brussels is a key factor in EU affairs and Sweden's largest overseas diplomatic mission. It handles the incoming documents from the Commission and dispatches them to Stockholm, participates with advice and knowledge in the consultations on up-coming Council negotiations, and sits in Council working group meetings when there is no representative from Stockholm. COREPER II and I meetings are always attended by the ambassador and his deputy. The Permanent Representation is headed by a top diplomat with considerable experience in EU affairs and a string of competent officials has secured a key role for the ambassador in Stockholm as a trusted adviser and source of insider information. The Permanent Representation played a key role during Sweden's two presidencies of the EU in 2001 and 2009, periods during which its personnel and budgetary resources were much enhanced. The Permanent Representation has been criticized for unnecessary compartmentalization between different divisions, explained by the fact that the chargés d'affaires are sent out from their 'home' ministries, are remunerated by them, and often stay in closer contact with their counterparts in the 'home' ministry than with colleagues at the Permanent Representation. Attempts have been made to break the rigid division between the sectoral units as it is seen as inefficient and cumbersome (Larue 2006).

Public authorities and agencies

There are about 200 public authorities and agencies in Sweden. They are responsible for the implementation and execution of policies decided by the government, and have considerable budgetary and personnel resources at their disposal. As the policy remit of the EU has enlarged, the involvement of public authorities and agencies has become increasingly crucial in regard to their duty to implement EU law and identify national legislation that is incompatible with European legislation. This has given them a large responsibility of interpretation as to what constitutes incompatibility in specific cases. Research has shown that, in the area of the internal market, public authorities and agencies are not well prepared for this kind of task as they have insufficient knowledge and understanding of the EU legal system based on case law and have no statutory right to refer an issue to the European Court of Justice (ECJ) for a preliminary ruling (Swedish Agency for Public Management 2007). Public authorities and agencies have become increasingly involved in EU policymaking through their participation in Council working groups, European agencies, preparatory forums in the Commission, and in the committees tied to the comitology system, including those that monitor the Commission's implementation legislation. Since accession, public authorities and agencies are systematically involved in all stages of policymaking, drafting, enacting and implementing EU legislation. Civil servants from public authorities and agencies have multiple points of access to the preparatory work on legislative proposals through their 'own' ministries as well as the EU network and committees. They represent Sweden at different levels in the Council and shape the implementation of specific measures on the ground as 'an extended arm' of European governance. The government has come to rely on the resources, technical knowledge, and expertise of the public authorities and agencies in EU policymaking and, although they in principle are subject to the same scrutiny as officials from the GO when representing Sweden in EU institutions and agencies, the government's ability to monitor their activities is not as effective as in the domestic setting. Public authorities' and agencies' intensified involvement in EU policymaking has altered the principle of separation between politics and implementation, and muddled the question of political responsibility. The wider consequences of this trend have been raised as parliament's constitutional prerogative to scrutinize public action covers the government but not public authorities and agencies. As the line between making and executing policy is blurred, it becomes more difficult to exercise political accountability in EU affairs (Reichel 2008).

Governance on the local and regional level

In Sweden, there are two sub-national levels of government—municipalities (*kommuner*) and regions (*län*)—with quite large internal differences as to their structure and competence. Over the fifteen years of EU membership, there has been a clear trend towards greater self-governance and intensified activity in Brussels and Stockholm to influence policies with sub-national impact. This development is gradual and by no means uniform, as sub-national authorities on both lower and intermediate levels have adopted different approaches to the opportunities offered by multi-level governance.

Sweden has 290 municipalities, which in European comparison are unusually large in geographical terms (Berg and Lindahl 2007). They have important competences and resources at their disposal in the right of imposition and autonomous decision making by directly elected councils (*kommmunfullmäktige*) and executive boards (*kommunstyrelse*). In the last decades, Sweden has experienced quite extensive devolution rendering municipalities responsible for the organization and delivery of most public services, such as education, child care, care for the elderly, social security, local infrastructure, environmental protection, and health and safety. As the scope of EU policies has grown considerably in the last decades, municipalities have become increasingly active in European policymaking to influence the orientation of EU policy (Berg and Lindahl 2007). As an indication, the number of municipalities with specific strategies for EU-related activities has increased from 25 per cent in

1996 to 40 per cent in 2006 (Berg 1999 and Johansson 2006, quoted in Berg and Lindahl 2007: 23). There are, however, big differences among municipalities regarding their ambition, investment, and ability to promote their interests in the EU. The most pronounced differences exist between the three big cities—Stockholm, Gothenburg, and Malmö—and countryside municipalities, as the former have stepped up their activities in recent years while the others are lagging behind. Active municipalities are more likely to express confidence in their ability to get their view across in Stockholm and Brussels, whereas the less ambitious municipalities take a more passive stance believing that lobbying activities are largely futile (Berg and Lindahl 2007). As a result of demands and opportunities of multi-level governance in the EU, many smaller and middle-sized municipalities cooperate regionally and some have set up permanent cooperative bodies (*samverkanorgan*) in order to pool resources and gain a stronger voice vis-à-vis national and European authorities.

Lobbying for regional interests in Stockholm and Brussels involves many actors on local and regional levels (Berg and Lindahl 2007). Sub-national authorities are represented in Brussels by twelve offices that group regions, municipalities, cities (Gothenburg and Malmö have offices of their own), and the Swedish Association for Local Authorities and Regions. These offices are particularly important in gathering information and setting up networks of contact within European institutions, in particular the European Commission's Directorate-General (DG) for Regional Affairs. Interestingly, the Committee of the Regions is not seen as a vital channel and only when a particular region or municipality has a representative on the committee is it seen as an important channel of influence. Regions and local authorities are also members of various European umbrella organizations for general or specific regional interests. As regional and local representatives have gained in experience, their involvement in such organizations has increasingly come to reflect their specific characteristics, for instance Sweden's three large cities feel more adequately represented by Eurocities than general umbrella organizations. On the national level, local and regional authorities have access to the GO, in particular the Ministry of Enterprise, Energy, and Communications, and, in Brussels, to the Swedish Permanent Representation which constitutes an important channel to knowledge, information, and contacts. A few interesting developments of multi-level governance should be mentioned. First, contacts with the GO have become more intensive in recent years, in regard to regional and cohesion policy, as the national level has reinserted its control over project and programmes through the national envelopes. Second, local and regional authorities do not always share the official positions in negotiations in the Council. For instance, the Swedish position advocating a zero increase of the EU budget is at loggerheads with the local and regional authorities' interests. Third, representatives of local and regional authorities witness a change in the nature of interaction with European institutions (the Commission) and national authorities to the effect that attempts to influence the content and orientation of policy has shifted to Brussels while attempts to influence the negotiations on the financial allocation to projects and programmes are increasingly directed at Stockholm.

Developments over the last decade show that the majority of Swedish local and regional authorities have become increasingly sophisticated in their attempts to influence EU policymaking. Sweden's EU membership has influenced sub-national governance in the direction of municipal cooperation through the creation of regional bodies regrouping substantial municipal competences and encouraged infra-national authorities to become increasingly active in EU affairs on both European and national levels.

Public Policy

Sweden's approach to EU public policy has always been quite paradoxical. On the one hand, Sweden had few problems adapting to EU legislation when it became a member, and in areas where adaptation was necessary it was generally because Swedish regulation was more advanced than in the EU. For instance in agriculture, a sector which had been deregulated in the decades preceding membership, national reforms had to be reversed. On the other hand, attempts to adopt a proactive stance in EU policymaking to influence the content and shape of policy was for a long time held back by a lingering suspicion of the underlying intentions of political integration. As a result, Swedish policy makers adopted a quite passive attitude, in stark contrast with the domestic criticism of many EU policies, particularly agriculture, social policy, and the budget. Today, there is little dispute about the existence of a European dimension in public policy. In the following, the analysis focuses on a few policy areas where the impact of Europeanization is strongly felt. For foreign policy, see 'Patterns of Sweden's Membership of the EU' above.

State Monopolies and European Market Integration

Some sectors of the Swedish economy have been traditionally shielded from the market forces for reasons of public health and safety, such as the distribution and sale of alcohol, the betting and gaming industry, and retail pharmacy, which were organized into state monopolies and used by the government as instruments of public policy. These arrangements have been deemed incompatible with EU competition rules, which forbid anti-competitive practices and protectionism in the internal market. However, the EU has no independent competence in the area of public health, and therefore the mediation between public health and safety concerns and free market forces is not ensured by deliberation amongst elected representatives but by default through the rulings of the ECJ laying down the principles and conditions for allowing or banning national measures with a potentially discriminatory impact.

The Swedish alcohol monopoly was one of the few sticking points in the accession negotiations of 1993–1994. At the time, the Commission pointed out that several aspects of the national alcohol policy were incompatible with EU law, in particular the regulation concerning travellers' imports of alcoholic beverages for private consumption and the Swedish Alcohol Retail Monopoly's market dominance. Since accession, Sweden's alcohol policy has undergone some significant changes prompted by actions taken by the Commission and the ECJ. The restrictions on travellers' private imports were abolished in 2004 and the Swedish Alcohol Retail Monopoly has been broken up through a deregulation of the import, wholesale, and production of alcoholic beverages. Today, only the retail monopoly remains but the monopoly has been forced to adopt more transparent and business-like practices (Hettne 2005; Cisneros Örnberg 2009). Moreover, alcohol taxes on certain beverages have been lowered and private purchases over the internet are no longer prohibited although the buyer is still liable to pay Swedish excise duty. On the whole, Swedish alcohol policy has become less restrictive and, some would argue, less effective from the perspective of public health. In order to counteract the loosening up of the alcohol monopoly, Swedish governments, supported by strong domestic civil society organizations, have become more active on the European level fighting for the introduction of alcohol abuse as a central concern in the EU's public health policy, supporting a strategy to reduce alcohol abuse among young people, and establishing the European Alcohol and Health Forum.

The case of the Swedish alcohol monopoly is an example of the pressure of compliance in regard to national public health policies, which operate in specific segments of the market. Because of its 'constitutional asymmetry', the EU has a tendency to prioritize market freedoms over societal concerns by leaving the task to the ECJ to strike the balance between the market and societal concerns. As Sweden has become aware of EU case law's impact on national economic structures, it has chosen to redefine the structures of the two remaining public health monopolies, the gaming and betting industry and retail pharmacy, to render them compatible with the EU's competition rules by revising national legislation in the case of the former and through a partial privatization in the case of the latter after a ruling of the ECJ found the pharmacy monopoly in breach of EU law.

The Environmental Policy

Sweden is considered a frontrunner in protecting the environment against the harmful effects of human activity. During the accession negotiations, it was recognized that a way had to be found to respect the EU *acquis* while at the same time allow Sweden to maintain a higher level of protection of the environment. Specific solutions were found on a case-by-case basis through transitional periods and flexible interpretations of EU legislation based on a political understanding that the EU would aim at reaching the Swedish level of environmental protection within a reasonable timeframe (Dinkelspiel 2009). Since becoming a member, Swedish governments have actively influenced the EU to adopt more ambitious and stringent environmental regulations: for instance, the Reach legislative package of 2006 regulating the use of chemicals, the directives on emissions standards and measures to curb acidic waste (Regeringskansliet 2005). Other noticeable developments spear-headed by Swedish governments are the EU's strategy for sustainable development and the inclusion of the environment as the Lisbon Strategy's third pillar at the time of the Swedish presidency of the EU in 2001 after strong personal involvement by the prime minister, Göran Persson (Ruin 2002). At the helm of the EU in the second half of 2009, the Right-wing government under Fredrik Reinfeldt promoted an ambitious EU policy on climate change, including leading the EU delegation in the negotiations on the UN Framework Convention on Climate Change at the Copenhagen summit in December 2009.

In the domestic political setting, an ambitious European environment policy has played an important role in making EU membership more palpable. Successive Swedish governments have argued in favour of EU membership by pointing out the necessity to tackle environmental problems on the European level through binding regulations and sanctions of countries that do not comply. In a similar fashion, the EU's ambitious stance on climate change also received wide political and popular support and has given EU proponents ammunition to argue that collective action on the European level provides a common platform to deal with the cross-border phenomenon and a louder voice on the international level. Environmental policy counts among the policies of the EU which has provided Swedish governments with an arena where traditional concerns can be pursued and a tangible example where the pro-EU elite can demonstrate the tangible benefits of EU membership to a sceptical domestic audience (Holmberg 2009).

The Welfare State

The impact of Europeanization on the Swedish welfare system is considered quite modest and mostly indirect in nature. The system's level of generosity has been maintained despite fears that pressure of tax harmonization would hollow out the safety net, and universal social provisions have remained largely intact although measures of targeted and means tested services have been introduced (Tallberg *et al.* 2010).

In the area of labour market policy, however, European integration has had a decisive albeit somewhat unexpected impact. The open nature of the Swedish economy has accommodated since the 1930s a specific model of labour market relations based on collective agreements between the social partners. Collective agreements are seen as one of the pillars of the Swedish social model and are held to reduce the level of conflict in the labour market. Labour market conditions are therefore in principle regulated by agreements between employers and trade unions with no a priori role for the state, in contrast to other member states where working conditions are set down in law. EU policymaking posed no problem as long as it concerned aspects of dismantling barriers to free trade (negative integration) but became a predicament when the EU began to regulate the conditions for the production of goods and services (positive integration). Therefore, when European regulation in the service sector grew, the traditional labour market organization in Sweden came under pressure. Just as in the case of the break-up of Swedish state-run monopolies, the supremacy of European law and the precedence given by the ECJ to the free circulation of factors of production over national practices have tested the boundaries between European and national norms.

It was precisely the issue of conflicting economic and social norms in the Laval ruling of 2007 (C-341/05, European Court of Justice) which highlighted incompatibility of national labour market conventions with the rules of European market integration. The case involved a dispute between the subsidiary of a Latvian company, *Laval un Partneri*, and the Swedish building workers' union over the conditions laid down in the collective agreement in force in the sector. As Laval refused to sign up to the agreement, the trade union put the building site in blockade and ultimately the company's Swedish operations went into receivership. As the case revealed a conflict of Swedish and European legal norms, the national labour court asked for a preliminary ruling from the ECJ. The court ruled in the employer's favour on the grounds that the demands of the Swedish trade unions were not supported by the rules laid down by the national legislation implementing the Posted Workers' Directive; the demands of the trade unions were excessive in relation to the provisions of the collective agreement in force; and the measures taken by the trade unions were not in proportion to the prejudice caused to the company. Furthermore, the court criticized the collective agreements in force in the sector as lacking in transparency thereby constituting an impediment for non-Swedish companies' ability to operate on the Swedish market. The court did not, however, question the legality of collective agreements or the right to take collective action which is enshrined in EU law. As a consequence of the ECJ's criticism, the government enacted a revision of the existing labour market legislation to make it compatible with EU law without changing the fundamental principles of the Swedish labour market model. The new law seeks to clarify the conditions that must be fulfilled before trade unions are allowed to take action in the event of a conflict with foreign companies operating in Sweden. The Laval case demonstrated that in order not to discriminate against economic actors from other EU member states the rules concerning collective agreements must be surrounded with greater certainty and predictability (SOU 2008). At the same time, the Swedish government was unwilling to restrict the traditional labour market model whose flexibility and consensual nature is seen as having worked in favour of the overall competitiveness of the Swedish economy.

Sweden in a Comparative Perspective

Sweden joined the EU in 1995 together with Austria and Finland. It initially adopted the more sceptical stance towards EU membership by staying outside the euro and taking a minimal approach to the issue of institutional reform. In terms of the nature of Euro-scepticism Sweden was often put in the same category as the UK. Despite the three newcomers in 1995 being bound by a policy of neutrality which had kept them outside any military alliance during the Cold War, the nature of their neutrality is different and that led them to adopt quite different positions also in regard to the CFSP.

Sweden shares a belief in a comprehensive welfare system and sustainable development with the other Nordic member states, Finland and Denmark, with which it also shares democratic traditions, values, and norms such as open society, transparency, and openness in public-making and gender equality. As an advocate of free trade and a supporter of an open, competitive, European market, Sweden has argued against state subsidies and protectionist measures thereby adopting a position close to that of the Netherlands and the UK.

In terms of coalition patterns in the Council of Ministers, research (Naurin and Lindahl 2008) shows that Sweden forms a cluster with the Northern member states, a pattern that has continued after the enlargement to the East. In many policy areas, in particular in those with a social, environmental, or normative content, Sweden most often forms coalition with Finland and Denmark while in areas linked to the internal market and in redistributive issues, including agriculture, Sweden will seek coalition with the Netherlands and the UK. Sweden, together with Denmark, was the member state that opposed most Council decisions between 2004 and 2006 in stark contrast with these countries' quite excellent implementation records (Hagemann and De Clerck-Sachsse 2007).

Conclusion

Sweden's involvement in the EU rests on pragmatic pursuit of national interests in the areas where European opportunity structures allow member states to influence the orientation of European policy and where the domestic political elite and public opinion expect changes to EU norms in order to reduce the perceived 'misfit' between European and domestic regimes. At the same time, Sweden has adapted without much ado to the obligations of membership and compliance to existing legislation has not posed a problem as Sweden has always been among the member states with the best record of implementation and enforcement of the *aquis*. Today, the area that causes concern is the strong impact of integration by law in labour market relations and in the area of public health and safety. In the latter area, Sweden has rather reluctantly complied with the rulings of the ECJ and adapted national legislation to European rules and a convergence to European norms is detectable in the areas that were previously dominated by state monopolies. The 'misfit' between national labour market conventions and the principle of free circulation of services and the posting of workers is more troublesome and has resulted in procrastination on behalf of the government and disquiet among the trade unions. It is emblematic of the Swedish reluctance to integration in the area of welfare that successive governments have promoted coordination of economic restructuring and social policy in the framework of the Lisbon Strategy through the Open Method of Coordination, based on voluntary convergence, not binding legislation.

In the fifteen years of membership, Swedish political, administrative, and organizational elites have undergone a process of socialization by which the increasing familiarity of Brussels policymaking has weakened the perception of exceptionalism in favour of a feeling of fitting in, giving rise to awareness of the opportunity structures existing on the European level. It is not only the parameters of membership per se which have influenced Sweden's relation to the EU as external developments have had a strong impact as well. Enlargement to the East influenced Swedish perceptions about the EU not only in the sense of de-dramatizing political integration, as its implications appear less ominous in a union of twenty-seven member states than with fifteen, but also in making good of the deeply felt rationale of the EU as a peace project assisting countries in their transformation to democracy and a market economy. Globalization of the economy, international security and the environment have strengthened the case for belonging to a regional organization, for pooling sovereignty with like-minded nations and for speaking with one voice on the international scene. Lastly, it should not be forgotten that Sweden adhered to the EU in the midst of a severe economic recession when the longevity of the Swedish economic and social system was in doubt. Today, the Swedish economic model is often put forward as an example of high economic growth and international competitiveness combined with a generous social safety net, a functioning public service, a clean environment and an advanced climate change policy. This has boosted the political and administrative elite's confidence in their ability to influence concrete policies and norms on the European level and reduced the public's concern about convergence to less attractive policy outcomes, whether real or perceived, on the European level.

 FURTHER READING

Literature on Sweden's membership in English is quite sparse. For an overview, see Lee Miles (2005) *Fusing with Europe? Sweden in the European Union*, Aldershot: Ashgate, and Lee Miles (ed.) (2000) *Sweden and the European Union Evaluated*, London: Continuum. Sweden's political system, including policymaking on European affairs, is explained in Henry Bäck and Torbjörn Larsson (2008) *Governing and Governance in Sweden*, Lund: Studentlitteratur. For the political dimension of coordination of EU affairs, see Persson (2007) and Johansson and Tallberg (2010).

184 Anna Michalski

WEB LINKS

Access to the Swedish government is available at **http://www.sweden.gov.se/**. Statistics Sweden publishes a wealth of data **http://www.scb.se/**. For studies of public administration see **http://www.statskontoret.se/**. The Swedish Association of Local Authorities and Regions see **http://english.skl.se/web/english.aspx**. Research institutes that publish in English see The Swedish Institute for European Policy Studies (SIEPS) **http://www.sieps.se/** and The Swedish Institute for Institute of International Affairs (SIIA) **http://www.ui.se/**.

REFERENCES

Andersen, K. (2001), 'Sweden: Retreat from Exceptionalism', in E. Zeff and E. Pirro, (eds), *The European Union and the Member States. Cooperation, Coordination and Compromise*, Boulder, CO: Lynne Rienner.

Bäck, H. and Torbjörn Larsson (2008), *Governing and Governance in Sweden*, Lund: Studentlitteratur.

Berg, L. and Lindahl, R. (2007), *Svenska Kommuners och Regioners Kanaler till Bryssel*, Stockholm: SIEPS.

Blomgren, M. (2009), 'Sweden', in *The Selection of Candidates for the European Parliament by National Parties and the Impact on European Political Parties*, Brussels: European Parliament.

Cisneros Örnberg, J. (2009), 'The Europeanization of Swedish Alcohol Policy', PhD thesis, University of Stockholm.

Danielsson, L. (2007), *I Skuggan av Makten*, Stockholm: Bonniers.

Dinkelspiel, U. (2009), *Den Motvillige Européen*, Stockholm: Atlantis.

European Commission (1995), *Eurobarometer. Public Opinion Analysis, No. 43*, Brussels, Directorate-General Communication.

European Commission (2005), *Eurobarometer. Public Opinion Analysis, No. 63*, Brussels, Directorate-General Communication.

European Commission (2010a), *Eurobarometer. Public Opinion Analysis, No. 73*, Brussels, Directorate-General Communication.

European Commission (2010b), *Eurobarometer. Public Opinion Analysis No. 72. National Report. Sweden*, DG Communication.

European Court of Justice, (2007), Laval un Partneri Ltd v. Svenska Byggnadsarbetarförbundet [*Laval*], C-341/05.

Hagemann, S. and De Clerck-Sachsse, J. (2007), *Decision-Making in the Enlarged Council of Ministers: Evaluating the Facts*, Brussels: CEPS.

Hettne, J. (2005), 'EG-domstolens nya syn på Handelsmonopol', in A. Meyrowitsch, E. Allroth, and J. Hettne, *EU och Svenska Monopol – Teori, Verklighet och Framtid*, Stockholm: SIEPS.

Holmberg, S. (2009), *EU allt mer accepterat*, Europapolitisk analys, No. 4, Stockholm: SIEPS.

Holmberg, S. (2010), 'Nu har en majoritet svenskar mentalt gått med i EU', *Europapolitisk analys*, No. 5, Stockholm: SIEPS.

Holmberg, S. and Oscarsson, H. (2008), *Regeringsskifte. Väljarna och valet 2006*, Stockholm: Nordstedts Juridik.

Johansson, K. M. (2008), 'Chief Executive Organization and Advisory Arrangements for Foreign Affairs: The Case of Sweden', *Cooperation and Conflict*, 43/3: 267–87.

Johansson, K. M. and Tallberg, J. (2010), 'Explaining Chief Executive Empowerment: EU Summitry and Domestic Institutional Change', *West European Politics*, 33/2: 208–36.

Johansson, K. M, Langdal, F., and von Sydow, G. (2010), 'Mellan Bryssel och Rosenbad: Ordförandeskapets Organisering', in R. Bengtsson (ed.), *I Europas tjänst. Sveriges Ordförandeskap i EU 2009*, Stockholm: SNS:s förlag.

Jungar, A-C. and Ahlbäck Öberg S. (2004), 'Are National Parliaments Lagging Behind? The Influence of the Swedish and Finnish Parliaments over Domestic EU Policies', in A. Ágh (ed.), *Post-Accession in East Central Europe: The Emergence of the EU 25*, Budapest: Hungarian Centre for Democracy Studies.

Larue, T. (2006), *Agents in Brussels. Delegation and Democracy in the European Union*, Umeå: Department of Political Studies.

Miles, L. (ed.) (2000), *Sweden and the European Union Evaluated*, London: Continuum.

Miles, L. (2005), *Fusing with Europe? Sweden in the European Union*, Aldershot: Ashgate.

Naurin, D. and Lindahl, R. (2008), 'East-North-South. Coalition-Building in the Council Before and After Enlargement', in D. Naurin and H. Wallace (eds), *Unveiling the Council of the EU: Games Governments Play in Brussels*, Basingstoke: Palgrave Macmillan.

Persson, T. (2007), 'Explaining European Union Adjustments in Sweden's Central Administration', *Scandinavian Political Studies*, 30/2: 204–28.

Regeringskansliet (2005), *Sverige och miljön efter 10 år i EU*, Stockholm: Miljö- och samhällsbyggnadsdepartementet.

Reichel, J. (2008), *Svensk livsmedelspolitick i EU – styrning och kontroll*, Stockholm: SIEPS.

Ruin, O. (2002), *Sveriges Statsminister och EU. Ett Halvår i Centrum*, Stockholm: Hjalmarsson & Högberg.

Statens Offentliga Utredningar (SOU) (2008), *Förslag till Åtgärder Med Anledning av Lavaldomen. Betänkande av Lavalutredningen*, SOU 2008:123, Stockholm: Fritzes.

Swedish Agency for Public Management (2007), *National Agencies in the Internal Market. Applying Free Movement*, Stockholm: Statskontoret.

Tallberg, J., Aylott, N., Bergström, C. F., Casula Vifell, Å., and Palme, J. (eds) (2010), *Europeiseringen av Sverige*, Stockholm: SNS Förlag.

 ENDNOTE

1. Sources: Regeringskansliets Årsberättelse 2009 (GO Annual Report 2009) **http://www.sweden.gov.se/content/1/c6/14/00/95/213731d0.pdf**. Arbetsgivarverket (Swedish Authority for Government Employers) **http://www.arbetsgivarverket.se/t/Page121.aspx** accessed on 27.9.2010

CHAPTER 8

Poland: An Awkward Partner Redeemed*

Nathaniel Copsey

■ **Summary**

After the fall of communism, Poland took an early decision in 1989 to place European integration at the centre of its plans for democratization and modernization. Actually joining the EU took far longer than anyone imagined possible, but Poland finally secured accession in 2004. A period of political and institutional adjustment followed, although it could be argued that the bulk of the EU's impact on Poland actually came in the long period of preparation for membership. Post-accession opinion in Poland on the EU was divided between an increasingly Europhile public and an occasionally Eurosceptic political class. This split was particularly obvious in the period 2005–2007. By the time of the Polish Presidency of the EU in 2011, however, Poland had largely shed its reputation for awkwardness and had notched up a few policy successes, notably in the field of relations with the Eastern neighbours.

Introduction

Poland joined the European Union on 1 May 2004 as the largest of the ten post-communist states that made up the fifth enlargement. The domestic political fall-out caused by the one-sided nature of the entry negotiations cast a long shadow over Poland's early years of EU membership. Following the election in 2005 of the Law and Justice-led coalition government, and of Lech Kaczyński as president soon after, Poland acquired the reputation of being an 'awkward partner' for the member states and institutions. Under the Kaczyński twins, in the eyes of its partners Poland often seemed socially conservative, nationalistic, and out of step with the Union's tradition of consensus-based decision-making. Donald Tusk's 2007–2011 Civic Platform-led administration was less socially conservative and employed a more nuanced rhetoric in defence of Polish interests. In consequence, by 2008 with the launch of the Eastern Partnership with Sweden, Poland was both successfully uploading new policy ideas onto the Union agenda and shedding its reputation as a somewhat touchy and difficult interlocutor.

This chapter has two main aims. First, it looks at how Poland came to join the European Union and its pattern of membership since then. Second, it looks at the impact of the European Union on domestic politics, public opinion, institutions, and public policy. It concludes with a few words of comparison between Poland and its Visegrád neighbours, the Czech Republic, Hungary, and Slovakia.

The Pattern of Relations with the EU 1989–2011

'Returning to Europe': European Integration in Poland 1989–2004

Poland's decision to choose European integration was taken almost immediately following the first democratic elections of June 1989, and on 19 September of that year Poland signed a Trade and Cooperation Agreement with the then European Communities. What followed was an exceptionally long and complicated period of negotiation with the EC and EU, at first for an Association or 'Europe' Agreement (signed on 16 December 1991) and subsequently for full membership (beginning on 31 March 1998, ending with the 12–13 December meeting of the European Council in 2002 and the signing of the Accession Treaty in Athens on 16 April 2003).

That the process of negotiating membership took so long was caused primarily by the increased—and increasing—volume of the *acquis communautaire*. Thus EU accession was a rapidly moving target that Poland, which was still reeling from the painful effects of the transition from a planned to market economy, struggled to keep up with. It is also sometimes forgotten that the member states did not make it clear until relatively late in the game that they were *definitely* going to enlarge to the East at all.[1] Moreover, in contrast to previous enlargements (e.g. Greece), applicants were required not only to transpose the *acquis* prior to accession, but their adequate implementation of the *acquis* was also to be verified by the European Commission.

Prior to EU accession, Poland often found itself unwillingly cast in its dealings with Brussels as a *demandeur*. It was a large, rather agricultural, uncompetitive, and poor post-communist state faced with the immense tasks of simultaneously creating a free market economy and liberal democracy governed by the rule of law at home, whilst struggling to extract concessions from its hard-headed west European neighbours abroad. Euro-Atlantic integration for Poland succeeded (it joined NATO in 1999), but the drawn-out period of tough negotiations, where inevitably the Polish team found themselves having to make most of the concessions, cast a shadow over the first years of Polish membership of the European Union. The one-sided nature of the negotiations helps to explain why the 2005–2007 Law and Justice-led post-accession government was relatively unconcerned about becoming a new 'awkward partner' for the other member states—and why so many otherwise Euro-enthusiast Poles supported the government's clumsily expressed and much reiterated pledge to defend what it saw as the national interest. Given the relatively short period that has elapsed since Poland joined the European Union in 2004, it is worth taking a brief detour in this section to look again at the substance of the negotiations between the two parties.

The Negotiations

The opening position of the European Union in accession talks is always 'the *acquis* and nothing but the *acquis*'. This stance was clearly laid out both in the Copenhagen criteria and in the negotiating directives given by the Council to the EU's negotiating team. The room for manoeuvre on the part of the EU negotiators was further restricted by the need for unanimity that is essential for the ratification of an accession treaty. Some chapters of the negotiations with Poland were particularly difficult to close, in particular:

- Agriculture, because of the size of the Polish agricultural sector, which despite contributing only 2.8 per cent of GDP (European Commission 1999) employed 26.7 per cent of the workforce in 1996 (European Commission 1996) creating financial problems for direct income payments to Polish farmers;

- Environment, because of the cost of implementing European standards in a short period of time—to give two examples here, Poland secured extra time, until 2015, to implement the Urban Waste Water *acquis* and the Landfill *acquis*, until 2012;

- Justice and home affairs, because of the difficulty of preparing adequate border controls—and of persuading EU member states to trust that the new member states were 'Schengen ready' (although Poland did not join the Schengen area until 2007);

- The free movement of people, mostly because the EU-15, with the exception of the UK, Ireland, and Sweden, were highly reluctant to open their markets immediately to Polish workers;

- The free movement of capital (including opening the agricultural land market to capital-rich foreign buyers);

- State aids and competition policy (for example, special economic zones);

- Financial questions because Poland was both very poor and large, and would thus merit a larger share of EU structural and cohesion funds—at the expense of previous recipients like Spain, Portugal, Greece, and Ireland; the issue of higher levels of Value Added Tax (VAT) on certain goods and increases in cigarette prices also proved to be a sticking point;

- Institutional questions because Poland was large and would require a similar number of votes in the Council of Ministers to Spain, a large number of MEPs and its 'own' Commissioner or even two—and all this was to be delivered at a time when Spain was trying to increase its relative voting weight in the Council of Ministers.

Thus despite the inflexible opening position of the member states, there was clearly some room for trade-offs to be made in negotiations. Crudely, this boiled down to less money from the CAP and European funds for Poland and other new member states in exchange for concessions such as temporary restrictions on the sale of farm land to foreigners and extra time to implement the *acquis* in a number of areas where the functioning of the internal market would not be too gravely impaired. To give some concrete examples of the bargains struck, on accession to the European Union in 2004, Poland's farmers would receive only 25 per cent of the direct income payment made to farmers in the EU-15, rising to 100 per cent by 2012. Labour markets in some member states would remain closed to Polish workers in the first instance—and right up until the 1 May 2011 limit in the case of Germany and Austria. The sale of agricultural land and forests in Poland to foreigners was restricted by up to twelve years until 2016. The Agenda 2000 financial package that was finally agreed between the member states in 1999 set out how enlargement was to be financed, and the rules were changed to ensure that EU-15 countries would continue to receive some Community assistance after the 2004 enlargement and a ceiling set on the maximum total appropriations from the EU budget that could be received at between 1.13 per cent and 1.19 per cent of GNP from 2000 to 2006 (European Commission 1997: 14). The Union probably made the better deal, but Poland's negotiators ultimately secured accession. Reaching any sort of agreement on accession was hailed as a great achievement for Polish diplomacy, but the question of whether the package agreed was the best that could have been negotiated was an issue to which political debate in Poland would return.

That the negotiations were one-sided did not escape the public's attention, and both the centre-Right Solidarity Electoral Action (*Akcja Wyborcza Solidarność*, AWS) coalition (1997–2001) and the Democratic Left Alliance (*Sojusz Lewicy Demokratycznej*, SLD) coalition (2001–2005) fretted about the concessions they had made. Headlines about 'the Germans returning' to buy the land they had been expelled from in 1945 or of Poles joining the European Union 'as second class citizens' led to a public information campaign that aimed to set the record straight, including a ten-part television series '*Negocjator*' ('Negotiator') presented by the author of this chapter on the details of the negotiations. In echoes of earlier fears about standardization of bananas, Polish citizens were reassured that they would still be able to buy traditional products, such as smoked unpasteurized sheep's cheeses (*oscypki*) following accession—although henceforth they would have to be shrink-wrapped to ensure compliance with the *acquis*. Despite everything, in the referendum on accession that followed the conclusion of negotiations, the Polish public voted overwhelmingly (77.5 per cent on a turnout of 59 per cent, which itself was high by Polish standards) for accession.

A New Awkward Partner? Relations with the EU 2004–2011

On 2 May 2004, Poland's discredited prime minister, Leszek Miller, stepped down some twenty-four hours after Poland had joined the European Union and handed over to the technocrat, Marek Belka, who presided over a caretaker administration in the run-up to the parliamentary elections that were held sixteen months later in September 2005. The first year of membership was relatively quiet as Polish officials learnt the rules of the Brussels game from the perspective of a member state, although it was already becoming clear that the provisions on qualified majority voting (QMV) in the draft Constitutional Treaty (CT) that was approved by the June 2004 European Council would not be acceptable to Poland. In 2003, Jan Rokita, the chair of Civic Platform's parliamentary grouping, memorably proclaimed that Poland must have 'Nice or Death!'. He was alluding to the fact that Poland, like Spain, had been allotted twenty-seven votes in the Council of Ministers to the twenty-nine apportioned to Germany by the Nice Treaty, despite the fact that its population was more than twice that of Poland. The ECT's double majority system required the support of at least 55 per cent of member states representing at least 65 per cent of citizens. This undermined the relative strength of Poland vis-à-vis the other member states considerably—although, of course, as is well known, the Council seldom takes a formal vote (Hayes-Renshaw *et al.*, 2006).

The 2005 parliamentary elections produced a long-forecast radical change with the post-communist SLD falling from first to fourth place in the polls and losing 75 per cent of its seats. The big surprise of the election was that the socially conservative centre-Right Law and Justice Party unexpectedly came in first place, twenty-two seats ahead of the second-placed liberal centre-Right Civic Platform. This upset the calculations of many that a so-called PO (Civic Platform)-PiS (Law and Justice) coalition would be formed of the two large centre-Right parties when Law and Justice decided to form a minority government, headed by Prime Minister Kazimierz Marcinkiewicz. In December 2005, the new government secured a hugely significant victory during the negotiations over the 2007–2013 EU budget. The British government (in the chair during the negotiations) had blocked a deal put forward during the 2006 Luxembourg Presidency worth 1.06 per cent of EU GDP and offered only 1.03 per cent of EU GDP. The compromise provided for a budget of 1.045 per cent of EU GDP, with Poland by far the largest beneficiary of EU cohesion funds, worth €59.7 billion from 2007–2013 (although the figure quoted widely and regularly by Danuta Hübner, when Polish Commissioner for Regional Policy, was €67 billion).[2]

Despite this early success, over the course of 2006 and 2007, Poland's credibility in the eyes of its European partners dropped, a process much hastened by the formation of a coalition government in July 2006 with the Catholic-conservative League of Polish Families and the populist Self-Defence, both of which parties were avowed Eurosceptics. This coalition also proved unworkable, all the more so after corruption and sexual harassment scandals broke within Self-Defence in late 2006. Eventually, Law and Justice was obliged to call early elections. By the time of the autumn 2007 parliamentary poll, Poland was widely portrayed in the Western media as the EU's new 'awkward partner', and as a liability in Brussels. The extent to which the responsibility for the negative perception of Poland in this period lies exclusively with the Law and Justice-led coalition or was more the product of a somewhat biased and ill-informed Western media is a matter of judgement. What is certain is that the Polish government lost control of its media and communications strategy—and this itself was a serious oversight.

It could be argued that there was a certain amount of substance behind the claims of intransigence and incompetence laid at the door of the Law and Justice government.

In November 2006, without prior warning, following a dispute with Russia over meat exports, Poland (together with Lithuania) vetoed the opening of negotiations with Russia on a replacement for the Partnership and Cooperation Agreement (PCA) with the EU. It is true that the then Commissioner for Trade, Peter Mandelson, had not leapt to the defence of the Poles in what was thought to be a politically-motivated trade dispute stemming from Russian irritation at Poland's role in Ukraine's Orange Revolution 2004, but what really rankled in Brussels was the lack of warning that the veto was about to be used. The government also dismissed or rotated a large number of policy grade civil servants and diplomats as part of its drive to remove communist-era placemen from post and prepare the ground for its 'Fourth Republic' project. This was part of a wider campaign against what the Law and Justice leadership termed the '*układ*', a network of politicians, businessmen, and public officials who, it was alleged, had conspired against the Polish people's collective interest since 1989. An immediate effect of this cull was to leave vacant a number of senior jobs in the Polish administration for long periods of time. One such case was the Polish Permanent Representative to the European Union, whose office remained unoccupied from 2006–2007; depriving the top level of Polish diplomacy in Brussels of a voice and the government in Warsaw of the necessary clear overview of European politics that it needed both to coordinate policy and to negotiate effectively with its partners.

Despite all this, the Law and Justice government's European policy record was a relatively minor issue in the 2007 parliamentary elections, although it was a contributing factor for the much larger question of the government's overall competence. Law and Justice's polarizing rhetoric was, after all, not limited to European and foreign policy questions. Donald Tusk's Civic Platform won the 2007 elections with 41.5 per cent of the vote to Law and Justice's 32.1 per cent—a good result for both parties in the circumstances. Civic Platform formed a coalition with the Polish People's Party (or PSL) and was welcomed with relief by Poland's European partners in Brussels. Over the course of the period 2007–2011, Poland's image in Brussels improved considerably and it even clocked up a few notable successes, particularly in putting forward the so-called Eastern Partnership for the EU's Eastern neighbours (see Copsey and Pomorska 2010 and forthcoming).

One problem that Civic Platform faced that had not troubled its predecessor in government was relations with the president (the twin brother of the leader of Law and Justice). In 2008, an embarrassing tug-of-war took place between President Kaczyński and Prime Minister Tusk over who represented Poland at the European Council. This culminated in two separate delegations arriving at the Council in Brussels on 15 October 2008 necessitating a game of musical chairs in the Council chamber where the finance and foreign ministers were obliged to leave the room to allow the president to take a seat next to the prime minister.[3] Although the primary responsibility for foreign affairs in the Polish Constitution is given to the government and foreign minister, the president 'represents' Poland abroad. The matter was settled in May 2009 when the Constitutional Court ruled that the president may himself decide whether to participate in the European Council, but it is the government who decides what the Polish position will be (Gazeta Prawna 2009). The Court also ruled that the president did not have the prerogative to conduct an independent foreign policy or to direct relations with international organizations. As the endgame of the negotiations on the Reform Treaty showed, however, President Kaczyński did not shrink from intervention in Polish European policy—even when his position was out of step with everyone else. Before concluding this overview of Poland's first few years of EU membership, the question of Poland's strong views on voting rights in the Council of Ministers is worth exploring in a little detail.

Nice or Death: Poland and Voting Weights in the Council of Ministers

Concerns about QMV in the Council of Ministers became something of a cause célèbre within Poland since the issue continued to crop up long after it had actually signed the CT following the IGC in June 2004. Between 2003 and 2007, voting weight seemed to acquire a truly totemic quality within Polish politics, not unlike the nature of political discussion about the British Budgetary Question within the UK—that is the issue seemed to grow out of all proportion to its objective significance. In 2007, immediately prior to the summit on the Reform Treaty, the Poles reopened the issue of voting rights by proposing the so-called 'square root' formula for the distribution of votes within the Council of Ministers. The formula proposed by Poland allotted each member state a number of votes based on the square root of its population, thus eighty-one million Germans would receive nine votes, sixty million Italians would receive seven or eight, and thirty-eight million Poles would receive six votes. But why was the Polish government so worried about this in the first place?

A first, and highly rational, explanation for why the Polish political class and government were so concerned about voting weights in the Council of Ministers is that the CT represented a clear reduction in the voting power of Poland relative to the other member states, particularly relative to the other large member states, as Table 8.1 shows.

Under the Treaty of Nice, the five largest member states were given more or less equal voting weight in the Council of Ministers. The four largest states, Germany, the UK, France, and Italy all received twenty-nine votes, despite Germany having a population around 130 per cent of that of the next three largest member states. Poland and Spain also benefited disproportionately from the voting of weights in the Council of Ministers with only two fewer votes than Germany—a country with a population around twice the size of that of Poland or Spain.

Poland and Spain had clearly received rather more than their fair share of votes under the Nice Treaty and it was natural that they wished to defend this, especially since, under the double majority (number of member states plus majority of population of the whole EU) system introduced by the CT, they lost the most power, as the

TABLE 8.1 Votes per member state with populations over twenty million under the Nice Treaty of 2001

Member state	Votes	Population (million)	Relative weight[1]
Germany	29	82.0	1.00
United Kingdom	29	59.4	1.38
France	29	59.1	1.39
Italy	29	57.7	1.42
Spain	27	39.4	1.94
Poland	27	38.6	1.98
Romania	14	22.3	1.78

Source: Treaty of Nice and author's own calculations.
[1] Votes are weighted relative to Germany's population, where Germany = 1. Thus, Poland, with a population of less than half of that of Germany, has almost the same number of votes with a relative weight of 1.98.

population rules favoured the large member states in general and Germany in particular—at the expense of Poland (Baldwin and Widgren 2004). What is less simple to explain is why Poland returned time and time again to the voting weights question, long after Zapatero had abandoned Spain's objections in 2004, especially since, as has been noted on many occasions (Hayes-Renshaw *et al.* 2006) the Council seldom votes, even on those issues where QMV is provided for—that is, unanimity remains the unofficial means by which most Union decisions are taken, a key element of the consensual nature of European Union politics. Nonetheless, it would be argued by some in Poland that, even if a formal vote is not taken, the relative voting weights are still considered and thus Poland could find itself outvoted. Ultimately, it is the perception rather than the reality of Poland being outvoted that matters most.

An explanation for Polish intransigence on voting weight could be that, like the United Kingdom, or indeed other member states, Poland did not trust its European partners and felt the need to have mechanisms to protect national interests that were seen as very different from those of other member states. It is true that Poland is sovereignty-sensitive, but so are other EU countries, such as Sweden, France, Ireland, and, of course, the UK. In Poland's case, the explanation for attitudes towards the issue of voting weights perhaps has much to do with the political culture of Poland and the legacy of the past.

History features fairly often in the speeches and writings of Polish politicians or analysts about the nature of European integration, usually in a way that refers to the 'righting of wrongs', or grievances, or making amends for past crimes. When Poland proposed the square root compromise for voting rights in the Council of Ministers, the President of Poland's then adviser on European affairs, Marek Cichocki, described the proposal as a 'Polish historical rebate . . . [for the fact that] for 50 years Poland for no fault of its own was outside EU integration'.[4] The implication appears to be made that Poland deserves compensation for historical wrongs: in this case for the post-1945 settlement by the United States, UK, and Soviet Union at Yalta which left Poland on the wrong side of the Iron Curtain with no input from a Polish delegation as to what should happen to Poland. Yalta may be the most recent occasion that decisions were taken about Poland's future without Polish participation, but it was certainly not the first occasion.

Such historical reasons are certainly a key factor in explaining—or at the very least in justifying—why Polish politicians (and officials) pressed so hard for extra guarantees and why they held the attitudes that they did towards the question of voting rights—after all it should be noted that the key net beneficiary from the CT was Germany, a country which the 2005–2007 government was highly suspicious of as a result of the shared past. Perhaps what truly mattered on this issue for the Polish elite was that Poland should lose voting weights in the Council of Ministers *relative to Germany*. The burden of history goes some way towards explaining why politicians on both the centre-Left and the centre-Right feel that they have to prove themselves as patriots and defenders of the national interest— although of course this is by no means unique to Poland. Polish politicians are capable of being patriotic and politically opportunist at the same time. Moreover, the singularity of the importance of historical factors for Poland should not be overplayed either. Other member states have similar problems, just as other member states share Poland's persistent belief that patriotism is not necessarily a bad thing.

The question of voting rights was finally settled in October 2008, when the Polish president negotiated a deal on voting rights to be added to the Lisbon Treaty that replaced the CT, using an amended version of the so-called Ioannina Compromise of 1994. Under the terms of the deal struck with President Kaczyński, the Nice Treaty voting system was extended until 2014. From 2014 to 2017, a member state will be able to ask for the Nice voting rules to be used if it faces being outvoted in the Council. Thus Poland won a seven-year stay of extension for the Nice voting system after the Lisbon Treaty came into effect on 1 December 2009. The Lisbon Treaty was ratified by the Polish Sejm on 1 April 2008, by 384 votes in favour and fifty-six against in the Sejm and seventy-four to seventeen in the Senate. The fifty-six deputies who voted against the treaty were all from the Law and Justice Party. President Lech Kaczyński delayed signing the Reform Treaty for almost as long as President Klaus of the Czech Republic, citing first the need for the Polish government to pass a Competences Bill[5] and subsequently the Irish 'no' in the referendum of 12 June 2008— despite the obvious fact that he himself had negotiated the extension of the Nice Treaty voting rules in Poland's favour.

In summary, voting weights in the Council of Ministers matter in Poland because the Nice Treaty rules were seen as a major achievement, because of sensitivity about loss of sovereignty, because of the lingering impact of the past and, more crucially, the lessons that should be learnt from a particular reading of history (i.e. stick together as a nation but be suspicious of your neighbours), and finally because the issue caught the public eye and became a benchmark for the patriotism of Polish politicians—that is, all politicians wanted to be seen to be defending the national interest at all costs.

Conclusions on the Pattern of Polish Relations with the EU 1989–2011

The Law and Justice-led government of 2005–2007 was anxious to draw a line under Poland's period as supplicant to the EU and adopted a robust line, vetoing the negotiations on a new PCA with Russia, and at one point threatening to invoke the Luxembourg Compromise to avoid being outvoted in the allocation of sugar beet quotas. It was also unconcerned at being in a minority of one and downright rude to its allies, such as Germany, which was even referred to on one occasion undiplomatically as a 'historical enemy'.

This polarizing 'if-you're-not-with-us-you're-against-us' style of governing fell out of fashion with the election of Donald Tusk and the Civic Platform-led coalition in 2007, although President Lech Kaczynski's outspoken views could be heard in the background. In autumn 2009, he refused to sign the Lisbon Treaty until the last minute, citing the initial Irish 'no'. On 10 April 2010, however, Lech Kaczyński's voice in Polish politics was silenced forever when he was killed, together with his wife and ninety-four others, in a plane crash whilst they were on their way to Smolensk for a commemoration of the seventieth anniversary commemoration of the Katyn massacre. In the presidential poll that followed, the aristocratic Civic Platform candidate, Bronisław Komorowski, beat Lech Kaczyński's twin brother Jarosław by 53 per cent to 47 per cent, which deprived Law and Justice of a power base at the heart of the Polish state.

Poland is both more ambitious in what it seeks to achieve from EU membership and more forthright in expressing its opinions than the other post-communist central European states that it, at times, purports (usually to their irritation) to lead. Several years after accession, perhaps as a result of the one-sided nature of the membership negotiations, and Poland's historical legacy of relative poverty vis-à-vis other European states, the Polish civil service retained a continuing notion of the EU as 'them' not 'us'—although perhaps they were not unique in this. This sentiment is bolstered objectively by Poland's absence from the euro area and the fact that it is unlikely to join it in the future. Nonetheless, there can be no question that Poland's remarkable political, economic, and social transformation since 1989 owes much to the exacting demands made by European integration. Poles are not simply richer as a result of EU accession, but have far greater opportunities, are far better governed, and live in far greater security than ever before. These facts have not escaped public opinion as the next section shows.

The Impact of EU Membership on Public Opinion and Political Parties

Public Opinion

According to the Eurobarometer, Polish support for EU membership (60 per cent) was more or less the same as the European average of around 54 per cent (Autumn 2009: No. 72), which marked a significant increase from the 42 per cent level of Polish support enjoyed by the EU at the time of accession in 2004 (see Figure 8.1). The proportion of Poles who believed that their country had benefited from EU membership was amongst the highest in the Union, at 74 per cent (Eurobarometer, Autumn 2009: No. 72), which was nearly twice the 40 per cent level at the time of accession. Such positive sentiments towards the Union on the part of the Polish population at large may at least in part be the result of the fact that EU membership coincided with a long economic boom (see Table 8.2), with the Polish economy even narrowly dodging recession during the great slump in the world economy of 2008–2009. Poles' enthusiasm for the EU may also be the result of the fact that they exhibit a much higher level of trust in EU institutions (the functioning of which additionally around 59 per cent of Poles say they understand) than national ones. Indeed, Poland joined the EU at a time when trust in politics was at an all-time low. In 2004, just 8 per cent of Poles claimed to trust the government (Eurobarometer, Autumn 2004:

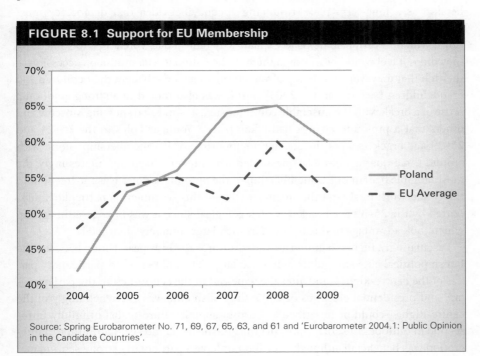

FIGURE 8.1 Support for EU Membership

Source: Spring Eurobarometer No. 71, 69, 67, 65, 63, and 61 and 'Eurobarometer 2004.1: Public Opinion in the Candidate Countries'.

TABLE 8.2 Economic growth, inflation, and unemployment in Poland 2004–2010

	2004	2005	2006	2007	2008	2009	2010
GDP Growth	5.30%	3.60%	6.20%	6.80%	5.10%	1.70%	3.80%
Unemployment	18.20%	16.50%	11.80%	8.30%	7.10%	9.10%	10.00%
Inflation	0.70%	3.40%	2.20%	1.30%	2.50%	4.20%	3.50%

Source: www.stat.gov.pl.

No. 62) and a risible 3 per cent of voters expressed confidence in political parties. By 2008, support for EU institutions such as the Commission or Parliament was at around 40–50 per cent of those polled, whilst trust in the Polish government had recovered to some 26 per cent of those questioned. Further proof that Poles appear at least to measure the effectiveness and legitimacy of the EU against a yardstick that is likely to include their national institutions is the fact that Poles were far more likely than the citizens of other EU member states to use adjectives like 'modern' or 'democratic' to describe the image of the European Union in their mind's eye (Eurobarometer Spring 2007: No. 67; see also Szczerbiak 2011).

Polish enthusiasm for the European project was rooted in the notion of EU membership as a long-term plan (trouncing Tocqueville's idea that democracy must always be about the present since voters are unconcerned by the vagaries of the future), which in turn also helps to explain why older Poles voted 'yes' to something they did not feel would be of use to them in the national referendum on accession—they felt that they were approving of something that would benefit their children and grandchildren (see Szczerbiak 2003). But it was also rooted in a strong emotional sense of a break with the miserable communist past—and also showing Moscow and others that a profound change had taken place.[6] Younger Poles in the 15–24 and 25–39 age brackets were the strongest supporters of EU membership, along with around three-quarters of those questioned with higher education. Interestingly, the most tangible benefit of EU membership in the opinion of Poles was the freedom to travel and work freely in other member states—this sentiment is particularly supported by the 25–39 age bracket, which is logical since it was of course this group which took advantage of this freedom in such large numbers after 2004.

Fascinatingly, there is a gulf in attitudes towards the European Union between the Polish political elite and public opinion at large. The political elite, particularly parties of the centre-Right—and after the wipe-out of the centre-Left in the parliamentary and presidential elections of 2005, the Polish elite was overwhelmingly of the centre-Right—could be described as Euro-pragmatist, Euro-realist or mildly Eurosceptic in outlook. In short, (most of) the Polish elite could see that European integration was beneficial, although they did not have a particularly strong sentimental attachment to the project as a whole. Polish public opinion, however, is strongly enthusiastic about the EU, with support levels for membership regularly topping 75 per cent compared to 49 per cent in France, 55 per cent in Germany, 37 per cent in Italy, and 36 per cent in the UK. This disconnect is further illustrated in the following section.

The EU in Polish Domestic Politics

Membership of the European Union appears to have had relatively little impact on Polish political parties or Polish domestic politics (on this see Szczerbiak and Bil 2009). No new parties have been formed to oppose the EU integration project nor have election campaigns been fought on 'European' issues. Whilst two of the major political parties of the past decade (Self-Defence and the League of Polish Families) did express Eurosceptic opinions, their electoral success in the early part of the 2000s was not evidence of a Eurosceptic reaction on the part of the Polish public, as shall be explained. This section begins with a very brief overview of the Polish party system in the 2000s before discussing the relative non-impact of the European Union on party politics and then turns to Polish public opinion and the EU.

The Polish party system, between the parliamentary elections of 2001 to the time of writing in 2010, consisted of six parties that contested and won seats in elections as follows: Civic Platform (*Platforma Obywatelska*); Law and Justice (*Prawo i Sprawiedliwość*); the Democratic Left Alliance (*Sojusz Lewicy Demokratycznej*); the Polish People's (or Peasant) Party (*Polskie Stronnictwo Ludowe*); Self-Defence (*Samoobrona*); and the League of Polish Families (*Liga Polskich Rodzin*), although the last two of these were wiped out in both the parliamentary elections of 2007 and the European elections of 2009. Table 8.3 shows their share of the votes in parliamentary and European parliamentary elections between 2001 and 2009. It should be underlined that there is no straightforward, single Left–Right cleavage based on attitude towards economic liberalism in Polish politics. In Poland, it could be said that there are effectively four axes along which the positions (ideologies is too strong a word) of political parties can be usefully mapped: a party's attitude towards the communist past; its stance on economic policy; its position on social norms; and its view of European integration.

Prior to joining the European Union in 2004, the three mainstream political parties: the Democratic Left Alliance, Civic Platform, and Law and Justice, were strongly pro-integration, especially the Democratic Left Alliance which exploited European integration as a modernizing narrative to help escape from its past as the successor to the Polish Communist Party (*Polska Zjednoczona Partia Robotnicza* or PZPR).[7] In the post-accession period, these three parties remained *largely* pro-European, although the centre-Right Law and Justice and Civic Platform both contained Euro-realist or Euro-pragmatist elements within them who lost some of their inhibitions about criticizing the EU once accession was assured. The SLD remained staunchly pro-European integration.

TABLE 8.3 Support for the main Polish political parties 2001–2009

Party name	Elections to Polish National Parliament (Sejm)			Polish elections to European Parliament	
	2001	2005	2007	2004	20.0009
Civic Platform (PO)	12.68%	24.10%	41.50%	24.10%	44.43%
Law and Justice (PiS)	9.50%	27.00%	32.10%	12.67%	27.40%
Union of Left Democrats (SLD)	41.04%	11.30%	11.00%	9.30%	12.34%
Polish People's Party (PSL)	8.98%	7.00%	8.90%	6.30%	7.001%
League of Polish Families (LPR)	7.87%	8.00%	1.30%	15.20%	n/a
Self-Defence	10.20%	11.40%	1.53%	10.80%	1.406%

Source: Państwowa Komisja Wyborcza, **http://www.pkw.gov.pl/**.

Although the two Eurosceptic, populist parties Self-Defence and the League of Polish Families won seats in national elections in both 2001 and 2005, according to Markowski and Tucker (2010) and Szczerbiak and Bil (2009), this cannot be interpreted as a result of their standing on a Eurosceptic platform. Only 4–7 per cent of voters rated the European issue as being salient to them in deciding how to vote, and the majority of supporters of all political parties (except the League of Polish Families) were supporters of EU membership. For example, in 2001 the largest number of Eurosceptic voters actually voted for the strongly pro-European SLD! Although the SLD was trounced in the 2005 election campaign, losing about three-quarters of its seats in the lower house of parliament (the Sejm), this was mostly the result of a series of corruption scandals and the fall-out from a failed healthcare reform.

European issues did, however, feature in the campaign that preceded the pre-term election of 2007, during which the Law and Justice government's handling of relations with the European Union came into question. The rhetoric and style of the incumbent government's European policy (along with that of the then Polish President Lech Kaczyński) had come under heavy criticism, particularly outside of Poland in the European media and within the Brussels village. The accusation was levelled against the government that Poland was becoming the European Union's new 'awkward partner' and that Polish influence vis-à-vis its European allies was greatly diminished—or worse, that the Polish government was becoming a laughing stock in Brussels. The government and its supporters argued that, in contrast to the humiliations of the pre-accession period, it was standing up for Poland, rather than giving in to policies not in the national interest and allowing Poland to be dominated by Germany.[8] This latter argument was part of Law and Justice's much wider critique of the post-communist Polish establishment and its call for the foundation of a 'Fourth Republic' free of the cronyism and corruption of the post-1989 Third Polish Republic.

To re-iterate, there is little evidence of the downward Europeanization of Polish domestic politics after 2004.

The Impact of EU Integration on Political Institutions and Governance

European Policymaking in Poland in the 2000s

Prior to EU accession, the coordination of EU policymaking in Poland was organized by three departments: the Ministry of Foreign Affairs (MSZ), the Office of the Committee for European Integration (UKIE), and the Office of the Prime Minister (KPRM) (Gwiazda 2006). Much of the heavy lifting was done by UKIE although accession negotiations were handled largely by the Office of the Chief Negotiator in the KPRM. In the case of the European Convention, the Polish position was put together by the MSZ. Following EU accession in 2004, and particularly after the change in government and president after 2005, this altered, albeit somewhat slowly. On 1 January 2010, UKIE merged with the MSZ—the precise rationale for its existence, preparing Poland for EU accession, having expired some time previously.

Although Article 133 of the Polish Constitution ascribes the role of 'representative of the state in foreign affairs' to the President of Poland, until the election of President Lech Kaczyński in 2005, this was not interpreted as giving the president much in the way of input in the determination of Poland's foreign policy. In consequence, Poland's centre-Left president between 1995 and 2005, Aleksander Kwaśniewski, played a limited role in formation of the government's position on the CT. To an extent, path dependency ensured that this non-partisan model of policymaking endured beyond Polish accession to the EU in 2004, although some areas of contestation between political parties existed on certain aspects of EU policymaking. President Lech Kaczyński interpreted the constitutional duties of the president in foreign policy differently from his predecessor and his position of refusing to sign the Lisbon Treaty was a reflection of this. In addition to the government and the civil service, the Polish Parliament, or Sejm, also has some input into the European policymaking process in Poland. In consequence, this section focuses on these three institutions.

The Polish Civil Service and Administrative Capacity

A factor of great importance in explaining Poland's ability to function effectively as a member state of the EU—indeed in some ways this is the crucial factor—is the administrative capacity of the Polish state. Given that the European Union is first and foremost a technocracy, the ability of a member state's civil service to coordinate European policy among line ministries is of vital importance, as is the quality of the diplomatic service that is tasked with negotiations in Brussels. In the first few years of Polish membership, the administrative capacity of the Polish state was considerably below what was needed, and it is this factor, combined with the somewhat Eurosceptic government rhetoric of the 2005–2007 period, that perhaps best explains the gaffes attributed to Poland in its early years of membership. Two of the most important explanations for Polish underperformance in administration are as follows.

First, membership produced a 'shock' to the Polish civil service, particularly in terms of the decision-making process and the professionalism and stability of the bureaucrats themselves (Grela 2003: 43). The shortcomings of the Polish institutions that created European policy included rivalry, doubling up of functions, faulty cooperation, a lack of any analysis of failures (Stemplowski 2004: 18), as well as a reluctance to share information with others (see Copsey and Pomorska 2010 and forthcoming). It might have been expected that the long and very complicated process of negotiations on accession, that the member states who joined in 2004 and 2007 had undergone, would equip them so well that their civil services would adapt swiftly and smoothly to the demands of membership, but this was not the case since there is a huge difference between doing as one is told by Brussels and actually being proactive in the European policymaking process. According to officials interviewed in Warsaw in May and June 2008, it took three or four years of membership for Poland to achieve what one official described as the necessary 'maturity' in the European Union to begin to even think about how to exercise an influence commensurate with Poland's size. One of the reasons was high rotation of the officials involved in the coordination of the European policy of Poland, as many left or were dismissed after the elections, or were employed by the European institutions at much higher salaries.

Second, policy coordination between line ministries in Warsaw was inadequate, indeed in the somewhat exaggerated words of one very senior official speaking in 2007, 'there is no policy coordination in Poland'. The changes in the overall coordination mechanisms after the accession were at first rather slow and aimed at adapting the existing institutional settings to the demands of membership, rather than creating a whole new system from scratch (for more on this, see Zubek 2005). The key element in Polish policy coordination was an absence of strategic deliberation at the highest government level about what Poland should be pushing for in the EU. As a result, the bi-weekly meetings to coordinate Poland's position in the Council of Ministers was a mechanistic exercise that was not rooted on coherent policy analysis and deliberation. To address this problem, a series of reforms were carried out, including the transfer of UKIE (*Urząd Komitetu Integracji Europejskiej* or the Office of the Committee for European Integration) to the Ministry of Foreign Affairs with full effect by 1 January 2010. An alternative solution mooted was the creation of a small European policy coordination unit within the Office of the Prime Minister, which would have had the advantage of prime ministerial backing in the arbitration and settlement of disputes between rival ministries, akin to the role played by the UK's Cabinet Office.

Polish performance did eventually improve and its image as a constructive partner in Brussels developed considerably, particularly after the 2007 election. By 2008 Poland could claim joint credit with Sweden for its initiative in helping to create an Eastern Partnership for the European Union (see Copsey and Pomorska forthcoming) and it was beginning to make its presence seriously felt as an important player in the Union. Many Polish shortcomings with regard to administrative capacity could be put down to inexperience.

The Role of the Sejm in the Making of Poland's European Policy

The Sejm is the preponderant chamber of Poland's bi-cameral parliament and, in consequence, it is vested with the lion's share of input into the European policymaking process. Parliament's control over the government in the field of European policymaking comes in two forms. First, the 'nuclear' option of a vote of no confidence in the government, which could, of course, be triggered by a European policy-related issue. It would be unusual for the government to be brought down in this way, but the option remains and is clearly more of an issue for governments with small majorities where oppositions feel they would benefit from pre-term elections. The second area of parliamentary control of European policymaking comes in the more prosaic form of the European Union Affairs Committee, which is the principal parliamentary committee concerned with the monitoring and oversight of the Polish government's activities at the European level.

The European Union Affairs Committee (EUAC) was established on 24 June 2004 for three main reasons: to monitor and oversee the Council of Minister's legislative powers at the EU level; to fulfil the requirement of the Polish Constitution (Article 95, chapter 2) that parliament should have control over the executive; and because similar committees exist in the national parliaments of other EU member states and the model seemed a good one for Poland. The EUAC does not transpose EU directives, rather its role is to compensate for the loss of parliament's legislative sovereignty as a result of accession to the EU. Its primary function is to oversee and scrutinize the Polish government's actions at the EU level.

The EUAC is intended to restore the separation of powers enshrined in the Polish Constitution (Article 10) and to help overcome the perceived democratic deficit that is alleged to result from the government-centred mode of policymaking that has tended to predominate in the European Union. Under the terms of the revised

Cooperation Act of 8 October 2010, the EUAC's opinions are supposed to form the basis for the Polish government's negotiating position on proposed EU legislation. Its decisions are in practice non-binding, although a representative of the Polish cabinet (Council of Ministers) is obliged to explain why the opinion of the EUAC is not being followed when there is a difference. Whether the EUAC succeeds in addressing the democratic deficit is therefore questionable for a number of reasons. First, it is dependent on the quality of deputies that sit on the committee, both in terms of intellectual firepower and in terms of their political punch. Given that the committee's members tend to be what could perhaps be termed 'second rank' politicians who do not hold important parliamentary posts, such as chairing other committees or leading parliamentary factions, there is a risk that the committee will not necessarily be composed of the best individuals. Moreover, given the extremely complex nature of European policymaking it is not clear that deputies will necessarily have the expertise needed to scrutinize legislation effectively.

The success of the Polish parliament in attempting to steer European policy is rather limited, although when some issues, such as the voting weights question, capture the media and public's interest, parliament tends to respond. In a sense, this is perhaps as it should be, since much of European policymaking is technocratic in nature and it is for parliament to intervene when it believes that it is in the public interest to do so—and perhaps this is the very essence of a body charged with powers of oversight rather than executive action.

The Impact of EU Membership on Public Policy

Compliance with EU Regulations and Directives

The issue of the uneven implementation of EU regulations and directives across the Union has long been of interest both to the European Commission and to academics. Prior to the 2004 accession, there were concerns that new member states such as Poland would reduce the speed and effectiveness with which rules were enforced as soon as the strict conditionality applied by the Commission was withdrawn. Preliminary evidence (Falkner et al. 2008; Falkner and Treib 2008) shows that although transposition[9] of EU directives is better than their implementation, this is not radically better or worse than in other member states of the Union.

Economic and Monetary Union (EMU)

In common with the other new member states, Poland committed to joining the single currency when it joined the European Union in 2004. Despite this, it did not actively pursue membership of the euro area in the post-accession period. The 2005–2007 Law and Justice-led government was distinctly lukewarm about joining the euro and President Kaczyński insisted that it would require a referendum of the

Polish people since a constitutional change would need to be made. Donald Tusk's 2007–2011 government was more positive about bringing Poland into the euro area and signalled his desire for Poland to join in 2011—without taking any serious action to bring this about.[10] At the time of writing, the Polish government has set a provisional target date for joining the euro area of 2015. However, in 2010 the only Maastricht Treaty criteria that Poland had met was the debt/GDP ratio, which came in at 54 per cent, 6 per cent below the 60 per cent ceiling. Were Poland to consolidate its budget, deflate the economy to keep inflation low, reduce the annual budget deficit to below 3 per cent of GDP, reduce its long-term interest rate to below 6 per cent, and join the Exchange-Rate Mechanism (now known as ERM-II), it could just about qualify for the 2015 date of entry. However, the fact that the government did not indicate when it would join ERM-II shows the relatively low priority that is given to euro area membership.

Structural and Regional Funds

In anticipation of substantial EU funding for development at the regional level, a territorial reform in 1999 brought Poland into line with many other EU member states and reduced the number of voivodships from forty-nine to sixteen. This created a clearer regional dimension of government. As a result of the budget deal negotiated by Prime Minister Kazimierz Marcinkiewicz in December 2005, Poland was slated to receive up to €67 billion worth of structural and cohesion funds from the European Union during the 2007–2013 financial perspective. In the eyes of many voters, this was the most tangible benefit of EU accession. The Polish European Commissioner from 2004–2009, Danuta Hübner, with whom this seemingly vast wave of money gushing into Poland became associated, consequently became one of the most popular politicians of the period, eventually topping the centre-Right Civic Platform party list for the European Parliament elections in 2009. It was hoped that structural and cohesion funds would drive forward the modernization of the Polish economy through the co-funding of much-needed infrastructure such as roads (especially motorways) and railways, and by subsidizing the training and re-skilling of the workforce along the road to the much-vaunted Lisbon-ready knowledge-based economy. It is too soon to say whether the structural funds in Poland have begun to meet their objectives, and there is a distinct lack of research on the actual impact of European funds (as distinct from other factors) in aiding economic development across the Union, but it is fair to say that Poland's infrastructure has benefited enormously from the capital injection that European funding has brought.

Europeanization of State Aids

As has been well-documented elsewhere (Schimmelfennig and Sedelmeier 2005; Gwiazda 2007), the effect of the European Union on domestic policies and policy-making in Poland, known as Europeanization, proceeded smoothly prior to EU accession. Although there was resistance on the part of domestic actors to EU policies, particularly in areas such as state aids, opposition could swiftly be overcome given the incentive that eventual accession to the Union provided. In the post-accession period, state aids were occasionally a source of tension between the Commission and Poland, notably in 2005 and 2006, when the Polish government was obliged to put together a credible plan for the future of Polish shipyards and the shipyards themselves required to repay several billion euros worth of aid already received. The case was particularly sensitive given that Poland's shipyards in Gdansk and Gdynia had an iconic political status as the birthplace of the independent Solidarity trade union in September 1980. The outcome of the dispute between the Polish government and the EU in this matter is perhaps testament to the even application of Community law in Poland since the Commission's decision appeared likely to lead to the closure of shipyards and the loss of jobs, notwithstanding the modest payouts that could be made under the Community's 'globalization readjustment fund'.

Polish Agriculture

The agricultural sector of the Polish economy benefited in a dramatic fashion after enlargement with the mean income of Polish farmers rocketing from 24 per cent to 54 per cent of the national average in just one year from 2004 to 2005. This was simply the result of the introduction of direct income payments—and is all the more extraordinary given that they were only at 25 per cent of the EU-15 level at the time. The size of the agricultural labour force continued to fall after accession to the Union, although it still employed around 16 per cent of the workforce full-time and around twice that percentage if part-time work is taken into consideration. Agriculture contributed only 4 per cent to Polish GDP in 2010 and although EU membership and the capital inflows that resulted from it increased productivity, it remained rather low in comparison with other member states. In the long-term, it is certain that the farmers' lobby in Poland (best represented by the PSL) and Polish governments from across the political spectrum will remain ardent supporters of the Common Agricultural Policy more or less as it stands today. Poland has no interest in renationalization of agricultural support since it does not wish to lose the valuable direct income payments. Nor does it seem likely that Poland will support the removal of price support for some types of agricultural produce from which Polish agriculture has benefited enormously since 2004.

Poland and EU External Policy: Relations with the Eastern Neighbours

Both before and since its accession to the Union, Poland had a strong interest in relations with the EU's neighbours in the East, especially the Eastern European Neighbourhood Policy (ENP) countries and Russia. Poland is an enthusiastic proponent of Ukraine's European integration and, together with some other central European states, the UK, and Sweden, has argued that Ukraine needs a membership perspective. Early Polish government initiatives in the field of relations with the Eastern neighbours bore fruit, such as the 2003 non-paper on the post-accession relationship between the EU and its Eastern neighbours—many of the ideas in this paper were integrated into the ENP. The joint Polish–Swedish paper on 'Eastern Partnership' in 2008 was indicative of a Polish desire to accelerate Ukraine's pace of European integration, as a test case for the other ENP countries. Poland is an enthusiastic proponent of enlargement to the East, particularly to Ukraine, Georgia, and Moldova (and also to Turkey and the Western Balkans).

Bilateral relations between Poland and Ukraine are closer than between any other two states lying on either side of the European Union's new Eastern border and since the mid-1990s they have forged a dynamic strategic partnership (Wolczuk and Wolczuk 2002). Poland's special role in Ukraine was highlighted during the Orange Revolution of 2004, when President Kwaśniewski so successfully used both his knowledge of Ukraine and close relations with Ukrainian politicians to help broker a peaceful settlement (Copsey 2005). In the first few years of membership at least, Poland has perceived itself as the member state best equipped to draw Ukraine closer to the EU.

With regard to two of Poland's other Eastern neighbours, Russia and Belarus, Poland's Eastern policy differs from that of many member states. First, Poland has sought to maintain dialogue with Minsk, despite the undemocratic and authoritarian practices of its president. However, Poland was relatively unsuccessful in persuading its partner member states of the importance of dialogue with the Belarusian government. Second, Poland's stance towards Russia, in common with many of the other post-communist new member states, but in contrast to other member states such as Germany or Italy, is generally more suspicious.

Given that Poland had long identified relations with the Eastern neighbours as the area of Union policy where it believed it had the most to contribute, the success of Polish diplomacy in the negotiations which led to the launch of the Eastern Partnership showed that by mid-2008 Poland had learnt important lessons about how to adapt, modify, and adjust national policy preferences in such a way that they could be rebranded as 'European' preferences and not 'Polish' preferences. In proposing the Eastern Partnership, Poland chose neutral, altruistic Sweden as its partner in presenting the proposal and put forward modest proposals that were harder for the other member states to oppose without seeming unreasonable.

In sum, the combined success of getting the Eastern Partnership on the Council agenda at the right moment, finding consensus between the member states, and winning the backing of the Commission was probably the greatest achievement of Polish diplomacy within the EU during its first few years of membership. Of course, it helped immensely that the Russian federation launched an attack on Georgia a few weeks after the proposal was put forward in 2008 which propelled relations with the Eastern neighbours to the top of the EU agenda. All the same, Russia's actions gave a degree of credibility to the Polish line on what kind of a relationship the EU should have with Russia and other post-Soviet states.

Comparisons with the Other Visegrád States

Poland's population is around 50 per cent larger than that of its three Visegrád neighbours (Czech Republic, Hungary, and Slovakia) combined. Apart from Poland, the Visegrád countries do not have, and will probably never have, the capacity to exercise influence in the EU in the way that we understood large, older member states such as France, Germany, or the UK to have done in the past. This emphatically does not mean that the Visegrád countries accept Poland's right to leadership of their regional group. Hungary is a former imperial power with a certain idea of itself and its place in the world. The Czechs and Slovaks also do not tend to appreciate their northern neighbour 'attempting to put on political weight'.

All the Visegrád countries struggled in the early years of membership to adjust to the demands that full participation in the EU brought. To date, only Slovakia has joined the euro area. In common with Poland, the administrative capacity of their national civil services was weak, as the Czech Presidency of the EU in 2009 showed to some extent. This in turn affected their negotiating strength within the EU system. There was much tough talk on the part of Visegrád politicians about the defence of their 'national interests', although in the absence of reliable cost–benefit analyses or policy impact studies they had no real means of knowing what these national interests actually were or should be.

Whilst there was little evidence across the Visegrád states of the Europeanization of their domestic politics, a few issues of purely local interest occasionally spilt onto the European agenda. Notable amongst these was the perennial issue of the alleged mistreatment of the Hungarian minority in Slovakia on the one hand, and Slovak allegations of insensitive, nostalgic Hungarian imperialism on the other. In August 2009, a one-day travel ban was issued by the Slovak government to prevent Hungarian President Sólyom from unveiling a statue of St Stephen (the first king of Hungary) in the Slovak town of Komárno. A few days later, an abortive attack was made on the Slovak Embassy in Budapest and the Slovak ambassador was intimidated. These relatively minor incidents perhaps serve best to illustrate an important wider point: that EU membership may not provide a vaccine against all nationalist sentiments, but it does at least prevent the escalation of bilateral tensions into anything more serious.

Conclusion

European integration played a crucial role in Poland's spectacularly successful transformation from communism to democracy and the market economy. The process took longer than anyone expected and Poland struggled to extract concessions from its hard-headed west European neighbours over the terms of accession. The one-sided nature of the negotiations with the EU was the cause of considerable resentment, and

Poland's natural desire to re-assert its authority after entering the EU meant that it acquired the reputation of being an awkward partner during its first few years of membership. In the period that followed Civic Platform's two successive election victories in 2007 and 2011, however, Poland showed its true colours as a mature and *communautaire* member state. In the second half of 2011, Poland ran a smooth and highly successful EU Presidency, which it could be argued symbolically marked the end of the long journey back to European normality that had begun in 1989.

FURTHER READING

Comprehensive studies focusing specifically on Poland in the EU in English remain hard to find at present but see Szczerbiak (2011) for an exception. On the negotiations between the EU and Poland, see Mayhew (1998, 2000). On Polish domestic politics and the EU, see Szczerbiak (2007) and Szczerbiak and Bil (2009). On Poland's performance as a member state within the EU see Copsey and Pomorska (2010, forthcoming). On Europeanization, see Gwiazda (2007) and on the transposition and implementation of the *acquis* see Zubek (2005). On comparisons with the Visegrád states see Malová *et al.* (2010).

WEB LINKS

http://www.poland.pl/ offers a basic guide to Polish affairs, including some information on its politics and system of government. Some information on Polish European policy is available in English from the Polish Ministry of Foreign Affairs website at **http://www.msz.gov.pl/index.php?document=2**. The Polish EU Presidency website gives an overview of the 2011 rotating Presidency at **http://pl2011.eu/**. Other good English-language sources of information include the business-oriented *Warsaw Voice* **http://www.warsawvoice.pl/WVpage/pages/index.php** as well as two of the main EU news portals which have good coverage of Poland–EU affairs **http://euobserver. com/** and **http://www.europeanvoice.com/**.

REFERENCES

Baldwin, R. and Widgren, M. (2004), 'Council Voting in the Constitutional Treaty: Devil in the Details', available at: http://hei.unige.ch/~baldwin/PapersBooks/Devil_in_the_details_BaldwinWid

Copsey, N. (2005), 'Popular Politics and the Ukrainian Presidential Election of 2004', *Politics*, 25/2: 99–106.

Copsey, N. and Pomorska, K. (2010), 'Poland's Power and Influence in the European Union: the Case of its Eastern Policy', *Comparative European Politics*, 8/3: 293–313.

Copsey, N. and Pomorska, K. (forthcoming), 'The Influence of Newer Member States in the European Union: The Case of Poland and the Eastern Partnership', *Europe–Asia Studies*.

Council of the EU (2008), 'Presidency Conclusions of the Brussels European Council 19/20 June 2008'; 11018/08.

Eurobarometer (2004–09), available at: http://ec.europa.eu/public_opinion/archives/eb_arch_en.htm.

European Commission (1996), *Eurostat Yearbook '96: A Statistical Eye on Europe*, Brussels: European Commission. These are available electronically at: http://epp.eurostat.ec.europa.eu/portal/page/portal/publications/eurostat_yearbook_2011/previous_editions.

European Commission (1997), 'Agenda 2000: The Challenge of Enlargement', COM (97) 2000, Available at: http://www.cvce.eu/content/publication/2005/7/1/353b1d52-69fb-43f4-9862-f949dcc3a4ef/publishable_en.pdf.

European Commission (1999), *Eurostat Yearbook '98/99: A Statistical Eye on Europe*, Brussels: European Commission. These are available electronically at: http://epp.eurostat.ec.europa.eu/portal/page/portal/publications/eurostat_yearbook_2011/previous_editions.

Falkner, G. and Treib, O. (2008), 'Three Worlds of Compliance or Four? The EU-15 Compared to New Member States' *Journal of Common Market Studies*, 46/2: 293–313.

Falkner, G., Treib, O., and Holzleithner, E. (2008), *Compliance in the Enlarged European Union: Living Rights or Dead Letters?* Aldershot: Ashgate.

Gazeta Prawna (2009), 'TK w sprawie sporu kompetencyjnego: prezydent sam decyduje o udziale w szczytach UE, rzad ustala stanowisko', available at: http://prawo.gazetaprawna.pl/artykuly/319182,tk_ws_sporu_kompetencyjnego_prezydent_sam_decyduje_o_udziale_w_szczytach_ue_rzad_ustala_stanowisko.html (accessed on 10 January 2010).

Grela, M. (2003), 'Polska w Unijnej Europie – Implikacje dla Polskiej Dyplomacji'. *Rocznik Strategiczny 2002/2003*, Warsaw: Wydawnictwo Naukowe Scholar, 37–44.

Gwiazda, A. (2006), 'Poland: The Struggle for Nice', in T. König, and S. Hug, (eds), *Policy-making Processes and the European Constitution: A Comparative Study of Member States and Accession Countries*, London: Routledge.

Gwiazda, A. (2007), 'Europeanization of Polish Competition Policy'. *Journal of European Integration*, 29/1: 109–31.

Hayes-Renshaw, F., Aken, Wim Van, and Wallace, H. (2006), 'When and Why the EU Council of Ministers Votes Explicitly', *Journal of Common Market Studies*, 44/1: 161–94.

Malová, D. Rybář, M., Bilčík, V., Láštic, E., Lisoňová, Z., Mišík, M. and Pašiak, M. (2010), *From Listening to Action. New Member States in the European Union*, Bratislava: Comenius University Press.

Markowski, R. and Tucker, J. (2010), 'Euroscepticism and the Emergence of Political Parties in Poland'. *Party Politics*, 16/4: 523–48.

Mayhew, A. (1998), *Recreating Europe: The European Union's Policy Towards Central and Eastern Europe*, Cambridge: CUP.

Mayhew, A. (2000), 'Enlargement of the European Union: An Analysis of the Nego-tiations with the Central and East European Countries', Sussex European Institute Working Paper, No. 39.

Schimmelfennig, F. and Sedelmeier, U. (eds) (2005), *The Europeanization of Central and Eastern Europe*, Ithaca: Cornell University Press.

Stemplowski, R. (2004), *Ksztaztowanie polskiej polityki zagranicznej. Wstęp do analizy*, Warsaw: Polish Institute of International Affairs.

Szczerbiak, A. (2003), 'The Polish EU Accession Referendum, 7–8 June 2003', Oppos-ing Europe Research Network Referendum Briefing No. 5, June.

Szczerbiak, A. (2007), 'Why Do Poles Love the EU and What do they Love About It? Polish Attitudes Towards European Integration During the first Three Years of EU Membership', Sussex European Institute Working Paper No. 98, November.

Szczerbiak, A. (2011), *Poland Within the European Union: New Awkward Partner or New Heart of Europe?*, Abingdon: Routledge.

Szczerbiak, A. and Bil, M. (2009), 'When in Doubt, (Re-)turn to Domestic Politics? The Non-Impact of the EU on Polish Party Politics', *Journal of Communist Studies and Transition Politics*, 447–67.

Wolczuk, K. and Wolczuk, R. (2002), *Poland and Ukraine: A Strategic Partnership in a Changing Europe?*, London: Royal Institute of International Affairs.

Zubek, R. (2005), 'Complying With Transposition Commitments in Poland: Collective Dilemmas, Core Executives and Legislative Outcomes', *West European Politics*, 28/3: 592–619.

ENDNOTES

* I would like to thank Vlado Bilcik, Tim Haughton, Karolina Pomorska, Alan Mayhew and Aleks Szczerbiak as well as the editors of this volume, Simon Bulmer and Christian Lequesne, for their insightful comments on earlier drafts of this chapter. Any remaining errors are, of course, the author's responsibility alone.

1. Although the Copenhagen European Council of 1993 had made it clear that the EU would eventually enlarge provided that the candidate countries met the criteria for membership.

2. 'Cohesion policy 2007–2013: Poland, the biggest beneficiary, has plan and priorities agreed with the Commission', available at: **http://europa.eu/rapid/pressReleases-Action.do?reference=IP/07/633&type=HTML&aged=0&language=EN&gui Language=fr**.

3. See: 'Polish President Wins EU Summit Bunfight', available at: **http://euobserver.com/9/26948**.

4. See Rettman, A. (2007) 'Poland to Fight for Square Roots in EU Treaty', available at: **http://euobserver.com/9/23808**.

5. This was supposed to set out clearly the respective responsibilities of the President and the Government.

6. I am grateful to Karolina Pomorska for this point.

7. The SLD made considerable efforts in the 1990s and 2000s to build bridges with West European social democratic parties through events like Tony Blair's London Progressive Governance conference in 2003, and its successor events around the world.

8. During the period of the Law and Justice-led coalition of 2005–2007, there was often a sense that the government was conflating the European Union and Germany. Neither Kaczyński twin was truly anti-European, but on many occasions Jarosław frequently

sounded anti-German, reflecting the attitude of an earlier generation's towards Poland's Western neighbour, which (whilst at least understandable in the context of German activities in Poland during the Second World War) was seriously out of step with accepted practice within the European Union. A point worth bearing in mind is that the Second World War and its impact looms larger and is much more present in the media and public and private life in Poland than in many other European countries.

9. EU regulations are directly effective and require no secondary domestic legislation to bring them into force within the member states. EU directives are binding as to the effect that is desired but leave it to the member states to decide how best a given directive's aims are to be reached, and thus further domestic legislation must be passed to bring a directive into full force.

10. Tusk made this speech on 10 September 2008, days before the collapse of Lehman Brothers that triggered the financial crisis. The pledge was subsequently modified to mean 'ready to join the euro' by 2011 and then quietly forgotten about entirely. See Financial Times, September 10 2008, available at: **http://www.ft.com/cms/s/0/6a6994b8-7f53-11 dd-a3da-000077b07658.html#axzz1JojGapfb**.

CHAPTER 9

Estonia: Excelling at Self-Exertion

Piret Ehin

▌ Summary

Estonia's dedication in pursuing integration with the EU reflects the small nation's quest to strengthen statehood in a complex international environment. In striving for maximum integration with Western institutions, Estonia has had few options but to diligently follow the rules—and hope that performance against objective criteria, not (geo)politics, determines the results. In the course of its post-communist transition, Estonia's homegrown reforms gradually gave way to policy change and institution building driven by EU accession conditionality. While adjusting national policy and institutions to EU templates has been difficult in some specific areas, the overall pattern of EU-Estonian relations is characterized by a high degree of congruence between EU and national interests and policy objectives. Estonia's track record as an EU member state suggests continued compliance with EU law and pre-accession demands. However, legal alignment has not always been accompanied by behavioural and attitudinal change.

Introduction

Within two decades of the collapse of the Soviet Union, Estonia's position in Europe has changed radically. In 1991, Estonia emerged from behind the Iron Curtain as a poor, peripheral, and obscure ex-Soviet republic. By 2011, Estonia had become one of the most integrated countries in Northern Europe in terms of membership in major international institutions and agreements. A member of both the European Union and NATO since 2004, Estonia acceded to the Schengen area in 2007 and to the Organization for Economic Cooperation and Development (OECD) in 2010. Having fulfilled the Maastricht convergence criteria amidst the global economic crisis, Estonia replaced its national currency with the euro on 1 January 2011.

The purpose of this chapter is to analyse the relationship between Estonia and the EU both before and after Estonia's accession to the union. In doing so, the chapter focuses both on the 'top-down' and 'bottom-up' aspects (see Börzel 2005) of the EU-Estonia interaction. In other words, it is concerned with the impact of European integration on domestic institutions, policies, and identities, while also enquiring about the principles and policy priorities that Estonia has sought to 'upload' to the EU arena. Because the EU's enlargement strategy and accession conditionality have been covered in detail elsewhere, the chapter places greater emphasis on Estonia's objectives and strategies as a candidate country and as an EU member state.

The chapter argues that Estonia's political elites have pursued European integration with a zeal that has, on several occasions, distinguished Estonia from the other candidate countries and new member states. Starting its quest for EU membership from a profoundly unfavourable position, Estonia has demonstrated a great capacity for self-exertion in complying with accession conditionality, striving to excel as a candidate country, and pushing for maximum functional integration once in the EU. This dedication, sustained through frequent changes of government, reflects the country's small size, understood both as a physical and a psychological condition, and the perceived vulnerability of the Estonian state in the face of external and internal threats. The country's geopolitical location and its history of foreign domination have not allowed its leaders and the public to take independent statehood for granted. While the collapse of the Soviet Union constituted a rare historical 'window of opportunity' to restore the Estonian state, rapid integration with the West became a key element in the imperative of 'ensuring the irreversibility of Estonia's independence'. Given a very strong domestic consensus on the strategic aims of democracy and a market economy, integration with the EU was largely congruent with the Estonian elite's state-building and transition strategies.

Because of the magnitude of changes that Estonia has experienced since regaining independence, assessing the role of the EU in the country's dramatic transformation is not an easy task. The drawn-out process of European integration has coincided—and been intertwined with—post-communist transition, state- and nation-building, Estonia's opening up to the world, and the broader process of globalization. In addition, the European Union has not been the only source of international influence in Estonia's state-building process. Compared to many other external actors and donors, including international organizations and foreign governments, it entered the picture relatively late, well after many of the formative decisions had been taken. Its influence, however, increased substantially over time and by the late 1990s, the EU had clearly established itself as the most important external agent driving domestic change. In light of the above, a study analysing the Europeanization of Estonia must allow for the possibility of complex interplay between external influence and homegrown orientations and reforms. Only a careful sector-by-sector analysis can distinguish which changes result from the 'transformative power of Europe', and which should be attributed to the influence of other domestic and external factors.

Overview of Estonia's Integration with the EU

Estonia is one of the smallest of EU member states. While the size of Estonia's territory (45,227 km²) is roughly comparable to that of the Netherlands or Denmark, the forested, sparsely inhabited country has a population of only 1.34 million. Among EU member states, only Cyprus, Malta, and Luxemburg are less populous. Located in Northern Europe on the shores of the Baltic Sea, Estonia is situated between greater powers that have ruled the country for most of modern history. While the Estonian culture has been shaped by centuries of contact with Western Europe as well as Russia, the Estonian language, unrelated either to Russian or to any of the major language families of Europe, constitutes the basis of a distinct cultural identity.

Today's Republic of Estonia conceptualizes itself as a restored state and claims legal continuity from the Republic of Estonia that was founded in 1918 and was occupied and annexed by the Soviet Union (USSR) in 1940. The incorporation of Estonia, Latvia, and Lithuania into the USSR was never recognized *de jure* by the majority of Western democracies. When the three Baltic states declared full independence from the Soviet Union in August 1991, international recognition—including by the European Communities and their member states—quickly followed.

Upon the restoration of independence, Estonia embarked on a radical reform programme, and is generally regarded as a model of a successful post-communist transition. Following the adoption of a liberal-democratic constitution, modelled after the constitutions of 1920 and 1938, the first democratic elections were held in 1992. The government of young reformers, led by Prime Minister Mart Laar, applied a shock therapy approach to economic restructuring and created a uniquely liberal tariff-free foreign trade regime. Soon, Estonia ranked among the leading post-communist countries in terms of per capita inflow of foreign direct investment. In 1992, Estonia became the first former Soviet republic to introduce its own currency—the kroon—which was pegged to the Deutsche Mark (since 1999, to the euro). While relations with Russia remained complicated, the country managed to free itself of Russian military bases by mid-1994. These reforms and developments made further steps towards integration with the European Union possible.

The EC/EU exerted a modest influence on Estonia's transition in the first half of the 1990s. Initially, its role was limited to supporting domestic reforms. In 1992, Estonia was included in the PHARE aid programme for the economic restructuring of Central and Eastern Europe. In 1993, the European Council in Copenhagen took a decisive step towards enlargement into Eastern Europe, declaring that 'the associated countries in Central and Eastern Europe that so desire shall become members of the European Union' (European Council 1993). The Council defined three criteria that applicants must meet to be invited to join the union. These included the stability of democratic institutions, a functioning market economy, and ability to take on the obligations of membership. In the same year, the Estonian government set up a working group to study the political, economic, social, legal, and financial implications of potential EU membership for Estonia. The final report identified a list of expected benefits, including increased security arising from closer economic and political ties to Western European countries, improved prospects for economic growth and modernization, access to advanced models for legislation and policy, as well as the reinforcement of Estonians' long-repressed European cultural identity. The process of weighing the pros and cons of possible accession culminated in Estonia submitting a membership application in 1995. By that time, a strong elite consensus on the desirability of EU accession had developed. This consensus was sustained throughout the accession period.

Estonia signed a free trade agreement with the EU in 1994. In contrast to the agreements concluded between the EU and the other post-communist countries, Estonia's agreement did not involve any transition periods. Because Estonia's liberal trade procedures did not include any import duties on industrial or agricultural products from any country, there was no need for a timetable to reduce customs tariffs. The Europe Agreement between Estonia and the EU—which provided a broader framework for cooperation—was signed in 1995, almost four years after Poland and Hungary had concluded their respective treaties.

Estonia's efforts aimed at securing an invitation to accession negotiations with the EU were significantly stepped up in 1996. The news that Estonia would not be included in the group of countries to join NATO in 1997 served as an immediate catalyst. The country's new foreign minister, Toomas Hendrik Ilves, argued that Estonia must focus on the European Union so as not to be left out of both enlargement processes (Sillaste-Elling 2009: 24). Although the prospect of receiving an invitation to EU negotiations seemed meagre, Estonia redirected its diplomatic resources and started to 'exert great efforts toward this end' (ibid.). The government drew up an Activity Plan for Joining the European Union and the civil servants laboured over providing answers to a 160-page questionnaire containing over a thousand detailed questions regarding Estonia's reform progress. In addition to the substantive preparations, Estonia carried out intense lobbying to convince EU officials and member states of its merits as a candidate country.

These efforts paid off. In 1997, the European Commission issued a positive opinion on Estonia's membership application and Estonia (together with Poland, Hungary, the Czech Republic, Slovenia, and Cyprus) was invited to start accession negotiations with the EU. The fact that the two other Baltic applicants—Latvia and Lithuania—were not included in the fast-track group caused some tensions in Baltic cooperation. However, the inclusion of Estonia demonstrated that the EU's door was open to countries of the former Soviet Union—something that, until then, had been subject to doubt. Accession negotiations between Estonia and the European Union lasted for five years and were completed in December 2002.

While the government made progress at the international negotiating table, problems appeared on the domestic front. With EU accession an imminent reality, public support for membership began to wane. A few years prior to accession, Estonia had some of the lowest levels of popular support for accession among all candidate countries. However, awareness and support-building campaigns run by the government, political parties, and various non-governmental organizations succeeded in reversing the trend. In the accession referendum, held on 14 September 2003, 66.8 per cent of the voters supported joining the EU. On 1 May 2004, Estonia became a full member of the EU together with nine other countries. Five weeks later, Estonian voters elected, for the first time, representatives to the European Parliament.

Accession to the EU provided an additional boost to the already fast-growing economies of the Baltic states. From 2000 to 2007, Estonia's real annual GDP growth averaged over 8 per cent. The global financial and economic crisis, however, affected the small, open Baltic economies particularly severely. In 2009, growth rates fell to -14 per cent in Estonia, -18 per cent in Latvia, and -15 per cent in Lithuania. Paradoxically, the worst economic crisis in the country's post-independence history offered a unique opportunity to realize a long-term aspiration. The recession brought down high inflation rates which had, during the boom years, prevented Estonia's accession to the euro-zone. In this context, qualifying for the euro hinged on Estonia's ability to keep its budget deficit within limits specified by the Maastricht criteria. By implementing ruthless budget cuts, the Estonian government was able to comply with the budget deficit criterion. The fruit of these efforts, the euro, replaced the kroon as Estonia's official currency on 1 January 2011.

Pattern of Relations with the EU

Pattern of Relations before Accession

Estonia commenced its quest for EU membership from a profoundly unfavourable starting position. While the Central and Eastern European (CEE) countries possessed at least the formal attributes of statehood, the Baltic states, as constituent parts of the Soviet Union, had to secure independence and build up basic state structures essentially from scratch before they could address the multitude of economic and social problems facing their societies (Lieven 1993: 100). As a result, they lagged several years behind the CEE countries in their reform efforts. Also, because the Baltic states stood closer to the epicentre of the earthquake that the collapse of the USSR represented, they were more severely affected by the ensuing chaos. The collapse of manufacturing and agriculture was more complete, output decline larger, and social problems more severe than in most CEE countries. By the time Estonia applied for EU membership, its GDP per capita stood at about a third of the EU average. Although the country had implemented ambitious reforms and achieved outstanding results on some fronts, it was far from having transcended the gloomy economic and social realities characteristic of early post-communism.

In addition, Estonia's geopolitical location and the complex legacies of Soviet occupation did not contribute to the country's attractiveness as a candidate for EU membership. Estonia shared a 334-kilometer border with the Russian Federation which opposed the inclusion of the Baltic states in NATO and the EU with varying levels of intensity throughout the 1990s and beyond. Estonia had an outstanding border dispute with Russia which the EU hardly wished to internalize given its commitment to building a single market surrounded by strong and stable external borders. Equally complex problems stemmed from the presence of sizable Russian-speaking minority populations in the Baltic states. As Soviet-era immigrants, who made up about a third of Estonia's population, were not automatically granted citizenship under Estonia's restitutionist citizenship policies, some 100,000 Russian-speakers had chosen Russian citizenship by the mid-1990s, while a large number did not apply for the citizenship of any country and thus became stateless persons with permanent residency in Estonia. The scope of the problem of statelessness in Estonia and Latvia remained unprecedented in the European context.

In addition to the multiple objective problems, Estonia had an image problem. Because of its absence from the map of Europe for a half-century, Estonia was largely unknown. Despite its radical break with the past, and an emerging national identity based on the negation of the Soviet experience, Estonia was viewed in European capitals as a former Soviet republic—a label with clear negative connotations, as well as potentially real political consequences in a context where the scope, timing, and limits of the EU's prospective Eastern enlargement remained hotly debated. The EU's early signals—or the lack thereof—seemed to confirm these anxieties. In 1993, the European Council in Copenhagen made no reference to the Baltic states or their prospects of becoming the associated countries that would be considered for membership, provided they fulfilled the membership criteria. Indeed, the EU decided to start free trade negotiations with Estonia, Latvia, and Lithuania and confirmed the prospects for concluding association agreements with them only after active lobbying by the Baltic governments (Kull 2009: 18).

These realities gave rise to an EU policy characterized by the following aspects. First, Estonia's strategy in the 1990s was based on doing its homework and excelling as a candidate country. In contrast to bigger powers, such as Poland, it had no other resources (e.g. size, location, political influence) to draw on. In addition, its perceived vulnerability and the precariousness of its statehood lent an expediency to its EU (and NATO) aspirations that bigger and more secure candidate countries lacked. The government set demanding timetables for the harmonization of Estonian legislation with the EU *acquis*. Preparing for periodic progress assessments by the European Commission, the Foreign Ministry 'placed great emphasis on polishing Estonia's overviews and on continually supplying the Commission with information that was as up to date and user-friendly as possible' (Sillaste-Elling 2009: 28). Indeed, driven by the fear of being left behind, Estonia tried to outperform other candidate countries and acquired, by the late 1990s, the reputation of being the 'top student' in the EU class. According to one diplomat, Estonia secured an invitation to the accession negotiations in 1997 'because we tried, in areas of importance to the EU, to be demonstrably better than the countries we thought were guaranteed an invitation' (Reinart 2009: 174).

Second, Estonia vehemently opposed the division of applicant countries into groups based on any other criteria than measurable progress in meeting the Copenhagen criteria. It contested attempts to classify the Baltic states with the other former Soviet republics, and strove for inclusion in the pre-accession framework on the same terms with the CEE countries. Estonian officials argued, with some success, that treating the Baltic states differently on account of their proximity to Russia or the history of Soviet occupation would amount to acknowledging spheres of influence.

Third, the Estonian government set out to improve the country's international image and launched a diplomatic and public relations campaign to 'sell' Estonia. In the period leading up to the negotiations, Estonian diplomats 'spent a great deal of their time battling prejudices and subjective opinions regarding Estonia' (Sillaste-Elling 2009: 29). In 1996, the government scrambled together resources to establish embassies in those European capitals that still lacked an Estonian representation. In the space of but a few months, Estonia opened missions in Dublin, the Hague, Athens, Lisbon, and Madrid. In the first half of 1997, Foreign Minister Ilves toured Europe, visiting eleven member states in six months (Sillaste-Elling 2009: 25).

In accession talks with the EU, Estonia followed the same diligent approach it had exhibited earlier, complying with accession conditionality and rarely questioning the rules. It requested transition periods or derogations only in a limited number of 'objectively difficult' areas where complying with the *acquis* either required very large investments or could have caused major political, economic, or social turbulence. The main stumbling block for Estonia in these negotiations was insufficient administrative capacity and a shortage of experts in a number of the specific policy areas discussed. Because of the small size of Estonia's civil service, a few ministerial officials often covered policy domains for which bigger countries employ entire departments.

Pattern of Relations after Accession

The double goal of acceding to the EU and NATO had dominated and defined Estonia's foreign and domestic policy for so long that the materialization of membership brought about a temporary confusion about what should constitute the country's new foreign policy objectives. After a short period immediately following accession, when political parties tried to outcompete one another in posing as the defenders of Estonia's national interests, Estonia settled on a strongly pro-European and integrationist strategy. It has been a staunch supporter of deeper integration and constitutionalization, as well as a firm proponent of further enlargement. Times of trouble for the EU do not seem to have weakened Estonia's pro-European resolve. For instance, the Estonian parliament ratified the Constitutional Treaty *after* it had been rejected by the French and Dutch publics in referendums. In 2010, Estonia's euro convergence efforts coincided with the spreading government debt crisis in the euro-zone that threatened the stability of the euro. The government led by Andrus Ansip pushed on, undisturbed by premonitions that Estonia was about to board a sinking ship.

Many observers have expressed concerns about the ability of the new member states to apply and enforce EU law, and some have doubted their continued commitment to European political norms once the carrot of membership 'has been offered and consumed' (Smith 2003: 133). Estonia's track record as a member state offers little support to these claims. There has been no roll-back on commitments made in the pre-accession period, both in terms of transposing and implementing the *acquis* as well as political conditionality. In particular, there has been no reversal of the liberalization of minority policies (e.g. simplification of the procedures for obtaining citizenship; softening of the Language Law) that occurred in the pre-accession period. This does not imply, however, that the complex task of societal integration has been completed. The shortcomings of Estonia's EU-backed minority integration efforts were amply demonstrated in the spring of 2007, when the government's decision to relocate a Soviet-era war monument from the centre of Tallinn led to massive riots by Russian-speaking youths in the Estonian capital, escalating into a major political crisis in Estonian–Russian relations. The EU's strong support to Estonia in this situation was a manifestation of precisely the sort of international solidarity Estonia had longed for, and appeared to boost domestic support for EU membership.

The fear that accession countries might lose reform momentum when no longer subject to accession conditionality appears equally unfounded in the Estonian case. The Estonian government willingly embarked on new conditional projects, such as Schengen and the euro, and has striven to earn the reputation of a rule-following, pragmatic, and reliable member state. The country has a strong track record in transposing EU directives into national law. Estonia's transposition performance in 2010 was above EU average on four of the nine indicators used to assess compliance by the European Commission, while falling below EU average on only one indicator (European Commission 2010). Estonia had no record of long overdue transposition, defined as a delay of two years or more. As of May 2010, the number of open infringement proceedings against Estonia was nineteen. This value clearly put Estonia at the lower end of the range, which varied from 111 cases in Belgium to thirteen in Cyprus (ibid.).

We can discern a fairly stable set of principles and policy preferences that the Estonian government has tried to 'upload' to the EU arena. These include, first of all, a commitment to pro-market economic policies and fiscal conservatism. Given this emphasis, Estonia's EU policies exhibit significant continuity from the neo-liberal economic formulas applied by the Laar government immediately after achieving independence. They also reflect the long-term domination of centre-Right parties in Estonian politics. In terms of specific EU issues and policies, Estonia's pro-market stance translates into prioritizing economic growth, competitiveness, and innovation, insisting on the simplification of the EU budget framework, and the need to adjust the Common Agricultural Policy to market rules. As a country that has pursued highly disciplined budgetary policies since independence, Estonia supports measures designed to strengthen the Stability and Growth Pact, including EU surveillance and coordination of national budgets. Under the broad heading of strengthening competitiveness, Estonia emphasizes the need to make better use of information and communications technologies, especially in relations between state institutions and citizens.

While Estonia's direct influence over EU policymaking remains limited, the country has sought to influence and inspire by example. During the euro-zone's debt crisis, the media portrayed Estonia as 'anti-Greece', distinguished by very low levels of public debt, a strong tradition of balanced budgets, a sizable stabilization reserve accumulated during periods of economic growth, and a seemingly limitless capacity of implementing fiscal austerity measures. In a country characterized by weak trade unions and a missing political Left, budget slashing at the onset of the recession brought no major strikes—indeed, the Estonian government's popularity remained significantly above EU average and even continued to increase. Estonia has also consciously cultivated an image of itself as a developed e-state, characterized by sophisticated and accessible internet-based services. Thus, Estonia has repeatedly made international headlines as the homeland of Skype, a pioneer in cyber defence, and the first country in the world to have instituted e-voting in national elections.

Another of Estonia's consistent preferences has been a 'principled' EU policy towards Russia. While Estonia has been a firm proponent of a common EU strategy towards Russia, it has argued that such a policy must reflect not just interests, but also values. In response to the often-heard calls to treat Russia 'as it is', Estonia's leaders have tried to remind their Western peers that Russia 'as it is' is a highly corrupt non-democracy with an appalling human rights record (Ilves 2008). Thus, Estonia has persistently criticized the EU's readiness to disconnect the building of the EU–Russia strategic partnership from the conditionality that is rigorously applied in relations with smaller countries in the EU's neighbourhood. More generally, it is now clear that the (partial and asymmetric) Europeanization of the historically burdened Baltic–Russian relationship has not helped the parties to 'put the past behind them', as optimistic end-of-history scenarios foresaw. Instead, some of the most dramatic clashes over history and memory have taken place after the enlargement of Western institutions. Indeed, Europeanization has allowed both parties to project old issues and antagonisms to new, more prominent arenas, and has intensified competition for the European recognition of conflicting historical narratives and concepts of 'self' (Berg and Ehin 2009).

On a related note, EU membership has clearly boosted Estonia's international 'action capacity' (Lamoreaux and Galbreath 2008) while also forcing it to look beyond its previously limited foreign policy horizons. Participation in the EU decision-making process routinely requires Estonia to take reasoned positions on issues that it previously regarded as being 'out of its range'. Membership has offered distinct opportunities to define a new foreign policy and an international identity that transcends the self-centred imperatives of achieving EU and NATO membership. Thus, Estonia has eagerly used the framework, discourse, and instruments of the European Neighbourhood Policy to promote democracy and reforms in the former Soviet Union, deriving a new sense of self-value from exporting its transition know-how and reform experiences to countries such as Georgia, Ukraine, and Moldova.

Impact of EU Membership on Public Opinion and Political Parties

In the domestic arena, the EU integration issue has been part of a complex dynamic between the Estonian political elite and the public. The attitudes of the Estonian public towards the EU have gone through rather dramatic changes. Roughly from 2001 to 2003, Estonia had some of the highest levels of public Euroscepticism among all candidate countries, as documented by the Eurobarometer surveys. With the accession referendum on the horizon, the political elite feared that stubborn voters would undermine a decade of efforts by vetoing accession.

The vast literature on the correlates of support for European integration suggests that attitudes towards the EU are complex, influenced by a range of factors including individual and collective utility calculations, perceived implications for national identity, cues picked up from political parties, as well as trust in domestic 'sponsors' of integration, primarily the national government. While the precise reasons for Estonians' cautious attitudes towards the EU in the pre-accession phase remain subject to debate, existing studies suggest that the low levels of public support in 2001–2003 reflected dwindling trust in the national government, concerns about the effects of accession for Estonia's sovereignty and culture, and a fear of price increases. While the elites regarded rapid integration with the West as an opportunity to bolster statehood, segments of the population resented elite eagerness in bending to the demands of Brussels, and argued that Estonia was heading from one union (the USSR) into another.

Eurosceptic mood was strongly present in the country's first-ever European Parliament elections, held in June 2004. Having secured a 'yes' to accession on the referendum, political parties could safely afford to flirt with Euroscepticism in an attempt to boost their electoral appeal among certain segments of the electorate. Many engaged in significant EU bashing. This, however, appeared to be a strategic miscalculation. With membership, the public mood had changed. In the EP polls, the voters overwhelmingly supported Toomas Hendrik Ilves, the country's former foreign minister distinguished by his EU expertise and strongly integrationist views.

Since Estonia became a full member of the EU, public support has steadily increased and, since 2007, it has been well above the EU average (see Figure 9.1). According to Eurobarometer surveys conducted between 2008 and 2010, some 70–80 per cent of Estonians believe that the country has benefitted from EU membership. The increase in support coincided with an economic boom that the country experienced during the first four years of EU membership. However, the EU-optimism of Estonians cannot be attributed to economic factors alone, as is evident from support rates well above the EU average in 2009 when the country was engulfed in one of the deepest recessions in the entire EU.

In the context of high public support for the EU, political parties have had few incentives to politicize Estonia's membership. Amidst the economic crisis, there were virtually no attempts to scapegoat the EU for the difficulties. To the contrary,

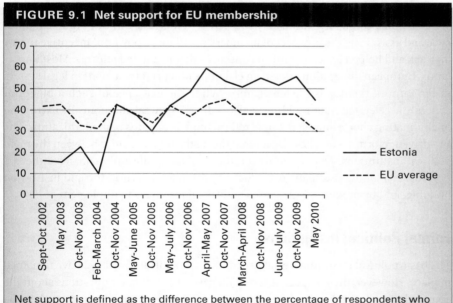

FIGURE 9.1 Net support for EU membership

Net support is defined as the difference between the percentage of respondents who think country's membership in the EU is (before accession: would be) a good thing and the percentage who think membership is a bad thing.
Q: *Generally speaking, do you think that (OUR COUNTRY)'s membership of the European Union is/ would be a good thing, a bad thing, or neither good nor bad?*

Source: Standard Eurobarometer 61–73, Candidate Countries Eurobarometer 2002, 2003.2 and 2003.4

many agreed with Prime Minister Ansip that without the EU, Estonia would be worse off. Eurosceptic forces were barely visible in the European Parliament election of 2009 which turned out to be a genuine 'second-order national contest' focusing on domestic, not European issues (Ehin forthcoming). Thus, the relatively strong presence of Eurosceptic forces in Estonian politics observed around the time of accession (Mikkel and Kasekamp 2008) seems to have been a temporary phenomenon. While the Estonian party system has not been reshaped by European integration, there is some evidence that ties to European party families and political groups have helped Estonia's weak political Left to reinvent itself. For instance, the Estonian Social Democratic Party has eagerly embraced the organizational and programmatic ideals of its partner parties in the EU (Johansson 2008).

Impact of European Integration on Political Institutions and Governance

The influence of European integration on Estonia's legal system and governance structures has been extensive. Following the restoration of independence, Estonia was faced with the immense task of building up a modern state virtually from scratch. While Estonia could have ultimately succeeded in this task without European influence and assistance, the prospect of membership offered a powerful incentive to stay on track and helped foster a political consensus that facilitated reforms. Most importantly, European integration offered an elaborate blueprint for a modern legal system in the form of the *acquis communautaire*. While the existence of such a blueprint certainly accelerated state-building, it also reduced national autonomy by narrowing or eliminating choice among possible reform models or paths of modernization. The EU-driven reform agenda has also altered the institutional balance between the main political institutions. Overall, however, the EU has significantly enhanced the 'action capacity' of the Estonian government by driving modernization and institution building, and by providing substantial additional resources to implement policy.

Formal Political Institutions

The basic political institutions established by the constitution of 1992 have remained in place. However, the prospect of accession gave rise to difficult questions about the compatibility of membership with the Estonian Constitution, which states that 'the independence and sovereignty of Estonia are timeless and inalienable', stipulates that legislative power rests with the *Riigikogu* (the national parliament), and assigns the exclusive right to issue currency to the Bank of Estonia. To avoid possible conflicts between the Estonian Constitution and European law, a constitutional amendment was prepared and approved by referendum on 14 September 2003. The amendment effectively acknowledges the supremacy of EU law, stating that, as of accession, the Constitution of Estonia applies taking into account the rights and obligations arising from the Accession Treaty. However, several legal experts regard the current solution as unsatisfactory and call for constitutional reforms that would bring the constitution into conformity with the reality of Estonia's membership in the EU.

As has often been noted, European integration tends to alter the institutional balance, strengthening the core executive at the expense of parliaments. The EU has even been accused of exporting aspects of its own democratic deficit to the accession countries (Grabbe 2001). The development of executive–legislative relations in Estonia during accession and following the attainment of membership offers some support to these arguments. Given the government's resolve to progress as quickly as possible in approximating EU legislation, the *Riigikogu* had to rapidly pass vast amounts of legislation in order not to become a bottleneck in the harmonization process. The imperative of meeting the targets stipulated in the executive-designed National Programme for the Adoption of the Acquis involved trade-offs between tempo and quality and tended to suppress political debate in the parliament. Critics argued that the role of the *Riigikogu* was limited to rubberstamping the accession policy of the government (Viks and Randma-Liiv 2005). Another problem was the concentration of EU-related information, technical expertise, and specialist knowledge in the executive. While the parliament's Committee on European Affairs, established in January 1997, was endowed with oversight functions, its ability to exercise control over the government's EU policy has been limited.

Finally, the influence of the EU is directly responsible for the creation of some new institutional bodies. In response to EU demands that Estonia adopt legislation on gender equality and general non-discrimination, the *Riigikogu* passed, in 2004, the Gender Equality Act, which created a special commissioner for gender equality. With the adoption of the new Equal Treatment Act in 2008 (after the European Commission had initiated infringement proceedings against Estonia because of a prolonged failure to comply with two important EU directives in the area), the commissioner's purview was extended to include all forms of discrimination. Reactions in the media, however, suggest that it will take time before the new institution acquires full legitimacy in the eyes of the public.

Policy Coordination

Integration with the European Union creates the need for effective policy coordination among ministries and government agencies. Estonia's domestic governance is relatively decentralized. This means that the individual ministries are endowed with significant EU-related responsibilities within their areas of competence. In the pre-accession period, these responsibilities included the harmonization of law, the implementation of the accession agenda, and advising the negotiation team on matters falling within their administrative purview (Viks and Randma-Liiv 2005). When preparing positions and decisions related to the European Union, the relevant ministers and ministries were expected to deal with the majority of EU issues in the same way as with domestic issues, as long as the steps taken remained in line with the government's general strategic objectives (Hololei 2009).

Although the position of a Minister of European Affairs was created in 1995, this arrangement was soon deemed ineffective, and responsibility for EU affairs was transferred to the prime minister. A high-level interministerial Council of Senior Officials (CSO) met regularly to develop EU strategy and review policy produced by sectoral working groups. The Office of European Integration (OEI) acted as a secretariat for the CSO and took care of day-to-day coordination. It led policy development in the approximation of legislation, identified technical assistance and training needs, and was in charge of activities designed to promote public awareness about the EU and Estonia's accession. While the Foreign Ministry remained in charge of the accession negotiations, the CSO and OEI provided input for the negotiations, ensured that information about obligations taken during the talks reached the ministries, and monitored the fulfilment of commitments. Other major elements of the system included the Estonian Mission to the EU, opened in November 1996, and the Committee on European Affairs in the Estonian Parliament, established in 1997.

Since accession, the prime minister has become the nucleus of the domestic coordination system, while the role of the Foreign Ministry has decreased. The government determines the political priorities and short-term objectives for each Presidency period. It also approves Estonian positions on EU legislative proposals and other major initiatives, as well as positions for EU Council meetings. The Coordination Council (an institutional heir to the CSO) remains the main body for interministerial cooperation. Individual ministries are responsible for preparing Estonian positions on EU legislative initiatives in their area of competence and defending these in the EU decision-making process. They are also responsible for the domestic implementation of EU law. The Permanent Representation of Estonia at the EU represents the government in the EU institutions. The role of the parliamentary Committee on European Affairs has become more institutionalized, and the committee has increasingly asserted itself in relations with the executive.

In the early days, the effectiveness of the coordination system was hampered by an insufficient formalization of procedures as well as a shortage of competent staff and a general lack of resources (Nunberg 2000: 211–6). In the longer term, however, the system has been deemed a success. Two factors in particular have contributed to its effectiveness. The first is stability: the lack of major overhauls allowed effective routines to develop and created confidence among domestic and external actors. Perhaps more importantly, a strong cross-party consensus on EU accession and 'strong political support for everything related to the EU accession' made all actors regard effective policy coordination as a top political priority (Hololei 2009: 98). Finally, the coordination mechanisms established for accession helped foster a broader coordination culture within Estonia's public administration (Viks and Randma-Liiv 2005), and served as a foundation for the establishment of new governmental structures for strategic long-term planning (e.g. the Strategy Unit in the Government Office).

Administrative Capacity

The third Copenhagen criterion—the ability to take on the obligations associated with EU membership—implied that accession countries had to adopt and implement over 80,000 pages of the *acquis communautaire* and develop the public services and public administration infrastructure necessary to support accession and membership. Among other challenges, they faced the task of developing effective systems for managing EU assistance.

Administrative capacity was the main stumbling block for Estonia in the accession process. In developing a professional and efficient public administration from the remains of the Soviet apparatus, the country faced a number of challenges including limited resources, significant human resource constraints, low qualification and high turnover of civil servants, and weak capacity for in-depth policy analysis (Randma-Liiv 2005; Nunberg 2000). A particular deficiency of the Estonian public administration in the 1990s lay in the weakness of regulatory and monitoring bodies—a peculiarity related to the country's thin welfare state and the relative lack of market intervention policies and mechanisms. On a positive note, however, the country had been relatively successful in shedding Soviet organizational and administrative culture. Because of a deliberate policy of the first post-independence governments to start administration building from a clean slate, Estonian civil servants were relatively young and an overwhelming majority of them had never worked in the Soviet administrative apparatus (Viks and Randma-Liiv 2005: 72). This discontinuity may help explain why Estonia has continuously ranked as one of the least corrupt countries in Eastern Europe.

While the EU paid great attention to the administrative capacity of the candidate countries, it did not provide a specific model for the organization of public administration (Viks and Randma-Liiv 2005: 74). Studies analysing foreign influence—and, specifically, the impact of the EU—on the modernization of Estonia's public administration suggest a complex dynamic involving a range of different actors. Overall, the major decisions 'about the design and operation of Estonian public administration have remained "home-grown"' (Randma-Liiv 2005: 484–5), although international influence has been strongly present at the level of individual programmes and policies. In the 1990s, Estonia received aid from a variety of donors, and many of the projects implemented included support and expertise for institution building. This diversity resulted in different ministries employing diverging, and occasionally, mutually incompatible models of administration. Since the late 1990s, Estonia's government institutions have become more proactive in selecting different country models and engaging in lesson drawing based on demand (Randma-Liiv 2005). The many demands and complex challenges associated with the accession process served as a catalyst for learning. In particular, the five years of negotiating accession have been regarded as the ultimate 'graduation test' for the Estonian civil service.

Another major test of public sector efficiency is the effective use of EU assistance. For the period of 2004–2006, Estonia was allocated some 800 million euros from the Structural Funds and the Cohesion Fund. The funding increased substantially under the 2007–2013 budgeting period, when the total allocation for Estonia for the seven-year period was over 3.4 billion euros (for comparison, the size of Estonia's annual national budget in 2010 was 5.4 billion euros). The main areas supported from the Structural Funds include environmental protection, transportation, entrepreneurship, research and development, and regional development. The value of EU structural policy is not limited to the direct results of the specific investment projects financed. Managing EU financial assistance has left a strong imprint on the administrative practices of the Estonian government. In particular, absorbing EU assistance has led to the introduction of strategic multiyear planning, the involvement of various interest groups in the shaping of governmental policy, improved interagency cooperation and increased transparency in the administration of financial resources (Mändmets 2009). While the central government has developed rather effective structures for managing EU funds, local governments continue to face numerous challenges in absorbing structural assistance such as low administrative capacity and problems meeting co-funding requirements. Because such problems stem, in part, from the very small size of Estonia's municipalities, the imperative of effectively using structural assistance has become an often-voiced argument for administrative-territorial reform.

Impact of EU Membership on Public Policy

While the EU's influence on Estonia's public policy has been undoubtedly extensive, the magnitude of change brought by European integration varies greatly across policy areas. The scope of domestic adjustments depends on the *thickness* or *thinness* of the *acquis* in the given policy domain, as well as the degree of congruence or 'misfit' between specific EU and national policies. This section will briefly consider three examples of how integration with the EU has affected Estonian public policy.

An example of a policy area marked by a high degree of congruence and complementarity between EU and Estonian policy objectives and measures is the Schengen acquis. The Schengen agreements, which were incorporated into the *acquis communautaire* in 1999, abolished checks on persons at the EU internal borders. To reduce the risks associated with the free movement of people, they created a number of compensatory mechanisms such as stronger controls at the external borders, the harmonization of visa, asylum, and migration policies, and enhanced cooperation between the police, immigration, and judicial authorities. For many candidate countries, implementation of the Schengen *acquis* implied a radical transformation of the liberal border regimes they had in place with neighbouring non-EU states, thus threatening good-neighbourly relations as well as the economic viability of border regions. In the Estonian case, however, Schengen was highly consistent with the general foreign policy orientation and security strategies pursued by the government since the early 1990s. After the restoration of independence in 1991, Estonia's Eastern border with the Russian Federation became laden with a range of functions crucial for consolidating sovereignty and statehood. A 'strong' Eastern border was seen as an important security prerequisite for completing the separation from Russia, guaranteeing territorial control, stopping illegal immigration, keeping out organized crime, preventing drug trafficking, and smuggling (Berg and Ehin 2006: 62). While the Estonian state began to demarcate the border immediately after achieving independence, and had introduced a complete visa regime already in 1992, building up a modern border infrastructure and services where none previously existed was an extremely costly undertaking. As the construction of the 'area of freedom, security, and justice' shifted to the centre of the policy agenda, the EU developed financial instruments to finance actions at its new external borders. Between 2004 and 2006, the EU channelled 77 million euros into upgrading and modernizing Estonia's border infrastructure and information systems, developing diplomatic and consular representations, and training border guards and customs officials. Thus, Estonia's accession to the Schengen area in 2007 represented an important landmark in bringing the physical realities on the ground into conformity with the mental maps of belonging and security that had guided Estonian foreign policy since independence.

An example of a 'misfit' between pre-existing Estonian practice and EU policy is trade policy. Following the restoration of independence, Estonia rapidly implemented one of the most liberal unilateral free trade regimes in the world. This rapid shift from 'high protection within the Soviet command economy to almost *complete free trade a la Hong Kong*' (Feldmann and Sally 2002: 79) clearly distinguished Estonia from other reformers in Central and Eastern Europe. Until 2000, the country imposed no import duties on any product imported from any country. Accession to the EU Customs Union, however, implied adhering to the EU's common external trade policy and applying the common external tariff. Harmonization with EU rules led to a complex 'multi-track' trade policy already in the late 1990s, when Estonia negotiated World Trade Organization (WTO) membership while holding EU accession talks. Following EU accession in May 2004, the external trade relations of Estonia with third countries became subject to the EU Common Commercial policy. As issues falling under this policy are the exclusive competence of EU institutions, Estonia gave up decision-making powers in this realm. All bilateral free trade agreements between Estonia and third countries were revoked. Overall, this made Estonia's trade policy markedly more regulated and protectionist. According to one source, Estonia had to introduce 10,794 new tariffs and adopt a number of non-tariff barriers, such as quotas, subsidies, and anti-dumping duties to comply with accession requirements (Tupy 2003: 2). Changes were greatest in the realm of agriculture where Estonia had to implement the whole arsenal of tariffs, price supports, export subsidies, and other measures associated with the Common Agricultural Policy.

Our final example focuses on an issue that has generated significant international interest as well as domestic controversy—i.e. EU influence on Estonian minority policies. Minority rights were a political condition of membership included in the Copenhagen criteria, and thus constituted an integral part of EU accession conditionality. When the EU included Estonia in the pre-accession framework, it began to monitor its policies towards ethnic minorities. However, it is important to note that by doing so, the EU was promoting a norm which is not codified in the *acquis* and thus has no basis in EU law (Sasse and Thielemann 2005: 660). Furthermore, minority rights is a relatively unclear norm which offers a wide room for interpretation: for instance, there is as yet no agreed international definition of what constitutes a national minority (Sasse 2005: 675). The definitional problems were amplified in the Baltic context where Soviet-era settlers constituted neither indigenous minorities nor immigrants in the usual sense of these terms. Finally, the political doctrine of legal restorationism embraced by the Estonian state and enshrined in its constitution effectively placed EU attempts to influence Estonia's minority policies in a 'legal straightjacket' (Pettai and Kallas 2009). Defining Estonia as a state that has been restored following a period of illegal occupation, this doctrine served as the basis for excluding Soviet-era settlers from citizenship. While the EU and its member states may not have liked its implications, they could hardly contest the doctrine of legal restorationism in principle—not least because it was entirely congruent with the West's long-term policy of non-recognition of Soviet annexation of the Baltic states.

Thus, instead of directly challenging Estonia's citizenship policy and its underlying principles, the EU tried to soften its effects. Indeed, EU carrots and sticks proved to be pivotal in bringing about a gradual liberalization of Estonia's minority policies. While Estonia had ignored repeated demands by the Organization for Security and Cooperation in Europe (OSCE) to grant citizenship to stateless children, it backed down once the European Commission raised the issue in its 1997 assessment of Estonia's membership eligibility. In other areas, such as language legislation, the EU succeeded in relating the status of minorities to the norm of non-discrimination which, in contrast to minority rights, has a strong basis in EU law. Importantly, the EU coupled its conditionality with generous financial assistance to measures designed to facilitate the integration of Russian-speakers into the Estonian society (primarily, Estonian language training). Yet, despite progress made in the naturalization of non-citizens, the Estonian government's programme of societal integration backed by EU efforts is now seen as a partial failure. Interethnic tensions loomed large in the 'Bronze Soldier' crisis of spring 2007, and since then, Russian-speakers' trust in the political institutions of the Estonian state has reached an all-time low. These developments have contributed to the likelihood that a significant number of Estonia's Russian-speakers will choose the strategy of 'exit,' now increasingly understood in terms of out-migration to other EU member states (Hughes 2005).

Conclusions

Although the Baltic countries account for a fraction of the EU economy and population, their inclusion in the EU was a 'high politics' decision with strong security and geopolitical implications—even when accession talks appeared to revolve around technical alignment in 'low politics' areas. Because European integration has been a game where much is at stake, Estonia tried hard to excel as a candidate country. Following accession, Estonia has been an unproblematic member state with a strong implementation record, and a 'pace-setter' among the new member states in terms of pushing for closer integration. Estonia's elites have submitted to the multiple conditionalities of accession, Schengen, and the EMU without protest. Indeed, successfully climbing the ladder rungs of various conditionalities has been a way for the small nation to achieve 'external valorization' of its 'qualitative virtues' (Goetschel 1998: 19) that, in turn, has helped boost Estonia's battered national ego. Estonia has, however, been very sensitive to signs that the rules are not applied in the same manner to big and small countries or old and new member states. Indeed, it can be argued that Estonia is a fan of clearly defined and evenly applied carrot and stick schemes that minimize the influence of politics. A small state like Estonia can master conditionality by self-exertion and cunning strategy, but has few means to correct the power imbalance that characterizes its interaction with bigger countries. The realization that big power politics represents the form of European decision making least conducive to its interests has turned Estonia into an avid supporter of supranational solutions and greater powers of the European Commission.

Estonia has been a step ahead of its Baltic neighbours in pursuing integration with the EU. In 1997, it was included in the first group of countries to start negotiations with the EU, while Latvia and Lithuania began accession talks only in 2000. In 2010, Estonia qualified for membership in the EMU, while Latvia's and Lithuania's accession to the euro-zone has been postponed. While Estonia has pursued more stringent budgetary policies than the other two, and was thus better positioned to weather the economic crisis, it has also had more luck in its bid to adopt the common currency. In 2006, Lithuania missed the Maastricht inflation criterion by 0.06 percentage points while fulfilling all other convergence criteria. Despite high hopes to the contrary, the EMU door remained closed.

Another important difference between Estonia and the other two Baltic states lies in the extent to which the political elites have been able to carry the public. Estonia has higher rates of popular trust in state institutions and higher levels of overall regime satisfaction than Latvia or Lithuania (Ehin 2007; TNS Opinion & Social 2010). There are also notable differences in how the Baltic publics assess their countries' membership in the EU. While both Estonia and Latvia had low support for prospective membership in 2001–2003, Estonia's public opinion turned strongly pro-EU after accession; while the Latvian public became increasingly pessimistic and now ranks among the most sceptical in the entire EU. The Lithuanian public is generally supportive of EU membership, although support is not as overwhelming as in Estonia. Thus, Estonia is distinguished from its Baltic neighbours by comparatively high levels of satisfaction with both the domestic political regime as well as the country's membership in the EU. One possible explanation for this observed divergence is the emergence of a 'virtuous circle' in Estonia where the perception of reform success translates into greater confidence in the elites that, in turn, lowers the political costs of carrying out new, potentially difficult reforms.

Not all is well, however. Beneath Estonia's image as a successful transition country and an international achiever lie a number of unresolved political, economic, and social problems, including poverty, inequality, and social and interethnic tensions (Lauristin and Vihalemm 2009). While Estonia's political elites have prioritized compliance with various EU conditionalities, ensuring the balanced development of the country may require shifting of attention to those areas of public policy where the *acquis* is thin and the transformative power of Europe limited.

 FURTHER READING

Comprehensive studies focusing specifically on Estonian–EU relations are hard to come by. A volume edited by Pettai and Zielonka (2003) offers a multi-faceted overview of the challenges faced by the Baltic states on their road to EU membership. Raik (2003) examines how EU integration influenced the construction of democracy in Estonia. A volume edited by Berg and Ehin (2009) examines the evolution of Baltic–Russian relations in the context of European integration. Various edited volumes include chapters dedicated to Estonia's relationship with the EU, such as Pettai and Kallas (2009) on the minority issue, or Mikkel and Kasekamp (2008) on party-based Euroscepticism. Finally, a highly informative collection of reflections and recollections by Estonian diplomats and officials directly involved in the EU accession process has been compiled by the Estonian Ministry of Foreign Affairs (2009).

 WEB LINKS

HTTP://estonia.eu/ is a general information gateway to Estonia state, society, economy, culture and science. The website of the Government Office of Estonia (**http://valitsus.ee/en/government-office**) contains useful information, including official documents, on the Estonian government's EU policy. The Press and Information section of the Estonian Ministry of Foreign Affairs website (**http://www.vm.ee**) contains press releases and Foreign Ministers' speeches since 1996. Detailed information on Estonia's changeover to the euro is available at **http://euro.eesti.ee/**.

ACKNOWLEDGEMENTS

Parts of this chapter are based on research supported by the Estonian Science Foundation (grant no. 7903).

REFERENCES

Berg, E. and Ehin, P. (2006), 'What Kind Of Border Regime is in the Making? Towards a Differentiated and Uneven Border Strategy', *Cooperation and Conflict* 41/1: 53–71.

Berg, E. and Ehin, P. (eds) (2009), *Identity and Foreign Policy: Baltic-Russian Relations and European Integration*, Farnham, Surrey: Ashgate.

Börzel, T. (2005), 'Europeanization: How the European Union Interacts with its Member States', in S. Bulmer and C. Lequesne (eds), *The Member States of the European Union*, Oxford: Oxford University Press, 45–69.

Ehin, P. (2007), 'Political Support in the Baltic States 1993–2004', *Journal of Baltic Studies* 38/1: 1–20.

Ehin, P. (forthcoming), 'Estonia', in D. Viola (ed.), *Routledge Handbook of European Elections* (London: Routledge).

European Commission (2010), *Internal Market Scoreboard No. 21*, Luxembourg: Publications Office of the European Union.

European Council in Copenhagen (1993), *Conclusions of the Presidency, 21-22 June 1993* (SN 200/93), available at http://www.europarl.europa.eu/enlargement/ec/pdf/cop_en.pdf (last accessed 7 January 2011).

Estonian Ministry of Foreign Affairs (2009), *Estonia's Way into the European Union* (Tallinn), available at http://web-static.vm.ee/static/failid/052/Estonias_way_into_the_EU.pdf (last accessed 22 September 2010).

Feldmann, M. and Sally, R. (2002), 'From the Soviet Union to the European Union: Estonian Trade Policy, 1991–2001', *The World Economy* 25/1: 79–106.

Goetschel, L. (1998), 'The Foreign and Security Policy Interests of Small States in Today's Europe', in L. Goetschel (ed.), *Small States Inside and Outside the European Union: Interests and Policies*, Boston: Kluwer Academic Publishers, 13–31.

Grabbe, H. (2001), 'How Does Europeanization Affect CEE Governance? Conditionality, Diffusion and Diversity', *Journal of European Public Policy* 8/6: 1013–31.

Hololei, H. (2009), 'Estonia's Preparations for Accession to the European Union 1995–2004: The Domestic Co-ordination System', in *Estonia's Way into the European Union*, Tallinn: Estonian Ministry of Foreign Affairs, 90–8.

Hughes, J. (2005), '"Exit" in Deeply Divided Societies: Regimes of Discrimination in Estonia and Latvia and the Potential for Russophone Migration', *Journal of Common Market Studies* 43/4: 739–62.

Ilves, T. H. (2008), 'The Challenge in Europe: Only Unified Can the West Defend Itself. But First it Must Heal the Transatlantic Rift', *Newsweek* 31 December 2008, available at http://www.newsweek.com/2008/12/30/the-challenge-in-europe.html (last accessed 9 January 2011).

Johansson, K. M. (2008), 'External Legitimization and Standardization of National Political Parties: The Case of Estonian Social Democracy', *Journal of Baltic Studies* 39/2: 157–83.

Kull, C. (2009), 'Relations between Estonia and the European Union in the Period Leading up to the Invitation to Accession Negotiations in 1997', in *Estonia's Way into the European Union*, Tallinn: Estonian Ministry of Foreign Affairs, 16–22.

Lamoreaux, J. W. and Galbreath, D. J. (2008), 'The Baltic States as "Small States": Negotiating the "East" by Engaging the "West"', *Journal of Baltic Studies* 39/1: 1–14.

Lauristin, M. and Vihalemm, P. (2009), 'The Political Agenda During Different Periods of Estonian Transformation: External and Internal Factors', *Journal of Baltic Studies* 40/1: 1–28.

Lieven, A. (1993), *The Baltic Revolution: Estonia, Latvia, Lithuania and the Path to Independence*, New Haven, CT: Yale University Press.

Mändmets, R. (2009), 'The Impact of European Union Financial Assistance on Estonia's Accession and the Lessons Learned', in *Estonia's way into the European Union*, Tallinn: Estonian Ministry of Foreign Affairs, 76–81.

Mikkel, E. and Kasekamp, A. (2008), 'Emerging Party-Based Euroscepticism in Estonia', in P. Taggart and A. Szczerbiak (eds), *Opposing Europe: The Comparative Party Politics of Euroscepticism: Case Studies and Country Surveys*, Oxford: Oxford University Press, 295–313.

Nunberg, B. (2000), 'Ready for Europe. Public Administration Reform and European Union Accession in Central and Eastern Europe', *World Bank Technical Paper 466*, Washington D.C.: World Bank.

Pettai, V. and Kallas, K. (2009), 'Estonia: Conditionality Amidst a Legal Straightjacket', in B. Rechel (ed.), *Minority Rights in Central and Eastern Europe: Success or Failure of EU Conditionality*, London: Routledge, 104–18.

Pettai, V. and Zielonka, J. (eds)(2003), *The Road to the European Union: Estonia, Latvia, and Lithuania*, Manchester: Manchester University Press.

Raik, K. (2003), *Democratic Politics or the Implementation of Inevitabilities? Estonia's Democracy and Integration into the European Union*, Tartu: Tartu University Press.

Randma-Liiv, T. (2005), 'Demand- And Supply-Based Policy Transfer in Estonian Public Administration', *Journal of Baltic Studies* 36/4: 467–87.

Reinart, V. (2009), 'Full Membership', in *Estonia's Way into the European Union*, Tallinn: Estonian Ministry of Foreign Affairs, 169–75.

Sasse, G. (2005), 'Securitization or Securing Rights? Exploring the Conceptual Foundations of Policies towards Minorities and Migrants in Europe', *Journal of Common Market Studies* 43/4: 673–93.

Sasse, G. and Thielemann, E. (2005), 'A Research Agenda for the Study of Migrants and Minorities in Europe', *Journal of Common Market Studies* 43/4: 655–71.

Sillaste-Elling, K. (2009), 'The Path to Receiving an Invitation for Accession Negotiations – the Critical Years of 1996–1997', in *Estonia's Way into the European Union*, Tallinn: Estonian Ministry of Foreign Affairs, 23–9.

Smith, K. (2003), 'The Evolution and Application of EU Membership Conditionality', in M. Cremona (ed.), *The Enlargement of the European Union*, Oxford: Oxford University Press, 105–40.

TNS Opinion & Social (2010), *Standard Eurobarometer 73: Public Opinion in the European Union*, available at http://ec.europa.eu/public_opinion/archives/eb/eb73/eb73_en.htm (last accessed 6 January 2011).

Tupy, M. (2003), 'EU Enlargement: Costs, Benefits, and Strategies for Central and Eastern European Countries', *Policy Analysis* 489, Washington DC: Cato Institute.

Viks, K. and Randma-Liiv, T. (2005), 'Facing the Challenges of EU Accession: Development of Coordination Structures in Estonia', *International Journal of Organization Theory and Behavior* 8/1: 67–102.

CHAPTER 10

Romania–Uneven Europeanization

Dimitris Papadimitriou and David Phinnemore

▌Summary

The road to EU membership in 2007 was a long and hard one for Romania, a country that struggled more than most after 1989 to overcome the legacies of the communist era and move beyond the faltering reform efforts of successive post-Ceauşescu governments. While public and political opinion remained solidly in favour of integration, and ultimately membership, institutional fluidity, poor administrative capacity, political factionalism, and corruption meant that processes of domestic adaptation faced significant challenges. Although the prospect of EU membership provided a strong and vital stimulus for reform, the resulting Europeanization was—and has remained—less than even and in many cases underdeveloped. Key obstacles to domestic reform have to varying degrees persisted post-accession and helped strengthen arguments that the EU admitted Romania prematurely. These obstacles have also hampered Romania's ability to define and upload its preferences into the EU policymaking process.

Introduction

The study of Romania's preparation for, and experience of, European Union (EU) membership offers a critical test case for the transformative effects of enlargement-led Europeanization. Romania, alongside Bulgaria, entered the EU on 1 January 2007, nearly three years later than the Central and Eastern European (CEE) 'front-runners', but well ahead of its Balkan neighbours whose EU membership ambitions still remain in limbo. Romania's delayed accession to the EU has reflected both the legacies of its incomplete post-communist transition and the country's uneven pattern of domestic reform since the early 1990s. At the same time, Romania's strategic importance—both in terms of its size and its geographical proximity to the conflicts of former Yugoslavia and Transnistria—produced powerful incentives for the EU to keep Bucharest on its 'enlargement radar'. The fact that Romania was often regarded as 'too big to fail' had important implications both for the projection of enlargement-led Europeanization (and the application of EU conditionalities within it) and the way in which adaptational pressures were internalized and mediated domestically. It also highlighted the highly politicized nature of the process of EU enlargement that went beyond the 'mechanical' transposition of EU rules in the applicant countries.

Romania's interaction with the EU over the past twenty years has been shaped by such contingencies. As the country's political elites have struggled to match their pro-EU rhetoric with a credible reform agenda, officials in Brussels have remained sceptical of Romania's ability to assume in full its EU membership responsibilities. This suspicion has necessitated a considerable degree of policy entrepreneurship on behalf of the EU in order to enhance its monitoring mechanisms and extend its conditionalities even after Romania's actual entry into the club. The introduction of 'post-accession conditionality' and the launch of the Cooperation and Verification Mechanism for the immediate post-accession period introduced a new dimension in the relationship between the EU and its member states that is likely to affect all future entrants.

Along with assessing the Europeanization effects associated with Romania's effort to begin and, later, complete its accession negotiations with the EU, this chapter will chart some of the early evidence of the impact of EU membership on Romania's politics and public policy. Through this analysis we aim to identify key factors that have affected both the 'production' and 'reception' of the Europeanization pressures associated with the EU's most recent enlargement. In doing so, we also seek to ascertain the extent to which Romania has been able to generate a consistent and sustainable momentum of domestic reform that will help the country complete—in both appearance and substance—its return to the European mainstream.

From Marginalization to Membership: The Changing Pattern of Romania's Relationship with the EU

Ever since the overthrow of its communist dictator, Nicolae Ceauşescu, in December 1989, the relationship between Romania and the EU has been a turbulent one. The country's transition to democracy has been delayed and idiosyncratic, shaped largely by the machinations of its reincarnated communist elites rather than a clear rupture with the previous communist order. The dominance of Ion Iliescu's National Salvation Front (FSN) over the domestic political scene during the first half of the 1990s was met with widespread scepticism in Brussels which often expressed open frustration with the slow progress of economic reform, and voiced concern over the commitment of Romania's ruling elite to democracy and human rights. As a result, the country's 'return to Europe' faced considerable complications which resulted in its effective separation—alongside Bulgaria—from the CEE 'frontrunners' of EU membership hopefuls. Evidence of this 'relegation' became apparent at an early stage with the later signing of a Europe (association) Agreement in February 1993 which, unlike similar agreements signed with Hungary, Poland, and Czechoslovakia in 1991, contained specific suspension clauses in case of human rights violations by the Romanian government (Papadimitriou 2002).

Despite the delay, the country's inclusion into the association process allowed the authorities in Bucharest to claim a victory of sorts; namely that Romania had remained on the radar of the EU as a potential candidate for membership. Yet, Romania's rapprochement with Brussels was driven primarily by security considerations rather than a recognition that the pace of domestic reform conformed to European expectations. The outbreak of the Yugoslav wars and their repercussions for the wider Balkans increased pressure on the EU to pursue an 'open door' policy as a means of stabilizing this volatile region. Romania and Bulgaria became the main beneficiaries of this imperative. Yet, the EU's deepening commitment to its eastwards enlargement—as demonstrated by the elaboration of the Copenhagen criteria in 1993 and the publication of the pre-accession strategy at the Essen European Council in 1994—failed to mobilize sufficient impetus for reform amongst Romania's ruling elites.

By the time the government of Nicolae Văcăroiu submitted the country's EU membership application in June 1995, Romania had very little to show to its European partners. Following months of political instability, a potential breakthrough was offered in late 1996 when the Party of Social Democracy in Romania (PDSR) (the successors to the FSN) was defeated—for the first time since 1989—in both presidential and parliamentary elections. The new political landscape—particularly the arrival of a new liberal-minded president, Emil Constantinescu—was warmly welcomed by EU member states and officials. Yet, as the new coalition government soon found itself paralysed by internal disputes and political miscalculations, earlier hopes for a rapid acceleration of the domestic reform process were dashed. The country's economic and political stalemate had become painfully apparent by the time the Commission, in 1997, published its opinions on the membership applications submitted by CEE governments. In its assessment of Romania's progress, the Commission concluded that the country did not meet the economic criteria set out at Copenhagen and was unlikely to do so in the medium-term. With regard to the political criteria, the Commission's assessment was ambiguous. While recognizing that, under the new government of Victor Ciorbea, democratic standards had improved, Romania was judged only to be 'on its way' (European Commission 1997: 114) to meeting the criteria, one of only two applicants not to be given an unequivocal green light in this area. The other was Slovakia.

Despite the protestations of the Romanian government over the EU's alleged discriminatory practices, the Commission's opinion was upheld by the Luxembourg European Council in December 1997 which formalized a 'two-tier' approach to the upcoming accession negotiations. As a result Romania—alongside Bulgaria, Latvia, Lithuania, and Slovakia—was placed on the backburner of the EU's enlargement process, having not been invited to open accession negotiations in March 1998.[1] The EU's Luxembourg decision dealt a major blow to the ambitions of Romanian political elites who had consistently failed to match their increasingly evident pro-EU rhetoric with the necessary actions on the ground. Romania's exclusion was also testament to the limitations of the EU's early enlargement strategy to penetrate the dense network of domestic 'veto points' that prevented the country from making a clean break from its communist past.

In the face of a weak domestic advocacy for reform, Romania's EU membership hopes were, once again, boosted by external events and wider security considerations (Phinnemore 2010). The outbreak of the Kosovo war in spring 1999, coupled with the arrival of Günter Verheugen as Commissioner for Enlargement in the autumn of that year, recast much of the EU's enlargement strategy in Central and Eastern Europe. The new Prodi Commission was now pointing to a 'greater awareness of the strategic dimension to enlargement' and called for a rethink of the 'two-tier' approach to the EU accession negotiations introduced at Luxembourg (European Commission 1999: 4). The Commission's new thinking and enhanced activism became a critical driving force behind the decision of the Helsinki European Council in December 1999 to open accession negotiations with Romania, alongside the other CEE applicants excluded at Luxembourg. Before the decision could be taken, however, Romania had to commit to improving its record in economic reform. As the Commission had recently noted, Romania was still not a functioning market economy. Moreover, the state of economic reform in Romania was 'very worrying' and had 'at best, stabilised' over the last year (European Commission 1999: 23). Romania would have to adopt a medium-term economic strategy—to be drawn up with significant external assistance—to address the country's macroeconomic problems. It also had to commit to the structural reform of its childcare institutions.

Commitments having been made, the Helsinki European Council announced the opening of accession negotiations in early 2000 and thereby, for the first time, offered Romania a credible membership perspective. The opening of accession negotiations in March 2000 appeared to have a galvanizing effect on its political elites, unleashing a momentum for domestic reform previously unseen in the country's post-communist history. Ironically, much of the drive towards the fulfilment of EU conditionalities, within the context of the accession negotiations, was provided by the PDSR, Romania's former reform 'pariahs' who had re-invented themselves as a mainstream social democratic party on a mission to capitalize on Romania's full integration into the EU. Indeed, under the premiership of Adrian Năstase (2000–2004) an ambitious—yet, often contested (see EU Membership and Public Policy below)— programme of domestic reform was launched aiming to secure full EU membership for Romania by 2007.

The reforms bore fruit and eventually, in October 2004, the European Commission recognized Romania as a 'functioning market economy'. This helped pave the way for the formal conclusion of the accession negotiations in December 2004. However, Romania's administrative capacity and political will to implement effectively the EU's *acquis* was openly questioned. In particular, a number of key areas of major concern were identified, including the government's Schengen Action Plan, the reform of the judiciary, anti-corruption measures, police reform, and state aids to its steel industry. To address these concerns, the EU introduced a range of enhanced conditionalities and additional instruments for monitoring compliance that had never previously been deployed in the context of EU enlargement. These included the introduction of super-safeguard clauses in the treaty governing Bulgaria's and Romania's accession to the EU. These provided the EU with the opportunity to postpone Romania's membership by one year if there were 'serious shortcomings' in the fulfilment of the country's obligations to the EU (Official Journal 2005: Article 39).[2] Whereas in the case of Bulgaria the activation of such a super-safeguard clause required a unanimous decision by the Council, Romania's clause could be triggered by a qualified majority of EU member states in specific instances. In addition, Romania's progress in the identified priority areas became the subject of intense scrutiny by the Commission, which produced three separate monitoring reports in the eighteen months between the signing of the Treaty of Accession on 25 April 2005 and the country's actual entry into the EU on 1 January 2007 (see Box 10.1).[3] Even though the EU agreed to admit Romania and Bulgaria as scheduled, concerns persisted about the need for judicial reform and improved efforts to root out corruption. Consequently, an unprecedented Cooperation and Verification Mechanism was introduced providing for continued Commission monitoring of both countries for compliance with a series of benchmarks in these areas. This monitoring process still remains in operation four years after Romania officially became a member of the EU (see Romania's EU Membership Experience in Comparative Perspective below).

Romania's accession to the EU has been the culmination of a long and often difficult relationship that was inextricably linked to the complexities of its post-communist

BOX 10.1	Romania: from marginalization to membership

February 1993:	Romania signs a Europe Agreement with the EU.
February 1995:	EU–Romania Europe Agreement enters into force.
June 1995:	Romania applies for EU membership.
July 1997:	Publication of the Commission Avis. Romania fails to meet the economic Copenhagen criteria and it is 'on its way' to meeting the democratic criterion.
December 1997:	The Luxembourg European Council does not invite Romania to begin accession negotiations with the EU.
November 1998:	Commission publishes first Regular Report on Romania. Six more follow (at yearly intervals).
December 1999:	The Helsinki European Council agrees to open accession negotiations with Romania.
February 2000:	Accession negotiations between the Commission and the Romanian government begin.
January 2002:	Romanian citizens gain visa-free access to the Schengen area.
March 2003:	Romania signs protocol governing accession to NATO.
May 2004:	EU enlarges to include ten new member states.
December 2004:	Romania's accession negotiations with the EU closed. The European Council sets 1 January 2007 as target date for accession.
February 2005:	Commission issues positive opinion on Romania's Treaty of Accession.
April 2005:	EP adopts Moscovici Report and approves Romania's accession to the EU.
April 2005:	Romania's Treaty of Accession into the EU is signed.
October 2005:	Commission publishes first Monitoring Report on Romania.
June 2006:	Commission publishes second Monitoring Report on Romania.
September 2006:	Commission publishes third Monitoring Report on Romania.
December 2006:	EP approves Leonard Orban as first Romanian member of the Commission
January 2007:	Romania accedes to the EU.
June 2007:	Commission publishes the first Cooperation and Verification report on Romania. Regular reports follow (at six-month intervals)

transition and the politicized nature of the EU's enlargement strategy. At one level, Romania's delayed and somewhat contested entry into the EU can be seen as a manifestation of its 'Balkan exceptionalism' and a testament to the resilience of its domestic 'veto points' in resisting the adaptational pressures of enlargement-led Europeanization. It is also arguable that the country's eventual membership of the EU has been primarily the result of wider security considerations (e.g. relating to the volatility in the Balkans) and the inclusive dynamics of eastern enlargement, rather than the outcome of a consistently applied process of conditionality (see Phinnemore 2010). Yet, the country's considerable progress in the aftermath of the Helsinki European Council decision also points to the significant pulling power of the EU and its empowering effects on domestic reform coalitions. In this sense the Romanian experience provides further evidence that EU conditionality works more effectively by reference to anticipated rewards rather than an opportunity for domestic elites to reflect on failure. In subsequent sections this chapter explores in more detail the extent to which a reform momentum emerged during Romania's pursuit of EU membership and has been sustained in the aftermath of the country's accession to the EU.

Public Opinion and Party Politics

Party political attitudes in Romania towards European integration and EU membership have evolved over the last twenty years from a state of apparent agnosticism through rhetorical and substantive enthusiasm to selective critical engagement with EU priorities. During the early post-communist period, Romanian political parties were clearly consumed by domestic agendas and generally paid little attention to European integration. A cross-party declaration supportive of eventual membership was adopted in 1995 but the commitment was more rhetorical than it was reflective of a substantive appreciation of what accession either required or entailed (Papadimitriou and Phinnemore 2008). Subsequently, particularly as avowedly more reformist governments took office after 1997, as public opinion showed itself to be overwhelmingly in favour of integration with the EU, and as Romania became involved in the EU's 'inclusive and evolutive' accession process, launched following the 1997 Luxembourg European Council, the country's political parties became more actively supportive of accession and vied to present themselves as pro-EU and pro-integration. Indeed, by the time they regained power in 2000, the former PDSR, and now Party of Social Democrats (PSD)—the successors to the National Salvation Front that had been responsible for the laboriously slow progress with economic and political reform during the first half of the 1990s—had not only declared its 'European vocation' but also adopted a distinctly more 'European' and pro-integration discourse. It would be under PSD stewardship of the country that most progress would be made with accession negotiations.

While the PSD's period in office has attracted harsh criticism of the levels of persistent corruption and allegations that Romanian politicians deceived the EU into believing that accession-related reforms were being pursued when in fact they were not (Gallagher 2009), it nevertheless delivered formal progress. The period also saw integration with the EU gain prominence in domestic politics, especially as the PSD sought unsuccessfully to capitalize on the progress in negotiations during the 2004 parliamentary and presidential elections. These took place as accession negotiations entered their final few weeks. Indeed news that the negotiations had been technically closed came coincidentally an hour before a live television debate between the two remaining candidates in the second round of the presidential election: Prime Minister Năstase (PSD), and Traian Băsescu of the Justice and Truth (DA) alliance of National Liberals (PNL) and Democrats (PD). Năstase nevertheless lost. Băsescu's victory led to the third alternation of power in post-communist Romania. It was therefore representatives of the new DA-led government that, once negotiations had been concluded in December 2004, assumed responsibility for implementing the necessary reforms to secure accession on 1 January 2007 and thereby avoid the possibility of a one-year delay.

Throughout this pre-accession period, Romanian public opinion remained the most optimistic about the benefits of membership. As late as autumn 2003, Eurobarometer was reporting that more than four-fifths of Romanians were anticipating that membership would be 'a good thing'. Only 10 per cent of respondents viewed the prospects of membership negatively (see Table 10.1). Few observers were therefore surprised that, when a package of constitutional reforms which included provisions allowing for accession to the EU and to the North Atlantic Treaty Organization (NATO) was put to a referendum in October, 89.7 per cent of voters gave it their backing. Much commentary at the time suggested that the figures reflected a high degree of naïve optimism about the benefits that would flow from membership. Indeed, as Romania entered the final stages of accession negotiations and the terms of membership became known, respondents became more cautious in expressing optimism. By the time the Treaty of Accession was signed in April 2005, the proportion of respondents who believed that membership would be a 'good thing' had decreased to 64 per cent. The figure remained high compared to public opinion in all other CEE states but nevertheless had declined, and significantly so by Romanian standards.

Nevertheless, at the time, accession to the EU retained widespread support both publically and among Romania's political parties. Such support was important for keeping the new government focused on pursuing reforms concerning the judiciary, the police, corruption, state aids, and the steel industry. Failure to meet obligations contained in the Treaty of Accession could have triggered a delay to the date of accession. Progress with reforms was such that accession did take place on 1 January 2007. It did so against a backdrop of increasingly acrimonious infighting within the government and especially between the prime minister, Călin Popescu-Tăriceanu (PNL), and the president, Băsescu. Indeed within a matter of months of gaining EU

TABLE 10.1 Romanian public opinion prior to EU membership

Membership viewed as:		2001	2002	2003	2004	2005	2006
		Autumn	Autumn	Autumn	Spring	Spring	Spring
'a good thing'	Romania	80	78	81	70	64	62
	Candidates	59	61	62	58	54 EU(25)	55
'neither good nor bad'	Romania	11	8	10	17	22	23
	Candidates	22	22	22	23	27 EU(25)	28
'a bad thing'	Romania	2	2	2	3	6	7
	Candidates	10	10	10	11	15 EU(25)	13

Note: Candidates = Candidate average including CEE countries, Cyprus, Malta and Turkey.

Sources: Candidate Countries Eurobarometer (2002:1; 2002:2; 2003:4; 2004:1) (via http://ec.europa.eu/public_opinion/cceb_en); Eurobarometer 65 (Spring 2006) and Eurobarometer 63 (Spring 2005) (via http://ec.europa.eu/public_opinion).

membership, the DA coalition had disintegrated. First the foreign minister was forced to resign, and then Tăriceanu dismissed the remaining PD members of his government. An important casualty was Monica Macovei, the minister of justice widely respected within the EU for her efforts to reform the Romanian judicial system and root out corruption more generally. Provoking a genuine constitutional crisis was the government's decision to seek the impeachment of the president.[4] In the absence of accession conditionality, political disorder now appeared to reign. The government certainly had no appetite for proceeding as planned with elections for Romania's thirty-five seats in the European Parliament (EP). These were postponed from May until November 2007.

The rescheduled EP elections provided little comfort for anybody concerned that the political chaos might alienate voters. Just under a quarter (24.96 per cent) of the electorate voted. Those who did turn out voted overwhelmingly for pro-EU parties following an election campaign which did at least focus in part on European issues (Maxfield 2008). Indeed the vote of the nationalist Greater Romania Party (PRM) fell to below 5 per cent and it therefore lost its presence in the EP.[5] The winner was Băsescu and the PD, which secured thirteen of Romania's thirty-five seats in the EP. The PSD gained ten seats pushing the ruling PNL into third place (see Table 10.2). Two years later, at the 2009 EP elections, the PD's share of the vote and MEPs dropped significantly despite a merger with the Liberal Democrats. The PSD increased its share of the vote by one-third. Notable gains were also registered by the Hungarian Democratic Union (UDMR) and the PRM. With the exception of the PRM gains, the results were similar to those in the parliamentary elections a year previously. The turnout in the EP election (27.7 per cent compared to 39.2 per cent) was, however, markedly lower, a reflection of electoral fatigue as well as a relatively quiet campaign, albeit one in which issues with a European dimension—global recession, economic migration, and Russia and Georgia—did feature (Maxfield 2009). The presence of such issues should not distract from the fact that the election focused more on domestic concerns than on EU policy matters. In this respect, the Romanian experience of EP elections is not dissimilar to the experiences of most other member states. Romania, nevertheless, does stand out with regard to the generally observable trend of increasing support for EU-critical or Eurosceptic parties. Although the PRM talks of a 'Europe of Nations' (Maxfield 2009), it, as the most obviously nationalist party in Romania, can hardly be regarded as Eurosceptic. Such parties do not exist in Romania, a reflection of the continued support for membership in the country.

Indeed, during the three years since accession, Romanian public opinion regarding membership has remained relatively stable with around two-thirds of respondents to Eurobarometer polls continuing to indicate that membership is both a 'good thing' and has benefited the country (see Table 10.3). Certainly until 2010, Romanian public opinion's support for membership remained well above the average for the EU as a whole. With the consequences of recession being felt, and reflective of a feeling that EU membership was not providing the protection from the global

TABLE 10.2 EP elections in Romania

	2007	2007		2009	
	Observer MEPs	%	Elected MEPs	%	Elected MEPs
Democrat Party (PD)	5	28.8	13	-	-
Liberal Democrats (PLD)		7.8	3	-	-
Democratic Liberal Party (PDL)		-	-	29.7	10
Social Democrats (PSD)	12	23.1	10	31.1	11
Conservative Party	2	2.9	0		
National Liberals (PNL)	6	13.5	6	14.5	5
Hungarian Democratic Union (UDMR)	3	5.5	2	8.9	3
Democratic Forum of Germans in Romania	1	-	-	-	-
Independent	1	-	-	-	-
Independent – László Tőkés	-	3.4	1	-	-
Independent – Elena Băsescu	-	-	-	4.2	1
Greater Romania Party (PRM)	5	4.2	0	8.7	3
Others	-	10.8	0	2.9	0
Total	**35**	**100.0**	**35**	**100.0**	**33**

Notes: PD and PLD merged in 2007 to create the Democratic Liberal Party; PSD ran a joint list with the Conservative Party in 2009.
Source: Maxfield 2007, 2009.

financial crisis many had hoped, support levels dropped by ten percentage points to come much closer to the EU average. The reality of EU membership being less than a panacea for the country's ills was evidently hitting home. All the same, the tendency was for mild agnosticism as opposed to opposition to EU membership. Only 11 per cent of respondents could bring themselves to say that membership was actually 'a bad thing'.

For many voters, the EU continues to offer a higher degree of stability than afforded by domestic politics. The 2008 election saw a fragile coalition of the new Democratic Liberal Party (PDL), which comprised the former PD and a number of

TABLE 10.3 Romania in the EU—public opinion

		2007	**2008**	**2009**	**2010**
		Spring	Spring	Spring	Spring
Membership viewed as:					
'a good thing'	Romania	67	64	66	55
	EU (27)	57	52	53	49
'neither good nor bad'	Romania	24	23	22	30
	EU (27)	25	29	28	29
'a bad thing'	Romania	5	6	6	11
	EU (27)	15	14	15	18
Country has:					
'benefited from membership'	Romania	69	65	63	56
	EU (27)	59	54	56	53
'not benefitted from membership'	Romania	13	15	19	26
	EU (27)	30	31	31	35

Sources: Eurobarometer 73 (Spring 2010); Eurobarometer 71 (Spring 2009); Eurobarometer 69 (Spring 2008); Eurobarometer 67 (Spring 2007) (via http://ec.europa.eu/public_opinion).

defectors from the PNL, and PSD take office. Within a year, however, the PSD had left the coalition. Political crisis ensued as Băsescu saw successive nominees for the post of prime minister rejected by parliament. Eventually the previous, and by now caretaker, prime minister, Emil Boc (PDL), was called on to form a minority government with the UDMR. Adding to the sense of perpetual political crisis was the disputed outcome of the Presidential election in December 2009. Contrary to most opinion and exit polls, Băsescu emerged the victor in the second round run-off against Mircea Geoana (PSD), Romania's foreign minister during the accession negotiations. The PSD maintained the result was rigged and set about challenging the result in the Constitutional Court. A partial recount ensued before the Constitutional Court rejected the PSD's request for a re-run.

The Romanian political scene since accession to the EU has been dominated by government instability and constitutional crises. While this has had no direct impact on party political and public attitudes towards the EU, it has severely undermined the capacity of successive governments to ensure that Romania meets its obligations as a member of the EU both generally and more specifically regarding judicial reform and the fight against corruption under the Co-operation and Verification Mechanism. Moreover, it has distracted attention away from efforts to gain from the opportunities afforded by membership to move from policy-taker to policy-shaper.

EU Membership and Public Policy

Both the management of the accession negotiations and the adjustment to the demands of EU membership have posed a major governance challenge for the Romanian authorities. The collapse of the Ceaușescu regime in 1989 left the country with a public administration starved of resources and expertise and ridden with corruption and favouritism. Romania's troubled transition to democracy ever since has been unable to create a conducive environment for much needed administrative reform at all levels of government. The extreme politicization of the civil service during the transition years has created major problems of institutional fluidity and a very high turnover of personnel. Despite strong EU pressure to insulate the public administration from the worst excesses of party political dominance, a number of high profile legislative initiatives in this direction have failed to produce the desired effects (Papadimitriou and Phinnemore 2008). As a result, the lack of transparent public policy rules and proper administrative oversight have created a fertile ground in which widespread corruption and instances of 'state capture' have been common occurrences.

A similar pattern of instability has also been witnessed at the very heart of the Romanian government. The process of coalition building—a key feature of all post-communist Romanian governments—against the background of a severely underdeveloped party system, has necessitated short term deals which produced paralysing effects for the government. This has been evident in the overwhelming experimentation with the size and structure of the Romanian Cabinet and the array of administrative bodies directly responsible to it (or personally to the PM). The many 'institutional houses' of the European policy portfolio (as part of the Foreign Ministry, the Ministry of Regional Development, as a separate Ministry of European Integration and, more recently, as an independent service under the PM) offer the most striking example in this respect. Since the early 2000s successive Romanian PMs have sought to address the centrifugal tendencies within their government through the establishment of stronger 'core-executive' institutions (such as Deputy PM offices, a Government Secretariat, and a Chancellery, to mention just a few), but the results have been rather disappointing in the face of coalition infighting and fundamental Cabinet disagreement over policy direction (OECD 2005).

Against this background, it is arguable that whereas the EU—both in the context of the accession negotiations and the post-accession period—has been able to discipline the agenda for domestic reform in terms of targets, it has been unable to change the underlying logic of Romanian public policymaking based on factionalism and 'closed' networks of power. The same also holds true with regard to the EU's effect on the heavily centralized nature of the Romanian state. In the run up to Romania's accession to the EU, a number of laws passed through parliament (1999, 2001, and 2004) aimed at decentralizing state power and preparing the country for the management of the EU's structural funds. Many of the new structures created, however, have been severely under-resourced and expertise on EU-related matters remains very limited (causing significant problems with the absorption of EU funds since 2007). In any event, few of these regional institutions were invested with sufficient powers to be able to claim either a meaningful representative function for the local people or strategic local resource to counter-balance the influence of the government in Bucharest (Turnock 2001).

Romania as a Policy Taker: Implementing the EU *Acquis*

Given the relatively short period of time since Romania's accession into the EU, a full assessment of its implementation record is not yet possible. In the yearly data on infringement proceedings against member states published by the Commission, Romania does not appear as one of the most frequent offenders. In 2009 Romania received twenty-nine formal notices and six reasoned opinions by the Commission whilst it was referred to the European Court of Justice just once (European Commission 2010c, statistical annexes I to III). These figures placed the record of the Romanian government half-way down the league of offenders amongst new EU entrants, which, as a group, fare considerably better than most of the EU's more established members.

The substantial discrepancies in the number of infringement proceedings between new and old member states may be partly explained by the nature of accession negotiations that led to eastern enlargement. Unlike previous enlargement rounds, the Commission's 'screening process' prior to the opening of each of the thirty-one chapters of accession negotiations subjected domestic legislation in the CEE countries to an unprecedented level of scrutiny. By the end of the accession process, the Commission's hard line over the granting of derogations from EU law had effectively ensured that the new member states had transposed the vast majority of the EU *acquis* well before they were actually admitted. The profound power asymmetries between the two negotiating parties ensured that the EU's wishes on this front met little opposition. The relatively 'thin' legal framework in most CEE countries (given its radical overhaul since the collapse of Communism) also provided fertile ground for the transformative power of enlargement-led Europeanization in re-shaping the legal underpinnings of public policy.

Yet, formal indicators on the implementation of EU law may obscure some of the limitations of enlargement-led Europeanization to change established 'ways of doing things'. Romania is a good example in this respect. The country's well-documented problems with corruption and the erratic administration of justice prompted the EU to launch the Cooperation and Verification Mechanism in 2007 as a means of applying pressure on the Romanian government to pursue further reforms in these areas post-accession. Although neither field officially forms part of the *acquis*, their all-encompassing effects on the functioning of the Romanian society and especially the country's public administration produced serious 'horizontal' problems for the implementation and upholding of EU law. In its regular reporting since the inception of the mechanism, the Commission has grown increasingly frustrated with the progress made by the Romanian authorities. A recent Commission report claimed that Romania has taken a number of backwards steps in this regard during the course of 2010 (European Commission 2010b).

The Romanian Economy: From Bust to Boom ... to Bust?

Romania's trajectory of economic transition since the early 1990s has broadly followed that of its democratic consolidation: uneven in its pace, and uncertain in its direction. At an early stage, the process of economic reform was shaped by the terrible legacies of the Ceauşescu regime and the unwillingness of the FSN to engage in a fundamental reconfiguration of the country's economic structures (and the political power associated with them). Subsequently, as the failures of economic gradualism became apparent, the appetite for change grew stronger, but its success was ultimately compromised by an unsuccessful policy mix, poor implementation and political infighting within successive coalition governments (Papadimitriou and Phinnemore 2008).

Romania's inclusion in accession negotiations in 2000 was arguably the single most important factor in kick-starting the process of previously stalled economic reform. By that time, the PDSR had returned to power with a dominant position in the Romanian parliament. Moreover, the new prime minister, Năstase, was keen to project his party's newly-found reform credentials and economic managerialism. Although his stewardship of the Romanian economy was not without its critics (particularly over his government's timidity to reduce the role of the state in the economy), the period 2000–2004 marked a significant improvement of all macroeconomic indicators and registered some of the highest GDP growth rates in Europe (see Table 10.4). It also paved the way for the Commission eventually recognizing Romania as a functioning market economy. By the time accession negotiations were concluded in December 2004, the Romanian economy was experiencing an unprecedented boom fuelled largely by domestic consumption and investment growth (assisted by an explosive expansion of credit).

The return to dysfunctional coalition politics following the 2004 election had an adverse effect on the Romanian economy. Although GDP growth remained strong during the first few years of EU membership, fiscal discipline was compromised, leading to a growing budget and a current account deficit problem. Early criticisms by both the International Monetary Fund (IMF) and the Commission (European Commission 2005: 29) were ignored by the Tăriceanu government amidst a rather misplaced euphoria that high GDP growth could mask the country's macroeconomic imbalances.

The structural weaknesses of the Romanian economy, however, became vividly exposed as the result of the global financial crisis in late 2008. As Romania's banking sector (90 per cent of which was under foreign ownership) experienced severe liquidity problems, lending to the private sector collapsed, leading to a rapid contraction of

TABLE 10.4 Romania: Main economic indicators (% of GDP, unless stated otherwise)

	1999	2000	2001	2002	2003	2004	2005	2006	2007	2008	2009	2010
GDP growth	-1.2	2.4	5.7	5.1	5.2	8.5	4.2	7.9	6.3	7.3	-7.1	0.8
Government borrowing	-4.4	-4.7	-3.5	-2.0	-1.5	-1.2	-1.2	-2.2	-2.5	-5.4	-8.3	-8.0
Inflation (HICP)	45.8	45.7	34.5	22.5	15.3	11.9	9.1	6.6	4.9	7.9	5.6	4.3
Current account balance	-4.1	-3.9	-5.6	-1.1	-4.9	-5.8	-8.9	-10.6	-13.6	-12.7	-4.2	-4.4
Unemployment rate	7.1	7.3	6.8	8.6	7.0	6.1	7.2	7.3	6.4	5.8	6.9	8.5
Domestic demand	-4.0	4.9	6.9	4.4	8.7	12.9	8.6	14.2	15.9	8.2	-14.4	0.6
Labour productivity growth	3.5	3.2	6.8	17.0	5.3	10.3	5.8	7.1	5.9	7.6	-6.2	2.5
External debt	21.7	22.5	25.7	24.9	21.5	18.7	15.8	12.4	12.6	13.3	23.7	n/a
Real effective exchange rate (1999=100)	100	129	142	116	118	112	148	159	189	192	180	n/a

Figures for 2010 are estimates.
Source: Eurostat.

the construction, manufacturing, and service sectors which had previously driven economic growth in the country. As a result, Romania's GDP fell by 7.1 per cent in 2009; the national currency (the *leu*) depreciated against the euro by nearly 30 per cent; and the capitalization of the Bucharest stock exchange decreased by over 80 per cent from its 2008 peak (see Table 10.4; International Monetary Fund 2009). With the Romanian economic bubble now burst, the government was left with no option but to seek external support. In May 2009, a financial assistance package worth €19.9 billion was agreed by the government and its major international creditors including the IMF (providing over half of the total assistance), the EU, and the World Bank (International Monetary Fund 2009). The conditionalities attached to this assistance brought a programme of severe cuts in wages (-25 per cent) and pensions (-15 per cent) which sparked a wave of protests in the spring of 2010). The Commission forecast Romania's return to modest GDP growth in 2010, although it warned that the key to economic recovery would be the government's ability to continue with its fiscal consolidation programme (European Commission 2010a: 132–4). This would be no small undertaking for Romania's fragile governing coalition.

Foreign Policy: Still to Shape EU Policy

In terms of foreign policy, there can be little doubt that the accession process transformed Romania's relations with its neighbours by promoting peaceful conflict resolution, cooperation, and interdependence (Bechev 2009). Since accession, however, Romania has been unable to fulfil its initial aspirations to shape EU policies both generally and regarding key neighbours such as Moldova and Ukraine. The same applies to the Black Sea where pre-accession Romanian-sponsored proposals for an EU 'Black Sea Strategy' (e.g. Asmus *et al.* 2004) were generally overlooked and instead the EU adopted a less substantial 'Black Sea Synergy'. Romania's limited impact on EU foreign policymaking can in part be attributed to the ambiguities surrounding the overall direction and substance of EU relations with these countries. As Bechev (2009) observes, however, it also reflects a combination of Romania's limited administrative capacity to define and upload its preferences into the EU policymaking process and unresolved issues in bilateral relations.

This combination has been particularly evident with regard to EU–Moldova relations, the promotion of which has long been a priority for Romania. However, bilateral relations between Bucharest and Chisinau remained strained for much of the second half of the 2000s as the presidencies of Vladimir Voronin in Moldova equated Romanian efforts to support the country's integration into the EU with a bid to undermine Moldovan statehood. Relations almost reached breaking point in April 2010 when Voronin accused the Romanian government of fomenting civil unrest in Chisinau following the Moldovan general election. The Romanian ambassador was expelled and visa requirements introduced for Romanian citizens. In response, the Romanian government further eased the requirements for Moldovans to obtain Romanian—and thus EU—passports, a move that simply intensified accusations from Voronin and his supporters that Romania was determined to undermine Moldova's independence. The easing caused concern among Romania's EU partners, in part because it was announced without any consultation, more importantly because of the potential it created for increased migration into the EU. Since the creation in August 2010 of a pro-EU 'Alliance for European Integration' government in Chisinau, relations have improved with the Romanian government providing technical, administrative, and political support to the new Moldova government. Its fragility, exacerbated by the failure to elect a president, has, however, meant that there has been only limited domestic capacity to make progress in pursuing closer integration. Four years of membership have seen Romania thwarted in its efforts to bring its north-eastern neighbour significantly closer to the EU.

The Moldovan case also reveals an appreciable willingness on the part of successive Romanian governments to prioritize bilateral relations over a collective EU approach to Chisinau. The domestic salience of relations with Moldova demands as much. The same can be said of Romania's outlier position on Kosovo, whose independence Bucharest refuses to recognize for fear that it will lead to intensified claims for territorial autonomy from ethnic Hungarians in Romania (Linden 2009). The possibility of granting autonomy remains a taboo domestically with many politicians and officials convinced of its destabilizing potential. Romanian governments would rather resist conforming to the majority position than risk a domestic political backlash and possible internal instability.

Romania's EU Membership Experience in Comparative Perspective

Many of the challenges that Romania has faced in coming to terms with EU membership have also been experienced to varying degrees by other 'new' members. But to what extent is the range of Romania's experiences peculiar to it or symptomatic of particular characteristics? Two obvious comparisons to make are with Poland, the other medium-sized CEE country that joined the EU as part of eastern enlargement, and Bulgaria, with which Romania has long been informally coupled throughout the process of integration with the EU and alongside whom Romania joined the EU in 2007. The Polish and Romanian experiences of membership offer interesting contrasts in terms of their respective successes in shaping EU policy and their willingness to doggedly pursue a national preference (see also Chapter 8). On the former, both Poland and Romania have suffered setbacks in their efforts to promote increased engagement with neighbours. The developments in the European Neighbourhood Policy (ENP), and in the EU's engagement with the Black Sea region, have fallen short of both countries' expectations, particularly as Ukraine and Moldova still lack anything approaching a clear membership perspective. However, whereas Poland has achieved some success in promoting an enhancement to the ENP through the Eastern Partnership initiative, and a more proactive EU stance towards Belarus, Romania has proved far less successful in increasing beyond 'synergy' the EU's engagement with the Black Sea region. In part this reflects varying domestic capacities to define and then upload realistic preferences. It also reflects, however, Poland's more effective pursuit of partners to promote initiatives. As Bechev (2009: 222) argues, Romania has failed to take 'decisive steps' in framing agendas and crafting coalitions. On the other hand, however, Romania has not sought to use its size and status as one of the larger 'new' member states to demand concessions from its fellow member states. By contrast, Poland in 2007 unsuccessfully threatened to veto progress towards the adoption of what became the Treaty of Lisbon. Its demand was the retention of an inequitable voting system that gave it almost a disproportionately large number of votes—twenty-seven compared to twenty-nine each for France, Germany, Italy, and the United Kingdom—despite having already agreed, in previous negotiations on the Constitutional Treaty, to abandon both it and an alternative 'square root' voting system. Romania has—so far at least—spared itself the political loss of standing that befell the Polish government in 2007.

Indeed Romania has generally adopted a low profile in EU debates. The same can be said of Bulgaria, which like Romania, has yet to develop the necessary administrative capacities and networks to be able to make a noticeable impact on EU policy-making. Neither, however, is wholly absent from policy-makers' thinking on the future of the EU. Both countries in fact continue to cause concern within the Commission and among other member states because of the limited progress that they have made in pursuing judicial reform and rooting out corruption. Hence questions continue to be raised about their respective capacities to assume their obligations as EU members. Indeed, in December 2010, these concerns led France and Germany to call for a postponement of any decision to admit Romania—and Bulgaria—to Schengen. The perception persists that they secured membership prematurely. Unless domestic reform records improve, such a perception threatens to stigmatize their membership for years to come.

In turn it has implications for the future of enlargement. Indeed, the abiding legacies of the 2007 enlargement to include Romania and Bulgaria are undoubtedly an increase in 'enlargement fatigue' and an evident tightening of the conditionality requirements would-be member states have to meet (İçener et al. 2010). Croatia and, to a lesser extent, Turkey have certainly had to meet greater demands as a consequence of negotiating EU membership in the shadow of Romania's accession. Moreover, Romanian membership of the EU has intensified debate about the consequences, particularly in the light of the furore in 2010 surrounding French moves to remove Roma from France, of granting free movement to the citizens of acceding states, and admitting these states to the Schengen area. It has also focused attention on the progress that acceding states have made in integrating marginalized and often disadvantaged minority groups, once again increasing the demands being made of would-be members before they can be admitted.

Conclusion

The Romanian case reveals a mix of results regarding the transformative effects of enlargement-led Europeanization. On the one hand, the prospect of gaining entry into the EU acted as a major driver for economic and political reforms in the country from the late 1990s onwards. Without the incentive of membership, the EU's conditionalities and its guidance—and irrespective of the criticisms regarding their deployment—economic and political reform in post-communist Romania is likely to have remained piecemeal and stalled. On the other hand, however, and as critics pointed out at the time, and most observers and EU officials have come to acknowledge since, there has often been a considerable mismatch between the commitment to reform and the reality on the ground. Notable examples include judicial reform and the combating of corruption where domestic resistance to the adaptational pressures emanating from the accession process has proved—and continues to prove—resilient. This has not only tarnished Romania's image within the EU, but it has also done little to assure doubters that high levels of popular support for EU membership reflect a genuine understanding of what membership entails or what is required of Romania to make a success—whether economically, politically, or socially—of being a member of the EU.

It is certainly too early in the country's membership to offer a definitive assessment of what sort of EU member Romania is or will be. The evidence so far suggests a country still coming to terms with the obligations and realities of membership and struggling to evolve from policy-taker to policy-maker. Much of this stems from underdeveloped institutional capacity and the tensions within the country's executive that have led to the initial years of membership being undermined by domestic political disfunctionality. Romania's efforts to present itself to other members as a reliable partner have been further constrained by its shaky record in complying with the demands emanating from the Cooperation and Verification Mechanism and concerns about its reaction to strategically important developments in its neighbourhood, such as Kosovan independence and the political uncertainties in Moldova. All this is not to deny that Romania has responded to Europeanization pressures associated with accession. It certainly has. Romania would not have been admitted to the EU otherwise. The first four years of membership have, however, very much confirmed that the extent of the country's Europeanization remains uneven and less developed than in many of the other participants in the EU's two-stage eastern enlargement. This has consequences not only for Romania but also the future of enlargement.

FURTHER READING

There are few comprehensive studies of Romania–EU relations. Papadimitriou and Phinnemore (2008) and Gallagher (2009) provide the most detailed academic analyses to date of Romania's accession to the EU. A special issue of the journal *Perspectives on European Politics and Society* (10:2, 2009) contains a number of articles examining the process and early years of accession. An edited volume by Phinnemore (2006), compiled shortly before accession, offers a range of perspectives on Romania and its forthcoming membership of the EU. On the post-communist period more generally, and Romania's efforts at reform in the context of European integration, see Pridham (2005), Gallagher (2005), and Light and Phinnemore (2001).

WEB LINKS

www.gov.ro is the homepage of the Romanian government and provides links to all ministries. The Ministry of Foreign Affairs website (**http://www.mae.ro/en**) contains some useful pages on Romania's position within the EU, as does the homepage of the Romanian Permanent Representation to the EU (**http://ue.mae.ro**) which offers links to more general information on Romania too.

REFERENCES

Asmus, R. D., Dimitrov, K., and Forbig, J. (eds) (2004), *A New Euro-Atlantic Strategy for the Black Sea Region*, Washington D.C.: The German Marshall Fund of the United States, http://209.200.80.89//doc/GMF_book.pdf.

Bechev, D. (2009), 'From Policy-Takers to Policy-Makers? Observations on Bulgarian and Romanian Foreign Policy Before and After EU Accession', *Perspectives on European Politics and Society*, 10/2: 210-24.

European Commission (1997), *Commission Opinion on Romania's Application for Membership of the European Union*, DOC/97/18, 15 July.

European Commission (1999), *Composite Paper: Reports on Progress Towards Accession of each of the Candidate Countries*, Brussels, 13 October.

European Commission (2005), *Romania: 2005 Comprehensive Monitoring Report*, Brussels, COM (2005) 534 final, 25 October.

European Commission (2010a), 'European Economic Forecast-Spring 2010', *European Economy*, 2/2010, Brussels.

European Commission (2010b), *Report on the Progress in Romania under the Co-operation and Verification Mechanism*, COM(2010) 401 final, 20 July.

European Commission (2010c), *27th Annual Report on Monitoring the Application of EU Law (2009), Statistical Annexes I to III*, COM(2010) 538, 1 October.

Gabanyi, A. U. (2005), *Rumänien vor dem EU-Beitritt*, Berlin: Stiftung Wissenschaft und Politik.

Gallagher, T. (2005), *Theft of a Nation: Romania since Communism*, London: Hurst and Co.

Gallagher, T. (2009), *Romania and the European Union: How the Weak Vanquished the Strong*, Manchester: Manchester University Press.

Içener, E., Papadimitriou, D., and Phinnemore, D. (2010), 'Continuity and Change in the European Union's Approach to Enlargement: Turkey and Central and Eastern Europe Compared', *Southeast European and Black Sea Studies*, 10/2: 207–23.

International Monetary Fund (2009), *Press Release*, No. 09/148, 4 May.

Light, D. and Phinnemore, D. (eds) (2001), *Post-Communist Romania: Coming to Terms With Transition*, Basingstoke: Palgrave Macmillan.

Linden, R.H. (2009), 'The burden of belonging: Romanian and Bulgarian foreign policy in the new era', *Journal of Balkan and Near Eastern Studies*, 11/3, 269–91.

Maxfield, E. (2007), 'Europe and Romania's Presidential Impeachment Referendum, May 2007', *EPERN Referendum Briefing*, No. 15, October, http://www.sussex.ac.uk/sei/.

Maxfield, E. (2008), 'The European Parliament Elections in Romania, November 24th 2007', EPERN *European Parliament Election Briefing*, No. 24, February, http://www.sussex.ac.uk/sei/

Maxfield, E. (2009), 'The European Parliament Elections in Romania, June 7 2009', EPERN *European Parliament Election Briefing*, No. 30, June (http://www.sussex.ac.uk/sei/.

OECD (2005), *Romania: Policy Coordination Assessment*, Support for Improvement in Governance and Management (SIGMA), Paris, June.

Official Journal (2005), *Act Concerning the Conditions of Accession of the Republic of Bulgaria and Romania and the Adjustments to the Treaties on which the European Union is Founded*, L 157, 21 June, 203–20.

Papadimitriou, D. (2002), *Negotiating the New Europe; the European Union and Eastern Europe*, Aldershot: Ashgate.

Papadimitriou, D. and Gateva, E. (2009), 'Between Enlargement-led Europeanisation and Balkan Exceptionalism: An appraisal of Bulgaria's and Romania's entry into the European Union', *Perspectives on European Politics and Society*, 10/2: 152–66.

Papadimitriou, D. and Phinnemore, D. (2008), *Romania and the European Union: From marginalization to membership*, London: Routledge.

Phinnemore, D. (2006), *The EU and Romania*, London: Federal Trust.

Phinnemore, D. (2010), 'And We'd Like to Thank . . .: Romania's Integration into the European Union, 1989–2007', *Journal of European Integration*, 32/3: 291–308.

Pridham, G. (2005), *Designing Democracy: EU Enlargement and Regime Change in Post-Communist Europe*, Basingstoke: Palgrave.

Turnock, D. (2001), 'Regional inequalities and regional development in post-communist Romania', in Light, D. and Phinnemore, D. (eds), *Post-Communist Romania: Coming to Terms with Accession*, Basingstoke: Palgrave, 150–74.

ENDNOTES

1. The CEE countries invited to open accession negotiations were the Czech Republic, Estonia, Hungary, Poland, and Slovenia. Cyprus was also invited.

2. All 2004 entrants (as well as Bulgaria and Romania) were also subjected to: (i) a 'general' economic safeguard clause (allowing EU member states extra protection for a period of up to three years after accession in case of 'serious deterioration in the economic situation of a given area'; and (ii) two 'specific' safeguard clauses relating to the internal market and third pillar issues (such as cooperation in criminal and civil matters) which allowed the Commission or individual member states (in the case of the JHA safeguard clause) to take 'appropriate measures' in cases where new member states failed to meet their EU obligations. For more details, see Gabanyi (2005) and Papadimitriou and Gateva (2009).

3. A similar number of reports were produced for Bulgaria.

4. The constitutionally required referendum took place in May. The result was a convincing victory—74.5 per cent vs. 24.8 per cent—for Băsescu (Maxfield 2007).

5. Prior to the election, Romanian voters were represented in the EP by observer MEPs. Of these, five came from the PRM. Their presence in the EP facilitated the creation of the short-lived right-wing Identity, Tradition and Sovereignty political group. Its demise was triggered by the departure of the PRM in November 2007.

CHAPTER 11

Contrasting States of Europeanization?

Simon Bulmer and Christian Lequesne

▌ Summary

This chapter reflects on the findings of the country-based chapters (2–10), seeking to identify and systematize recurrent themes. First, it reflects on the contribution of Europeanization as an analytical tool for understanding EU member state relations on a country-by-country basis. It then explores emergent themes and issues. The country chapters were organized by enlargement round, so the significance of timing of accession is considered for the Europeanization experience. At the same time, but not consistently, timing has often interacted with a geographical focus to each enlargement wave, such as the southern enlargements of the 1980s or the eastern enlargement of 2004. Are there different geographical experiences of Europeanization across the EU? This question is related to another argument relevant to the Europeanization literature, namely that there are different 'worlds of compliance' across the EU. A further consideration is whether size matters. Is the Europeanization experience different for large states rather than small states? Alternatively, is it the embeddedness of member states' political systems that plays a role, making a state with a considerable history of continuity more resistant to change than transitional states? Finally, what is the role of the real impacts of the EU versus the perceived ones and, indeed, the discourse which frames the Europeanization experience? After exploring these issues we create a bridge through to the thematic chapters of Part III by identifying different impacts along the dimensions of politics, polity, and policy.

Introduction

The EU member states display considerable diversity, as has been seen in the preceding chapters. It is evident from quantitative indicators such as their population, geographical area, their political system, and economic size and wealth (see Table 11.1). It is also clear from more qualitative indicators discussed in the preceding chapters, such as the degree of Euroscepticism in the party system, trends in public opinion as well as patterns of institutional adaptation or the challenges posed by EU policy for existing domestic practice. The chapters thus reveal the contrasting 'states of Europeanization' present in the EU. The diversity is even greater, in fact, as the smallest member state in our coverage is Estonia, which is three times larger than Malta in population terms and many times larger in area. If we could have covered all twenty-seven states we would have found elements of diversity that go beyond that revealed in the chapters. For instance, for Cyprus the de facto partition of the country, where the Turkish-controlled area in the north has declared itself to be the Turkish Republic of Northern Cyprus but has only been recognized by Turkey, looms very large in its relationship with the EU. However, rather than trying to list all the distinguishing features of the twenty-seven member states, the task here is to find some way of reflecting on this diversity that can help 'position' the Europeanization of *any* member state, whether covered specifically in this volume or not.

Conceptual and Theoretical Insights

In reviewing the analytical agenda in Chapter 1 we referred to James Caporaso's (2007) identification of three 'worlds' of regional integration theory, namely integration theory, governance, and Europeanization. This book is especially concerned with the third of these but the others have also been present in the background of the country chapters, so let us take each in turn.

Whilst all member states will defend their national interests in different ways and at various times, it is none-the-less possible to regard some states as more willing to support neo-functionalist methods than others. Germany, France, and the UK exhibit this contrast well. The Nazi experience and wartime defeat made West Germany willing to embrace neo-functional integration as a way of creating a new era of Franco-German peace, and Europeanization was a specific consequence of that decision to integrate into the West. France, by contrast, has been more schizophrenic in its support for neo-functionalism, as Olivier Rozenberg spelt out in Chapter 3. It has been a major advocate of integration in the early years, with the Schuman Plan and proposals for the European Defence Community (EDC). In more recent decades, French governments developed the Franco-German reflex of advocating more integration, such as through the monetary integration proposals that fed into the Maastricht Treaty. Equally, it was the French National Assembly which rejected the EDC in 1954. It was President de Gaulle who resisted neo-functionalism and supranationalism in the 1960s on the grounds that the nation state was central to his efforts to rebuild French prestige after the collapse of the Fourth Republic; and French voters rejected the Constitutional Treaty in 2005. This schizophrenia is less evident in the approach of successive UK governments, which consistently have favoured both a more intergovernmental EU and an associated discourse of protecting national interests and preserving national sovereignty (see Chapter 5). Even under Labour Prime Minister Tony Blair (1997–2007), when the UK government pursued a relatively pro-integrationist approach, the justification for this 'utilitarian supranationalism' (Bulmer 2008; see also Chapter 5) was that it was explicitly in the national interest. Of course, West Germany's support for neo-functionalist solutions could also be seen as in its national interest, but a discourse of this form would have been counterproductive in the immediate post-war period and, in any case, was also highly problematic because of the division of Germany until 1990.

If these three large states serve as markers in relation to integration in broad terms, we can find so-called red lines—issues where each member state will defend its national interest—when we explore the detail of specific policy or institutional issues. Spain and Poland have both been very insistent on 'supersizing' their voting weights in the Council in order to set themselves apart as 'largish' member states (see Chapters 6 and 8 respectively). Ireland has been insistent on having the freedom to set low rates of corporation tax—even when under pressure to change this stance in negotiations over reducing its sovereign debt during the euro-zone crisis—because this is an important way to attract corporate investment into the Republic. For Germany, sound money and financial discipline have been concerns that have recurred in negotiations of the EU medium-term budget (the 'financial perspective') as well as in the euro-zone crisis. The Cyprus Problem, Luxembourg's savings banks, the UK's insistence on maintaining passport controls, in France agriculture (or what Olivier Rozenberg terms in Chapter 3 an 'ambitious' Common Agricultural Policy), the Greek position on Macedonia, Spanish insistence on generous cohesion policy funding, and high Danish environmental standards are amongst the issues on which the respective state has placed great emphasis on its national interests. Five member states (Spain, Slovakia, Cyprus, Romania, and Greece) refuse to recognize Kosovo's independence on an EU-wide basis, principally on the grounds that it might give oxygen to secessionist groups or minorities at

TABLE 11.1 Member state indicators in the EU-27

Member state	Accession date[1]	Population (million)	Area (km²)	Political system	GDP current prices €1 000	GDP per capita in PPS[2]	Euro-zone state?	Votes in Council	MEPs elected 2009[3]
Austria	1995	8.3	83,870	Federal republic	286	126	Yes	10	17
Belgium	1952	10.7	30,528	Constitutional monarchy	354	119	Yes	12	22
Bulgaria	2007	7.6	111,910	Republic	36	44	No	10	17
Cyprus	2004	0.8	9,250	Republic	17	99	Yes	4	6
Czech Republic	2004	10.5	78,866	Republic	149	80	No	12	22
Denmark	1973	5.5	43,094	Constitutional monarchy	236	127	No	7	13
Estonia	2004	1.3	45,000	Republic	14	64	Yes	4	6
Finland	1995	5.3	338,000	Republic	180	115	Yes	7	13
France	1952	64.3	550,000	Republic	1,933	108	Yes	29	72
Germany	1952	82	356,854	Federal republic	2,477	118	Yes	29	99
Greece	1981	11.2	131,957	Republic	227 (P)	90 (P)	Yes	12	22
Hungary	2004	10	93,000	Republic	97	65	No	12	22
Ireland	1973	4.5	70,000	Republic	156	128	Yes	7	12
Italy	1952	60	301,263	Republic	1,556	101	Yes	29	72

Latvia	2004	2.3	Republic	65,000	18	51	No	4	8
Lithuania	2004	3.3	Republic	65,000	28	57	No	7	12
Luxembourg	1952	0.5	Constitutional monarchy	2,586	40	271	Yes	4	6
Malta	2004	0.4	Republic	316	6	83	Yes	3	5
Netherlands	1952	16.4	Constitutional monarchy	41,526	588	133	Yes	13	25
Poland	2004	38.1	Republic	312,679	354	63	No	27	50
Portugal	1986	10.6	Republic	92,072	173 (P)	80	Yes	12	22
Romania	2007	21.5	Republic	237,500	124	46	No	14	33
Slovakia	2004	5.4	Republic	48,845	66	74	Yes	7	13
Slovenia	2004	2	Republic	20,273	35	85	Yes	4	7
Spain	1986	45.8	Constitutional monarchy	504,782	1,051	100	Yes	27	50
Sweden	1995	9.2	Constitutional monarchy	449,964	347	123	No	10	18
United Kingdom	1973	61.7	Constitutional monarchy	244,820	1,706	112	No	29	72

Population and area data compiled from the Europa website: http://europa.eu/about-eu/countries/index_en.htm. GDP data (January 2012) from Eurostat webs ite: http://epp.eurostat.ec.europa.eu/portal/page/portal/eurostat/home/(P) denotes provisional.

[1] Accession to the EC/EU or, for founder-members, to the European Coal and Steel Community.

[2] Purchasing power standards, (December 2011 data); EU-27 = 100.

[3] Some adjustments to the figures were introduced by the Lisbon Treaty but had not been implemented at the time of writing.

home. And whilst most if not all of the above 'national interests' are material in nature, the construction of interests can owe as much to discourse as material interests, as British concerns with sovereignty or French concerns over the Services Directive with the symbolic figure of the 'Polish plumber' reveal (Grossman and Woll 2011).

The governance turn is amply represented in the country chapters. Our guidance to contributing authors requested them to go beyond considering the impact of Europeanization on government and government policy. Contributions have focused on how other institutions (parliament and sub-national government, in some cases also the judicial structure) have adapted, alongside parties and public opinion. The opportunities offered by Europeanization extend more widely to a possible reconfiguration of relations between government and civil society or to the impact on established patterns of policymaking with socioeconomic actors (such as on Austria's long-standing tradition of corporatism: see Falkner and Laffan 2005: 220). Thus, changing patterns of governance at the EU level can impact upon the (horizontal) state-society boundary at member state level. Similarly, the EU's more multi-levelled nature can impact upon the vertical distribution of authority within member states, such as with the German Länder seeking, through ratification of the Maastricht Treaty, to recover powers previously lost to the EU, or the Spanish Autonomous Communities seeking to strengthen their voice in EU policymaking, with Catalonia and the Basque Country usually at the fore of such moves. Yet the incentives offered to sub-state government by the EU, namely through its structural funds, do not automatically lead to the emergence of an effective tier of regional governance, as the Romanian case revealed (see Chapter 10; for further discussion, see Chapter 16).

These observations about governance tie in with the three hypotheses that predated the Europeanization literature: that the EU strengthens the state; that the EU stimulates a new multilevel politics; and that the EU transforms governance in the member states. The first hypothesis was consistent with liberal intergovernmentalism. It is certainly true that executives were strengthened in their relations with domestic parliaments but, in several members, sub-state government has sought to recover powers lost to central government (Belgium, for instance; also see previous paragraph on Catalonia and the Basque Country). Evidence to make a decisive judgement on whether the EU has rewritten the boundary between the state and socioeconomic actors and civil society is insufficient in this book or in the literature more generally. What is clear, however, is that EU membership has transformed member-state governance. As a first step, 'the state' itself needs to be opened up in order to see some of the transformation (Bulmer and Burch 2009: 204–7). Diplomacy is no longer the preserve of diplomats in foreign affairs ministries, since EU policy is more 'intermestic' in character. Brigid Laffan (2005) has highlighted the emergence in central governments of groups of boundary managers and boundary spanners: officials in the relevant coordination bureaus in the home capital as well as the officials in the permanent representations in Brussels. Heads of government (or state) have found summitry in the EU to be time consuming, and possibly reinforcing a presidentialization of domestic politics and a centralization within government. At the same time, virtually all government ministers—even interior ministers—have found that EU meetings are part of their schedule. The status of foreign ministries within home governments has also been challenged by the widening of EU business across the activities of government and the centralization around the chief executive representing the state in the European Council.

These observations are confined to the transformation of central government. Beyond that there are changes to the functioning of parliament, local and regional levels of governance, parties, interest groups, and so on. Quite simply, the EU changes the political opportunity structure. As Darren McCauley has shown (2011), the effects have reached social movements, such as the campaign against genetically modified organisms, providing them with new options for 'bottom-up' Europeanization. It therefore seems clear that the EU has 'transformed governance' (hypothesis 3) but it is more debatable about it having created a multilevel politics (hypothesis 2). On the one hand, Ian Bache (2008) has argued that there is some evidence of such an outcome and in particular in the UK. Francesc Morata (Chapter 6) examines the interrelationship between the challenges to the Spanish state from above and below, including the multilevel politics. However, the evidence from recent accession states is very mixed and suggests that such an outcome is dependent upon some pre-existing features; trying to invent them in connection with the EU structural funds may be unsuccessful, at least in the short- to medium-term, as the Romanian case illustrates (Chapter 10). These conflicting findings are analysed further by Peter Bursens in Chapter 16.

Moving away from this narrower focus on multilevel politics, have the country chapters chimed in other ways with the conceptual and theoretical debates in the Europeanization literature? Our examples have highlighted some cases where EU membership has been linked with other motivations and processes that raise the classic problem of whether to attribute the outcome to Europeanization alone. The southern enlargement was associated with embedding democracy, joining the European mainstream, and modernization. The outcomes have, of course, differed between the states concerned (see Hibou 2005 comparing Greece and Portugal; Chapter 6 in this volume on Spain). Has the wide-scale acceptance of Europeanization across the Spanish political spectrum been facilitated by the perception that it was intrinsic to economic and social modernization? And, if so, was this modernization a separate (but perhaps inseparable) independent variable driving the process? Or was it a discourse of modernization that facilitated adaptation to the EU. The answer would require a larger project of original research than is at hand in this volume, but to highlight the question is to identify some of the problems facing Europeanization research. In the aftermath of the euro-zone crisis, the risk for Greece is that the painful period of economic adjustment, together with the serious political and social consequences, is associated amongst its public with the EU (and specifically Germany) rather than other key policy drivers, notably domestic administrative weakness, the financial markets, and the International Monetary Fund. Regardless of the causes of the crisis in Greece, the Europeanization of its austerity programme risks becoming perceived as imperialism.

This issue of disaggregating different independent variables is also present in central and eastern Europe (CEE)—and for that matter West Germany and Italy—where EU membership also followed the democratization process in relatively short order. In the CEE states and the Baltic republics, Europeanization was not just about embracing the EU but also about another identitive matter, namely laying to rest a period under Soviet domination. Piret Ehin's account of Estonia's political elites' zealous pursuit of European integration as part of seizing a rare historical opportunity to restore statehood is particularly striking (Chapter 9). However, as noted in Chapter 1, EU-ization and Europeanization risk being conflated. Thus, on a visit to the University of Malta in October 2011 Simon Bulmer was informed in the Department of Maltese Studies that the Europeanization of the island occurred with the arrival of the Normans in the late eleventh century, thus chiming with the historical sociological analysis of Trine Flockhart (2010). The overlap between Europeanization and EU-ization may therefore be context-specific.

One final observation concerning the Europeanization of the member states at a macro level is that it is quite difficult to provide a framework to encompass the multiple dimensions of EU impact, across polity, politics, and policy. The notion of fit/misfit may well work for policies, or some of them (see Chapter 15) but there is no EU template for politics and polity, and consequently the terms fit and misfit do not suit. Perhaps the only way in which the situation can be captured at macro level is through exploring the 'congruence' between the EU and individual member states (see Bulmer and Jeffery 2010 for a comparison of Germany and the UK). It is worth underlining that this macro level is important because maladaptation to the EU in one sphere of the domestic political system—whether it be because of persistent party-political divisions over membership such as in the UK or owing to a failure to make all the necessary reforms as in Romania—can have a system-wide impact. The most likely consequence, as revealed by these two examples, is a weakening of the capacity to upload domestic policy preferences to the EU level.

We turn now to other empirically-based comparative observations on member state adaptation to the EU.

Timing of Accession

The organizational logic of Chapters 2–10 is by enlargement round. Is it therefore possible to observe that the timing of accession matters? Certainly, the later the enlargement, the bigger the EU's policy inheritance and so-called *acquis communautaire*. Consequently, the corpus of EU rules and policy commitments has been greater with each accession and, on the face of it, the challenges have become more onerous. As Papadimitriou and Phinnemore note in Chapter 10, the feeling that Romania (and Bulgaria) may have secured accession prematurely has resulted in raising the conditionality requirements for Croatia and Turkey. The contrast for recent accession states is therefore greatest with the founder members that played the role of decision-*makers* rather than that of decision-*takers*. However, the fact that the *acquis communautaire* and other policy commitments have been larger with each policy round does not automatically mean that the accession adjustment is larger with each enlargement round. This situation was illustrated with the 1995 accession of Austria, Finland, and Sweden. These states had all been adjusting to the single market through membership of the European Economic Area (EEA) prior to acceding to the EU. Consequently, the challenge of accession was lessened. This circumstance could be repeated should EEA member Iceland successfully negotiate terms of accession and ratify them.

A more general observation about the timing of accession is simply to underline that accession states have to accept the rules applying when they join. If the rules have an adverse effect—as the shape of the Common Agricultural Policy and the EU's budgetary system did for the UK—it may be a long time before any significant reform can be achieved, given that unanimity is typically needed to unravel pre-existing policy. In this particular case, the material financial consequences for the UK—even allowing for the rebates negotiated from the 1980s—has fuelled party-political divisions and contributed to a continuing Eurosceptic discourse. Policy misfit arising from being a latecomer can therefore have a wider impact on Europeanization across the political system.

Timing can also be significant in another sense, namely in respect of circumstances in the acceding state. The UK joined at the time of the oil crisis, and the associated performance in the domestic economy did not demonstrate benefits of membership whilst the politics of membership were highly contested. Sweden, as Anna Michalski points out, joined at a time when its economy was in recession. Public opinion became more favourably disposed to integration with the passage of time as the practical policy benefits emerged and concerns about the EU's impact on the welfare state and its distinctive normative foreign policy were allayed. Hence shifts in public opinion towards greater support for EU membership are not simply the product of events at the EU level. The tempo of Europeanization might well be dictated by domestic events (see Bulmer 2009: 317–9), whether this relates to the impact on public opinion, the central government (where an election may act as trigger for administrative or policy reform to better align with EU practice), or elsewhere in the political system.

The Worlds of Membership

Apart from the temporal aspect of the accession rounds, in many cases they have had a geographical dimension as well (referred to here as the 'worlds' of membership). The 1973 enlargement was perhaps the least striking in this regard and tends not to have a label. The central factor was the UK and states with key trading links, Denmark and Ireland. The southern enlargement of 1981 and 1986 self-evidently entailed a clustering of accession states even if only Portugal and Spain were in close proximity. The 1995 enlargement brought in Austria, Finland, and Sweden from the European Free Trade Association, and is known as the EFTA enlargement. Again, this is not a perfect clustering in geographical terms. However, just as Greece, Spain, and Portugal were countries that had recently made the transition to democracy from military or authoritarian rule and were much less economically developed than the European Community norm, so the EFTAns were well-established democracies with advanced economies. They had grown closer to the EU via the EEA but the end of the Cold War removed prior political inhibitions to membership that arose from their commitment to neutrality. The 2004 and 2007 rounds are often abbreviated to eastern or central and eastern European enlargement. Of course, Malta and Cyprus of the 2004 accession states did not fit the implied geographical clustering, whilst Romania and Bulgaria (2007) were stretching it too. Nevertheless, if Cyprus and Malta are set aside, the common features of this cluster of states were their recent transition to democracy following the fall of the Iron Curtain and the collapse of the Soviet Union, and the creation of market economies. As with the southern European states, there were potential barriers to Europeanization associated with pre-existing administrative systems that pre-dated liberal democracy, the reshaping of economies emerging into an open capitalist system, and the near absence of provision in some areas of public policy, notably the environment. The different experiences of the Europeanization of the Polish, Estonian, and Romanian administrative structures are evident from Chapters 8–10. Strikingly, Estonia appears to have made the swiftest transition in the public administration of these states despite having been part of the Soviet Union, whilst the troubled transition to democracy in Romania has been a particular problem for adapting to EU membership. The so-called 'new' member states cannot be approached as a single block. Each state has distinctive characteristics that result in a different relationship with the European Union.

Klaus Goetz (2007) has explored Europeanization and territorial groupings, drawing attention to the relative lack of comparative (rather than single country) analyses of Europeanization. He refers to 'families of nations' arguments that highlight geographical, linguistic, cultural, and historical commonalities (see also Castles 1993). Such groupings are typically reflected in discussions on research design in comparative EU policy analysis, where the selection of a western and southern European, along with a Nordic and CEE state tends to be seen as the basis of a representative sample.

In a notable analysis of EU public policy compliance, Gerda Falkner and her associates explored the worlds of compliance in the EU, including after the 2001/2004 enlargements, initially identifying three (see Falkner *et al.* 2005; Falkner *et al.* 2007). In later work Falkner and Treib (2008) suggested the existence of four worlds of compliance:

- the world of law observance, typically characterized by a commitment to compliance overcoming domestic objections, with Demark, Finland, and Sweden as exemplars;
- the world of domestic politics, where domestic concerns may prevail in any clash with the need to comply with the EU, resulting in instances of non-compliance, e.g. Austria, Belgium, Germany, the Netherlands, Spain, and the UK;

- the world of transposition neglect, where national arrogance over 'superior' domestic legislation or administrative inefficiency may result in failure to transpose EU requirements, e.g. France, Greece, Luxembourg, and Portugal; and

- the world of dead letters, where politicized transposition and administrative shortcomings may result in compliance in terms of the statute books but with no real enforcement at street level or in the domestic court system.

This classification derived from work on EU labour law, so the four 'worlds' are not necessarily generalizable. In any case, other 'worlds' are relevant to Europeanization. In the domain of social policy, Esping-Andersen's (1990) three worlds of welfare capitalism may be used to explore the EU's comparative effect on member states. Similarly, national models of capitalism (see Hall and Soskice 2001; Menz 2005; also Vivien Schmidt's Chapter 17 in this volume) form a reference point in studies of whether the EU has led to convergence in the national political economies.

A further geographical dimension of Europeanization has been the way in which neighbouring areas have become subject to EU policy initiatives aimed at political stability, security, and economic cooperation in the vicinity of member states. Examples include initiatives in the Mediterranean that were especially promoted by Spain (and France), notably the Euro-Mediterranean Partnership (or Barcelona Process, initiated in 1995), bringing together the states bordering the Mediterranean; the northern dimension that was pushed by Sweden and Finland and then by the Baltic accession states for cooperation with neighbouring countries surrounding the Baltic, and including Iceland and Norway; Romania's promotion of Black Sea cooperation; and ad hoc initiatives, such as Poland's towards the Ukraine, the Polish–Swedish initiative on an Eastern Partnership, and Romania's relationship with Moldova (see the respective chapters). These relationships have the potential to extend European policy principles—both political and economic—to neighbouring states, with accession of a new state, or states acting giving the impulse for the initiative. Enlargement can also have such indirect Europeanization effects beyond the immediate neighbourhood; for example, bringing many former British colonies into the EU's development policy framework, in which those of France and the Netherlands were already prominent, or adding new areas of interest to EU foreign policy cooperation, notably Latin America upon the accession of Spain and Portugal.

Size

Size is another potential factor in Europeanization (see Table 11.1 for data). Archer and Nugent (2006) have considered whether the size of member states makes a difference to the kind of the role they can play in the EU. They note (2006: 6) that size is not simply a matter of territory and population but also of how resources are managed by the state and of how size is perceived both inside and outside the state. For instance, Poland is perceived by a majority of its elites as a 'big' state in Central

Europe, with a regional role to play. They also suggest that a state's size has to be understood in historical, geographical, and cultural context. Equally, they note that the EU modulates the effects of size through its rules requiring unanimity for key issues and through, for instance, the over-representation of small states in Council voting. These issues are taken further by Baldur Thorhallsson (2006) in reviewing the parameters of size and generating two scales for locating states: an action competence continuum and a vulnerability continuum (see also the country chapters in *Journal of European Integration* 2006).

Size also has relevance to how the EU impacts on individual member states. Morata (Chapter 6) and Copsey (Chapter 8) have noted how Spain and Poland are especially sensitive to having strong representation in the Council to designate they are not small states. Beyond these cases the importance of size is less explicitly invoked in Chapters 3–10. However, the size of the UK and France has also been expressed in other ways relating to Europeanization. Successive governments have sought to emphasize that the UK is a global *and* European power, typically expressed through trying to balance a 'special relationship' with the United States. For instance Tony Blair attempted to position the UK as a bridge between the USA and the EU (see Chapter 5). This policy impacted at times on the 'fit' between British foreign policy objectives and those of the CFSP, notably with the invasion of Iraq in 2003. For France, analogous challenges have been posed. Françoise de la Serre (1996: 34) identified the foreign policy challenge as being 'Europeanization versus the concern for rank'. Like the UK, France has preferred an intergovernmental CFSP. It sought to guard its legacy of Gaullist policy in having close relations with Arab states, and it also sought to keep its policy activities in much of Francophone Africa a *domaine réservé*, excluded from the CFSP. Thus France and the UK have demonstrated on occasion that they have, by virtue of size and legacy, 'other options' beyond the CFSP. They have also exploited the size of their military expenditure to play a key role in the shaping of the EU's Common Security and Defence Policy. However, the importance of understanding size in context is demonstrated by Germany which, despite its size—whether before unification or subsequently—has only very rarely departed from the common EU approach expressed through European Political Cooperation and, following the Maastricht Treaty, the CFSP. Germany's decision in December 1991 to recognize Slovenia and Croatia ahead of EC-wide agreement was notable for its breach of multilateralism (Crawford 1996). However, this did not prove to be as significant a departure in German foreign policy as some realist analysts thought (see Crawford 2007: 58–60 for discussion). Nevertheless, a more self-confident Germany has emerged, particularly from the Red-Green coalition government under Gerhard Schröder (1998–2005) onwards, as Timm Beichelt argues (Chapter 4). Schröder was more willing to 'go solo', notably in conducting bilateral relations with Russia independently of the EU. The Christian Democrat/Free Democrat coalition's refusal in 2011 to endorse collective action over Libya was another such manifestation of not following EU policy.

Small states, by contrast, often have much reduced scope for solo policy dé-marches and, indeed, welcome the enhanced capacity for international action that Europeanization affords them (see Chapter 9). Even so, just as Germany does not conform to the situation where large member states may have foreign policy options outside the EU, so a country like Cyprus, owing to its internal divisions, may prove difficult to align on some foreign policy issues, most notably relating to Turkey. Finally, if small states have the option of alliances to resist (or promote) Europeani-zation, the reality of over sixty years of European integration is that the Franco-German alliance (i.e. of two large states) has been the most important one for uploading policy to the EU level. The fifth enlargement to CEECs in 2004 and 2007 has, however, reduced the possibilities for the big member states to exercise leader-ship in the EU. As a French Permanent Representative to the EU has argued, the Council and the COREPER with twenty-seven representatives look more like an 'as-sembly of joint owners'. However, quantitative studies have shown that a Council with twenty-five member states is not taking decisions less efficiently than a Council with 15 member states (Best *et al.* 2008).

Embeddedness

Another potential domestic factor that shapes the Europeanization of individual states is the domestic embeddedness of the political and economic systems. Of the large member states, Britain has had the longest-standing continuity in its political system (even if some of the narratives about this conflate English circumstances with those of the UK). National and parliamentary sovereignty—terms used by poli-ticians in the UK attempting to restrict the impact of the EU—can be traced back to myths surrounding, respectively, English territorial integrity (external sovereignty) and parliamentary authority in relation to the monarch (internal sovereignty). These myths date back to events in the sixteenth and seventeenth centuries (Wallace 1986: 382–4). By contrast, a significant number of states have joined supranational inte-gration following transition from non-democratic rule: Germany and Italy; Greece, Spain, and Portugal; the ten CEE states that joined in 2004 and 2007. These states were all enduring transitions of varying kinds. Precisely because these states were at a time of political and economic transition, the hypothesis would be that they were willing to embrace Europeanization as a route to political and economic stability and perhaps a new (or renewed) identity.

However, beyond generalized observations such as these, the crudeness of the hypothesis can be observed in the differential trajectories of accession states. Whilst sovereign debt problems in Spain have arisen primarily from a construction bubble, Greece's fiscal crisis has arisen from a failure to observe the rules of mon-etary union as well as a failure to introduce administrative reform amongst a range of other factors. In short, whilst states in transition have an opportunity to embrace

Europeanization—taking advantage of a range of reform opportunities—there is no guarantee that they will be seized or that the reforms will take root.

Impacts, Perceived Impacts, and Discourse

Whilst most of the observations above have related to different aspects of the material impact of Europeanization upon the member states, matters of perception, discourse, and identity are also significant. The country chapters have revealed a varying performance amongst the member states in trying to align national interests with European integration. Until the Schröder coalition government, German politicians scarcely uttered the expression 'national interests'; his predecessor, Helmut Kohl, saw the EU as a 'Schicksalsgemeinschaft' (a community of destiny). In the UK, to take a contrasting case, even the most pro-European prime minister, Tony Blair, failed to find an effective narrative to align British interests with integration. The English press, moreover, has a strong record in shaping a Eurosceptic discourse, as Daddow (2007) has argued. France, by contrast, has managed to reflect the schizophrenia revealed in Chapter 3 by Olivier Rozenberg. French politicians—including the same ones!—can have a positive narrative of '*Europe puissance*' (power through Europe) together with another narrative on the defence of *souverainisme*, i.e. autonomy from the EU.

German concerns about sovereignty follow a completely different route, being the domain of constitutional-legal discourse. The Federal Constitutional Court has pronounced (in its judgement on the Maastricht Treaty) that the member states are the 'masters of the treaties' (*Herren der Verträge*). This posture is more intergovernmental than pre-existing mainstream views towards the EU in the German political elite. The German judicial system has come to police the boundaries of Europeanization and, remarkably, has through its Maastricht and Lisbon judgements, given politicians in Berlin the powers to do so even though there had been no clamour for them at the federal level. Following the Maastricht Treaty, the Länder governments have also sought to resist EU intrusions into their areas of authority by demanding that the EU treaties contain a catalogue of competences (*Kompetenzkatalog*); something finally achieved in the Lisbon Treaty. Two separate discourses have developed in Germany about protecting authority, and both have been couched in constitutional-legal terms.

Once again, this can only be an illustrative view of a wider point in evidence in the country chapters: that politicians' and governments' narratives of integration matter. That all the Spanish parties seem to be able to find a modernization narrative in European integration is striking. The Polish narrative, by contrast, is less uniform and at times coloured by historical references. These are all cases illustrating the diverse forms of narrative that shape the experience of Europeanization across the EU. Just as with the material expressions of Europeanization in the member states, so the discursive framing of Europeanization displays considerable diversity as well.

Impact on Politics, Polity, and Policy

The diversity of responses across the member states can also be organized around the classic disaggregation of the political system into politics, polity, and policy. In some member states, such as the UK, the EU remains a divisive force in party politics, whereas Sweden has seen a gradual de-politicization of the issue (Chapter 7). Public opinion's support for the EU is variable from state to state. The convergent and divergent impacts of Europeanization on 'politics' are now carried forward in the next part of the book in the chapter on political parties by Robert Ladrech (Chapter 13) and that addressing the response to Europeanization of interest groups and social movements by Sabine Saurugger (Chapter 14). The country chapters have revealed variation in response amongst governments, such as the effect in Sweden on its distinctive form of agency government. All national parliaments have struggled to find their place in the EU policy cycle but some have been more effective than others. Hussein Kassim explores the impacts on executives, parliaments, and the court systems (Chapter 12). The EU also has an impact on sub-national governance (Chapter 16), a theme that has been especially apparent in the chapters on Germany and Spain. The Europeanization of public policy is interpreted in Chapter 15 through setting up an analytical framework, since the intersection of twenty-seven states and multiple policy areas amounts to a massive potential policy impact arising from the EU that cannot be covered in a single chapter. Rather, Bulmer and Radaelli set up a default framework that can be applied to explore the Europeanization of public policy, whatever the policy, whichever the member state. Finally, the issue of the EU's impact on the member states' political economies is examined in Chapter 17.

Conclusion

Chapters 3–10 have revealed a strong sense of diversity across the member states. The literature on Europeanization has often insisted too much on the convergence of policy, politics, and polity. By focusing first on the member states it has been possible to observe also national differences and idiosyncrasies: the contrasting states of Europeanization. The differential impact is strengthened by a further feature of integration that has not been discussed in detail but must be recalled, namely the increasing tendency of the EU towards differentiated integration (Piris 2012). The membership of the eurozone is one manifestation (see Table 11.1). Irish and British opt-outs from the passport-free Schengen zone are another. The British and Czech opt-outs from the 2012 Treaty on Stability, Coordination, and Governance in the Economic and Monetary Union (the fiscal union treaty) are another but there are more beyond these illustrations. The task of the chapters in Part III of the book is to explore this subject matter further, but from a different, thematic, perspective.

FURTHER READING

Apart from the subsequent thematic chapters in the volume, other comparative analyses synthesizing thematic work on Europeanization can be found in Graziano and Vink (2007) and Ladrech (2010). Cowles *et al.* (2001) and Featherstone and Radaelli (2003) are also recommended. Some of the member states not covered in this volume were covered in Bulmer and Lequesne (2005). An alternative review of the member states that does not place Europeanization as prominently as our own collection is Zeff and Pirro (2006).

WEB LINKS

There is no website dedicated to thematic analyses of Europeanization. However, a good source of scholarship that brings together several series of working papers, including specifically on Europeanization is available at **http://eiop.or.at/erpa/**.

REFERENCES

Archer, C. and Nugent, N. (2006), 'Introduction: Does the Size of Member States Matter in the European Union?', *Journal of European Integration*, 28/1: 3–6.

Bache, I. (2008), *Europeanization and Multilevel Governance: Cohesion Policy in the European Union and Britain*, Lanham, MD: Rowman and Littlefield.

Best, E., Christiansen T., and Settembri, P. (eds) (2008), *The Institutions of the Enlarged European Union. Continuity and Change*, Cheltenham: Edward Elgar.

Bulmer, S. (2008), 'New Labour, New European Policy? Blair, Brown and Utilitarian Supranationalism', *Parliamentary Affairs* 61/4: 597–620.

Bulmer, S. (2009), 'Politics in Time Meets the Politics of Time: Historical Institutionalism and the EU Timescape', *Journal of European Public Policy*, 16/2: 307–24.

Bulmer, S. and Burch, M. (2009), *The Europeanisation of Whitehall: UK Central Government and the European Union*, Manchester: Manchester University Press.

Bulmer, S. and Jeffery, C. (2010), 'Does Congruence Matter? Germany and Britain in the European Union', in S. Bulmer, C. Jeffery, and S. Padgett (eds), *Rethinking Germany and Europe: Democracy and Diplomacy in a Semi-Sovereign State*, Basingstoke: Palgrave Macmillan, 113–38.

Bulmer, S. and Lequesne, C. (2005), *The Member States of the European Union*, Oxford: Oxford University Press.

Caporaso, J. (2007), 'The Three Worlds of Regional Integration Theory', in P. Graziano and M. Vink (eds), *Europeanization: New Research Agendas*, Basingstoke: Palgrave Macmillan, 23–34.

Castles, F. (1993), 'Introduction', in F. Castles (ed.), *Families of Nations: Patterns of Public Policy in Western Democracies*, Aldershot: Dartmouth Publishing, xiii–xxiii.

Cowles, M. G., Caporaso, J., and Risse, T. (eds) (2001), *Transforming Europe: Europeanization and Domestic Change*, Ithaca, NY: Cornell University Press.

Crawford, B. (1996), 'Explaining Defection from International Cooperation: Germany's Unilateral Recognition of Croatia', *World Politics*, 48/4: 482–521.

Crawford, B. (2007), *Power and German Foreign Policy: Embedded Hegemony in Europe*, Basingstoke: Palgrave Macmillan.

Daddow, O. (2007), 'Playing Games with History: Tony Blair's European Policy in the Press', *British Journal of Politics and International Relations*, 9/4: 582–98.

de la Serre, F. (1996), 'France: The Impact of François Mitterrand', in C. Hill (ed.), *Actors in European Foreign Policy*, London: Routledge, 19–39.

Esping-Andersen, G. (1990), *The Three Worlds of Welfare Capitalism*, Cambridge: Polity.

Falkner, G. and Laffan, B. (2005), 'The Europeanization of Austria and Ireland: Small can be Difficult?', in S. Bulmer and C. Lequesne (eds), *The Member States of the European Union*, Oxford: Oxford University Press, 209–28.

Falkner, G. and Treib, O. (2008), 'Three Worlds of Compliance or Four? The EU-15 Compared to New Member States', *Journal of Common Market Studies*, 46/2: 293–313.

Falkner, G., Hartlapp, M., and Treib, O. (2007), 'Worlds of Compliance: Why Leading Approaches to European Union Implementation are only "Sometimes-True Theories"', *European Journal of Political Research*, 46/3: 395–416.

Falkner, G., Treib, O., Hartlapp, M., and Leiber, S. (2005), *Complying with Europe: EU Harmonisation and Soft Law in the Member States*, Cambridge: Cambridge University Press.

Featherstone, K. and Radaelli, C. (eds) (2003), *The Politics of Europeanization*, Oxford: Oxford University Press.

Flockhart, T. (2010), 'Europeanization or EU-ization? The Transfer of European Norms across Time and Space', *Journal of Common Market Studies*, 48/4: 787–810.

Goetz, K. (2007), 'Territory', in P. Graziano and M. Vink (eds), *Europeanization: New Research Agendas*, Basingstoke: Palgrave Macmillan, 73–87.

Graziano, P. and Vink, M. (eds) (2007), *Europeanization: New Research Agendas*, Basingstoke: Palgrave Macmillan.

Grossman, E. and Woll, C. (2011), 'The French Debate on the Bolkestein Directive', *Comparative European Politics*, 9/3: 344–66.

Hall, P. and Soskice, D. (eds) (2001), *Varieties of Capitalism: The Institutional Foundations of Comparative Advantage*, Oxford: Oxford University Press.

Hibou, B. (2005), 'Greece and Portugal: Convergent or Divergent Europeanization?', in S. Bulmer and C. Lequesne (eds), *The Member States of the European Union*, Oxford: Oxford University Press, 229–53.

Journal of European Integration (2006), 'Special issue' (Does the Size of Member States Matter in the European Union?), 3–120.

Ladrech, R. (2010), *Europeanization and National Politics*, Basingstoke: Palgrave Macmillan.

Laffan, B. (2005), 'Managing Europe from Home: Impact of the EU on Executive Government: A Comparative Analysis', Dublin: Dublin European Institute, available at: http://www.oeue.net/papers/acomparativeanalysis-theimpact.pdf, accessed 26 February 2012.

McCauley, D. (2011), 'Bottom-up Europeanization Exposed: Social Movement Theory and Non-State Actors in France,' *Journal of Common Market Studies*, 49/5: 1019–42.

Menz, G. (2005), *Varieties of Capitalism and Europeanization: National Response Strategies to the Single European Market*, Oxford: Oxford University Press.

Piris, J. C. (2012), *The Future of Europe. Towards a Two-Speed EU?*, Cambridge: Cambridge University Press.

Thorhallsson, B. (2006), 'The Size of States in the European Union: Theoretical and Conceptual Perspectives', *Journal of European Integration*, 28/1: 7–31.

Wallace, W. (1986), 'What Price Independence? Sovereignty and Interdependence in British Politics', *International Affairs*, 62/3: 367–89.

Zeff, E. and Pirro, E. (2006), *The European Union and the Member States*, 2nd edn, Boulder, Co.: Lynne Rienner.

PART III

Europeanization

CHAPTER 12

Europeanization and Member State Institutions

Hussein Kassim[1]

▮ Summary

The impact of the EU on domestic institutions has been complex and far-reaching. The effect on central governments, as both actors and organizations, has been the most dramatic and is the most ambivalent: Union membership imposes constraints and burdens that are often onerous, but at the same time afford new opportunities and make available new resources. Integration has reinforced the decline of national legislatures, while national courts at all levels have assumed new functions and become part of a wider Community of law. At the same, the precise effects of the EU have varied cross-nationally as the demands of membership have interacted with differing constitutional arrangements, legal traditions, and political cultures. Moreover, the EU's domestic impact is only one half of the story. National institutions—governments, parliaments, courts—have left their mark on the EU and determine to a large extent the capacities of the Union as a system.

Introduction

Membership of the EU has far-reaching consequences for national institutions, which it embeds in a 'system of shared decision-making and collective governance' (Laffan *et al.* 2000: 74). It imposes obligations, requires continual adjustment, and makes continual demands on their operation. Although political debate (and much of the academic literature) focuses on the constraints that Union membership imposes, integration has also created 'new structures for opportunity' (Hix and Goetz 2000: 12), new possibilities to influence the economic and political environment in Europe, and a new space for political action above and beyond the national level (Favell 1998).

This chapter examines the impact of European integration on executives, parliament, and the courts, and their interaction with the Union.[2] It puts forward three arguments. The first is that, though national institutions have responded to the demands of membership, the impact of the EU has been differential. As Olsen has observed (2007: 239):

[S]tructural diversity persists among the core domestic institutions in spite of increasing contact and competition between national models. There has been no general trend towards isomorphism and no significant convergence towards a common institutional model homogenizing the domestic structures of the European states . . . [E]stablished domestic patterns have been resilient but also flexible enough to cope with changes at the European level, and no new and unified model of dealing with Union matters has emerged. In general, EU arrangements have turned out to be compatible with the maintenance of distinct national institutional arrangements.

The second argument is that national context matters. National differences are evident both in the EU's impact on member state institutions and their interaction with the Union (Rometsch and Wessels 1996, Wessels *et al.* 2003a). The effects of membership have varied according to, for example, the structure of the domestic polity, the dominant policy style, and popular and elite attitudes towards integration. These factors also account for why the EU's penetration of domestic systems has created very different structures of opportunity between member states.

Finally, and less of an argument than a reminder, the relationship between the EU and the member states does not work only in one direction. The top-down dynamic is an important dimension of integration, but the bottom-up flow is no less significant. Not only can national influences be detected in the design of EU bodies, but member state institutions are players at the EU level (in other words, the Union is not exogenous to national political systems[3]), they have a considerable impact on the operation of EU institutions and the Union as a system more broadly (Metcalfe 1992).

National Governments and the EU

Although they are widely regarded to have been the 'winners' of European integration, membership of the EU has affected governments as actors and as organizations. In a long-standing debate about the first, intergovernmentalists (Moravcsik 1993, 1998; Milward 2000; Hoffmann 1966, 1982) argue that governments not only control, but are strengthened by, European integration, while neofunctionalists (Haas 1958, Stone Sweet and Sandholtz 1998), new institutionalists (Pierson 1996, Pollack 1997) and multilevel governance theorists (Marks *et al.* 1996) acknowledge the power of national governments, but emphasize the constraints imposed on them by the Union. In regard to governments as organizations, there is general agreement that the EU has led to 'a shift in the internal national balance of powers towards governments and administrations' (Wessels *et al.* 2003b: xvi) and away from parliaments. However, the effects of the EU on relations between ministers and bureaucrats, between ministers, especially the PM and others, and administrations more broadly are less clear-cut.

In the interaction between member states and the EU, national governments are the most powerful member state institutions in Brussels. They also dominate, even if they do not absolutely control, the relationship between the Union and the national polity, as well as domestic EU policymaking.

The Impact on National Governments

Most scholars agree that, while EU membership imposes significant constraints on governments,[4] the Union avails them of important benefits and it has brought about 'a shift in the internal national balance of powers towards governments and administrations' (Wessels *et al.* 2003b: xvi). Membership enables governments to achieve collectively what they can no longer achieve individually. The EU is an instrument for managing the externalities that arise from regional interdependence (Moravcsik 1993, 1998), a standing forum where transnational concerns can be addressed without the need to incur set-up costs each time a new problem arises, and a system in which entrepreneurial governments can gain economic advantage by exporting policy preferences to their EU partners. Where they succeed as 'policy leaders' (Héritier *et al.* 1996) in the EU, governments ensure that the policies pursued in the rest of the Union are favourable to their own constituencies.[5]

At home, governments are strengthened by the 'nesting' of the domestic arena inside the EU framework. In this 'two-level game' (Putnam 1988), governments can appeal to the constraints imposed by other states as a justification for presenting a limited set of policy options at home.[6] EU membership increases the government's control over domestic agendas. EU decision making favours the executive, accentuates the information asymmetries that advantage the executive, and strengthens the ideological justifications for government policy (Moravcsik 1994; see also 1993:

473–524). In some member states at certain periods, governments are able to override domestic opposition by citing the demands made by Brussels (Smith 1997). However, since Maastricht, as 'Europe' has become a salient domestic issue and popular opinion more Eurosceptic, this possibility is less often available.

EU constraints on governments take various forms. As treaty signatories, member governments accept the primacy of EC over national law (Raunio and Hix 2000: 154), and all existing and future Community legislation. They submit to the obligation to agree common policies and to participate in joint action of varying forms. As the EU's competencies have expanded, policies grown and jurisprudence developed, the scope for discretionary action on the part of member states has diminished. In signing the treaties, governments also agree to share decision-making authority with other governments and with the supranational institutions. They share executive power with the European Commission, and legislative power with the European Parliament and the Council of Ministers (Hix 1999: 25, 32, 56). Both the Commission and the European Court of Justice exercise important powers that undermine 'member state institutional autonomy' (Schmidt 1999: 20). The Commission's near-monopoly over policy initiation, its strategic location in the policy process, and the privileged access to information which it enjoys give its considerable leverage in decision making. The court, meanwhile, through the constitutionalization of the treaties—a process that was neither anticipated nor supported by the member states—has created a Community legal system, which significantly restricts the actions and choices available to national governments (see discussion on national courts under Interaction with the EU below). Indeed, Keohane and Hoffmann conclude that '[o]f all Community institutions, the court has gone furthest in limiting national autonomy by asserting the principles of superiority of Community law and of the obligation of Member States to implement binding acts consistent with Community Directives' (1991: 278). Both institutions were created by member states to act in their interests (see Moravcsik 1993, 1998; Pierson 1996; Pollack 1997; see also Kassim and Menon 2003a), but as their experience with the court illustrates government 'principals' have found it difficult either to prevent their 'agents' from developing or acting on their own preferences, or to reassert their control once agents have 'shirked' or 'drifted' (Pierson 1996; though see Kassim and Menon 2003b).

Nor does their greater influence over decision making since Maastricht (Kassim and Menon 2003b) compensate for the loss of policy control that governments have experienced. Collectively, governments may sit at 'the decision making centre of the Community' (Wessels 1991) and, arguably, they remain 'masters of the Treaty' (Wessels 2001), but individually their influence over the pace of integration or the determination of EU policy is limited—a trend that successive treaties reforms have only strengthened. Qualified majority voting (QMV) has been extended to an increasingly wide number of policy areas. Under the Lisbon Treaty, QMV has become the default decision rule in the Council. With the national veto effectively obsolete, governments must forge 'winning coalitions' or a blocking minority if they are to exert any influence over final outcomes.

EU membership is also demanding in institutional terms. The EU political system is a challenging environment in which to operate. The complexity, fluidity, and fragmentation of EU institutions, the Union's organizational density and complex procedures, and the breadth of its policy agenda make 'Brussels' extremely difficult for governments to negotiate, particularly in the absence of the resources (authority, agenda control, party discipline, established networks, and administrative traditions) that enable them to dominate the domestic arena (Wright 1996; Kassim *et al.* 2000). Second, membership makes exacting demands on human resources. Governments must routinely find the personnel to attend myriad meetings in the Council and elsewhere. When they hold the rotating Council Presidency, moreover, they must find the extra resources necessary to manage stewardship of the EU's legislative agenda. Third, the institutional costs of membership are substantial. National administrations have had to put in place systems to manage their input into EU decision making. The importance of 'getting it right in Brussels' in order to ensure that favourable outcomes are secured and damaging outcomes avoided creates a strong incentive to establish effective mechanisms. All EU member states have put in place an apparatus to fulfil this purpose, though managing coordination at, and between, national and EU levels is a source of considerable strain, exacerbated by the different, often contradictory, logics that prevail in each arena (Wright 1996).

The EU has had a major impact on member state bureaucracies. With membership, the latter become part of the EU administration. As well as their national responsibilities, ministries assume the task of implementing and enforcing EU rules. Given the range of EU activity and the magnitude of its output, this is a formidable task, involving adjustment costs,[7] the application of unfamiliar instruments or the introduction of measures that may not be compatible with traditional policy orientations. EU-induced administrative change is most dramatic in the case of acceding states, who must not only incorporate the *acquis communautaire*, but must demonstrate the capacity to administer and enforce EU rules.[8] At the same time, EU membership creates new structures of opportunity for national ministries, making available options that would not exist otherwise. One possibility is captured by Derlien's notion of 'vertical brotherhoods' (2000: 59), the linkages, and thereby the channels of possible influence, that connect officials in line ministries with their counterparts at the EU level.

Adjustment by national administrations to the demands of EU membership is, however, only one side of the story. The relationship between the EU and state bureaucracies runs in two directions. For example, not only do EU institutions bear the imprint of national administrative traditions (Stevens and Stevens 2000), but national administrations are a ubiquitous presence in the EU system (Kassim and Wright 1991; Kassim 2003). Moreover, the functioning of EU institutions, most notably the Council, is dependent on the speed and effectiveness of national administrations. More broadly, since the EU depends on national administrations for the implementation and enforcement of Union legislation, the administrative capacity of the EU as a system is determined by the capacities of national bureaucracies.

Weaknesses in the latter are likely to impair the Union's overall effectiveness (Metcalfe 1992; see also Spanou 1998). More specifically, how EU policy is enacted on the ground is, to a large extent, conditional on member state bureaucracies. Dimitrakopoulos (2008) has shown, for example, how the institutions of central government can steer the implementation of EU policy.

National administrative policies implemented since the 1980s have also influenced developments at the EU. The creation of national agencies by European states has made possible the development of networks of regulators as a second-best strategy for ensuring the coherent implementation of EU rules across the territory of the Union (Sutherland 1992). More broadly, agencification has been a key development in the transformation of the executive order in Europe. Egeberg (2006) and Curtin and Egeberg (2008) have argued that national agencies, operating at arm's length from ministries and with dual loyalties—they are responsible for implementing EU and national rules—have developed autonomous links with supranational institutions. These linkages create new organizational entities, thereby transforming the Westphalian order of states and challenging traditional conceptions of accountability.

Despite some commonalities of response and strategy, EU impact has not produced administrative convergence between the member states.[9] The impact of 'Europe' has been 'differential' (Héritier *et al.* 2001). In many of the older member states, national administrations had long-established traditions and characteristics, in some cases, centuries before the advent of European integration. It is not surprising therefore that they reacted very differently in the face of demands imposed by European integration. Drawing on sociological institutionalist premises, but consistent also with historical institutionalism, Dimitrakopoulos and Pappas offer a persuasive explanation for the continuation of differences in the face of common obligations and external pressures. They argue that administrative change in response to the pressures of EU membership has been 'incremental', 'path dependent . . . along the lines of previously established patterns', and driven by 'learning', whereby 'member states come to identify the pressure that they face, but then go on to "respond" *individually*' (2003: 442).

Finally, there are two unresolved debates concerning the EU's impact within the executive (Goetz and Meyer-Sahling 2008). The first concerns whether the EU's effects have been experienced differently by the political and the administrative elements. As Goetz and Meyer-Sahling (2008: 13) observe: 'The very intensive engagement of national officials in EU policymaking is well documented (e.g. Wessels, Maurer, and Mittag 2003) as are the socialising effects of regular participation in EU policy-making bodies.' However, there is little research as yet to suggest that the EU has created a 'mandarin's paradise' that has enabled bureaucrats systematically to evade ministerial control (though see Larsson and Trondal 2005). The second focuses on the impact within the cabinet. One long-standing view (Andeweg and Irwin 1993: King 1994), recently updated (Johansson and Tallberg 2008), is that EU summitry and the need to coordinate (Kassim *et al.* 2000) has strengthened the prime minister within the cabinet. However, research on EMU emphasizes the power of the finance ministry as an additional pole within the government (Dyson 2002: Bulmer and Burch 2001).

Interaction between National Governments and the EU

In the interaction between the EU and the member states, central government is the dominant actor in representing national interests in Brussels and in defining and delivering policy responses to EU initiatives.[10] The national coordination systems put in place by the member states share several features:

- heads of government play a central role and have, with the strengthening of the European Council, become increasingly involved in EU policymaking;

- foreign ministries remain influential, but are increasingly overshadowed by prime ministers, challenged by finance ministers, and by-passed by line ministries;

- interdepartmental coordination in EU matters is managed by specialist mechanisms, such as the European Committee of the Council of Ministers, KERM (Poland), Committee for the EU (Czech Republic), the Coordination Council (Estonia), the Inter-ministerial Committee on European Integration (Hungary), central units for coordination include the European Secretariat of the Cabinet Office (UK), the Secretariat General for European Affairs, SGAE (France), the Office of the Committee on European Integration, UKIE (Poland), and the State Secretariat for Integration and Foreign Economic Relations, SSIEER (Hungary);

- dedicated EU policy units have been set up in line ministries;

- all member states maintain a permanent representation in Brussels, which is the main locus for national coordination at the EU level.

However, there are also significant differences (see Table 12.1 for selected states in comparison). While in some member states (e.g. Denmark, Hungary, Latvia, Portugal, Spain), the foreign ministry is the leading actor, elsewhere responsibility is shared with the economics or finance ministry (e.g. Germany, Greece) or with the Prime Minister's Office (Estonia, Italy, Lithuania).[11] In some countries, there is no clear division of labour. For example, in Poland, although the main coordinating committee, KERM, is chaired by the minister for foreign affairs, its vice president is appointed by the PM, and the PM attempts to influence the action of the UKIE, even though the latter is formally subordinate to the Ministry of Foreign Affairs (MFA) (Novak-Far 2008). In addition, in semi-presidential systems—notably, France and Lithuania—the PM may have day-to-day responsibility for central coordination, but presidents may become involved in high level EU negotiations, intervene in salient areas, or be called upon to arbitrate in controversial dossiers.

There is also significant variation between member states in the role, authority, and importance of inter-ministerial committees, the status and composition of the central coordinating unit, and the part played by line ministries also varies (Kassim and Dimitrov 2008). Variation is additionally to be found in the role, responsibilities, and influence of the Permanent Representation. Those of Hungary and Lithuania are especially influential; Latvia's is less so. Beyond these institutional differences, the extensiveness of consultation with interest groups and social partners varies markedly. In the UK, ministries frequently involve stakeholders, but consultation is ad hoc. In Sweden, the Czech Republic, and Latvia consultation tends to be more formal.

More generally, there are two points of contrast between older and newer member states, i.e. the EU-15 and the countries who joined the Union in 2004 and 2007. First, national coordination systems in the latter have tended to be less stable. Although it is not unusual for newer member states to review and revise their coordination arrangements shortly after joining, political factors have produced a degree of instability in some central and East European states. In Hungary, Poland, and Latvia, for example, the locus of central coordinating responsibility has been politicized and personalized, so that alternation in government has led to changes in the coordination architecture. This is partly because of the prevalence of coalition government, partly because of the absence of the tradition of an independent civil service, and partly because of an initial decentralizing response to practices of the communist era, but later learning about the benefits of centralization. Holding the Council Presidency is often an important and formative experience for new member states that has frequently led to a shift towards a more centralized approach to the coordination of EU policy once the presidency has come to an end. Second, there is a stronger emphasis on the implementation of EU policy in the new member states than in the old—a legacy of the long process of closely supervised accession.

Fundamentally, national coordination systems vary along two main dimensions (see Table 12.2). The first is the nature of the coordination ambition. Some countries attempt to monitor Commission activity and intervene on all fronts, while others concentrate attention on areas that are salient domestically. The second is the extent to which decision making is centralized. Simplifying, these differences reflect different national attitudes towards integration—countries which have a preference for intergovernmentalism are more likely to adopt a comprehensive (defensive) strategy—and features of the domestic polity—directive coordination—is only possible in a strongly centralized state; a more decentralized, even ministerial, approach to coordination is likely to be found where coalition governments are common or in federal states (Kassim 2003).

Parliaments and the EU

With few exceptions, the consensus in the literature is that national parliaments have been among the 'losers' of integration (Maurer and Wessels 2001a; Maurer 2001; Maurer 2002; see also Raunio and Hix 2000). Parliaments lack influence both

TABLE 12.1 Key features of national systems for the coordination of EU policy: selected member states

	Role of lead department	Central coordinators	Coordinating structures – political level	Coordinating structures – administrative level	Involvement of subnational authorities	Involvement of social partners and/or interest groups
Austria	Lead ministry sets policy	PM's office coordinates European Council preparation	Federal Government	Weekly coordination meetings, involving responsible departments	Länder involved in weekly coordination meetings	Social partners involved in weekly coordination meetings
Belgium	Lead ministry drafts policy	Permanent Representation Directorate for European Integration and Coordination in Ministry of Foreign Affairs	Cabinet (or cabinet sub-committee on foreign policy)	Inter-departmental conferences (sectoral)	Direct participation of regions and communities in coordination processes	Interest groups lobby governmental actors involved in coordination
Czech Republic	Lead ministry drafts policy	Unit of the Minister for European Affairs, PM's office	Government Committee on the EU	Committee on the EU	Depends on issue; mediated via Ministry for Regional Development	Tripartite meetings in Ministry of Labour and Social Affairs
France		SGAE in PM's office	Inter-ministerial Committee on Europe, which meets monthly; Issues not resolved by SGAE referred to Interministerial Committee chaired by adviser to PM or President	SGAE	Very limited	Very limited

(continued)

TABLE 12.1 (*continued*)

	Role of lead department	Central coordinators	Coordinating structures – political level	Coordinating structures – administrative level	Involvement of subnational authorities	Involvement of social partners and/or interest groups
Germany	Lead ministry drafts policy	Responsibility divided between Economics Ministry and Foreign Ministry; Chancellor is ultimate authority		Meetings of directors-general and monthly meetings of secretaries of state discuss issues that cannot be resolved by lead ministry	Twice yearly meetings between Federal and Lander EU coordinators	Involvement on informal basis
Hungary	Lead ministry drafts policy	State Secretariat for Integration and Foreign Economic Relations (SSIEER)	Cabinet of the Government for European Affairs, chaired by the Minister without portfolio	Inter-ministerial Committee for European Coordination, with 48 interdepartmental working groups; outstanding matters referred to Conference of State Secretaries		Consultation with line ministries
Poland	Lead ministry drafts policy	Office of the Committee on European Integration (UKIE)	Committee on European Integration at the ministerial level (KIE)	European Committee of the Council of Ministers (KERM)	Informal involvement	Informal involvement

Spain	Lead ministry drafts policy	State Secretariat for Foreign Policy and the European Union (SSEU), located in the Foreign Ministry	Consejo de Ministros (Cabinet), chaired by PM's office	Interdepartmental Commission for European-related Economic Affairs, Delegated Commission for Economic Affairs	Representative of the regions attached to the Permanent Representation	
Sweden	Lead ministry prepares first policy draft	The Secretariat of EU coordination, one of three units in PM's office		EU committee composed of secretaries of state, in which all departments represented Government		Informally by individual ministries
United Kingdom	Lead ministry proposes policy position	European and Global Issues Secretariat (EGIS) in the Cabinet Office, FCO and UK Permanent Presentation	European Affairs Committee	Weekly meeting between Head of European Secretariat and UK Permanent Representative. Ad hoc meetings arranged by EGIS	Coordination with the devolved authorities takes place within Joint Ministerial Committee Europe	Informal consultation of stakeholders by individual ministries

Source: Kassim *et al.* (2000, 2001); Batory (2012), Beyers and Bursens (2011); Gärtner *et al.* (2011), Kabele (2012); Kassim *et al.* (2011).

TABLE 12.2 National Coordination Systems of the EU-27: classification by ambition and distribution of power

	Coordination ambition	Distribution of power
Austria	Comprehensive	Decentralized
Belgium	Comprehensive	Decentralized
Bulgaria	Selective	Decentralized
Cyprus	Selective	Decentralized
Czech Republic	Comprehensive	Centralized
Denmark	Comprehensive	Centralized
Estonia	Selective	Decentralized
Finland	Comprehensive	Centralized
France	Comprehensive	Centralized
Germany	Comprehensive	Decentralized
Greece	Comprehensive	Decentralized
Hungary	Comprehensive	Decentralized
Ireland	Selective	Centralized
Italy	Comprehensive	Decentralized
Latvia	Comprehensive	Centralized
Lithuania	Comprehensive	Centralized
Luxembourg	Selective	Centralized
Malta	Selective	Centralized
Netherlands	Comprehensive	Decentralized
Poland	Comprehensive	Centralized
Portugal	Selective	Centralized
Romania	Selective	Decentralized
Slovakia	Comprehensive	Decentralized
Slovenia	Comprehensive	Decentralized
Spain	Selective	Centralized
Sweden	Comprehensive	Centralized
United Kingdom	Comprehensive	Centralized

Sources: Kassim (2000, 2003); Laffan (2006); Gärtner *et al.* (2011).

as players at the EU level and as domestic actors in national EU policymaking (Maurer 2001). At the same time, it is rarely argued that the EU has been a factor contributing to the decline in legislatures The concentration of expertise in the executive and strong party discipline are generally identified as the sources of parliamentary weakness since 1945. Their influence is as evident in EU policymaking as it is elsewhere. In terms of interaction, the ability of national parliaments to influence governments in matters of EU policy varies between member states, but is generally limited, even if institutional arrangements have been strengthened since Maastricht (O'Brennan and Raunio 2007: 9).

The Impact on National Parliaments

The most obvious impact of EU membership on national parliaments has been the workload generated by Union business. The volume is significant, but EU work is also complex and technical. More broadly, the effects of the Union's development and operation has been to weaken parliaments. '[P]arliaments have lost out due to the transfer of policymaking powers and . . . in particular legislative powers to the EU level' (Goetz and Meyer-Sahling 2008: 6; see also Schmidt 1999). Not only has decision making in important areas been taken out of the hands of national parliaments, but, because the EU is structurally embedded in the domestic systems, their ability to control their governments has also been diminished (Raunio and Hix 2000: 154). Parliaments 'are now operating in a situation where the source of legislation is partially external, and where they cannot legally bring about any alternation in the *acquis* or even promote alternative policies or laws which could conflict with those of the EU' (Newman 1996: 189, cited by Raunio and Hix 2000: 154). Second, as noted above, the EU privileges executives over legislatures in the domestic arena. Although parliaments have established oversight mechanisms to scrutinize the action of ministers, governments benefit from key advantages. Third, parliaments lack the resources, the presence in Brussels, and the independence necessary to exert meaningful control over the executive.

Two further observations are, however, important. First, all parliaments have established dedicated procedures in response to EU membership.[12] These were upgraded in the 1980s and enhanced in the 1990s (Raunio and Hix 2000; Maurer 2002; Maurer and Wessels 2001b; O'Brennan and Raunio 2007). In the wake of Maastricht, committees were strengthened, many following constitutional change aimed at enshrining parliamentary oversight.[13] The driving force, according to Raunio and Hix was 'the desire by non-governing parties and backbench parliamentarians to redress the "information gap" between governing elites and the parliamentary rank-and-file' (2000: 163). As a result, the position of parliaments was improved 'through more effective overall scrutiny of government, particularly better access to information' (ibid.).[14]

Second, some parliaments have fared better than others. 'Path dependence' is again in evidence with the effects of integration on legislatures varying according to their strength in the domestic polity (Dimitrakopoulos 2001b; also see Norton 1996: 187–9). The effect of integration in countries where the legislature is weak or subordinate (e.g. in France) has been felt less intensely than those where the parliament is strong (e.g. in Denmark and Italy). Meanwhile, in the UK, which is distinguished by the principle of parliamentary sovereignty, the impact has been especially dramatic (Craig 1991).

Interaction with the EU

Although networking between national parliaments has been formalized since the late 1980s, and the scope for direct intervention has increased with the 'early warning system' introduced by the Lisbon Treaty (see later in this section), interaction between national parliaments and the EU remains largely indirect. The involvement of national parliaments in EU business takes place within a domestic setting and is limited to three functions: treaty ratification, the transposition of EU legislation, and scrutinizing government. The room for manoeuvre with respect to the first two is limited (Maurer 2002: 6–7). Ratification is a strong power, but parliaments can only answer 'yes' or 'no', and casting a negative vote would be to choose the nuclear option. With regard to transposition, meanwhile, parliaments can be circumvented by government. Dimitrakopoulos (2001a) shows, for example, how governments use delegated legislation to by-pass parliament.

In respect of government scrutiny, the presence of European Affairs Committees in all member state parliaments should not be allowed to obscure significant cross-national variation in formal arrangements, still less their operation,[15] or their legal basis (see Table 12.3).[16] The two most important choices concern the type of control imposed on ministers and the organization of committee responsibilities in relation to oversight. With regard to the first, there are two main models (Kiivers 2006: 54–7; COSAC 2007:7–9).[17] The mandate-giving system is based on arrangement in the Danish Folketing. Ministers must seek *ex ante* approval from the Europe Committee for the positions they intend to take in upcoming meetings of the Council, and are bound by its decision. This model was adopted in several states on joining the EU in 1995 and 2004. In the document-based system, pioneered by the UK House of Commons, legislative proposals from the EU are sent to the European Affairs Committee with an accompanying memorandum that sets out the position that the relevant minister intends to take. The committee can put questions to the minister or ask for information to be disclosed, and may decide to refer the issue for debate. The parliament may decide to adopt a resolution. Crucially, ministers are not permitted to give their consent to measures in the Council until scrutinized by parliament.

Second, there is considerable variation in the organization of parliamentary oversight. Not only does the status, composition, and competence of the European Affairs Committee differ between parliaments,[18] but the extent to which the expertise of sectoral committees is called upon and how also varies. In Denmark, overlapping committee membership furnishes the European Affairs Committee with specialist

TABLE 12.3 European Affairs Committees in the EU-27

Member state	Name of committee(s)	Date established	Composition
Austria – *Nationalrat*	Main Committee on EU Affairs Standing Subcommittee on EU Affairs	1995/2000	27 Members. 17 Members.
Austria – *Bundesrat*	EU-Committee	1996	14 Members.
Belgium – *Chambre des représentants* – *Sénat*	Federal Advisory Committee on European Affairs	1985/1990	30 Members: 10 Senators, 10 MPs, and 10 (Belgian) MEPs.
Bulgaria – *Narodno sabranie*	Committee on European Affairs and Oversight of the European Funds	2001	18 Members.
Cyprus – *Vouli ton Antiprosopon*	Committee on European Affairs	1999	10 Members.
Czech Republic – *Poslanecká sněmovna*	Committee for European Affairs	2004	15 Members. Composition reflects party balance.
Czech Republic – *Senát*	Committee on European Union Affairs	1998	9 Members. Composition reflects party balance.
Denmark – *Folketing*	European Affairs Committee	1972	17 Members.
Estonia – *Riigikogu*	European Union Affairs Committee	1997	15+ Members.
Finland – *Eduskunta*	Grand Committee	1994	25 Members and 13 substitutes.
France – *Assemblée nationale*	Committee on European Affairs	1979	48 Members. Composition reflects party balance.

(continued)

TABLE 12.3 (*continued*)

Member state	Name of committee(s)	Date established	Composition
France – *Sénat*	Committee for European Affairs	1979	36 Members. Composition reflects party balance.
Germany – *Bundestag*	Committee on the Affairs of the European Union	1991/1994	33 Members of the *Bundestag* and 15 (German) MEPs.
Germany– *Bundesrat*	Committee on European Union Questions	1957/1965	17 Members. One member from each state.
Greece – *Vouli ton Ellinon*	Special Standing Committee for European Affairs	June 1990	31 Members.
Hungary – *Országgyülés*	Committee on European Affairs	1992	21 Members. Composition reflects party balance.
Ireland – *Houses of the Oireachtas*	Joint Committee on European Union Affairs	1995/2011	9 Members of the *Dáil Eireann* and 5 Members from the *Seanad Eireann*.
Italy – *Camera dei Deputati*	Committee on EU Policies	1971/1990	44 Members.
Italy – *Senato della Repubblica*	14th Standing Committee on EU Policies	1968/2003	27 Members.
Latvia – *Saeima*	European Affairs Committee	1995/2004	17 Members. Composition reflects party balance.
Lithuania – *Seimas*	Committee on European Affairs	1997	15–25 Members. Composition reflects party balance.

Luxembourg – *Chambre des Députés*	Committee for Foreign and European Affairs, for Defence, for Cooperation and for Immigration	1989	11 Members. Composition reflects party balance.
Malta – *Kamra tad-Deputati*	Standing Committee on Foreign and European Affairs	1995/2003	9 Members.
Netherlands – *Tweede Kamer*	Committee on European Affairs	1986	27 Members. All parties in House are represented.
Netherlands – *Eerste Kamer*	Committee for European Co-operation Organizations	1970	27 Members.
Poland – *Sejm*	European Union Affairs Committee	1992/1997/2001/ 2004	No more than 44 Members (10% of the *Sejm*). Composition reflects party balance.
Poland – *Senat*	European Union Affairs Committee	1991/2004	18 Members (no formal limit).
Portugal – *Assembleia da República*	Committee on European Affairs	1980/1988	21 Members. Composition reflects party balance.
Romania – *Camera Deputaților*	Committee on European Affairs	1995/2006/ 2011	25 Members.
Romania – *Senatul*	Committee on European Affairs	1995/2006/2011	11 Members.
Slovakia – *Národná rada*	Committee on European Affairs	2004	11 Members. Composition reflects party balance.
Slovenia – *Državni zbor*	Committee for EU Affairs	April 2004	14 Members. Composition reflects party balance.

(continued)

Table 12.3 *(continued)*

Member state	Name of committee(s)	Date established	Composition
Slovenia – *Državni svet*	International Relations and European Affairs Commission	1993	10 Members: interest groups representatives.
Spain – *Cortes Generales*	Joint Committee for the European Union	1986/1994	43 Members.
Sweden – *Riksdag*	Committee on EU Affairs	1994	17 Members and 42 alternates. (All sectoral committees are represented).
United Kingdom – *House of Commons*	European Scrutiny Committee	1974	16 Members. Composition reflects party balance.
United Kingdom – *House of Lords*	European Union Committee	1974	18 Members plus 52 on seven sub-committees of the Committee.

Source: Conference of Parliamentary Committees for Union Affairs – available at **http://www.cosac.eu/en/info/scrutiny/eac/For_more_info/ (accessed 31 January 2012).**

expertise. Documents are distributed to sectoral committees and the European Affairs Committee consults them where it finds that a proposal violates subsidiarity.[19] In Finland, by contrast, the Grand Committee for European Affairs delegates scrutiny to the sectoral committees, views the reports that they submit, and on that basis decides whether to question ministers and to issue a negotiating mandate. A third approach is taken in the UK House of Commons, where sifting is performed by European Standing Committees, each of which specializes in particular policy domains. Fourth, in the Bundestag, the European Affairs Committee is responsible for cross-departmental issues, but coordinates and deliberates with the relevant sectoral committees. Finally, in the Dutch Lower House and in the two houses of the French parliament, the sectoral committees are responsible for scrutinizing EU proposals, but the European Affairs Committee in the first and the European Affairs Delegations in the second assist and coordinate. As Kiivers (2006: 23) observes, this variation 'along the centralization-decentralization line illustrates that institutional and procedural adaptation reflects the way in which European affairs are qualified: as quasi-domestic affairs, foreign affairs or a sui generis hybrid with a bit of both'.

As a number of authors have shown, the formal powers available to parliaments are not necessarily accurate indicators of parliamentary control.[20] Auel and Benz (2005: 388) argue convincingly that it is important to 'look beyond the formal institutions and to take the strategies into account, which parliamentary actors develop to deal with their power or lack of'. Evidence from Hungary, Latvia, and Slovakia also suggests that parliamentarians may elect not to use the powerful sanctions at their disposal. In their study of the Austrian parliament—another parliament with strong control mechanisms—Pollack and Slominski (2003) show how the use of sanctions, such as mandating ministers, can be counterproductive. Tight control can restrict a minister's room for manoeuvre in the Council as negotiations reach the endgame and can leave the national delegation sidelined. In practice, parliamentarians deploy other mechanisms to influence the government's position. Benz (2004) shows, similarly, that Danish MPs recognize that mandates are an inflexible instrument and potentially counterproductive. They too have developed other strategies for exerting influence. While behavioural factors—interactions within and between parties, relations between government and opposition, and contacts between MPs and legislators at the EU level—and attitudes—the extent to which parliamentarians are prepared to invest in developing the necessary expertise—need to be incorporated in any metric of parliamentary influence, comprehensive data not yet available.

Accounting for cross-national variation in the arrangements put in place by national parliaments is not straightforward. Dimitrakopoulos (2001b) draws on historical institutionalism to explain the responses of three parliaments in terms of incremental adaptation and path dependence. Other authors, including Raunio and Hix (2000), and Holzacher (2005) look respectively to inter-and intra-party relations and single- or multi-party government. Perhaps the most imaginative approach is that undertaken by Bergman (1997), who tests five explanatory factors, including political culture, public opinion, federalism, frequency of minority governments, and evidence of strategic action. He concludes that all have some impact, but that political culture, with a north–south division running across Europe, can explain much of the variation in scrutiny arrangements.

At the EU level, national parliamentarians lost an organic link with the Community in 1979 when the direct election of the European Parliament was instituted, but since the late 1980s the view that national parliaments should have greater involvement within the EU has become increasingly salient. In response to the Community's growing importance, the presidents of national parliaments agreed in 1989 to meet regularly, and in the same year the Conference of Representatives of European Affairs Committees (COSAC) was founded.[21] Shortly thereafter, the EU issued a formal encouragement to national parliaments in declarations attached to the Treaty on European Union (TEU). Declaration 13 called for a strengthening of legislatures at the domestic level, Declaration 14 for a collective role for national parliaments at the EU level. The first was followed by action at national level, as discussed above, and by EU institutions. The European Council and Parliament amended their internal rules so as to recognize national parliaments and COSAC as consultative bodies in the EU decision-making process (Maurer 2002: 21). Then, in 2006, following the 'Barroso initiative', the Commission agreed to send its proposals directly to national parliaments (Chalmers *et al.* 2010: 129). The following year, a Protocol on National Parliaments, attached to the Treaty of Amsterdam, identified which documentation was to be supplied to parliaments. The Lisbon Treaty expanded these provisions further. Article 12 stipulates that, 'National Parliaments contribute actively to the good functioning of the Union: (a) through being informed by the institutions of the Union and having draft legislative acts forwarded to them in accordance with the Protocol on the role of national Parliaments in the European Union'.[22]

Defining a collective role for national parliaments has proved a more difficult undertaking, not least because of the fundamental questions it posed.[23] The form that 'a collective role' might take (see Maurer 2002: 11–13, 27–29), the identification of a rationale for such a development (Kiivers 2006), and how conflict with the mandate of national governments on the one hand and the European Parliament on the other could be avoided were apparently intractable. A partial answer emerged in the Constitutional Convention, where delegates proposed rights for national parliaments to veto legislative texts. The proposal was diluted in the Constitutional Treaty, but strengthened in the Lisbon Treaty. Lisbon instituted two procedures:

- a 'yellow card' procedure whereby legislative proposals are transmitted to parliaments, which then have eight weeks to decide whether they comply with the principle of subsidiarity and to submit a reasoned opinion to the Presidents of the Parliament, Council and Commission. Each parliament has two votes and if eighteen of the fifty-four votes question the compliance of the proposed measure, the institution that introduced it can decide to maintain, amend, or withdraw it.

- an 'orange card' procedure whereby if the Commission originates a proposal in response to which a majority of national parliaments submit reasoned opinions, the Commission is obliged to review the proposal. Should the Commission decide to maintain the draft, it would have to refer it to the Council and the European Parliament, and avoid a situation where either fifty-five per cent of the Council or a simple majority of MEPs took the view that the text did not comply with the principle of subsidiarity.

Experience of the first year of the Lisbon Treaty's operation suggests that, even if in the longer term the new procedures are likely to increase networking between parliaments and strengthen the role of COSAC, the new prerogatives granted to national parliaments have, in the words of one commentator, seemed to be more 'paper tigers' than 'sleeping beauties' (Kaczynski 2011). As the same author observes, '[t]he first year of using the procedure shows that the existing forms of cooperation [between parliaments] are either too weak or poorly used. Only 59% of the scrutiny processes initiated were completed on time within the eight-week period. Only eight national chambers completed their procedures in all cases for which they initiated the subsidiarity control. Twelve others had significant problems with less than half of initiated subsidiarity controls being completed on time. Three of them have not completed a single process they started!' (Kaczynski 2011: 11).

Though strictly speaking the right of referral does not create a collective role for national parliaments, and is limited to subsidiarity considerations alone, it may ultimately strengthen their position vis-à-vis EU decision making. As yet, the contention made by Chalmers *et al.* (2010) that, even where formal thresholds are not met, it is unlikely that the EU would proceed with a proposal if a significant number of parliaments query its compliance, has not been properly tested.

National Courts

The constraints imposed on national governments by the EU's development as a 'Community of law' have already been noted, but the legal systems of the member states have also been significantly affected. National courts have been drawn into a Community-wide legal order with the European Court of Justice (ECJ) at its apex and converted into enforcers of EU law. At the same time, they have participated in, and contributed to, albeit with varying levels of enthusiasm, the creation and development of this system.

Impact on National Courts

The founding treaties imposed a new set of responsibilities on national courts. While the ECJ was to be responsible for resolving legal disputes at the Community level—those that arise between EU institutions and the member states, and between member states—national courts were entrusted with the task of ensuring member state conformity with EU law (Stone Sweet 1998). Moreover, '[i]n its jurisprudence, the court has sought to enlist national judges in a working partnership to construct a constitutional, rule of law Community . . . [whereby], national judges become agents of the Community order' (Stone Sweet 1998: 163–4), as 'Community judges'. The court relied heavily on the willingness of national judges to follow its rulings, but also to use the Article 234 [ex. 177] 'preliminary ruling' procedure,[24] which permits a national court to request the ECJ's opinion when a case raises an issue that requires interpretation of the treaty. '[N]ational courts and the European Court are thus integrated into a unitary system of judicial review' (Weiler 1991: 2420).

Fundamental changes have also resulted from 'constitutionalization', the process whereby 'the EC treaties evolved from a set of legal arrangements binding upon sovereign states, into a vertically integrated legal order that confers judicially enforceable rights and obligations on all legal persons and entities, public and private within EC territory' (Stone Sweet 1998: 160). As a consequence, and in contrast to the doctrine of *lex posteriori*, according to which in international law treaty obligations can be overridden by laws that are subsequently adopted by the legislature, national judges 'treat EC law as if it were a source of law that is superior to, and autonomous from, national statutes, and capable of being applied, directly, within the national legal order, by national judges' (Stone Sweet 1998:161). However, national courts take contrasting views on the two principles, enunciated by the court in two leading cases, *Van Gend en Loos v. Nederlandse Administratie der Belastingen*, and *Costa v. ENEL*,[25] on which the Community of law is founded. The first is the doctrine of *direct effect*, whereby Community legal norms grant individual citizens rights that can be invoked against their own governments in national courts. The second is the doctrine of *supremacy*, according to which any Community norm takes precedence over any national law that conflicts with it, whether or not that law was adopted before or after the Community norm.

Though they differ in their reasoning and in the terms on which they accepted these principles, national courts have in general responded positively to the ECJ's 'gambit' (Stone Sweet 1998).[26] Of the many explanations put forward to account for the willingness of the national courts in this regard (Mattli and Slaughter 1998b; Craig 2003), two are particularly persuasive and can be seen as complementary. The first is the 'judicial empowerment thesis', associated with Stein (1981) and Weiler (1991, 1994), which asserts that 'judges work to enhance their own authority to control legal . . . outcomes, and to reduce the control of other institutional actors' (Stone Sweet 1998: 164). The second is an approach consistent with neofunctionalist arguments (see Burley and Mattli 1993; Stone Sweet 1998), which contends that, once the court provided them with the opportunity, private actors pursued their interests before national courts, using Community norms to challenge national laws through the preliminary ruling procedure. The power of national courts was increased as cases involving direct effect and supremacy were pleaded before them, turning them into Community courts in their own right. Lawyers specializing in EC law were 'willing advocates' in the process (Craig 2003: 32).[27]

The bases on which national courts have accepted the supremacy of EU law and the terms of its application vary significantly (Mattli and Slaughter 1998a, 1998b; Craig 2003).[28] Courts in Belgium and the Netherlands based their judgements on reasoning that is close to the ECJ's own; namely, that 'by creating a Community of unlimited duration, having . . . powers stemming from a limitation of sovereignty, or a transfer of powers from the States to the Community, the Member states have limited their sovereign rights, albeit within limited fields, and thus have created a body of law which binds both their nationals and themselves'.[29] In France, by contrast, the highest civil court, the Cour de Cassation, accepted the supremacy of Community law in 1975, but based its decision on Article 55 of the French Constitution, which recognizes the superior authority of treaties or agreements duly ratified. The highest administrative court, the Conseil d'Etat, did not reach this conclusion until 1990, while the Conseil Constitutionnel ruled in 1992 that there are limits to France's acceptance of supremacy. In Italy, the Constitutional Court initially held that where two norms clashed the one that was adopted later in time should take precedence—this was the decision which led eventually to the ECJ's ruling in the *Costa* case—but modified its position in 1984, when it recognized the primacy of Community legislation, where no threat is posed to the fundamental values of the Constitution.

In Germany, the Federal Constitutional Court (FCC) first accepted the ECJ's claim, but retreated in 1974 on the grounds that the transfer of competence to an international organization must not contravene the underlying principles of the Basic Law. Its concern about the protection of the rights of individuals was linked to the absence of a codified charter at Community level). However, in 1986, the FCC ruled that so long as the EC ensured effective protection of fundamental rights, the FCC would no longer review Community legislation against the Basic Law. Since then, however, in its 1993 'Maastricht judgement', the FCC has ruled that the Basic Law limits the transfer of powers to the EC and that it (the FCC) has the power to declare acts of the EC *ultra vires* where they stray beyond it. More recently, in its ruling on the Lisbon Treaty of 30 June 2009, the FCC specified the areas where competences cannot be transferred and thereby held out the possibility of further review (Auel and Baquero Cruz 2010). Finally, although in the UK the doctrine of direct effect was accepted by British courts on accession to the Community, supremacy was problematic because it conflicted with parliamentary sovereignty. Since any treaty given force by being incorporated in an Act of Parliament could be superseded by any later Act of Parliament, the 1972 Act of Accession was apparently as vulnerable as any other Act. The leading decision was made in 1990. Following a reference from the House of Lords, the ECJ ruled in *R. V Secretary of State for Transport, ex p. Factortame Ltd (no. 2)* that the Merchant Shipping Act of 1988 was in breach of EU law. The

House of Lords accepted this judgement, arguing that there was no conflict with parliamentary sovereignty, because in adopting the 1972 Act the UK parliament had accepted the EU legal system of which the supremacy doctrine is a part. It followed that any future parliament could repeal the 1972 Act.

The development of a EU system of law has had a major impact on national legal systems and on national courts. Kelemen (2011) has argued recently that the effects may be even more considerable than hitherto understood. He contends that, as a result of its fragmented institutional structure and the priority ascribed to market integration, EU policy makers have been compelled to adopt detailed rules that are judicially enforceable, backed by public enforcement litigation and opportunities for private litigation. The consequence is the rise of 'Eurolegalism', a European version of the adversarial legalism that has long characterized the US and in contradistinction to which regulatory law in Europe had been defined. Competition policy, an area of core Community competence, which has become increasingly juridified and where recent reforms have decentralized private enforcement to national courts, and encouraged private litigation before national courts (Peyer 2010),[30] offers but one example of this trend (Kelemen 2011: 144; Peyer 2010).

The above discussion makes it clear that the EU has not only had an impact on national courts, but that national courts were key actors in extending the EU system of law and key agents in its administration. They 'asked questions which the Commission or a member state would never ask', enabling the ECJ 'to comment on national policy and to expand the reach and scope of European law' (Alter 2001: 22). At the same time, the conditions according to which national courts have accepted the supremacy doctrine, especially the FCC's Lisbon ruling, suggests that there may be a point beyond which they will not view further transfer of competencies as constitutional.

Interaction with the EU

At the heart of the EU's legal order is a 'set of institutionalised dialogues between supra-national and national judges' (Stone Sweet 1998: 305). The interchange has become increasingly intense, particularly since the late 1970s.[31] In the 1980s, the number of references for preliminary ruling per annum fell below the 100-mark only once, and for much of the 1990s was consistently above 140 (Stone Sweet and Brunell 1998: 74). By 2010, the figure was 385 (ECJ 2011: 1) However, beyond a general increase across time and the older members making more references in each period than the member states that joined later, there are significant differences in the extent to which national courts use the Article 234 system. Explaining cross-national variation has so far proved elusive (although see Stone Sweet and Brunell 1998; Chalmers 2000), but Hix (1999: 114) makes two interesting observations. First, with each enlargement, the larger member states made more references than the small states—France, Germany, and Italy made more than the Benelux countries, the UK more than Denmark and Ireland, and Spain more than Portugal. Second, UK courts make relatively few references (see Golub 1996).

Conclusion

The impact on national institutions of their imbrication in a system of collective governance has been far-reaching. Domestic institutions have assumed new tasks, responsibilities, and obligations. In some areas, their freedom of action has been circumscribed, but these losses must be set against the new opportunities that have been created and the new channels of influence that have opened.

The impact of integration has not been uniform, however, and there is no sign of 'ever greater convergence' or homogeneity. Although in some respects central governments feel their constraints more keenly than other bodies, they are also the most powerful actors within the EU system and have greater opportunities to pursue their favoured projects. National courts have assumed a new function as part of the system of Community law to which they belong, while sub-national governments have experienced both the effects of regulation and the opportunities deriving from the territorial redefinition that has taken place in the Union. Only national parliaments seem to have registered no benefit. Despite a strengthening of oversight arrangements since Maastricht, and the new procedures to police subsidiarity introduced by the Lisbon Treaty, they remain marginal actors in relation to EU affairs at both Union and national levels. Their inability to scrutinize governments effectively raises important questions about accountability and the democratic credentials of national EU policymaking systems (see Katz 1999).

National differences are also evident. Differences in the way that constitutions allocate power and responsibility between branches of governments domestically, produce a pattern of strong national differentiation in terms of the resources available to institutions and their vulnerability to encroachment by the EU. These factors affect both the inclination and the capacity of domestic institutions to mobilize. This point is illustrated well by the experiences of national parliaments, where in general the more powerful they have been in the pre-existing domestic system, the more assertive and influential they have been able to be in relation to the EU.

Finally, while attention in the EU literature, particularly on Europeanization, focuses on the implications of action in Brussels for domestic actors, it should not be forgotten that national institutions play an important part not only in shaping outcomes at the EU level, but also in determining the capacities—administrative, legal, and political—of the Union as a system. The functioning of EU institutions and the ability of the Union to deliver along all three dimensions depend, fundamentally, on the operation and effectiveness of member state bodies at both EU and domestic levels.

FURTHER READING

In a literature that has become increasingly voluminous over the past decade, Wessels *et al.* (2003c) provide a comprehensive, if now somewhat dated, examination of the impact of the EU on member state institutions, while Graziano and Vink (2007) offer a useful conceptual analysis of Europeanization, as well as helpful overview chapters on how the EU has affected institutions in national polities. On individual institutions, the review of literature on the EU's impact on parliaments and executives by Goetz and Meyer-Sahling (2008) is excellent. Goetz (2000) offers one of the few conceptual discussions of how executives have been affected by the EU, the executive transformation thesis elaborated by Egeberg (2006) is an important perspective on the interaction between EU and national developments, while Dimitrakopoulos and Pappas (2003) and Page (2003) take very different approaches to the Europeanization of national administrations. O'Brennan and Raunio (2007), Auel and Benz (2005), Maurer (2001, 2002), Maurer and Wessels (2001b), and Raunio and Hix (2000) are the best places to begin reading on national parliaments. On national courts, Craig (2003) and Slaughter *et al.* (1998) are extremely valuable—the first a single chapter overview, the latter a landmark text. Kelemen (2011) is an important recent addition to the literature. On the interaction between the EU and national levels, see Kassim and Dimitrov (2008).

WEB LINKS

There are few websites on the Europeanization of member state institutions, but contributions to the Convention on the Future of Europe at **http://european-convention. eu.int/** highlight institutional dynamics. The member governments all have websites, although there is no gateway to all of them. The national parliaments' websites can be accessed via the COSAC site, **http://www.cosac.eu/en/mailbox/parliaments/**.

REFERENCES

Alter, K. (1998), 'Who are the "Masters of the Treaty"? European Governments and the European Court of Justice', *International Organization*, 52/1: 121–47.

Alter, K. L. (2001), *Establishing the Supremacy of European Law*, Oxford: Oxford University Press.

Andeweg, R. and Irwin, G.A. (1993), *The Government and Politics of the Netherlands*, Basingstoke: Macmillan.

Auel, K. and Baquero Cruz, J. (2010), *Karlruhe's Europe*, Studies and Research 78, Paris: Notre Europe, http://www.notre-europe.eu/uploads/tx_publication/Etud78-Karlsruhe_sEurope-en_01.pdf.

Auel, K. and Benz, A. (eds) (2005), *The Europeanisation of Parliamentary Democracy*, London: Routledge.

Batory, A. (forthcoming 2013), 'The National Coordination of EU Policy in Hungary: Patterns of Continuity and Change', *Public Administration*.

Benz, A. (2004), 'Path-Dependent Institutions and Strategic Veto Players: National Parliaments in the European Union', *West European Politics*, 27/5: 875–900.

Bergman, T. (1997), 'National Parliaments and EU Affairs Committees: Notes on Empirical Variation and Competing Explanations', *Journal of European Public Policy*, 4/3: 373–87.

Beyers, J. and Bursens, P. (2011), 'Domestic European Policy Coordination and Informational Lobbying. How EU Policies get Politicized in Belgium', unpublished mimeo.

Bulmer, S. and Burch, M. (2001), 'The Europeanization of Central Government: The UK and Germany in Historical Institutionalist Perspective', in: G. Schneider and M. Aspinwall, (eds), *The Rules of Integration: Institutional Approaches to the Study of Europe*, Manchester: Manchester University Press, 73–98.

Burley, A. M. and Mattli, W. (1993), 'Europe before the Court: A Political Theory of Legal Integration', *International Organisation*, 47/1: 41–76.

Chalmers, D. (2000), 'The Positioning of EU Judicial Politics within the United Kingdom', in K. H. Goetz and S. Hix (eds), 'Europeanised Politics? European Integration and National Political Systems', special issue of *West European Politics*, 23/4: 169–210.

Chalmers, D., Davies, G., and Monti, G. (2010), *European Union Law. Text and Materials*, Cambridge: Cambridge University Press, second edition.

Claes, D. H. (2002), 'The Process of Europeanization—The Case of Norway and the Internal Energy Market', University of Oslo: ARENA Working Papers, WP 02/12.

Community and European Affairs Committees of Parliaments of the European Union (COSAC) (2007), 'Eighth bi-annual report: Developments in European Union Procedures and Practices Relevant to Parliamentary Scrutiny', Prepared by the COSAC Secretariat and presented to: XXXVIII Conference of Community and European Affairs Committees of Parliaments of the European Union 14–15 October.

Craig, P. (1991), 'Sovereignty of the UK Parliament after *Factortame*', *Yearbook of European Law*, 11: 221–55.

Craig, P. (2003), 'National Courts and Community Law', in J. Hayward and A. Menon (eds), *Governing Europe*, Oxford: Oxford University Press, 15–35.

Curtin, D. and Egeberg, M. (2008), 'Tradition and Innovation: Europe's Accumulated Executive Order', *West European Politics*, 31/4: 639–61.

Dehousse, R. (1988), 'Completing the Internal Market: Institutional Constraints and Challenges', in R. Bieber and R. Dehousse (eds), *1992: One European Market?: A Critical Analysis of the Commission's Internal Market Strategy Strategy*, Baden-Baden: Nomos.

Derlien, H-U. (2000), 'Germany', in H. Kassim, B. G. Peters and V. Wright (eds), *National Coordination of EU Policy: The Domestic Level*, Oxford: Oxford University Press, 54–78.

Dimitrakopoulos, D. G. (2001a), 'The Transposition of EU Law: "Post-Decisional Politics" and Institutional Autonomy', *European Law Journal*, 7/4: 442–58.

Dimitrakopoulos, D. G. (2001b), 'Incrementalism and Path Dependence: European Integration and Institutional Change in National Parliaments', *Journal of Common Market Studies* 39/3: 405–22.

Dimitrakopoulos, D. G. (2008), *The Power of the Centre. Central Governments and the Macro-implementation of EU Public Policy*, Manchester: Manchester University Press.

Dimitrakopoulos, D. G. and Pappas, A. G. (2003), 'International Organizations and Domestic Administrative Reform', in B. G. Peters and J. Pierre (eds), *Handbook of Public Administration*, London: Sage, 440–50.

Dyson, K. (2002), 'Introduction: EMU as Integration, Europeanization, and Convergence', in K. Dyson (ed.), *European States and the Euro. Europeanization, Variation, and Convergence*, Oxford: Oxford University Press, 1–27.

Egeberg, M. (ed.) (2006), *The Multilevel Union Administration: The Transformation of Executive Politics in Europe*, Basingstoke: Palgrave Macmillan.

European Court of Justice (2011), 'Statistics Concerning Judicial Activity in 2010: References for a Preliminary Ruling Have Never Been Dealt With so Quickly', Press release no. 13/11, 2 March.

Favell, A. (1998), 'The Europeanisation of Immigration Politics', *European Integration On-line Papers* (EIoP), 2:10 at http://eiop.or.at/eiop/texte/1998-010a.htm

Fischer, A., Nicoloet, S., and Sciarini, P. (2002), 'Europeanisation of a Non-EU Country: The Case of Swiss Immigration Policy', *West European Politics*, 25/4: 143–70.

Garrett, G., and Weingast, B. R. (1993), 'Ideas, Interests and Institutional Constructing of the EC's Internal Market', in J. Goldstein and R. Keohane (eds), *Ideas and Foreign Policy*, Ithaca, NY: Cornell University Press, 173–206.

Gärtner, L., Hörner, J., and Obholzer, L. (2011), 'National Coordination of EU Policy: A Comparative Study of the Twelve "New" Member States', *Journal of Contemporary European Research*, 7/1: 77–100, available at: http://www.jcer.net/index.php/jcer/article/view/275.

Goetz, K. H. (2000), 'European Integration and National Executives: A Cause in Search of an Effect', in K. H. Goetz and S. Hix (eds), 'Europeanised Politics? The Impact of European Integration on Domestic Politics', special issue of *West European Politics*, 23/4: 211–31.

Goetz, K. H. and Meyer-Sahling, J-H. (2008), 'The Europeanisation of National Political Systems: Parliaments and Executives', *Living Reviews in European Governance*, 3: 2 http://europeangovernance.livingreviews.org/Articles/lreg-2008-2/.

Golub, J. (1996), 'The Politics of Judicial Discretion: Rethinking the Interaction Between National Courts and the European Court of Justice', *West European Politics*, 19: 360–85.

Graziano, P. and Vink, M. (eds) (2007), *Europeanization: New Research Agendas*, Basingstoke: Palgrave Macmillan.

Haas, E. B. (1958), *The Uniting of Europe*, Stanford: Stanford University Press.

Héritier, A., Knill, C., and Mingers, S. (1996), *Ringing the Changes in Europe*, Berlin: Walter de Gruyter.

Héritier, A., Kerwer, D., Knill, C., Lehmkuhl, D., Teutsch, M. and A. C. Douillet (2001), *Differential Europe. The European Union Impact on National Policymaking*, Lanham, MD: Rowman & Littlefield.

Hix, S. (1999), *The Political System of the European Union*, Basingstoke: Macmillan.

Hix, S. and Goetz, K. H. (2000), 'Introduction: European Integration and National Political Systems', in K. H. Goetz and S. Hix (eds), 'Europeanised politics? The Impact of European Integration on Domestic Politics', special issue of *West European Politics*, 23/4: 1–26.

Hoffmann, S. (1966), 'Obstinate or Obsolete? The Fate of the Nation State and the Case of Western Europe', *Daedalus*, 95: 892–908.

Hoffmann, S. (1982), 'Reflections on the Nation State in Europe Today', *Journal of Common Market Studies*, 21: 21–37.

Johansson, K. M. and Tallberg, J. (2008), 'Explaining Chief Executive Empowerment: European Union Summitry and Domestic Institutional Change', paper presented at the Fourth Pan-European Conference on EU Politics, Riga, 25–27 September.

Kabele, J. (2012), 'The Czech Coordination System of EU Policy (2003–2007)', under review.

Kaczynski, P. (2011), *Paper tigers or sleeping beauties? National parliaments in the post-Lisbon European Political System*, CEPS Special Report, Brussels: CEPS, February.

Kassim, H. (2003), 'The National Co-ordination of EU Policy: Must Europeanisation Mean Convergence?', in K. Featherstone and C. Radaelli (eds), *The Politics of Europeanisation: Theory and Analysis*, Oxford: Oxford University Press, 83–111.

Kassim, H. and Dimitrov, V. D. (2008), 'National Coordination of EU Policy in the "New" Member States: A Comparative Perspective', under review.

Kassim, H. and Menon, A. (2003a), 'The Principal-Agent Approach And The Study Of The European Union: Promise Unfulfilled?', in E. Jones and A. Verdun (eds), 'Political Economy and the Study of European Integration', special issue of *Journal of European Public Policy*, 10/1: 121–39.

Kassim, H. and Menon, A. (2003b), 'Les Etats membres de l'UE et la Commission Prodi', *Revue Française de Science Politique*, 53/4: 491–510.

Kassim, H. and Stevens, H. (2010), *Air Transport and the European Union: Europeanization and Its Limits*, Basingstoke: Palgrave Macmillan.

Kassim, H. and Wright, K. (2009), 'Bringing Regulatory Processes Back In: Revisiting the Reform of EU Antitrust and Merger Control', *West European Politics* 32/4: 738–55.

Kassim, H. and Wright, V. (1991), 'The role of national administrations in the Decision-Making Processes of the European Community', *Rivista Trimestrale di Diritto Pubblico*: 832–50.

Kassim, H. with Dittmer-Odell, M. and Wright, N. (2011), 'The Internal Coordination of EU Policy Coordination in the United Kingdom', report prepared for the Federal Chancellery of Austria, December.

Kassim, H., Menon, A., Peters, B. G., and Wright, V. (eds) (2001), *The National Coordination of EU Policy: the European level*, Oxford: Oxford University Press.

Kassim, H., Peters, B. G., and Wright, V. (eds) (2000), *The National Co-ordination of EU Policy: The Domestic Level*, Oxford: Oxford University Press.

Katz, R. S. (1999), 'Representation, the Locus of Democratic Legitimation, and the Role of the National Parliaments in the European Union', in R. S. Katz and B. Wessels (eds), *The European Parliament, the National Parliaments and European Integration*, Oxford: Oxford University Press, 21–44.

Kelemen, R. G. (2011), *Eurolegalism. The Transformation of Law and Regulation in the European Union*, Cambridge, MA: Harvard University Press.

Keohane, R. O. and Hoffmann, S. (1991), 'Institutional Change in Europe in the 1980s', in R. O. Keohane and S. Hoffman (eds), *The New European Community*, Boulder, Colorado: Westview Press, 1–40.

Kerremans, B. (2000), 'Belgium', in H. Kassim, B. G. Peters, and V. Wright (eds), *The National Co-ordination of EU Policy: The Domestic Level*, Oxford: Oxford University Press, 182–200.

King, A. (1994), 'Chief Executives in Western Europe', in I. Budge and D. McKay (eds), *Developing Democracy*, London: Sage, 150–62.

Kiivers, P. (2006), *The National Parliaments in the European Union: A Critical View on EU Constitution-Building*, The Hague: Kluwer Law International.

Knill, C. (2001), *The Europeanisation of National Administrations*, Cambridge: Cambridge University Pres).

Laffan, B., O'Donnell, R., and Smith, M. (2000), *Europe's Experimental Union*, London: Routledge.

Larsson, T. and, Trondal, J. (2005), 'After Hierarchy? The Differentiated Impact of the European Commission and the Council of Ministers on Domestic Executive Governance', ARENA Working Papers, No. 22 (Oslo: ARENA).

Lippert, B., Umbach, G., and Wessels, W. (2001), 'Europeanization of CEE Executives: EU Membership Negotiations as a Shaping Power', *Journal of European Public Policy*, 8/6: 980–1012.

Marks, G., Hooghe, L., and Blank, K. (1996), 'European Integration from the 1980s', *Journal of Common Market Studies*, 34/3: 341–78.

Mattli, W. and Slaughter, A-M. (1998a), 'Revisiting the ECJ', *International Organization*, 52/1: 177–209.

Mattli, W. and Slaughter, A-M. (1998b), 'The Role of National Courts in the Process of European Integration: Accounting for Judicial Preferences and Constraints', in A-M. Slaughter, A. Stone Sweet, and J. H. H. Weiler (eds), *The European Court and National Courts–Doctrine and Jurisprudence*, Oxford: Hart, 253–76.

Maurer, A. (2001), 'National Parliaments in the European Architecture: From Latecomers Adaptation to Permanent Institutional Change', in A. Maurer and W. Wessels (eds), *National Parliaments on their Ways to Europe: Losers or Latecomers?* Baden-Baden: Nomos Verlagsgellschaft, 27–76, available on-line at http://aei.pitt.edu/archive/00001476/.

Maurer, A. (2002), *Les rôles des Parlements nationaux dans l'Union européenne: Options, Contraintes et Obstacles*, contribution to the Convention on the Future of Europe, available on-line at http://europa.eu.int/futurum/documents/other/oth010302_fr.pdf.

Maurer, A. and Wessels, W. (2001a), 'Main Findings', in A. Maurer and W. Wessels (2001), *National Parliaments on their Ways to Europe: Losers or Latecomers?* Baden-Baden: Nomos Verlagsgellschaft, 17–26, available on-line at http://aei.pitt.edu/archive/00001476/.

Maurer, A. and Wessels, W. (2001b), *National Parliaments on their Ways to Europe: Losers or Latecomers?* Baden-Baden: Nomos, available on-line at http://aei.pitt.edu/archive/00001476/.

Metcalfe, L. (1992), 'International policy coordination and public management reform', *International Review of Administrative Sciences*, 60 271–90.

Milward, A. S. (2000), *The European Rescue of the Nation-State* 2nd edn., London: Routledge.

Moravcsik, A. (1993), 'Preferences and Power in the European Community: A Liberal Intergovernmentalist Approach', *Journal of Common Market Studies*, 31/4: 473–524.

Moravcsik, A. (1994), 'Why the European Union Strengthens the State: Domestic Politics and International Cooperation', CES Working Paper Series, No. 52, Center for European Studies, Cambridge, MA, http://www.ces.fas.harvard.edu/publications/docs/pdfs/Moravcsik52.pdf.

Moravcsik, A. (1998), *The Choice for Europe. Social Purpose and State Power from Messina to Maastricht*, Ithaca, NY: Cornell University Press.

Newman, M. (1996), *Democracy, Sovereignty and the European Union*, London: Hurst and Company.

Norton, P. (1996), 'Conclusion: Addressing the Democratic Deficit', in P. Norton (ed.), *National Parliaments and the European Union*, London: Frank Cass, 177–93.

Novak-Far, A. (2008), 'Coordination of EU policy in Poland', under review.

O'Brennan, J. and Raunio, T. (eds) (2007), *National Parliaments within the Enlarged European Union: From Victims of Integration to Competitive Actors?* London: Routledge.

Olsen, Johan P. (2007), *Europe in Search of Political Order: An Institutional Perspective on Unity/Diversity, Citizens/Their Helpers, Democratic Design/Historical Drift and the Co-Existence of Orders*, Oxford: Oxford University Press.

Page, E. C. (2003), 'Europeanization and the Persistence of Administrative Systems', in J. Hayward and A. Menon (eds), *Governing Europe*, Oxford: Oxford University Press, 162–76.

Peyer, S. (2010), 'Myths and Untold Stories-Private Antitrust Enforcement in Germany', ESRC Centre for Competition Policy, ESRC Centre for Competition, CCP Working Paper 10–12.

Pierson, P. (1996), 'The Path to European Integration: A Historical Institutionalist Analysis', *Comparative Political Studies*, 29/2: 123–63.

Pollack, M. A. (1997), 'Delegation, Agency and Agenda Setting in the European Community', *International Organization*, 51/1: 99–134.

Putnam, R. D. (1988), 'Diplomacy and Domestic Politics: The Logic of Two-Level Games', *International Organization*, 43/2: 427–60.

Raunio, T. and Hix, S. (2000), 'Backbenchers Learn to Fight Back: European Integration and Parliamentary Government', in K. H. Goetz and S. Hix, (eds), 'Europeanised Politics? The Impact of European Integration on Domestic Politics', special issue of *West European Politics*, 23/4:142–68.

Rideau, J. (1972), 'Le rôle des Etats Membres dans l'application du droit communautaire', *Annuaire Français De Droit International* 18: 864–903.

Rometsch, D. and Wessels, W. (eds) (1996), *The European Union and member states. Towards institutional fusion?*, Manchester: Manchester University Press.

Sasse, C., Poullet, E., Coombes, D., and Deprez, G. (1977), *Decision Making in the European Community*, New York: Praeger.

Schimmelfennig, F. and Sedelmeier, U. (2002), 'Theorising EU Enlargement–Research Focus, Hypotheses, and the State of Research', *Journal of European Public Policy* 9/4: 500–28.

Schimmelfennig, F. and Sedelmeier, U. (eds) (2005), *The Europeanization of Central and Eastern Europe*, Ithaca, NY: Cornell University Press.

Schmidt, V. (1999), 'European "Federalism" and its Encroachments on National Institutions', *Publius: The Journal of Federalism*, 29/1: 19–44.

Slaughter, A-M., Stone Sweet, A., and Weiler, J. H. H. (eds) (1998), *The European Court and National Courts–Doctrine and Jurisprudence*, Oxford: Hart, 305–30.

Smith, M. P. (1997), 'The Commission Made Me Do It: The European Commission as a Strategic Asset in Domestic Politics', in N. Nugent (ed.), *At the Heart of the Union: Studies of the European Commission*, New York: St Martin's Press, 167–86.

Spanou, C. (1998), 'European Integration in Administrative Terms: A Framework for Analysis and the Greek Case', *Journal of European Public Policy*, 5/3: 467–84.

Stein, E. (1981), 'Lawyers, Judges and the Making of a Transnational Constitution', *American Journal of International Law*, 75/1: 1–27.

Stevens, A. and Stevens, H. (2000), *Brussels Bureaucrats?* Basingstoke: Palgrave Macmillan.

Stone Sweet, A. (1998), 'Constitutional Dialogues in the European Community', in A-M Slaughter, A. Stone Sweet and J. H. H. Weiler (eds), *The European Court and National Courts–Doctrine and Jurisprudence*, Oxford: Hart, 305–30.

Stone Sweet, A. and Brunell, T. L. (1998), 'The European Court and the National Courts: A Statistical Analysis of Preliminary References, 1961–95', *Journal of European Public Policy*, 5/1: 66–97.

Stone Sweet, A. and Sandholtz, W. (1998), 'Integration, Supranational Governance, and the Institutionalization of the European Policy', in W. Sandholtz and A. Stone Sweet (eds), *European Integration and Supranational Governance*, Oxford: Oxford University Press, 1–26.

Sutherland, P. (1992), 'The Internal Market after 1992: Meeting the Challenge', Report to the EEC Commission of the High Level Group on the Operation of the Internal Market, Brussels.

Weiler, J. H. H. (1991), 'The Transformation of Europe', *Yale Law Journal*, 100/8: 2405–83.

Weiler, J. H. H. (1994), 'A Quiet Revolution: The European Court of Justice and its Interlocutors', *Comparative Political Studies*, 26/4: 510–34.

Wessels, W. (1991), 'The EC Council: The Community's Decision making Center' in R. O. Keohane and S. Hoffmann (eds), *The New European Community*, New York: Westview, 133–54.

Wessels, W. (2001), 'Nice Results: The Millennium IGC in the EU's Evolution', *Journal of Common Market Studies*, 39/2: 197–219.

Wessels, W., Maurer, A., and Mittag, J. (2003a), 'The European Union and the Member States: Analysing Two Arenas Over Time', in W. Wessels, A. Maurer, and J. Mittag (eds), *Fifteen into One? The European Union and its Member States*, Manchester: Manchester University Press, 3–28.

Wessels, W., Maurer, A., and Mittag, J. (2003b), 'Preface and Major Findings', in W. Wessels, A. Maurer, and J. Mittag (eds), *Fifteen into One? The European Union and its Member States*, Manchester: Manchester University Press, xii–xvii.

Wessels, W., Maurer, A., and Mittag, J. (eds) (2003c), *Fifteen into One? The European Union and its Member States*, Manchester: Manchester University Press.

Westlake, M. (1994), A *Modern Guide to the European Parliament*, London: Pinter.

Wright, K. (2008), 'European Commission Opinions to National Courts in Antitrust Cases: Consistent Application and the Judicial-Administrative Relationship', paper for the ECPR Standing Group on the European Union, Fourth Pan-European Conference on EU Politics, 25–27 September, University of Latvia, Riga.

Wright, V. (1996), 'The National Co-ordination of European Policy-Making Negotiating the Quagmire', in J. Richardson (ed.), *European Union. Policy and Policy-Making*, London: Routledge, 148–69.

 ENDNOTES

1. The author would like to thank Vanessa Buth, PhD candidate at UEA, for her contribution as a research assistant to this chapter.
2. The EU's impact is also felt beyond its borders. For its effects on Central European states before they became EU members, see Lippert *et al.* (2001), and for its impact on non-members, see Fischer *et al.* (2002) on Switzerland and Claes (2002) on Norway.
3. I am grateful to Dionyssis G. Dimitrakopoulos for this formulation.
4. Only intergovernmentalists would dispute that EU membership constrains member governments.
5. The case of aviation liberalization offers a spectacular example. After it had exhausted bilateral possibilities, the UK sought to multi-lateralize its liberal aviation policy via the EC (Kassim and Stevens 2010).
6. The fact that negotiations can take place behind closed doors, at the margins of meetings or in corridors, allows governments to press for measures that they would not be prepared to support publicly.
7. As Knill (2001: 214-5) notes, where a regulation calls for a specific administrative style, such as regulatory intervention, or for administrative interest mediation, domestic arrangements will have to be adjusted.
8. This was already a challenge in the 1980s. Greece had to establish a department for overseas development, while Portugal created an environment ministry. For the countries of Central and Eastern Europe, the level of adjustment was unprecedented (see Schimmelfennig and Sedelmeier 2002, 2005).
9. With respect to the former, it might have been expected that the ECJ-upheld principle of institutional autonomy (Rideau 1972), 'the right of member states to perform the tasks that stem from membership of the EU on the basis of their own constitutional rules' (Dimitrakopoulos 2001a: 444) would lead to significant differences between the way that EU law is transposed in member countries. However, as Dionyssis Dimitrakopoulos has argued, 'analysis of the national mechanisms and procedures . . . demonstrates remarkably similar patterns' (ibid).
10. Belgium is to some extent an exceptions, since in principle the six sub-national authorities are co-equal partners of the federal government (Kerremans 2000).
11. Between 2003 and 2006, Hungary's MFA coexisted uneasily with a minister without portfolio for EU coordination, who headed a new European Affairs Office in the PM's office and whose responsibilities included the development of a national coordination plan, structural funds, and the horizontal coordination of EU matters across the administration (Batory 2012).
12. The Six had rather rudimentary systems, where parliamentary committees commented ex post on annual government reports (Sasse *et al.* 1977: 78). Denmark and the UK gave considerably more power to their parliaments on entering the EEC in 1973.

13. France and Germany changed their constitutions in 1992. Belgium, Finland, Austria, the Czech Republic, Slovenia, and Hungary also amended their constitutions to allow for parliamentary oversight (Kiivers 2006: 59).

14. Indeed, 'in some countries', they contend, 'European integration has been a catalyst in the re-emergence of parliaments' (2000: 143).

15. In Austria, members of the main parliamentary committee and party leaders enjoy the right to attend cabinet meetings where EU matters are discussed (Maurer 2002: 21).

16. Most are based on statute. The Danish mandate system is based on convention.

17. The parliaments of Estonia, Hungary, and Lithuania and the Dutch *Tweede Kamer* combine elements from both models.

18. MEPs are represented in committees in the Belgian federal parliament, the German Bundestag, and the Greek and Irish legislatures (Raunio and Hix 2000: 157).

19. A similar system applies in the Swedish *Riksdag*, though sectoral committees follow EU developments independently.

20. For example, in the Danish case, the minister only needs to avoid a majority vote against the position he or she proposes. Ninety per cent of the time, the minister secures his or her desired outcome.

21. On the eve of the Maastricht IGCs, what turned out to be a one-off conference of parliaments (the *Assises*) took place in Rome (Westlake 1994).

22. The Protocol on National Parliaments was amended at the time of the Lisbon Treaty.

23. See Kiiver (2006) for a reflection on these issues.

24. Federico Mancini and David Keeling summarize, as follows: 'If the doctrines of direct effect and supremacy are . . . the "twin pillars of the Community's legal system", the [preliminary ruling] reference procedure . . . must surely be the keystone in the edifice; without it the roof would collapse and the two pillars would be left as a desolate ruin' (quoted in Alter 2001: 209).

25. Cases 26/62 [1963] ECR 1 and 6/64 [1964] ECR 585) respectively.

26. One effect, as Alter (2001: 218) points out, was increased workload: '[A]llowing private litigants access increases the number of actors who can raise legal challenges, and thus the number of cases a court has to hear' (Alter 2001: 218).

27. The 'inter-court competition' approach, developed by Karen Alter (1998), argues that different courts have different interests in legal integration and that lower courts are more likely to use ECJ jurisprudence as a way of asserting their power vis-à-vis higher courts, whereas higher courts have an interest in 'thwarting the expansion and penetration of EC law into the national legal order' (Alter 1998: 242; see also Dehousse 1988: 140). For a different view, which emphasizes the power of the member states in relation to the ECJ, see Garrett and Weingast (1993).

28. Mattli and Slaughter (1998a, 1998b) have suggested that the timing and scope of acceptance has been influenced by three factors: national policy preferences concerning the desirability of European integration; national legal culture (e.g. professional values, modes of legal reasoning, understanding of the role of courts in relation to legislative bodies, etc.); and specific national legal doctrines (e.g. monism or dualism). However, they concede that these factors do not provide a wholly satisfactory explanation.

29. The quotation is from the case *Costa v. ENEL*, case 6/64 [1964] ECR 585.

30. See Wright (2008) for discussion of one of the consequences of this development. See Kassim and Wright (2009) for a discussion of the reform.

31. For a study of preliminary references by topic between 1961 and 1995, see Stone Sweet and Brunell 1998.

CHAPTER 13

Europeanization and Political Parties

Robert Ladrech

▌ Summary

Political parties are indispensable to the functioning of the member states of the EU. They are key actors in the national-supranational nexus of EU politics, and the extent to which they have been influenced by the EU is of keen interest to scholars and practitioners alike. However, unlike domestic institutions and policies, national parties are not embedded in a formal relationship with the EU. Consequently, Europeanization dynamics arising from 'goodness of fit' or a legally dominant role of the European Commission in their activities are not especially helpful. Nevertheless, parties at the national level as well as their 'agents' at the European level—Euro-parties and European Parliament party groups—have exhibited evidence of an EU influence. This chapter highlights the ways in which the EU and parties interact and produce changes. The chapter distinguishes different types of change, causal mechanisms, and discusses the differences between parties and the EU in both older and newer member states.

Introduction

Political parties are key actors in the domestic politics and governance of EU member states. As such, party positions on European integration in general, and EU policies in particular, can have indirect effects on EU inter-governmental bargaining and decision making as well as on the process of 'bottom-up' Europeanization (see Graziano and Vink, Chapter 2). However, in attempting to understand the impact of the EU on domestic political parties, the 'top-down' Europeanization perspective is usually employed. This being said, linking domestic party change and Europeanization is a relatively recent scholarly pursuit, and the analytical lens continues to be refined. Unlike Europeanization research into institutional and policy change, national parties are not intimately intertwined with EU institutional decision-making procedures nor are they directly (and legally) involved in policy making. This has meant, from a methodological standpoint, that the mechanism of change employed to explain adaptational responses in these other dimensions is not so easily transferable to the case of parties. Nevertheless, certain identifiable political dynamics have emerged about the relations between domestic parties and the EU that characterize the ways in which domestic parties, in older and newer member states, experience change that at least in part is attributable to the influence of the EU. This chapter first describes the different partisan actors that operate in the multi-level system of domestic and EU politics. Next, the chapter explains the manner in which domestic political parties can be said to have 'Europeanized', paying attention to arguments regarding the complexity of correctly attributing a causal link to the EU. The chapter also makes explicit the differences between parties in older and newer member states. Finally, the chapter concludes with a discussion of the wider effects on domestic politics of party Europeanization.

Parties in the European Union

Party actors can be grouped into four categories: national, sub-national or regional, transnational, and parliamentary groups in the European Parliament. The first category is the most familiar to students of partisan and electoral politics, coalition government formation, party government, etc. National parties contest elections from which the victor(s) form the government and hold responsibility for policy development and implementation, including interacting with the various institutions of the European Union. The second category consists of regional parties, whose political relevance mostly depends on national electoral rules and the form of territorial representation (i.e. unitary or federal state). The third category is populated by transnational party federations (also referred to as 'Euro-parties'), party family-specific organizations that operate as a European–level organizational nexus for the promotion of policy ideas and exchange (Johansson and Zervakis 2002; Ladrech 2000; Van Hecke 2004), involving national party leaders at periodic summits (usually coinciding with European Council summits, though the frequency has grown over the past ten years) as well as national and EP party delegates to Euro-party congresses and national party officers such as an International or European affairs secretary. These Euro-parties help to organize so-called caucuses among ministers belonging to their respective party family before Council of Minister meetings and increasingly, especially the centre-Right and centre-Left Euro-parties, prepare special policy-oriented summits of party leaders and other relevant national party personnel. To date, five party families have organized a Euro-party, with varying degrees of institutionalization and coordination: the European Left Party, the European Green Party, the Party of European Socialists, the European Liberal Democrat and Reform Party, and the European People's Party. Finally, the fourth category consists of the parliamentary groups within the European Parliament, usually having, again, a party family basis (i.e. one of the five Euro-parties). The influence of national delegations within Euro-parties varies greatly, with some parties occupying a substantial leading role, for example the German Christian Democratic Union (CDU) in the European People's Party. Interest in deepening European transnational cooperation and size of EP delegations often explains this role. Another perspective linking three types of party formation (excluding the regional) is to consider the transnational and European Parliamentary arenas as extensions of national party activity, as in most cases a major national party is both a member of a Euro-party as well as having a delegation in a European Parliamentary group (Hix and Lord 1997). In the case of regional parties, although many have joined a parliamentary group, a transnational party federation has not been organized, owing to their wide variation in political ideology. Nevertheless, as the case below suggests, even regional parties use Europe as a resource to influence national politics, though again this varies in relation to major national party position Hepburn (2010). As an example, the British Labour Party is a member of the Party of European Socialists as well as having a national delegation within the European Parliament's Progressive Alliance of Socialists and Democrats group. Exceptions to this tri-partite multi-level partisan activity are primarily parties on the far Right and far Left. On the far Right, a transnational party federation does not exist and the EP's Europe of Freedom & Democracy group does not include all possible such parties (for example, it includes the Danish People's Party and the Italian *Lega Nord*, but not the French *Front National* nor the Austrian Freedom Party, members of whom are classified in the EP as 'non-attached'). Explanations for the lack of transnational organization by many of the far Right range from their lack of national governmental experience, disparate domestic strategies, and numerical insignificance in the European Parliament (Almeida 2010; see also Fennema and Pollmann 1998; Mudde 2007). On the far Left, there is the European Left Party (Euro-party), and a parliamentary group, the Confederal Group of the

European United Left/Nordic Green Left (GUE/NGL). However, the membership is not completely synonymous between the two groups; for example, an important party in Sweden, the Left party (Vänsterpartiet), is a member of the EP group but not the Euro-party. From the perspective of a Europeanization research agenda, the question is then two-fold: are these extra-national party formations a result of Europeanization and second, more importantly, in what ways are national parties themselves impacted, if at all, by EU influence?

Euro-parties and EP Parliamentary Groups

Establishing the causality of the EU in party change is a significant methodological challenge, for separating domestic from international influences can be a complex affair (Haverland 2007). Nevertheless, in the case of the first set of party actors under review, Euro-parties and EP parliamentary groups, counterfactual reasoning would lead to the obvious conclusion that if the EU did not exist neither of these two actors would have a purpose. The complementary question is, then, what actually triggers their creation? In the case of Euro-parties, preparation for the first directly elected European Parliament in 1979 launched a phase of cross-national networking among the three major party families of the day—social democrat, Christian democrat, and liberal—to form transnational parties in readiness for a putative European level party system that might arise from an elected European level parliamentary arena (Pridham and Pridham 1981). From an organizational or developmental perspective, these Euro-parties remained essentially very loose confederations until the late 1980s, when, in response to the resurgence in the European integration process beginning with the Single European Act (SEA), an organizational enhancement of their decision-making processes occurred (Johansson and Zervakis 2002), mimicking in certain ways the institutional development of the EU institutions (for example, qualified majority voting, as a rule, was adopted in light of the rule change in the Council of Ministers). From a Europeanization research perspective, explaining why national parties expended resources to create Euro-parties—which involved the recruitment of staff and amendment of rules to accommodate MEPs in party decision-making bodies—can be explained as a case of institutional isomorphism, rather than a 'goodness of fit' mechanism of change as employed in other dimensions of Europeanization research (Börzel and Risse 2006). In the 'misfit' hypothesis, pressure to conform to legally binding EU policies, or to re-organize part of a ministry for resource developmental purposes, etc., assumes that the actor or policy is engaged in a relationship in which the EU plays a substantial, if not hierarchically dominant, role. Whether making small adjustments or major adaptation, the Europeanization perspective understands domestic change in relation to the *impact* or *influence* of the EU on domestic decision and policy making. As national parties are neither 'down-loaders' of EU policy, in any direct sense that impacts their organization and activities, nor is the EU in any way a supplier of resources that can give parties any competitive edge in domestic politics, the concept of misfit is not really applicable as an explanation for the timing and type of change with regard to Euro-parties. A better explanation is a form of institutional isomorphism, in which the interaction of national party delegates holding an EC/EU portfolio, which increased over time from the late 1980s onward, demonstrated a sharing of best practice, with select parties providing a vanguard role. Supporting this explanation is the timing of Euro-party expansion and development alongside the specialization of party international secretariats in which a separate 'Europe' secretary was created, as well as the formation of national parliamentary committees or sub-committees on European affairs (again, some parliaments having created such committees upon joining the EC, e.g. Denmark and the UK). In the wake of the SEA, numerous member states created such committees (in this case best practice may also have been spread through meetings of national parliament representatives and the European Parliament under the auspices of Conference of European Affairs Committees of the Parliaments of the European Union (COSAC), launched in 1989—see Chapter 12). Institutional (organizational) isomorphism, in which organizations that interact on a regular basis tend to become alike, a more sociological explanation based on horizontal means of Europeanization in which 'there is no pressure to conform to EU policy models' (Radaelli 2003: 42), leads to a more likely causal connection. Börzel (2005) points to a number of diffusion mechanisms in regard to institutional isomorphism, and the mechanism of 'imitation' seems most appropriate to explain the development of Euro-parties. When applied to national polities, imitation is understood to mean that member states 'emulate a model recommended by the EU to avoid uncertainty (*imitation*)' (ibid.: 57). Adapting this mechanism to parties, it becomes clear that the primary responsibility of Euro-party membership, as well as that of a national party Europe secretary, is to provide information to the leadership bodies of the party. In other words, the role of these positions is to reduce the degree of uncertainty that may emanate from the arenas in which the party is not fully engaged. In the specific case of the Party of European Socialists and the European People's Party, competition between the two was also a contributing factor in their organizational development, although national party leaders ultimately had to sanction any fundamental changes.

European Parliament party groups (see Box 13.1), like Euro-parties, are staffed by individuals chosen through national party mechanisms of recruitment, and are then elected in campaigns primarily resourced by national parties. Once formed, though, EP party groups exist in a supranational parliamentary arena, with its own rules and resources, separate from the main activities of their principal, the national party (Kreppel 2002; Hix *et al.* 2007). National parties participate in European elections in order to gain representation in the EP so as to influence decisions that may have a direct impact on the member state. That is to say, the extent to which national parties exert direct influence on the activities of their delegation in the EP is related to the nature of EU policies and issues in which the delegation can influence the party group position, specifically matters that are especially pertinent for a particular member state. In this sense, MEP's represent the early warning

BOX 13.1	Number of MEPs by member state in EP party groups (January 2011)

EP Party Groups:

GUE/NGL: Confederal Group of the European United Left/Nordic Green Left

Greens/EFA: Greens/European Free Alliance

S&D: Socialists and Democrats

ALDE: Alliance of Liberals and Democrats for Europe

EPP: European People's Party

ECR: European Conservatives and Reformists

EFD: Europe of Freedom and Democracy

1. Belgium: Greens/EFA (4); S&D (5); ALDE (5); EPP (5); ECR (1)

2. Bulgaria: S&D (4); ALDE (5); EPP (6)

3. Czech Republic: GUE/NGL (4); S&D (7); EPP (2); ECR (9)

4. Denmark: GUE/NGL (1); Greens/EFA (2); S&D (4); ALDE (3); EPP (1); EFD (2)

5. Germany: GUE/NGL (8); Greens/EFA (14); S&D (23); ALDE (12); EPP (42)

6. Estonia: Greens/EFA (1); S&D (1); ALDE (3); EPP (1)

7. Ireland: GUE/NGL (1); S&D (3); ALDE (4); EPP (4)

8. Greece: GUE/NGL (3); Greens/EFA (1); S&D (8); EPP (8); EFD (2)

9. Spain: GUE/NGL (1); Greens/EFA (2); S&D (21); ALDE (2); EPP (23)

10. France: GUE/NGL (5); Greens/EFA (14); S&D (14); ALDE (6); EPP (29); EFD (1)

11. Italy: S&D (22); ALDE (6); EPP (35); EFD (9)

12. Cyprus: GUE/NGL (2); S&D (2); EPP (2)

13. Latvia: GUE/NGL (1); Greens/EFA (1); S&D (1); ALDE (1); EPP (3); ECR (1)

14. Lithuania: S&D (3); ALDE (2); EPP (4); ECR (1); EFD (2)

15. Luxembourg: Greens/EFA (1); S&D (1); ALDE (1); EPP (3)

16. Hungary: S&D (4); EPP (14); ECR (1)

17. Malta: S&D (3); EPP (2)

18. Netherlands: GUE/NGL (2); Greens/EFA (3); S&D (3); ALDE (6); EPP (5); ECR (1); EFD (1)

19. Austria: Greens/EFA (2); S&D (4); EPP (6)

20. Poland: S&D (7); EPP (28); ECR (15)

21. Portugal: GUE/NGL (5); S&D (7); EPP (10)

22. Romania: S&D (12); ALDE (5); EPP (14)

23. Slovenia: S&D (2); ALDE (2); EPP (3)

24. Slovakia: S&D (5); ALDE (1); EFD (1)

25. Finland: Greens/EFA (2); S&D (2); ALDE (4); EPP (6); EFD (1)

26. Sweden: GUE/NGL (1); Greens/EFA (3); S&D (5); ALDE (4); EPP (5)

27. United Kingdom: GUE/NGL (1); Greens/EFA (5); S&D (13); ALDE (12); ECR (25); EFD (11)

Number of national party delegations in EP party groups (January 2011)

GUE/NGL: Confederal Group of the European United Left/Nordic Green Left (13)

Greens/EFA: Greens/European Free Alliance (14)

S&D: Socialists and Democrats (27)

ALDE: Alliance of Liberals and Democrats for Europe (19)

EPP: European People's Party (26)

ECR: European Conservatives and Reformists (8)

EFD: Europe of Freedom and Democracy (9)

system role that Euro-parties play to a lesser degree (Ladrech 2007). It could be argued that mainstream national parties could not afford to ignore participation in EP elections, whereas small or new parties, for whom entering a national parliament can be difficult—because of percentage thresholds, type of electoral system, etc.—have found election to the EP an alternative parliamentary platform in terms of holding elected office. Certainly the resources that are available to national delegations that are part of a party group, for example Green parties in the 1990s or post-communist parties in the 2000s, can be crucial for party development. In this sense, for this category of party, elections to the EP do represent a resource or political opportunity structure. For small, marginal, or newly created domestic parties, the European Parliament represents a means by which to establish an echelon of elected officials and gain or increase a financial resource base. Even larger parties may, at times, seek to influence their respective EP group to reflect domestic political realities, such as the change of name of the Socialist Group to the Progressive Alliance of Socialists and Democrats, reflecting the changes within the Italian party system, in particular the change of name by the Left Democrats to simply the Democrats in 2009.

In general, though, the Europeanization literature follows the top-down approach when party analysis is concerned, and therefore the prime focus has been upon national parties operating in their domestic political system. The question is, then, does the EU impact these parties in some form?

Europeanization and National Parties

At the outset of this chapter it was noted that a methodological issue arising from any attempt to bring a Europeanization perspective to national party analysis is the simple fact that unlike domestic policy and institutions, there is not an institutional or direct relationship between EU decision making and policy outputs and individual national parties. This has meant that translating the misfit hypothesis as a mechanism of change is not so straightforward in establishing a causal link between the EU and domestic party change. Nevertheless, Mair (2007b) has helped to clear the conceptual terrain by proposing a *direct* and *indirect* manner in which the EU impacts parties. The EU is said to directly affect national parties by virtue of its existence—i.e., there are elections to the European Parliament which necessitate recruiting candidates, creating a manifesto, and amending party organization rules to allow for MEP participation in leadership bodies and other decision-making venues such as party conferences, etc. Additionally, and perhaps more importantly in terms of domestic politics in general, Mair states that the EU may stimulate the creation of new parties—most likely anti-EU oriented—and opinion (politicized) within existing parties. One can add to this list, as Ladrech (2002) suggested, at least five areas in which party change may have links to EU influence: organizational, programmatic, party system or patterns of party competition, government-party relations, and relations beyond the national political system (i.e. with Euro-parties). Indeed, evidence has been provided, for parties in both older and newer EU member states, for changes in organization, both structural, e.g. new offices and rule changes, as well as behavioural, i.e. leadership efforts to contain or manage dissent. Programmatic change, as measured in party manifestos, programmes, and other party documents, has also been a line of research, and the study of Euro-parties and their national principles has developed over the years (see Introduction above). Below is a list of examples, by no means exhaustive, cited in the literature on Europeanization and party change. They encompass parties in both older and newer member states.

- Organizational change: new positions such as Europe Secretary; rule changes such as voting rights for MEPs in national party congresses and leadership bodies; internal dissent on EU policies prompting factionalism.

- Programmatic change: explicit stance on European integration in campaign manifestos and programmes; change in policy positions, including the formation of new positions on policies introduced by the EU.

- Pattern of party competition: new parties entering electoral politics and parliament; divisions within parties affecting campaign strategy.

- Party government relations: changes in or pressures on party discipline of the party(ies) in government over EU policy issues.

- Relations beyond the national political system: changes in membership in EP parliamentary parties and/or transnational party federations; initiatives at the EU level on policy issues.

These examples of domestic party activity linked to the EU are a result of adaptation—misfit as a mechanism of change—but also institutional isomorphism, an imitation of so-called 'pioneer' parties in matters of organization, e.g. the establishment of EU-related positions. As for justifying a misfit explanation for aspects of party change described above—when national parties are not intimately involved in a direct relationship with EU decision-making processes or policy development—a sociological institutionalist approach appears most relevant, as party actors are reacting to perceptions of pressure on party activity. Before turning to an explanation of how misfit as a mechanism of change might work in the case of national parties, presenting Mair's argument relating to an *indirect* impact of the EU upon parties—and its alleged effects—is in order, as it has the potential for generating much more profound effects on national political systems in general.

According to Mair (2000, 2007a, 2007b) and others (e.g. Bartolini 2005), the transfer to, or even sharing of, national policy competence with the EU, especially since the increased pace of European integration from the mid-1980s onward, has had a subtle effect upon the legitimacy of national party government. The argument is as follows: the less control a national government has over a range of domestic policies, the less policy 'substance' there is over which parties can compete. On the one hand, the transfer of policy issues to the EU results in their de-politicization (as they become simply a matter of technocratic problem-solving, only occasionally politicized in Council deliberations). The effect of this 'hollowing out' of party government responsibility is not only reflected in fewer issues over which parties may compete against each other, or can legitimately promise voters, but it may have the wider effect of rendering national government impotent in the eyes of the electorate, and this may, in turn, promote widespread popular disenchantment and/or de-politicization. The effect is, for Mair, two-fold; first, the nature of party competition is altered, and second the legitimacy of party government is compromised. Thus the EU may be said to indirectly impact national parties. To the extent party actors perceive this indirect pressure, and lay the blame for voter frustration at the door of the EU, this indirect pressure can produce changes in party activity much as a misfit mechanism of change based on a sociological institutionalist understanding.

Europeanization, Misfit, and Party Change

A Europeanization approach must establish the basis upon which the EU can be considered a causal factor in the changes described above, as well as to conceptualize an appropriate mechanism of change. It is not enough to simply provide descriptive accounts of change, but to explain how the EU comes to exert an influence on actors for whom the EU is removed from the central arena of their activities, the national political and party system. Minor organizational changes have been credited to a simple form of copying other party management techniques of EU issues as well as producing positions to fill EU and EP posts, what Börzel (2005: 59) might label *absorption* ('incorporate European requirements into their domestic institutions and policies without substantial modifications of existing structures and the logic of political behaviour'). However, apart from this type of change, which includes relations with member EP groups and transnational party federations, there is a common denominator triggering changes in other areas, such as programme, internal relations, relations between government and party, and even the party system. In this respect, a Europeanization perspective can provide insights into party behaviour and change. The common denominator is a perception among party members, from the leadership to activists, that core party policies and principles are or may be threatened by changes instigated by the EU. The reaction or subsequent response to this state of affairs is what drives changes in these areas, and also allows a misfit explanation as a causal mechanism. The misfit hypothesis in the case of institutional adaptation understands change as a result of coercion, normative pressure, regulatory competition, etc. In the case of parties, the diffusion of new EU norms, rules, and practices, which are perceived to be in opposition to core party principles and policies, represent the misfit pressure; how an individual party responds depends on a variety of factors, both party-structural as well as the pattern of party competition. For example, in member states in which the EU's competition policy has been responsible for influencing policy developments, such as deregulating certain industries or cutting back on the amount of state aid, many Left-of-centre parties have had to grapple with domestic political pressure to protect public sector jobs (a major constituency) while at the same time avoid undermining the legitimacy of the EU itself—as most social democratic parties are supportive of the general thrust of European integration. As for party-structural factors, in parties where the more electorally-minded wing of the party dominates party strategy, i.e. the parliamentary party, dissent is compartmentalized and channelled into avenues that do not upset internal party equilibrium, for example at a party congress or a special thematic conference. Where the extra-parliamentary body is roughly equal to, or even dominant, the party leadership is obliged to compromise over demands for distinctive policy positions or even agree to an internal referendum, as in the case of the French Socialist Party in December 2004 in relation to the national referendum on the Constitutional Treaty called by President Chirac in early 2005.

This 'party-policy misfit' tension manifests itself in mainstream parties in the following ways:

  a) Party manifestos and programmes—the political dynamic represented in debate over whether to make explicit references to EU policies and the party's own position, and this calculation may be influenced by the salience of the EU itself in the domestic political system, or the position of competing parties, especially where an anti-EU party is prominent (Steenbergen and Scott 2004);

b) For parties in which the more electoral-oriented parliamentary party is not dominant, a party-structural feature for example in the French Socialist Party, *party leaderships* are obliged to compromise with party activists in terms of programmatic statements, positions on EU referendums such as the 2005 Constitutional Treaty, etc.;

c) Party government relations—where a major step forward in a member state's integration into EU institutions and policy areas is contested within the party, its representatives in government are less certain of securing success, for example the case of the Swedish Social Democrats and the referendum on joining the single currency in 2003 (Aylott 2005);

d) The constraints identified by Mair resulting from indirect EU influence may initiate *new policy developments*, whether derived from an EU policy direction or wholly domestic, to replace the absence of some traditional policy pursuits.

In all of these examples, the response to a perception of threat to party relevance is conditioned by the balance of power in a party, so a variable response may be explained by party-specific and party systemic factors. It may also be the case that apparent quiescence over EU issues masks internal dissent that is skilfully managed by a party leadership, where open conflict risks upsetting a party's voter base by sending mixed cues (Gabel and Scheve 2007). Whether by a direct or indirect manner, the EU penetrates domestic political systems and many political parties experience a low level of pressure/misfit because of the policy orientation of the EU. Some policy areas stimulate reactions from certain sets of party families, for example economic policy has more of an impact on Left-of-centre parties, while post-2004 enlargement and related immigration policies are highlighted by Right-of-centre parties (Hooghe and Marks 2009).

The EU does have an impact on domestic political parties, but it is more accurate to say that its influence—to disrupt internal party equilibrium, to generate policy developments, 'inspire' the creation of new parties, etc.—is linked to key events in both national electoral cycles as well as that of the EU. These occasions can be opportunities for some parties while for others seen as potentially divisive. EU treaty changes require national ratification, and in some member states a referendum is constitutionally mandated (although there are cases where ratifications have been held as political choice, for example France in 1992 (Maastricht Treaty) and 2005 (Constitutional Treaty) (see Oppermann 2010; Shu 2008). Joining the EU and joining the euro-zone have been other EU-explicit occasions where political mobilization opportunities have taken place, and governing parties in particular have been at risk of being at the receiving end of anti-incumbency sentiments, whatever the exact detail of the EU proposition. In such cases, party leaderships try to exert their authority over their party so as not to produce a picture of internal division. At times this does not succeed—the Swedish Social Democrat party leadership countenanced a separate 'yes' and 'no' campaign in 1995 (Aylott 2002), while pressure from mid-level party elites in 2004 elicited leadership backing for an internal party referendum within the French Socialists on the position for the party on the Constitutional Treaty referendum (Wagner 2008). In national electoral cycles, usually elections to the national parliament, it is rare that EU issues occupy centre-stage, but again in order to avoid directly highlighting a party's support for potentially divisive EU policies, party leaderships strive to eliminate discussion on EU affairs from their campaign as much as possible—unless there are clear electoral dividends, e.g. to embarrass a competitor party experiencing such internal problems. As most centre-Left and centre-Right parties in the EU are broadly supportive of the EU policy orientation, it underscores the general 'silence' of the EU as an issue between mainstream parties at national elections, leaving the terrain to far Left or far Right parties of varying Eurosceptic persuasions. The impact of the EU is therefore critical at certain points in national electoral calendars, and although not a 'relationship' as such, does represent the key political moments when the EU and domestic party politics intersect.

Party Politics and the EU, East and West

Much of the literature that has developed around the issue of Europeanization and political parties has focused until recently on the parties of the older member states (EU-15). One of the clear differences between older and newer (post-2004) member states' party politics is the degree of institutionalization of parties and party systems, or the difference between mature and consolidating political systems. This general characteristic has thrown up some differences in the impact of the EU on both sets of parties. In the *older* member states, parties and patterns of party competition preceded membership in the EU, and in many cases centre-Left and centre-Right parties preceded the establishment of the European integration process itself. The result of this simple fact is that the identity of parties, the relations between parties and voters, the channels between party and government, as well as with other organized interests in society—for example business associations and trade unions—all of these relationships constitute a domestic web of political dynamics with their own logic and factors which explain changes in electoral results, system stability or instability, etc. The political science literature on party change in Western Europe, which dates roughly from the late 1960s and early 1970s, analyzed parties in the then European Community member states as well as in non-member states (e.g. Austria and Sweden). Some of the key issues were changes in party competition because of the rise of new parties such as the greens in the latter 1970s and 1980s, the decline of voter turn-out in national elections, ageing of party members and problems of recruitment, and so on. Until the late 1980s, the European integration process and its policy outputs did not intrude into the domestic competitive political sphere or were regarded as foreign policy by most parties (this view continues to be held in many parties). The EU, consequently, was not a factor in domestic party politics (exceptions were the Danish Social Democrats in the 1970s and the British Labour and Conservatives parties in the 1980s and 1990s). The national governments represented via their leaders in the European Council, and in many cases founding member states, portrayed EC/EU membership as a beneficial pursuit and took a non-partisan attitude toward the integration process, thus deflecting internal party debate—such as it may have developed in the 1970s and 1980s—from wider party concerns, especially party competition (Gaffney 1996). More vocal and concerted policy concerns within mainstream parties began developing in the early 1990s in the wake of the Maastricht Treaty (1992), especially in reaction to plans for a monetary union (see Notermans 2001 for debates within social democratic parties). Government–opposition dynamics, national election cycles, counter-arguments regarding the political benefits of monetary union, etc., were deployed by party leaderships to contain the unease articulated by factions within parties. Consequently, the general picture for the majority of parties, especially parties of government, apart from selected episodes of internal disgruntlement with an EU initiative, was a widespread quiescence over EU matters. As Poguntke *et al.* (2007) concluded, much of the internal organizational change related to EU party roles and offices was relatively minor and certainly did not produce any new power centres within parties.

To say that the party-political landscape in the older EU member states did not reflect much of an impact by the EU would be misleading, however, as one of most visible changes in party politics was the rise of Eurosceptic parties and opinion among electorates. Though parties whose overriding identity was based on a Eurosceptic stance, such as United Kingdom Independence Party (UKIP) in the UK, have not achieved a breakthrough at the national level, many other parties of the far Right have adopted Eurosceptic positions, and have been able, in selected cases, to exert influence on a minority or coalition government regarding EU policies, for example the Danish People's Party, the Freedom Party (FPÖ) in Austria, or the Party of Freedom (PVV) of Geert Wilders in the Netherlands. Perhaps more significantly, Eurobarometer and other surveys have tracked a general decline in public support for further European integration (an especially potent constraint on national governments following failed referendums in the 2000s in Ireland, France, and the Netherlands). Still, except for a few older member states, the party-political landscape remains immune from EU influence, apart from the cyclical nature of elections and the occasional EU treaty change or major initiative (the Services directive of 2006 triggered a mobilization in opposition by Western trade unions, Left-leaning MEPs, and some parties on the Left, such as the French Socialists). The conclusion that the EU has not had any major impact on the formal structure of parties and their classic operation remains valid, but the automatic support—or at least lack of opposition—by national electorates for further strides forward in European integration can no longer be taken for granted (Van der Eijk and Franklin 2007). Furthermore, from a Europeanization perspective, key EU initiatives such as EMU have generated a 'party-policy misfit' which has impacted selected parties.

Parties in the newer or *post-communist* member states have had a fundamentally different experience in relation to the EU, and one that includes more varied evidence of its influence. The literature on the impact of the EU on post-communist transition and consolidation, and parties in particular, has concerned itself with questions of democratization, the transfer of EU norms to political actors, party development factors deriving from EU political conditionality in general, and the contribution of transnational party federations in particular. A singular difference between the experiences of parties in the older member states and post-communist parties is the fact that, for the most part, any EU influence detected in the activities of older parties had occurred *after* the country's entry into EU membership; whereas in the case of post-communist parties, EU influence has probably been at its most potent *during* the accession process, from the early to mid-1990s until membership in 2004. Political conditionality, as chapters in this volume on post-communist member states attest, induced institutional, policy, and behavioural changes in aspirant states, with the goal of EU membership sought by most political actors as well as the electorate. A combination of self-motivation and EU directions for change, encapsulated in the negotiations and evaluation with each state of the various chapters of the *acquis communautaire*, explains how change was produced. As for political parties, the new political landscape differed in many fundamental ways from that of the older member states. To begin with, a competitive party system had been absent since soon after the end of World War Two (and only a few East European countries actually had any experience in parliamentary democracy during the inter-war period in the first place). Thus an absence of knowledge and skills for competitive campaigning, party manifesto and programmatic development, as well as financial and infrastructural resources, were in short supply. Also characterizing the party terrain of most post-communist states was the presence of the communist successor party, a political organization for whom material resources were not in short supply, as they usually inherited the assets of the formerly-governing party organization. Not all successor parties followed a social-democratization process (Ishiyama 2006), and those that did not, i.e. remained hostile to EU membership and the 'marketization' of society, constituted a small niche on the extreme end of the emerging party systems. Where successor parties remained 'unrepentant', new social democratic parties were created. Another set of new parties were those that asserted a link with pre-communist era parties, such as a farmers/peasants party, monarchist, or even a liberal party. The Centre and Right-wing of many emerging party systems also witnessed newly established parties, conservative, and in some cases Christian democratic, but also nationalist. Finally, 'parties-in-exile' from the pre-WWII period returned and exercised some limited influence in (re-)establishing some parties, notably in some Baltic states. Thus, the first decade or so of the post-communist period witnessed an effervescence of political party formation, some disappearing after one or two elections (Lewis 2001).

Under such conditions, and with most governments in the area having signalled by the mid-1990s their intention of securing membership into the EU as soon as possible, the EU played a far different role in party development and party politics in general. First of all, the weakness of new parties, not just in material terms but also with regard to campaign and organizational expertise, lack of a stable voter base, and minimal number of members—many new parties were formed 'in parliament' and thereafter sought members—meant that they were responsive to the efforts of Western transnational party federations (Euro-parties) in their attempt to recruit new member parties. In these cases, particularly involving the social democratic, liberal, and conservative/Christian democratic Euro-parties, a party-oriented form of political conditionality was activated, as potential member parties were evaluated in terms of their organization principles, policies, and commitment to fair and free competitive politics (Pridham 2001; Spirova 2008). Thus Euro-parties assisted in the wider effort to transmit EU norms into new post-communist parties, policy positions, and, in some cases, expertise with regard to modern, Western-style party organization and campaigning. Euro-parties, therefore, were a factor of influence to at least some degree in terms of party development in post-communist states, and assisted in the shaping of party policy and government relations with the EU. However, it may be more accurate to state that this influence waned *after* accession, and the example of the Slovakian centre-Left party direction—Social Democracy (Smer-SD)—leading a government coalition consisting of two extreme Right-wing parties in 2006, despite the protest of the Party of European Socialists, demonstrated perhaps the loosening of external constraints on post-communist parties (or the diminishing of 'external europeanization', Agh 2007).

Apart from 'unreconstructed' communist parties, opposition to EU influence—or Euroscepticism in its varying degrees—has also characterized many post-Communist parties, and not simply at the extremes of the party system. As a major centre-Right party, the Czech Civic Democratic Party (ODS) is as Eurosceptic in its rhetoric as the British Conservative Party, both being parties of government. On the other hand, the Polish PiS has evolved in its degree of hostility to the EU, seen by some as a change in domestic electoral strategy after its competitor, Civic Platform, came to power—this was reflected in the softening of its opposition to ratifying the Lisbon Treaty (Dakowska 2010; Szczerbiak 2008). The Polish Peasants' Party (also known as the Polish People's Party, PSL) has also evolved, from suspicion and scepticism about the benefits to its members from joining the EU to general support, linked perhaps to the flow of EU regional and CAP resources. This instrumental use of the EU as an issue in domestic party strategy is underlined by Neumayer (2008), who suggests that a more relational approach to account for patterns of party competition better explains post-communist Euroscepticism (see also Taggart and Szczerbiak 2004).

Two comparative studies on the impact of the EU on post-communist parties have arrived at somewhat similar conclusions. A special issue of the *Journal of Communist Studies and Transition Politics* (2009), edited by Haughton, and a volume edited by Lewis and Mansfeldová (2006) judged the EU to have been the cause of only minor changes in the political development trajectory of post-communist parties, though each recognizes some common factors, such as the role of Euro-parties (specifically, only on those parties which were able to establish a membership link with a Euro-party). Haughton concludes that the impact and role of the EU 'is better encapsulated in the metaphor of the conductor or the fellow passenger. In the former cases, the conductor ensures that the passengers have paid the fare and abide by the rules . . . by imposing sanctions or applying moral pressure . . .'. In 'terms of party politics it may be better to see the EU's influence as a lively, talkative and large fellow passenger in the compartment, seeking to influence the other passengers' behaviour through engagement and force of argument . . .' (2009: 424). From a Europeanization perspective, although post-communist parties, especially those with members in the European Parliament, did establish specialist positions on EU affairs—in fact borrowing this organizational feature from established Western parties (a case of institutional isomorphism)—the EU certainly had an indirect effect on these parties. While evidence of some policy transfer has occurred, expedited by Euro-parties during the pre-accession period, the EU's assertion of a post-communist liberalized political economy, transmitted through the various chapters of the negotiations of the *acquis communautaire*, established the parameters of policy and partisan competition in the nascent political and party systems. There is also evidence, again during the phase of negotiations with the EU, of parties in various member states agreeing not to make the substance of negotiations a matter of partisan competition in parliament, thereby ensuring a more rapid parliamentary approval of the application process (Grzymala-Busse and Innes 2003). The high point of EU influence on post-communist parties was the pre-accession period ending in 2004, and as these party systems have matured, the issue of the EU's influence on parties in the east may come to resemble that of parties and party systems in the west (Whitefield and Rohrschneider 2009). Also, as in the case of parties in older member states, explaining the variable impact of the EU in post-communist states is similar, i.e. domestic factors such as public opinion toward the EU, the number of parties in a party system, as well as whether or not a Eurosceptic party has 'blackmail potential' (Sartori 1976), etc., are variables in a Europeanization analysis.

Conclusion

The European Union in both older and newer member states, is of limited impact in the day-to-day functioning of parties, whether it is in terms of their internal organizational power structures and programmatic development, in patterns of domestic party competition, or in the operation of party government, from coalition-building to relations between various actors in public office. Nevertheless, minor organizational changes—similar for most parties, such as a specific portfolio on EU affairs, rules changes allowing MEP's representation, and a vote in national party congresses and leadership bodies, etc.—have been common. More variable has been the nature of programmatic responses to EU policies, electoral strategies and the degree of internal dissent that must be managed by party leaderships. The factors that explain the differential impact of the EU on parties are similar to those in wider arguments about Europeanization, e.g. the role of political leadership, different organizational structures, cycles of reform, and public opinion (in particular the level of Euroscepticism). Tracing changes in party organization, policy, and behaviour to EU influence, i.e. the issue of causality, is a complex task whether in older or newer member states. By distinguishing an EU direct and indirect impact on political parties, a Europeanization approach can analyze in a more precise manner different or discrete types of party change, thereby also ranking change in terms of significance to party goals, etc. The EU's influence, in both east and west, may be more significant in the long run in terms of its indirect impact on the patterns of party competition because of the downloading of EU policies—more intense in the post-communist pre-accession period than any experience in the west, but nevertheless a dynamic that has implications for the democratic constitution of member states in which competition over vital public policy issues is a hallmark of liberal democracy. Whether the legacy of de-politicizing areas of public policy results in a growing public disenchantment with 'politics as usual', reflected in diminishing support for mainstream parties, might be an unintended consequence of the narrowing parameters of party government.

FURTHER READING

One of the first sustained, book-length analyses of Europeanization and political parties specifically evaluates the impact of the EU on party organization (Poguntke *et al.* 2007). While not employing a strict Europeanization approach, nevertheless a comprehensive analysis of the development patterns of Euro-parties is presented by Hanley (2008). Ladrech (2009) presents an overview of the literature on Europeanization and parties. There is a growing literature on the EU and post-communist parties, with Vachudova (2008) evaluating the significance of EU influence before and after accession, and Fink-Hafner (2008) specifically employing a Europeanization approach to the party politics in three aspiring EU members in the Western Balkans.

WEB LINKS

The five Euro-parties discussed in the chapter all have a website, with links to each of their member national parties and, where applicable, to their respective EP party group:

European Left Party **www.european-left.org**

Party of European Socialists **www.pes.org**

European Green Party **http://europeangreens.eu**

European Liberal, Democrat and Reform **www.eldr.org**

European People's Party **www.epp.eu**

REFERENCES

Agh, A. (2007), *Eastern Enlargement and the Future of the EU27*, Budapest: Together for Europe Research Centre, Hungarian Academy of Sciences.

Almeida, D. (2010), 'Europeanized Eurosceptics? Radical Right Parties and European Integration', *Perspectives on European Politics and Society*, 11/3: 237–53.

Aylott, N. (2002), 'Let's Discuss This Later: Party Responses to Euro-Division in Scandinavia', *Party Politics*, 8/4: 463-81.

Aylott, N. (2005), 'Lessons Learned, Lessons Forgotten: The Swedish Referendum on EMU of September 2003', *Government & Opposition*, 40/4: 540–64.

Bartolini, S. (2005), *Restructuring Europe: Centre Formation, System Building, and Political Structuring Between the Nation State and the European Union*, Oxford: Oxford University Press.

Börzel, T. (2005), 'Europeanization: How the European Union Interacts with Its Member States', in S. Bulmer and C. Lequesne (eds), *The Member States of the European Union*, Oxford: Oxford University Press, 45–69.

Börzel, T. and Risse, T. (2006), 'Europeanization: The Domestic Impact of European Union Politics', in K. E. Jørgensen, M. A. Pollack, and B. Rosamond (eds), *Handbook of European Union Politics*, London: SAGE, 483–504.

Dakowska, D. (2010), 'Whither Euroscepticism? The Uses of European Integration by Polish Conservative and Radical Parties', *Perspectives on European Politics and Society*, 11/3: 254–72.

Fennema, M. and Pollmann, C. (1998), 'Ideology of Anti-Immigrant Parties in the European Parliament', *Acta Politica*, 33/2: 111–38.

Fink-Hafner, D. (2008), 'Europeanization and Party System Mechanics: Comparing Croatia, Serbia and Montenegro', *Journal of Southern Europe and the Balkans*, 10/2: 167–82.

Gabel, M. and Scheve, K. (2007), 'Mixed Messages: Party Dissent and Mass Opinion on European Integration', *European Union Politics*, 8/1: 37–59.

Gaffney, J. (1996), *Political Parties and the European Union*, London: Routledge.

Grzymala-Busse, A. and Innes, A. (2003), 'Great Expectations: The EU and Domestic Political Competition in East Central Europe', *East European Politics and Societies*, 17/1: 64–73.

Hanley, D. (2008), *Beyond the Nation State: Parties in the Era of European Integration*, Basingstoke: Palgrave Macmillan.

Haughton, T. (2009), 'Driver, Conductor or Fellow Passenger? EU Membership and Party Politics in Central and Eastern Europe', *Journal of Communist Studies and Transition Politics*, 25/4: 413–26.

Haverland, M. (2007), 'Methodology', in P. Graziano and M. Vink, (eds), *Europeanization: New Research Agendas*, Basingstoke: Palgrave Macmillan, 59–70.

Hepburn, E. (2010), *Using Europe: Territorial Party Strategies in a Multi-Level System*, Manchester: Manchester University Press.

Hix, S. and Lord, C. (1997), *Political Parties in the European Union*, Basingstoke: Macmillan.

Hix, S., Noury, A., and Roland, G. (2007), *Democratic Politics in the European Parliament*, Cambridge: Cambridge University Press.

Hooghe, L. and Marks, G. (2009), 'A Postfunctionalist Theory of European Integration: From Permissive Consensus to Constraining Dissensus', *British Journal of Political Science*, 39/1: 1–23.

Ishiyama, J. (2006), 'Europeanization and the Communist Successor Parties in Post-Communist Politics', *Politics and Policy*, 34/1: 3–29.

Johansson, K. M. and Zervakis, P. (2002), *European Political Parties between Cooperation and Integration*, Baden-Baden: Nomos Verlagsgesellschaft.

Journal of Communist Studies and Transition Politics, (2009), Special issue: 'Does EU Membership Matter? Party Politics in Central and Eastern Europe'.

Kreppel, A. (2002), *The European Parliament and Supranational Party System: A Study in Institutional Development*, Cambridge: Cambridge University Press.

Ladrech, R. (2000), *Social Democracy and the Challenge of European Union*, Boulder: Lynne Rienner Publishers.

Ladrech, R. (2002), 'Europeanization and Political Parties: Towards a Framework for Analysis', *Party Politics*, 8/4: 389-403.

Ladrech, R. (2007), 'Europeanization and national party organization: Limited but Appropriate Adaptation?', in T. Poguntke, N. Aylott, E. Carter, R. Ladrech, and K. R. Luther, (eds), *The Europeanization of National Political Parties: Power and Organizational Adaptation*, Abingdon: Routledge, 211–29.

Ladrech, R. (2009), 'Europeanization and Political Parties', *Living Reviews in European Governance*, 4/1: 1–19, www.livingreviews.org/lreg-2009-1

Lewis, P. (2001), *Party Development and Democratic Change in Post-Communist Europe: The First Decade*, London: Cass.

Lewis, P. and Mansfeldová, Z. (eds) (2006), *The European Union and Party Politics in Central and Eastern Europe*, Basingstoke: Palgrave Macmillan.

Mair, P. (2000), 'The Limited Impact of Europe on national party systems', *West European Politics*, 23/4: 27–51.

Mair, P. (2007a), 'Political opposition and the European Union', *Government and Opposition*, 42/1: 1–17.

Mair, P. (2007b), 'Political Parties and Party Systems', in P. Graziano and M. Vink, (eds), *Europeanization: New Research Agendas*, Basingstoke: Palgrave Macmillan, 154–66.

Mudde, C. (2007), *Populist Radical Right Parties in Europe*, Cambridge: Cambridge University Press.

Neumayer, L. (2008), 'Euroscepticism as a Political Label: The Use of European Union Issues in Political Competitions in the New Member States', *European Journal of Political Research*, 47/2: 135–60.

Notermans, T. (2001), *Social Democracy and Monetary Union*, Oxford: Berghahn Books.

Oppermann, K. (2010), 'Plebiscitary Politics and European Integration: Juxtaposing a Defensive and an Offensive Case for Pledging EU Referendums', paper presented a the Fifth Pan-European Conference on EU Politics, June, Porto, Portugal.

Poguntke, T., Aylott, A., Carter, E., Ladrech, R., and Luther, K. R. (eds) (2007), *The Europeanization of National Political Parties: Power and Organizational Adaptation*, Abingdon: Routledge.

Pridham, G. (2001), 'Patterns of Europeanization and Transnational Party Cooperation: Party Development in Central and Eastern Europe', in P. Lewis, (ed.), *Party Development and Democratic Change in Post-Communist Europe*, London: Cass, 178–98.

Pridham, G. and Pridham, P. (1981), *Transnational Party Co-operation and European Integration*, London: Allen and Unwin.

Radaelli, C. (2003), 'The Europeanization of Public Policy', in K. Featherstone and C. Radaelli, (eds), *The Politics of Europeanization*, Oxford: Oxford University Press, 27–56.

Sartori, G. (1976), *Parties and Party Systems: A Framework for Analysis*, Cambridge: Cambridge University Press.

Shu, M. (2008), 'Referendums and the Political Constitutionalisation of the EU', *European Law Journal*, 14/4: 423–45.

Spirova, M. (2008), 'Europarties and Party Development in EU-candidate States: The Case of Bulgaria', *Europe-Asia Studies*, 60/5: 791–808.

Steenbergen, M. and Scott, D. (2004), 'Contesting Europe? The Salience of European Integration as a Party Issue', in G. Marks and M. Steenbergen (eds), *European Integration and Political Conflict*, Cambridge: Cambridge University Press, 165–92.

Szczerbiak, A. (2008), 'Opposing Europe or Problematizing Europe? Euroscepticism and "Eurorealism" in the Polish Party System', in A. Szczerbiak and P. Taggart, (eds), *Opposing Europe? The Comparative Party Politics of Euroscepticism, vol. 1, Case Studies and Country Surveys*, Oxford: Oxford University Press.

Taggart, P. and Szczerbiak, A. (eds) (2004), 'Contemporary Euroscepticism in the Party System of the EU Candidate States of Central and Eastern Europe', *European Journal of Political Research*, 43/1: 1–27.

Vachudova, M. (2008), 'Tempered by the EU? Political Parties and Party Systems Before and After Accession', *Journal of European Public Policy*, 15/6: 861–79.

Van der Eijk, C. and Franklin, M. (2007), 'The Sleeping Giant: Potential for Political Mobilization of Disaffection with European Integration', in W. Van der Brug and C. Van der Eijk, (eds), *European Elections and Domestic Politics: Lessons from the Past and Scenarios for the Future*, Notre Dame, Indiana: University of Notre Dame Press, 189–208.

Van Hecke, S. (2004), 'A Decade of Seized Opportunities: Christian Democracy in the European Union', in E. Gerard and S. Van Hecke (eds), *Christian Democratic Parties in Europe Since the End of the Cold War*, Leuven: Leuven University Press, 269–95.

Wagner, M. (2008), 'Debating Europe in the French Socialist Party: The 2004 Internal Referendum on the EU Constitution', *French Politics*, 6/3: 257–79.

Whitefield, S. and Rohrschneider, R. (2009), 'The Europeanization of Political Parties in Central and Eastern Europe? The Impact of EU Entry on Issue Stances, Salience and Programmatic Coherence', *Journal of Communist Studies and Transition Politics*, 25/4: 564–84.

CHAPTER 14

The Europeanization of Interest Groups and Social Movements

Sabine Saurugger

▌ Summary

European integration has influenced interest groups and social movements since the beginning of the process in the 1950s. However, influence has not been uniform—transformation has been induced by other elements such as globalization or the transformation of the state. While these factors are important, this chapter aims to systematize the influence stemming from the European level. More generally, it attempts to offer answers to the questions of what has changed and what are the elements of change? The chapter thus relates the transformation and variables when analyzing the change in interests, strategies, and internal organizational structures of interest groups and social movements, both in the 'old' and 'new' member states.

Introduction

Interest groups as well as social movements are key actors in contemporary democracies. As such, they are influenced by European integration processes and debates. New opportunities and policies posed by the EU may trigger a process of change for interest organizations and social movements. Empirical evidence shows that farmers' unions, environmental organizations, women's lobbies, chemical industries, or banks have chosen to represent their interests in Brussels and have integrated European policies, programmes, and legal constraints into their domestic interest representation strategies. Thus, while Europeanization is not a natural or immediate response of interest groups and social movements (Ladrech 2005: Beyers and Kerremans 2007), all groups are at one point concerned by the European construction process. The aim of this chapter is to present an analysis of the process of change or non-change that interest groups and social movements have undergone.

There is a general consensus that the impact of European integration is a differential one: no one single interest intermediation type, nor collective action form has emerged to date. At the same time, some empirical regularity exists in the fact that all interest groups as well as social movements are increasingly summoned to coordinate their interest representation at different levels of EU governance.

In order to better grasp the dynamics of interest group and social movement Europeanization at the national level, this chapter addresses three more general issues identified by the literature on Europeanization (Börzel 2005): the dimensions of domestic interest group and social movement change, the mechanisms of group change, and the outcomes of domestic change. The dimensions of change in this chapter refer to the interests and strategies of groups and social movements on the one hand, and their internal organizational structures on the other hand. The mechanisms of change with regard to these actors refer to coercion, in which the EU proscribes or imposes a model, or normative diffusion/learning, where interest, strategies, and organizational structures of groups are gently nudged into transforming incrementally. Finally, the outcomes of change with regard to interest groups and social movements are differentiated and range from adaptation to rejection.

This chapter aims to present the main forms of Europeanization of groups and social movements that have emerged in this context and to illustrate these through empirical studies. It will start with the debate on the definition of these actors before concentrating more precisely on the change in actors' interests as well as action repertoires including groups' relations with state actors. Finally, the chapter will attempt to open up the black box of interest groups and social movements and present the transformations their internal structures have undergone on account of European integration processes.

Interest Groups vs Social Movements?

Before analyzing the results of research undertaken on the Europeanization of interest groups and social movements, it is crucial to define these notions in the context of European integration. This chapter considers 'non-state actors' as a more generic term, thus referring to interest groups and social movements as synonymous notions (Saurugger 2012b). The distinction in the literature is often based on an implicit assumption—taken mainly from the discourses of 'civil society organizations'—according to which the term 'interest groups' refers to activities carried out by groups defending economic and selfish interests, whereas 'morally good actors' such as social movements defend the common good. As Beyers *et al.* (2008: 1110) contend,

Literatures that use these labels [social movement, advocacy, civil society] go to great lengths to avoid the 'interest group' label because they associate the term with selfish inside lobbying (usually conducted by narrow economic or sectional interest). . . . [T]he SMO [social movement organization] label is used by scholars to study allegedly different forms of contentious politics with a focus on political opportunity structures as well as the process of identity formation and the mobilization of resources in SMO's.

However, empirical research on these actors' action strategies and target institutions has shown how similar 'social movements' and economic interest groups strategies actually can be. Both frame their interests in terms of the common good, both have specific interests to defend (the smallest common denominator being their survival), both target all European institutions: the European Commission, the European Parliament, or the Council/European Council. In this sense, interest representation refers to 'all efforts to push public policy in a specific direction on behalf of the constituencies or a general political idea' (Beyers *et al.* 2008: 1106).

Two elements are of specific importance when defining non-state actors: strategies or action repertoires, on the one hand, and the degree of organizational structuring, on the other. In turn, the strategies of non-state actors to represent their interests can roughly be divided into inside and outside strategies. Inside strategies refer to semi-institutionalized action repertoires in which expertise and knowledge seem particularly important. Here, well organized and highly centralized collective actors are thought to be more generally present than loose networks which are considered more prominent in the use of outside strategies such as protesting or, more generally, non-institutionalized forms of claim making. This chapter argues, by contrast, that both types of actors—interest groups and social movements—use these action repertoires interchangeably. Groups such as farmers' unions or Greenpeace have access to inside as well as outside lobbying. However, while an organization such as Business Europe (the European federation of industrialists) may almost exclusively use inside lobbying, social movements such as marches by the unemployed usually refer

> **BOX 14.1**   **Interest groups and social movements—a definition**
>
> Interest groups and social movements are entities whose aim is to represent the interests of a specific section of society. Their action strategies and degree of organization must be placed on a continuum from loose to very organized, and from informal and formal consultation to protest movements. These elements thus do not allow the clear distinction of interest groups from social movements.

to protest strategies. It is, therefore, more useful to apply a continuum reaching from protest movements to institutionalized inside lobbying open to all groups and social movements than to introduce a clear distinction between them.

The notion of an organized group is the second central term in collective action studies. In this sense, social movements and interest groups are organizations. They have either formal signed-up members or informal supporters who routinely show up to assist their organization (for a detailed debate on this issue see Maloney and Jordan 1997). However, it is important not to overestimate this organizational principle in general, and at the EU level in particular. Empirical research has shown that social movements or latent groups can be highly organized and hierarchically structured and thereby only distinguishable from interest groups by name (Balme and Chabanet 2002). In a similar way to the typology of action repertoires, the organizational structure of groups must be placed on a continuum of more or less structured situations. Thus a number of transnational non-governmental organizations (NGOs) are structured like real companies. On the other hand, as David Coen (1997) contends, firms act increasingly often as if they were interest groups at the EU level. Using the degree of organization as a criterion to define interest groups in the EU can therefore be misleading.

These preliminary conceptual clarifications are of particular importance when dealing with the Europeanization of these actors whether they are called economic interest groups, firms, diffuse interest groups, NGOs, social movements, or foundations.

Europeanization of Interests and Strategies

There seems to be agreement amongst scholars working on non-state actors in the EU that resources as well as the domestic national institutional context determine whether national interest groups Europeanize their lobbying strategies or not (Klüver 2010). In other words, the structural embeddedness of groups has significant explanatory power for Europeanization. While there is no agreement on the question of whether interest groups, social movements, or state actors either gain or lose from European integration, scholars share the idea that, more or less deeply, all groups are affected by European integration processes.

Two bodies of research have developed on this particular aspect. On the one hand are scholars working with interest intermediation categories such as pluralism, neo-corporatism, or statism, who analyze whether these have changed (Schmidt 1996: Falkner 2000: Grossman 2004: Eising 2009). On the other hand, we find a group of scholars developing new categories of group adaptation, based on research undertaken in the field of social movements.

State-group Relations

The ever deepening integration over the last fifty years has brought new research questions onto the agenda focusing on the instruments interest groups use in the policy-making processes of the EU's multilevel governance system. Based on comparative politics, the debate is centred on the qualification of interest intermediation systems as either pluralist (highlighting competition amongst interest organizations), neocorporatist (stressing negotiations among governmental actors and peak organizations), or statist (underlining the hierarchy among state and non-state actors) (see Table 14.1) (see also Eising 2008; Streeck and Schmitter 1999).

Research by a number of scholars has found that different interest groups have experienced biased access to European institutions, leading these scholars to characterize the EU system as a form of 'elite pluralism' (Coen 1997; Eising 2008). Others have argued that examples for both neocorporatism and pluralism can be found at the EU level. By the mid-1990s, this typology characterizing a state level interest intermediation structure shifted to the policy level. Scholars of the EU working on collective action no longer considered states to be the organizational model for interest group intermediation, but concentrated instead on the different forms of

TABLE 14.1 Interest representation modes

Mode of interest intermediation	Role of public authorities	Role of non-state actors	Dominant action repertoires
Statist	Statist state: organizes interests	Weak: fragmented and poorly organized	Conflict and confrontation; clientelism
Pluralist	Regulatory state: registers demands issues by non-state actors	Medium: high degree of professionalization, service providers for members	Formal and informal consultation, expertise
Neocorporatist	Mediating state: strong presence, organizes interaction between state and non-state actors	Strong: very organized, hierarchically structured, representation monopoly	Formal negotiations, participation in policy making

relations between groups and the state in specific policy areas (see Smith 1993). Thus, some policy areas may be highly pluralistic (e.g. environmental policy) while others may exhibit corporatist tendencies (e.g. agriculture). In statist policy areas—particularly numerous in France, Britain, and Greece—state actors have traditionally provided interest groups with little access or influence in policy formulation, but as Schmidt (2006: 672) notes, 'have accommodated them in implementation, either by making exceptions to the rules as often as not or limiting the number of rules to allow self governing arrangements'. However, only in exceptional cases do interest groups adapt extremely marginally to the multilevel decision-making process. Such a case can be found in the example of the French farmers' union whose organizational structures and lobbying strategies adapted very slowly, relying for a long time solely on their national governments. In policy fields where neocorporatist structures prevail, interest groups have similar difficulties adapting to the multilevel EU framework, except in cases where governments establish EU coordinating structures which include major interest groups as applies in Austria or Sweden. Finally, interest groups in pluralist policy fields adapted rather rapidly to become the main interlocutors in the specific policy field—as illustrated in the example of the Netherlands (Wilts 2002).

The limits of categorization

Working with these categories leads to serious problems when qualifying the degree of Europeanization of non-state actors at the domestic level. As Eising (2008) notes, a number of studies using these typologies come to conflicting conclusions. Vivien Schmidt (1999) analyzes the repercussions of the EU on the domestic modes of interest intermediation in France, Germany, the United Kingdom, and Italy. She finds that quasi-pluralistic patterns are prevalent at the EU level and argues that German corporatism fits this mode better than the statism that she identifies in the UK, Italy, and France. Consequently, adaptation pressures—and difficulties—would be greater in this group of countries than in Germany.

Maria Green Cowles (2001) arrives at fundamentally different results in her study of the impact which EU foreign trade policy-making in the Transatlantic Business Dialogue (TABD) has on national industry federations. She characterizes the EU mode as a form of 'elite pluralism' because, in the context of the TABD, large firms have a direct say in the formulation of EU foreign economic policy. The author argues that this elite pluralism poses a greater challenge to associations socialized in German corporatism and French statism than to those that are used to British pluralism. Cowles finds empirical support for her argument in the German and British cases and contends that the French industry association has actually been empowered on the domestic level because of its involvement in the TABD negotiations.

Schneider *et al.* (2007) come to a different conclusion again. In analyzing domestic pre-negotiations of EU legislation in fifteen EU member states, the authors argue that the interaction between government agencies, interest groups, and parties is largely statist (*étatiste*), insofar as interest groups are very much dependent on state actors to influence or even participate in the debate. This conclusion is convincing when considering that a majority of EU member states have more or less centralized national coordination structures. Thus, while interest groups want to defend their corner, national governmental actors act as the ultimate arbiter in domestic pre-negotiations. It is only at the agenda-setting phase that resourceful interest groups have the possibility of circumventing the state. And it is here where groups used to pluralist or semi-pluralist policy areas have a competitive advantage and do not need to operate via national governments. These conclusions reflect more generally the idea that inside a specific public policy area interest intermediation types may converge, whereas, system-wide, these types increasingly diverge. This '*inter-system convergence*' in specific policy areas as a consequence of Europeanization goes hand in hand with '*intra-system divergence*' which is because of the 'coexistence of different types of policy networks within the same political system' (Falkner 2000: 94).

In a valiant attempt to find a solution to these conflicting findings, Eising (2004, 2009) argues that the degree of initial similarity between the interest intermediation type prevalent at the EU and the national level does not necessarily lead to a situation where groups stemming from a pluralist intermediation system would have easier access at the EU level to a policy area characterized by a pluralist intermediation mode than those stemming from a neocorporatist member state. According to Eising (2004), two factors shape interest representation in a multilevel setting: groups' internal governance capacities and domestic opportunity structures. Internal governance structures refer to negotiation capacities of interest groups, i.e. their capacity to mediate between competing demands of members and state, and engage in self-regulation. Organizational resources, on the other hand, refer to money, time, expertise, and sustained effort. However, interest groups are constantly embedded in social relations and depend on routine exchanges with established domestic partners.

Taking these variables into account, and going beyond the classic distinction between pluralist, neocorporatist, and statist interest intermediation structures, Eising identifies five types of interest group Europeanization:

1. Multilevel players (more active and present throughout the entire policy cycle at both the EU and national levels);

2. EU players (very active at the EU level, but few contacts at the national level—absent during implementation phase);

3. Traditionalists (concentrate mainly on the national level, also sometimes active at the EU level);

4. Occasional players (obtain all information at the national level);

5. Niche organizations (hardly active during the policy cycle).

In comparing Germany, Britain, and France, he finds the largest group of multilevel players (29 per cent) in Germany, 22.1 per cent of multilevel players in Britain, and only 14.2 per cent of multilevel players in France. All three countries, however, still have a high level of Traditionalists (25–35 per cent), and all have very few EU players (1–6 per cent). Eising concludes that interest groups that specialize in the representation of interests are in a better position to reconcile the conflicting demands of state actors, on the one hand, and of members of these organizations, on the other; and to act better in a multilevel setting than those that specialize in other tasks—such as coordinating market activities, providing services, issuing licenses, resolving disputes, or gathering and providing market information.

In concentrating more strongly on internal factors than does Eising (2004), but not contradicting his research results, Beyers and Kerremans (2007) argue that size or resources do not necessarily matter when interest groups aim to Europeanize. On the contrary, financial resources can backfire: dependency on government subsidies restrains Europeanization. What matters is the relationship between interest groups and member constituencies as well as the policy sector. The authors show that, in policy sectors where EU competencies are weak or non-existent, interest groups are less inclined to Europeanize because they are still able to fulfil many of their political goals at the domestic level. Thus instead of pursuing a logic of influence, in other words looking for influence at the European Union level, interests groups—both public and private—follow a logic of the immediate environment, which refers to membership dues, domestic policy environment, dependence on government subsidies.

Europeanization of 'new' member states

In the new member states, the use of traditional interest intermediation categories is not widespread, and for good reason. As has been underlined (Howard 2003: Perez-Solorzano Borragan 2005: Mudde 2007), post-communist societies are the result of a systemic change leading to a transition in political, economic, and social affairs. Most observers agree, however, that the role of the state has a continued relevance in post-communist settings. Although a large number of interest organizations emerged after the opening up of the political system in 1989, in particular in the field of public interest groups such as NGOs or associations more generally, the state plays a prominent role in the management of day-to-day politics. It seems that corporatist arrangements have become the norm in the relationship between the state and economic interest groups such as industrial associations and trade unions. Thus, for industrial and business associations, peak level tripartite structures and parliaments are the main institutionalized channels for interest intermediation, allowing governments, trade unions, and employers' associations to remain in rather continued contact despite infrequent agreement. However, these structures are considered to be particularly weak and inefficient. This can be linked to the weakness of both employers' associations and trade unions, whose negative image amongst the citizens continues in most member states, except in Poland (Avdagic and Crouch 2006).

European integration has also required interest groups to redirect their access points towards the European affairs services of ministries in post-communist EU member states. Thus, the Polish Chamber of Commerce and the Economic Chamber of the Czech Republic have both adapted their internal structures to the new European environment by creating committees for European affairs which provide information about European institutions and policies, represent the country's business sector in Brussels, and cooperate with European business organizations. Parallel to these national adaptation processes, business associations and trade unions also have developed institutionalized as well as non-institutionalized contacts with EU institutions and EU interest group federations. These so-called Eurogroups have developed specific support and training programmes, financed by the European Union to transfer knowledge and organizational know-how to Central and Eastern European interest groups (Perez-Solorzano Borragan 2005; Parau 2009). The tasks performed by interest group offices in Brussels stemming from the new member states are similar to those performed by their counterparts from the old member states: informing their members at the national level about EU legislation, funding opportunities, and relevant developments in EU policies; representing their members in Eurogroups; providing members with specific services, and organizing EU policy training sessions for their members in Brussels.

Public interest groups, associations or NGOs, on the contrary, do not fit into this description. Their Europeanization was less a transformation of already existing structures and interests, or of their relationship with the state, than their pure and simple creation. As data from the World Values Survey show, the average figure for organizational membership per person is relatively low (0.91) in post-communist countries as compared to older democracies (2.39) (Howard 2003: 62; see also Balme and Chabanet 2008). As in old member states, the influence of European integration on interest groups is indirect. Foreign donors, such as the George Soros foundation, or EU federations, such as ECAS (European Citizen Action Service), were and remain eager to supply financial assistance to public interest groups, seen as an instrument to promote grass roots democracy in the new member states. These funds offered an incentive to establish a NGO as a secure source of income in an environment where living costs and unemployment were rising as a result of economic liberalization. At the same time, however, three main factors explain the rather low level of organizational membership: a general mistrust of any kind of public organization, a general satisfaction with one's own social network, and disappointment in the developments of post-communism (Howard 2003).

Public interest groups in Central and Eastern European countries, instead of 'fitting' the classical typology of the pluralist-neocorporatist divide were affected both by external factors linked to their countries' membership of the European Union and the politics of transition based on overcoming or, better, working through, the communist heritage. Thus these groups had to absorb both domestic and EU institutional and policy norms (Ladrech 2010).

These results, both in old and post-communist EU member states, show that national opportunity structures still act very significantly as a condition on how interest groups and social movements transform their interest representation strategy. Europeanization research on interest groups underlines that interest groups have been created at the national level and remain part of their national political arenas where they continue to represent their interests (Beyers and Kerremans 2007: Eising 2009: Klüver 2010; but also more generally Ladrech 2005, 2010). Their ties bind them to the national level and are part of the environment that allows them to develop their strategies.

While the debate based on the traditional interest intermediation typology is of continued relevance in research into Europeanization, another typology, linking interest groups and social movements together, has made its way into collective action research on Europeanization.

Beyond the Pluralist-neocorporatist Divide

At the beginning of the 2000s, an increasing number of scholars crossed the long-standing divide between interest group and social movement studies and analyzed the transformation of their action repertoires and strategies in the EU comparatively (Balme and Chabanet 2002). These scholars argued that four types of transformations through European integration processes might be identified for interest groups and advocacy organizations: internalization, externalization, supranationalization, and transnationalization (see Table 14.2). The first mode, *internalization,* refers to the development of local or national mobilizations around European policies. Dialogue between national or local interest and advocacy groups helps to influence national European policy making. However, these mobilizations and action repertoires remain concentrated at the national level, mostly directed towards national public opinion and government. The second mode of Europeanization of collective action is *externalization.* Here, national non-state actors directly contact European political actors, side-stepping the national level in order to represent their specific interests. Balme and Chabanet argue that this strategy is generally reserved for groups with substantial financial resources, such as firms. *Supranationalization,* the third mode of

---

TABLE 14.2 Forms of Europeanization

Modes of Europeanization	Dynamics
Internalization	Groups and movements concentrate their activities at the domestic level
Externalization	Groups and movements side-step the domestic level and directly 'go to Brussels'
Supranationalization	Movements and groups establish federations or confederations of groups at the European level to influence the EU level directly
Transnationalization	Transformation of national actors into global actors (examples: Amnesty International, Greenpeace)

change, corresponds to the institutionalization of European confederations or federations of national non-state actors at the EU level. It is the mode describing the emergence of most 'Eurogroups', as European confederations of national federations are called in Brussels, such as Business Europe (Union of Industrial and Employers' Confederations of Europe, formerly UNICE), COPA (Committee of Farmers' organizations in the EU) or EFPIA (European Federation of Pharmaceutical Industry Associations). Finally, *transnationalization* refers to a profound transformation of national actors which become transnational actors, such as Greenpeace or Amnesty International.

Empirical research in this context reveals a rather neat differentiation between policy sectors. With regard to the environment and migration in particular, scholars stress the weak externalization or transnationalization of contentious events. Protesters rather turn to national governments and act only exceptionally at the European level (Rootes 2008; Rucht 2001). In the field of environmental protection, while non-state actors were quicker than many other organized interest groups to address the European level, as environmental issues encourage transnational perspectives, they are facing a more severe problem today. A number of movements resist this Europeanization, in the name of purity of purpose. Except for the very salient and transnationalized groups at the EU level, such as Greenpeace and Friends of the Earth, they concentrate on the national level. In the field of immigration movements, scholars also observe the relative scarcity of these network activities in Brussels.

The social and gender policy fields, however, are in a different position. The European Women's Lobby, created in 1990, developed into an agency representing women's interests, well recognized by European institutions. Following the debates about the implementation of the Maastricht Treaty and the increasing disapproval of the EU among women in particular, a window of opportunity opened during the years leading to the 1997 Amsterdam Treaty. However, this opportunity to intervene sometimes runs into difficulties stemming from the heterogeneity of member states' political structures (Helfferich and Kolb 2001). The national women's movements attract media attention through petitions and public marches and, at the same time, contact national representations of member states. Similar strategies can be found in the case of the European Trade Union Confederation (ETUC) (Erne 2008). In the framework of the fragile European Social Dialogue, the ETUC relies on Commission initiatives as national trade unions working with the ETUC mostly formulate domestic demands. While there has been more union transnationalization in the European labour movement than expected, the pattern is ambiguous. The ETUC has strengthened and professionalized in response to market integration, but still strongly relies on national trade unions to put forward its demands to national governments. European collective bargaining at the sectoral and company level is still weak.

More recently, evidence has shown that social movements seek to represent their interests at the EU level in order to circumvent limited political opportunities at the domestic level (Balme and Chabanet 2008). While referred to as exceptional events during the 1990s, illustrated by the European marches of the unemployed and the strike at Renault's Vilvoorde factory in Belgium, triggered by the decision of the Paris-based Renault headquarters to close the Belgian plant, social movements became increasingly visible in the 2000s. These activities, though temporary, can now be found increasingly often in the wake of European Council meetings, where anti- and alter-globalization movements—the latter seeking to change globalization according to their values rather than opposing it—organize in networks, protest and counter-events (Della Porta and Tarrow 2005). Here we clearly observe the exceptional construction of a European public space. Marks and McAdam (1996) are correct in reasoning that, when non-state actors encounter EU institutions, they model their behaviour around techniques of interest representation that are accepted by European officials instead of engaging in more contentious behaviour. But not all actors adapt their strategies and action repertoires. This argument is developed by McCauley (2011) when he argues that social movements are more often 'out of focus' when attempting to influence the specific European level opportunity structures, than 'out of reach'. In other words, they do not always strategically exploit attractive opportunity structures. Ideology and usage opportunities of these structures are important factors for explaining the transformation, or non-transformation, of groups.

Thus, the influence of European integration on the behaviour of non-state actors, while important, varies according to political fields. The main conclusion is that political opportunity structures at the EU level lead to very specific strategies that interest organizations must adopt in order to influence policy making. This behaviour is closer to lobbying and bargaining than it is to protest strategies. Case studies consistently underline the difficulties for, and in some cases the unwillingness of, social movements to adopt the most efficient action repertoires in order to influence European decision making (Beyers 2004: Della Porta 2007).

Internalization Strategies in Central and Eastern Europe

With regard to public interests in Central and Eastern European (CEE) member states, protest strategies are even less prominent. While the political opportunity structures of the EU generally decrease the number of protest movements at the EU level, CEE public interest groups protest even less in the new member states. At the EU level, this can be explained by the absence of a political interlocutor whose re-election at the European level might be jeopardized by a broad protest movement, a situation leading to an internalization strategy amongst public interest groups in old member states., This is surprising in the light of the role that social movements played during the final year of communist regimes (Mudde 2007: Ladrech 2010). Grassroots movements in new member states can be seen partially as 'window dressing movements' linked to the self-identification of executives of the new member states with certain elements of the advocacy network, reinforced by a general concern for their external reputation (Parau 2009). Nevertheless, change in the political regimes of CEE states after 1989 was both an opportunity and a constraint for public interest groups, and social actors more generally. Their adjustment to the new system was contingent upon the advent of democratic institutions and practices that opened a space for public debate (Devaux 2008). Support from international actors, however, was central in order to transfer the financial resources necessary to function. These actors were not only European institutions or Eurogroups, as we have seen earlier, but also American or EU member state foundations.

The situation in Central and Eastern Europe is based on the complex relationship between authoritarian regimes and the so-called 'civil society' (generally understood in its Hegelian definition as collective actors neither part of the state, nor the market, nor private life). While public and private interest groups or 'civil society' in general had difficulty emerging as freely as in liberal democracies, some scope for the establishment of interest groups existed. Thus, the Hungarian regime under Kadar allowed for a certain level of associative freedom as long as it was not explicitly anti-communist (Mudde 2003). In Czechoslovakia, state-controlled environmental associations were established as a consequence of the transnational debate on environmental protection at the beginning of the 1970s, strongly linked to the events organized in the framework of the United Nations, and more precisely the influential 1972 Stockholm conference held by the UN on environmental issues. However, these associations were established by the government and led by members of the Czechoslovakian Communist party nomenklatura. 'The regime canvassed citizen participation [. . .] in nature programmes, portraying "care" for nature as a way of furthering "democracy"' (Devaux 2008: 213). Authorizing further freedom would have led to an acute questioning of the political system and to profound change in one direction or another.

The transformation of these interest groups into the professional groups they are today, however, was largely influenced by Western donors and associations, which leads Cas Mudde (2003: 164) to take a particularly critical position. He argues that the efforts of 'civil society' are negligible in CEE countries 'because the many NGOs so often hailed in Western policy circles and academia, i.e. the pro-Western, liberal democratic groups, have few if any ties to the national grass roots, and communicate mainly if not exclusively with their international (i.e. Western) donors'.

More detailed micro-sociological studies allow an insight into the nitty-gritty of these transformations. Without questioning the critical stance of civil society scholars working on CEE countries today, Sandrine Devaux (2008) adopts a long-term perspective and convincingly argues that effective mobilization of public interest groups is possible only when there exists a functioning 'public space'. At the same time, research on Europeanization of interest groups in the 'new' member states underlines the limits of the Europeanization hypothesis: transformation and change of interest intermediation structures and interests is not only on account of European integration, but to other factors beyond Brussels and Strasbourg, such as the influence or transfer (Bulmer and Padgett 2005) of instruments, ideas, or financial resources.

Resistance

While change in non-state actors' strategies and interests has been analyzed in a large number of studies, as we have seen, few studies have centred on non-change: either passive (inertia) or active (resistance) among interest groups. However, European integration has also led to the development of attitudes of rejection of European integration, in the sense that non-state actors use European integration to develop an anti- or transformative-European discourse that helps them to redefine their preferences and relationships with the state. In the French context this research has shown how interest groups use this discourse to reinforce their position in the national context and play a role in political representation.

Representation seems to be 'in trouble' in contemporary liberal democracies, both in the sense of effectiveness (*for* the people) and participation (*by* the people). This crisis of representation is characterized by 'parties in decline and representation on the rise' (Berger 2006: 280). The decline in party membership and the rise in participation in associations suggest that activists prefer to participate in a context where they have more voice and closer, less hierarchical relationships with others. Instead of disappearing, political engagement is transformed and forcefully uses European integration to establish itself through contentious politics. In France, this action repertoire is still particularly well developed. Data stemming from the World Values Survey has shown that over three quarters of all French citizens have joined in some protest activity, signing a petition, demonstrating, or striking (Balme and Chabanet 2008).

Criticism of neoliberal European integration has been used by a large number of these non-state actors either to boost their appeal with the population or to establish themselves. Indeed, French trade unionism offers an appropriate illustration of this (Saurugger 2007). While traditional French trade unions, confronted by the decrease in union membership, started adapting to European integration during the 1980s, in the sense that they participated in the negotiation processes at the EU level through the ETUC, new trade unions emerged on the basis of their refusal to participate in what they see as a non-democratic consultation process. The emergence of the *SUD union* (*Solidaires, Unitaires et Démocratiques*) is one of the most significant examples. SUD was born from internal opposition within the CFDT (*Confédération française démocratique du travail*), from officials who had joined the trade union in 1968 from the extreme Left. This opposition was a result of the CFDT's attempt to evolve and change after François Mitterrand came to power in 1981, to adopt a more cooperative negotiation style in order to become the primary partner of public authorities and employers. The CFDT quickly gave rise to other alternative unions and became one of the major forces of the so-called 'group of ten' founded in 1981 as a federation of independent unions. This group focuses on the same issues promoted by the CFDT during the 1970s: self-management, anti-capitalism, feminism, and opposition to the perceived liberal free market ideology of the EU.

Parallel to these developments in French trade unionism, a certain number of organizations emerged in the 1990s using European integration as a scapegoat to attract broad support: the 'sans' (the withouts). There are especially the sans-emploi (without jobs), the sans-logis (without homes), and the sans-papiers (without papers), who materialize in associations such as Droits devant!!, AC! (Acting against unemployment), DAL (the right for housing), or APEIS (association for employment, information, and solidarity of unemployed and vulnerable workers) (Agrikolianski et al. 2007). Those movements fight the extreme fragmentation of society and defend human rights and fundamental social rights, such as housing, jobs, etc. The emergence of these developments at the domestic level is generally linked to the neoliberal European integration process. The main political actor in France opposing the so-called neoliberal European integration process is ATTAC (an association seeking tax levies on financial transactions to aid citizens), founded in 1998 by a coalition of Left-wing intellectuals, trade unions, newspapers, and civic action associations. Its 'politics against global markets' attitude has played a highly visible role in international demonstrations (McCauley 2011).

At the same time, another form of protest movement using the rejection of European integration as leverage for its development emerged in European member states. Here, the main issue is sovereignty. For the defenders of sovereignty, the bottom line of their activities is the control of borders. Brussels' decisions are seen as lacking legitimacy and must be rejected with force. In the field of social movement protest activities, one particular example is hunters' associations. Confronted with the EU's environmental legislation to regulate hunting periods, these agrarian groups have been amongst the most active opponents of European integration. In France, their action repertoires are numerous and have even gone so far as to transform the main movement, Chasse Pêche Nature et Traditions (CPNT), created in 1989, into a political party, which did very well in the 1999 European parliamentary elections, winning six seats. However, they lost them again in the 2004 elections. Established initially to counter European directives attempting to regulate hunting seasons, CPNT broadened the scope of its activities to protest at food regulations and public health norms. This allowed them to find new members and supporters of their demands in France. Their rejection of European integration, although used as a justification of their existence, is more general. The EU is generally described as Eurocratic and a cold monster that citizens cannot understand, whose bureaucrats ignore the political, social, and economic realities of the domestic level. Similar arguments can be found in the fields of social movements that emerged in the three referendum campaigns to ratify the constitutional (France and Netherlands) in 2005 and the subsequent Lisbon Treaty (Ireland) in 2009. European integration was the reason for establishing these movements, or the reason for reinforcing their position in the public arena.

These examples illustrate that this form of Europeanization—the use of their opposition to European integration to establish and legitimize non-state actors' mobilization at the domestic level—is linked less to policy sectors than to characteristics of non-state actors and the transformation of democratic systems.

Organizational Structures

At the European level, the hypothesis that European non-state actors model their behaviour around the techniques of interest representation that are fostered by European officials seems to have gained large acceptance (Marks and McAdam 1996; for an overview see Saurugger 2012a). In order to gain access and eventually to exert influence, interest groups are, however, also under pressure to adapt their internal organizational structures. This can be seen both with regard to their recruitment strategies as well as with the bureaucratic structures that allow them to manage the financial funds obtained from EU donors, and most generally, the Commission.

Europeanization of Recruitment Strategies

Empirically, illustrations of this assumption can be found in a number of case studies of European interest groups. The recruitment logic of interest groups at the European level seems to correspond more to a career-centred logic than to an activist one. The example of the European Women's Lobby shows, after the gradual retreat of the founding mothers, the emergence of a frontier between elected representatives and staff members. This frontier results from the establishment of a meritocratic recruitment procedure. Associational 'civil servants' seem to emerge (Cavaille 2004: 13).

In the field of trade unions, this institutional professionalization has led to considerable criticism of 'high level unionism' or 'elite and expert unionism' (Gobin 1997). The European trade unionists are considered to be the new elite, integrated in the universe of European high-ranking civil servants and other professionals. Here we observe a form of competition between different modes of trade unionism which calls the legitimate basis of unionism into question. Thus, interest groups and 'civil society organizations' are set up in the EU political spaces as 'political sites of contestation, in which actors are strategically constructing bounded fields of social power in their own right, at the same time as building successful and well-paid careers in these emerging professions' (Favell 2007: 127).

Similar observations can be found in the field of business interest groups in globalized politics and the European Union (Streeck and Schmitter 1999; Ronit and Schneider 2000; Lahusen 2004; Streeck et al. 2006). The question here centres implicitly or explicitly on identifying how interest associations manage the 'two logics': that derive from their membership, on the one hand, and that driven by the wish for influence on politics, on the other (Streeck and Schmitter 1999). The profound social change triggered in past decades by economic and political internationalization raises the issue of how interest groups cope with an increasingly complex environment, in terms both of membership and political decision-making institutions. Justin Greenwood (2002) more precisely questions the degree of governability of EU business associations appreciating the influences exerted by the institutional environment in which they act. Greenwood comes to the conclusion that associations need to be independent from their members in order to bring value to them. Those that are too closely controlled by their members become a mouthpiece for their short-term demands, while those who have acquired some autonomy from their members' demands have the flexibility to participate in policy making with EU institutions.

This phenomenon is not only visible in old member states or at the EU level. Devaux (2008: 220) argues that Czech interest groups active in the field of environmental protection are representative of the way associations have developed since the early 1990s, and which has led to increased professionalization. Professionalization takes the form of creating salaried staff positions and specifically recruiting young staff with university training in the management of voluntary organizations and in specific policy areas, such as environmental law. It is, however, important to note that the career logic does not systematically replace the activist logic in interest group structures both at the EU and the domestic level, as these groups combine amateur and professional dimensions. In a number of groups—farmers, the European Women's Lobby, and trade unions—activists still form the majority of the elected representatives. It is in the secretariats that we see a professionalization of non-state actors, where individuals move from group to group in order to pursue their career path. This phenomenon seems to be gaining momentum. Beyond the realm of European integration, Martens (2005, 2006) has convincingly argued that the professionalization of Human Rights NGOs has led to their increasing significance in international relations more generally. However, there might be a legitimacy problem stemming from this process: if they have become more influential, they have, at the same time lost part of the representative character they claimed to possess in order to gain a legitimate place in transnational governance structures.

Europeanization of Funding

Funding and patronage are the second element leading to professionalization via European integration. The EU has provided significant levels of funding to many public interest groups. A recent study shows, more generally, that the Commission's funding decisions reflect its goals of supporting supranational EU 'civil society organizations': in particular EU integration groups, European youth, education and intercultural exchange groups as well as citizenship, democracy promotion, and education groups. The findings also show, however, that when it comes to societal cohesion, the Commission's funding practices are not in line with its rhetoric. Rather than equal funding across members states, or extra support for the organized civil society in the new member states, it is the oldest and wealthiest members that are receiving the largest numbers of grants and the greatest amounts of funding (Mahoney and Beckstrand 2008).

These funding requirements have, however, equally transformed the groups' accounting structures (Sanchez-Salgado 2007). It is particularly external funding structures, especially those of the European Commission, which transform internal interest group structures and make them more professionalized. While this influence was already visible before 1999, the European Commission—in particular after the 1999 resignation of the Santer Commission because of alleged internal fraud— now requires specific managerial and organizational abilities on the part of the groups it is funding. Thus funded groups had to adapt rapidly in terms of functional requirements. These transformations are, however, value loaded.

New public management ideas can also be observed with regard to the internal organization structures of interest groups. The diffusion of management techniques usually takes place through training seminars, either set up by international or national organizations, or by partnerships with existing university training schemes established by the non-state actors themselves. Thus the European Commission has financed a number of programmes (such as PACO—Support Programme for Co-finance schemes) with the aim of improving the quality of proposals submitted by public interest groups to the Commission. The CONCORD network (*Confederation d'ONG pour l'aide d'urgence et le développement*) develops very similar training schemes or capacity building working groups with EU and non-EU funding (Sanchez-Salgado 2007). Public donors thus define the conditions governing how the resources have to be managed.

This debate more generally refers to the question of a democratic paradox: the higher the degree of professionalization, the higher the odds that interest groups gain access to European institutions. Thus, the greater the reliance on 'technical' knowledge and skills, the greater the probability that the decisions made may be 'better'. However, at the same time, these results will be decreasingly understood as politically relevant both to the groups' members as well as to the public at large. Increasing professionalization also involves the transformation of power relations between elected members and grassroots activists and the secretariat, and increasing external—public as well as private—funding.

By studying NGOs in the development policy domain at the EU level, Alex Warleigh found (2001: 623) that the secretariats of these organizations dominated the agenda-setting processes. Instead of fostering participation amongst citizens, they made 'little or no efforts to educate their supporters about the need for engagement with EU decision makers'. This is a contradiction of social capital claims and more particularly the fact that the participation of the 'civil society organizations' would lead to an increase in the democratic legitimacy of the decision-making processes (Castiglione *et al.* 2008: part II). The social capital expectation is that groups should be open, with transparent decision-making processes and an accountable and responsive leadership in order to promote democracy itself.

Like Skocpol (2003) in the American case, Maloney and Jordan (1997) have shown for Great Britain that professionalized and bureaucratized interest groups

staffed by communications experts, lawyers, and lobbyists are increasingly supported by sophisticated fund-raising departments and management structures.
Grassroots members of public interest groups, or the so-called 'civil society organizations', have become cheque-book participants. The number of members has
also increased dramatically over the last twenty years, and it is these numbers
which are used by professional groups in their argumentation about representativeness in politics. These numbers are used to compare the number of members
of political parties and those of large 'civil society organizations', leading to the
idea of the decline of the political party and the creation of alternative modes of
participation.

Thus, in order to represent interests in the realm of the EU, groups and social
movements transform their internal organization structures. This process can be
induced through informal pressures by EU institutions, perceived as incentives to
recruit lobbying professionals, or through formal requirements as in the field of
funding opportunities initiated by the EU. However, these processes, while not only
linked to European incentives, but to the transformation of the global political system in general, question a number of democratic aims the EU has fostered since
1990, such as representativeness and participation. The Europeanization of interest
groups and social movements thus not only leads to the study of issues such as interests, strategies, or internal organizational structures, but also questions the transformation of democratic political systems more generally.

Conclusion

The Europeanization of interest groups and social movements follows a very similar
pattern to that of public policies: it is highly differentiated, according to public policy areas, group types, and national origins. The change of direction 'towards Brussels', however, is not automatic (Ladrech 2010). Targeting the European institutions
is a bonus rather than an alternative, as interest groups are embedded in national
political opportunity structures and thus consider national governments and national political actors more generally as the main interlocutors. Critical resource
dependency is one of the central arguments explaining this phenomenon. The aim
of this chapter was to illustrate this diversity by insisting on the change observed in
the interests of interest groups, the type of relationship the groups have with the
state and, finally, the internal organization structures of groups. Well-established
and structured groups with strong links to the state either do not adapt or their adaptation is still strongly influenced by national characteristics. Latent groups or non-
state actors whose legitimacy is in decline use the European integration process to
establish or re-establish themselves.

A number of general lessons can be drawn, however, when reviewing the literature
on the influence of European integration on interest groups and social movements:

1. Research on CEE interest groups, however patchy, shows the difficulties when using the concept of Europeanization as the explaining factor of change. Interest group interests, action repertoires, relations with political actors, or internal organizational structures are not only adapted because of European pressure, be it coercive or soft. The transition period, internal developments, and the influence of international non-EU donors and foundations have led to a different pattern, where causality in change is difficult to establish. Influence is more diffuse and diverse: the end of communist regimes opened a large spectrum of external as well as internal influences.

2. European integration is not only a constraint, but constitutes also a resource for a number of interest groups, most generally social movements critical of European integration. These actors use European integration to set up their own identity to create or renew their constituency. Resistance to European integration is a key element to be taken into account which allows analysis to go beyond studies concentrating on Euroscepticism.

3. The Europeanization of interest groups through coercion is less widespread, except in the field of adaptation processes arising from funding possibilities at the EU level, than through learning or strategic adaptation processes.

4. Finally, while both interest groups and social movements are confronted with similar incentives stemming from the European level, social movements remain largely confined to the domestic level. This phenomenon arises because the main action repertoire used by social movements, namely protesting in Brussels, is less efficient given the absence of direct electoral accountability of actors at the EU level. Electoral accountability can be found in the domestic realm, but is limited to the European Parliament at the EU level. The complexity of holding accountable a specific member of the EP is such that protest movements have rather limited impact at that level.

It is thus necessary to conclude by stating that there is a rather limited Europeanization of interest groups and social movements. Domestic opportunity structures, or more generally, the embeddedness of non-state actors in the national realm still accounts, in both quantitative as well as qualitative case studies, for a large proportion of their strategies, interests, and action repertoires.

 FURTHER READING

Recommended for further reading are the most recent introduction to lobbying in the EU by Coen and Richardson (2009), as well as the more conceptual special issue of West European Politics edited by Beyers *et al.* (2008). More specifically on the Europeanization of interest groups and social movements see Eising (2009), Balme and Chabanet (2008), as well as the older, but excellent Imig and Tarrow (2001) on contentious politics in Europe or Della Porta and Tarrow (2005) on transnational protest more generally.

WEB LINKS

The most relevant websites are those of individual non-state actors. However, a very good starting point is the European Commission Civil Society Website (**http://ec.europa.eu/transparency/civil_society/**) as well as the website on the Transparency Initiative (**http://ec.europa.eu/transparency/eti/index_en.htm**) where the register on European interest representatives can be found (**https://webgate.ec.europa.eu/transparency/regrin/welcome.do?locale=en#en**). A crucial website for references is **http://www.euractiv.com/** which offers information on all policy issues as well as position papers on these issues stemming from key stakeholders.

REFERENCES

Agrikolianski, E., Fillieule, O., and Sommier, I. (eds) (2007), *Généalogie du Movement Antiglobalisation en Europe. Une Perspective Compare*, Paris: Karthala.

Avdagic, S. and Crouch, C. (2006), 'Organized Economic Interests: Diversity and Change in an Enlarged Europe', in P. M. Heywood, E. Jones, M. Rhodes, and U. Sedelmeier (eds), *Development in European Politics*, Basingstoke: Palgrave Macmillan, 196–215.

Balme, R. and Chabanet, D. (2002), 'Action Collective et Gouvernance de l'Union Européenne', in R. Balme, D. Chabanet, and V. Wright (eds), *L'action Collective en Europe. Collective Action in Europe*, Paris: Presses de Sciences Po, 21–120.

Balme, R. and Chabanet D. (2008), *European Governance and Democracy. Power and Protest in the EU,* Lanham: Rowman and Littlefield.

Berger, S. (2006), 'Representation in Trouble', in P. Culpepper, P. Hall, and B. Palier (eds), *Changing France. The Politics that Markets Make*, Basingstoke, Palgrave Macmillan, 276–91.

Beyers, J. (2004), 'Voice and Access: Political Practices of European Interest Associations', *European Union Politics*, 5/2: 211–40.

Beyers, J. and Kerremans, B. (2007), 'Critical Resource Dependencies and the Europeanization of Domestic Interest Groups', *Journal of European Public Policy*, 14/3: 460–81.

Beyers, J., Eising, R., and Maloney, W. (eds) (2008), 'The Politics of Organised Interests in Europe: Lessons from EU Studies and Comparative Politics', *West European Politics*, 31/6: 1103–302.

Börzel, T. (2005), 'Europeanization: How the European Union Interacts with its Member States', in S. Bulmer and C. Lequesne (eds), *Member States of the European Union*, Oxford: Oxford University Press, 45–76.

Bulmer, S. and Padgett, S. (2005), 'Policy Transfer in the European Union: An Institutionalist Perspective', *British Journal of Political Science,* 35/1: 103–26.

Castiglione, D., van Deth, J., and Wolleb, G. (eds) (2008), *The Handbook of Social Capital*, Oxford: Oxford University Press.

Cavaille, A. (2004), 'Au Nom des Femmes: Trajectoires Sociales et Carrières Associatives au Lobby Européen des Femmes', Paper presented at the workshop 'Société Civile Organisée et Gouvernance Européenne', IEP de Strasbourg, 21–23 June.

Coen, D. (1997), 'The Evolution of the Large Firm as Political Actor in the European Union', *Journal of European Public Policy*, 4/1: 91–108.

Coen, D. and Richardson, J. J. (eds) (2009), *Lobbying the European Union: Institutions, Actors and Issues*, Oxford: Oxford University Press.

Della Porta, D. (2007), 'The Europeanization of Protest: A Typology and Empirical Evidence', in B. Kohler-Koch and B. Rittberger (eds), *Debating the Democratic Legitimacy of the European Union*, Lanham: Rowman and Littlefield, 189–208.

Della Porta, D. and Tarrow, S. (eds) (2005), *Transnational Protest and Global Activism*, Lanham: Rowman and Littlefield.

Devaux, S. (2008), 'Building Social Cause in Post-Communist Countries: Ecological Politics in the Czech Republic', in J. Pickles (ed.), *State and Society in Post-Socialist Economies,* Basingstoke: Palgrave Macmillan, 208–28.

Eising, R. (2004), 'Multi-level Governance and Business Interests in the European Union', *Governance: An International Journal of Policy, Administration and Institutions* 17/2: 211–46.

Eising, R. (2008). 'Clientelism, Committee, Pluralism and Protests in the European Union: Matching Patterns?', *West European Politics,* 31/6: 1166–87.

Eising R. (2009), *The Political Economy of State-Business Relations in Europe*, London: Routledge.

Erne, R. (2008), *European Unions, Labor's Quest for a Transnational Democracy*, Ithaca: Cornell University Press.

Falkner, G. (2000), 'Policy Networks in a Multi-Level System: Converging Towards Moderate Diversity?', *West European Politics*. 23/4: 94–120.

Favell, A. (2007), 'The Sociology of EU Politics', in K. E. Joergensen, M. Pollack, and B. Rosamond (eds), *The Handbook of EU Politics*, London: SAGE.

Gobin, C. (1997), *L'Europe Syndicale: Entre Désir et Réalité*, Bruxelles: Ed. Labor.

Green Cowles, M. (2001), 'The Transatlantic Business Dialogue and Domestic Business-Government Relations', in M. Green Cowles, J. Caporaso, and T. Risse (eds), *Transforming Europe: Europeanization and Domestic Change*, Ithaca, NY: Cornell University Press, 159–79.

Greenwood, J. (2002), *Inside the EU Business Associations*, Basingstoke: Palgrave Macmillan.

Grossman, E. (2004), 'Bringing Politics Back In: Rethinking the Role of Economic Interest Groups in European Integration', *Journal of European Public Policy*, 11/4: 637–54.

Helfferich, B. and Kolb, F. (2001), 'Multilevel Action Coordination in European Contentious Politics: The Case of the European Women's Lobby', in Imig, D. and Tarrow, S. (eds), *Contentious Europeans. Protest and Politics in an Emerging Polity*, Rowman and Littlefield, 143–61.

Howard, M. M. (2003), *The Weakness of Civil Society in Post Communist Europe*, Cambridge: Cambridge University Press.

Imig, D. and Tarrow, S. (eds) (2001), *Contentious Europeans: Protest and Politics in an Emerging Polity*, Lanham: Rowman and Littlefield.

Klüver, H. (2010), 'Europeanization of Lobbying Activities: When National Interest Groups Spill Over to the European Level', *Journal of European Integration*, 32/2: 175–91.

Ladrech, R. (2005), 'Europeanization of Interest Groups and Political Parties', in S. Bulmer and C. Lequesne (eds), *Member States of the European Union*, Oxford: Oxford University Press, 317–37.

Ladrech, R. (2010), *Europeanization and National Politics*, Basingstoke: Palgrave Macmillan.

Lahusen, Christian (2004), 'Joining the Cocktail Circuit: Social Movement Organizations at the EU', *Mobilization*, 9/1: 55–71.

Mahoney, C. and Beckstrand, M. J. (2008), 'Following the Money: EU Funding of Civil Society Organizations', Paper prepared for presentation at Cornell University's Center for European Studies, EU Research workshop, 25 October, Ithaca, NY.

Maloney, W. A. and Jordan, G. (1997), *The Protest Business. Mobilizing Campaign Groups*, Manchester: Manchester University Press.

Marks, G. and McAdam, D. (1996), 'Social Movements and the Changing Structure of Political Opportunity in the European Union', *West European Politics*, 19: 249–78.

Martens, K. (2005), *NGOs and the United Nations – Institutionalization, Professionalization and Adaptation*, Basingstoke: Palgrave Macmillan.

Martens, K. (2006), 'Institutionalizing Societal Activism into Structures of Global Governance – Amnesty International and the UN System', *Journal of International Relations and Development* 9(4): 371–95.

McCauley, D. (2011), 'Bottom-Up Europeanization Exposed: Social Movement Theory and Non-state Actors in France', *Journal of Common Market Studies*, 49/5: 1–24.

Mudde, C. (2003), 'Civil Society in Post-communist Europe. Lessons from the "dark side"', in P. Kopecky and C. Mudde (eds), *Uncivil Society? Contentious Politics in Post-communist Europe*, London, Routledge, 157–70.

Mudde, C. (2007), 'Civil Society', in S. White, J. Batt, and P. G. Lewis (eds), *Developments in Central and East European Politics 4*, Basingstoke: Palgrave Macmillan, 213–28.

Parau, C. (2009), 'Impaling Dracula: How EU Accession Empowered Civil Society in Romania', *West European Politics*, 32/1: 119–41.

Perez-Solorzano Borragan, N. (2006), 'The Europeanisation of Interest Representation in the new EU Member States from ECE. NGOs and Business Interest Associations in Comparative', Paper presented at the 3rd ECPR Conference of Europeanists, Budapest.

Ronit, K. and Schneider, V. (2000), *Private Organizations in Global Politics*, London, Routledge.

Rootes, C. 2008, 'Acting Locally: The Character, Contexts and Significance of Local Environmental Mobilizations', in C. Rootes (ed.), *Acting Locally: Environmental Campaigns and Mobilizations at the Local Level*, London: Routledge, 2–21.

Rucht, D. 2001, 'Lobbying or Protest? Strategies to Influence EU Environmental Policies', in D. Imig and S. Tarrow (eds), *Contentious Europeans. Protest and Politics in an Emerging Polity*, Lanham: Rowman and Littlefield, 125–42.

Sanchez-Salgado, R. (2007), *Comment l'Europe Construit la Société Civile*, Paris: Dalloz.

Saurugger, S. (2007), 'Differential Impact: Europeanising French Non-State Actors', *Journal of European Public Policy*, 14/7,:1079–97.

Saurugger, S. (2012a), 'The Professionalization of EU's Civil Society. A Conceptual Framework', in J. van Deth and W. Maloney (eds), *New Participatory Dimensions in Civil Society: Professionalization and Individualized Collective Action*, London: Routledge.

Saurugger, S. (2012b), 'Interest Representation and Advocacy within the European Union: The Making of Democracy?', in B. Reinalda (ed.), *Ashgate Research Companion to Non-State Actors*, Aldershot: Ashgate.

Schmidt, V. (1996), *From State to Market?: The Transformation of French Business and Government*, Cambridge, Cambridge University Press.

Schmidt V. (1999), 'La France Entre l'Europe et le Monde: Le Cas des Politiques économiques Nationales', *Revue Française de Science Politique*, 4 (1): 49–78.

Schmidt, V. A. (2006), *Democracy in Europe. The EU and National Polities*, Oxford: Oxford University Press.

Schneider, G., Finke, D. and Baltz, K. (2007), 'With A Little Help from the State: Interest Intermediation in the Domestic Pre-Negotiations of EU Legislation', *Journal of European Public Policy*, 14/3: 444–59.

Skocpol, T. (2003), *Diminished Democracy: From Membership to Management in American Civic Life*, Norman: University of Oklahoma Press.

Smith, M. J. (1993), *Pressure, Power and Policy. State Autonomy and Policy Networks in Britain and the United States*, Pittsburgh: University of Pittsburgh Press.

Streeck, W. and Schmitter, P. (1999), 'The Organization of Business Interests: Studying the Associative Action of Business in Advanced Industrial Societies', *MPIfG Discussion Paper 99/1*, Köln, Max-Planck-Institut für Gesellschaftsforschung.

Streeck, W., Grote, J., Schneider, V. and Visser, J. (eds) (2006), *Governing Interests: Business Associations Facing Internationalization*, Oxford: Routledge.

Warleigh, A. (2001), 'Europeanizing Civil Society: NGOs as Agents of Political Socialisation' *Journal of Common Market Studies*, 39/4: 619–39.

Wilts, A. (2002), 'Strategies of Business Interest Associations in the Netherlands and Germany: European Priorities or Domestic Concerns?', *Politique européenne*, 7: 96–115.

CHAPTER 15

The Europeanization of Member State Policy

Simon Bulmer and Claudio M. Radaelli

▌ Summary

Europeanization has had a profound impact upon the public policy functions of the member states. However, the impact has not been uniform. Member states have lost much of the scope for independent action in some areas, such as trade policy or, for euro-zone members, monetary policy. In others, the effect has been much more fragmented: on areas such as health care or education. Between these two extremes lie the majority of policy areas. In reviewing this subject matter we explore the dynamics of Europeanization: what are the processes involved and the effects produced? We then relate the processes and effects to categories of policy in order to map the Europeanization of public policy.

Introduction: Why Europeanization?

Over the last two decades, the Europeanization of member states' policy has been a burgeoning research topic (see Chapter 2 this volume; Further Reading below). Some aspects of Europeanization research are a simple re-branding of classic research themes. However, there are also substantive reasons for the growth of interest in this topic. They derive both from the evolution of European integration and from the internal dynamics of research agendas in political science and public policy analysis. Let us look at the changing nature of integration in the European Union (EU) first and then consider the internal dynamics.

There are at least five macro-dynamics in 'the real world out there' prompting a redirection of the intellectual debate toward Europeanization. One was the institutionalization of the single market and the Lisbon Agenda, originally defined in 2000 and recently re-launched as 'Europe 2020' (European Commission 2010a). Although the EU is, in a sense, still completing the internal market (Howarth and Sadeh 2010; Monti 2010), the sheer volume of EU directives, regulations, and jurisprudence affecting domestic markets increased dramatically from the Single European Act (1986) onwards (see Fligstein and McNichol 1998: 75–85). The Lisbon Agenda added an ambitious project, arguably a 'governance architecture' (Borras and Radaelli 2011), to increase competitiveness by connecting the single market to several policy initiatives for growth and jobs in a socially cohesive sustainable economy. The single market project has also spun-off into a regulatory reform agenda branded with the label 'smart regulation'. That is, regulation itself should stimulate growth and competitiveness, as well as deliver on participatory governance (European Commission 2010b).

The second reason was the advent of Economic and Monetary Union (EMU). Not only has EMU created a single currency and interest rate regime across participant member states (the euro-zone) but it has heightened still further the degree of interdependency amongst other policies, most importantly macroeconomic and fiscal policies (Dyson 2008). As with the single market, the Europeanization of member states' monetary and fiscal policies continues to develop. Notably, the financial crisis that started in 2007 had ramifications for both the EU and the euro-zone. The process started in 2010 with the Greek debt crisis that entailed a rescue plan in May, repeated in 2012, with similar bail-outs needed for Ireland (November 2010) and Portugal (May 2011), whilst Spain and Italy have been notable in undertaking austerity plans designed to pre-empt a crisis. Such concerns about public finances in the euro-zone have resulted not only in the creation of an ongoing European Stability Mechanism but also proposals for far-reaching reforms to the governance of the euro-zone to ensure stronger discipline over members' public finances and a rescue fund. Specifically, the March 2012 fiscal pact—officially known as the Treaty on Stability, Coordination and Governance in the Economic and Monetary Union—strengthens the Europeanization of Euro-zone states' public finances.

Yet, Europeanization is not simply the product of integration at EU level. A third macro-dynamic factor that ran parallel to the creation of the single market was an emergent pattern of regulatory competition. The conflicts over the Services Directive (Nicolaïdis and Schmidt 2007) are the clearest example of how narratives of more or less unfair regulatory competition can capture the political attention. Europeanization may thus be a process whereby national policies adjust to seek competitive advantage within a broad EU policy context. In other words the adjustment of national policy is not simply to some EU requirement but, in this case, to a market dynamic unleashed by the global economy but 'framed' by a set of EU rules.

Fourth, if the single market and monetary union played a prominent role in advancing interest in the Europeanization of member states' policies, analogous developments in other policy areas soon captured the attention of political analysts. Environmental policy (Börzel 2002; Jordan and Liefferink 2004); cohesion policy (Bache 2008); immigration policy (Ette and Faist 2007), and foreign policy (Rieker 2006; Wong 2006) are amongst other areas that have prompted Europeanization research.

A final key dynamic arose from the process of enlargement (Grabbe 2006). This process continues, since negotiations are under way with candidate-states, whilst further applications are pending. Nor is this process entirely predictable, as was demonstrated in the aftermath of the financial crisis when Iceland rapidly moved from a content member state of the European Economic Area to a candidate-state for full EU membership. Negotiations with candidate countries can be seen as a colossal exercise in policy transfer, whereby the EU exports its legislative rules (the *acquis communautaire*). At the same time, enlargement also sets political and legal standards, namely the 1993 Copenhagen criteria, that candidate-states must meet with regard to the rule of law, democracy, human rights, and having a functioning market economy. In the process of enlargement, not only does the EU engage in a formidable export of its regulatory pillar, it also seeks to transfer the normative pillar (see Laffan 2001 on the relations between these pillars of the EU). In this sense, enlargement may be seen as the largest-scale example of Europeanization. The 'Europeanization effect' is very strong externally—at least until accession, at which point the process becomes internal.

The accumulated effect of these developments prompts the question: what is left for national public policy? Virtually every policy area is now affected to a greater or lesser extent by the EU. The ramifications of this development reach well beyond the bounds of this chapter. They include, not least, the question 'what is left to be decided by national politics and, specifically, domestic elections' (see also Chapter 13)? The room for autonomous domestic policy choices is constrained by Europeanization, although it is still considerable (Schmidt 2002). At the same time, the room for open, democratic engagement with EU-level policy choices is narrow, since public opinion and European elections are focused overwhelmingly on member state politics. This political asymmetry is a major reason for concern about the adverse effects of Europeanization on democracy in Europe (Mair 2001). Others have argued that

Europeanization has created a democratic deficit in the member states, since political leaders have lost a legitimizing discourse that would make domestic adjustment to EU policy acceptable to their citizens (e.g. Schmidt 2006).

Looking at these changes arising from European integration, it is little surprise that there has been an increased academic interest in Europeanization (Exadaktylos and Radaelli 2009 for a review of highly-cited articles). Having spent intellectual energy in seeking to understand the 'nature of the beast', that is, the nature of European integration, political scientists realized that a EU political system is in place, produces decisions, and impacts on domestic policies in various guises. Hence the focus shifted to studying those impacts.

Europeanization raises some fundamental questions that are found in the discipline of politics more broadly. How can Europeanization be modelled? What are the causal mechanisms that help explain the way the EU impacts upon member state policy? This approach is challenged by other political scientists who adopt a more reflexive form of political analysis. For instance, the boundaries between cause and effect, and independent and dependent variables are blurred, as is demonstrated in Tanja Börzel's discussion of Europeanization as uploading and downloading (see Börzel 2002, 2005). How to model the impact of European integration on domestic policy and its causal mechanisms, knowing that, at the same time, domestic politics is a major factor at work in EU political change (Olsen 2002)? Europeanization may also take less measurable forms, such as through policy discourses. Modelling Europeanization faces two additional challenges. First, neither the EU nor the member states are static, so Europeanization is a matter of reciprocity between moving features. Second, the attribution of domestic change to the EU is not always easy, since globalization is also a force at work in many areas of policy.

Types of Europeanization

Having explained why Europeanization of policy is a hot topic, we need to understand it. Elsewhere in this volume a range of definitions has been utilized (see Introduction and Chapter 2). In this chapter we understand it in a relatively broad manner, as set out in Box 15.1. This definition is important because it identifies a

---

BOX 15.1   **A definition of Europeanization**

Europeanization consists of processes of (a) construction, (b) diffusion, and (c) institutionalization of formal and informal rules, procedures, policy paradigms, styles, 'ways of doing things', and shared beliefs and norms; which are first defined and consolidated in the EU policy process and then incorporated in the logic of domestic (national and subnational) discourse, political structures, and public policies.

number of features of Europeanization that we will deploy in the empirical part of the chapter. It highlights three particular features of Europeanization:

- It can derive from different stages and forms of the policy process: policy formulation (construction); embedding policy into practice (institutionalization); and in a much less structured manner (diffusion), where the EU's role may be quite limited.

- Europeanization is not simply about formal policy rules but about less tangible aspects, such as beliefs, values and norms.

- The concept of Europeanization is about the *impact* of European policy within member states. It thus entails two steps: adoption at EU level and then incorporation at the domestic level. The former step alone is only part of the story. That is why Europeanization and EU policymaking are distinct from each other conceptually.

How can we move from these preliminary observations to something more analytical: something that allows us to explain the dynamics of the Europeanization process? One way is to look at the different modes of EU policymaking, as identified in the existing literature.[1] However, these modes have not been devised with Europeanization in mind. Our preference is to devise a typology that is built on analytical categories which target the research questions of this field of research.

Drawing upon the work of Scharpf (1997), Knill (2001), and Bulmer and Padgett (2005), we identify four characteristic patterns of governance in the EU (also see Knill and Lehmkuhl 2002). As with any framework with only four patterns, we should point out that this simplifies what is a more complex situation. We then seek to identify the analytical core, the mechanisms of Europeanization and the explanatory factors that apply to each of the four patterns. Later in the chapter we go on to utilize these categories to explain 'the real world' of the Europeanization of member state policy. Let us look at each of the four patterns of governance in turn.

Governance by Negotiation

The EU is in a constant state of negotiation across multiple policy areas: everything from fisheries through foreign policy to immigration. The EU's authority varies considerably across the range of policy areas: from having exclusive authority (for instance, on the customs union) to having limited coordinating power (such as on employment policy). Indeed, one of the contributions of the Lisbon Treaty was to spell out the exact powers of the EU in a 'catalogue of competences' (see Box 15.2). However, in each case where the EU takes a decision—whether legally binding or a mere declaration—it is the culmination of a process of negotiation.

How does governance by negotiation relate to Europeanization? The answer to this question lies in the fact that European policy does not emerge from thin air but derives from a process, namely that of negotiation. As noted in the definition above, Europeanization is predicated upon an initial step whereby anything from 'hard'

BOX 15.2	The EU's catalogue of competencies

Areas of exclusive competence

Customs union

Competition rules for the internal market

Monetary policy for those states in the euro-zone

Conservation of marine biological resources under the common fisheries policy

Common commercial policy

Where an international agreement is necessary to enable the Union to exercise its internal competence.

Areas of shared competence

Internal market

Aspects of social policy

Economic, social and territorial cohesion

Agriculture and fisheries (except marine conservation – see above)

Environment

Consumer protection

Transport

Trans-European networks

Energy

Area of freedom, security and justice

Aspects of public health safety

Research, technological development and space

Development and humanitarian aid

Areas of policy coordination

Member states' economic policies

Member states' employment policies

Member states' social policies

Areas of supporting, coordinating, or supplementary action

Protection and improvement of human health

Industry

Culture

Tourism

Education, vocational training, youth and sport

Civil protection

Administrative cooperation

The common foreign and security policy

'The Union shall have competence . . . to define and implement a common foreign and security policy, including the progressive framing of a common defence policy'.

Note: The listing is summarized from Articles 3–6, Treaty on the Functioning of the European Union (TFEU). The CFSP provisions derive from Article 2, TEU.

---

legal instruments through to 'soft' norms 'are first defined and consolidated in the EU policy process' (see Box 15.1). The member governments are central to this process, but of course negotiation also involves lobbyists and the input provided by the institutions of the EU. As noted by Tanja Börzel (2002, 2005), at this stage actors seek to 'upload' their preferences. National policy models or rules are inserted into EU-level negotiations, with the most likely outcome being a synthesis, although very occasionally one delegation may be especially influential. More typically, however, EU policy templates are a synthetic construction arising from Commission proposals, different national approaches, country-block coalitions, and the inevitable horse-trading during negotiations.

In the initial negotiating phase, namely where policy is under construction, the explanations for the extent of Europeanization lie in the extent of convergence of preferences on the part of the member states, the voting rules in the Council, and the learning that takes place over repeated sessions of negotiation. The potential for the Europeanization of national policy is greatest where the member governments are able to agree policy because their interests converge. It is also greatest where they are encouraged by Council rules to avoid unanimous voting and the use of national veto power. Finally, repeated negotiations may encourage the construction of a shared understanding of the issues. Some policy areas require several rounds of legislation as part of a process of building up a shared understanding of new arrangements, for instance in the case of air transport liberalization's three packages (Armstrong and Bulmer 1998: 169–97). The creation of a shared understanding of policy through learning on the part of the participants is important for the potential for the success of Europeanization when policy comes to be put into practice. In the absence of such a shared understanding, the prospects for Europeanization of national policy are likely to be much weaker. There are also cases in which negotiation takes a lot of time and ultimately fails, yet some domestic actors involved in EU negotiations may have changed their policy beliefs and some elements of domestic policy may have changed in anticipation of the expected content of EU policy. To illustrate, in tax policy there have been changes of domestic policy originated by new ideas aired in EU negotiations. These negotiations have so far failed to produce a comprehensive EU corporate tax system—yet they have re-oriented domestic policy (Radaelli 1997).

We have included negotiation in the chapter for the sake of completeness in understanding the process. However, we are not suggesting that Europeanization is synonymous with European integration or EU policymaking. Rather, we are making clear that the process of agreeing EU policy is a necessary first step with the prospect, later in the policy process, that a change in policy will ensue at the member state level. If member state policy is to be Europeanized, EU policy must have an impact at the domestic level. In moving to this next stage in the policy process, we explore the different patterns of governance whereby EU policy is put into practice at domestic level: governance by hierarchy and facilitated coordination.

Governance by Hierarchy

Governance by hierarchy relates to those circumstances where the supranational institutions have a considerable amount of power delegated to them. The institutions concerned are the Commission, the Council, and the European Court of Justice (ECJ). At the end of the negotiation phase of governance (see previous section above) the Council typically has agreed European legislation which needs to be put into practice in the member states. A set of 'command and control' mechanisms comes into play at this stage. These mechanisms derive from the uniquely supranational character of the EU and help to ensure that agreements are put into effect by the member states. The enforcement mechanisms are designed to build trust by limiting the scope for individual states to cheat on the negotiated agreements. In a wider sense, hierarchy is a shadow that steers the behaviour of actors in different circumstances—as a rule-bound context, a threat, opportunity, or expectation of future gains and losses (Schmidt 2000; Börzel 2010). The exact character of the mechanisms and the consequent explanations of the dynamics of Europeanization vary according to what are known as positive and negative integration (Pinder 1968). We explore each of these in turn.

Positive integration

Positive integration requires the introduction of an active, supranational policy. Typically, the EU has negotiated a policy template, and the task is to put it into operation in the member states. In economic policy areas, positive integration often entails market-correcting rules. That is to say, policy is designed to limit damaging effects of market processes: through pollution control, social policy, regional policy, veterinary policy to accompany the Common Agricultural Policy (CAP), and so on. In policy areas such as these, the EU has to go through often arduous negotiations in order to agree the policy rules. But what is of key interest here is that the agreed policy template has to be 'downloaded' to the member state level. The Commission has to ensure that legislation is properly implemented, and it can refer laggard governments to the ECJ if necessary. The supremacy of European law is indicative of the hierarchical nature of arrangements. There is a pronounced coercive dimension in these arrangements, and it is the member governments that have to ensure that market-correction is put into practice effectively.

Negative integration

By contrast with positive integration, negative integration relates to areas where the removal of national barriers suffices to create a common policy. National legislation is often not required to put policy into practice. Indeed, in some cases, even European legislation is unnecessary since the rules may be embedded in the treaties themselves. The Commission is delegated extensive powers and the jurisprudence of the ECJ can be relied upon to enforce the framework of rules, such as those set down in the supranational treaties. Negative integration is typically concerned with 'market-making'. In other words, EU-level rules are designed to allow the efficient functioning of the market. A classic case is the EU's competition policy, which specifies what is admissible in terms of mergers or joint ventures between companies, pricing and market-sharing agreements between them, and so on. Where there is doubt about the admissibility of an arrangement, the companies concerned must seek approval from the competition authorities. Similar arrangements obtain in the single market, where discrimination by nationality is outlawed, whether through physical barriers (border controls), fiscal ones (tax regimes), or technical ones. In particular sectors of the economy, special rules may be needed in order to facilitate 'market-making'. Thus, special policy arrangements were needed initially for areas such as telecommunications, energy, air transport, postal services, and so on. However, the aim was to enable markets to function subject to oversight, normally by the Commission.

The market that is created in this way has two dimensions. It is, first, a market amongst economic actors. Second, it is a market amongst differing national regimes. If the UK regime for the new media, for instance, is perceived as creating a better environment for the flourishing of business, then other member states may find they have to adjust their national set of rules to prevent companies re-locating. In short, the market-making character of negative integration creates a much more horizontal process of policy adjustment associated with Europeanization. In negative integration it is the competition amongst rules or amongst socioeconomic actors that accounts for Europeanization rather than the need for national policy to comply with EU policy templates, as under positive integration.

Facilitated Coordination

Facilitated coordination relates to areas where decisions are not (or are only negligibly) subject to European law; where unanimity applies and consensus is impossible to achieve; or where the EU is simply an arena for the exchange of ideas. In practice, these circumstances apply where the Open Method of Coordination (OMC) operates, such as in the European Employment Strategy (as to the achievements of the OMC, the jury is still out, see Kröger 2009; Borras and Radaelli 2010). It also operates in foreign and security policy. In these areas, agreements predominantly take two forms: political declarations, for instance by the European Council, or 'soft law'. Soft law relates to rules of conduct that are not legally enforceable, but nonetheless have a legal scope in that they guide the conduct of the institutions, the member states, and other policy participants (Wellens and Borchardt 1980: 285; see also Snyder 1994).

Whichever of these forms the agreements take, the supranational institutions have very weak powers: they cannot act as strong agents promoting Europeanization. Nevertheless, that does not mean that no Europeanization takes place, but simply that it is much more voluntary and non-hierarchical. If the member states cannot reach an agreement on policy, such as occurred in 2003 with foreign policy owing to the fundamental divisions on how to deal with the Iraqi regime of Saddam Hussein, then policy is not Europeanized. However, whilst many commentators have focused on the institutional shortcomings of the CFSP, a strong 'coordination reflex' (procedural learning) developed (for example see Glarbo 1999: 643–5) and in some areas of policy a shared set of policy understandings has emerged, for instance over the Palestinian issue. Similarly, the exchange of practice on employment policy may lead to the cross-fertilization of ideas and learning. This is why this form of policy is concerned with the convergence of ideas. The lack of supranational powers in these policy areas explains the predominantly horizontal pattern of Europeanization, which may result in the learning of shared policy principles.

To summarize this section, we have identified three modes of governance in the EU, and they intersect with different types of policy to produce different mechanisms of Europeanization (see Table 15.1). These mechanisms may be vertical (uploading or downloading) or horizontal. In other words, Europeanization follows no single 'logic'.[2]

Understanding the Dynamics of Europeanization

We now turn our attention to the *interpretations* of the dynamics of Europeanization. At this stage we omit detailed consideration of Europeanization by negotiation. Although some earlier understandings of Europeanization focused on the development of institutions at EU level (see Olsen 2002), in the present context such an understanding is essentially synonymous with EU policymaking: a topic which has been covered extensively elsewhere (for example, see Wallace *et al.* 2010). An absence of learning at this stage of the policy process—that is of all the member states developing a shared understanding of policy goals—may store up problems such that the Europeanization process is more fragile later on. We also draw attention to the evidence from some areas of market integration that the process of EU-level policy negotiation may bring forward domestic reforms already under consideration. There was evidence of this Europeanization effect in the liberalization of the telecommunications and electricity sectors, where some states accelerated domestic reform in order to synchronize it with EU policy developments (see Bulmer *et al.* 2003). The main effects of Europeanization, however, are felt in connection with the three following patterns of adjustment.

Goodness of Fit

Let us start with the 'goodness of fit' argument, which was first developed by Risse, Cowles, and Caporaso (2001). They argued that, in order to produce domestic effects, EU policy must be somewhat difficult to absorb at the domestic level. If the policy of country A fits in well with EU policy, there will no impact: things can go on as they were before. At the other extreme, where country A has a policy which is completely different from the EU policy, it would be almost impossible to adapt to Europe. They argued that the impact of Europeanization would be most pronounced in cases of moderate goodness of fit (Börzel and Risse 2003; Cowles *et al.* 2001). Domestic institutions play a key role in absorbing, rejecting, or domesticating Europe. Indeed, the 'goodness of fit' explanation is rooted in new institutionalist approaches to political behaviour.

We argue that the 'goodness of fit' argument is valid under certain conditions (namely, the presence of EU policy templates or models). As such, it best applies to one type of policy—positive integration—rather than offering a general explanation. 'Goodness of fit' assumes a clear, vertical, chain-of-command in which EU policy descends from Brussels into the member states. Domestic institutions are like rigid posts channelling the impact of Europe. But we know of cases in which EU policy has been an absolute innovation for domestic institutions. EU environmental policy started before Spanish environmental policy became a reality (see Chapter 6). The same applies to the transfer of competition policy to some of the states which joined in 2004. To speak of 'goodness of fit' between EU policy and non-existent domestic policy is unconvincing.

More importantly still, the 'goodness of fit' explanation may be a special case rather than a general explanation. As shown by Mark Thatcher (2004), in the case of telecommunications, governments have been under little adaptational pressure from EU regulation. Yet they have used European policy to justify and legitimate change. Governments already seeking reform have been able to use European policy as an opportunity, rather than responding to a 'pressure'. The effects are not captured by the 'goodness of fit' argument. European policies can be exploited by national actors engaged in policy reforms even if European and national arrangements are compatible (Héritier and Knill 2001). Adaptational pressure is not a necessary condition for Europeanization to cause domestic change.

Other authors have observed that adaptational pressure is not the best predictor of how a country responds to Europeanization. A country can be under strong adaptational pressure, yet it can implement EU policy without too many problems, as shown by the implementation of the packaging waste directive in the UK (Haverland 2000). The facilitating factor in this process is the presence or absence of institutional veto points (see Haverland 2003). Institutional veto points available to those opposing EU policy can make Europeanization very problematic even in the case of low adaptational pressure. Conversely, in the absence of veto points and supporting formal institutions, it is quite possible for large adaptational steps to be taken.[3]

TABLE 15.1 Governance, policy, and the mechanisms of Europeanization			
Mode of governance	**Type of policy**	**Analytical core**	**Main mechanism**
Hierarchy	Positive integration	Market-correcting rules; EU policy templates	Vertical (downloading)
Hierarchy	Negative integration	Market-making rules; absence of policy templates	Horizontal
Facilitated coordination	Coordination	Soft law, OMC, policy exchange	Horizontal

The 'goodness of fit' interpretation works well in cases where EU policy prescribes a model or a template of how a country should go about putting policy into practice. However, one drawback of the 'goodness of fit' explanation is that it is couched in a 'vertical' (chain-of-command type) view of Europeanization. It best corresponds, therefore, to governance by hierarchy and patterns of positive integration. But, as Table 15.1 indicates, this represents only one of the mechanisms of Europeanization, so what of the horizontal variants?

Regulatory Competition

One of these variants is regulatory competition in the shadow of EU negative integration. In this case, a policy template is either absent or plays a limited role. A range of actions (such as discrimination against other EU nationals or companies) are prohibited by EU law and some key principles are established by the jurisprudence of the ECJ, most importantly mutual recognition. Countries can play the regulatory competition game in different ways. They can be more or less aggressive, for example. But this game is always 'horizontal'; that is, one country versus the others in the 'race' for highly skilled labour and capital. Fitting in with EU models plays a limited role.

Despite the importance often attributed to regulatory competition, the fact is that studies of competition amongst rules have been few and far between (Radaelli 2004). Indeed, there are some significant problems to be tackled in conducting such projects. Arguably the most significant is to isolate the impact of European market rules from those emanating from the global economy. Let us take a hypothetical example of how Europeanization impacts upon regulatory competition in the telecommunications sector. Two counter-arguments would need to be isolated first of all, namely: (a) competition amongst rules is a product of global regulatory competition, and the EU does not matter; (b) national traditions of regulation are so embedded in their domestic context that adaptation may not give rise to convergence, whether in response to EU or global stimuli (see as illustrations Héritier *et. al.* 2001; Teubner 2001). Without being able to isolate these other explanations it would be difficult to demonstrate that Europeanization is the explanation for regulatory competition in the first place.

In reality, what we find in seeking evidence of the impact of Europeanization upon competing regulatory regimes is pretty mixed. A well-established literature sets out how the EU, through its internal market programme, provided for mutual recognition (see, for instance, Egan 2001). However, the impact of mutual recognition on (competing) regimes of national standards has received much less treatment. In those sectors, such as telecommunications or electricity, where specific legislation was introduced to facilitate liberalization, we find Europeanization studies concentrating on the policy templates that were introduced with a view to phasing in competition rather than on any competition amongst rules subsequently unleashed (Schneider 2001; Héritier *et al.* 2001; Bulmer *et al.* 2003). In one of the rare exceptions, Susanne Schmidt explores the consequences of opening up the internal market to competition in the insurance and road haulage sectors (Schmidt 2002). Her findings are that there has been relatively little use of regulatory competition in these sectors. In her case-study states (France and Germany) she found that liberalization of the sectors had led to major domestic change but found little evidence of competition amongst rules. Our evidence-base on this form of Europeanization remains limited. Jabko (2006) makes the important point that the creation of markets in Europe has been accompanied by the emergence of regulatory powers in Brussels. Hence market-making and institution-building are two faces of the same process of integration.

Learning

Learning is an important dimension in all stages of Europeanization, including negotiation. However, it becomes an especially important feature where the EU does not work as a law-making system but, rather, as a platform for the convergence of ideas and policy transfer between member states. This is especially the case with the OMC. However, intergovernmental forms of EU policymaking are decades old and soft law has been known to legal scholars for a long time (Snyder 1994). Indeed, the OMC itself, as defined by the Lisbon Council in the year 2000, was more an attempt to provide a definition to modes of policy coordination that emerged in different policy areas in the 1990s than a dramatic innovation.

The OMC is a means of spreading best practice and achieving convergence towards the EU's goals. The idea is to use the EU as a transfer platform rather than a law-making system. Thus, the OMC should assist member states in developing their own policies. As such, it eschews the vertical imposition of models coming from Brussels, placing greater emphasis on horizontal mechanisms of governance. The 'method' is defined by the following characteristics: EU guidelines combined with specific timetables; action to be undertaken at the national and regional level;

benchmarking and sharing of best practice; qualitative and, when appropriate, quantitative indicators; 'period monitoring, evaluation, and peer review organized as mutual learning processes' (Presidency Conclusions, Lisbon European Council, 23–24 March 2000). OMC introduced into the political sphere some of the practices of the business sector, such as benchmarking. In some policy areas (that is, immigration and social policy) the method works in conjunction with traditional EU legislative instruments. In other areas, however, the method enables the EU to enter new policy domains, where no legislation is operating and where the member states think that there is no scope for legislative action at the EU level.

Scholars looking at the OMC as a governance architecture stress its potential for policy learning (Hartlapp 2009). Arguably, the major impact of this mode of policy-making is at the ideational level. Policy-makers engage in the definition of criteria of best practice and, as in the case of taxation, worst practice. They also accept the principle of peer review of their policies. Criteria and peer review are fundamental instruments of ideational convergence. In areas in which it is either impossible or politically too sensitive to say what the EU 'model' should be, policy-makers seek to develop some ideas of how to improve their policies and notions of good and bad policy. They develop common benchmarks. They also elaborate a common vocabulary. Thus in areas previously impenetrable to Europeanization, 'communities of discourse' emerge, with their own vocabulary, criteria, and belief systems.

After the term OMC was coined, it received a great deal of attention as an innovative form of governance. It has even been understood as part of a wider pattern of 'experimentalist governance' in the EU (Sabel and Zeitlin 2008, 2010). However, longer-standing patterns of intergovernmental policymaking have been subject to similar dynamics. Like the OMC, they feature a prominent role for national ministers and officials, with the supranational institutions playing a relatively small role. European law is largely absent as a policy instrument, with 'soft law' and political agreements predominant. Similarly, there are relatively discrete communities of policy-makers concerned with a particular set of issues. Whether it be CFSP, judicial cooperation, or policy on social inclusion, the same largely horizontal dimension applies to the Europeanization process. In other words, if Europeanization occurs, it is a process of learning amongst national elites. The EU provides the arena. Indeed, the cooperation need not be across all EU member states but can as easily occur within smaller groupings of member states, as in the Schengen process, both when it was outside the treaties prior to the Amsterdam Treaty and when inside the formal EU framework thereafter (den Boer and Wallace 2000; Monar 2002: 188).

With the OMC and with intergovernmentalism it is unclear whether these patterns of governance are a stepping stone towards deeper integration in the form of governance by hierarchy. That occurred when, respectively, some aspects of the Schengen Treaty were brought into the Treaty of the European Community under the terms of the 1997 Treaty of Amsterdam (see Monar 2002), and when the steps were taken to create EMU. However, whilst the Lisbon Treaty did transfer judicial and police cooperation to the mainstream 'Union method' of policymaking, CFSP remains apart.

Whether the process is intergovernmentalism or the OMC, the basic premise of learning is that ideational convergence will produce policy change at the domestic level. The EU thus serves as a platform for learning about policy and good policy practice. Then—the argument continues—policy-makers with the same 'Europeanized' ideas will learn and change their domestic policies accordingly. Of course, policy-makers can also learn without the EU, for instance through other international organizations. However, in the absence of collective learning platforms, policy-makers typically learn through crisis and sustained policy fiascos. The advantage of learning platforms such as the OMC is that they can enable policy-makers to learn ahead of failure (Hemerijck and Visser 2001).

The relationship between ideational convergence, learning, and policy change is rather problematic. Thus, a major project reached the conclusion that redistributive and deeply entrenched problems, and more generally a prisoner's dilemma situation, limit the effectiveness of new modes of governance (Héritier and Rhodes 2010).

People may adopt the same language and talk in terms of the same criteria without necessarily taking the same decisions. To make things more complicated, decisions may not be followed by actions, or may be followed by unforeseen actions, 'deviant' administrative behaviour, and 'creative' bottom-up interpretations of decisions (Brunsson 1989; Pollitt 2001). The 'linear causal relationship between the formation of a European ideational consensus and local action' has also been questioned by projects on areas outside the OMC, such as regional policy (Kohler-Koch 2002).

A decade after the 2000 Lisbon European Council, when the OMC became the discourse for policy coordination, the jury is still out on the results achieved. In abstract terms, the potential of the OMC is all in terms of creating ideational convergence and learning (with the aspiration of improvement to domestic policy); not necessarily in terms of creating the basis for hard law in the future. The OMC should not be seen as a poor substitute (under conditions of political necessity) for hard law, but as a radically different way forward for Europeanization. Those who criticize the OMC for its lack of sanctions do not understand its mechanisms. The method is based on changes in the cognitive frameworks used by policy-makers to understand and assess reality. This potential for learning does not hinge on sanctions but on conviction. A separate, empirical question concerns whether learning actually occurs (Hartlapp 2009).

An important observation made by Kenneth Armstrong (2010: 145) is that there is no single OMC approach. So, whilst in our schema displaying different mechanisms of Europeanization it may appear that way, in reality the precise mechanisms vary between each individual OMC. Moreover, each individual OMC has changed over time. For instance, the 2005 re-launch of the Lisbon Agenda on competitiveness brought change to some of the individual OMCs. Martin Lodge's analysis (2007) of the OMCs in pensions and the information society argues that no noticeable modification of behaviour could be discerned at national level. Kenneth Armstrong's analysis of the social inclusion OMC identified a stronger Europeanization effect on the UK policy process—by bringing in non-governmental actors—than in respect of the policy environment or strategy (2010: 187). The results of the learning mechanism may therefore be limited.

Researching Europeanization

What we have established thus far in this chapter is that Europeanization is more variegated in nature than in initial understandings. However, this inevitably comes at a cost: that of simplicity. Owing to its variegated character it is not easy to provide a single research strategy or analytical framework to analyze the impact of Europeanization on different types of policies. The first type of policy—positive integration—lends itself to research designs informed by new institutionalism (Bulmer 2007). This is the predominant framework deployed in the first major collection of studies of Europeanization, although the role of domestic actors is also taken into account (Cowles *et al.* 2001). Institutions are seen as mediating pressures from the EU and shaping the consequent impact in terms of domestic change. A similar admixture of institutional and actor-centred analysis is to be found in the study by Héritier *et al.* of the EU's impact on domestic transport policy across the member states (2001). In the case of negative integration, where we have limited policy templates, a similar approach can be pursued. However, in view of the expected impact here of a competition amongst rules, it would seem particularly appropriate to apply a more rationalist framework, emphasizing the strategic calculations of actors in responding to the opportunities available to them in the context of liberalized markets. The third type of policy, facilitated coordination, is arguably the most difficult to assess. Research strategies on this type need to be extremely sensitive to the local context. They also need to avoid the fallacy of assuming a linear relationship between the emergence of ideas of good practice or policy at the EU level and domestic policy change. The question is how does one know if changes in domestic policy are the result of the engagement in the European policy process and not the product of other variables at work at the domestic or global level?

The more traditional forms of intergovernmental cooperation are perhaps easier to research by process tracing, monitoring shifting national policy positions in light of repeated negotiations within, say, CFSP on some aspect of foreign policy, such as the Middle East. This task has been attempted by Alistair Miskimmon and William Paterson (2003) in respect of German foreign and security policy during the 1990s. Their framework comes from the same institutionalist tool-kit as that used by Cowles *et al.* (2001), but includes cognitive dimensions too. This use of the cognitive dimension forms a bridge with some of the considerations which come into play when exploring Europeanization in the OMC.

When it comes to isolating the impact of Europeanization upon policy areas covered by the OMC, one needs a focus on the local level, not on Brussels. The idea is to look at the problems, resources, and ideas most relevant to policy-makers 'at the hub of the problem' and then to examine to what extent the ideational resources made available by the OMC do or do not matter in the games domestic actors play.

It is important to be alert to the contextual variables at work in Europeanization processes and to the possibility of looking for Europeanization beyond the narrow space of EU policymaking processes. This is a difficult task. Bilateral relationships, notably between France and Germany, have served to generate policy models or ideas that have then been adopted at EU level. And, one of the most interesting findings of research on the Europeanization of policies in candidate countries is that the EU is only one of the actors promoting Europeanization. Organizations such as the Council of Europe are also deeply involved (perhaps to a higher degree than the EU) in the transfer of European models (Harcourt 2003).

Breaking down complex policies into smaller units of analysis (component dependent variables) alongside rigorous process tracing is a useful research strategy. Exadaktylos (2010) identifies those micro-level pressures that trigger Europeanization or detects the presence of other explanatory factors of domestic or global dimensions. However, any emphasis on identifying mechanisms of Europeanization should not neglect the interpretive dimension of politics. Thus, EU policy discourses or narratives may also trigger adjustments. In addition, as Woll and Jacquot have argued (2010), domestic 'usages of Europe' (that is, who uses the EU for domestic policy change, how and why?) may be as or more important than top-down mechanistic responses. The interpretivist approach to usages of Europe found early application in the work of Hay and Rosamond (2002) in interrogating the relationship between globalization, Europeanization, and domestic policy choices:

- Is Europeanization a defensive response to globalization (in this case understood as 'Americanization')?

- Is Europeanization (as opposed to globalization) a convenient discourse for legitimizing domestic reform (for a critical opinion see Schmidt 2006)? Put another way, is Europeanization a manifestation of globalization?

- Or is it a 'mix' of both of these that is dependent on the particular circumstances within individual member states?

The Europeanization of public policy can take different forms. In principle, it can impinge on all the basic elements of the policy process, such as actors, resources, and policy instruments. Additionally, Europeanization can affect the policy style, for example by making it more or less conflictual, corporatist, or pluralist, or more or less regulative. This kind of effect potentially has major implications, such as by rebalancing the power of national policy actors and policy-makers. Finally, it can impact on the cognitive and normative dimensions. Changes of cognitive and normative frames (Surel 2000) may trigger transformative effects on all the elements of policy. For example, they may alter the interpretation of a political dilemma facing a political party. Or they may impact on the perception of what is at stake in a policy controversy. They may even transform the interests and preferences upon which negotiations are structured. Policy discourses can be decisive in terms of securing legitimacy for choices in line with EU policy (Schmidt 2001). To conclude, research designs should be clear on the type of impact that is to be measured. They should distinguish between impacts on the elements of the policy process, impacts on cognitive and normative frames (a topical issue for research on the OMC), and impacts at the level of actual policy results (or, simply, what goes under the label 'policy change').

Enlargement

Enlargement is a special case of the Europeanization of public policy that deserves brief attention. The enlargement process is characterized by the asymmetry of power—rooted in the conditionality of accession—between the EU and candidate countries. The major mechanisms of policy transformation in candidate countries include the provision of models, financial and technical aid, advice and twinning, and benchmarking (Grabbe 2003). All three types of policy portrayed in Table 15.1 are involved in these mechanisms. The EU has made use of asymmetric power to Europeanize the policies of candidate countries. Yet the use of power is also constrained by uncertainty, as shown by Grabbe (2003). There is uncertainty about the content of the EU policy agenda in areas such as social policy, justice and home affairs, and taxation. There is uncertainty about whom to satisfy: the Commission, the Council, or specific governments. And there is uncertainty about standards and thresholds, that is, what degree of compliance will really count as the candidates 'meeting the EU conditions' in the economic domain?

The predominant explanation for Europeanization in candidate countries has centred on conditionality (see Schimmelfennig and Sedelmeier 2007). This argument posits that 'the key condition for the success of Europeanization is whether the EU sets its rules as conditions for countries with a credible membership perspective' (Schimmelfennig and Sedelmeier 2007: 92). In much of this work two competing hypotheses have been tested. The first is a rationalist institutionalist 'external incentives' explanation: that the lure of EU membership brings about policy and other adjustment on the part of the applicant states. The second emphasizes domestic dynamics of adjustment brought about by lesson-drawing and social learning. Schimmelfennig and Sedelmeier (2004, 2005) have concluded that the external incentives account is the more persuasive one. For Woll and Jacquot (2010), by contrast, both of these logics are top-down in nature, whereas their emphasis is upon the usages of Europe by domestic actors: something which is also possible in an applicant state such as Turkey. These propositions suggest that there may be greater scope for domestic contestation in adapting for EU membership than previously assumed in the literature.

Empirical Overview

How can we bring together the analytical discussion in this chapter with some suggestive characterization of the Europeanization of member state policy? We cannot possibly do this in great detail, given that there are twenty-seven member states,

TABLE 15.2 Europeanization and policy illustration		
Type of policy	**Illustrative policy areas**	**'Default' explanation of Europeanization**
Positive integration	Environment, social policy, EMU, CAP	Goodness of fit
Negative integration	Internal market in goods and services, utilities sectors (for example telecommunications, electricity), corporate governance	Regulatory competition
Coordination	CFSP, OMC policies (for example employment, social inclusion, pensions, enterprise policy, asylum policy)	Learning

each with a different story in many different policy areas. Detailed accounts must be the province of case studies (see the reviews of the policy literature in Graziano and Vink 2007: chapters 15–24). Thus, we seek to map our typology onto the EU's policy areas by way of concluding (see Table 15.2).

- Positive integration, with its utilization of policy templates to achieve market-correcting goals, has the most coercive form of Europeanization. Backed up by European law, measures have a formal expectation that they will be put into effect in the member states. Amongst the policy areas concerned are the CAP, EMU (for euro-zone countries), and social and environmental policies. In each case the supranational character of policy provides the adjustment pressure behind adaptation. The potential for regulatory intrusion is high. In these cases the goodness of fit argument seems to be the default interpretation: how well does the EU policy template match up with the existing domestic policy? What adjustments are necessary?

- Negative integration uses policy templates in a limited sector-specific way. They are designed to bring about an internal market of the kind that exists in the general market for goods and services as a result of the treaties. Here also European legal measures spell out policy requirements. However, regulatory intrusion is less than in positive integration, since the whole idea of policy is to allow markets to function. In the transitional phase of legislation, some member states will be faced with the need to adjust policy following the goodness of fit explanation. However, once the transition is complete, regulatory competition should become the key dynamic. Member states (or even sub-national entities) will seek to position themselves competitively. The internal market and the utilities sectors (telecommunications, transport, electricity) should be exemplars here.

- Coordination comes about in those policy areas where the EU is itself weak, thus severely limiting the scope for coercion. Policy is made through intergovernmental negotiations or looser exchanges. Legal measures are downplayed in favour of political declarations, targets, and so on. A whole host of policy areas is covered by the term coordination, including developments under the OMC, (economic policy, employment policy, social inclusion, research and development, and so on) plus conventional intergovernmentalism, as exemplified by the CFSP. In such cases, the process is essentially horizontal and dependent on learning. In older forms, the learning is typically part of agreeing a European policy intergovernmentally. In the OMC, the learning is much more ad hoc, with the EU serving as an arena within which member governments may find policy solutions to domestic problems.

Our brief section on empirical illustration must carry with it a health warning. First, despite the greater clarification of competences through the Treaty on the Functioning of the European Union (see Box 15.1), there is no clear delineation of responsibilities between the EU itself and the member states *by policy area*. Consequently, it is quite difficult to assign some policy areas to one of our three categories. Taxation policy, for instance, entails some elements of positive integration (for example regarding Value Added Tax regimes), some competition amongst national regimes in accordance with negative integration (for example on savings or corporation taxation), and a means of monitoring *harmful* tax competition through coordination. Another illustration is environmental policy, where there is a mix of policy instruments, including directives and non-binding codes. In some cases, therefore, it is the *policy issue* rather than the policy area that is the more suitable basis for classification. Second, we underline that Table 15.2 refers to the *default* patterns of Europeanization. As we already noted in discussion above, deviant cases will always exist. In addition, variegation exists within the modes of governance, especially hierarchy and facilitated coordination. Third, although most of the empirical research on the Europeanization of public policy is concerned with the degree of change in domestic public policy, there is another important effect on policymaking styles and structures. Europeanization effects vary depending on whether a country (or a sector within a country) is pluralistic, corporatist, or *dirigiste* (Schmidt 2006). Recent evidence on different policy sectors suggests that Europeanization has weakened corporatist styles in countries like Belgium, and even outside the EU, as shown by Switzerland (Fontana 2011). Thus, it is useful to specify whether the Europeanization effects concern policy outcomes or policymaking styles and structures.

Conclusion

Over the last decade, the EU's impact has become a focus of attention for academic scholars, taking the debate beyond its long-standing concerns with (largely 'bottom-up') processes of integration and policymaking. The EU has had a very significant impact upon the policies of the member states. It has also impacted upon near-neighbours, such as states in the European Economic Area, and outside Europe, for instance on the recipients of aid programmes. This chapter, however, has been concerned only with member and accession states.

Empirical studies in this field can be organized in various ways: by the member state or by the policy/issue area concerned. In this chapter we have not sought to concentrate on summarizing empirical studies, for that would probably result in a bewildering array of findings. Instead we have sought to concentrate on the dynamics, processes, and effects involved by developing typologies and classifications derived from patterns of governance within the EU. We have argued that governance by negotiation—the agreement on EU policy—bears upon the Europeanization process. The identification of a set of 'default' explanations of Europeanization effects draws upon analytical and empirical work in the area. With the ongoing institutional and policy reform process over the period from the Single Act of 1986 to the fiscal pact of 2012, not to mention successive waves of enlargement, studying the empirical effects of the Europeanization process looks likely to be a similarly long-term pursuit on the part of students of the EU.

FURTHER READING

A first important step in exploring Europeanization is to consider how the term is utilized (see Olsen 2002; Radaelli and Pasquier 2007). For broad reviews of the Europeanization literature, see Featherstone (2003) and Graziano and Vink (this volume; 2007). Börzel and Risse (2007), Exadaktylos and Radaelli (2009), Ladrech (2010), Graziano and Vink (2007: Chapters 15–24) and Ladrech (2010: Chapter 8) give extended discussion of the literature on the Europeanization of member state policy. Exadaktylos and Radaelli (2012) provide different examples of how to deal with the challenge of establishing causality in Europeanization processes.

On different modes of policymaking in the EU, see Wallace (2010), Scharpf (1999), Héritier and Rhodes (2010), and Bulmer and Padgett (2005). Sabel and Zeitlin (2008, 2010) consider 'experimentalist governance' in the EU, where horizontal patterns of Europeanization, such as through the OMC, are prominent. On the OMC there is a collection of empirical and theoretical papers available on the EIoP web-based journal (Kröger 2009). Schimmelfennig and Sedelmeier (2007) and Schimmelfennig (2007) serve as an entry-point for the literature on Europeanization and enlargement, Dyson (2008) for the impact of the Euro on domestic policy and state structures.

WEB LINKS

There are few websites devoted to Europeanization as such. However, both ARENA in Oslo and Queen's University Belfast hosted online papers related to the subject. These and other series on the EU may be accessed through the following online portal: **http://eiop.or.at/erpa/**. The project New Modes of Governance, now concluded, provides a portal with access to several studies that intersect the key themes of this chapter, see **http://www.eu-newgov.org/**.

REFERENCES

Armstrong, K. (2010), *Governing Social Inclusion: Europeanization Through Policy Coordination*, Oxford: Oxford University Press.

Armstrong, K. and Bulmer, S. (1998), *The Governance of the Single European Market*, Manchester: Manchester University Press.

Bache, I. (2008), *Europeanization and Multi-level Governance: Cohesion Policy in the European Union and Britain*, Lanham: Rowman and Littlefield.

Borras, S. and Radaelli, C. M. (2010), 'Recalibrating the Open Method of Coordination: Towards Diverse and More Effective Usages', Swedish Institute of European Policy Studies, WP SIEPS 2010:7, Stockholm, www.sieps.eu.

Borras, S. and Radaelli, C. M. (2011, forthcoming), 'The Politics of Governance Architectures: Creation, Change and Effects of the EU Lisbon Strategy', *Journal of European Public Policy*, 18/4: 463–606.

Börzel, T. (2002), 'Pace-Setting, Foot-Dragging, and Fence-Sitting: Member State Responses to Europeanization', *Journal of Common Market Studies*, 40/2: 193–214.

Börzel, T. (2005), 'How the European Union Interacts with its Member States', in S. Bulmer and C. Lequesne (eds), *The Member States of the European Union*, 1st edn, Oxford: Oxford University Press, 45–69.

Börzel, T. (2010), 'European Governance: Negotiation and Competition in the Shadow of Hierarchy', *Journal of Common Market Studies*, 48/2: 191–219.

Börzel, T. and Risse, T. (2003), 'Conceptualising the Domestic Impact of Europe', in K. Featherstone and C. M. Radaelli (eds), *The Politics of Europeanization*, Oxford: Oxford University Press, 57–80.

Börzel, T. and Risse, T. (2007), 'Europeanization: The Domestic Impact of European Union Politics', in K. E. Jørgensen, M. Pollack, and B. Rosamond (eds), *Handbook of European Union Politics*, London: SAGE Publications, 483–504.

Brunsson, N. (1989), *The Organization of Hypocrisy. Talk, Decisions and Actions in Organizations*, Chichester and New York: John Wiley and Sons.

Bulmer, S. (2007), 'Theorizing Europeanization', in Graziano, P. and Vink, M., *Europeanization: New Research Agendas*, Basingstoke: Palgrave Macmillan, 46–58.

Bulmer, S. and Padgett, S. (2005), 'Policy Transfer in the European Union: An Institutionalist Perspective', *British Journal of Political Science*, 35/1: 103–26.

Bulmer, S., Dolowitz, D., Humphreys, P., and Padgett, S. (2003), 'Electricity and Telecommunications: Fit for the European Union?', in K. Dyson and K. Goetz (eds), *Germany, Europe and the Politics of Constraint*, Oxford: Oxford University Press, 251–69.

Cowles, M. G., Caporaso, J., and Risse, T. (eds) (2001), *Transforming Europe: Europeanization and Domestic Change*, Ithaca NY and London: Cornell University Press.

den Boer, M. and Wallace, W. (2000), 'Justice and Home Affairs: Integration through Incrementalism?', in H. Wallace and W. Wallace (eds), *Policy-Making in the European Union*, 4th edn. Oxford: Oxford University Press, 493–519.

Dyson, K. (ed.) (2008), *The Euro at Ten: Europeanization, Power and Convergence*, Oxford: Oxford University Press.

Egan, M. (2001), *Constructing a European Market*, Oxford: Oxford University Press.

Ette, A. and Faist, T. (2007), *The Europeanization of National Policies and Politics of Immigration: Between Autonomy and the European Union*, Basingstoke: Palgrave Macmillan.

European Commission (2010a), *Governance, Tools and Policy Cycle of Europe 2020*, Brussels: European Commission.

European Commission (2010b), *Smart Regulation in the European Union*, COM(2010) 543 final, Brussels: European Commission, 08 October.

Exadaktylos, T. (2010), 'The Europeanization of National Foreign Policy: The Case of Greek and German Foreign Policies vis-à-vis the Eastern Enlargement of the European Union', University of Exeter, PhD thesis.

Exadaktylos, T. and Radaelli, C. M. (2009), Research Design in European Studies: The Case of Europeanization, *Journal of Common Market Studies*, 47/3: 507–30.

Exadaktylos, T. and Radaelli, C. M. (2010), 'Causal Explanation in Studies of Europeanisation', *Political Methodology Working Paper Series of the Committee on Concepts and Methods of the IPSA*, 28. http://www.concepts-methods.org/working_papers/20100317_40_PM_28_Exadaktylos_&_Radaelli.pdf.

Exadaktylos, T. and Radaelli, C. M. (eds) (2012), *Research Design in European Studies*, Basingstoke: Palgrave Macmillan.

Featherstone, K. (2003), 'In the Name of Europe', in K. Featherstone and C. M. Radaelli (eds), *The Politics of Europeanisation*, Oxford: Oxford University Press, 3–26.

Fligstein, N. and McNichol, J. (1998), 'The Institutional Terrain of the European Union', in W. Sandholtz and A. Stone Sweet (eds), *European Integration and Supranational Governance*, Oxford: Oxford University Press, 59–91.

Fontana, M. C. (2011), 'Europeanization and Domestic Policy Concertation Inside and Outside the EU. A Comparison of Belgium and Switzerland', University of Lausanne, PhD dissertation.

Glarbo, K. (1999), 'Wide-awake Diplomacy: Reconstructing the Common Foreign and Security Policy of the European Union', *Journal of European Public Policy*, 6/4: 634–51.

Grabbe, H. (2003), 'Europeanisation goes East: Power and Uncertainty in the EU Accession Game', in K. Featherstone and C. M. Radaelli (eds), *The Politics of Europeanisation*, Oxford: Oxford University Press.

Grabbe, H. (2006), *The EU's Transformative Power: Europeanization Through Conditionality in Central and Eastern Europe*, Basingstoke: Palgrave Macmillan.

Graziano, P. and Vink, M. (2007), *Europeanization: New Research Agenda*, Basingstoke: Palgrave Macmillan.

Harcourt, A. (2003), 'The Regulation of Media Markets in Selected EU Accession States in Central and Eastern Europe', in *European Law Journal*, 9/3: 316–40.

Hartlapp, M. (2009), 'Learning About Policy Learning. Reflections on the European Employment Strategy', *European Integration Online Papers-EIoP*, 13.

Haverland, M. (2000), 'National Adaptation to European Integration: The Importance of Institutional Veto Points', *Journal of Public Policy*, 20/1: 83–103.

Haverland, M. (2003), 'The Impact of the EU on Environmental Policies', in K. Featherstone and C. M. Radaelli (eds), *The Politics of Europeanisation*, Oxford: Oxford University Press, 203–21.

Hay, C. and Rosamond, B. (2002), 'Globalisation, European Integration and the Discursive Construction of Economic Imperatives', *Journal of European Public Policy*, 9/2: 147–67.

Hedström, P. (2005), *Dissecting the Social. On the Principles of Analytical Sociology*, Cambridge, Cambridge University Press.

Hemerijck, A. and Visser, J. (2001), 'Learning and Mimicking: How European Welfare States Reform', typescript.

Héritier, A. and Knill, C. (2001), 'Differential Responses to European Policies: A Comparison', in Héritier, A., Kerwer, D., Knill, C., Lehmkuhl, D., Teutsch, M., and Douillet, A-C. (2001), *Differential Europe. The European Union Impact on National Policymaking*, Lanham MD: Rowman and Littlefield., 257–94.

Héritier, A. and M. Rhodes (eds) (2010), *New Modes of Governance in Europe*, Basingstoke: Palgrave Macmillan.

Héritier, A., Kerwer, D., Knill, C., Lehmkuhl, D., Teutsch, M., and Douillet, A-C. (2001), *Differential Europe. The European Union Impact on National Policymaking*, Lanham MD: Rowman and Littlefield.

Howarth, D. and T. Sadeh (2010), 'The Ever Incomplete Single Market: Differentiation and the evolving Frontier of Integration', *Journal of European Public Policy*, 17/7: 922–35.

Jabko, N. (2006), *Playing the Market: A Political Strategy for Uniting Europe, 1985–2005*, Ithaca, NY: Cornell University Press.

Jordan, A. and Liefferink, D. (eds) (2004), *Environmental Policy in Europe: The Europeanization of National Environmental Policy*, London: Routledge.

Knill, C. (2001), *The Europeanisation of National Administrations. Patterns of Institutional Persistence and Change*, Cambridge: Cambridge University Press.

Knill, C. and Lehmkuhl, D. (2002), 'The National Impact of EU Regulatory Policy: Three Mechanisms', *European Journal of Political Research*, 41/2: 255–80.

Kohler-Koch, B. (2002), 'European Networks And Ideas: Changing National Policies?', *European Integration on line Papers* (EIoP) vol. 6/6, http://www.eiop.or.at/eiop/texte/2002–006a.htm.

Kröger, S. (2009), 'The Open Method of Coordination: Underconceptualisation, Overdetermination, Depoliticisation and Beyond', *European Integration online Papers (EIoP)*, 13/5, http://eiop.or.at/eiop/texte/2009-2005a.htm.

Ladrech, R. (2010), *Europeanization and National Politics*, Basingstoke: Palgrave Macmillan.

Laffan, B. (2001), 'The European Union Polity: A Union of Regulative, Normative, and Cognitive Pillars', *Journal of European Public Policy*, 8/5: 709–27.

Lodge, M. (2007), 'Comparing Non-Hierarchical Governance in Action', *Journal of Common Market Studies*, 45/2: 343–65.

Mair, P. (2001), 'The Limited Impact of Europe on National Party Systems', in K. H. Goetz and S. Hix (eds), *Europeanised Politics? European Integration and National Political Systems*, London: Frank Cass, 27–51.

Miskimmon, A. and Paterson, W. (2003), 'Foreign and Security Policy: On the Cusp Between Transformation and Accommodation', in K. Dyson and K. Goetz (eds), *Germany, Europe and the Politics of Constraint*, Oxford: Oxford University Press, 325–45.

Monar, J. (2002), 'Institutionalizing Freedom, Security and Justice', in J. Peterson and M. Shackleton (eds), *The Institutions of the European Union*, Oxford: Oxford University Press, 186–209.

Monti, M. (2010), *A New Strategy for the Single Market. At the Service of Europe's Economy and Society*, Brussels: European Commission, ec.europa.eu/bepa/pdf/monti_report_final_10_05_2010_en.pdf.

Nicolaïdis, K. and Schmidt S. K. (2007), 'Mutual Recognition "on Trial": The Long Road to Services Liberalization', *Journal of European Public Policy*, 14/5: 190–207.

Olsen, J. (2002), 'The Many Faces of Europeanization', *Journal of Common Market Studies*, 40/5: 921–52.

Pinder, J. (1968), 'Positive Integration and Negative Integration: Some Problems of Economic Union in the EEC', *The World Today*, 24/3: 89–110.

Pollitt, C. (2001), 'Convergence: The Useful Myth?', *Public Administration*, 79/4: 933–47.

Radaelli, C. M. (1997), 'How does Europeanization Produce Domestic Policy Change? Corporate Tax Policy in Italy and the United Kingdom', *Comparative Political Studies*, 30/5: 553–75.

Radaelli, C. M. (2004), 'The Puzzle of Regulatory Competition', *Journal of Public Policy*, 24/1: 3–23.

Radaelli, C. M. and Pasquier, R. (2007), 'Conceptual Issues', in Graziano, P. and Vink, M., *Europeanization: New Research Agendas*, Basingstoke: Palgrave Macmillan, 35–45.

Rieker, P. (2006), 'From Common Defence to Comprehensive Security: Towards the Europeanization of French Foreign and Security Policy', *Security Dialogue*, 37/4: 509–28.

Risse, T., Cowles, M. G., and Caporaso, J. (2001), 'Europeanization and Domestic Change: Introduction', in Cowles, M. G., Caporaso, J., and Risse, T. (eds), *Transforming Europe: Europeanization and Domestic Change*, Ithaca NY and London: Cornell University Press, 1–20.

Sabel, C. and Zeitlin, J. (2008), 'Learning from Difference: The New Architecture of Experimentalist Governance in the EU', *European Law Journal*, 14/3: 271–327.

Sabel, C. and Zeitlin, J. (eds) (2010), *Experimentalist Governance in the European Union: Towards a New Architecture*, Oxford: Oxford University Press.

Scharpf, F. W. (1997), *Games Real Actors Play. Actor-Centred Institutionalism in Policy Research*, Boulder CO: Westview Press.

Scharpf, F. W. (1999), *Governing in Europe: Effective and Democratic?*, Oxford: Oxford University Press.

Schimmelfennig, F. (2007), 'Europeanization Beyond Europe', *Living Reviews in European Governance*, http://europeangovernance.livingreviews.org/Articles/lreg-2007-1.

Schimmelfennig, F. and Sedelmeier, U. (2004), 'Governance by Conditionality: EU Rule Transfer to the Candidate Countries of Central and Eastern Europe', *Journal of European Public Policy*, 11/4: 661–79.

Schimmelfennig, F. and Sedelmeier, U. (2005), *The Europeanization of Central and Eastern Europe*, Ithaca, NY: Cornell University Press.

Schimmelfennig, F. and Sedelmeier, U. (2007), 'Candidate Countries and Conditionality', in Graziano, P. and Vink, M., *Europeanization: New Research Agendas*, Basingstoke: Palgrave Macmillan, 88–101.

Schmidt, S. (2000), 'Only an Agenda Setter? The European Commission's Power Over the Council of Ministers', *European Union Politics*, 1/1: 37–61.

Schmidt, S. (2002), 'The Impact of Mutual Recognition—Inbuilt Limits and Domestic Responses to the Single Market', *Journal of European Public Policy*, 9/6: 935–53.

Schmidt, V. (2006), *Democracy in Europe: The EU and National Polities*, Oxford: Oxford University Press.

Schmidt, V. (2001), 'The Politics of Economic Adjustment in France and Britain: When Does Discourse Matter?', *Journal of European Public Policy*, 8/2: 247–64.

Schneider, V. (2001), 'Institutional Reform in Telecommunications: The European Union in Transnational Policy Diffusion', in Cowles, M. G., Caporaso, J., and Risse, T. (eds), *Transforming Europe: Europeanization and Domestic Change*, Ithaca NY and London: Cornell University Press, 60–78.

Snyder, F. (1994), 'Soft Law and Institutional Performance in the European Community', in S. Martin (ed.), *Essays in Honor of Emile Noel*, Dordrecht and London: Kluwer, 197–225.

Surel, Y. (2000), 'The Role of Cognitive and Normative Frames in Policymaking', *Journal of European Public Policy*, 7/4: 495–512.

Teubner, G. (2001), 'Legal Irritants: How Unifying Law Ends up in New Divergences', in P. Hall and D. Soskice (eds), *Varieties of Capitalism. The Institutional Foundations of Comparative Advantage*, Oxford: Oxford University Press, 417–41.

Thatcher, M. (2004), 'Winners and Losers in Europeanization: Reforming the National Regulation of Telecommunications', *West European Politics*, 27/1: 29–52.

Wallace, H. (2010), 'An Institutional Anatomy and Five Policy Modes', in H. Wallace, M. Pollack, and A. Young (eds), *Policymaking in the European Union*, 6th edn., Oxford: Oxford University Press, 69–104.

Wallace, H., Pollack, M., and Young, A. (eds) (2010), *Policymaking in the European Union*, 6th edn., Oxford: Oxford University Press.

Wellens, K. and Borchardt, G. (1980), 'Soft Law in European Community Law', *European Law Review*, 14/5: 267–321.

Woll, C. and Jacquot, S. (2010), 'Using Europe: Strategic Action in Multi-level Politics', *Comparative European Politics*, 8/1: 110–126.

Wong, R. (2006), *The Europeanization of French Foreign Policy: France and the EU in East Asia*, Basingstoke: Palgrave Macmillan.

⁂ ENDNOTES

1. One categorization of policymaking is that proposed by Helen Wallace, and comprising five variants: the Community method, the EU regulatory model, multilevel governance, policy coordination and benchmarking, and intensive transgovernmentalism (Wallace 2010: 90–103).

2. We use the term 'mechanism' here in a broad sense (Hedström 2005). On mechanisms at work in Europeanization see Knill and Lehmkuhl (2002), Exadaktylos and Radaelli (2010).

3. The role of veto players is acknowledged in later versions of the 'goodness of fit' explanation. See Börzel and Risse (2003).

CHAPTER 16

Europeanization and Sub-national Authorities

Peter Bursens

▌ Summary

The Europeanization of sub-national authorities (SNAs) can be broken down to the effect of EU membership on the policies, politics, and polity of SNAs. With respect to *policies*, the scarce literature available suggests that SNAs implement EU legislation in diverse ways according to the varying national contexts. The *politics* dimension discusses the impact on EU policy coordination mechanisms, domestic horizontal and vertical relations, and actors' preferences and strategies. This chapter finds limited but differential impact, mediated by domestic institutions. *Polity* effects are analysed against the background of the question whether the EU empowers or weakens the regional level. Again the impact is found to be rather modest, mediated by the national contexts and with substantial variation between (old and new, centralized and federal) member states, generally finding that strong regions are further empowered. The chapter concludes with some remarks regarding the analytical approaches and the variables used in the research on the Europeanization of SNAs.

Introduction

This chapter follows the volume's understanding of Europeanization defining it as the impact of the EU upon the SNAs of the member states. How did SNAs adapt to European integration? How did SNAs react to the fact that the countries they are part of are member states of the European Union? The Europeanization of SNAs has not (yet) developed into a separate research agenda. Rather, a series of regional dimensions has been touched upon, without so far being embedded in an encompassing framework. Nevertheless, a substantial body of literature discussing various aspects of regional adaptation to the EU has been published since the beginning of the 1990s. This chapter presents an extensive overview of the theoretical and empirical contributions of this literature.

There have been two previous overviews of European impact on SNAs. In the first edition of *The Member States of the European Union*, Kassim (2005) devotes some attention to SNAs in his chapter on the Europeanization of member states' institutions. Next to tackling national executives, parliaments, and courts, Kassim briefly touches upon the European impact on sub-national government (2005: 303–07). Reviewing the literature in 2005, he lists three major empirical conclusions, pointing to the effect on the policies, politics, and polity of SNAs. First, European integration alters (loosens) the relationship between regional and central authorities as the latter are no longer the only superior authorities SNAs have to take into account (a polity effect). Second, European integration touches upon the competencies of SNAs (a policy effect), most notably through regional policies, triggering SNAs to seek direct and indirect influence in EU decision making (a politics effect). Third, the literature points to a differential impact of the EU, affecting powerful SNAs the most. At the same time, these powerful SNAs also have the most resources to restore the balance, resulting in varying degrees of involvement of SNAs in EU policymaking.

The Graziano and Vink (2006) edited volume *Europeanization: New Research Agendas* contains a chapter on state structures which reviews the literature dealing with the adaptation of domestic institutional organization to European integration (Bursens 2006). With regard to the involvement of SNAs in national EU policymaking, Bursens concludes that there is empirical evidence of a strengthening of the regional level, whereby especially strong 'constitutional regions' have been able to become influential players in national EU policymaking (a politics effect). With respect to the impact on domestic intergovernmental relations, the literature up to 2006 reveals a moderate but differential impact, again suggesting that especially strong SNAs have been able to use the EU in order to strengthen their position vis-à-vis the central level (a polity effect).

Both review chapters are only partial discussions. So far, the literature lacks a systematic and overarching assessment of the impact of the EU on SNAs. Keating (2008a and 2008b) comes close to this in a *West European Politics* review article and *Regional and Federal Studies* special issue. His main conclusion is that the impact of the EU regional policies and regional cooperation schemes upon regional power has been limited. This chapter seeks to verify this conclusion by an extensive overview of the literature discussing the relation between the EU and SNAs. The remaining sections will deal with the impact of the EU on regional policies, on the position of SNAs in national politics, and on the polities of the member states. By dealing with these three dimensions we supersede what Carter and Pasquier (2010: 302) call the 'deterministic approach', which exclusively focuses on the issue of empowerment or disempowerment of regions (polity). Indeed, studying Europeanization of SNAs should be completed with attention for other dimensions such as Europeanization of political procedures, cognitive processes (politics), and contents of policies. Although the border between the politics and polity dimension is sometimes thin, disentangling them will bring us further than studies which do not make the distinction (not even implicitly), mix them up, or tackle both dimensions at the same time. The distinction between the three dimensions also has analytical advantages as it allows for a more precise delineation of independent, intermediating, and dependent variables. The last section presents an assessment of the research agenda so far and presents some possible future avenues.

SNAs in the EU

What kind of SNAs are we dealing with in this chapter? The EU's NUTS classification (Nomenclature of Territorial Units for Statistics) is a useful point of reference. The NUTS classification divides the EU into territorial units for the purpose of gathering statistics, making socioeconomic analyses, and developing regional policies. Although it is based on economic parameters, also linguistic, cultural, and ethnic regions can be traced back by this system. NUTS 1 points to major socioeconomic regions, NUTS 2 to basic regions for the application of regional policies, and NUTS 3 to small regions for specific diagnoses. The empirical literature reviewed in this chapter mainly deals with NUTS 1, sometimes with NUTS 2 regions (see Table 16.1). This is a pragmatic delimitation. It falls beyond the scope of this review to present a definition of 'a sub-national authority' or even 'a region', keeping in mind that even Marks *et al.* (2008) take such a pragmatic approach in their landmark overview of regional authority. One consequence of this option is that the chapter does not deal with the Europeanization of local authorities. Although the literature on that topic is far more limited, the empirical findings are very much in line with the conclusions drawn regarding SNAs (cf. the last section of this chapter).

Europeanization of SNA Policies: Implementation of EU Policies

Understanding Europeanization as domestic adaptation following EU membership, the Europeanization of policies boils down to the question: to what extent and how has European integration triggered change in the content of national policies? Much

TABLE 16.1 Sub-national authority structures in the EU

	NUTS 1		NUTS 2		NUTS 3		LAU 1		LAU 2	
BE	Gewesten / Régions	3	Provincies / Provinces	11	Arrondissementen / Arrondissements	44	-		Gemeenten / Communes	589
BG	Rajoni	2	Rajoni za planirane	6	Oblasti	28	Obshtini	264	Naseleni mesta	5329
CZ	Území	1	Oblasti	8	Kraje	14	Okresy	77	Obce	6249
DK	-	1	Regioner	5	Landsdeler	11	Kommuner	99	Sogne	2148
DE	Länder	16	Regierungs-bezirke	39	Kreise	429	Verwaltungsge-meinschaften	1457	Gemeinden	12379
EE	-	1	-	1	Groups of Maakond	5	Maakond	15	Vald, linn	227
IE	-	1	Regions	2	Regional Authority Regions	8	Counties, Cities	34	Electoral Districts	3441
GR	Groups of development regions	4	Periferies	13	Nomoi	51	Demoi, Koinotites	1034	Demotiko diamer-isma, Koinotiko diamerisma	6130
ES	Agrupacion de comunidades Autonomas	7	Comunidades y ciudades Autonomas	19	Provincias + islas + Ceuta, Melilla	59	-		Municipios	8111
FR	Z.E.A.T + DOM	9	Régions + DOM	26	Départements + DOM	100	Cantons de rattachement	3787	Communes	36683
IT	Gruppi di regioni	5	Regioni	21	Provincie	107	-		Comuni	8101
CY	-	1	-	1	-	1	Eparchies	6	Dimoi, koino-tites	613

(continued)

Table 16.1 (*continued*)

	NUTS 1	NUTS 2	NUTS 3	LAU 1	LAU 2
LV	*1* –	*1* –	*1* *Reģioni*	6 Rajoni, republikas pilsētas	33 Pilsētas, novadi, pagasti — 527
LT	*1* –	*1* –	*1* Apskritys	10 Savivaldybės	60 Seniūnijos — 518
LU	*1* –	*1* –	*1* –	1 Cantons	13 Communes — 116
HU	*3* *Statisztikai nagyrégiók*	*7* *Tervezési-statisztikai régiók*	*7* Megyék + Budapest	20 Statisztikai kistérségek	168 Települések — 3152
MT	*1* –	*1* –	*1* Gżejjer	2 Distretti	6 Kunsilli — 68
NL	*4* *Landsdelen*	*12* Provincies	*1* COROP regio's	40 -	Gemeenten — 443
AT	*3* *Gruppen von Bundesländern*	*3* Bundesländer	*9* Gruppen von politischen Bezirken	35 -	Gemeinden — 2357
PL	*6* *Regiony*	*6* Województwa	*16* Podregiony	66 Powiaty i miasta na prawach powiatu	379 Gminy — 2478
PT	*3* Continente + Regioes autonomas	*3* Comissaoes de Coordenaçao regional + Regioes autonomas	*7* Grupos de Con-celhos	30 Concelhos-Municipios	308 Freguesias — 4260
RO	*4* *Macroregiuni*	*4* Regiuni	*8* Judet + Bucuresti	42 -	Comuni + Municipiu + Orase — 3174

SI	-	1	Kohezijske regije	2	Statistične regije	12	Upravne enote	58	Občine	210
SK	-	1	Oblasti	4	Kraje	8	Okresy	79	Obce	2928
FI	Manner-Suomi, Ahvenananmaa /Fasta Finland, Åland	2	Suuralueet / Storområden	5	Maakunnat / Landskap	20	Seutukunnat / Ekonomiska regioner	77	Kunnat / Kommuner	416
SE	Grupper av riksområden	3	Riksområden	8	Län	21	-		Kommuner	290
UK	Government Office Regions; Country	12	Counties (some grouped); Inner and Outer London; Groups of unitary authorities	37	Upper tier authorities or groups of lower tier authorities (unitary authorities or districts)	133	Lower tier authorities (districts) or individual unitary authorities; Individual unitary authorities or LECs (or parts thereof); Districts	443	Wards (or parts thereof)	10664
EU27		97		271		1,303		8,397		121601

Source: **http://epp.eurostat.ec.europa.eu**, © European Union, 1995–2012.
Adapted from Eurostat table at: **http://epp.eurostat.ec.europa.eu/portal/page/portal/nuts_nomenclature/correspondence_tables/national_structures_eu**, accessed 13 March 2011.
Key: **BE**: Belgium, **BG**: Bulgaria, **CZ**: Czech Republic, **DK**: Denmark, **DE**: Germany, **EE**: Estonia, **IE**: Ireland, **GR**: Greece, **ES**: Spain, **FR**: France, **IT**: Italy, **CY**: Cyprus, **LV**: Latvia, **LT**: Lithuania, **LU**: Luxembourg, **HU**: Hungary, **MT**: Malta, **NL**: Netherlands, **AT**: Austria, **PL**: Poland, **PT**: Portugal, **RO**: Romania, **SI**: Slovenia, **SK**: Slovakia, **FI**: Finland, **SE**: Sweden, **UK**: United Kingdom. **LAU**: local administrative unit; **NUTS**: Nomenclature of Territorial Units for Statistics.

research in this area falls under the heading of implementation and compliance studies (see Bulmer and Radaelli in this volume for an overview). Implementation research has mainly focused on how the central level of member states deal with EU legislation. In several member states, however, SNAs have become key players in the process of implementing EU policies (Borghetto and Franchino 2010). It is therefore somewhat surprising that so little literature explicitly focuses on the involvement of SNAs in the implementation of EU policies: even overview articles such as the contributions of Sverdrup (2007) and Treib (2008) hardly touch upon how SNAs deal with the implementation of EU policies.

Also, Sturm and Dieringer (2005: 285–87) are surprised by the lack of specific literature dealing with the Europeanization of regional policies. From what is available, they suggest a diverging impact of the EU on SNAs. This differential impact is confirmed by Borghetto and Franchino (2010) who focus more explicitly on the role of SNAs in the implementation of EU directives. They find substantial variation in regional involvement in several ways: SNAs are more involved in some policy fields (notably environment, social policy, public procurement) than in others and—not surprisingly—they are more involved in strongly decentralized states than in other states. In addition, they also find considerable differences of involvement within the category of decentralized states.

The most prominent way SNAs pop up in implementation literature is as one of the variables influencing national implementation processes. In this respect, SNAs are often regarded as veto-players, potentially hampering the smooth implementation of EU policies in federal or decentralized member states. Falkner *et al.* (2005) for instance allocate all federal and decentralized states (except Italy) to the category of 'the world of domestic politics', suggesting that the national constellation of actors and preferences, including intergovernmental relations, is largely responsible for the mediocre implementation record. Borghetto and Franchino's review (2010) points to several explanations: unwillingness of regions to implement EU policies that come about without their involvement, an institutional misfit between EU requirements and domestic procedures, and a policy misfit between EU and domestic policy instruments.

Bache and Conzelmann (2008: 136–7) mention one other way in which regional policies are relevant. In a study on the UK, they find 'clear efforts on the side of the government to design regional policies in a way to make them attractive as co-financing instruments of the structural funds'. Again, this study reveals more about how a national government strategically uses the regional level than about the impact of the EU on the policies. In addition, they also conclude that the European impact should not be overstated as 'central government has been instrumental in shaping developments rather than simply succumbing to adaptational pressure'.

In short, the scarce literature on the Europeanization of SNA policies reveals that regions deal differently with EU policies and that this divergence is caused by the different national contexts.

Europeanization of SNA Politics: EU Impact on Regional Actors and Institutions

Europeanization of the politics dimension of SNAs is defined as the impact on national political actors and procedures. Does the EU alter preferences and strategies of domestic political actors? Does the EU trigger changes in member states' institutional settings and decision-making mechanisms? The politics dimension covers different aspects: the establishment of EU policy coordination mechanisms, the effects on existing horizontal and vertical actor relations, and the effects on actors' preferences and strategies.

A first well documented dimension deals with domestic EU policy coordination (Kassim *et al.* 2000; Wessels *et al.* 2003; Zeff and Pirro 2006). Descriptions of national coordination mechanisms often also deal with regional involvement. In his overview chapter, Bursens (2006) starts from the observation that European integration has not only transferred competences to the EU from the national level, but also from the regional level of member states. The result was that strong regions had more to lose than weak regions, who did not possess many competences anyway. Therefore, the impact of European integration on regions with legislative power was much more substantial. At the same time, however, these strong regions already had a powerful position within the domestic constitutional order before the EU came along. They quite often, therefore, had the means to strike back and win an influential role in the domestic coordination of EU policies. German and Austrian Länder (Jeffery 1996; Dyson and Goetz 2003) and Belgian Regions and Communities (Beyers and Bursens 2006) are the most obvious examples of influential players in domestic EU policymaking, but also Spanish Autonomous Communities (Closa and Heywood 2004) and some British devolved authorities (Giddings and Drewry 2004; Bulmer *et al.* 2006) have been able—albeit to a lesser extent—to gain access to domestic EU policy coordination as partial compensation for having lost competences to the European level. Empirical evidence from these member states all points in the direction of a variety of participation modes of regions in domestic formulation of EU policies.

A second, rather under-researched aspect, is the Europeanization of intergovernmental relations within member states. Some contributions examine whether EU membership and, more specifically, EU regional policy affect the number of actors involved in domestic decision making. The general trend is a vertical and horizontal proliferation of actors. National regional policies are no longer solely run by elected and democratically legitimated actors at the national level, but increasingly also by regional actors (especially in federal member states), administrative actors (civil servants, agencies), and semi-private and private actors (experts, interest groups). Thielemann (2002: 61) discusses the reforms of the domestic German regional policy framework and concludes that this has been strongly influenced by European regional policy development principles. He argues that the European partnership principle has triggered increased participation of sub-national and semi-public actors in the European policy process, weakening the gatekeeping role and policy autonomy of central government. Fargion *et al.* (2006) deal with the Europeanization of territorial representation in Italy. They find a differential impact of EU structural funds. Northern Italy witnessed a 'considerable reshaping of representation' (Fargion *et al.* 2006: 777–80), favouring non-elected officials and well organized interest groups, expertise becoming a crucial resource. In Southern Italy, politicians stay in charge but often seem unable to employ the necessary innovation and expertise.

We can conclude by saying that structural funds, and Europeanization at large, have played a role in reshaping the mechanisms of representation and the configuration of actors involved in their management. However, the European influence over such a reshaping process has been filtered by concurrent processes of change at the domestic level and internal mediating factors at the national and regional level (i.e. the pre-existing styles of decision- and policy-making, and the characteristics and attitudes of the political and bureaucratic actors involved in the programming and management of structural funds) (ibid.: 780).

Clearly, Europe has delivered the possibilities to build territorial channels of representation but only rarely leading to the creation of solid partnerships between public and private actors. Also, Bache (2008: 152) suggests a vertical and horizontal effect. From his (comparative) study on the Europeanization of the UK, he concludes that cohesion policy has strengthened the regional level (vertical effect) because it triggered the establishment of regional administrative institutions and processes (even in centralized states). Bache also discerns a horizontal effect as the principles of programming and partnership, inherent in cohesion policies, have triggered cross-sectoral engagement and interdependence. 'Overall, there is an evident trend toward greater domestic multi-level governance that has been encouraged and incentivized by EU cohesion policy' (Bache: 2008: 81). He adds that 'in federal states, multi-level interactions and regionalization were intensified, but without transformative effects' (2008: 83). Bache and Conzelmann equally find 'enhancement of the regional tier, the emergence of more partnership-oriented, inter agency work at and between several territorial levels' (Bache and Conzelmann 2008: 136).

In Central and Eastern European member states, the impact on political life is more profound. Studying Poland, Czech Republic, and Slovakia, Scherpereel (2010) finds that EU norms, incentives, and discourses, transmitted through EU cohesion policy, have become deeply embedded in the identities and strategies of Eastern European officials. He describes impact on regional actors' strategies, the size and shape of regional structures, workloads and orientations of regional bureaucrats, and patterns of interaction linking public institutions to societal actors, especially after accession took place (Scherpereel 2010: 46). Baun and Marek (2006) find an ambiguous impact of the EU in the Czech Republic: At the polity level, they see the creation of new regional authorities, while at the politics level, they find a centralization of the accession process and of the management of regional policies (which is a general conclusion of the enlargement literature). Such centralization tendencies are even present in federal member states: Beyers and Bursens (2006) found forms of centralization of administrative-bureaucratic processes in Belgium because of the country's involvement in European decision making.

A third body of literature examines whether the EU affects domestic actors' preferences and strategies. With respect to preferences, the literature seems to suggest that EU membership has a positive but limited effect on the demands for self-government. The argument is that the EU triggers preferences towards autonomy because of using institutional factors (EU offering institutional targets such as through the structural funds), economic factors (EU reducing costs of self-government), and symbolic factors (EU causes less identification with the state) (Dardanelli 2005b: 8–9). With respect to Central and Eastern European Countries (CEECs), Baun and Marek (2006: 410) argue that, in the long term, the impact of the EU is expected to be much greater as the newly established regional structures trigger self awareness (e.g. elected councils, political parties' positions become pro-regionalization) and assertiveness of regions because the regionalization has changed the constellation of political forces and has altered the preferences of political actors.

A related question is whether regional actors make strategic use of the EU in order to reach certain goals. One of the factors explaining a positive outcome to the Scottish devolution referendum in 1997 (as opposed to 1979) is the European dimension (Dardanelli 2005a).While in 1979 elites failed to frame self-government in a European context, hence making the public fear independence, in 1997 the political elites exploited the European dimension, raising support for independence (Dardanelli 2005b: 20, 2009): the 'Yes' camp succeeded in framing the devolution positively in the broader European framework in 1997. In other words, political parties can exploit the European dimension to pursue strategic goals in competition between parties: the Scottish National Party (SNP) and Labour used the EU to play down the fear, triggered by the Conservatives, for independence. Likewise, Murphy (2007: 310) concludes on Northern Ireland that: 'the impact of the EU has not been emphatic, rather subtle and discrete in both nature and extent'. New sub-national institutions have been influenced, actors explicitly consider the EU dimension, and some adaptation takes place on the part of parties and interest groups. Beyers and Bursens (2011) discuss the changing preferences of political parties in the Belgian case. They argue that the existing heterogeneity between regions means that regions are affected differently by European economic integration. To offer an answer to this heterogeneity, regional political elites are to some extent reliant on federal policy. However, if achieving a federal consensus on measures to make regions more competitive or dealing with specific regional social needs becomes more difficult, regional political elites become increasingly motivated to conduct policies themselves, to strive for more autonomy and pursue their own economic and social policies, according to what the median voters in their region prefer.

Concluding, EU regional policies and the establishment of all sorts of cooperation mechanisms (INTERREG programmes—EU funded cooperation schemes between regions of neighbouring countries, networks of regions and cities) have triggered learning processes among SNAs. It changed the way regions 'are doing things' (Goldsmith 2003: 129). Bache and Conzelmann (2008: 136) found '[. . .] the emergence of more partnership-oriented, inter agency work at and between several territorial levels, and the incorporation into domestic governance of practices first developed in EU programmes'. However, the impact is rather varying: learning seems to be evolving from 'strategic' and 'rational' to 'deep' in old member states, while it remains more 'strategic' in CEECs (Bache 2008: 82); effects regarding horizontal relations at the sub-national level are more frequent in old and federal member states than in CEECs and statist political systems (Bache 2008: 83). The variation is attributed to a range of intervening variables which affect the learning: some are typical for the policy area (the amount of funding money at stake, the practices of planning and evaluation), others are related to a number of domestic institutional features: the level of formal institutional development, the cohesiveness of policy networks and the prominence of political entrepreneurship. In short, EU impact on SNA politics is limited to a framing effect (no deep impact) and differs largely because of the varying domestic institutional features.

Europeanization of SNA Polities: EU Impact on Territorial Reorganization

Europeanization of the polity points to adaptations in the core of the constitutional set-up of member states. With respect to SNAs, it deals with the creation of regional entities or regional arrangements, shifts in the interregional balance of competences, and shifts in power balance between the central and regional level. Most literature on the Europeanization of SNAs deals with the polity dimension, discussing several aspects.

The research on the Europeanization of SNAs took off around the mid nineties, after the EU had responded to regional realities in the Maastricht Treaty (for instance through the establishment of the Committee of the Regions). It was also the time when EU regional policies were being fully implemented. Two strands of literature turned their attention to the relationship between the EU and the regional level in the member states.

It was, first of all, in this sphere that Marks, Hooghe and Blank developed their model of multi-level governance (Marks et al. 1996). They argued that European integration weakened the national level because central governments were, to a varying extent, challenged in their monopolistic relations with the EU (Hooghe 1996). Smyrl (1997) came to similar conclusions finding variation in the political impact of EU regional policy on the powers of regions, reflecting the political and administrative differences in the member states. More concretely, Smyrl found that empowerment of regions was conditional on timely policy entrepreneurship of regional elites and on the pre-existence of a regional policy community concerned with regional development.

During the late nineties, a parallel literature on regionalism developed. Authors such as Jeffery, Jones, and Keating, primarily interested in the growing relevance of the regional level, were forced to take the EU level on board (Jones and Keating 1995; Jeffery 1996, 1997; Tömmel 1997; Keating 1998). Taking stock of this literature, Jeffery's (2000) expectations for regional empowerment were rather high. Based on a comparison between German, British, and Spanish regions, he concludes that regions, although to a diverging degree, have undermined the central government monopoly over European integration policy. He rather optimistically forecasts that they will gain ever relatively stronger positions against central government in the years to come. Not all authors believed in such a bright future for the regional level, however. Bache (1998) concludes that regional policy does not lead to empowerment of SNAs but rather expects that the central government remains in charge as a flexible gate-keeper. He explicitly downplays the multi-level governance literature expectations (see above all Hooghe 1996) and speaks of multi-level participation, minimizing the real influence of SNAs. Likewise, Goetz (1995) argues that Europeanization does not alter the structure of German federalism, but only the balance of power between the Bund and the Länder.

Later empirical research within the Europeanization literature seems to confirm the broad lines of the more optimistic expectations, but not without adding a whole series of nuances. The following paragraphs deal with these findings. As the literature reveals a different impact of the EU on old member states and on those that joined the EU in 2004/2007, these two groups are discussed separately.

Old Member States: Domestically Driven and Divergent Territorial Change

As Europeanization of the polity refers to the question whether the EU triggers changes in the territorial arrangements of its member states, the first states to look at are obviously the ones with a federal set-up (Belgium, Germany, Austria) and those on the way to decentralization and devolution (Spain, UK). The main question brought forward in the literature is whether European integration increases or decreases the autonomy of the regional level. The starting point is that regions in federal and strongly decentralized states lost power and policy discretion because some, or even many, of their competences are transferred to the common European level. Confronted with this evolution, regions have sought ways to compensate for this loss. Those regions who already enjoyed a strong position (German and Austrian Länder, Belgian Regions and Communities, and Spanish Autonomous Communities) were especially able to restore the balance. Most of these compensations can be situated within the politics sphere, such as opening lobbying bureaus in Brussels, forging transnational alliances and trying to influence domestic European policy-making. Constitutional changes were very scarce: examples are minor constitutional changes in Germany (e.g. Article 23 of the Basic Law) (Jeffery 2003; Sturm and Dieringer 2005) and the drafting of a Cooperation Agreement with quasi constitutional status in Belgium (Beyers and Bursens 2006). With respect to the UK, Bache reports nuanced conclusions with respect to the impact of the EU on the devolution process (Bache 2008: 152). Likewise for Spain: Bache and Jones (2000) mention the establishment of formal procedures for regional participation in the EU policy process, but with limited implications for the level of autonomy, mainly because of diverging interests among regions. In short, the literature on federal and decentralized states does not find any hollowing out of the central level on account of European integration, but rather some sort of transformation of state sovereignty. The pre-existing balance of power between the centre and the regions is a crucial explanation for the variation in regional empowerment (Börzel 1999; Dobre 2005; Bache and Jones 2000: 19).

Assessments of the regional adaptation in centralized states are more scarce, but the findings go in the same direction: different outcomes of regionalization reforms can be attributed to the different domestic institutions and interests. In some states there was no impact at all. Magone (2001) examines the Portuguese case and even speaks of resistance: there was no territorial change, because politicians did not see the necessity and public support was absent. Kettunen and Kungla look at Estonia and Finland and conclude that EU influence is filtered by the existing regional policy legacy, the number of veto-points and the interest constellation at the national level (Kettunen and Kungla 2005: 358–9) (see also Héritier et al. 2001). In Estonia, they find weak Europeanization of sub-national structures, more a centralization than a decentralization to meet the EU requirements of management of the structural funds. Kettunen and Kungla explain this by the absence of wide domestic support for regionalization to overcome the institutional veto-points. The Finnish adaptation to European requirements was more in favour of the regions, attributed to earlier evolutions towards empowering regions, but the central government kept a central position. In short, the EU does not seem to be able to change existing power constellations in unitary states.

CEECs: Accession Triggers Differential Territorial Adaptation

There is a surprisingly large body of literature covering the Europeanization of CEECs both pre- and post-accession. Many of these studies also tackle the regional dimension. Quite often, the starting point is the assumption that the Commission has an interest to foster territorial reorganization, along NUTS lines, as empowerment of regions is a way to by-pass the member state level (Sturm and Dieringer 2005: 281). Although some scholars dispute that the Commission actively sought to disempower the member state level in this way, it cannot be denied that the new member states restructured their territorial organization in the years before accession took place. Several authors point out that EU pre-accession programmes triggered new institutions for territorial development (Bruszt 2008: 609). Discussing the Hungarian case, Palné Kovacs argues that, in preparing for EU accession and above all for the management of structural funds, the EU has triggered formal and systemic changes (Palné Kovacs *et al.* 2004). Also Brusis (2002) considers the EU a catalyst for territorial reform (what he calls a process of re-regionalization) in CEECs. Czernielewska *et al.* (2004: 492) write that '[i]t is clear that institutional reforms and extensive administrative restructuring have been strongly influenced by considerations related to the need for compliance with the EU'.

Most authors discussing CEECs consider conditionality as the prime driver of Europeanization. The argument is quite straightforward: the EU sets conditions for accession which applicant states have to comply with. Responding to this conditionality, CEECs have incorporated the *acquis communautaire* in their national legal order and have set up institutions to guarantee full implementation of EU policies. However, regional policy is crucially different from single market or environmental legislation. It is a thin area of conditionality as there is no standard model of regionalization. In addition, the Commission evolved from a more normative concern to introduce territorial reform in CEECs that would foster democracy towards a more functionalist and technocratic concern of sound management of structural funds, the latter often implying that a centralized approach would be better in terms of available capacity (Hughes *et al.* 2004a: 167–8). In other words, because of power asymmetry, the CEECs had to react to the conditionality, but the conditionality itself was rather weak leaving room for domestic settings to intervene and eventually resulting in divergent outcomes.

Hughes *et al.* (2004a: 169) summarizes this process as follows:

The outcome of the interactions over these policy areas appears to have been more strongly affected by path-dependent factors in the domestic political settings in the CEECs than the explicit/formal or implicit/informal conditionality emanating from the Commission.

Several domestic intervening variables pop up from the literature. First, many authors point to the importance of historical legacies. Czernielewska *et al.* (2004: 492) argue that a culture of distrust, a lack of social capital and cooperative culture, political clientelism, and low levels of institutional performance shaped the regionalization process in CEECs. Ferry and McMaster (2005: 32) ascribe the different impact in Poland and Czech Republic in setting up arrangements for administering structural funds to different domestic regional policy traditions and institutional arrangements, in particular the pre-existing balance of centre–region relationships. Likewise, Brusis (2002) points out that the outcomes of regional reform in CEECs can be explained by domestic institutional legacies, policy approaches of involved actors, and the influence of ethnic/historical regionalism. Also Camyar (2010) mentions the different reformist legacies in CEECs as a crucial intervening variable for CEEC administrative reforms, including territorial reorganization.

Next to historical legacies, the political constellation at the time of accession also intervenes in the enactment and implementation of regional reform. Several authors point to the crucial role of domestic party politics (Brusis 2006; O'Dwyer 2006; Ferry and McMaster 2005). Studying the Czech Republic, Poland, and Slovakia, O'Dwyer claims that the EU opened up 'a critical juncture for reform [. . .] a useful pretext for reforms that allowed domestic political forces, in particular governing party coalitions, to shape regional institutions in their own interests' (O'Dwyer 2006: 222).

In the end, divergent domestic contexts intervene in the Europeanization process and trigger differential outcomes. Poland and the Czech Republic witnessed a democratized and decentralized variant of regional self-government, including elected regional councils (Hughes *et al.* 2004a: 169; Baun and Marek 2006), to the cost of bureaucratic expansion favouring political parties in the coalition in Poland, and without negative effects because of stable and strong coalition in the Czech Republic (O' Dwyer 2006: 222). Decentralization was much more modest in Slovakia (Hughes *et al.* 2004a; O'Dwyer 2006; Czernielewska *et al.* 2004). Regionalization in Hungary, the Baltic States, and Slovenia was little more than an administrative-statistical operation with unelected regional authorities and centralized management (Hughes *et al.* 2004a: 169). With respect to Lithuania, Maniokas (2008: 122) even argues that, in preparation for the management of the structural funds, a centralized mechanism at central government level was created, reducing the likelihood of involving regional actors and the creation of a new viable regional layer of government.

In short, nearly all CEECs created new or reactivated existing regional authorities (Bruszt 2008: 609) but the EU must rather be considered a catalyst for these reforms ('an additional rationale', (Brusis 2002)) instead of the prime driver. Territorial reform in CEECs has not been determined by demands of European integration but rather by different domestic politics and capacities and historical legacies (Keating and Hughes 2003: Goldsmith 2003). 'On balance, domestic institutional choices made during the early transition period outweigh and actually constrain the importance of external factors during enlargement' (Hughes *et al.* 2004a: 8). In terms of outcomes, regions with existing institutional and financial resources have become stronger partners while weaker regions have become more marginal (Ferry and McMaster 2005: 35). As the reforms in CEECs are quite young, one could wonder about the long term effects. The answer to this question is related to the evaluation of the depth of the reforms. Some argue that the EU has only triggered formal changes in terms of institution building, but that institutional thickness prevents profound changes (Palné Kovacs *et al.* 2004, discussing the Hungarian case). Also Sturm and Dieringer (2005: 290) see no core impact, but only formal change (establishment of regional institutions), more symbolic, not resulting in real regional power (perhaps with the exception of Poland). Baun and Marek (2006: 410), on the contrary, expect that in the long term the impact will be much greater as the new structures trigger self awareness (e.g. elected councils, political parties' positions become pro-regionalization) and assertiveness of regions, because regionalization has changed the constellation of political forces and has altered the preferences of political actors.

Modest and Differential Impact

The most important conclusion covering all dimensions of Europeanization is the limited and differential impact of European integration. Regardless of the theoretical approach used, all empirical findings so far point in the direction of robust national territorial arrangements and continuous divergence between the member states.

With respect to the Europeanization of *policies*, the literature comes to the rather trivial conclusion of varying involvement of SNAs in the implementation process: the more legislative and executive competencies a region has, the more EU legislation is transposed by the regional level. In addition, the scarce literature specifically dealing with the regional level confirms the main conclusions of the general compliance literature: SNAs comply with EU legislation in varying degrees with the differences largely attributable to the varying domestic contexts. Moreover, explaining the different national implementation records, many authors explicitly point to SNAs acting as veto-players which delay or hamper smooth transposition.

Regarding the Europeanization of the politics and polity dimensions, two opposite lines of argumentation are put forward (Bourne 2003; Carter and Pasquier 2010). The decentralization or empowerment narrative argues that European integration has created opportunities for the regional level to the detriment of the central national level. Multi-level governance will grow and regions will be empowered because supranational actors and regions build alliances to the detriment of central governments, because the introduction of governance concepts by the European Commission fosters the role of regions and because of the introduction of legal tools such as partnerships. The centralization narrative, on the contrary, claims that European integration entails a transfer of previously regional policies to the European level, downgrading regions to become implementing actors of EU policies and reducing their policy autonomy as they are hardly compensated by access to EU policymaking or to domestic EU policy formulation. This disempowerment is caused by the institutional bias of the EU, preferring member states above regions. It is correct that competences of both levels are transferred to the EU, but the central level remains in power through its position in the Council and even gains power over regional competences.

Both hypotheses have been tested extensively in the literature. With respect to various aspects of the *politics* dimension, the EU seems to have a clear differential impact. Comparative analyses of national EU policy coordination mechanisms reveal an increased involvement of SNAs, with especially strong regions having been able to conquer an influential role in domestic EU policy formulation. In terms of EU impact on the internal relations between domestic policymaking actors, both a vertical and a horizontal effect can be discerned: both SNAs and private actors have become more involved in domestic politics. Many authors point out, however, that more involvement or participation does not necessarily mean increased impact or enhanced influence, the latter being only the case for regions that already had a strong position in the domestic constellation. A last aspect of the politics dimension points to the cognitive learning process of SNAs: the literature describes several examples of regions and regional actors changing their preferences (cf. Belgium) or using the EU in a strategic way (cf. the UK).

The most obvious way to test the empowerment thesis is looking at the *polity* effects of the EU. A distinction should be made here between states already members of the EU before 2004 and those that joined the EU since 2004. Territorial changes in 'old' member states were found to be rather rare, especially in the more centralized states. In federal and devolved member states, SNAs often tried to restore the territorial balance that had been disturbed by the transfer of competencies to the European level. However, these adaptations hardly ever altered the core features of the constitutional setting and were, in all cases, in line with the already existing territorial organization. The impact of the EU on the CEECs was somewhat more profound. Driven by the mechanism of conditionality, CEECs often upgraded or even created regional authorities in order to become eligible for EU funding programmes. Similar to the older members, the changes in the new member states were also shaped by the different historical legacies, hence resulting in diverging territorial settings.

Bache and Conzelmann summarize it quite nicely when they conclude that the impact of the EU should not be overstated, '[. . .] central government has been instrumental in shaping developments rather than simply succumbing to adaptational pressure' (2008: 136). True, territorial reform and regionalization took place, but the EU's role was generally qualified as secondary to sticky domestic dynamics (Hughes *et al.* 2004b). Hence, 'The homogenization or harmonization of domestic practices across Europe is not a realistic expectation' (Bache and Marshall (2004: 2)). Amidst all this variation, one more general conclusion stands out: supporting the claim that the EU is some kind of catalyst, all empirical findings conclude that already strong regions seem to be even further empowered by the European context they operate in. Clearly, European integration has not had a deep impact on territorial restructuring in the member states. As Goldsmith rightly points out, 'territorial restructuring is only partially triggered by European integration' (2003: 118–20). There are indeed all kinds of policies directed from the European level to the sub-national level. But sub-national government has also been confronted with two other challenges. From below, there is a process of regionalism with regions seeking autonomy, mainly in federal states. From the central level, there is a process, mainly in centralized states, of granting regional and local authorities more responsibility in certain policy areas.

Conclusion: Assessing Past and Future Research Avenues

As Dardanelli (2005b) points out in his literature review, all empirical findings reveal some kind of impact of European integration on the regional level, but there is no agreement on the intensity or the direction of the impact. So far, the variation in domestic contexts was identified as an empirical explanation for the differential outcome. However, the diverging conclusions on empowerment of the regional level can also be attributed to the diverging research designs. The literature reviewed in this chapter indeed uses different theoretical approaches, dependent and independent variables.

An interesting conclusion in this respect is that those authors using the argumentation of socialization and learning see more influence from the European level than those arguing along rational choice lines. Consider the following two examples. Pasquier (2005: 296) defends the existence of a process of cognitive Europeanization, i.e. a process in which 'knowledge about policies, administrative arrangements, institutions etc. in one time and/or place is used in the development of policies, administrative arrangements, institutions in another time and/or place'. He argues that regional actors become socialized in a European model of regional development and adapt new 'ways of doing things' at the regional level, in accordance to their regional goals. Basically applying Radaelli's argument about Europeanization as socialization, Pasquier claims that regions 'Europeanize without EU legislation', hence they go through a learning process that eventually produces structural changes in the territorial governance of the EU member states. The result is considerable impact of the EU: the creation of similar policy levels despite a very different tradition of territorial organization in different member states. Sedelmeier, on the other hand, uses rational choice argumentation to interpret his more modest conclusions. 'The lack of impact of the EU fits well with the expectations of rationalist institutionalism. The acquis does not prescribe decentralisation and the devolution of powers to the regional level, but merely the establishment of statistical units for the purpose of administrating the allocation of structural funds' (2006: 16). In other words, regional actors shape regional policy within the margins of European requirements but following the domestic institutional context.

Dissatisfied with such contradictory findings, Bourne (2003: 603–7) uses an analytical framework that combines rational choice elements with sociological elements, hence including interests, ideas, and institutions in one model. Although this is a promising avenue, the application of the model to five dimensions of the Basque Autonomous Community still delivers ambiguous results (both disempowerment and no effect). Such findings lead Bache (2008: 162–3) to argue that there is evidence of both redistribution of power resources and learning, hence indicating that both rational and sociological paradigms must be combined in a clever way to get a full grasp of the Europeanization process.

A second reason why empirical findings seem to be contradictory is the variation in the dependent variable. Murphy (2007: 295) presents quite a long list of how the dependent variable (adaptation) is conceptualized when examining the Europeanization of SNAs: political structures and political institutions (changes in parliament, executive, public administration), policymaking processes (changes in the behaviour of policymaking actors, policy styles, instruments and resources), changes in intergovernmental relations, adaptations by political parties and interest groups, cultural developments (changes in discourse, evolving norms and values, attitudes to identity). Clearly some refinement is needed on the side of the dependent variable if we want to compare the results of the numerous studies conducted so far. This chapter tried to do so by reorganizing the existing literature into the traditional distinction between policies, politics, and polities. However, if the future research agenda on the Europeanization of SNAs wants to deliver comparable results, far more agreement is needed on the conceptualization of the dependent variable(s).

Third, as the literature seems to agree that the domestic context can be considered as an important intermediating variable, filtering the impact of European integration on SNAs, an exhaustive inventory and categorization of these variables would be more than welcome. Sturm and Dieringer (2005: 281) present perhaps the most complete list so far: the power of existing institutions, the cultural identity, strength of national veto-players, the degree of political mobilization for or against certain issues or organizational innovations, and the degree to which institutional and social change in the national context is path-dependent. The overview presented in this chapter, however, makes clear that many other authors use many other variables, hampering the development of a cumulative research agenda on the Europeanization of SNAs.

By way of conclusion, Pitschel and Bauer (2009: 328) rightly claim that, so far, 'little accumulation of knowledge seems to have taken place'. A more encompassing use of approaches and variables is a prerequisite for this. The research agenda on SNAs does not have to reinvent all this, as there already exist similar codifications in the broader Europeanization research (see Chapter 2, this volume).

 FURTHER READING

Literature discussing the Europeanization of SNAs is embedded in the general framework of the Europeanization research agenda. Chapter 2 of this volume as well as Featherstone and Radaelli (2003) and Graziano and Vink (2006) provide excellent overviews of the Europeanization framework. Keating (2008a and b) presents a historical overview of the regional dimension in the European Union. The *Regional and Federal Studies* special issue (2008 18/2–3), edited by Marks *et al.* contains abundant empirical material on regional authorities, both within and outside the EU. A well elaborated application of the Europeanization framework on the regional dimension is provided by Bache (2008). Examples of case studies include Beyers and Bursens (2006) on Belgium, Dardanelli (2005b) on the UK, and Hughes *et al.* (2004a) on CEECs.

WEB LINKS

The Marks *et al.* dataset on Regional Authority is accessible through the personal pages of Gary Marks (**http://www.unc.edu/~gwmarks/data_ra.php**). Data on European Regions is also available on the website of the EU (**http://europa.eu**), see especially the NUTS classification **http://epp.eurostat.ec.europa.eu/portal/page/portal/nuts_ nomenclature/introduction** and the pages on regional policy (**http://ec.europa.eu/ regional_policy/index_en.htm/**). By far the most scholarly articles on SNAs and the EU have been published in Regional and Federal Studies (**http://www.tandf.co.uk/ journals/titles/13597566.asp**).

REFERENCES

Bache, I. (1998), *The Politics of European Union Regional Policy: Multi-Level Govern-ance or Flexible Gatekeeping?*, Sheffield: Sheffield Academic Press.

Bache, I. (2008), *Europeanization and Multilevel Governance*, Lanham, MD: Rowman and Littlefield.

Bache, I. and Conzelmann, T. (2008), 'EU Structural Funds and Domestic Governance and Policy in Britain', in T. Conzelmann and R. Smith (eds), *Multi-level Governance in the European Union: Taking Stock and Looking Ahead*, Baden Baden: Nomos, 124–41.

Bache, I. and Jones, R. (2000), 'Has EU Regional Policy Empowered the Regions? A Study of Spain and the United Kingdom', *Regional and Federal Studies*, 10/3: 1–20.

Bache, I. and Marshall, A. (2004), 'Europeanization and Domestic Change: A Govern-ance Approach to Institutional Adaptation in Britain', *Queen's Papers on Europeaniza-tion*, No 5, Belfast: Queen's University.

Baun, M. and Marek, D. (2006), 'Regional Policy and Decentralization in the Czech Republic', *Regional and Federal Studies*, 16/4: 409–28.

Beyers, J. and Bursens, P. (2006), 'The European Rescue of the Federal State. How Europeanization Shapes the Belgian State', *West European Politics*, 29/5: 1057–78.

Beyers, J. and Bursens, P. (2011), 'Towards a Multilevel Welfare State? On the Relative Autonomy of Regional Social Policy', in B. Cantillon, P. Popelier, and N. Mussche (eds), *The Multilevel Welfare State*, Antwerpen: Intersentia, 45–66.

Borghetto, E. and Franchino, F. (2010), 'The Role of Subnational Authorities in the Im-plementation of EU Directives', *Journal of European Public Policy*, 17/6: 759–80.

Börzel, T. (1999), 'Towards Convergence in Europe? Institutional Adaptation to Europe-anization in Germany and Spain', *Journal of Common Market Studies*, 37/4: 573–96.

Bourne, A. K. (2003), 'The Impact of European Integration on Regional Power', *Journal of Common Market Studies*, 41/4: 597–620.

Brusis, M. (2002), 'Between EU Requirements, Competitive Politics and National Traditions: Re-creating Regions in the Accession Countries of Central and Eastern Europe', *Governance*, 15/4: 531–59.

Brusis, M. (2006), 'The Instrumental Use of European Union Conditionality: Regionalization in the Czech republic and Slovakia', *Eastern European Politics and Societies* 19/2: 291–316.

Bruszt, L. (2008), 'Multi-level Governance – the Eastern Versions: Emerging Patterns of Regional Developmental Governance in the New Member States', *Regional and Federal Studies*, 18/5: 607–27.

Bulmer, S. and Lequesne, C. (eds) (2005), *The Member States of the European Union*, Oxford: Oxford University Press.

Bulmer, S., Burch, M., Hogwood, P., and Scott, A. (2006), 'UK Devolution and the European Union: A Tale of Cooperative Asymmetry?', *Publius: The Journal of Federalism*, 36/1: 75–93.

Bursens, P. (2006), 'State Structures', in. P. Graziano and M. Vink, (eds), *Europeanization: New Research Agendas*, Basingstoke: Palgrave Macmillan, 115–27.

Camyar, I. (2010), 'Europeanization, Domestic Legacies and Administrative Reforms in Central and Eastern Europe: A Comparative Analysis of Hungary and the Czech Republic', *Regional and Federal Studies*, 32/2: 137–55.

Carter, C. and Pasquier, R. (2010), 'The Europeanization of Regions as "Spaces for Politics": A Research Agenda', *Regional and Federal Studies*, 20/3: 295–314.

Closa, C. and Heywood, P. (2004), *Spain and the European Union*, London: Palgrave Macmillan.

Czernielewska, M., Paraskevopoulos, C., and Szlachta, J. (2004), 'The Regionalization Process in Poland: An Example of "Shallow" Europeanization', *Regional and Federal Studies*, 14/3: 461–95.

Dardanelli, P. (2005a), 'Democratic Deficit or the Europeanisation of Secession: Explaining the Devolution Referendums in Scotland', *Political Studies*, 53: 320–42.

Dardanelli, P. (2005b), *Between two Unions. Europeanisation and Scottish Devolution*, Manchester: Manchester University Press.

Dardanelli, P. (2009), 'Europeanization as Heresthetics', *Party Politics*, 15/1: 49–68.

Dobre, A. M. (2005), 'Europeanisation and Domestic Territorial Change: The Spanish and Romanian Cases of Territorial Adaptation in the Context of EU Enlargement', *Journal of Southern European and the Balkans*, 7/3: 351–66.

Dyson, K. and Goetz, K. H. (2003) (eds), *Germany, Europe and the Politics of Constraint*, Oxford: Oxford University Press.

Falkner, G., Treib, O., Hartlapp, M., and Leiber, S. (2005), *Complying with Europe. EU Harmonisation and Soft Law in the Member States*, Cambridge: Cambridge University Press.

Fargion, V., Morlino, L., and Profeti, S. (2006), 'Europeanisation and Territorial Representation in Italy', *West European Politics*, 29/4: 757–83.

Featherstone, K. and Radaelli, C. (eds) (2003), *The Politics of Europeanization*, Oxford: Oxford University Press.

Ferry, M. and McMaster, I. (2005), 'Implementing Structural Funds in Polish and Czech Regions: Convergence, Variation, Empowerment?', *Regional and Federal Studies*, 15/1: 19–39.

Giddings, P. and Drewry, G. (eds) (2004), *Britain in the European Union*, London: Palgrave Macmillan.

Goetz, K. H. (1995), 'National Governance and European Integration: Intergovernmental Relations in Germany', *Journal of Common Market Studies*, 33/1: 91–116.

Goldsmith, M. (2003), 'Variable Geometry, Multilevel Governance: European Integration and Subnational Government in the New Millennium', in K. Featherstone, and C. Radaelli (eds), *The Politics of Europeanization*, Oxford: Oxford University Press, 112–33.

Graziano, P. and Vink, M. (eds) (2006), *Europeanization: New Research Agendas*, Basingstoke: Palgrave Macmillan.

Héritier, A., Kerwer, D., Knill, C., Lehmkuhl, D., and Teutsch, M. (2001), *Differential Europe: New Opportunities and Restrictions for Policy-Making in Member States*, Berlin: De Gruyter.

Hooghe, L. (ed.) (1996), *Cohesion Policy and European Integration: Building Multi-Level Governance*, Oxford: Oxford University Press.

Hughes, J., Sasse, G., and Gordon, C. (2004a), *Europeanization and Regionalization in the EU's Enlargement to Central and Eastern Europe*, London: Palgrave Macmillan.

Hughes, J, Sasse, G., and Gordon, C. (2004b), 'Conditionality and compliance in the EU's Eastward Enlargement: Regional Policy and the Reform of Sub-National Government' *Journal of Common Market Studies*, 42/3: 523–51.

Jeffery, C. (1996), 'Towards a "Third Level" in Europe? The German Länder in the European Union', *Political Studies*, 44: 253–66.

Jeffery, C. (ed.) (1997), *The Regional Dimension of the EU*, London: Cass.

Jeffery, C. (2000), 'Sub-National Mobilization and European Integration', *Journal of Common Market Studies*, 38/1: 1–24.

Jeffery, C. (2003), 'The German Länder: From Milieu-Shaping to Territorial Politics', in K. Dyson and K.H. Goetz (eds), *Germany, Europe and the Politics of Constraint*, Oxford: Oxford University Press, 97–108.

Jones, B. and Keating, M. (eds) (1995), *The European Union and the Regions*, Oxford: Clarendon Press.

Kassim, H., Peters, B. G., and Wright, V. (eds) (2000), *The National Co-ordination of EU Policy. The Domestic Level*, Oxford: Oxford University Press.

Kassim, H. (2005), 'The Europeanisation of Member States Institutions', in S. Bulmer and C. Lequesne (eds), *The Member States of the European Union*, Oxford: Oxford University Press, 285–317.

Keating, M. (1998), *The New Regionalism in Western Europe: Territorial Restructuring and Political Change*, Cheltenham: Elgar.

Keating, M. (2008a), 'Thirty Years of Territorial Politics', *West European Politics*, 31/1-2: 60–81.

Keating, M. (2008b), 'A Quarter Century of the Europe of the Regions', *Regional and Federal Studies*, 18/5: 629–35.

Keating, M. and Hughes, J. (2003) (eds), *The Regional Challenge in Central and Eastern Europe. Territorial Restructuring and European Integration*, Brussels: PIE - Peter Lang.

Kettunen, P. and Kungla, T. (2005), 'Europeanization of Sub-national Governance in Unitary States: Estonia and Finland', *Regional and Federal Studies*, 15/3: 353–78.

Magone, J. (2001), 'The Transformation of the Portuguese Political System: European Regional Policy and Democratization in a Small EU Member State', in K. Featherstone and G. Kazamias (eds), *Europeanization and the Southern Periphery*, London: Frank Cass, 119–140.

Maniokas, K. (2008), 'Preparation of Structural Funds and Europeanization', in. T. Conzelmann and R. Smith (eds), *Multi-level Governance in the European Union*, Baden Baden: Nomos, 114–23.

Marks, G., Hooghe, L., and Blank, K. (1996), 'European Integration from the 1980's: State-centric versus Multi-level Governance' *Journal of Common Market Studies* 34/3: 341–78.

Marks, G., Hooghe, L., and Schakel, A. (2008), 'Measuring Regional Authority', *Regional and Federal Studies*, 18/2–3: 111–21.

Murphy, M. C. (2007), 'Europeanization and the Sub-National Level: Changing Patterns of Governance in Northern Ireland', *Regional and Federal Studies*, 17/3: 293–315.

O'Dwyer, C. (2006), 'Reforming Regional Governance in East Central Europe: Europeanization or Domestic Politics as Usual?', *Eastern European Politics and Societies*, 20/2: 219–53.

Palné Kovács, I., Paraskevopoulos, C. J., and Horvath, G. (2004), 'Institutional Legacies and the Shaping of Regional Governance in Hungary', *Regional and Federal Studies*, 14/3: 430–60.

Pasquier, R. (2005), 'Cognitive Europeanization and the Territorial Effects of Multi-Level Policy Transfer: Local Development in French and Spanish Regions', *Regional and Federal Studies*, 15/3: 295–310.

Pitschel, D. and Bauer, M. (2009), 'Subnational Governance Approaches on the Rise – reviewing a decade of Eastern European Regionalization Research', *Regional and Federal Studies*, 19/3: 327–47.

Scherpereel, J. A. (2010), 'EU Cohesion Policy and the Europeanization of Central and East European Regions', *Regional and Federal Studies*, 20/1: 45–62.

Sedelmeier, U. (2006), 'Europeanisation in New Member and Candidate States', Living Reviews in European Governance 1/3: http://www.livingreviews.org.lreg-2006-3.

Smyrl, M. E. (1997), 'Does European Community Regional Policy Empower the Regions?', *Governance*, 10/3: 287–310

Sturm, R. and Dieringer, J. (2005), 'The Europeanization of Regions in Eastern and Western Europe: Theoretical Perspectives', *Regional and Federal Studies*, 15/3: 279–94.

Sverdrup, U. (2007), 'Policies', in P. Graziano and M. Vink (eds), *Europeanization: New Research Agendas*, Basingstoke: Palgrave Macmillan, 197–211.

Thielemann, E. R. (2002), 'The Prize of Europeanization: Why European Regional Policies Are a Mixed Blessing', *Regional and Federal Studies*, 12/1: 43–56.

Tömmel, I. (1997), 'The EU and the Regions: Towards a Three-tier System or New Modes of Regulation', *Environment and Planning C: Government and Policy*, 15/4: 413–36.

Treib, O. (2008), 'Implementing and Complying with EU Governance Outputs', *Living Reviews in European Governance 3/5:* http://www.livingreviews.org/lreg-2008-5.

Wessels, W., Maurer, A., and Mittag, J. (eds) (2003), *Fifteen into One? The European Union and its Member States*, Manchester, Manchester University Press.

Zeff, E. E. and Pirro, E. B. (eds) (2006), *The European Union and the Member States*, Boulder: Lynne Rienner.

CHAPTER 17

The Europeanization of National Economies?

Vivien A. Schmidt

▋ Summary

With the ever-quickening pace of European monetary and market integration, epito-
mized by the completion of the Single Market project in 1992 and the inception of the
Single Currency in 1999, the European Union has sought to build a single European
economy out of the diverse national economies of its member states. The main questions addressed in this chapter are: How successful has the EU been in promoting this
goal? How much convergence has occurred among EU member states, and how much
divergence remains? What impact has the economic crisis beginning in 2008 had on
the EU and its member states?

This chapter answers these questions by examining the development of Europe's
national economies from the post-war period until today. The chapter begins with a
discussion of the impact of globalization and Europeanization on post-war varieties of
capitalism and then considers the changes from the 1970s up to and including the economic crisis in the three West European capitalisms plus the new East European capitalism. The chapter concludes by speculating on future patterns of political economic
development in the European Union in light of the crisis.

Introduction

Before the economic crisis as much as subsequently, globalization has attracted the headlines as the primary cause of the major economic changes in advanced industrialized countries. It has often been characterized as a juggernaut sweeping away national differences, with the competitive pressures resulting from the internationalization of the financial markets and trade ensuring the replacement of national varieties of capitalism with a one-size-fits-all neoliberal version; with the rise of supranational trade organizations and treaties undermining national sovereignty by reducing government autonomy in decision making and control over economic activities in the national territory; and with the circulation of neoliberal ideas pushing out contrary views and eliminating differences between governments of the Right and Left.

But if all this were true for globalization, then it would have to be doubly true for Europeanization. This is because European integration, as a regional variant of globalization, has gone much further in terms of the Europeanization of financial markets and trade, of the Europeanization of decision making, and of the circulation of neoliberal ideas than anything linked to globalization. But Europeanization has not been subject to the same polemics or confrontations as globalization—we do not find the same numbers of demonstrators at the European Council meetings that we find in Seattle, Genoa, or Copenhagen, nor of pamphlets and books on the evils of Europeanization to match those on globalization. Why? Because Europeanization has brought significant economic enhancement along with competition, with the Single Market and the Single Currency providing greater economic stability and growth than might have been the case if European countries had been subject to globalization alone. Moreover, in exchange for the loss of governmental autonomy and control, European member states have gained a kind of shared supranational authority and joint control that goes way beyond anything experienced by countries that are part of only global or other regional trade associations. Finally, as a set of ideas, Europeanization offers different rationales for change from those for globalization, serving as a positive reference in the national discourse to legitimize reform as well as an empowering force for national actors seeking such reform—although it has also served national politicians as a blame-shifting device for unpopular reforms, and social movements as an increasing focus of concern.

As a regional variant of globalization, the experience of the EU can tell us much about the potential challenges for advanced industrialized democracies worldwide if and when global and other regional institutions reach the level of maturity of EU ones. For Europe itself, it already tells us that whatever the pressures for convergence, countries will remain highly differentiated. In consequence of common EU policies and an integrating European economy, as this chapter argues, national government policies—although more similar as a result of monetary convergence, financial market liberalization, business deregulation, labour market decentralization, and welfare state rationalization—are not the same. National business practices, although more competitive in inter-firm relations and more dependent upon the financial markets for capital, continue to differ. And national labour relations, although more flexible and decentralized, remain highly differentiated.

This chapter will show that national political economies, despite all moving toward greater market orientation, continue to be distinguishable into not just one neoliberal version of capitalism, as much of the globalization literature has assumed (for example Ohmae 1990), nor towards two varieties, as firm-centred approaches to capitalism suggest (Hall and Soskice 2001a), but at least three varieties of capitalism in Western Europe, differentiable along lines of development from the original post-war models (Schmidt 2002; Coates 2000), plus arguably a fourth variety for Central and Eastern Europe. Liberal market economies such as Britain, and Ireland to a lesser extent, with post-war market-driven inter-firm relations and market-reliant management–labour relations assured by a 'liberal' state, have gone even further in this direction. The economic crisis hit these countries very hard, largely as a result of the ever-greater role for the financial markets and the credit-fuelled growth that produced their massive housing bubbles. Coordinated market economies such as Germany, as well as the smaller West European countries such as the Netherlands, Sweden, Denmark, Finland, Belgium, Luxembourg, and Austria, with post-war collaborative inter-firm relations and cooperative labour–management relations facilitated by an 'enabling' state, have retained their overall outlines, despite changes at the edges. The economic crisis has been less severe in these countries, partly as a result of their greater reliance on value-added manufacturing for export-led growth and the benefits of coordinated wage restraint by the social partners. State-influenced market economies such as France, Italy, Spain, Portugal, and Greece, with the post-war 'interventionist' state organizing inter-firm collaboration, directing business investment, and imposing management–labour cooperation,[1] have transformed themselves—but nevertheless remain distinguishable from both liberal and coordinated market economies as a result of the continued defining role of the state. The economic crisis has had a differentiated impact here, owing in part to whether the state played an enhancing or hindering role with regard to economic activity. This made the crisis not too bad for France, pretty bad for Italy, and downright ugly for Portugal, Spain, and Greece, the last of which has been at the centre of the sovereign debt crisis from 2010.

The central and east European countries (CEECs), with communist command and control economies from the post-war years up until the fall of the Berlin Wall in 1989, naturally underwent revolutionary change, subsequently becoming what could be characterized as a fourth variety of capitalism. These dependent market economies are largely driven by outside forces, whether capital coming from global as much as European sources or regulation coming from the EU, despite significant differences among them in the role of the state and the interrelationships of business and labour. The economic crisis also affected these countries differently owing to a mix of factors, including foreign-denominated loans and state mismanagement, with some such as Poland, the Czech Republic, Estonia, Slovenia, and Slovakia not too hard hit by contrast with Bulgaria, Lithuania, Latvia, Hungary, and Romania, the last three of which had to go to the International Monetary Fund (IMF) for a bailout following the inception of the economic crisis in 2008.

Challenges of Globalization and Europeanization to Post-war Varieties of Capitalism

In the post-war period, from the end of the Second World War through to the early 1970s, all European countries flourished, relatively little affected by external pressures, whether in the Western European democracies, the Eastern European communist dictatorships, or the Southern European authoritarian dictatorships. All such countries were busy rebuilding after the devastation wrought by the war, with their populations experiencing massive improvements in their standards of living and much more disposable income, whatever their economic management systems and their relative competitiveness. Growth, which had been essentially flat taken on average from just prior to the First World War to the end of the Second World War, skyrocketed along with GDP per capita by comparison with the previous period (see Figure 17.1). This was the case not only for the West European countries but also East and Southern European countries, although they remained below the West in terms of GDP per capita.

In the West of Europe, countries developed in a situation of 'embedded liberalism' (Ruggie 1982)—with the protective barriers of capital exchange controls, fixed but adjustable exchange rates, and optional barriers to trade enabling them to consolidate very different capitalist systems of economic management and development. While monetary policy was not a defining characteristic of any particular variety of capitalism, ranging as it did from 'hard' to 'soft', government policies, business practices, and labour relations were. Typically, in 'liberal market economies', the government role was hands-off, capital came from the financial markets, business practices were competitive and contractual, and labour relations fragmented; in 'coordinated market economies', the government role was 'enabling', capital came from the banks, businesses were cooperative, and labour coordinated (Hall and Soskice 2001a); and in 'state-influenced market economies', the government role was interventionist, capital came from the state, business was state led, and labour relations state organized (Schmidt 2002) (see Table 17.1). In all three varieties of capitalism, the welfare state was also slowly developing, albeit differently, with liberal market economies having liberal welfare states with low levels of benefits and services; coordinated market economies dividing between the conservative welfare states of continental countries with reasonably high levels of benefits, but low levels of services, and the social democratic Nordic welfare states with the highest levels of benefits and

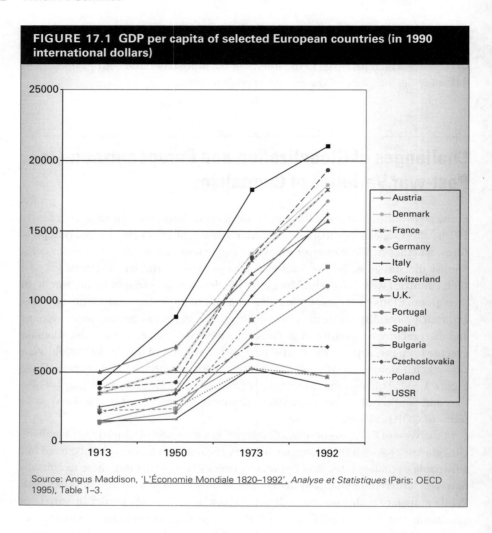

FIGURE 17.1 GDP per capita of selected European countries (in 1990 international dollars)

Source: Angus Maddison, 'L'Économie Mondiale 1820–1992', *Analyse et Statistiques* (Paris: OECD 1995), Table 1–3.

services; and state-influenced market economies with conservative welfare states, although France also developed high levels of public services akin to the Nordic states while the Southern European countries tended to have the lowest benefits and services.[2]

In the East of Europe, countries such as Poland, Czechoslovakia, Hungary, Romania, and (as part of the Soviet Union) the Baltic states, had a very different trajectory from the West. They developed reasonably similar socialist command and control economies behind the protective barrier of the Iron Curtain and under the watchful eye of the Soviet Union, as their interventionist states centrally organized the distribution systems, owned all businesses, and controlled labour. In the South of Europe, by contrast, Spain, Portugal, and Greece developed under authoritarian dictatorships with state-controlled market economies in which their

TABLE 17.1 Characteristics of the post-war varieties of capitalism (1950s–1970s)

Market economies	Liberal (UK, Ire)	Coordinated (Ger, Dk, Sw, Aus, Bel, NL)	State-influenced (Fr, It)
Monetary policies	Soft	Hard to Soft	Soft
Government role	Liberal	Enabling	Interventionist
Business	Arbitrator	Facilitator	Director
Labour	Bystander	Bystander (Ger) or co-equal (Sw, DK, NL)	Organizer
Business relations	Competitive	Cooperative	State-led
Inter-firm	Contractual	Mutually reinforcing	State-mediated
Investment	Capital markets	Banks	State
Time-horizons	Short-term	Long-term	Medium-term
Goals	Profits	Firm value	National priorities
Industrial relations	Fragmented	Coordinated	State-organized
Mgt–labour	Adversarial	Cooperative	Adversarial
Wage-bargaining	Market reliant	Coordinated	State imposed

interventionist states centrally controlled business and organized corporatist labour–management relations.

All of the seemingly unrestrained growth that began in the early post-war period was to be severely challenged beginning in the early 1970s. For Western and Southern Europe, the challenges began with the collapse of the Bretton Woods system of fixed exchange rates based on the dollar, which ushered in an era of floating exchange rates. This was followed by the first oil crisis in the mid-1970s, which brought the sudden fivefold rise in the price of crude oil, and then by the second oil crisis in the late 1970s, all of which together produced growing currency volatility, rising inflation, and declining competitiveness. The specific challenges of the 1970s, moreover, were followed from the 1980s onwards by two other sets of economic challenges, which can be summed up in two words: globalization and Europeanization.

For Eastern European countries, with currencies tied to the rouble rather than the dollar and sheltered from the oil crisis by Soviet oil, the moment of reckoning came later—beginning in the 1990s. This is when the end of communism spelled the collapse of their command economies and led to their precipitous conversion to market economies, subject to the twin forces of globalization and Europeanization.

As an economic challenge, globalization can be defined most succinctly as the competitive pressures stemming from the rising internationalization of national

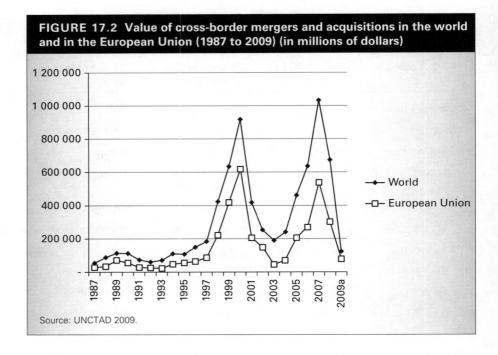

FIGURE 17.2 Value of cross-border mergers and acquisitions in the world and in the European Union (1987 to 2009) (in millions of dollars)

Source: UNCTAD 2009.

markets for goods, capital, and services. Notably, the European Union has been a central player in globalization. For one, the European Union's share of cross-border M&As (mergers and acquisitions) has across time generally been 50 per cent or more of that of the world as a whole (see Figure 17.2). By 2006, moreover, the EU could claim to be the world's biggest trader, with its percentage of trade with the external world at 17.1 per cent, slightly above the US at 16 per cent, as well as China at 9.6 per cent and Japan at 6.6 per cent (Eurostat 2007). In 2000 alone, moreover, EU member states were responsible for 67 per cent (US$770 billion) of world FDI outflows and attracted 50 per cent (US$617 billion) of world inflows. Significantly, intra-European investment was a major component of such flows, since 50 per cent of the outflows were to other member states and 80 per cent of the inflows were from other member states. All of this points to the fact not only that European Union member states have been active participants in globalization, but also that Europeanization has been part and parcel of globalization—and arguably a greater force for change in EU member states than globalization itself.

Europeanization has entailed massive changes for member state economies, including integrating national markets for goods, capital, services, *and* labour in a single market—and not simply opening to external competition—in addition to eliminating national currencies in favour of a single currency, the euro. As a result, it has often intensified the competitive pressures from globalization as it has added its own specifically European pressures. For example, the phased elimination of capital controls beginning in the 1980s together with the deregulation of the rules limiting financial market access and tradable instruments has opened up EU member states to intra-European competition on top of the global competition in the capital markets. Moreover, the end to tariff barriers between European countries by 1969 made European countries even more susceptible to rising competition in European product markets than they would have been had they only been subject to the tariff reductions related to the GATT (General Agreement on Tariffs and Trade) agreements. Subsequently, growing product market integration related to the reduction of non-tariff barriers through harmonization and mutual recognition in the Single Market programme only intensified competition, as did deregulation first in competitive industrial sectors and then, increasingly in the 1990s, in public utilities and infrastructural services such as telecommunications and electricity. Deregulation in the latter case not only opened up formerly closed sectors to global as well as European competition, but also threatened deep-seated notions about public interest obligations in some member states (especially France). Finally, European monetary integration, beginning with the European Monetary System (EMS) in 1979, culminating in the European Monetary Union (EMU) in the late 1990s, with the introduction of the euro in 2002, has only added to the competitive pressures economically—by providing greater transparency in prices while reducing the costs of cross-border transactions—at the same time that it has institutionally put pressure on national budgets to remain within the parameters of low inflation, low deficits, and diminishing debt set by the Stability and Growth Pact (SGP).

Europeanization has not just been a conduit for globalization. It has also served as a shield against it, by reducing European member states' exposure to the volatility of the international currency markets through European monetary integration, by improving EU member states' international competitiveness through the economies of scale afforded by the single market and the discipline of monetary integration, and by providing protection through the common agricultural policy (CAP), anti-dumping measures, and common industrial policies. Moreover, its cohesion and structural funds have provided less developed European countries and regions with significant amounts of money to promote economic development and modernization, something that proved decisive in the case of Ireland, enabling it to go from one of the poorest and least developed of West European countries to one of the richest (until the financial crisis in 2008).

Only in the labour and social policy arenas have member states been left to cope largely on their own with social security deficits, unemployment, and/or poverty in a climate of budgetary austerity—which was itself intensified by the 1990s belt-tightening related to meeting the convergence criteria for EMU—continued in the 2000s as part of the SGP—and was further exacerbated in the aftermath of the 2010 sovereign debt crisis. Moreover, it is primarily in this arena that member states also run the risks of regulatory competition. This is because the 'negative integration' represented by the 'market-creating' policies of liberalization and deregulation that follow from the treaties, in the absence of 'positive integration' from 'market-correcting' measures through agreement by member states on common policies, can lead to rising pressures for reductions in such things as payroll taxes and labour protections in order to increase countries' attractiveness to investors and national firms' competitiveness (Scharpf 2000a). For a time in the 2000s, common efforts through the 'open method of coordination' (OMC), following the Lisbon and Luxembourg Summits, sought to address these issues—although here, too, the focus was more on market creation—by finding ways to promote labour market flexibility—than on market correction—by arriving at common solutions, say, to the crisis of pensions systems. What is more, national labour and social systems found themselves under increasing attack by EU Commission initiatives such as the proposed services directive in 2005, which privileged home country rules for service workers' pensions and wage rates in host countries—watered down after much social mobilization and EP intercession, but only after becoming a cause célèbre of the anti-ratification forces in the French Referendum on the Constitutional Treaty. ECJ cases have also raised problems, as in its decisions based on freedom of movement to curtail national unions' rights to strike in the Laval and Viking cases. Although these could be seen positively from a EU level perspective as promoting a 'Polanyian,' market-correcting governance for all Europeans (see e.g. Caporaso and Tarrow 2008), it can just as readily be seen negatively from a national level perspective as a neoliberal post-Polanyian destruction of national labour relations and welfare systems (Höpner and Schäfer 2007). And certainly there can be no question that the pressures for neoliberal reform of national labour and welfare systems have only been further exacerbated by the austerity measures imposed subsequent to the euro-zone crisis, in particular in Southern Europe and Ireland.

Europeanization, in short, has exerted even greater pressures on EU member states than globalization, given that it adds institutional pressures for policy adjustment to the economic ones. But although governments may all have adopted similar policies within a narrower range, they have still exercised choice not only in the timing of reform but also in its content. Because political actors with different ideas about what constitutes appropriate kinds of change have grafted such policy reforms onto their often very different national varieties of capitalism, significant differences remain in the EU member states' economic systems. As a result, although the patterns of interaction between government, business, and labour have certainly changed appreciably from those of the post-war period, the imprints of the past have nevertheless been important influences on the present, so much so that we can continue to identify liberal, coordinated, and state-influenced market varieties of capitalism in the West of Europe, and, as of the 1990s, a new dependent market variety of capitalism in the East. Within the varieties of capitalism, however, the trajectories of change also vary. This is because of a range of factors, including countries' differing levels of vulnerability to global and European economic forces, the degree of fit (or misfit) of governments' policy initiatives with long-standing policies and preferences; the political interactions and institutional arrangements that affected governments' capacity to reform; and the legitimizing discourses that enhanced governments' reform capacity by persuading the public not just of the necessity of change in light of the failure of long-standing policies to solve the economic problems, but also of its appropriateness in terms of national values (Schmidt 2002: Chapter 2). These factors together help explain the differences in how, why, and when EU member states reformed their national economies.

Money and Macroeconomic Policy

The first major crisis related to globalization—which was to find a remedy in Europeanization—was focused on money and on macroeconomic policy. In the 1970s, as the first oil crisis hit, countries faced a choice between 'hard' money policies focused on maintaining the real value of currencies by fighting inflation through higher interest rates and reduced government spending, even if this meant momentarily rising unemployment and diminishing business investment. Or they could follow 'soft' money policies which allowed inflation to rise in efforts to maintain employment and investment. In both cases, the worst of the problems of either unemployment or inflation were largely avoidable if the unions engaged in wage moderation (see Scharpf 2000b).

Germany was the first to choose hard money policies. As early as 1974, the Bundesbank tightened monetary policy and essentially forced the unions to agree to wage restraint as the way to reduce escalating unemployment. The turn to monetarism fitted with the Bundesbank's traditional preference for stability and its focus on the fight against inflation above all else—with German memories of the hyper-inflation of the interwar years still fresh. The non-accommodating monetary policy worked, however, only because of the capacity of the 'social partners'—business and labour— to deliver on wage moderation in this coordinated market economy, which they did by 1976. Switzerland, also a coordinated market economy, was the only other European country to choose a hard money policy at this time, although coordinated Denmark ended up with an imported hard money policy because of its currency's peg to the Deutschmark.

All the other EU member states chose to continue with soft money policies via Keynesian reflation and increased government spending in efforts to maintain employment and encourage investment. For most such countries, however, this proved only a short-term fix—or no fix at all. Liberal Britain ended up, arguably, in the worst shape. In a situation of rising inflation, the government did not have the capacity to impose wage moderation, nor could the unions ultimately ensure it—given its fragmentation and adversarial relationship with business. The result, after a short period of 'incomes policy' in the shadow of an IMF bailout, was exploding wages, double-digit inflation, and major strikes, followed by Margaret Thatcher's victory in 1979 and the country's embrace of monetarism.

Following the second oil crisis in the late 1970s, the turn to monetarism appeared almost inevitable in an environment of rising real interest rates and growing costs of public debt, with tighter monetary policies from the now monetarist US Federal Reserve Bank. Moreover, the creation of the EMS in 1979—the joint initiative of France and Germany to regain control in the face of increasing currency volatility— only added to that inevitability. By 1981, just about all EU member states had shifted to monetarist policies except for France, which instead in 1981, under the newly elected socialist government, instituted counter-cyclical Keynesian reflation plus re- newed state *dirigisme* in industrial policy through large-scale nationalization and extensive industrial restructuring. By 1983, however, confronted with double-digit inflation, runaway spending, and declining business competitiveness, as well as faced with having to pull out of the EMS, President Mitterrand completely reversed course, imposing the 'great U-turn' to monetarism and to the policy of 'competitive disinflation' focused on damping inflation and keeping the franc strong. After this, the only countries that continued with Keynesianism were coordinated market economies outside the EU—Austria for a time, and Sweden until the early 1990s. This is when the bursting of a housing bubble sent Sweden's economy tumbling, and to recover it Sweden switched to monetarism and petitioned to join the EU.

By the 1990s, the focus turned to the establishment of the single currency, with most member states having signed up to the Maastricht Treaty but certainly not all (i.e., Britain and Denmark, which negotiated opt-outs, and Sweden, which did not negotiate an opt-out when it joined the EU in 1995, but nevertheless has not become a member of EMU). The Maastricht criteria targeting a budget deficit of no more than 3 per cent of GDP, a public debt approaching 60 per cent of GDP, and an infla- tion rate no more than two points higher than the lowest rate among member states, and in any case at or below 3 per cent, forced all signatories to the treaty to focus on their budgets. Most instituting austerity measures that generally sought to reduce public spending, in particular in terms of the welfare state, which was also the sub- ject of independent concerns about its sustainability given negative projections about demographics into the twenty-first century.

The route to monetary union, moreover, was fraught with difficulty. In the early 1990s, speculation against monetary union sparked two monetary crises that in- volved major runs on European currencies, the first of which in September 1992 pushed a number of countries out of the Exchange Rate Mechanism (ERM) of the EMS, including Italy and Britain, which, having suffered the worst single loss in monetary history, of around 3 trillion pounds, left, not to return. The second mon- etary crisis in August 1993 pushed even more member states out of the ERM, nearly destroying the EMS altogether, and forcing the widening of the band of fluctuation allowed within the ERM. But the French currency held good, helped by the German Bundesbank, thereby reinforcing France's commitment to monetary integration de- spite the economic costs related to the deepening recession caused by Bundesbank interest rates set to control German inflation. For Italy, getting back into the ERM and then joining EMU became a major rallying point for the reform of the country's public finances and welfare system, with national leaders' communicative discourse to the public focused on the blow to national pride if Italy, as one of the founding members of the EU, was not to be able to join the single currency—and Spain was! This was reinforced by a coordinative discourse with the social partners that emphasized the appropriateness, and not just the necessity, of welfare reform in terms of intergenerational solidarity, and was shored up by a 'tax for Europe' portrayed as 'the last ticket for Europe' (Radaelli 2002). Greece, joining two years after the euro was established, in 2001, also seemed to have performed miracles of fiscal consolidation and general belt-tightening, although it turns out, as it admitted a few years later, that it had falsified the data in order to qualify.

Once the single currency came into being—as the banking currency in 1999, as money used by the public in 2002—the major fears seemed over since it proved itself to be a credible international currency. The transition from national monies to the euro was very smooth, with no panics and no major problems in any member states. The fact that the currency's value was initially very low, although of concern to some, was a boon to exports. Its later overvaluation, reaching briefly even US$1.60 to the euro in April 2008, was more problematic, as have been the fluctuations in value since the inception of the sovereign debt crisis in 2010.

The economic crisis beginning in 2008 tested the euro-zone most severely. But whereas it passed the test in 2008 with flying colours in response to the banking crisis—as the ECB intervened in coordination with other central banks to stabilize world currency markets while the member states, led by the UK and France, followed by national actions to rescue banks—and then in response to the crisis in the real economy—through the injection of major stimulus spending into the economy—it barely passed in response to the sovereign debt crisis. The EU delayed much too long in taking action when Greece was under immense market pressure because of fears of a sovereign debt default. And as the EU dithered, largely because the German government resisted taking action, the problem festered while the costs of Greek government borrowing went up and up. Market distrust became such that, even once the EU approved a loan of 110 billion euros (of which 30 billion came from the IMF) on 3 May 2010, it was not enough to calm the markets, now worried about the sovereign debt default of other Southern European member states plus Ireland (by now aptly named the PIIGS—Portugal, Ireland, Italy, Greece, and Spain). The EU was therefore forced six days later to come up with the 750 billion euro loan guarantee fund, the European Financial Stability Facility (EFSF—of which 250 billion euros came from the IMF), because of the continued slide in the value of the euro on worries about the contagion effects on other Southern European countries with fragile finances. And subsequently, largely at the urging of the EU Commission, pushed by Germany, all euro-zone members—but especially the Southern European countries—engaged in major 'fiscal consolidation,' instituting massive across-the-board budgetary cuts in efforts to reduce national budget deficits very quickly. Whether austerity will solve the problems of the EU, let alone re-launch growth, is open to debate, however. While EU leaders as a group seemed to be convinced that austerity was the answer to the demands of the markets, many economists questioned this, concerned that with all countries tightening their belts at the same time, recession was a more likely outcome than growth, and that default on some debt was in any case a certainty—and so did the markets, which continued to hammer the weaker EU member states. After the Greek loan in May 2010 came the Irish bailout by the EFSF in December 2010, with Portugal under extreme pressure also to go to the EFSF by the end of March 2011 with Greece granted a second loan bailout by winter 2012.

Political Economic Adjustment in Liberal Market Economies

Beginning in the mid to late 1970s, the shift in monetary policies was only the first in a wide range of economic reforms that governments sought to institute in response to the deteriorating economic climate caused by the two oil crises and the increasing competition in capital and product markets. But some countries—and in particular Britain—went a lot further a lot faster a lot earlier than others, anticipating many of the liberalizing and deregulatory initiatives of the EU that were to follow. As a result, it was little affected by many EU policies other than those that, though often modelled on British policy, instituted statutory rules in place of the voluntary ones.

Prime Minister Thatcher, elected on a platform focused mainly on instituting monetarist macroeconomic policy, went on to impose radical neoliberal reforms across policy arenas. These ensured that Britain's 'liberal' market economy would only become more liberal. She eliminated most protectionist barriers to trade, which left British industry to sink or swim against global competition—mainly to sink, or to be acquired by foreign investors. Privatization was extensive and highly laissez-faire, with companies freely floated on the stock market that had been liberalized with the 'big bang' of 1986. Deregulation served as an accompaniment to privatization, replacing voluntary self-governing arrangements and informal government–industry relationships with independent regulatory agencies to supervise the financial markets and the privatized public service industries such as telecommunications, gas, and, later, the railways. The result was a more truly hands-off government relationship with business not only through the sell-off of public enterprises and the proliferation of regulatory agencies, but also through massive cuts in ad hoc subsidies to industry.

Business, as a result of all of these changes, became more competitive as well as even more market-driven than in the past. The liberalization of the capital markets intensified inter-firm competition and imposed greater pressures on firms for corporate performance in increasingly short time horizons. Moreover, Thatcher's labour policies, which crushed the unions, together with better human resources management practices (typically following the Japanese model), virtually neutralized the employees, largely putting an end to the adversarial, strike-ridden relationships of the past (Howell 1999). This also ensured that by the mid-1990s, Britain had largely solved its high unemployment problems as well as having its social security deficits under control. Labour traded job availability for the job security of the past, although it also had lower wages.

In all of these reforms, Thatcher benefited from the institutional arrangements of the 'Westminster model' and political interactions that insulated her from electoral sanctions, given a divided and unelectable opposition. Her capacity to reform was also enhanced by a legitimizing discourse that invoked not just the necessity of neoliberal reform—that 'there is no alternative', or 'TINA'—but also its appropriateness—that this was the way to encourage individual responsibility and entrepreneurship (see Schmidt 2000). But public acceptance as well as economic turn-around did take a while. And although Mrs Thatcher's policy programme set the stage for the dramatic economic recovery, the price was high with respect to the rise of poverty (Rhodes 2000). Moreover, Mrs Thatcher was unable to institute significant welfare reform, although she did manage to reduce benefits to single mothers and dependent children (Pierson 1994).

It took the arrival in power of New Labour, under Prime Minister Tony Blair, in the late 1990s to reform the welfare state as well as to address the problems of poverty. The New Labour government's discourse trumpeted the ability of the 'third-way' to solve these problems by promoting greater social equality and opportunity through market-oriented methods such as welfare-to-work and youth employment programmes. Moreover, at the same time that Blair embraced neoliberal approaches to unemployment, he did reintroduce some positive rights and job protections for workers, along with a minimum wage for the first time in British labour history as well as the acceptance of the EU Social Chapter (Rhodes 2000). Importantly, although problems of poverty persisted, the government significantly increased the levels of social transfer in Britain 'by stealth' (i.e. without talking about it so as not to alienate its middle class support). The result was that by the mid-2000s Britain's levels of poverty after social transfers were on a par with those of continental European countries, thus lending credence to the government's claims that it was attempting to create an 'Anglo-social' model in emulation of Sweden (see Figure 17.3).

Notably, the only other European liberal market economy, Ireland, was at the bottom of the class with regard to poverty after social transfers. In other ways, however, Ireland was remarkable for its departure from the expected liberal hands-off state and radically decentralized labour relations. From the mid to late 1980s onwards, its state-led economic development programme—focused on attracting FDI—made it look more like French *dirigisme* in the post-war years, and its cooperative state-led labour market coordination made it look more like post-war Scandinavian corporatism (Hardiman 2004; Teague and Doneaghy 2004). Its wage-bargaining system was a highly organized, deliberative process involving a 'four room' negotiating procedure—including not only the main employer and trade union associations in the main room but also a business room, a farming room, and a community room representing the voluntary and community sector. This system worked admirably well until the

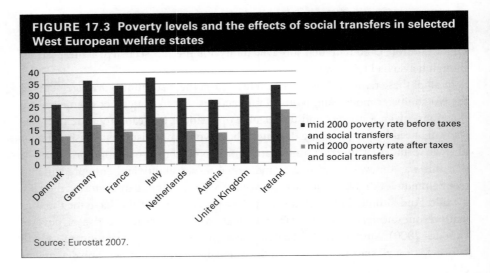

FIGURE 17.3 Poverty levels and the effects of social transfers in selected West European welfare states

- mid 2000 poverty rate before taxes and social transfers
- mid 2000 poverty rate after taxes and social transfers

Source: Eurostat 2007.

economic crisis, at which point the government abandoned any semblance of state-led concertation as it sought to impose drastic cuts in wages—public sector pay was cut by 15 per cent on average—and in welfare benefits as part of a painful fiscal adjustment programme in response to the crash of the credit-fuelled decade-long property boom.

The economic crisis hit Ireland very hard. The collapse of major banks followed by government rescue in 2008 left the country in the deepest recession of any advanced economy (according to the IMF). By the beginning of 2010, it had the highest deficit in the euro-zone, revised upwards in the autumn to over 32 per cent from the predicted, already high, 11.5 per cent, plus an unemployment rate of close to 14 per cent. By the end of 2010, it had to go to the EFSF, thereby submitting itself to EU and IMF tutelage as it sought to impose even greater budgetary austerity. Elections in February 2011 led to the fall of the Fianna Fáil government, blamed not just for having failed to regulate the banks effectively but also for having saddled the country with the banks' bad debts. The new government came to power hoping to negotiate a change to the high interest rates of the EFSF loan, but failed in its first such attempt because it was not willing to give up the low corporate tax rate that the Irish are generally convinced is their only hope to attract foreign direct investment, and thereby to ensure growth. By 2012, however, Ireland had returned to healthy growth, led by its export sector, although unemployment and poverty remained serious problems, as did massive emigration. The government had also begun to look for ways to get out of at least some of the massive debt burden, incurred when the government promised to guarantee the banks at the height of the 2008 crisis.

Britain during this same period had not suffered nearly as much, despite the bursting of its own massive credit-fuelled housing bubble. As a bigger country with greater resources and its own international currency, in 2008 Prime Minister Gordon Brown was able reflate the economy while stabilizing the banks in the seemingly full confidence of the financial markets. But despite the continued confidence of the markets, the newly elected Conservative–Liberal Democrat coalition government of David Cameron pledged to make swingeing public spending cuts of upwards of 30 per cent. This was motivated as much by conservative ideology—that budget deficits are bad—as by concern that the markets could turn on the UK at any point, given its high deficit. By winter 2011, however, the economy's unexpected drop in rate of growth, together with the pain linked to budget cuts, prompted many to question the wisdom of the government's extremely rapid programme of deficit reduction. Moreover, the economic outlook had not brightened all that much by 2012.

Political Economic Adjustment in Coordinated Market Economies

The coordinated market economies were in very different places in the 1970s with regard to their coordinating ability as well as their economic outlooks. While most of the smaller West European countries had to reform on an on-going basis, Germany seemed insulated from most problems until the 1990s, following the 1989 fall of the Berlin Wall.

Germany, having responded to the first oil crisis with a non-accommodating monetary policy and accommodating unions, managed to weather the recession linked to the second oil crisis reasonably well. In consequence, it felt little challenge to its traditional policies and preferences in the 1980s, and so it did little to reform its business or labour policies, although it did tighten social expenditures. Its moment of reckoning came with German unification, which was extremely costly, in particular because of the political decision to convert the East German mark on a one-to-one basis with the West's. This only added to the costs resulting from the collapse of the East German economy, which engendered an immense transfer of wealth from West to East—to the tune of approximately US$100 billion a year—and the exponential rise in unemployment and social security deficits (Streeck 1997). In the face of these costs as well as the growing pressures of international competition and EU regulation, Germany seemed to have little choice but to liberalize. In addition to the massive privatization programme in East Germany, monopolistic public service providers in telecommunications and air and rail transport were at least partially privatized and opened to competition, while highly regulated markets, such as the stock markets, electricity, and road haulage were deregulated in conjunction with EU directives. Notably, EU rulings against Germany in competition policy, which initially appeared to jeopardize the 'enabling' role of *Länder* governments with regard to the provision of subsidies to business (for example the Volkswagen case), as well as the role of the regionally based public sector banks in the social market economy, were resolved in symbiosis with the EU (Smith 2001).

All of these reforms, together with the demands of competition and the pressures for corporate performance in the financial markets, helped loosen the traditional closeness of firms' networked-based relations. Since the mid-1990s, inter-firm relations have become less cooperative and mutually reinforcing, as firms have been putting the squeeze on suppliers and subcontractors to cut costs while maintaining quality. Moreover, the close ties between business and banks have been loosening as the largest firms have internationalized and listed their shares on the international financial markets, while the big banks have moved into international finance by buying British and US investment banks. The banks, thanks to the 2002 elimination of the 50 per cent capital gains tax, have also been divesting themselves of the holdings of poorly performing firms while managing the rest on the basis of 'shareholder value' principles. This said, hostile takeovers remain the exception in Germany, given that the bulk of equity continues to be concentrated in the hands of German banks as well as industrial enterprises (Vitols 2005). What is more, the bedrock of the system, the regional banks and small- and medium-sized firms, remained solid up until the economic crisis, despite challenges to the public status of the regional banks by EU competition policy as well as international competitive pressures. By 2010, however, there was a move to consolidate the regional banks, many of which are too weak in the new climate.

But while the country did go ahead with deregulation and privatization of business, Germany was largely stymied with regard to reforming the structure of work and welfare until the mid-2000s. Labour resisted attempts to institute greater labour market flexibility, more differentiated wages, or a reduction in the generosity of publicly funded pensions that were viewed as property rights, and could not agree with business on reform (Thelen 2001). The labour market became increasingly flexible nevertheless, also as a result of deals outside the formal negotiating process, so much so as to develop an insider/outsider problem that saw large parts of the labour force outside the traditional corporatist arrangements and employed in low-paid, often temporary or part-time jobs—generally women, immigrants, and youth. As to welfare reform, by the mid-2000s, the Schröder government had passed the Hartz IV reforms, substantially cutting the duration of unemployment benefits and the generosity of social assistance. Although Chancellor Schröder did this without much legitimizing communicative discourse to the general public, and to plummeting popularity ratings, the coordinative discourse among social partners and with parliament was reasonably successful, largely because of the 'ideational leadership' provided by particular ministers in Schröder's government (Stiller 2010) which in turn helped create a 'reform coalition' that agreed to a package of reform mixing positive and negative effects (Häusermann 2008).

All of these reforms put Germany in a very good position when the economic crisis hit. Chancellor Merkel's resistance to following Britain and France on the fiscal stimulus, on the grounds that 'Germans save', did not stop her from ultimately spending every bit as much, if not more, including on a very effective programme of 'short-time work', which encouraged firms to not to lay off their skilled workers but instead to reduce their working time with government compensation on wages, social contributions, and retraining. By 2010, with the sovereign debt crisis, Germany's continued high economic performance enabled it to take the moral high ground as it led the move to budgetary austerity across the EU, insisting that the only road to sound finances was to follow its own belt-tightening example. The fact that it would have to provide the largest amount of collateral for the EFSF also played a major role, in particular given the hostility of the German public to any possibility of a 'transfer union'. This is why Chancellor Merkel insisted on a number of successive agreements meant to reinforce euro-zone members' commitments to fiscal austerity. These culminated in the 'fiscal compact' that the UK vetoed as a treaty in December 2011, forcing the twenty-five countries that ultimately agreed to sign it into a multilateral treaty outside the formal EU architecture.

The smaller coordinated market economies of Western Europe also weathered the crisis rather well because they, too, had reformed extensively. But although they reformed more steadily over a longer time period than Germany, their reforms did not negatively affect the coordinating ability of business and labour quite as much as Germany, while their welfare systems remained more generous.

The Netherlands, the poster child for 'corporatism' in the 1950s and 1960s, had been a basket case in the 1970s, as all semblance of labour–management cooperation fell apart while the economy spiralled downwards. In the early 1980s, however, the government managed to bring the unions and management to the table with a discourse that threatened that it would impose its own wage restraint policies on the social partners if they did not come to agreement among themselves. The result was the Waasenaar agreement of 1981, which ushered in an era of labour peace along with much greater labour market flexibility that brought on what came to be described as the 'Dutch miracle' (Visser and Hemerjick 1997). However, this also led to the Netherlands having the lowest rate of working hours among West European countries, plus lower incomes, in particular for outsiders with part-time jobs. This said, the governments have also maintained a generous basic pension with top-ups for those with incomplete work histories, thereby ensuring that the Netherlands, once categorized as a conservative welfare state, is often now listed alongside Scandinavian social democratic welfare states like Sweden or Denmark on measures of redistribution and equality.

With regard to the labour market, however, Dutch 'flexicurity' was outdone by the Danish, given labour market policies in which workers accept easy hiring and firing by business in exchange for generous unemployment compensation. These long-standing policies, joined in the 1990s by active labour market policies for retraining and decentralized bargaining flexibility within a still centrally coordinated system, ensured the country very low rates of unemployment along with wage restraint, all of which together gained it renown as the 'Danish Miracle'. All the Scandinavian countries, moreover, managed to rationalize the welfare state in the 1990s and 2000s without seriously affecting pensioners' income, and were able to reduce the generosity of social assistance programmes without reneging on commitments to equality, universality, or solidarity. Their corporatist social partnerships also seem to have better weathered the internationalization of their major corporations than Germany (Pontusson 2011).

Political Economic Adjustment in State-Influenced Market Economies

The state-influenced market economies underwent the greatest amount of political economic adjustment among West European countries. While democratic transitions in Spain, Portugal, and Greece transformed state-controlled markets under authoritarian dictatorships, liberalizing reforms in France and Italy transformed their state-led market economies of the post-war period. The reforms themselves came at different times and were successful to varying degrees.

France began its major reforms in 1986 under a newly elected 'neoliberal' conservative government, with the 'little bang' of the liberalization of the financial markets in 1986 accompanied by the privatization of public enterprise, which continued intermittently, but increasingly, through the 1990s under the Left as well. Unlike in Britain, such privatization focused primarily on public enterprises in the competitive sector, and was highly *dirigiste* in approach, as the government decided how a controlling portion of the shares were to be distributed among a hard core of investors in order to provide privatized firms with stable leadership and protection against hostile takeovers and foreign acquirers (Schmidt 1996). Deregulation in a wide range of industrial sectors complemented privatization, and substituted more arms' length relationships by way of regulatory agency and incontrovertible law for the closer, more accommodating relationships between ministry and industry of the past. Deregulation of the labour markets, finally, which began in 1982 with laws that established more direct worker–management dialogue, culminated by the end of the decade in the government's abandonment of the entire system of state organized wage-bargaining (Howell 1992). The resulting radical decentralization of wage-bargaining brought with it a decline in union membership from around 25 per cent in the 1960s down to around 9 per cent by the mid-1990s and 7 per cent today—along with the end to strikes and job actions in all but a small (but strategic) part of the public sector.

With the retreat of the state, French firms have become much more autonomous than in the past. Although privatization was intended to reproduce the German networked pattern of corporate governance, it produced only a very pale imitation of this which started breaking apart in the mid to late 1990s, as hardcore investors sold and foreign institutional investors—mainly North American pension funds—bought (Schmidt 1996). But although French firms are more financial market driven, they are much less exposed to the pressures of the financial markets than the British because of the more concentrated share-ownership of French firms, and they are much more autonomous than their German counterparts, who are more constrained by boards of directors, networked relationships, and employees. This said, although French businesses lack the deep network linkages of coordinated Germany, they are, nonetheless, more interconnected than the British by way of informal networks based in CEOs' shared elite state education and career paths, and through the vertically integrated relationship, or *partenariat*, of large firms with their suppliers (Schmidt 1996, 2002; Hancké 2001). These ties among big business elites based on state-related training and experience create a closeness that has its equivalent in the family-based ties of big business in state-influenced Italy and Spain.

But although French business was much more autonomous and government much less interventionist as a result of all these reforms, the state did not entirely give up on seeking to influence business or labour where it saw fit. Although it left the fate of most firms to the markets, it still bailed out the biggest of failing industries, albeit under the increasingly watchful eye of the EU Commission, as in the case of the Crédit Lyonnais in the early 2000s, and interfered in M&As where it was concerned about 'strategic' national interests, including the yogurt-maker DANONE.

In addition, the state was forever tinkering with the industrial relations system and the welfare state. While governments of the Right sought to liberalize the labour markets with regard to hiring and firing, work conditions, and working hours—as in Prime Minister de Villepin's abortive attempt in 2006 to increase flexibility with a two year probationary contract for youth employment, which was greeted by massive demonstrations—the Left sought to 'moralize' them, as in the Jospin government's initiative on the thirty-five hour work week in the late 1990s. The welfare state was also a target for reform. But while private sector pension reform passed in 1993, largely because Prime Minister Balladur engaged in a coordinative discourse with the social partners, the attempt to institute a similar reform in the public sector and to eliminate the special regimes of railroad workers in 1995 led to massive strikes that paralysed the capital for over three weeks, mainly because Prime Minister Juppé failed to communicate either with the public or the social partners. It was not until 2003 that the Raffarin government brought public sector pensions in line with private sector ones, with an extensive coordinative discourse between government and social partners.

By 2007, then, just before the crisis hit, France had incrementally reformed across areas, and was in comparatively good shape. Once the crisis hit, France exercised leadership on the European and world stage in promoting neo-Keynesian policies and pro-active state intervention to save the banks and then the real economy via a big stimulus package. France itself, however, beyond the stimulus, needed to do relatively little by comparison with countries with major housing bubbles like Ireland, the UK, and Spain, or with massive budget deficits like Greece. All in all, it had a pretty good crisis, despite the downgrading of its triple A rating in early 2012. By contrast, Italy had a pretty bad one, but nothing like Spain's, which was downright ugly, let alone that of Greece.

Greece's problem was an extremely high deficit that had accumulated in the early to mid-2000s, but which the ruling conservative party had hidden and lied about, only to be discovered by the newly elected socialist government. This, combined with a population that shirks paying taxes, has rigid labour markets, closed, protected professions, and a public administration that lacks capacity and is riddled with corruption, makes reform difficult but absolutely imperative given the pressures from markets, worried about sovereign debt default, and the terms of the Greek loan bailout, monitored under the watchful eyes of the EU and IMF.

Spain's main problem was not bad economic management—much the contrary, since just before the crisis it was being touted as a model for Southern European countries, with its deficit under control and its debt comparatively low. For Spain, the crisis brought the bursting of a gigantic housing bubble, in which construction represented 60 per cent of GDP, and the subsequent collapse of the big banks, forcing the government to take on massive debt to shore them up. Because of the continued weakness of its banking sector—in particular the smaller savings banks—along with its excessively high deficit, once the Greek-related sovereign debt crisis hit, Spain became a major target of the markets, although it remained less consistently in their line of fire than Portugal.

Italy's problem was its high public debt—although because much of this at the onset of the crisis was held by Italian citizens, it was not as vulnerable to the markets as the other PIIGS—and its increasing loss of competitiveness as a result of the lack of reform in the 2000s. Italy had had an impressive burst of reform in the 1990s, as the state overcame its earlier paralysis in the early years of the 'Second Republic', when the end of the Cold War led to the collapse and subsequent renewal of the Italian party system. This is when privatization and deregulation began for real under technical and centre-Left governments, as did reforms of pension systems and labour markets. But all such reforms slowed once Berlusconi came into power as of 2001. Nonetheless, big business outside of the nationalized sector, more autonomous than state-led French business, given a predominance of family-owned private firms and the state's lack of leadership, only increased its autonomy with privatization and deregulation. Business relations with labour also improved significantly—but in this case followed a completely different course from that of France, and more like in Spain.

Instead of the radical decentralization of the labour markets, as in France, both Italian and Spanish states stepped in to institute a kind of state-led corporatism, through greater business–labour coordination by way of a kind of macro-concertation between employers, unions, and governments (Hancké and Rhodes 2005; Royo 2002). Although both Italy and Spain engaged in such social pacts, Spain's were arguably more successful over the long term. Whereas in Italy, success in sustaining social pacts came only in the 1990s, in Spain social pacts worked from the late 1970s to the mid-1980s, collapsed after 1986, and re-emerged in the mid-1990s. Moreover, while in Italy social pacts have always depended on positive government action to promote them—explaining the success of centre-Left governments in the 1990s, the failure of the Berlusconi government in the 2000s—this has not always been the case in Spain, where a number of pacts have been signed without the government (Royo 2008).

For all state-influenced market economies then, what defines them in terms of their political economic institutions in contrast to liberal and coordinated market economies is the central role of the state, and how business and labour depend upon the state to solve their coordination problems. In consequence, a key factor in the differential political economic success of these countries is the capacity of the state to govern—both in terms of political actors' ability to exercise leadership and the probity and competence of the administration. This has been demonstrated most notably by the change in leadership in Italy. The appointment of Mario Monti as Prime Minister at the head of a 'technical' government, precipitated by the resignation of Berlusconi, has been followed by a range of much needed reforms of business and labour regulation as well as the pension system—which has also markedly improved the markets' views, as evident from the significant drop in 'spreads' in interest rate between Italian and German bonds.

Political Economic Adjustment in Dependent Market Economies

The changes in the East of Europe were naturally much more dramatic than any in the West. The fall of the Berlin Wall in 1989 led to revolutionary transformation of the economies of CEECs, with the transition from command economies to capitalist economies. The transformations led to significant differences among CEECs in the role of the state, the organization of business, and the coordination with labour. But most were united by one main characteristic: the dependence upon foreign capital for investment and growth and the dependence upon supranational institutions—in particular the European Union in the accession process—for regulatory direction and crisis support. This is why, although some scholars have called the CEECs 'hybrids', while others referred to them as systems of 'embedded neoliberalism', as these countries seek to create institutions of social protection even as they follow the neoliberal tenets (Cernat 2006; Bohle and Greskovits 2007), the most recent label of 'dependent market economy' seems to do best in highlighting the way in which most of these countries operate (Nölke and Vliegenthart 2009; see also Orenstein 2010) even though the term is usually restricted to the Visegrád countries of Poland, Hungary, Czech Republic, and Slovakia.

The collapse of communism led to a major transformation of the role of the state, from strong centralized state imposing policy and coordination on business and labour to weak state taking policy direction from the EU and managing the move from communist to capitalist enterprise. But although the state was weak, business and labour were generally even weaker, with unions and business associations fragmented and civil society organizations not very well developed in most CEECs. In consequence, the state's transformation in the 1990s into a strong regulative power in most countries was not balanced out by non-state actors, which entailed that market-making reforms in Eastern Europe often came without the market-correcting social policies found in the West (Bruszt 2002). This can be especially problematic where corruption is rampant, as in Bulgaria and Romania, or where the government mismanages and then 'lied morning, noon and night' about it, as admitted by the Hungarian Prime Minister himself immediately following his re-election.

While privatization, deregulation, and liberalization became the watchwords across the CEECs as these countries reformed following the advice of international organizations such as the IMF, the World Bank, and the EU (Epstein 2008), states proceeded in different ways at different rates. Although most countries underwent an overnight transformation, some went through a shock therapy conversion to capitalism, whereas others took the transition period more slowly. Some, like Poland, engendered a 'big bang' in political economic reform, liberalizing prices and shifting macroeconomic policy very quickly, while others were slower—some so slow, in fact, that they experienced an anti-democratic backlash, as in Bulgaria (Ekiert 2003; Aslund 2002). All experienced transition related recessions, from which many took a decade or longer to emerge as they privatized many if not most of their formerly state-owned industries—with West European firms often the acquirers—and deregulated various sectors of their economies. Moreover, they have all been subject to the discipline of the euro-zone monetary policies, either because they have already entered, the cases of Slovenia, Slovakia, and Estonia, or because they are in the antechamber, and peg their currencies to the euro. Most of their labour-management systems bear some resemblance to the corporatist relations of coordinated market economies, with consultative tripartite institutions, but labour tends to be weak, in particular in sectors where foreign multinationals are predominant, so that agreements tend to be dominated by management (Crowley 2005). The welfare system has naturally also been transformed since the communist welfare system died, along with guaranteed jobs and pensions. Although there is great diversity in welfare provisions, most CEECs tend to resemble a somewhat less generous version of the conservative continental welfare state, in particular with regard to pensions and social services (Cerami and Vanhuysse 2009).

What distinguishes the CEECs' dependent market economies is first and foremost the fact that foreign capital in the form of financial and direct investment—rather than financial markets, bank-firm networks, or autonomous firms—essentially drives economic decision making. The most productive of economic enterprises, whether banks or manufacturing firms, are most often foreign- owned or dominated. Because of this, governments are concerned primarily with maintaining an environment attractive to such enterprises, by preserving the country's cost advantages, based on low waged, highly skilled workers, and by constraining consumer demand, at the same time that they have to be careful to manage the capital inflows—a major problem for Hungary and the Baltic states in particular (Orenstein 2010). Another aspect of the dependent market economy is the importance of outside supranational organizations for their internal governance of the economy. CEECs have been especially dependent on the EU, in particular early on, whether through the conditionality of joining or the requirement that they accept all the *acquis communautaire* in the accession process; on the IMF, when in need of a bail-out to avoid default; on the credit-rating agencies that influence whether capital will flow to them; and on neighbouring West European countries, whether Sweden for the Baltics, Germany for Poland and the Czech Republic among others, or Austria for Hungary and Slovenia.

Finally, just as most CEECs began to achieve high rates of growth and productivity, with major gains in national standards of living, the global crisis hit. Some countries managed to weather the storm reasonably well—Poland in particular, the only European country that did not go into recession in 2009. But for those countries most reliant on foreign direct investment, with high rates of borrowing in euro-denominated bonds, the crisis spelled disaster, as they found themselves highly vulnerable to economic downturn and capital flight (Orenstein 2009). For Hungary, Romania, and Latvia, the difficulties of servicing their debts and the dangers of sovereign debt default meant that they had to turn to the IMF. And, because they chose not to give up their currencies' peg to the euro (encouraged in this by the EU Commission), they could not devalue their currencies in order thereby to grow their way out of recession via less expensive exports and lower comparative labour costs. Instead, they had to cut spending in the public sector, closing schools and hospitals, reducing benefits, public sector salaries and pensions, and raising taxes. Thus, at a time when the rest of Europe, and in particular the richer countries, were encouraged to spend, spend, spend to avoid recession and maintain employment, the East European countries in trouble were plunged into deepening recessions and rising unemployment. The result has been increasing differentiation among CEECs, with some becoming more and more prosperous, such as Slovenia, Poland, and the Czech Republic, and others languishing, in particular countries subject to harsh budgetary austerity regimes like Hungary, Romania, and Latvia.

Conclusion

All European countries were faced with major economic challenges, beginning in the 1970s with the end of the Bretton Woods System, and the two oil crises that followed in the 1980s and 1990s bringing growing competitive pressures in the capital and product markets from global and European forces, as well as growing institutional pressures from the EU. And all adapted and adjusted their systems in a more market-oriented direction in response. But these responses remained nationally specific and path-dependent. The liberal market economies of Anglophone Europe engaged in radical therapy that brought the system closer to the liberal capitalist ideal,

TABLE 17.2 Changes in models of capitalism in the 2000s				
Market economies	Liberal (UK/Ire)	Coordinated (Ger, Dk, Sw, Aus, Bel, NL)	State-influenced (Fr, It, Sp, Port, Gr)	Dependent (Pol, Baltics, Hu, Cz, Sl, Sk, Bu, Ro)
Monetary policies	Hard	Hard	Hard	Hard
Government roles	More liberal	Still 'enabling'	Enhancing/ hindering	Most liberal
Business	More Arbitrator	Still facilitator	Arbitrator or intervener	Arbitrator
Labour	More of a bystander	Still bystander (Ger) or coequal (e.g. Sw)	New bystander or state-led corporatism	Bystander
Business relations	Competitive	Cooperative	Competitive	Competitive
Inter-firm	Contractual	Less mutually reinforcing	Autonomous	Contractual
Investment	Capital markets	Firm, capital markets, banks	Firm, capital markets	Foreign capital markets, FDI
Time-horizons	Short-term	Less longer-term	Less medium-term	Short-term
Goals	Profits	Firm value and profits	Firm value and profits	Profits
Industrial relations	Market reliant	Still coordinated	Market reliant	Market reliant
Management– Labour	Neutral	Still cooperative	Neutral	Neutral
Wage-bargaining	Radically decentralized (UK) or state-led coord (Ire)	Still coordinated	Radically decentralized (Fr) or coordinated (Sp/It in 1990s)	Somewhat coordinated

with government policies even more arms' length and liberal, business practices even more competitive, and labour relations either more market reliant, as in the UK, or more coordinated by the state, as in Ireland. The coordinated market economies of continental and Nordic Europe, instead, saw little deep-seated change in their capitalist coordination, even if the closeness of network-based business practices may have begun to loosen and the cooperativeness of coordinated labour relations begun to lessen as governments struggled to facilitate adjustment—albeit more so in Germany than in the smaller West European countries. The state-influenced market economies of France and Southern Europe generally went much farther than either liberal or coordinated market economies, transforming themselves with the move away from state-led capitalism. But while the state retreated as it established greater autonomy for business and greater flexibility for labour, it still has a role to play, which may be more enhancing for the social partners and the economy, generally the case of France and arguably Spain, or hindering because of state incapacity and corruption, as in Italy (until the Monti government in late 2011) and Greece (see Table 17.2). Finally, the dependent market economies of Central and Eastern Europe underwent revolutionary transformation, going from communism to a capitalism that is best defined by the importance of outside influences, such that foreign capital coming in through the financial markets or direct investment are defining forces, as are supranational organizations, and in particular the EU.

Europeanization, even more so than globalization, has had a major impact on the four varieties of capitalism. There has undoubtedly been some convergence in practice, brought about by the single market rules and EMU. However, as this chapter has revealed, the practice of capitalism remains distinct between the four varieties, rooted as they are in historical trajectories or pathways. Hence, while economic integration in the EU has promoted convergence, much like the picture for member state institutions (see Chapter 12), no single European model has supplanted distinct national practice.

The economic crisis, finally, rather than representing a force for greater convergence, has produced just the opposite. Although all member states instituted austerity budgets in 2010 in response to the market pressures building up during the sovereign debt crisis, the deepness of the cuts has varied within as well as across varieties of European capitalism. Moreover, the differentials in economic performance are certainly growing not only between the North and the South, but also within Central and Eastern Europe. The question for the European Union is whether, in a region aspiring to further integration under a single currency in a single market, these kinds of divergences will not ultimately thwart that very aspiration.

FURTHER READING

The literature on globalization is vast. For a moderate view of its impact, see Held *et al.* (1999). For a general book on the political economy of the European Union, see McCann (2010). For different takes on the varieties of capitalism in Europe, for two varieties see Hall and Soskice (2001b), for three see Schmidt (2002), and for a fourth in Eastern Europe see Nölke and Vliegenthart (2009). Dyson (2002) is important for examining the impact of the euro on the member states. See Ferrera (2005) for the impact of the EU on the welfare state.

WEB LINKS

There is no immediately obvious website on the political economy of the EU and its member states. However, the European Central Bank is of central importance **http://www.ecb.int**. Similarly, the EU's own portal is an important source for identifying the European policy developments that impinge on the member states **http://www.europa.eu**. For more analytical perspectives, see the **http://eiop.or.at/erpa/** portal of online papers, especially the series of the Max Planck Institute for the Study of Societies (MPIfG) Cologne.

REFERENCES

Aslund, A. (2002), *Building Capitalism: The Transformation of the Former Soviet Bloc*, Cambridge: Cambridge University Press.

Bohle, D. and Greskovits, B. (2007), 'Neoliberalism, Embedded Neoliberalism, and Neocorporatism: Paths towards Transnational Capitalism in Central-Eastern Europe', *West European Politics* 30/3: 443–66.

Bruszt, L. (2002), 'Making Markets and Eastern Enlargement: Diverging Convergence'? *West European Politics*, 25/2: 121–40.

Caporaso, J. and Tarrow, S. (2008), 'Polanyi in Brussels: European Institutions and the Embedding of Markets in Society', *RECON Online Working Paper* 2008/01. www.reconproject.eu/projectweb/portalproject/RECONWorkingPapers.html

Cerami, A. and Vanhuysse, P. (2009), *Post-Communist Welfare Pathways: Theorizing Social Policy Transformations in Central and Eastern Europe*, Basingstoke: Palgrave Macmillan.

Cernat, L. (2006), *Europeanization, Varieties of Capitalism, and Economic Performance in Central and Eastern Europe*, Houndmills: Palgrave Macmillan.

Coates, D. (2000), *Models of Capitalism: Growth and Stagnation in the Modern Era*, Cambridge: Polity Press.

Crowley, S. (2005), 'Overshooting the Mark: East European Labor, Varieties of Capitalism, and the Future of the European Social Model', paper prepared for presentation at the annual conference of the American Political Science Association, Washington, DC, 31 August–4 September.

Dyson, K. (ed.) (2002), *European States and the Euro*, Oxford: Oxford University Press.

Ekiert, G. (2003), 'Patterns of Post-Communist Transformation in Central and Eastern Europe', in G. Ekiert and S. E. Hanson (eds), *Capitalism and Democracy in Central and Eastern Europe*, Cambridge: Cambridge University Press, 89–119.

Epstein, R. (2008), *In Pursuit of Liberalism: International Institutions in Postcommunist Europe*, Baltimore, MD: Johns Hopkins University Press.

Ferrera, M. (2005), *The Boundaries of Welfare*, Oxford: Oxford University Press.

Hall, P. and Soskice, D. (2001a), 'Introduction', in P. Hall and D. Soskice (eds), *Varieties of Capitalism: The Institutional Foundations of Comparative Advantage*, Oxford: Oxford University Press.

Hall, P. and Soskice, D. (2001b), *Varieties of Capitalism: the Institutional Foundations of Comparative Advantage*, Oxford: Oxford University Press.

Hancké, B. (2001), 'Revisiting the French Model: Coordination and Restructuring in French Industry', in Hall, P. and Soskice, D., *Varieties of Capitalism: the Institutional Foundations of Comparative Advantage*, Oxford: Oxford University Press.

Hancké, R. and Rhodes, M. (2005), 'EMU and Labour Market Institutions in Europe: The Rise and Fall of National Social Pacts', *Work and Occupations*, 32/2: 196–238.

Hardiman, N. (2004), 'Which Path? Domestic Adaptation to Economic Internationalization in Ireland', paper prepared for delivery to the National Meetings of the American Political Science Association (Chicago, Ill, 2–5 September).

Häusermann, S. (2008), 'What Explains the "Unfreezing" of Continental European Welfare States? The Socio-structural Basis of the New Politics of Pension Reforms', Paper presented at the annual meeting of the American Political Sciences Association, Boston, 28 August–3 September.

Held, D., McGrew, A., Goldblatt, D., and Perraton, J. (1999), *Global Transformations: Politics, Economics and Culture*, Stanford CA: Stanford University Press.

Höpner, M. and Schäfer, A. (2007), 'A New Phase of European Integration: Organized Capitalisms in Post-Ricardian Europe', *MOIFG Discussion Paper* No. 2007/4. http://ssrn.com/abstract=976162.

Howell, C. (I992), *Regulating Labor: The State and Industrial Relations Reform in Post-war France*, Princeton: Princeton University Press.

Howell, C. (1999), 'Unforgiven: British Trade Unionism in Crisis', in A. Martin and G. Ross (eds), *The Brave New World of European Labour*, New York: Berghahn.

McCann, D. (2010), *The Political Economy of the European Union*, Cambridge: Polity Press.

Nölke, A. and Vliegenthart, A. (2009), 'Enlarging the Varieties of Capitalism: The Emergence of Dependent Market Economies in East Central Europe', *World Politics*, 69/4: 670–702.

Ohmae, K. (1990), *The Borderless World: Power and Strategy in the Interlinked Economy*, New York: Harper Business.

Orenstein, M. (2009), 'What Happened in East European (Political) Economies: A Balance Sheet for Neoliberal Reform', *East European Politics and Societies* 23: 479–90.

Orenstein, M. (2010), 'Economic Crisis and Varying State Responses in Poland and Hungary', paper presented at the American Political Science Association Annual Meetings, Washington, DC, September.

Pierson, P. (1994), *Dismantling the Welfare State: Reagan, Thatcher and the Politics of Retrenchment in Britain and the United States*, Cambridge: Cambridge University Press.

Pontusson, J. (2011), 'Once Again A Model: Nordic Social Democracy in a Globalized World', in J. Cronin, G. Ross, and J. Shoch (eds), *What's Left of the Left: Democrats and Social Democrats in Challenging Times*, Durham, NC: Duke University Press.

Radaelli, C. (2002), 'The Italian State and the Euro', in Ken Dyson (ed.), *The European State and the Euro*, Oxford University Press: Oxford.

Rhodes, M. (2000), 'Restructuring the British Welfare State: Between Domestic Constraints and Global Imperatives', in F. W. Scharpf and V. A. Schmidt (eds), *Welfare and Work, Vol. II*, Oxford: Oxford University Press.

Royo, S. (2002), *'A New Century of Corporatism?' Corporatism in Southern Europe, Spain and Portugal in Comparative Perspective*, Westport, Conn., London: Praeger.

Royo, S. (2008), *Varieties of Capitalism in Spain*, Basingstoke: Palgrave Macmillan.

Ruggie, J. (1982), 'International Regimes, Transactions, and Change: Embedded Liberalism in the Postwar Economic Order', *International Organization*, 36: 379–415.

Scharpf, F. W. (2000a), *Governing in Europe*, Oxford: Oxford University Press.

Scharpf, F. W. (2000b), 'Economic Changes, Vulnerabilities, and Institutional Capabilities', in F. W. Scharpf and V. A. Schmidt (eds), *Welfare and Work In the Open Economy. Vol. I: From Vulnerability to Competitiveness*, Oxford: Oxford University Press.

Schmidt, V. A. (1996), *From State to Market? The Transformation of French Business and Government*, New York and London: Cambridge University Press.

Schmidt, V. A. (2000), 'Values and Discourse in the Politics of Welfare State Adjustment', in F. W. Scharpf and V. A. Schmidt (eds), *Welfare and Work, Vol. I*, Oxford: Oxford University Press.

Schmidt, V. A. (2002), *The Futures of European Capitalism*, Oxford: Oxford University Press.

Schmidt, V. A. (2005), 'The Europeanization of National Economies?', in S. Bulmer and C. Lequesne (eds), *The Member States of the European Union*, Oxford: Oxford University Press.

Schmidt, V. A. (2009) 'Putting the Political Back into Political Economy by Bringing the State Back Yet Again', *World Politics*, 61/3, 516–548

Smith, M. (2001), 'Europe and the German Model: Growing Tensions or Symbiosis?', *German Politics*, 10/3: 119–40.

Stiller, S. (2010), *Ideational Leadership in German Welfare State Reform*, Amsterdam: Amsterdam University Press.

Streeck, W. (1997), 'German Capitalism: Does It Exist? Can It Survive?', in C. Crouch and W. Streeck (eds), *Political Economy of Modern Capitalism*, London: SAGE.

Teague, P. and Donaghey, J. (2004), 'The Irish Experiment in Social Partnership', in H. Katz, W. Lee, and J. Lee (eds), *The New Structure of Labour Relations: Tripartism and Decentralization*, Ithaca: Cornell University Press, 10–36.

Thelen, K. (2001), 'Varieties of Labor Politics in the Developed Democracies', in Hall, P. and Soskice, D., *Varieties of Capitalism: the Institutional Foundations of Comparative Advantage*, Oxford: Oxford University Press.

Visser, J. and Hemerijck, A. (1997), *A Dutch Miracle, Job Growth, Welfare Reform and Corporatism in the Netherlands*, Amsterdam: Amsterdam University Press.

Vitols, S. (2005), 'Changes in Germany's Bank-Based Financial System: Implications for Corporate Governance', *Corporate Governance: An International Review* 13/3: 386–96.

 ENDNOTES

1. One caveat: until the mid to late 1970s, we need to distinguish between democratic state-influenced market economies like France and Italy and authoritarian state-controlled market economies encompassing the other Southern Mediterranean countries.

2. For further detail on the post-war West European varieties of capitalism, see Chapter 16 of the first edition of this book (Schmidt 2005).

Conclusion

Simon Bulmer and Christian Lequesne

▌ Summary

Europeanization is not just a matter for the existing member states, but is also relevant because of the continued attraction of European Union membership to other states waiting in the wings. We briefly review the current applicant states, and the ways in which the Europeanization literature can be applied to candidates, before turning to the issue of how enlargement impacts upon the functioning of the EU. Finally, we highlight the impact of Europeanization upon states in the EU's neighbourhood.

Introduction

In the previous parts of this book the theoretical, country-based, and thematic aspects of Europeanization have been explored. However, one further aspect requires attention: that is the relationship between issues discussed earlier in the volume and enlargement, a key dynamic in European integration. In Chapter 1, devoted to an initial exploration of Europeanization, we referred to Johan Olsen's 'mapping' of the research area, and specifically one strand that he referred to as 'changes in external boundaries' (Olsen 2002: 923–4). In this Conclusion, we devote attention to this variant of Europeanization in the context of enlargement, with brief reference to the near-neighbourhood policy.

Enlargement as a Matter for Europeanization

Enlargement as a matter for Europeanization research arises from the fact that the EU is a polity with flexible boundaries. According to Article 49 of the TEU, 'any European state [. . .] may apply to become a member of the Union'. In June 1993, in the context of the anticipated enlargement to the CEECs, the Copenhagen criteria were spelt out. Under the criteria, candidate states must have:

- stable institutions that guarantee democracy, the rule of law, human rights, and respect for and protection of minorities;
- a functioning market economy, as well as the ability to cope with the pressure of competition and the market forces at work inside the Union; and
- the ability to assume the obligations of membership, in particular adherence to the objectives of political, economic, and monetary union.

The end of the Cold War had a serious impact on the enlargement of the EU. From twelve member states in 1989, the number increased to twenty-seven by 2007. As of spring 2012, five countries have candidate status for EU membership: Iceland, the former Yugoslav Republic of Macedonia, Montenegro, Serbia, and Turkey. Another state, Croatia, has already completed bilateral negotiations with the EU and is considered to be an acceding country. The Croatian population agreed on membership by 66 per cent in a referendum which took place on 22 January 2012. Once the existing member states have ratified the accession treaty, Croatia should become the twenty-eighth member state of the EU on 1 July 2013. Three other states of the Western Balkans—Albania, Bosnia and Herzegovina, and Kosovo—are potential candidates for EU membership. This status means that the EU has promised them the prospect of membership. Having an EU with thirty-five member states in 2025 is thus not a purely theoretical perspective, and makes the comparative study of the member states and accession states even more relevant. In broad terms, the challenge for would-be member states (and for scholars analysing this process through the prism of Europeanization) is fourfold.

Attractiveness of the EU for the European States

First, it invites scholars to continue research on the attractiveness of the EU, especially when common sense focuses a lot on the economic recession and the political crisis of the EU. The choice to apply for membership of the EU can be the result of different incentives: to consolidate economic reforms, the search for geopolitical stability, and also a quest to share democratic values. In the case of the CEECs, research has demonstrated that the application of the liberal democratic agenda was an important incentive for the elites of the candidate countries to join the EU (see Schimmelfennig and Sedelmeier 2005; Lavenex and Schimmelfennig 2009). The reason for the EU's attractiveness is very similar for the pro-reform elites of the Western Balkans (see Pickering 2011). As democracy has always been an important conditionality for the EU, enlargement remains probably the most efficient 'carrot' to make democratic rules effective in countries which have experienced a transition from authoritarian regimes (see Lavenex 2004). Of course, in the case of Iceland, the improvement of democratic stability is not the incentive for membership. The main reason is the search for an anchor to enable Iceland to move beyond its severe economic crisis. It is however not certain if the Icelandic population, when asked in a referendum, will ratify the membership of the EU. This first set of observations thus stresses the importance of continued research on the attractiveness of the EU to potential additional member states. It is also important not to forget the particularity of each candidacy for membership of the EU.

Impact of the EU on Candidate Countries

Second, the prospect of further enlargements confirms the importance of looking carefully at the impact of the EU on domestic institutions and policies in candidate states. First, there is the question of how to analyse the impact of the EU on candidate states. This debate has largely centred around the idea of conditionality: that candidate states have to meet specific criteria, as discussed above, in order to conclude negotiations. Two contending dynamics have been set out to explain the process whereby candidate states respond to this conditionality (see Schimmelfennig and Sedelmeier 2006: 108–9). One dynamic, based on rationalist institutionalism, sees the process being driven by the external incentives offered by EU membership, and how this offers rewards for the necessary adaptation to domestic rules and legislation so that they are EU-compliant. Another dynamic, based on sociological institutionalism and constructivism, considers the socialization processes associated with candidacy and whether they may result in identity change in the states concerned. This research agenda gained a lot of momentum with the 2004/2007 enlargements, and especially in light of the major transitions that had to be made in the CEECs.

Each candidate state has to go through pre-accession adaptation. The machinery of government has a foretaste of dealing with the EU from the inside while organizing itself for the accession negotiations. At the heart of its work is considering the necessary legislative and policy adaptation to pre-existing practices. Domestic parliaments and subnational governments engage with these negotiations as best as they can. Political parties consider their policy on membership and the terms of accession. Interest groups and other civil society organizations have to consider the organizational implications posed by potential accession. The domestic legal system has to consider the implications. The EU offers pre-accession assistance to help with some of the adjustments. The actual character of the adjustment reflects the particularities of the member state concerned. As Chapters 3–10 revealed, the member states have adapted in distinct ways to the common challenges posed by EU membership. However, whilst each state has its own historical trajectory, its patterns of governance and party politics are not beyond comparison. Patterns of adaptation are identifiable when member states' experiences are viewed thematically, as Chapters 11–17 showed. Hence there are options for candidate states to learn from existing members about the options for parliamentary scrutiny of EU legislation, for instance, or for EU policy coordination in central government. In short, the particularities of each candidate state does not mean that its adaptation cannot be compared, whether by those charged with the adaptation or those seeking to analyse it.

As more states join the EU, the diversity of decision-making and policy-making practices will also increase. An enlargement to Iceland, for instance, would reinforce the issue of parliamentary control over EU policies at the domestic level. In the case of the Western Balkans, policy implementation will be an important issue, as these countries still have limited administrative resources and weak civil societies. After the first enlargement to CEECs in 2004, scholars showed that the Czech Republic, Hungary, Slovakia, and Slovenia did not transpose the EU policies less efficiently than the so called 'old' member states (see Falkner *et al.* 2008; Falkner and Treib 2009). However, scholars also observed that a good level of transposition of EU policies in these 'new' member states does not necessarily translate into strong enforcement by the administrative actors. In their search for a typology, Falkner *et al.* (2008) called this situation the 'world of dead letters'. As we can expect the same kind of trends in the countries of the Western Balkans, European Commission officials and scholars alike will be looking at the enforcement of EU policies by local administrations and economic actors, and not just at the transposition of legal obligations by central parliaments and administrations. The lobbying by non-governmental actors and civil societies in favour or against the enforcement of EU policies will also remain a relevant topic on the research agenda.

Member States Within the EU Institutions

Third, future enlargements raise questions about the role of member states within the EU institutions. Scholarly research has shown that the move from fifteen to twenty-five member states in 2004 had no direct impact on the decision-making speed of the Council of Ministers (see Deloche *et al.* 2006; Best *et al.* 2008). However, the doubling of member states has shifted the negotiations more from the formal political settings to the preparatory bodies working in closed circles, such as the Council working groups and the Committee of Permanent Representatives, COREPER. There is a clear contradiction between these trends and the request on the part of the EU electorate for more transparency in decision making. Enlargements tend also to reinforce the intergovernmental dynamic within the EU institutions. In the Commission, for instance, having one commissioner per member state has increased the propensity of each commissioner to speak on behalf of 'his/her' member state, despite the provisions of the EU treaties for the independence of the commissioners. This situation will remain as such at least until November 2014, when a reform could possibly introduce a number of commissioners lower than the number of member states. All these evolutions should be carefully studied not only within the Commission, but also the European Parliament and the European Court of Justice. On the policy side, the reluctance of the current member states to increase the EU budget will also have an impact on the future allocation of policy expenditure. The EU is more a regulatory state than a welfare state, such that it distributes modestly through policy delivery (see Majone 1996). New member states of the Western Balkans, considering their low GDP, could expect to benefit significantly from the funds devoted to the Common Agricultural Policy and the Cohesion Policy. How would the current members of the EU, such as Poland, accept the shift of expenditure away from themselves towards the newcomers? Budgetary politics will remain a crucial issue for the member states in the future.

Towards More Differentiation

Finally, new enlargements will reinforce debates, both amongst practitioners and scholars, about the role of institutional and policy differentiation in the EU. The Treaty of Lisbon has increased the possibilities for using the mechanism of 'enhanced cooperation' for EU policies and has extended the procedure to the European Security and Defence Policy. In recent years, the procedure has only been used twice: once to bypass Swedish opposition to EU rules on cross-border divorce, and a second time to overcome disagreements with Italy and Spain on an EU patent law. The management of the euro-zone and of the Schengen Agreements on the free movement of people are also examples of policy differentiation. The increase of diversity resulting from new enlargements will reinforce these trends towards more differentiation. Some analysts would argue that a 'two-speed' EU, allowing an inner core of member states to move towards closer economic and political union, is the only scenario to protect the EU as a whole in the future (see Piris 2012). The debate is not at all new. In 1994, the German Christian Democratic Party already proposed the creation of a 'hard core' ('Kerneuropa' in the German language) around a limited number of members of the future euro-zone. At the time, the suggested exclusion of Italy and Spain under this 'Schäuble/Lamers proposal' created a lot of discontent in Rome and Madrid. In fact, any member state wanting to participate in an EU policy has difficulty in accepting exclusion, even on a temporary basis (see Lequesne 2012). The new member states are generally sensitive to this issue, as they had to accept the entire *acquis communautaire* in the negotiations for membership. On the other hand, differentiation appears the only way to move forward for some older members of the club. This contradiction will become more acute if some EU member states propose a post-Lisbon agenda with new institutional and policy reforms.

Europeanization Without Membership

The Europeanization of a state does not depend on becoming an EU *member* state or the preliminary step of becoming a candidate state. The EU has created a relationship of interdependence with its neighbourhood in such a way that has sometimes contributed to the Europeanization of third states. Norway and Switzerland are good examples of European states which are Europeanized, or more precisely 'EU-ized', even if they formally remain outside the EU. In both cases, EU membership has been proposed by national politicians but has lacked sufficient support from the electorates. Nevertheless, because of their strong level of economic interdependence with the EU, Norway, through the European Economic Area, and Switzerland, through a set of bilateral agreements, have already enforced most of the EU regulations and standards on the internal market. Both countries are also members of the Schengen Agreements and apply the same policies on migration and visa delivery as the majority of the EU member states. Membership and Europeanization are thus not necessarily congruent processes (see Schwok 2010). The European Neighbourhood Policy (ENP), which the EU has developed since 2004 to spread peace and democratic stability to its Eastern and Southern neighbours, also offers scope for Europeanization without membership. In 2004, the President of the EU Commission, Romano Prodi, presented the new ENP as 'everything but institutions', even for the European states like Ukraine or Moldova which could aspire to be potential candidates to the EU. If research on the domestic conditions for the implementation of EU norms in ENP states reveals the need for further investigation (see Delcour and Tulmets 2008), scholars have also observed that the promotion of democracy appears more hazardous when the carrot of membership is missing (see Schimmelfennig and Scholtz 2008; Lavenex and Schimmelfennig 2009). By contrast with the situation relating to enlargement, conditionality remains loose and puts the ENP more in the category of a classic external policy. There is also a broad agenda for research to demonstrate that the impact of 'Normative power Europe', whereby the EU exports a set of democratic values to other states (see Manners 2006), is dependent upon a series of domestic institutional conditions in the neighbourhood countries.

Conclusion

The enlargements of the EU emphasise the relevance for EU scholars and students to link the study of EU politics to a comparative study of the European politics and policies of each member state. The exercise was obviously easier when Helen Wallace wrote *National Governments and the European Communities* (Wallace, 1973), because the number of member states was far more limited. However, the importance of studying EU member state relations appears to be even more important with twenty-seven member states, along with the analytical perspective offered by Europeanization. EU studies and comparative European politics cannot be separate. It requires scholars who can investigate the domestic politics of the member states, ideally in the original languages of the countries. Neglecting the national level in any analysis of the EU can only lead scholars and students to grasp a very partial picture of how the EU as a whole operates.

FURTHER READING

For a review of analytical approaches to the study of enlargement, see Schimmelfennig and Sedelmeier (2006). The impact of the enlargement upon the EU's institutions is considered in Best *et al.* (2008) and Diedrichs *et al.* (2011). Falkner *et al.* (2008) explore the issue of policy compliance in the CEECs, prompting questions of a similar kind in future for the Western Balkans. Delcour and Tulmets (2008) review the EU's foreign policy impact in its 'neighbourhood'. For a recent review of the prospects for a two-speed Europe, see Piris (2012).

WEB LINKS

General information on enlargement is available on the website of the Commission DG enlargement at **http://ec.europa.eu/enlargement/**. For ENP, see the website of the European External Action Service at **http://eeas.europa.eu/enp/**. Most of the ministries of Foreign Affairs of the candidate and neighbouring countries provide information (sometimes translated into English) on their negotiations with the EU. See also the specific websites of the Permanent Delegations of the candidate and neighbouring countries to the EU, as well as the websites of the EU Delegations in the candidate and neighbouring countries.

REFERENCES

Best, E., Christiansen, J., and Settembri, P. (eds) (2008), *The EU Institutions of the Enlarged EU: Continuity and Change*, Cheltenham: Edward Elgar.

Delcour, L. and Tulmets, E. (eds) (2008), *Pioneer Europe?: Testing EU Foreign Policy in the Neighbourhood*, Baden –Baden: Nomos.

Deloche, F., Dehousse, R., and Duhamel O. (eds) (2006), *Elargissement: Comment l'Europe s'adapte?*, Paris: Presses de Sciences Po.

Diedrichs, U., Reiners W., and Wessels W. (eds) (2011), *The dynamics of change in EU governance*, Cheltenham: Edward Elgar.

Falkner, G. and Treib, O. (2009), 'Three Worlds of Compliance or Four? The EU-15 compared to New Member States', *Journal of European Public Policy*, 46/2: 293–313.

Falkner, G., Treib, O., and Holzleithner, E. (2008), *Compliance in an Enlarged Europe: Living Rights or Dead Letters*, Aldershot: Ashgate.

Lavenex, S. (2004), 'EU External Governance in "Wider Europe"', *Journal of European Public Policy*, 11/4: 680–700.

Lavenex, S. and Schimmelfennig, F. (2009), 'EU Rules Beyond EU Borders: Theorizing External Governance in European Politics', *Journal of European Public Policy*, 16/6: 791–812.

Lequesne, C. (2012), 'Old Versus New', in E. Jones, A. Menon, and S. Weatherill (eds), *Oxford Handbook of the European Union*, Oxford: Oxford University Press, 267–77.

Majone, G. (1996), *Regulating Europe*, London: Routledge.

Manners, I. (2006), 'Normative Power Europe Reconsidered: Beyond the Crossroads', *Journal of European Public Policy*, 13/2: 182–99.

Olsen, J. (2002), 'The Many Faces of Europeanization', *Journal of Common Market Studies*, 40: 5: 921–52.

Pickering, P. P. (2011), 'The Constraints in European Institutions' Conditionality in the Western Balkans', *Europe – Asia Studies*, 63/10: 1939 – 44.

Piris, J-C. (2012), *The Future of Europe: Towards a Two-Speed Europe?*, Cambridge: Cambridge University Press.

Schimmelfennig, F. and Scholtz, H. (2008), 'EU Democracy Promotion in the European Neighbourhood. Political Conditionality, Economic Development and Transnational Exchange', *European Union Politics*, 9/2: 187–215.

Schimmelfennig, F. and Sedelmeier, U. (eds) (2005), *The Politics of European Union Enlargement: Theoretical Approaches*, London: Routledge.

Schimmelfennig, F. and Sedelmeier, U. (2006), 'The study of EU Enlargement: Theoretical Approaches and Empirical Findings', in M. Cini and A. Bourne (eds), *Palgrave Advances in European Union Studies*, Basingstoke: Palgrave Macmillan, 96–116.

Schwok, R. (2010), *Suisse – Union Européenne: l'Adhésion Impossible*, Lausanne: Presses polytechniques et universitaires romandes.

Wallace, H. (1973), *National Governments and the European Communities*, London: Chatham House.

▌ INDEX

QM LIBRARY
(MILE END)